LARBI SADIKI

The Search for Arab Democracy

Discourses and Counter-Discourses

Columbia University Press
New York

Columbia University Press
Publishers since 1893
New York

Printed in India

Library of Congress Cataloging-in-Publication-Data

Sadiki, Larbi.
The search for Arab democracy : discourses and counter-discourses / Larbi Sadiki.
p. cm.
Includes bibliographical references and index.
ISBN 0-231-12580-1 (cloth : alk. paper)–ISBN 0-231-12581-X (pbk. : alk. paper)
1. Democratization–Arab countries. 2. Democracy–Arab countries. 3. Islam and politics–Arab countries. 4. Arab countries–Politics and government–1945- . I. Title.
JQ1850.A91 S235 2001
321.8'0917'4927–dc21
2001042519

Columbia University Press books are printed on permanent and durable acid-free paper.

c 10 9 8 7 6 5 4 3 2 1
p 10 9 8 7 6 5 4 3 2 1

CONTENTS

PREFACE AND ACKNOWLEDGEMENTS

Searching for Arab democracy is part of a broader cultural project. No single book can possibly do justice to the themes expounded within this book. The lines of inquiry followed in its eight chapters have been gestating for more than ten years—since my first interview in 1992 in Amman with political activists and parliamentarians from the then newly-resurgent Muslim Brotherhood. Ten years later, and armed with literally hundreds of interviews from around the Arab World, my search for Arab democracy is no closer to conclusion. Two more books on similar themes are in progress. What is fascinating about this challenging enterprise is the hybridity that increasingly resonates through the discourses and counter-discourses of Islam and democracy. This in-between-ness is as true of al-Fārābī and Averroes as it is of Khayr al-Dīn or al-Kawākibī. Other contemporary voices, religious and secular, are no exception. Thus what is "Arab", "Muslim", "democratic" is never single or fixed. Professor Fouad Ajami is right in depicting the Arab predicament, like those of many developing societies, as being an alternation "between the quest for the Occident's power and success and the desire to retreat to their own universe, to try to find their own values, to rebel and say no to those who judge and penetrate".* My inquiry shows that hybridity is the order of the day: Arabness, Islam and democracy are fluid, indeterminate and up for grabs. What may be labelled "Occidental" and "Oriental" are enmeshed in discourses and counter-discourses of self–other definitions and imaginings in a world noted for the diversity of voices caught in numerous crises of paradigms, identities, difference, indifference, intolerance, belligerence, Manicheanism, ignorance, poverty, marginalisation, oppression, misrepresentation, fanaticism and of missionary zeal, both religious and secular. So speaking of the "Occident's power", of Arabs or the set of "values" or the "universe" they seek retreat into as single or fixed is today open for interrogation.

* Fouad Ajami, *The Arab Predicament: Arab Political Thought and Practice since 1967* (Cambridge and New York: Cambridge University Press, 1992), p. 251.

In researching and writing *The Search for Arab Democracy* I have benefited from a number of distinguished scholars and colleagues. Their minds, in the form of constructive feedback, often challenged me to think harder, more critically and more creatively. In some instances I succeeded; in others I may not have done so. Gratitude goes especially to Jim George for his unfailing support since the inception of this project. He taught me to appreciate and deploy critical theory. I was fortunate to benefit from his mentoring both during my doctoral years at the Australian National University (ANU) and as a lecturer in Arab and Islamic Studies after my doctorate. He was a source of intellectual stimulation to a small group of dedicated young scholars at the ANU: Roland Bleiker, Tony Burke, David Kennedy, Rodney McGibbon and Paul Rutherford. They have all enabled me through the long discussions we had in the late 1990s to question foundationalism. Together we debated Foucault, Lefort, Connolly, Walker and Ibn Khaldūn. Professor Bryan Turner, now of the University of Cambridge, was most helpful in sharing his ideas on Orientalism with me in the course of a visiting fellowship to Deakin University in 1996. I am indebted to Professor Michael Hudson, Centre for Contemporary Arab Studies, Georgetown University, for a number of insightful and long discussions on democracy in his Copenhagen flat during April 1999 whilst we were both visiting fellows at the Carsten Neibuhr Institute for Near Eastern Studies, Copenhagen, University of Denmark. Professor Hudson's work on the question of democracy has inspired my work greatly. Rachel Bloul (Sociology, ANU) and Jan Jindy Pettman (Women's Studies, ANU) offered useful comments. Stephanie Lawson, now at the University of East Anglia, offered encouragement and insights. Both at the ANU and at the University of Exeter I ran courses on "Understanding Islam and the West" and "Understanding Islam and Democracy in the Arab World". I am indebted to a number of students whose passion for dialogical thinking and questioning made classroom practice not only a critical and interactive opportunity for co-learning, but also an enjoyable experience. They are too many to be listed exhaustively. I especially thank Doug Sturkey, Catherine Kawazoe, Bartek Razewlski, Jason Hinder, Yusuf Ibrahim (now adviser to the Somali President), Vanessa True, Michelle Paterson, Maree Fudge and Rachel Gittings (ANU). Of my students at the University of Exeter, I would like to mention: Brieg Powel, Jodie Baker, Ruth

Woodward, Jana Beyreuther, Laura Rodriguez, Christine Taylor, George Koukoudakis, Samantha Broad, Fabrizio Harley, Emma Brook, Andrew Nozensky, Helen Fry, Kasia Zielinska, Naz Khan, Hannah Morris and Fiona McKinstrie. Thanks are due to the Centre for Arab and Islamic Studies, especially its director, Professor Abdullah Saeed in Melbourne, for giving me two fellowships in 2001 and 2002, thus providing me with individual time to refine the text. Equally, two visiting fellowships in 2001 at the ANU's Centre for Educational Development and Academic Methods have been most valuable in preparing the manuscript. In particular, I express my gratitude to Robin Collins whose computer skills were vital for sending the manuscript to the publishers. I thank Bela Malik for her editorial inputs. Comments by anonymous referees have been most useful. Finally, I acknowledge the editors of the *Arab Studies Journal* and *Orient* for allowing me to reproduce very short tracts from two articles I published respectively in vol. 6, no. 1 (spring 1998) ["To Export or not to Export Democracy to the Arab World: The Islamist Perspective", pp. 60–73] and in vol. 39, no. 1 (January 1998) ["Occidentalism: The 'West' and 'Democracy' as Islamist Constructs", pp. 103–20].

I have used full diacritical marks in my transliteration, indicating the Arabic guttural *'ayn* ['] and the *hamzah* ['] thus and using [¯] over a vowel to indicate that it is long. In some instances, assimilation of the definite article [al-] before the *qamariyyah* has been used, such as in the phrase *al-risālatu 'l-nabawiyyah*. Given the abundance of Arabic terms used in the text, a glossary is appended to help access the text.

All the people listed have in different ways made the appearance of this book possible. But I alone bear full responsibility for any shortcomings in it.

I thank Professors Jim Piscatori (Oxford), David Armstrong, Stephen Wilks, and Ian Hampsher-Monk (Exeter) for their mentoring; Bill Tupman, Bice Maiguashca, Nathan Widder for their friendship.

Exeter, England, July 2003 LARBI SADIKI

GLOSSARY

'abīd	slaves
'ādah	a custom
'adl	justice
aghlabiyyah	parliamentary majority
aḥādiyyah	homogeny, singularity
'ahdu 'l-amān	covenant of Social Peace in Muḥammad Bey's Tunisia, 1860s
ahlu 'l-ḥadīth	the traditionalists or literalists
ahlu 'l-ḥall wa 'l-'aqd	literally, "those who loosen and bind", in reference to the learned scholars
ahlu 'l-ra'y	the rationalists, in reference to exegetes
ahwā'	whims
al-aḥwāl al-shakhṣiyyah	personal status
'ā'ilah	family
al-'ā'ilāt	refers to powerful families in whose hands economic and political power is concentrated in many Arab States
al-'ajz	impotence
akhlāq	ethics
'ālam	world
'almāniyyah	secularism
'amal	praxis
'amālah	subservience
amīru 'l-mu'minīn	the commander of the faithful
al-amr bi al-ma'rūf wa al-nahy 'an al-munkar	enjoining the good and preventing the reprehensible
ansinah	humanism, a term that recurs in the Islamists' discourse

ʿaqlānī	rational
aqalliyyah	minority of votes
ʿaṣabiyyah	a term used by Ibn Khaldūn by which he means tribal kinship, solidarity
aṣālah	authenticity
ashrāf	noblemen in al-Kawākibī's discourse
aslamah	Islamisation
ʿaṣru 'l-nahḍah	the liberal age of Arabic thought, as rendered by Albert Hourani
aʿyān	notables
azamāt	plural of *azmah*, crises
azmah	crisis
ʿawlamah	globalisation, a recent coinage also known by the term "*kawkabah*"
bābu 'l-ijtihād	gate of *ijtihād*
badāwah	nomadism or desert culture
al-badīl	the alternative, a term that refers to the Islamists' programme
al-baḥth ʿani'l-dhāt	it can mean soul-searching. It is rendered here as self-defining
barlamān	parliament, a direct borrowing from English and French
bāṭin	sub-textual or inner meaning
bayʿah	oath of allegiance, the act by which power is legitimately invested in a leader
buʾar thaqāfiyyah	cultural holes, in the parlance of Ḥanafī
dalālah	signifier
Dār al-amān	abode of safety
dār al-ḥarb	territory of unbelief
dar al-Islām	abode of Islam
daʿwah	literally the call, in reference to the act of summoning people to Islam, missionary call practised today, for instance, by the apolitical religious group al-daʿwah wa'l-tablīgh
dawlah	state

dawlatu 'l-qānūn	State of Law, a term that recurs in the political rhetoric of many an Arab state
dīmuqrāṭiyyah ḥaqīqiyyah	genuine democracy
al-dīmuqrāṭiyyatu 'l-ṣaḥīḥah	true or genuine democracy
al-dīmuqrāṭiyyatu 'l-shaʿbiyyah	people's democracy in the discourse of Kamāl Junblāṭ, the late Lebanese Druze leader
dīmuqrāṭiyyah	democracy, a direct borrowing from English and French
dīn	religion
fāḍil	virtuous, especially in reference to rule or government
failasūf	philosopher
falāsifah	plural of *failasūf*, philosophers
falsafah	philosophy
farāgh	empty space, absence, the term that best captures Lefort's notion of absence
fardiyyah	individualism
fasād	decay and corruption
al-fasādu 'l-dīmuqrāṭi	democratic decay
fawḍa	disorder
al-fikru 'l-dīnī	religious rationality in the discourse of Abū Zayd
fiqh	jurisprudence
fitnah	conflict, schism, discord
fitnah	a form of temptation or a test to the devouts (e.g. women, children and wealth)
fiṭrah	human nature
fiṭriyyah	natural and intuitive
al-gharb	the West
gharīb	foreign
ghazw fikrī	cultural invasion, in the parlance of Islamists; can be rendered as 'cultural imperialism'
ghulb	political preponderance in Ibn Khaldūn's discourse

ghuluww	religious extremism in the interpretation of the sacred texts
al-ḥaḍar	sedentary culture
ḥaḍārah islāmiyyah	Islamic civilisation
ḥadāthah	modernity
ḥadīth	the Prophet's traditions as reported through known transmitters, ranging from the strongly reliable to the unverifiable
ḥākimiyyah	God's sovereignty
ḥalaqah	a link; can also mean a circle of interactive learning
al-ḥall	the solution, specifically refers to the Islamists' political programmes
ḥarām	all that is considered, by way of a direct Qur'ānic text, to be forbidden or unlawful
ḥasanāt	merits or virtues, also known as *maḥāsin*
al-ḥayāt	the herenow, life
haymanah	hegemony
ḥiwār	dialogue
ḥizb	political party
ḥudūdu Allāh	Allah's sanctioned limits
ḥuqūq	singular of *ḥaqq*, divine right or truth, rights
ḥuqūq shar'iyyah	legitimate rights, or Godly-sanctioned rights
ḥurriyah	freedom
ḥurriyatu 'l-fikr	freedom of inquiry
huwiyyah	identity
'ibādāt	worship
al-idāratu 'l-dīmuqrāṭiyyah	democratic administration, a term coined by al-Kawākibī
al-idh'ān	conformity
iḥtisāb	accountability in Khayr al-Dīn's political thought
iḥtishām	modesty
ijtihād	the exercise of independent reasoning
ijtihādāt	plural of *ijtihād*, diverse attempts at deploying independent reasoning

ijtimāʿ	association as elaborated by Ibn Khaldūn in his *Prolegomenon*
ʿilm	knowledge or learning, including scientific knowledge; also known as *maʿrifah*
iltiḥām	coalescence in Ibn Khaldūn's discourse
iltizāmāt	singular of *iltizām*, commitments or obligations
imām	prayer leader; also means learned scholar or leader of a religious community
imāmah	Imamate, as in rulership
al-imāmu 'l-ghā'ib	the Hidden Imam, in reference to the Shīʿ ite eschatological leader whose awaited return from his long occultation is one sign of doomsday
imān	faith
al-imāratu' l-kubrā	the greater governance
iḥtifāẓ	preserving foundational or useful elements within Islam
imtilāku 'l-ḥaqīqah	possession or monopoly of truth
inghilāq	closure
insān	human being
intikhabāt	elections
iqāmat al-dawlah	the founding of the state
iqlāʿ	take-off, in a developmental sense
ishtirākiyyah	socialism
iṣlāḥāt	plural of *iṣlāḥ*, reforms
islāmiyyāt	Islamist feminists
islāmiyyūn	Islamists
iṣlāḥ	reform
isnād	chain of authority, in reference to the transmitters of *ḥadīth*
istibdād	despotism, a key term in al-Kawākibī's discourse
istighrāb	one meaning of this term is the act of seeking the "West", "Occidentalism", a term coined by Ḥasan Ḥanafī

istiḥsān	justice-driven legal exercise with judges seeking a favourable ruling in Islamic schools of law other than their own, a practice exercised by Ḥanafī jurists, for instance
istiṣlāḥ	seeking all that is consistent with the public good
istiqlāl	independence
istishrāq	Orientalism
itmāmu makārima 'l-akhlāq	bringing to perfection noble traits, which has its origin in a *ḥadīth*
ʿitq	emancipation of slaves
al-ittikāliyyah	dependence
jāhiliyyah	pagan ignorance, describing both a state of unbelief as well as the historical period before Islamic
jamāʿatu'l-muslimīn	another term referring to the Muslim community
al-jamāhiriyyah	the state of the masses, which claims to restore political authority to the people, is specific to Libya where it was introduced in 1977
jihād	often essentialised to mean martial struggle but, as an act of striving, it can take spiritual and peaceful forms
jinsiyyah	nationality
jumhūriyyah	republic
kalām	literally speech, refers to medieval dialectical theology
kāmil	literally, wholesome or complete, i.e. perfect
kawkalah	"Coca Cola-isation", used by Islamists, for instance, in reference to globalisation
Khawārij	Seceders, those who literally "go out" of the community of the faithful. Specifically, the term refers to an early Islamic sub-sect who withdrew support for the fourth Caliph in the Battle of Siffīn. They were egalitarian and meritocratic, considering all pious Muslims eligible for the office of Imām. But they were also extremist in

	that they considered non-members of their sect to be non-believers.
khawf	fear
khayru ummah	morally sublime Muslim community
Khubz	bread
Al-khulafā'u 'l-rāshidūn	the rightly-guided Caliphs
khurūj	secession
khuṣūṣiyāt	specificities
kufr	blasphemy, unbelief; sometimes it is referred to by the word *ilḥād*, atheism
ladhdhāt	pleasures
al-lijānu' l-sha'biyyah	people's committees, in theory, they are grass-roots fora for deliberation and decision-making, which help translate people's power into action
al-madaniyyah	civility
madhhab	rite or school of jurisprudence; the plural is *madhāhib*
madīnah	city; also the name of the second holiest city in Islam
al-madīnatu 'l-fāḍilah	the virtuous city in al-Fārābī's parlance
al-madīnatu 'l-jamā'iyyah	a concept that belongs to al-Fārābī; it approximates the notion of democracy according to many students of this Muslim philosopher, such as Muḥsin Mahdī
madinatu 'l-karāmah	timocracy, a concept that belongs to al-Fārābī
madīnatu 'l-khissah	plutocracy, in al-Fārābī's discourse
madīnatu 'l-taghallub	tyranny, al-Fārābī's term
madrasah	literally school; also, a moral and educational beacon or lighthouse
maghzā	significance
al-manhaju 'l-ilāhī	Godly path
al-manhaju 'l-Islāmī	Islamic way or programme
al-manhaju 'l-waḍ'ī	man-made path
maqālāt al-islyāmiyyīn	the Islamists' Theses
al-ma'rūf	the good

maṣāliḥ	political interests or expedience
al-mashrū'u 'l-Islāmī	the Islamist project
mashūrah	another term for consultation, used in al-Ṭahṭāwī's discourse
maṣlaḥah	public interest
al-mas'ūliyyatu'l-jamā'iyyah	mutual obligation
mawālī	clients in the sense of the power base supporting a state according to Ibn Khaldūn
millet	religious community under the Ottomans
al-mithāq al-waṭanī	the National Charter, introduced in a number of Arab States with the aims of ordering power-sharing and the conditions of democratic transition as well as national reconciliation in other instances
mu'āmalāt	profane dealings
mu'assasāt	institutions
mu'assasāt dustūriyyah	constitutional institutions
al-mudunu 'l-jāhilah	ignorant states, in al-Fārābī's discourse
mufassirūn	Exegetes, jurists or expounders of Islamic orthodoxy
mujaddid	one who renews or innovates
mujtahid	the person who applies *ijtihād*
munāẓarah	medieval Arabo-Islamic forum in which the learned engaged in dialogical co-learning; used here to denote a process of dialogical contests as well as a shared space for co-learning
munāẓarāt	plural of *munāẓarah*
al-munkar	the reprehensible
Al-Muqaddimah	*The Prolegomenon*, title of Ibn Khaldūn's celebrated work
murakkab al-naqṣ	inferiority complex
musāwāt	equality
muṣliḥ	reformer
al-musta'mir	the *colon*, the occupier
mustashriq	practitioner of Orientalism, Orientalist
mustaḍ'afūn	the downtrodden in Imām Khomeini's discourse

mustakbirūn	a term used by Imam Khomeini to refer to arrogant supremacists, especially the two superpowers in the 1980s
mu'tamar	conference, congress
al-mu'tamarātu' l-sha 'biyyah	popular congresses, claimed to be one mechanism for direct self-government in Libya
muwāṭanah	citizenship
muwāṭin	compatriot or citizen
nahḍah	Renaissance
nahḍāwiyyūn	advocates of an Arab Renaissance
namūdhaj	model
naz'ah	instinct
nazāhah	probity
niẓām	system
niẓāmu 'l-shūrā	Islamic consultative system
nubuwwah	prophecy in Shaḥrūr's discourse
qaḍiyyah ḥaḍāriyyah	civilisational question
al-qānūn	the law
qawmiyyah	pan-nationalism
qiyam	values
Qur'ān	literally means recitation, the Holy Book of Islam
ra'īs	president, ruler or leader
al-ra'iyyah	the populace
al-rajulu' l-urūbbī	the European man
raqābah	the act of keeping rulers accountable
al-ra'y wa 'l-ra'yu 'l-ākhar	the opinion of the "self" and the "other", a phrase which captures the principle of tolerance of difference and diversity of ideas; it is used by both Arab Islamists and secularists
al-risālah	the message of the Prophet Muḥammad in Shaḥrūr's discourse
al-risālatu 'l-nabawiyyah	Prophetic message
rudhūkh	subordination
sa'ādat al-dārayn	happiness in this life and the hereafter

sa'adatu 'l-dunyā	this-worldly happiness
al-sa'ādatu 'l-haqīqiyyah	supreme happiness in al-Fārābī's discourse
ṣaḥwah islāmiyyah	literally Islamic awakening in reference to Islamic resurgence, Islamic revival
al-salafu 'l-ṣāliḥ	the pious ancestors, the righteous forebears
sayṭarah	domination
shahawāt	desires, including carnal, wants
al-shakṣiyyah al-islāmiyyah al-'arabiyyah	Arabo-Islamic identity, a term that recurs in Islamist discourses
sharī'ah	Islamic law
shar'iyyah	legitimacy
al-shar'iyyatu 'l-dustūriyyah	constitutional legitimacy
Sharq	east
shūrā	consultation
al-shūrā 'l-aristuqrāṭiyyah	aristocratic *shūrā* in al-Kawākibī's discourse
shudhūdh	sexual perversity
shumūliyyah	all-inclusiveness
shuyū'iyyah	communism
ṣirā'	struggle
siyādatu 'l-qānūn	the Rule of Law, a term that recurs in the political discourse of reforming Arab regimes
sulṭān	ruler, a form of monarchical head of state; the title was used by the Ottomans. It is still used in Oman and Brunei
Sulṭawiyyah	hegemony, authoritarianism
al-ta'addudiyyah	pluralism
al-ta'addudiyyatu 'l-ḥizbiyyah	multipartyism
ṭā'ah	obedience
ta'āwun	cooperation
taba'iyyah	dependence
tabarruj	flaunting, especially of beauty
al-ṭabī'ah	nature
tadbīr	governing, managing

tadrīj	gradualism, advocated by al-Kawākibī for the sake of a sustainable process of political reform
tafriqah	divisiveness
tafsīr	exegesis
taghrīb	Westernisation
taghrīb thaqāfī	cultural Westernisation
tahāfut	incoherence, a term associated with the great Muslim theologian al-Ghazālī (d. 1111)
taḥarrur	emancipation
taḥlīl	the act of making something permitted or lawful
taḥqīqāt	analyses
taḥrīm	the act of forbidding or prohibition
taḥṣīlu 'l-sa'ādah	attaining happiness in al-Fārābī's discourse,
tajāwuz	discarding and surpassing that which is irrelevant in al-Turābī's discourse
tajdīd	renewal, innovation, a term popularised in the 1980s by the Sudanese Islamist ideologue, Ḥasan al-Turābī
tajhīl	relegation to the realm of pagan ignorance, a frequent practice in many extremist Arab Islamist movements, which are influenced by the known work, *Signposts*, by Sayyid Quṭb
takfīr	relegation to the realm of unbelief, has a similar usage as *tajhīl* for many extremist Islamists
takrīm	ennobling, in reference to human beings
al-talfīq	the syncretic reference to all schools of jurisprudence within Islam as advocated by al-Kawākibī.
tamaddun	urbanisation, another term used by Ibn Khaldūn
tamyīz 'unṣurī	racism, racial discrimination
tanshi'ah	socialisation
tanẓīmāt	Ottoman institutions, systems, of which Khayr al-Dīn was a strong advocate
taqlīd	recourse to the authority of Muslim forebears
taqwā	piety
tarāḥum	mutuality

tarbiyah	education, a strong theme in Islamist discourses
Taʿrīb	Arabisation
tasalluṭ	domination
tasāmuḥ	tolerance
ta'ṣīlu 'l-maʿrifah	Islamisation of knowledge
tathqīf	acculturation
tawāzun	equilibrium
tawfīq	harmonisation
tawḥīd	unity of God, Unitarianism, monotheism
ta'wīl	allegorical exegesis. A similar term is *taḥrīf*, distortion of textual meaning
tazwīr	fraud
thabāt	permanence or fixity in al-Turābī's discourse
al-dhāt	subject
turāth	cultural heritage
ʿuḍwiyyah	membership
ʿulamā'	the learned scholars; singular is *ʿālim*
ūlū 'l-amr	those in charge, in reference to the rulers, and more broadly to those in possession of a type of knowledge or power, economic, political or intellectual
ummah	the Islamic community
Ummu'l-kitāb	The Book in Shaḥrūr's discourse
ʿUmrān	a Khaldūnian term, often rendered as civilisation but may also mean development or modernity
al- ʿumrānu 'l-siyāsī	used in this text to refer to the notion of political development
unthawiyyah	feminism
ʿurūbah	Arabness
uṣūl	those core elements considered foundational to Islam
waqf	religious endowment, also known by the plural noun, *awqāf*
waṭan	homeland

waṭaniyyah	patriotism
al-wāzi'	restraint, a notion used by Khayr al-Dīn
wiṣāyah	guardianship
ẓāhir	literal or explicit meaning
zakāt	obligatory alms giving, one of the five pillars of Islam
zīnah	make-up
zuhd	asceticism
ẓulm	injustice

1
CONTESTING DEMOCRACY
DISCOURSES AND COUNTER-DISCOURSES

"… There are three things that Arab societies need in varying degrees. To some, these things appear to be a kind of superficial luxury because they are values and not material things. In reality, the need for these things has become urgent…For, no developed society has achieved material advancement without the prevalence of values, institutions and systems which facilitate such advancement on a solid foundation. These three internal challenges…Arabs must attain…are democracy, rationality and legitimacy."— Aḥmad Bahā'u al-dīn[1]

"Amongst the factors that have, in varying degrees, militated against the institutionalization of democracy in the Arab consciousness and tarnished its reputation were Arab parliamentary experiments marked by malpractice…This notwithstanding, the corruption of specific parliamentary experiences and the inherent flaws within democracy itself, no matter how great, should not be used as an excuse to desecrate democracy. For there is no alternative to it but despotism and dictatorship. There is no third option: there are only either the flaws of democracy or the flaws of despotism and dictatorship."— Muḥammad ʿĀbid Al-Jābirī[2]

At the turn of the millennium, no concept is more on the agenda of discussion than democracy. Democracy has indeed returned.[3] Like

[1] Aḥmad Bahā'u al-dīn, *Sharʿiyyatu 'l-sulṭah fi 'l-ʿālami 'l-ʿarabī* [*Legitimacy of Political Power in the Arab World*] (Cairo: Dar Al-Shuruq, 1984), pp. 6–7.

[2] Muḥammad ʿĀbid Al-Jābirī, "Al-mas 'alatu 'l-dīmuqrāṭiyyah wa 'l-awḍāʿu 'l-rāhinah fi 'l-waṭani 'l-ʿArabī" [The Democratic Issue and the Present Conditions in the Arab Homeland], *al-Mustaqbal al-ʿArabī*, no. 157 (March 1992), p. 11.

[3] The re-emergence of scholarly debate on the question of democracy is marked by the fecund literature on the subject. For Arab sources see Burhān Ghalyūn *et al.* (eds), *ḥawla al-khiyār al-dīmuqrāṭī: dirāsāt naqdiyyah* [*On the Democratic Option: A Critique*]

postmodernism and Islamism, it is in vogue. The schisms over its various aspects continue to occupy scholarly debates. Similar polemics are likely to dominate the discourse on *dīmuqrāṭiyyah* (democracy) in the Arab world. Democracy continues to dominate minds across languages and cultures. It is being appropriated by a wide range of discourses, voices and struggles. What is democracy? Which democracy? Whose democracy? Is it possible for a concept, ideal and system that elicits virtually universal interest to have any claim to singularity? In a multicultural world, can democracy's universalism withstand the plurality of particularisms?

Although the ensuing analysis partly addresses these questions, it does not pretend to offer answers, especially at a historical moment when democracy is fiercely contested. The contestability of democracy goes in tandem with the eruption of the democratic discourse globally. This contestability, which raises legitimate questions about its foundations, coincides with another historical moment marked by democracy's rising global appeal. If Westerners themselves rethink democracy, they cannot baulk at Muslims or Arabs, amongst others, doing their own questioning of democracy, its foundations, assumptions and justifications. Central to this discussion is the foregrounding of anti-foundationalist perspectives. Democracy, to deserve the epithet democratic, has to be defoundationalised if it is to be relevant for the multitude of world cultures and peoples, many of whom are

---

(Beirut: Markiz dirasat al-wihda al-ʻarabiyyah, 1994); Fahmī Huwaydī, *Al-'Islamu wa 'l-dīmuqrāṭiyyah* [*Islam and Democracy*] (Cairo: Markiz al-Ahram, 1993); Ḥāfiẓ, Ṣalāḥ al-dīn, *Ṣadmatu 'l-dīmuqrāṭiyyah* [*The Shock of Democracy*] (Cairo: Sina Li-Nashr, 1993); Saʻad al-dīn Ibrāhīm (ed.), *Al-taʻaddudiyyatu' l-siyāsiyyah wa 'l-dīmuqrāṭiyyah fī 'l-waṭani 'l-ʻarabī* [*Pluralism and Democracy in the Arab Homeland*] (Amman: Arab Thought Forum, 1989); Ṣālah Ḥasan Sumay, *ʻAzmatu 'l-ḥurriyyatu' l-siyāsiyyah fī 'l-waṭani 'l-ʻarabī* [*The Crisis of Political Freedom in the Arab Homeland*] (Cairo: Al-Zahra' li 'l-Iʻlām al-ʻArabī, 1988); ʻAlī al-dīn Hilāl *et al.*, *Al-Dīmuqrāṭiyyah wa ḥuqūqu 'l-insān fī 'l-waṭani al-ʻarabī* [*Democracy and Human Rights in the Arab Homeland*] (Beirut: Markiz Dirasat al-Wihdah al-ʻArabiyyah, 1986); and Fu'ād Bīṭār, *Azmatu 'l-dīmuqrāṭiyyah fī 'l-ʻālami 'l-ʻarabī* [*The Crisis of Democracy in the Arab World*] (Beirut: Dar Birayt, 1984). See also Geraint Parry and Michael Moran (eds), *Democracy and Democratization* (London: Routledge, 1994); Ross Harrison, *Democracy* (London: Routledge, 1993); David Held (ed.), *Prospects for Democracy* (Cambridge: Polity Press, 1993); John Dunn (ed.), *Democracy: The Unfinished Journey 508 BC to AD 1993* (Cambridge University Press, 1992); John Mathews, *The Age of Democracy* (Melbourne: Oxford University Press, 1989); Philip Green (ed.), *Key Concepts in Critical Theory: Democracy* (Atlantic City, NJ: Humanities Press, 1993) and the special issue of *Political Studies*, XL (1992).

striving to found good government in their societies. They all clamour for good government, seizing on the current historical moment of democratic diffusion in many parts of the world. To this end democracy is stressed in this book as an *ethos of anti-foundationalism*, indeterminacy and contingency.

THE DEMOCRATIC PROBLEMATIQUE: ABSENCE NOT PRESENCE

The current historical moment of anti-foundationalist interrogation of democracy and indeterminacy has made it propitious for "subaltern" discourses and counter-discourses of democracy to become more vociferous. The democratic problematique in the Arab Middle East (AME) is most noted for the neglect of the question of democracy and the scant attention accorded to Arabo-Islamic views on it. It is only recently that scholars working on the Middle East have "discovered" Arab democracy after its neglect for the greater part of this century. At least three factors lie behind this major neglect: the persistent "Orientalisms" which see democracy as being more irrelevant than relevant to the Arab world; the "policy Orientation" of area studies, funded by Western powers keen to learn about "the behaviour of political elites" and to advance their economic interests; and the scholarly obsession with the Arab–Israeli conflict to the detriment of the study of other important questions.

The study of Arab democracy has recently come into vogue, moving from near occultation to prominence.[4] It is the contestability of

4 Examples of these are: Heather Deegan, *The Middle East and Problems of Democracy* (Boulder, CO: Lynne Rienner, 1994); Elie Kedourie, *Democracy and Arab Political Culture* (Washington, DC: The Washington Institute for Near East Policy, 1992); Ghassan Salamé (ed.), *Democracy Without Democrats? The Renewal of Politics in the Muslim World* (London: I.B. Tauris, 1995); Augustus R. Norton (ed.), *Civil Society in the Middle East* (Leiden: E.J. Brill, 1995/1996); Rex Brynen, Bahgat Khorany and Paul Noble (eds), *Political Liberalization and Democratization in the Arab World*, vol. 1 (Boulder and London: Lynne Rienner, 1995); and Ellis Goldberg *et al.* (eds), *Rules and Rights in the Middle East: Democracy, Law and Society* (Seattle: University of Washington Press, 1993). Democracy features almost everywhere. It is being related to almost all other important issues of the day, for example concerning gender relations, minorities and human rights, and, recently, the Arab and Palestinian-Israeli conflict and the faltering peace process, e.g., Mark Tessler and David Garnham (eds), *Democracy, War and Peace in the Middle East* (Bloomington and Indianapolis: Indiana University Press, 1995).

democracy—not its uncontested utility—that is particularly difficult to deal with in an Arab political setting. One major difficulty lies in the absence of any kind of substantively systemic linkage with democratic rule. The absence of democracy in the Arab region complicates further the definitional problems of an essentially contested theory.[5]

Despite the expanding corpus of books on democracy in the Middle East, which no doubt furthers our understanding of the nature and scope of Arab political liberalisations, the scholarly enterprise is not as illuminating as might be hoped. This may be because of the uncritical reliance on Eurocentric definitions of "democracy", on the one hand, and the preoccupation of many Orientalists with the defence, for instance, of individualism and secularism as prerequisites for democracy, on the other. In either case, there is a lack of concern for specificity and context. Not much attention has been given to the current state of the debate on democracy in the Arab world. Narratives by Arabs themselves do not feature much in scholarly debates of democracy in the Arab Middle East. Islamists, for instance, are often studied as abstracts. The diglossia of democratic discourse in the Arab world, owing to the duality of secularist and Islamist political configurations, is unresearched.

But the fact that democracy has been noted by its absence rather than presence does not mean democracy carries no meanings for Arab Middle Easterners. Democracy primarily exemplifies freedom from fear. That is, fear not just in the sense Samir al-Khalil describes in *The Republic of Fear*,[6] but also, and most importantly, fear from the threats of uncertainty (psychological), hunger and unemployment (economic marginalisation), silence (cultural obscurantism), disenfranchisement (political), injustice (legal), and patronage clientelism

[5] One definition of democracy by Larry Diamond, Juan J. Linz and Seymour Martin Lipset states that it is: "a system of government that meets three essential conditions: meaningful and extensive competition among individuals and organized groups (especially political parties) for all effective positions of government power, at regular intervals and excluding the use of force; a 'highly inclusive' level of *political participation* in the selection of leaders and policies, at least through regular and fair elections, such that no major (adult) social group is excluded; and a level of *civil* and *political liberties*—freedom of expression, freedom of the press, freedom to form and join organizations—sufficient to ensure the integrity of political competition and participation." See their *Politics in Developing Countries: Comparing Experiences with Democracy* (Boulder, CO: Lynne Rienner, 1990), pp. 6–7.

[6] Samir al-Khalil, *The Republic of Fear* (Berkeley: University of California Press, 1989).

(social). The Arab individual has encountered nationalism through marginalisation, from the periphery of the various circles of power—political, economic, informational, legal, cultural and social—and of concentric relations of power resulting from its uneven distribution in most Arab societies.

The corollary is disillusionment punctuated by crises of legitimacy and moments of social upheaval. No disillusionment is greater than that with the emancipatory project of national independence. The liberation movements of the 1950s and 1960s and the avant-garde elites who spearheaded these struggles embarked on hegemonic and homogenising politics that defeated the promise of newly found *ḥurriyah* (freedom) and *istiqlāl* (independence). Indigenous governance took many forms of exclusionary politics: revolutionary one-man or one-party rule (Iraq, Egypt, Algeria, Libya), traditional clan-based systems (Arab Gulf states), pseudo-liberal regimes (Lebanon, Tunisia), and pseudo-constitutional monarchy (Morocco). The nuances are not always clear. The common denominator is that Arab governments lacked popularly based legitimacy. *Sulṭawiyyah* (hegemony) and *aḥādiyyah* (homogeny) have been the currency of rule, not legitimacy. Hegemony has meant that the state is the centre of all circles of power. Homogeny has entailed the emasculation of all rival centres of power and the cancellation of all available political identities, visions and programmes.

Thus, while diverse epistemic communities continue to be entangled in discourses aimed at disentangling the *essentially contested* concept of democracy, Arab nationals, like hundreds of millions of powerless human beings, need not say or do much to substantiate why democracy is a widely *uncontested ideal*. The often violent, corrupt, unjust and non-representative political orders they have known spurred them, even if intuitively, to aspire to democracy. Millions of these human beings do not have to articulate eloquently the conventional wisdom on democracy developed by academic "temples of wisdom". Nor do they have to justify convincingly how they come to see "democracy" as an uncontested good. Nothing can be more eloquent or convincing than personal experience with authoritarianism. Nothing can be more relevant. It is the violence of the past that makes democracy relevant for the future. Thus, whereas at the academic and scholarly levels democracy may be contested for different reasons, at the popular levels democracy is aspired to for one simple reason: that it may make the state and officialdom accessible as well as relevant to their lives in a positive way rather than in a negative way. Generally, people's intuition about democracy in the Arab Middle East, including amongst highly educated interviewees and democratic activists, does not therefore revolve around some abstract or idealistic notion of self-rule. Rather, it has to do with an expectation that authority's overriding objective must be the service of the people and people's equal and easy access to such a service.

Indeed, it is the practical relevance of good government to the daily lives of any citizenry anywhere which seems to be occluded in most discourses of democracy. From Hellenic times down to the present, it seems that democracy has mostly been a narrow conception at least in two ways: the philosophers and seminal thinkers who constructed it; and the "publics" they constructed democracy for. The former proposition is self-evident. Democracy has been conceived over millennia in the minds and works of dozens of intellectually gifted males. The latter suggestion requires a brief elaboration. Athenian democracy was the privilege of male citizens, those who made up Aristotle's *societas civilis* (civil society) or *res publica* (political society). Liberal democracy privileges nationals, discriminating, to cite one example, against minorities and non-nationals, as well as private proprietors. Other marginalised "publics", such as females, have not fared better than ethnic minorities or foreigners, something feminist scholars, for instance, have highlighted in their criticism of liberal contractual theories of political community from the seventeenth and eighteenth centuries. The "universality" of political community and citizenship has always been premised on the inequality of other realms and "publics" within it: the *oikos*, a lower stratum charged with catering for the affective and productive needs of those above it, in Greece; and until recently, women, amongst others, in liberal democracies.

FOCUS AND PURPOSE

With these difficulties in mind, this study is designed to fill such obvious gaps in the existing literature. It builds on the analyses of existing fine works as well as on others in the fields of comparative development and critical theory. The book uses primary material from the author's interviews with Islamists; it highlights Arab writings on democracy; makes extensive reference to Arab women's perspectives, including Islamist women; and looks at the politics of identity and moral protest. One goal of this book is to explore democracy in a variety of discourses and counter-discourses, dominant and marginalised, top-down and bottom-up, Occidental and Oriental, and masculine and feminine. Specifically, it will focus on what is referred to here as "marginalised publics"; that is, Islamists and women. Nevertheless, the discourses of the ruling elites are not omitted. The marginalised "publics" that this book draws on to analyse the problem of democracy have occupied a peripheral space in politics. They may be considered to belong to the realm referred to in Anglo-American political thought as civil society, *societas civilis* in Aristotelian parlance. But this is not a civil society in a Western sense even if a measure of political liberty constitutes one of its central impulses. For instance, it is not guided by voluntary association for defending individual interests such as property. Nor is it a voluntary association by a growth-induced "democratisation" and "middle class", a problematic categorisation that defies definition and whose criteria in terms of income may raise more questions than provide answers. "Middle class", at least as can be gleaned from the economic status of interviewees, whose narratives are drawn on in this book, is more of a reference to a high level of political consciousness than a financial stratum. At one extreme of the range of this "middle class" are those interviewees who live on modest handouts given to political refugees in Europe (e.g. members of the exiled al-Nahḍah of Tunisia in the United Kingdom and France). At the other are some high-salaried professionals (interviewees from Egypt, Sudan and Jordan). By drawing on these peripherally situated "publics", to avoid the term "middle class", the analysis also reproduces the liberal bias that only a highly educated, politically conscious, and organised social agency can apply pressures for political reform and change. What justifies the deployment of self-representative narratives from the margins is that at a time when democracy in the AME has begun to attract scholarly attention, very little has been done to present a map of the discursive terrain of democracy by non-state actors.

The book therefore asserts that the departure point for treating a contested and problematic question like democracy in an Arabo-Islamic context must be an exploration of how Arabs themselves understand, imagine and view democracy. The perspectives of the ruling elites, women and Islamists are exposed and compared. Although a late "discovery", democracy, which is often presented as an "oxymoron" in relation to the Arabo-Islamic context, was known to medieval Arab and Muslim philosophers. A look at al-Fārābī, the tenth-century Arab-Muslim logician and philosopher (known as the second teacher—Aristotle being the first), and his idea of the "virtuous city", shows that there is nothing "oxymoronic" about democracy in relation to Arabs or Muslims. That Aristotle and Plato along with the Hellenic legacy are today alive in the West is partly due to Arab and Muslim philosophers.

Since the AME constitutes the main reference point of this work, the understanding of democracy postulated here goes beyond its ideal-typical definitions. It takes into account the current Anglo-American theorising of democracy in post-foundationalist terms, so that Arab understandings of democracy need no longer be grounded in Western foundations. This book not only questions democracy's Western foundations but also problematises many of the axioms of Orientalism, raising questions as to the Eurocentric nature of a range of key political concepts, including "democracy", and their consequent utility in the study of Arab and Muslim politics. It consults a wide range of Arab sources neglected by existing literature on Arab democracy and democratisation. More importantly, it draws on interviews conducted by the author with Islamists from four leading movements in the Arab region: the Muslim Brethren in Egypt; The Islamic Action Front, the political arm of the Muslim Brethren in Jordan; the exiled Tunisian al-Nahḍah led by Rāshid al-Ghannūshī; and the National Islamic Front in Sudan of Ḥasan al-Turābī (al-Turābī and al-Ghannūshī are among the leading theoreticians of contemporary Islamism).

Factoring such marginalised narratives in a work on democracy in the AME is essential. This book is about the quasi-discursive explosion of democracy in the Arab world. Unpacking such an explosion is no easy task. Two reasons explain this: the short history of democratic reforms and the contestability of democracy. The two dominant paradigmatic approaches vying for ascendancy, religious and secular, are fiercely contesting each other's hermeneutics of Islam and imaging of democratic politics. Since the "death of God" in the West, liberal democracy has, more or less, assumed the role of a new religion, and the nation-state has become quasi-transcendental. This "death" has no analogue in the Middle East. Thus, the blurring of religion and politics is a fixture of politics in the Middle East even in states governed by self-professed secularists or self-consciously Westernising and modernising elites. This is as true of Atatürk's Turkey as it is of Bourguiba's Tunisia. A form of modified secularism, one that is distinct from French Laicism or other types of Anglo-American secular politics, has been the hallmark of political systems in the region. Essentially, it is one of political control over religion instead of religious management of politics. Hence, the disestablishment of religion by delimiting it institutionally has not necessarily led to secular politics.

The question of democracy is therefore doubly complicated in the AME. The role of religion in public affairs has not diminished despite its disestablishment in many Muslim countries. Today, there is a contest within a contest. The contest over "which" democracy, "whose" democracy and "how much" democracy takes place within an already existing and hotly debated contest over "which", "whose" and "how much" "islam", as opposed to "Islam",[7] must be given preeminence in the political and the cultural sphere. Just as there is a "Democracy" and "democracies," there is an "Islam" and "islams". There is an "Ideal" at the core of "Democracy" and "Islam". The various attempts at living up to the "Ideal" of each is what gives rise to a diversity of "objectified" "democracies" and "islams" at this historical juncture. "Objectification", as elaborated by Eickelman, entails a dynamic process leading to questions about the nature and relevance of an ideal to peoples' lives, which, in turn, leads to a diversity of interpretations and understandings of such an ideal.

In this fluidity, the normative claims of Western democracy have not gone unchallenged. But the democratic ideal has. Here lies the democratic paradox: democracy is an essentially contested concept; yet, it is globally marvelled at as an uncontested ideal, including in the AME. The democratic ideal has a global appeal amongst citizens in the established democracies of the West and "denizens" in many non-Western countries where democratic government is cosmetic or still in its infancy. At the core of this global appeal are shared dreams and fears. Most notably, the dream to be free, and the fear of

[7] For more on the notions of "Islam" and "islam" see Dale F. Eickelman, *The Middle East: An Anthropological Approach* (Englewood Cliffs, NJ: Prentice Hall, 1989), pp. 255–63.

oppression. Just as freedom is thought to be essential for a human being's capacity to be "ennobled" and to lead a dignified life, oppression is feared as the one evil standing in the way of the fulfillment of humanity and dignity. In the modern Arab Middle East, the various stories of nation-statehood have unravelled more by way of oppression rather than freedom. Initially, oppression by the colonisers over the colonised; and, after independence and the emergence of the nation-state system, by indigenous rulers over their subjects. It is not surprising then that democracy has captivated millions of minds and hearts in this region.

A significant question about the nature of democracy at a time when its ideal has travelled globally concerns the "unfixing" of democracy and of "fixed" readings and understandings of it. As the democratic ideal becomes appropriated globally, the interpretation of democracy is bound to be decentred and pluralised. At issue here is not whether democracy can flourish outside its culturally specific Western milieu or stands much chance for cohabitation with non-Western cultures and knowledge practices. This angle has racist overtones. The more important question is about whether democracy has what it takes to be amenable to decentring or destabilising without losing its moral potency. Equally important, therefore is the question of whether the "unfixing" of democracy, by opening it to non-fixed interpretations and understandings, can be matched by similar processes of "unfixing" in its new milieu.

THE DEMOCRATIC DEBATE

Democracy, that "honorific" term, has never been easy to unpack. It is widely contestable and manifestly polymorphous. In his fine work, *The Theory of Democracy Revisited*,[8] Giovanni Sartori brings to the fore the various interrelated strata of complexity—historical, etymological, epistemological, semantic, conceptual, and empirical—pertinent to the much used key-concept, democracy. In the light of his work, it is doubtful whether, in analysing democracy, the risk of reductionism is escapable. Scholars seem only to agree on the etymology of the word. *Demokratia* is the Greek composite of *demos*, people, and *kratia*, from the verb, *kratieen*, to rule. While literally

8 Giovanni Sartori, *The Theory of Democracy Revisited* (Chatham, NJ: Chatham House Publishers, 1987).

'rule by the people' was the ideal of Athenian democracy, practically, even in the Greek *polis*, only a very good approximation of that ideal was possible.[9] Athenian democracy with its political equality and rationality might have typified what Aristotle refers to in his *Politica*, in 334 BC, "the form of government…in which every man, whoever he is, can act best and live happily."[10] In practice, however, even Athenian democracy was imperfect. It was patriarchal and exclusive—not for women, slaves and foreigners. Sartori poignantly identifies the inherent dichotomy between concept and reality in all democracies: "No [all-inclusive] democracy has ever existed nor is likely to exist."[11]

Despite its imperfections, democracy as a form of government is still valued as the best system for regulating state–society relations. Many of its students regard it as a facilitator of the expression and application of public preferences and choices. Others promote its virtues of solving contending interests peacefully, and of delineating legal and constitutional boundaries for official and public behaviour. No virtue is perhaps greater than democracy's inner pluralism and versatility. This is a valuable asset for democrats everywhere. For, democracy is not only inherently versatile, but versatility is also inherently democratic. This is why democracy can easily be stressed above all else as an "ethos of pluralisation", in the words of William Connolly,[12] and of anti-foundationalism. There is much significance in this at a time when there is a globally growing chorus of voices against misrule, human rights abuses, corruption and man-made misery. The affirmation of such an ethos will more likely than not predispose democrats from non-Western cultures and from all sorts

[9] In Athens in the fifth century BC, the prototype of direct democracy was conceived. An institutionalised framework for a functioning direct democracy was in place. The *ekklesia* was the Popular Assembly (ibid., p. 22), to which all adult male citizens belonged and where they convened ten times a year to address public affairs. A non-elected 500-man council, divided into ten sub-councils, was entrusted with actual governing, with crucial matters (war, peace) being referred back to the assembly. Specialised courts administered a justice system in which citizens staffed juries—the largest of which comprised 500. Many citizens were office-holders in the administrative system.

[10] Aristotle, *The Politics*, ed. by Stephen Everson (Cambridge University Press, 1988).

[11] Ibid.

[12] William E. Connolly, *The Ethos of Pluralization* (Minneapolis: University of Minnesota Press, 1995).

of political backgrounds to put stock in democracy, thus boosting the search for good government around the world. As an idea geared towards the building of open societies, democracy understood as a *defoundationalising ethos* entails predisposition to openness. Hence Sartori notes that "the concept of democracy is entitled to be diffuse and multifaceted."[13] If democracy *is* entitled to be diffuse, it is because it *can* be diffuse. This is a kind of an inner democracy within the concept of democracy. More importantly, if democracy is entitled to be diffuse and multifaceted, then it is entitled to be multicultural. That is, democracy *can* be multicultural. It is for all cultures to adopt and adapt. Effecting a kind of transfiguration from monoculturalism to multiculturalism holds the key to democracy's wide adoption and adaptation.

But adapting democracy is not tailoring it to the whims of dictators. Being variable and inherently plural, democracy is an ethos that rejects the violence of exclusion through fixity, hegemony and homogeny. There is no oneness about it. David Held's categorisations in his *Models of Democracy* demonstrate this point emphatically. Besides the two prominent and rival forms of democracy, the liberal and civic republican, Held problematises the normative and institutional criteria of seven other models.[14] Democracy does not come from one mind, from one historical period, or from one polity. The assertion that it is the political-end product (to-date) of Western civilisation is perhaps irrefutable. Athenian democracy, the Renaissance, the European Reformation and the Age of Reason form part of Western civilisation's political heritage. But Western civilisation is part of human civilisation. Hence those monopolistic claims that democracy is an exclusively Western by-product are both exclusionary and ethnocentric. This apologetic logic has been applied within and without the West to justify the rule of dependent despots. Non-Western peoples should neither cringe, nor grant the West monopoly over the practice of democracy.[15]

13 Aristotle, *The Politics*, p. 3.

14 David Held, *Models of Democracy* (Cambridge: Polity Press, 1996).

15 See B.K. Nehru, "Western Democracy and the Third World", *Third World Quarterly*, 1 (April 1979), pp. 53–70. In this article the author gives evidence to support his contention that Western democracy is not suitable for developing countries. For a response to Nehru, see W.H. Morris-Jones, "The West and the Third World: Whose Democracy, Whose Development?" *Third World Quarterly*, 1 (July 1979), pp. 31–42.

The practice of modern democracy accounts only for a short period of human history.[16] In the interlude, between the time when Athens fell and Athenian democracy ceased to exist and the late eighteenth and nineteenth centuries (which marked the beginning of democratic gestation in the United States, Great Britain and Switzerland), no democracy in the Western sense had existed. During that interlude, rule was oligarchic, princely, monarchical, imperial or Sultanic. In the immediate aftermath of the Second World War, the number of countries qualifying as democracies was limited;[17] and some democracies were exclusionary.[18] Democracy, in the variety of its immature forms, is even more recent in the Arab world. Judged by various criteria, especially the criterion of whether a state bestowed political and civil liberties, Arab countries mostly failed to show on the lists of democratic political systems. In one survey, which categorised less developed countries' political systems on the basis of competitiveness and modernity, only Lebanon's was classified as competitive. Those of Algeria, Jordan, Morocco, Somalia and Tunisia were considered semi-competitive. Others such as in the former United Arab Republic (the union of Egypt and Syria between 1958 and 1961), Iraq, Libya, Sudan, Saudi Arabia and Yemen were considered authoritarian.[19] Based on the holding of elections, only Egypt of all Arab countries qualified as an "electoral democracy" in 1986 along with 30 other Third World countries.[20] In the Freedom House survey of political rights and civil liberties for 1986–7,[21] which uses Western electorally-based criteria, not a single Arab country was classified as "free". Most were "partly free". In short, no single Arab country can yet be classified as a democracy.

Although democracy is a positive concept based on positive principles such as moral egalitarianism and self-determination, underlying

16 Arend Lijphart, *Democracies: Patterns of Majoritarian and Consensus Government in Twenty-One Countries* (New Haven: Yale University Press, 1984), p. 37.

17 Ibid., p. 38.

18 Adult suffrage was not, for instance, available for Swiss women. In Australia, aborigines were not enfranchised until the 1960s and voting, for them, became compulsory only in 1983.

19 Gabriel A. Almond and James S. Coleman (eds), *The Politics of the Developing Areas* (Princeton: New Jersey, 1960), p. 534.

20 Richard L. Sklar, "Development Democracy", *Contemporary Studies in Society and History*, 29 (October 1987), p. 692.

21 See Raymond D. Gastil, *Freedom in the World: Political Rights and Civil Liberties 1986–1987* (New York: Greenwood Press, 1987), pp. 30–4.

it is a set of pessimistic assumptions about human nature. Socrates, in *Plato's Republic*, warns of the dangers of "those commoner natures" and "their evils" to cities and state—defeating them requires the unity of philosophers and kings.[22] Machiavelli's counsel to statesmen, in his *Discourses*, is to always assume that "all men are bad".[23] Hobbes, in *The Citizen*, voices a similar cynicism about people's "brutish" and "nasty" dispositions, which, without "fear of some coercive power", would put self-preservation out of reach.[24] It is this preservation of life, liberty and property that Locke, in *Two Treatises of Government*, sees as a worthy cause for people to give up their freedom in the state of nature.[25] Rousseau's *Social Contract* extols the virtues of democratic society based on equality and justice, to curb "unbridled passions" and the "evils" and conflicts in society.[26] Distributive justice, as Hume asserts in *Political Essays*, is the driving moral force behind the creation of the "political society" without which no peace and safety are possible.[27] Jefferson, in *On Democracy*, intimates the dangers of tyranny and oppression and sees, in education and the enlightenment of the people, deterrents against them. Counterbalancing this pessimism, however, is the optimistic assumption that people are not "accident-prone" or "automata", but rather beings capable of rationality,[28] the kind of rationality that makes them favourably inclined towards democratic association.

Finally, democracy is not a panacea. In a world of imperfect political systems, democracy stands out.[29] The "oldest" democracy, the

[22] Plato, *The Republic of Plato*, trans. by Francis McDonald Cornford (New York: Oxford University Press, 1945).

[23] Niccolo Machiavelli, *The Discourses of Niccolo Machiavelli*, trans. by Leslie Joseph Walker and Cecil H. Clough (London: Routledge, 1991).

[24] Thomas Hobbes, *De Cive*, ed. by Howard Warrender (Oxford University Press, 1983).

[25] John Locke, *Two Treatises of Government*, 2nd edn, ed. by Peter Laslett (Cambridge University Press, 1967).

[26] Jean-Jacques Rousseau, *The Social Contract*, trans. by M. Cranston (Harmondsworth: Penguin Books, 1975).

[27] David Hume, *Political Essays*, ed. by Knud Haakonssen (Cambridge University Press, 1994).

[28] Thomas Jefferson, *Democracy*, ed. by Saul K. Padover (New York: Appleton-Century, 1939).

[29] As put by two analysts, "democracy seems likely to be superior to other forms of collective decision making". See Geoffrey Brennen and Loren Lomasky, *Democracy and Decision: The Pure Theory of Electoral Preference* (Cambridge University Press, 1993), p. 198.

United States, is also the world's largest debtor nation and millions of its citizens are hungry and homeless. Democracy may not mean freedom from hunger, but it holds the promise of freedom from tyranny. Pennock correctly observes: "Democracy is not an absolute guarantee that human rights will be protected and human interests advanced, but it is the best guarantee we have."[30] Democracy may not eradicate what has been described as "physical misery", but it does enhance the citizenry's psychological quality of life. It also presents the people with the ways and means to fight physical misery (e.g. through social pluralism, free association and self-help organisation). Legal curbs against unfettered state power help minimise illtreatment while self-government helps maximise self-respect.[31]

Any unpacking of democracy must be prefaced with two important observations. The first being that having flourished in the West, especially in the post big wars period in Europe and North America, democracy's best critics are mostly Western or are based in the West (e.g. including scholars of non-Western origins). There is no bias intended here against non-Westerners. Clearly, democratic "imperfections", "shortcomings" or "lacunae" are clearer to those who have had the full advantage of observing democracy's operation directly. Viewed from a broader perspective, the vigorous discourse on democracy underscores the crisis of governance in pre-industrial and post-industrial societies. It is not, therefore, fortuitous at all that the most ardent calls for what Keane calls "more and better democracy",[32] and what Przeworski and others call "sustainable democracy"[33] are originating in the West. *The Idea of Democracy*, edited by Copp, Hampton

30 Roland Pennock, *Liberal Democracy: Its Merits and Prospects* (New York: Rinehart Company, 1950), p. 108.

31 Ibid., pp. 107–108.

32 John Keane, *Democracy and Civil Society: On the Predicaments of European Socialism, the Prospects for Democracy, and the Problem of Controlling Social Political Power* (London and New York: Verso, 1988), p. x. Keane's arguments for "more better democracy" is worth producing here: "I reject the narrow complacency of those who consider democracy as simply government by means of party competition, majority rule and the rule of the law. The subject encompasses much more than this. It extends from topics such as sovereignty, revolution, ideology and the threats to civil and political liberties posed by 'invisible' state power, neo-conservatism and regimes of the Soviet type, to a cluster of new issues, including the restructuring of the global economy, the gradual poisoning of the ecosystem, the decline of party politics and the emergence of social movements."

33 Adam Przeworski *et al.*, *Sustainable Democracy* (Cambridge University Press, 1995).

and Roemer, is illustrative of the ongoing debate on democracy in a changing world.[34] Equally important, in the fine collection of essays, *Deliberative Democracy*, Jon Elster and his co-authors convincingly argue for new forms of democracy that go beyond periodic voting.[35]

Epitomising the tense contestability of democracy is the strong passions—fear of democracy, fear for democracy and outright cries of triumphalism—evoked by the scholarly discourse. Consider, for instance, the inputs of two contemporary American academics, Graham E. Fuller and Francis Fukuyama. Of democracy, Fuller writes, "[d]emocracy is a superb form of government—the most desirable in human history. But it contains its own serious pitfalls…"[36] In contrast to Fuller's circumspect assessment of democracy, Fukuyama brings all history and all ideology to a halt, declaring that "…at the end of the twentieth century, it makes sense for us once again to speak of a coherent and directional history of mankind that will eventually lead the greater part of humanity to liberal democracy."[37] Fukuyama's faith in history having a linear, and not, for instance, a circular,[38] trajectory is not widely shared. His assertion about the sound economic performance of capitalist authoritarianism is confusing: "[t]here is considerable empirical evidence to indicate that market-oriented authoritarian modernisers do better economically than their democratic counterparts."[39] Autocratic 'rentierism' has thus far survived in the Arab Gulf, sustaining "oil-garchies" in power. Liberal democracy is not yet in sight. Then it is neither the end of history, nor of ideology. Cries of triumphalism by the American "philosophical right" are perhaps premature.

Generally, the critiques of liberal democracy by Heidegger[40] and Nietzche[41] continue to inspire those scholars whose analytical

[34] David Copp, Jean Hampton, and Jhon E. Roemer (eds), *The Idea of Democracy* (Cambridge and New York: Cambridge University Press, 1993).

[35] Jon Elster (ed.), *Deliberative Democracy* (Cambridge University Press, 1998).

[36] Graham E. Fuller, *The Democracy Trap* (New York: Dutton, 1991), p. 2.

[37] Francis Fukuyama, *The End of History and the Last Man* (London: Penguin Books, 1992), p. xii.

[38] For a brief critique of Fukyama's conception of "The End of History" see Fuller, *The Democracy Trap*, pp. 16–18.

[39] Fukuyama, *The End of History*, p. 123.

[40] Luc Ferry and Alain Renaut, *Heidegger and Modernity*, trans. by Franklin Philip (Chicago: University of Chicago Press, 1990).

[41] William E. Connolly, *Political Theory and Modernity*, (Oxford and New York: Basil Blackwell, 1988); see also Mark Warren, *Nietzsche and Political Thought* (Cambridge, MA: MIT Press, *c.* 1988).

methodologies are influenced by their schools of thought. Foucault,[42] whose writings neither attempt nor form a cogent political theory, is interpreted by the expounders of his legacy to indicate, *inter alia*, his suspicions of the state (and the over-emphasis of the state) through which forms of subjectivity are defined, and through his rejection of a single notion of citizenship or individuality—the ways in which individuality is understood and constructed are different. The discussants of liberal democracy comprise many women whose critiques contribute to the understanding of political community and citizenship—Hanna Arendt,[43] Iris Young[44] and Anne Phillips[45], amongst others. The scope here is limited to a sample of some of the criticisms pertinent to the questions raised by a few of these thinkers. The main point worth reiterating is that the criticisms imparted by these discourses of interrogation of democratic political community and citizenship take their meanings from specific inadequacies or flaws that cause marginalisation and subjection, processes that clearly reverse the democratic ideals of inclusion and universality of rights.

Non-Westerners, though, have partly encountered Western democracies through colonial hegemony, in the past; and since independence, these democracies have been noted for their active sponsoring of subversion or indifference to authoritarian rule in many countries and regions of the South. Therefore one of the most recurring criticisms of democracy by non-Westerners is this contradictory aspect of the democratic project. However, this criticism is not uncommon in Western analyses of democracy. The other observation relates to the fact that critical perspectives on democracy are entangled with a plethora of discourses, from feminism to postmodernism. The section below attempts to unpack democracy through the various critical discourses which are vital for understanding the context and contestability of democracy. In so doing, the aim is to highlight the anti-foundationalist critiques of democracy rather then dwell on those amply rehearsed elsewhere.

[42] Graham Burchell, Colin Gordon and Peter Miller, *The Foucault Effect: Studies in Governmentality* (University of Chicago Press, 1991); Mitchell Dean, *The Constitution of Poverty: Toward a Genealogy of Liberal Governance* (London: Routledge, 1991).

[43] Hanna Arendt, *The Human Condition* (University of Chicago Press, 1958).

[44] Iris M. Young, "Polity and Group Difference: A Critique of the Ideal of Universal Citizenship", *Ethics*, 99 (1989), pp. 250–74; Iris M. Young, *Justice and the Politics of Difference* (Princeton University Press, 1990).

[45] Anne Phillips, *Democracy and Difference* (Cambridge: Polity Press, 1993).

DISCURSIVE CONTEXT

The contesting of democracy in the AME does not happen in a vacuum. This contesting, which can be mapped out here only very generally, needs to be situated within the Western context given the fact that the origins of democracy in both theory and practice are Western. What is evident in the West is the challenge to the dominant discourses of democracy by newly emerging counter-discourses. Thus the "eruption" of democracy has brought to the fore both new and old schisms and what Schmitter calls "dangers and dilemmas".[46] In late modernity, the contestability of democracy has become very acute. In order to understand this contestability, it is imperative to present a map of the vast analytical and theoretical terrain of the democratic debate put forth by a number of discourses. Linking the critiques of democracy to their paradigmatic discourses is done with the objective of not banalising their power and specificity. The analytical terrain consists of old and new lines of interrogation focusing on issues concerning the breadth, depth, institutions and values of democracy. More recent lines of interrogating democracy have been able to raise "destabilising" questions in a globalising, feminising and pluralising historical context. In effect, these more recent questions have, more or less, radicalised the democratic debate. Metaphorically, in relation to the Enlightenment project (the baby), the questions posed do not stop at "throwing the bathing water"; they go further, suggesting a kind of "sanitisation" of the "baby". For, these new questions boldly interrogate the whole Enlightenment package and its attendant rationality, re-reading its democratic component, anew. This questioning has a tinge of apostasy to it. This coincides with a time in which certainty in the realm of knowledge-making is up for grabs.

New polemics

The new polemics are today radically altering the parameters within which the rethinking of democracy must take place, pushing contestability to new frontiers. The discourses entangled with this kind of radicalisation are too numerous to be examined here. But four "isms"—feminism; postmodernism; global solidarism and reformism; and

[46] Philippe C. Schmitter, "Dangers and Dilemmas of Democracy", *Journal of Democracy*, 5 (April 1994), pp. 57–74.

multiculturalism/cosmopolitanism—constitute the matrices within which the radicalisation of the democratic debate and the polemics resulting from them have been moulded. Each of these destabilising discourses constitutes a response to a set of pressures, strains or challenges presented respectively by patriarchy, Enlightenment Humanism, globalisation and uniculturalism. All four call into question the rationalisation or routinisation of inequality in democracy, a system that idealises inclusiveness. All four seek to destabilise a fixed *logos*, a centre, that produces markers of exclusion or hierarchy on which self-other oppositions rest. Feminism jostles with androcentric politics; postmodernism joins issue with fixity and with post-Enlightenment rationality; global solidarism and globally radical reformism interrogate state-centrism and territorial political cartographies; and multiculturalism targets ethnocentrism. Democratisation of democracy is at the core of each one of these four discourses. They all, directly and indirectly, and in varying degrees, open up ways for reimagining political community and space, and identity. These openings and reimaginings threaten the dominant *logos* of masculinity, rationality, raciality and territoriality. Together, they are bent on undoing the post-Enlightenment templates of knowledge and practice that frame democratic politics.

Feminism and postmodernism, however defined, being two powerful paradigms of contemporary critical thought on democratic theory and polity, are engaged in defoundationalising these templates. If Foucault's texts critique the over-emphasis of the state and its subjectivist nature, those by feminist critics point to the over-emphasis of the male. Anne Phillips foresees the end of gendered politics and gendered democracy, with their inherent inequalities between the sexes, in the redefinition of citizenship and in the revamping of representativeness so as to equalise between men and women.[47] Iris Young, acknowledging and challenging the exclusiveness of politics to dominant groups and the limits of the "common good" given the compound of group identities, differences and interests in society, makes a case for a cosmopolitan democracy in which the partiality of representation and justice, and the cultural oppression of the disempowered and the invisible, cease.[48] A common theme that runs

47 Anne Phillips, *Engendering Democracy* (Cambridge: Polity Press, 1991); also by Anne Phillips, "Must Feminists Give up on Liberal Democracy?" *Political Studies*, 40 (1992), pp. 68–82.

48 Young, *Justice and the Politics of Difference*.

through feminist scholarship is the questioning of the private–public division which domesticates women effectively leading to their exclusion from political participation. This scholarship decries the depoliticisation of the domestic sphere, the private household space to which women are confined. Male-centred politicisation and political activity in the public sphere have been made possible by this depoliticisation. These power relations have been a function of the household sexual division of labour favouring males whose share of the domestic production and reproduction has generally been close to nought.[49] The public–private dualism is one of many hierarchical and male centred oppositions—political-personal, spirit-body, reason-emotion—that feminist discourses have sought to combat and undo.[50] Feminist deconstruction and reconstruction, as put by Angela Miles, aim at "developing new political forms that reflect [feminists'] holistic values [by] integrat[ing] these oppositions as part of their struggle to build a new world."[51] Thus, some feminist discourses make the democratisation of democracy incumbent on dispelling the myth that the private sphere is apolitical and on challenging the conventional divide between private and public arenas operating in most democracies. The divide doubles the inequality of women, in the household and in public space, reducing them personally and politically. Unlike Pateman, Young or Phillips, Miles does not explicitly engage with the issue of democratising democratic politics. But she voices opposition to the reductionisms found in Western democracies, and articulates a practical vision whereby women get to be unburdened from unfair household overwork not only with a view to "engag[ing] in what are currently male-associated activities, but also so that women's life-oriented work and concerns can become the organizing principles of the whole society." The feminist perspective is discussed further in chapter 6.

The renewed interest in democracy and democratic thought has coincided with the recent rise and high intellectual profile of the latest "ism"—postmodernism (understood as a self-reflective, tolerant and critical attitude, not as a historical stage or period). In fact, the rise of postmodernism has galvanised the defenders of democracy,[52]

[49] Phillips, *Engendering Democracy*, pp. 97–8.

[50] See Angela R. Miles, *Integrative Feminisms: Building Global Visions, 1960s–1990s* (London: Routledge, 1996), pp. xi–xii.

[51] Ibid., p. xii.

[52] Thomas L. Pangle, *The Ennobling of Democracy* (Baltimore and London: Johns Hopkins University Press, 1992).

amongst others,[53] into alarmist frenzy, and a critical and reformist rediscovery of democracy. A fine embodiment of such a response is *The Ennobling of Democracy* by Thomas Pangle. He writes:

> I mean to sound an alarm of what I see to be the civic responsibility, the spiritual deadliners, and the philosophic dogmatism of this increasingly dominant trend of thinking. I wish to help rescue the genuinely galvanizing spiritual, moral, and civic challenges of our question-ridden age from what I fear may be the banalizing and belittling effects of the new philosophic elite.[54]

Hence to be rescued are those "all-powerful philosophic pillars of [Western] modernity",[55] "by reappropriating classical civic rationalism…a framework that integrates the politically most significant discoveries of modern rationalism into a conception of humanity that does justice to the whole range of the human problem and the human potential…"[56] Central to this is "the protection of human rights and of self-government in constitutional mechanisms and civic practices unknown to classical republic theory."[57] Despite definitional complexities and ambiguities, postmodernism, a critical worldview directly or indirectly related to the eclectic foundational conceptions of Nietzsche, Heidegger, Foucault, Derrida and Lyotard, amongst others, can, for the purpose of this analysis, be summed up by the following: 1) A diverse, seminal and critical interpretation of modernity. These philosophic critics contend "that rationalism is incapable of providing an acceptably profound, diverse, 'creative' and 'historical' account of what is truly human."[58] Postmodernism is a critical perspective and knowledge practice that attempts to respond to the inadequacies of rationalism. It seeks to re-read the human experience, re-affirming its history and its diversity. Thus it opens up a discursive space for "decentering", and for the resistance of "othering" and "worlding". 2) While the postmodernist worldview looks critically at "Enlightenment rationalism", its exclusions, its "homologising

53 Ernest Gellner, *Postmodernism, Reason and Religion* (London: Routledge, 1992); see also Alex Callinicos, *Against Postmodernism: A Marxist Critique* (Cambridge: Polity Press, 1989).

54 Pangle, *The Ennobling of Democracy*, p. 5.

55 Ibid., p. 3.

56 Ibid., p. 7.

57 Ibid., pp. 7–8.

58 Ibid., pp. 4–5.

egalitarianism", and its "biased universalism",[59] it does not reject Enlightenment nor does it shun democracy. Rather, it redefines them in such a way that it does more than just expand the democratic ethos:

> Its aim is…to alert us to that which in principle escapes our empathy and understanding; to invoke a nonrational dimension immune to rationalization. The political purpose of this account is not to render dialogue impossible, but to show it as irretrievably rent by myriad dislocations and exclusions (linguistic, cultural, unconscious)…It subverts our faith that finally, and in the last instance, otherness can be domesticated because there is a kernel of rationality at the heart of alterity on which basis it might be brought to the negotiating table.[60]

3) The notion of pluralism that the postmodernist perspective implies is not fixated on power distribution in the conventional sense—procedure.[61] It seeks to deconstruct not only the discourses and practices that create privilege and exclusion but also the systems of knowing and knowledge that underpin them. Hence,

> For postmodernists discourse is problematic insofar as it structures privilege and exclusion, a will to mastery which operates through the silences and oppositions that structure meaning, while for democrats discourse means dialogue, conversation and a will to inclusion and consensus via communicative transparency. In other words, for the former discourse is a site for political intervention; for the latter it is only a means to political resolution.[62]

4) As a critical worldview postmodernism has neither a cohesive political theory of its own nor a single postmodernist position on democracy. There is, however, a postmodernist perspective on the problematic of democracy:

> A democracy consistent with a postmodern ethic…must engage in the "permanent critique" of a rationality such as this [modern-scientific rationalism,

[59] Diana Coole, "Wild Differences and Tamed Others: Postmodernism and Political Theory", paper from the workshop on Citizenship and Plurality, 2–8 April 1993, University of Leiden, the Netherlands, p. 2.

[60] Ibid., p. 3.

[61] Jim George, "Realist 'Ethics', International Relations and Postmodernism: Thinking Beyond the Egoism-Anarchy Thematic", paper prepared for the 36th Annual Convention of the International Studies Association, Chicago, IL, 21–25 February, 1995, p. 33.

[62] Coole, "Wild Differences and Tamed Others", p. 3.

structuralist determinism...], and it must do so in ways that go beyond the instrumental tinkering with the rules and procedures of the system, while supporting those reforms which allow for enhanced "thinking space" and for positive self-reflective political practice. It must do so for the sake of a democratic ethos, acknowledged by Foucault as systematically stifled by modernism, thus it must do so for postmodern emancipatory purposes, which cannot be constrained by foundationalist logics of "rational action", or by fixed, universalist invocations of the "art of the possible".[63]

The problematisation and contestation of democracy is also a response to the sweep of globalisation and transnational forces and actors on an unprecedented scale. Territorial, cultural, economic and political borders have manifestly been rendered porous as a result of the onslaught of globalisation. At one level, globalisation has meant diffusion of democratic discourses; but, at another, globalisation has engendered undemocratic practices, especially via the control of an unaccountable minority of business and entrepreneur elites over the lives and livelihoods of a huge majority of human beings. Globalisation, which by no means is an even, positive, integrative or irreversible process,[64] has accelerated the dialectics of deterritorialisation and territorialisation, localisation and delocalisation. Gidden's definition of globalisation describes an "intensification of worldwide social relations which link distant realities in such a way that local happenings are shaped by events occurring many miles away and vice versa".[65] One significant element which is missing in definitions of globalisation, especially in relation to dialectics of exchange, is that of contestation. Nothing perhaps illustrates this point more potently than the delocalisation of democracy from its particularistic and specific milieu, the West, and its localised renderings in its new milieu (examples of this contestation relate to Islamist renderings of democracy in chapters 6 and 7).

But more to the point, the discussion of democracy in the context of globalisation considers at least two other types of contestation: the meaning of territorial democracy in an age of proliferating forces which operate above the nation-state; and the viability of democratic norms, procedures and institutions in inter-state relations. The traditional systemic link between territorial cartography and political

[63] George, "Realist 'Ethics', International Relations and Postmodernism", p. 33.

[64] John Gray, *False Dawn: The Delusions of Global Capitalism* (London: Granta Books, 1998), pp. 55–60.

[65] Anthony Giddens quoted by John Gray in ibid., p. 57.

community is under duress. Questions are being asked about the meaning of "sovereignty" in a world in which transnational corporations (TNCs) and multinational corporations (MNCs) are increasingly operating outside the ambit of national jurisdictions. The popularly unelected managerial and executive boards running TNCs and MNCs wield substantial power, often to the point of influencing decision-making and policy choices of elected political leaders. Their clout can be felt equally in powerful and weak as well as democratic and non-democratic states. Also, it can be more influential and immediate than that of voters to whom democratic leaders and parliaments are supposedly accountable. This is probably one aspect of the adverse effects of globalisation on democracy. An advantage of globalisation is the rise of globally integrated visions, struggles and identities operating above the state. These agents and vehicles of global social engineering are to some extent democratising the world by way of pluralisation and broader participation. This is exemplified by the globalised solidarities around issues concerning the environment, indigenous rights, human rights and women's empowerment (for the last, see chapter 6).

The challenge to territorial democracy by transnational forces and intensified globalisation has spawned movements of global radical reformists and global solidarists. The latter take the form of transnational/hybrid identities and struggles which seek to mobilise and organise both below the state, in a localised fashion, and above the state, in a globalised way. This newly-emerging model of resistance and emancipation by previously marginalised identities and collectivities is today relatively and unwittingly marginalising the territorial state. Communities and identities are progressively acquiring resilience in the face of regulative territorial power through an increasing capacity to by-pass the nation-state, by shifting their struggles back and forth between the communal village and the global village. In the communal village, people-centred and directed self-help is taking many forms (e.g. consumer cooperatives, people's banks, self-employment). In the global village, people-to-people links, solidarities and identities have become adept at setting the political and moral agenda by way of getting their causes heard and canvassed globally, with NGOs, UN and member states' involvement (e.g. indigenous rights, human rights, women's empowerment). Local problems are forcing searches for global solutions mediated by globally-oriented identities and moralities. In this respect, feminists, amongst others, are seeking global solidarities transcending territorial boundaries. Hence Miles speaks of "integrative feminisms". Only by being integrative can they be "transformative feminisms". Integral to integrative feminisms is the "affirm[ation] [of] the work, characteristics, and concerns that are relegated to women, marginalised, and trivialised in industrial, patriarchal society".[66] Central to transformative feminisms is "not only [to] name and resist diverse women's oppression, but also name and affirm diverse women's strengths and worth".[67]

However, globalisation may have undermined territorial democracy and popular sovereignty.[68] That is not to say that the state is about to disappear. Hence a great deal of contestation focuses on institutional renewal of democracy in a way that brings back civil society and active citizenship. Hirst, for instance, criticises the fiscal, distributional and organisational limitations of democracy, social and liberal, in their Keynesian and monetarist forms, rejecting both "state collectivism" and capitalistic individualism.[69] Hence his "associationalism"[70] or "associative democracy" as an alternative project for social organisation. Whilst he acknowledges the democratic values of human welfare and liberty, he rejects the nation-state as the context within which democracy can be maximised, stressing the primacy of "voluntary and democratically self-governing associations".[71] In the same vein, Dryzek adds his *Discursive Democracy* to the democratisation of democratic discourse, insisting on institutional reformation and widespread public debate so that decision-making is not insulated within the bureaucracy and technocracy.[72]

Perhaps, thus far, the most systematic response to the challenge mounted by globalisation to territorial democracy is led by a committed

66 Miles, *Integrative Feminisms*, p. xii.

67 Ibid., p. xii.

68 An excellent collection of articles dealing with this question is by Anthony McGrew (ed.), *The Transformation of Democracy* (Cambridge: Polity Press, 1997).

69 Paul Hirst, "Associational Democracy" in Held (ed.), *Prospects for Democracy*, pp. 112–35; Paul Hirst, "Associative Democracy", *Dissent*, 41 (spring 1994), pp. 241–7.

70 Hirst defines it as: "a normative theory of society the central claim of which is that human welfare and liberty are both best served when as many of the affairs of society as possible are managed by voluntary and democratically self-governing associations" in his "Associational Democracy", p. 112.

71 Ibid., p. 112.

72 John S. Dryzek, *Discursive Democracy: Polities, Policy, and Political Science* (Cambridge University Press, 1990).

team of globally radical reformists. This team comprises scholars such as David Held, Richard Falk, Daniele Archibugi, James Roseneau and other co-authors of two fine works outlining their project of radical reformism of democracy, locally and globally: *Cosmopolitan Democracy* and *Reimagining Political Community*.[73] Like Held's other work on this question,[74] the gist of the collaborative project is to reassess democracy creatively in the context of the pressures that the weakening "Westphalian order" is undergoing and of the asymmetries spawned by globalisation.[75] By so doing, Held and his co-authors indirectly capture the often-overlooked essence of changing politics where national democracy can no longer be uncoupled from regional and global democracy. Hence, the democratisation of the latter equals democratisation or re-democratisation of the former. In this respect, Held proposes more accountable, and even international, relations via regional parliamentarisation and pluralisation of the interdependent and, at the same time, competing "sites of power".[76]

The treatment of the question of globally democratic renewal in the works by Held and his co-authors is both systematic and sophisticated. Its sophistication lies in its cross-disciplinary and holistic approach of their proposed cosmopolitan democracy. Six interconnected processes sum up the conditions for the viability of cosmopolitan democracy. The leading process is that of democratisation as can be gleaned by the definition of cosmopolitan democracy:

> [A] model of political organization in which citizens, wherever they are located in the world, have a voice, input and political representation in international affairs, in parallel with and independently of their own governments...[It] entails a substantive process rather than merely a set of guiding rules. For the distinctive feature of democracy is...not only a particular set of procedures (important though this is), but also the pursuit of democratic values involving the extension of popular participation in the political process.[77]

[73] Daniele Archibugi and David Held (eds), *Cosmopolitan Democracy: An Agenda for a New World Order* (Cambridge: Polity Press, 1995); Daniele Archibugi, David Held and Martin Köhler (eds), *Re-imagining Political Community: Studies in Cosmopolitan Democracy* (Cambridge: Polity Press, 1998).

[74] David Held, "Democracy: From City-States to a Cosmopolitan Order?" in Held (ed.), *Prospects for Democracy*, pp. 13–52.

[75] Ibid., pp. 25–44. See also, David Held, "Democracy and Globalization", *Alternatives*, 16 (1991), pp. 201–208.

[76] David Held, "Sites of Power, Problems of Democracy", *Alternatives*, 19 (spring 1994), pp. 221–36.

[77] See Daniele Archibugi and David Held (eds), "Editors' Introduction", *Cosmopolitan Democracy*, p. 13.

Three processes directly intertwine with the normative standards elicited in the above definition: harmonisation, institutionalisation and pluralisation. One idea that resonates through the newly-expanded anthology of essays on cosmopolitanism and democracy and its 1995 precursor is the parallelism between the transnational and state systems. The former is not intended to cancel or compete with the latter. Democratically, they are understood to feed into one another. This is a point well elucidated by Daniele Archibugi for whom one merit of cosmopolitan democracy is to promote good government between and within states as well as globally.[78] The increased interdependence in the international system justifies national, international and transnational deepening of democracy. Mindful of this interdependence, Rosenau's notion of "global governance" encompasses systems of rule and control from the family to the UN. He justifies his broad definition, correctly noting that "in an ever more interdependent world where what happens in one corner at one level, may have consequences for what occurs at every other corner and level."[79] Similarly, Archibugi and Held stress the point that democracy inside states will most likely be attainable if democracy is the norm in the world order.[80]

Institutionalisation is addressed, for instance, by Held whose illustration of institutional features is quite comprehensive. He foresees the creation of global institutions geared for global governance: global parliament, New Charter of Rights and deliberative assemblies.[81] Pluralisation is self-evident in most contributors' discussion of cosmopolitan democracy and of global governance. Hence Falk's notion of "global civil society", which has the potential to embody the principle of dispersed publics and active citizenship that are in a position to ensure that cosmopolitan democracy at all levels is of such depth, breadth and quality as to be viable.[82] A fifth process is

[78] Daniele Archibugi, "Principles of Cosmopolitan Democracy" in Daniele Archibugi, David Held and Martin Köhler (eds), *Re-imagining Political Community*, pp. 209–12.

[79] James N. Roseneau, "Governance and Democracy in a Globalizing World" in ibid., p. 29.

[80] See Daniele Archibugi and David Held (eds), "Editors' Introduction" *Cosmopolitan Democracy*, p. 14.

[81] David Held, "Democracy and Globalization" in Daniele Archibugi, David Held and Martin Köhler (eds), *Re-imagining Political Community*, p. 25.

[82] Richard Falk, "The World Order between Inter-State Law and the Law of Humanity: The Role of Civil Society Institutions" in Daniele Archibugi and David Held (eds), *Cosmopolitan Democracy*, pp. 163–79.

that of legalisation. One of the legal standards that Falk proposes is that of the "Law of Humanity" the advancement of which necessitates a dependable agent, "transnational social forces", or a global civil society—that is, the moral forces constitutive of an alternative "globalisation-from-below".[83] The Law of Humanity, which Falk reads in international legal texts such the Universal Declaration of Human Rights, the Treaty on the Non-Proliferation of Nuclear Weapons, the Nuremberg Principles, and the Preamble of the UN Charter, has the potential of providing the emerging global civil society with the instrumentality of representing its voices and influencing the policy agenda at all levels. But legalisation can work subversively in the international arena, as the essay by Crawford and Marks shows, by entrenching a culture of indifference towards non-democracy.[84] Nonetheless, Falk's proposed legalisation is symbiotic with humanising political order, nationally and transnationally.

The last process is no less humanising: pacification of interstate relations. It is introduced by Norberto Bobbio. In the grand scheme of international relations the thesis on the "peaceableness" of democratic states stands out as an area where contention is mammoth.[85] A gamut of interrelated propositions with implications for the Arab milieu, notwithstanding their controversial nature, surrounds this question. Theorising about the supposed nexus between war making and authoritarianism, and between democracy and non-violence, tends to be reductionistic. For it obscures the strategic connection between liberal democracy with its inherently materialistic ethos, the military and its circuits of power and industrial complexes. Whilst democracies have not generally, especially in the post-Second World War period, dealt belligerently with one another, "the[ir] liberal

[83] Ibid., pp. 170–1.

[84] James Crawford and Susan Marks, "The Global Democracy Deficit: An Essay in International Law and its Limits" in Daniele Archibugi, David Held and Martin Köhler (eds), *Re-imagining Political Community*, pp. 72–90.

[85] See Rudolf J. Rummel, "Libertarianism and International Violence", *Journal of Conflict Resolution*, 27 (March 1983), pp. 27–71; compare Rummel's thesis of correlation between democracy and non-belligerence with the dissenting argument put by Jack Vincent, "Freedom and International Conflict: Another Look", *International Studies Quarterly*, 31 (March 1987), pp. 103–12. For an analysis of how the discourse on the link between democracy and war-making applies to the Middle East see Robert L. Rothstein, "Democracy and Conflict" in Edy Kaufman, Shukri B. Abed and Robert L. Rothstein, *Democracy, Peace and the Israeli-Palestinian Conflict*, (Boulder, CO: Lynne Rienner, 1993), pp. 17–40.

democratic 'peace' may be tied to the very tendency of hegemonic leadership to successfully organize and incorporate, above all, liberal democratic states in a strategic-military order".[86] Bobbio, though fully aware of the un-answerability of his hypothetical linkage between peace and a globally democratised system, raises a set of important questions to validate further the merits of cosmopolitan democracy.

There is a great deal of serious pace-setting being done by the authors of cosmopolitan democracy. They put forth a multidimensional and multilevelled programme of democratising democracy that is challenging to territorial thinking, being and doing. Democracy is usually conceptualised traditionally and narrowly in a fashion presupposing the nation-state. Whilst impressively sophisticated, imaginative and committed, the project will be seen by many as utopian. But a more serious problem with the project is its Western authorship. This makes cosmopolitan democracy another world scheme filtered through Westerners whose intellectual integrity and international citizenship are beyond questioning. The moral and humanist underpinnings of the project will strike a chord with many struggles in North and South. But many publics, especially in an Arabo-Islamic setting, will have qualms about a project that has a manifestly secular morality informing its ideas. The pluralising ethos of the project has not been demonstrated tangibly; it refers to West-ocentric laws and systems but not to the laws and ways revered by indigenous peoples around the world, Jews, Muslims, Hindus or others. However, the humility to learn imbues the project, which is, after all, still continuous. Nowhere is that humility more apparent than in its opening of a space of contestation, never foreclosing other possibilities or the debate at hand, a stance akin to that of postmodernism. Like postmodernism, the project opens up a space of contestation without placing itself above contestation.

Another space of contestation regards the politics of difference versus the politics of universalism in consolidated and established democracies. This contestation, which finds its strongest expression in the works of Will Kymlicka,[87] gives another slant to the debate of

[86] Robert Latham, "Democracy and War-Making: Locating the International Liberal Context", *Millennium: Journal of International Studies*, 22 (summer 1993), p. 164 (pp. 139–64). See also, Robert C. Johansen, "Military Policies and the State System and Impediments to Democracy" in Held (ed.), *Prospects for Democracy*, pp. 213–34.

[87] Will Kymlicka, *Multicultural Citizenship: A Liberal Theory of Minority Rights* (Oxford: Clarendon Press, 1995); Will Kymlicka, *The Rights of Minority Cultures* (Oxford University Press, 1995).

democracy in a globalising world. Kymlicka does this by considering the internal implications for universalistic citizenship and democratic political community in the multicultural societies of the West. Permanent and temporary, legal and illegal migratory movements of peoples and cultures, especially from the impoverished South to the richer North, will remain a fixture in a world in which globalisation is being intensified. But politics of identity is of concern not only to cultural and ethnic minorities but also to women.

In this respect, contesting democracy revolves around the important issue of representation of difference. Classically, liberal democracy designates political identity and community membership on the basis of an egalitarian formula, "one person, one vote". In theory, at least, democratic citizenship is synonymous with equality of rights and responsibilities of the voting public irrespective of their colour, sex, or ethnicity. In practice, however, democratic citizenship has historically placed a few limitations on its ideal of universalism. Being territorialised, it is never been available to non-nationals. Its private–public divisibility has for a long time meant that "one individual, one vote" meant "one *man*, one vote"; and, in the same vein, the evolution of citizenship has until very recently been a case of "one *white* individual, one vote", excluding indigenous populations in countries such as the United States and Australia. In other words, the democratic project was, throughout its formative years, and still is in some countries (Switzerland) engendered in a gendered (e.g. exclusionary of women), racialised (e.g. exclusionary of blacks, Indians) and ethnicised (e.g. exclusionary of migrant minorities) fashion. Democratic citizenship has almost been a quasi-contradiction in terms: a notion of inclusiveness valorising pluralism and aiming at equality that operationally is about integrating or assimilating difference, rather than representing it, into a homogenised nationalist identity. In effect, this has been a trivialisation of sexual, racial, ethnic and other forms of difference.

Thus, at the centre of the equality–difference debate, especially within the body of social theory by a variety of feminists, is a critical rethinking and redefining of universalistic citizenship and equality of rights. Two issues stand out. One is that equality's frame of reference is faulty if it upholds male-oriented values or criteria of political participation and community membership. At stake is not the commonality of frame of reference. Rather, and this is the second issue, it is that equalisation must entail recognition and representation of differences, not their oppression and dissolution. For, under a male-centred equality, as has been the case under democratic citizenship, only one hegemonic and homogenising difference is tolerated: manly difference. By the standard of a dominant male-difference, universalistic citizenship is in effect assimilation into a political order in which equality, right, responsibility and identity are constituted in the image of men. Iris Young proposes that righting this wrong entails a rethinking of the standards of equal participation. For equal participation to be realised, oppression of difference must cede to representation of difference; and, more importantly, given the inevitability of difference and specificity of identity, the right to group representation must become naturalised in the political process.[88] The underlying idea behind this reasoning is that if difference makes for distinct identity, then, distinct identity must make for different or special treatment as the only form of just treatment in a democracy.

Departing from Young's key idea of group-specific rights for the purpose of representing difference, Kymlicka puts liberal notions of political community and equal rights to the litmus test: representing distinct cultures of national minorities and polyethnic groups. Kymlicka's contestation of liberalism's capacity to rethink its model in relation to the politics of cultural difference merits attention. Recently, the Balkans and Europe were in the midst of an ugly conflict legitimised by fear for the fate of the Albanian minority in Kosovo threatened by the dominant Serb majority. This ugly conflict follows the Bosnian war with all of its atrocities committed to defend or oppose culturally-based territorial and self-determination claims. Rwanda's multiethnic society has revealed the ugly face of intolerance of difference with tragic losses within the warring Hutu and Tutsu sides. The contestation is therefore timely, shattering the "silence" of Western political thought on the issues Kymlicka raises and examines.[89] Western political tradition has operated on the basis of two assumptions. The one regarding the "ideal[isation] of the polis in which fellow citizens share a common descent, language, and culture",[90] is by any accounting unrealistic in today's multicultural

[88] Iris M. Young, *Justice and the Politics of Difference* (Princeton University Press, 1990).
[89] Kymlicka, *Multicultural Citizenship*, p. 2.
[90] Ibid., p. 2.

Western societies. The other, a presumptuously optimistic or confident assumption, concerns the ideal that universalistic citizenship bestows upon individuals, regardless of race, sex, or creed, the full gamut of rights required to fulfill all sorts of needs, including those having to do with culture and ethnicity.[91] Kymlicka brings to the fore an important distinction: cultural fulfillment under the liberal paradigm is very much a privatised affair[92] premised on an important principle: separation of state and ethnicity. Accordingly,

> The members of ethnic and national groups are protected against discrimination and prejudice, and they are free to try to maintain whatever part of their ethnic heritage or identity they wish…But their efforts are purely private, and it is not the place of the public agencies to attach legal identities or disabilities to cultural membership or ethnic identity.[93]

The case for separation of state and ethnicity is overstated. Most states of the world are, in line with majoritarianism, run by a dominant difference, ethnic, linguistic, cultural and so forth. A two-fold objective guides Kymlicka's enterprise. First, he insists that no comprehensive theory of justice can obtain without a differential treatment whereby separate ethnic and national minorities are granted culturally-based group rights currently unavailable in democracies. A moral imperative underlies this objective. That is, to go beyond multiculturalism as a cosmopolitan celebration of diversity through gastronomy. Kymlicka is serious about some form of group-specific institutionalised empowerment epitomised by "group-differentiated rights or special status for minority rights", in conjunction with universal rights available in democratic states.[94] He actually speaks of the creation of "distinct and institutionally complete societal cultures", by which he means "a full range of social, educational, economic, and political institutions, encompassing both public and private life".[95] This imperative is itself underlined by Kymlicka's conviction that the standard democratic model of political community found in the West will remain discriminatory without the provision of such rights. The second objective is to affirm that self-determination and freedom are not separable from cultural embeddedness.[96]

91 Ibid., p. 107.
92 Ibid., p. 78.
93 Ibid., pp. 3–4.
94 Ibid., p. 6.
95 Ibid., p. 78.
96 See ch. 5 in ibid.

More specifically and emphatically, Kymlicka argues that freedom depends on culture.[97] This he justifies by employing the notion of "societal cultures", the repertoire of common historical narratives, language, values, institutions and practices that any distinct group taps into for the purpose of self-fulfillment, privately and publicly, in every domain of social life.[98] Cultural deracination, such as via immigration, for a national minority or an ethnic identity does not entail cultural erosion. For, the shared memories, language and values, travel with migrants into the new homeland. But the "institutionalised practices" do not travel. So, cultural deracination regards the uncoupling of the shared memories and values from the social practices within which theory were nurtured, acquired meaningfulness, produced and reproduced, learnt, transmitted, assessed and reassessed, and modified.[99] Because self-fulfillment cannot happen without cultural embeddedness, Kymlicka argues that it is then very natural for immigrants to aspire to "re-create these practices in their new country".[100] The liberal tradition itself affirms the naturalness of cultural aspiration and founds individuality and individual autonomy on the basis of cultural embeddedness:

> It may seem paradoxical for liberals like Rawls to claim that the bonds to one's culture are "normally too strong to be given up". What has happened to the much vaunted liberal freedom of choice? But Rawls' view is in fact common within the liberal tradition…The freedom which liberals demand for individuals is not primarily the freedom to go beyond one's language and history, but rather the freedom to move around within one's societal culture, to distance oneself from particular cultural roles, to choose which features of the culture are most worth developing, and which are without value.[101]

In line with the above, Kymlicka contends that individual freedom, embedded in the liberal tradition, comes with the exercise of choice in conceptualising direction and purpose in life as well as conceptualising "the good life".[102] Moreover, the exercise of choice and conceptualisation of the good are themselves embedded in societal cultures. For, societal cultures are the framework within which

[97] Ibid., p. 75.
[98] Ibid., pp. 76–80.
[99] Ibid., p. 77.
[100] Ibid., p. 78.
[101] Ibid., pp. 90–1.
[102] Ibid., p. 80.

choices are exercised and they are the ultimate frame of reference within which the good is defined. They provide the options from which to choose as well as give them meaning, Kymlicka points out.[103] Therefore, for Kymlicka, cultural embeddedness and freedom are mutually reinforcing. Immigrants' access to differential treatment giving them access to their societal cultures harnesses individual autonomy in their search for the good. In other words, group-specific rights of the kind he proposes do not threaten mainstream society or the dominant culture; rather, they empower new citizens with the means to be fulfilled culturally and politically. The inextricability of culture and freedom resides in the fact that, in their quest for the good life, immigrants access not only democratic rights of non-discrimination, enabling them free and unhindered access to their cultural frames of reference and the institutions undergirding them. They also get to question and revise the values and conventions within their own societal cultures in considering the spectrum of options before them, leading them to develop individual autonomy. This inextricability is at the heart of Kymlicka's theorising for a liberal justice:

> For meaningful individual choice to be possible, individuals need not only access to information, the capacity to reflectively evaluate it, and freedom of expression and association. They also need access to a societal culture. Group-differentiated measures that secure and promote this access may, therefore, have a legitimate role to play in a liberal theory of justice.[104]

Kymlicka's advocacy of group-specific rights as one way of securing equal participation is of immense importance not only in a democratic society but also in democratising societies. Electoral processes in some parts of the Arab Middle East are already moving in this direction. Differential treatment may be inevitable if minorities' differences are to be represented rather than oppressed—the Kurds, Berbers and others in the Middle East. It may be the only way to level the field. Group rights are not alien to Islam or to the Islamic world. The Ottoman *millet* (religious community) system operated quite smoothly for close to 400 years. Under it, coexistence was made possible by the freedom of worship accorded to all religious communities. As Kymlicka observes, besides being a strategy for maximising

[103] Ibid., p. 83.
[104] Ibid., p. 84.

justice, special treatment may be one way of preventing future conflict and social upheaval. The question introduced by Kymlicka addresses democracy's ability to incorporate and cope with cultural difference. In recognising this potential, he has challenged the conventional wisdom that cultural homogeneity is a prerequisite for democracy. His line of questioning, like those by feminists, postmodernists and global radical reformists, points to an increasing tendency towards defoundationalising democracy.

WORDS AND WORLDS

No culture contents itself with repeating borrowed foreign ideas or concepts. To parrot a foreign concept, especially when it comes to an unavoidably relative and value-laden term like democracy, is to clutter reality and overlook specificity. The city-state democracy that thousands of years ago flourished in Athens cannot be replicated in either meaning or practice. The essence of democracy in Hellenic antiquity was, more or less, a system of direct self-government by a select male citizenry—no more than 5,000—who can easily fit in a city square or a stadium for deliberations. Nothing akin to the democracy of the *polis* can be staged in modern-day Mexico City, New Delhi, Beijing, Tokyo or Cairo. Greek democracy has travelled to the modern era but not intact. What was for the Greeks a signifier of male citizenry's direct self-government is in its Western incarnation, representative government. The linkage is one of "homonymy not homology".[105] Just as democracy's modern incarnation differs from the version of its Greek inventors, it cannot be expected to travel from its Western milieu, where it has been refigured, to an Arabo-Islamic milieu unedited. In fact, democracy does not cease to undergo change upon change necessitated by crossing borders of time, place, culture, language, and of technology (fifty years hence, the internet, for instance, may reconstruct democracy and democratic procedures). It is this dynamic of change, not of fixity, that is at the core of rethinking democracy as a pluralising ethos.

Since antiquity the power of the pen or of the word has been politically and socially vital. Hence the Hellenic notion of king-philosophers which had analogues in many other cultures and civilisations such as

[105] Sartori, *The Theory of Democracy Revisited*, p. 178.

in imperial China—sage-kings. In pre-Islamic Arabia, poets were the mouthpieces of their tribes. In Islamic Arabia it was the expounders of Islamic orthodoxy—the literati—that formed a quasi-"temple of wisdom" whose exegetical expertise often served to underwrite dynastic rule—the sword. This active interaction between knowledge and power has for long occupied a seminal position in human agency, evolution and history. The Qur'ān refers to knowledge as *sulṭān* (king)—knowledge is king. Moreover, it ranks the learned above those who are not.

Just as power and knowledge articulate each other, so do language and power. In fact, language and power not only articulate one another, they also validate one another. Language is more than a vehicle for transmitting knowing practices; it is a form of knowledge and, by extension, a form of power. Language and discourse engender power. That is, whilst power has to have structural prerequisites, it cannot have its claims validated and even legitimated, sustained and reproduced without discursive and linguistic prerequisites or mechanisms. Accordingly, wording entails "worlding" (a term made popular by Jan Pettman in her work *Worlding Women*, by erecting barriers of discrimination and separation and the creation of separate worlds)[106] and worlding necessitates wording. The way language grips on to the world is the way speakers of any language cut up the world.

The discursive scene in the Arab world is crowded. Perhaps no word describes such a crowding more than *tahāfut*, not in the sense of incoherence but rather in terms of variety and cacophony of voices. The medieval jurist, al-Ghazālī, coined the term to refer to the dense discursive terrain of his time and the disputations and arguments between the defenders of philosophy and of orthodoxy that resulted from them. The discursive binary of philosophy and orthodoxy has a contemporary analogue in the diglossia of national-secular and vernacular narratives. The jostling between these two discourses has been apparent in the Arabo-Islamic world since the colonial period and has continued unabated in the postcolonial era. The diglossic stand-off revolves around a solution–problem dialectic, spawning a zero-sum power game between modernity and tradition, itself a polar opposition invented by a Western straight-line imagining of

[106] Jan Pettman, *Worlding Women: A Feminist International Politics* (St Leonards, NSW: Allen Unwin, 1996).

politics and change. The national-secular narrative's imagining of the ideal polity is founded on the premise that modernity holds the key solution to the acquisition of such "goods" as development, progress or democracy. In other words, by-passing tradition is simply to avoid the key stumbling block—problem—to their acquisition. For the vernacular discourse, tradition is an essential repertoire with many relevant and useful resources for progress or development.

Postcoloniality is, amongst other things, a diglossically discursive site with fierce contestations between seemingly irreconcilable imaginings of community and identity. The "glossia" of modernity taps into the knowledge practices, epistemological artefacts or conceptual resources and technological acquisitions borrowed from or introduced by the West for the elaboration and defence of their imaginings and visions. The glossia of tradition deploys the epistemological, cultural, conceptual and linguistic storage in its duel with the former. For the greater part of the postcolonial period, the prevailing community and identity have been heavily informed by the imagining of the dominant discourse, which is ethnonationalist and secular. Deviation from or non-conformism to its norms has often translated into degrees of marginalisation and even of loss of freedom, if not life. Deviation or non-conformism to the vernacular narrative, one which is far from being naturalised as the dominant ideology or praxis of political power, has, from the margins of political power, but not of public discourse, been no less punitive and oppressive. Its practice of *tajhīl* (relegation to the realm of pagan ignorance) or *takfīr* (relegation to the realm of unbelief) is emblematic of its oppressive *modus operandi*. Both then are noted for their fixity and singularity, which cannot but augur ill for democratic politics.

What is certain in the jostling between these two rival narratives is their non-neutrality. Hence their non-neutral political languages. Therefore, one point to note in looking at the relationship of language and power is that language is never neutral. In this context language cannot be separated from reality as the positivists tend to think.[107] Both Shapiro and Fairclough, following Foucault, observe that the use of language is determined by discourse. That is what Foucault calls "orders of discourse". Orders of discourse refer to, or recognise, interdependent networks of discourses and the structure

107 Michael Shapiro, *Language and Political Understanding* (Michigan: UMI Out-Of-Print Books on Demand, 1981), p. 24.

of these discourses. One example of a discourse is that of the policeman/witness relationship given by Fairclough. Here the discourse structures the relationship, with the police dominating the interview, often cutting the witness off in mid-sentence, in order to extract the relevant information. The discourse in this instance allows the policeman to dominate and requires the witness to submit.[108] What this indicates is that discourse often distributes power to one party over another—at the same time that it engenders empowerment it engenders disempowerment. Shapiro gives another example of how the professional discourses of medicine or law allocate control to doctors or legal practitioners and deny them to their clients.[109] In this sense, "discursive practices" are considered "political practices".[110] In the same vein, Fairclough argues that the orders of discourse are ideologically restructured by the dominant societal powers in order to preserve their domination. He remarks:

> Orders of discourse embody ideological assumptions, and these sustain and legitimise existing relations of power. If there is a shift in power relations through social struggle, one can expect transformation of orders of discourse. Conversely, if power relations remain relatively stable, this may give a conservative quality to reproduction.[111]

Consideration of wording and worlding is essential not only for understanding the dynamics of power allocation and denial, but also for the purpose of making political analysts and theorists take language more seriously, argues Shapiro. For, he reasserts the Foucauldian idea that discursive practices must not be regarded as "denotional tools for discovering aspects of experience". Rather, he adds, they are "representations" of power relations.[112] Foucault takes discursive practices as his primary unit of analysis. They are the practices which determine what is legitimate knowledge, action and so forth. As Shapiro notes, they

> [D]elimit the range of objects that can be identified, define the perspectives that one can legitimately regards as knowledge, and constitute certain kinds of persons as agents of knowledge, thereby establishing norms for developing conceptualisations that are used to understand the phenomena which

108 Norman Fairclough, *Language and Power* (London: Longman, 1989), p. 18.
109 Shapiro, *Language and Political Understanding*, p. 23.
110 Ibid., p. 129.
111 Fairclough, *Language and Power*, p. 40.
112 Shapiro, *Language and Political Understanding*, p. 140.

> emerge as a result of the discursive delimitation…When we…review the set of constructs relating to conduct…in a language, we are viewing…the horizons of possible speech [and]…of possible actions. The possibilities of action, then, exist in the language of a culture, and the actions that actually emerge are presented as a result of the controlling interpretations, those with general legitimacy.[113]

Words and their masters create worlds. Revelation has done so for millennia. So has philosophy. The humanist narrative of civilisationism and progress extended the coloniscrs' grasp over global power and reduced their colonised subjects to misrepresented contrasts. By putting the "goods" of their discursive practices—modernism, liberty, democracy, development, progress, nationalism, secularism—in the minds and lives of their subjects, they reordered the worlds around them by expanding their power at the expense of their subjects. The categories of powerful and powerless they created through their discursive practices destabilised the indigenous discursive scene. The inheritors of the colonial discursive practice have grasped the colonisers' lesson in the control and denial of power through words. Thus they set out to assign the secular-national project a discursive function for the valorisation of the "goods" of modernism and progress, essentially indigenising the structures of domination and the knowledge practices informing them. As wording became Westernised, worlding became oppressive of and disempowering to the vernacular narrative.

The secular-national discourse takes recourse to the Western model, its institutions, proceduralism and developmentalism. The vernacular discourse reverts to the example of the forebears. The former leans towards "Western-ism", seeking to emulate the West and model polity, society and economy on European and North American examples. The latter leans towards atavism, attempting to re-enact the irrecuperable Medinan model of the seventh century. These two dominant narratives are not merely pitted against each other, but also, and increasingly, they are at variance with a variety of syncretic and hybrid discursive practices which are increasingly asserting themselves—women's struggles, anti-authoritarian solidarities and other new social movements, religious and secular. These emerging narratives are carving common spaces for dialogism and shared struggles against the extremes of Western-ism and atavism. Definitely, many

113 Ibid., p. 130.

an Islamist and human rights activism can be situated m[illegible] in the problem–solution dialectic characteristic of the binary polarity between the avid Westernisers and their rival traditionalists.

The discursive terrain is thus becoming polyglossic. In the midst of the ongoing *tahāfut* of these discursive practices, words map out, construct and order worlds of imaginings, being, thinking and acting. Through them reality is made and remade, new and old narratives are interpreted and meanings are assigned. Democracy within this *tahāfut* is either transcribed as an essential item of civility and progress that must be emulated, rendered as "alien" and, subsequently, rejected, something atavistic knowledge practices would do, or is reworked by syncretic narratives through readings that tend to be congenial to but critical of both democracy's Western origins and of the indigenous cultural and linguistic repertoire.

As a signifier, democracy entered the Arab Middle East through loss of freedom to the colonial powers and afterwards through the emergence of the nation-state system. But by travelling from its Western setting to the Arab Middle East, the signifier got disembodied and its signification got subsequently disembedded. That is true at least of the atavistic and syncretic narratives which interrogate or destabilise original significations according to their imaginings of community and identity. By rejecting democracy, for instance, an atavistic narrative may render democracy as totally alien, relegating it to the realm of "otherness". A syncretic narrative, on the other hand, may seek accommodation and negotiation with both the modern and the traditional. As a signifier, democracy may be assigned a signification that rereads it as equivalent to an existing conceptual resource within the repertoire of tradition. Islamists and secularists converge in this regard. Islamists render democracy as the equivalent of shūrā (consultation); whereas the secularists, such as during the height of Arab socialism in the 1960s and 1970s, read socialism in Islam. For the Westernisers, and with the benefit of hindsight of more than 40 years of independence, democracy has served no more than a rhetorical device to exclude the "enemies" of democracy, of progress and of national unity.

Hence words delineate discursive boundaries which cut up and create worlds. These worlds are set apart by divergent knowledge practices, modes of identification, imagining of politics, moral systems and their underpinning ideals. Words can serve to stress uniqueness or accentuate commonality; they can also cement self-imagining to a long by-gone past or connect them to a more recent one. By way of signification, modernity and tradition become forms of referencing or filters for rendering and reading all sorts of signifiers, especially in a globalising world where the travel of such signifiers covers vast areas in relatively short time. Democracy is one of those signifiers the signification of which is bound to yield many readings in a variety of multicultural and multilinguistic settings. Like any global "good", once departed from its original setting, it becomes open to endless and relentless filtering, rendering, deconstructing, rethinking or contesting before it is brought to life again either as an assimilated or disowned item. From this perspective, to say that words cut up or create worlds is to say not only that identity is inextricably linked to language, but also that identity is linguistically constituted. Thus Charles Taylor grounds human agency and identity in language.[114] That is, the narratives that result from them as well as beliefs and values that weave them into human existence and identity.

Filtering precedes appropriation, assimilation or rejection. By filtering is meant a reading of imports (such as "democracy") through the filters of tradition or modernity. In this process, democracy gets delocalised from the global "market" of ideas, and then filtered before it is localised. Just as the process of filtering begins with vetting delocalised "goods", that of localisation ends with authorisation and legitimation of the newly-acquired "goods" often with new meanings. But rejectionism can be another outcome. This only serves to stress the point that globalisation, namely, the diffusion of democratic discourses, is not a one-way flow. Delocalised "goods" or "ideas" are filtered through local conventions and norms as well as the indigenous vernacular and they are authorised in a way that accords with them. But being largely diglossic societies, the process of filtering in the Arab Middle East is two-fold. One form of filtering is incubated in the matrix of religious, cultural and linguistic tradition. In the Arab world, the main claimants of the mantle of tradition are the voices of resurgent Islam and Arabophony. Often after going through the filter of this tradition, democracy is syncretically read as *shūrā* and consensus is read as *ijmāʿ*, and so forth. The second filter is that of "Anglophony" or "Francophony", the forces of Westernisation and the inheritors of the postcolonial state. Through their filter,

114 Charles Taylor, *Human Agency and Language* (Cambridge University Press, 1996).

democracy is often read as proceduralism. Having set themselves on a supposedly linear course of progression toward emulating or replicating the goals of the Western "miracle", Westernising elites read delocalised goods—development, democracy, nationalism—filtered through their own matrix of political and ideological conventions as antitheses of readings through the filter of Arabophony. Thus the binary oppositions, differentiating Occident from Orient, democracy from despotism, and reason from religion, which characterise the globally-hegemonic discursive practices of Western Humanism, exist in microcosmic forms in many a local scene in postcolonial societies.

The study of Arab and Middle Eastern politics not only lags behind theoretically but also linguistically. Students in the field have almost invariably paid little or no attention to language. The language of Western social science cannot be assumed to be always adequate to address political, social and economic phenomena in the region. It is neither unproblematic nor neutral, that is, value-free or apolitical. Democracy or pluralism, for instance, have come to occupy a central place in recent political and social discourse on the Arab world. They are accepted in general language as concepts, notions and ideas needing no special explanation. Yet there is ample evidence to the contrary from different Arab contexts.

Three caveats regarding the problem of setting out Arabic terms in English are in order. First, certain terms and phrases defy accurate translation. These terms are set down in transliteration, presenting them at their first appearance with a periphrastic translation. There are many phrases and Arabo-Islamic concepts where any English term would sacrifice the semantic richness of the original. Second, there is the problem of the deceptive appearance of neologisms and calques. Even direct calques must not be expected to give direct equivalence to their European counterparts—they take on a life of their own in Arabic. For example, the term *dīmuqrāṭiyyah* itself does not have the same resonance as its Western referent, the semantics of which it is supposed to carry.

Third, there is the metaphorical and etymological environment of Arabic words which can never be conveyed through translation. Many political terms in everyday use in English are drenched in Western metaphors, deriving especially from the Greek. "Government" refers to the rudder of a ship. The entire complex of metaphors deriving from "the ship of state" has no corresponding metaphors in

Arabic. The Arabic term *siyāsah* in its origin refers to the grooming of horses. This is mentioned simply to underline the problems in rendering Arabic political writings in English.

The term *dīmuqrāṭiyyah* is a straight calque from the French (*démocratie*) or English (democracy). Strangely, however, the term was not calqued until the nineteenth century. Nor was it a direct transfer from the Greek, given that medieval Arab and Muslim philosophers manifested a deep interest in Hellenic philosophy, especially through the translations of some of the works by Aristotle and Plato, for instance. Greek philosophy influenced the "Muslim mind", encouraging the deployment of the tools of "reason" as opposed to the scriptural sources in all sorts of *taḥqīqāt* (analyses). The term *dīmuqrāṭiyyah* is a gerund whose voice (active or passive) and aspect (complete or incomplete) is underdetermined. This is owed to one of the plasticities of Arabic that it can take any word. The introduction of *dīmuqrāṭiyyah* to Arabic is significant in three ways. First, it indicates, at least obliquely, a perceived lack in the Arabic lexicon. Secondly, this is strange historically given the equations put forward for democracy and *shūrā*. Thirdly, with its introduction it has to jostle with concepts like *ijmāʿ*, another hotly-disputed item in the lexicon.

The concepts "Islamism", "secularisation", "secular" and "Middle East" must also be considered in order to settle on workable definitions. Despite the wide use of the latter, "no standard boundary delimitation exists by which a 'Middle East' region can be precisely located geographically".[115] Simply put, "Middle" of where? "East" of what? The term is applied freely by various disciplines—for anthropologists it is "a culture area extending from Morocco to Timbuktu".[116] More importantly, it is a nineteenth-century Western coinage, and inevitably a political term. The term "Arab Middle East" (AME) will, for the lack of a better term, recur in this book to refer to the Arab regional subsystem (all members of the Arab League) and who "are bound by geographic contiguity and who share similar linguistic, cultural, historical and social properties".[117] But its use must not be read as one way of hiding or overlooking the Arab world's diversity. The concluding chapter attends to the fluidity and

115 Fawaz A. Gerges, "The Study of Middle East International Relations: A Critique", *British Journal of Middle East Studies*, 18 (1991), p. 209.

116 Ibid.

117 Ibid., p. 210.

the multilayered nature of identity; Arab identity is no exception. Hodgson and Hentsch ascribe many disadvantages to the term "Middle East", vague and ethnocentric respectively. Thus the latter opts for the term "Mediterranean Orient" to refer to the Arab world plus Turkey and Iran.[118] The former uses the more self-explanatory term "Nile to Oxus".[119] Neither is adopted here. "Secularisation" and "secular" are amongst the pathologies of "modernity". Both tend to be elusive for historically they have changed from neutral meanings denoting a demarcation of jurisdictions between the civil and ecclesiastical to ones conveying negative ideas ranging from a rupture and clash between the sacred/religious, on the one hand, and the worldly/secular, on the other. The interpretations and the precepts of the two on questions ranging from ethics to politics seemed indefinitely irreconcilable leading, as Chadwick points out, to the sacking of religion from worldly affairs.[120] This was not the final position as, with the Reformation, religion came to be rehabilitated in mundane affairs, but to a point.[121] "Secularisation" refers to that process of disestablishing religion ideologically and institutionally. Loen describes the whole momentum of secularisation and de-sacrilisation as a "historical process by which the world is de-divinised".[122]

In the Arabo-Islamic setting, as Piscatori notes, a "*de facto* secularism has often developed in Islamic history".[123] But the notion of secularism under the Abbasyds as well as the Umayyads has recently been questioned and debunked in Muhammad Qasim Zamman's *Religion and Politics under the Early ʻAbbāsyds*.[124] Generally, Islam has been interpreted in simplistic terms of "traditionalism" and "anachronism" positing it against modernisation.[125] The position taken in

[118] See Thierry Hentsch, *Imagining the Middle East*, trans. by Fred A. Reed (Montreal and New York: Black Rose Books, 1991), p. xi.

[119] Marshall G.S. Hodgson, *The Venture of Islam: Conscience and History in a World Civilization*, vol. I, *The Classical Age of Islam* (Chicago and London: University of Chicago Press, 1977), pp. 60–2.

[120] See Owen Chadwick, *The Secularisation of the European Mind in the Nineteenth Century* (Cambridge University Press, 1975), p. 17.

[121] Ibid., p. 8.

[122] Arnold E. Loen, *Secularization: Science without God?* (London: SCM Press, 1967), p. 7.

[123] James P. Piscatori, *Islam in a World of Nation-States* (Cambridge University Press, 1988), p. 117.

[124] Muhammad Qasim Zamman, *Religion and Politics under the Early ʻAbbāsyds: The Emergence of the Proto-Sunnī Elite* (Leiden and New York: E. J. Brill, 1997), pp. 70–118.

[125] Ibid.

this book neither considers religion to be an antiquated worldview nor that it "stultifies public life and that modernity, or the process of development, requires secularism".[126] With regard to the debate about secularisation in the AME, the view adopted here is that it should not be a "stark choice of 'Mecca or mechanisation".[127] Secular models (Marxist and Liberal) are being questioned in a world where re-sacralisation of polity, society and economy in many parts of the world is manifesting itself via revivalist phenomena ranging from Christian tele-evangelisms, liberal theology, Sikh activism to Arab Islamisms.[128] Therefore secularisation or secularism, be they atheistic or anti-religion, are rejected here. They are not understood here in terms of a dichotomy or hostility between the religious and the secular—that they are mutually exclusive. By "secular" and "secularisation" is meant the neutral and non-antagonistic separation of religion and politics.[129]

Coming only late to the AME, antagonism between the religious and the secular has unfolded with Western secularist paradigms in sectors of the social sciences based on deterministic and evolutionary premises whereby modernisation, industrialisation and urbanisation render religion either irreversibly redundant or privatised. No term in Arabic has existed to describe the phenomenon of the separation of the religious and the secular. The term *'almāniyyah* is a neologism coined in the late-nineteenth century in response to the French term "*laïcisme*", appearing first in the dictionary *Muḥīṭ Muḥīṭ* written by a Christian Lebanese teacher, Bouṭrous al-Bustānī.[130] *'Almāniyyah* as

126 Ibid., p. 118.

127 Ibid.

128 Revival and revivalism are defined in a variety of ways. Piscatori notes that it "would be misleading if their use implied that Muslims have only recently rediscovered their faith and dusted off the Quran…In addition the idea of revival would be misleading if it implied that the more pronounced zeal and visibility of Muslims today are novel." See Piscatori, *Islam in a World of Nation-States*, p. 24. J.C. Vatin, quoted by Emmanuel Sivan, describes Islamic revivalism as "An evident regeneration of culture, a profound renewal of religiosity, a political exploitation of the Islamic vocabulary that use it to reinforce their legitimacy and strengthen their power, and a use of religion by a political opposition that is often left with no other means of expression." See his *Radical Islam: Medieval Theology and Modern Politics* (New Haven: Yale University Press, 1985).

129 'Abd-Allah Nu'mān, *Al-ittijāhātu 'l-'almāniyyah fī 'l-'ālami 'l-'Arabī* [*Seçular Trends in the Arab World*] (Junih, Lebanon: Dar Nu'man li 'l-Thaqafah, 1990), pp. 13–15.

130 Ibid., p. 13.

a descriptive nomenclature lacks in precision for being a neologism for a borrowed European idea. Etymologically, there is no Arabic verb root for *'almāniyyah*—"*'almana*", the word for "secularise", is non-existent in Arabic (it has been derived from *'ālam* (world).

ABOUT THIS BOOK

The enterprise at hand aims to capture an excitingly historical moment in Arab societies. There seems to be a momentum spear-headed by reforming "publics" within and without ruling elites which is directed at steering Arab societies towards more open polities. This more recent momentum is relatively less xenophobic and more engaging with ideas of and by the "other" than its predecessors. Its diminishing cultural autarchy is manifest in the wide appeal the ideal of democratic government enjoys amongst reforming publics, secular or religious, and statist or societal. This is not to say that "deterritorialisation" has replaced "territorialisation" in the realms of culture or knowledge. Rather, at this historical moment there seems to be greater confidence to engage with the question of "democracy", and share in its ideal and experience. Through this boldness, even from religious actors, authenticity, identity, and polity are being reconfigured and reimagined without excessive fear of cultural dissolution or dilution. The oppositions and dichotomies have not completely disappeared; but the search for democracy in the Arab Middle East is fervid.

This should come as no surprise. At the turn of the new century, the Arab Middle East is not out of step with history: mobile telephones and satellite dishes can be found in desert dwellings; the internet—even deep in the North African Sahara, *les bureaux d'informatique* and *les publinets* such as in Tunisia are mushrooming; millions of non-Arab expatriates live in the Arab Gulf and close to 20 million Arab expatriates or Western citizens of Arab backgrounds live in Europe, South and North America and in Australasia; and the Arab region is more plugged into the international economy than ever before with three Arab countries (Egypt, Morocco and Tunisia) having separate association agreements with the European Union and with others seeking similar arrangements. Nothing therefore can reverse the migratory and cross-fertilisation tides of peoples and ideas. Democracy and democrats are unstoppable. The official and unofficial, religious and secular "publics" that are today enmeshed in the search for good government realise that without democratic rule they will remain delegitimised (state actors) or powerless (non-state actors). This historical moment in this region coincides with an equally exciting moment of flux with respect to the kind of knowledge practices that animate ideas, ideals and strategies about political community, identity and authority globally. More importantly, it is a moment in which "fixity" in every sense of the term is being challenged. In late modernity, fixity, whether as meanings of permanence, rigidity, immutability, invariability or of singularity cannot cohabitate with the democratic ethos of indeterminacy. Not even democracy itself can pretend to be democratic if it continues to be imagined as "fixed": a project that is animated only by monoculturally post-Enlightenment dogmas (individualism, secularism); and one that presupposes the presence of certain market preconditions. In this moment of indeterminacy, the study of democracy and democratisation in the Arab Middle East foregrounds many important questions.

This book comprises eight chapters. This introductory chapter and the next seek to capture the contestability of democracy by way of unpacking its many renderings and by looking at how it is being defoundationalised. This defoundationalising has some analogue in objectified Islam. This theme is explored in chapter 2 to show that the coincidence of the refashioning of democracy as an anti-foundationalist ethos and of Islam as communicative tradition with ample potentialities for renewal bodes well for good government. The question of foundationalism represents the focal point of analysis in this chapter. It looks at foundationalist and anti-foundationalist and post-foundational inputs into the democratic debate. This is necessitated by the linguistic and cultural complexities of applying democracy and the democratisation paradigm to non-Western settings. Against the backdrop of the cultural and civilisational hubristic contestations and debates, Western and Arabo-Islamic, it works out an understanding of democracy in which culture and democracy stand a good chance of becoming mutually reinforcing rather than mutually exclusive. Central to that understanding is that the ethos of democracy with its indeterminacy rejects a fixed and single source of power, creating potentialities for defoundationalising democracy and pluralising its interpretation and adoption globally. Sensitivity to cultural specificity must not disown or compromise democracy; and sensitivity to democracy must not translate into it being a "fixed" framework, that is, an exclusionary and an ethnocentric project. In a multicultural world democracy must be diffuse.

Chapters 3 and 4 should be read in conjunction. Here analysis turns to questions of discursive formations of democracy in the Occident and in the Orient. The discussions of democracy in these two chapters, respectively on Occidentalist and Orientalist representations, are important debates underlying not only the question of democracy but also the overarching project of modernity and the encounter between West and East. Chapter 3 attends to the proposition that "Occidentalism" is the complement of "Orientalism", with the aim of exploring the linkage between processes of Orientalisation and Occidentalisation. It looks at constructions and images of the "West" and "democracy" in Islamist discourses. One reason for focusing on this question is to provide a degree of symmetry in the debate about Orientalism. The chapter illustrates Occidentalisations about democracy and the West through extracts from interviews conducted by the author with Islamists. It avoids essentialising Islamists as anti-democratic or anti-Western. One important conclusion is that Islamist Occidentalist modes of discourse are bifurcated, pointing to both fascination with and denunciation of the "West" and of "democracy". Deploying Said's thesis on Orientalism, as a style of Western discourse premised on a feeling of positional superiority, chapter 4 explores Orientalisations about Arabs and Islam with regard to democracy. It highlights the undercurrent of superiority in discourses of democracy and modernity by some Westerners in their relations with their Oriental objects. This it does through the images (such as notions of "Oriental despotism") and the image formulators (from Weber to Huntington). However, Orientalists are not always Western; hence "Oriental Orientalism" is touched upon, showing the discursive linkage and power relations between Westerners and Westernisers.

In any discourse, it is necessary to ask "who is doing the 'speaking', discoursing or representing?" chapters 5, 6 and 7 provide answers to the question of *who* is doing the speaking and *what* they "speak". Arab Middle Eastern peoples must not be abstracted in discussions of democracy. Chapter 5 introduces readers to Arab narratives of good government, past and present, showing that there has been continuous discourse, mostly for, but also against, democracy. Although nuanced, Arab notions and conceptions of democracy point in one direction: the search for *al-dīmuqrāṭiyyatu 'l-ṣaḥīḥah* (genuine democracy). The search for good government from the time of al-Fārābī to the present is shown to have constituted an endless series of efforts to harmonise the Greek *polis* with the Muslim *madīnah* (city), renewal with imitation, reason with revelation, cultural authenticity with modernity, the individual with society and the national with the pan-Arab.

Breaking with the Orientalist conventional wisdom that Arab women are an oppressed lot, silenced and inactive, chapter 6 proves the opposite. It analyses the perspectives of Islamist and secularist women on democracy, with emphasis placed on Islamist female activists a number of whom were interviewed for this work. While bound by the common goal of achieving greater participation in public life and realising a form of "non-gendered" or "degendered" good government, the narratives by these women reveal a kind of diglossia: unlike Islamist women, the democratic ideas and vocabulary of secularist women are represented by loan words, neologisms and direct translations. Generally, the discourse of the secularists is bound to a culture and to a knowledge practice other than the local ones. Islamist activists' discourse is bound to a culture that reveres Islamic values of community, piety, humanity, morality and justice which they claim lay at the heart of their faith.

Chapter 7, which surveys Islamists' inputs on the question of democracy, opens up a new set of vexing questions about the factors that constrain democratic transition. It analyses the extent to which claims can be made that a causal relationship of sorts exists between Western governments' close ties with Arab regimes and the persistence of authoritarian rule. Evaluation of the history of involvement by a number of Western powers in the Arab Middle East points to its subversive effects on the democratisation of the Arab world. Today the connection between Arab autocrats and Western democrats is stronger rather than weaker. The second segment of this chapter examines the specific role of the West (i.e. governments and interests of both the United States and Europe) in helping create conditions for democratic development. Here attention is given to Islamist perspectives on external relations with the West in the quest for good government and improved human rights in the AME. Contemporary Islamists tend to follow the same itinerary as earlier Islamist reformers, rejecting all Western political interference in this region.

The last chapter asserts that the possibility toward a new being, communication across difference and a shared space between islams and democracies emerges by moving from fixed and single tests to contests and from text to context.

On both normative and descriptive grounds, it can be said that democracy is contested. Marx called it capitalist democracy. *Economic democracy* was considered the remedy. Pareto held that democracy was no more than a sham which he called *plutodemocracy*.[131] According to another perspective, there is some validity in the view that some democracies are *dysfunctional*, having the form but not the substance.[132] This, however, does not imply duplicating the defects of democracy by Arabs searching for good government. Nor should it mean developing a capitalist or industrial-based democracy. Most importantly, it should mean engaging in their own contestation of democracy at a time when Islam itself is in the midst of a dynamic process of contestation and renewal, as shall be argued in the next chapter. Only through questioning and revising can the twin search for democracy and Islamicity lead to cultural pluralism and syncretism. Questioning and revising is inherently democratic as well as Islamic. Only thus will Muslims and Arabs owe a new basis for renewal and dialogism with the West and Western democracy to their capacity to open up common spaces with the "other" and create sites for continuous contestation, unfixity, multipolarity and political pluralism.

131 Vilfredo Pareto, *The Transformation of Democracy* (New Brunswick: Transaction Books, 1984); see also S.E. Finer, "Pareto and Pluto-Democracy: the Retreat to Galapagos", *The American Political Science Review*, 62 (June 1968), pp. 440–50.

132 Maurice Rotstein, *The Democratic Myth* (Florham Park Press, 1983), p. 9.

2

DEFOUNDATIONALISING DEMOCRACY AND THE ARABO-ISLAMIC SETTING

> "For fourteen centuries Islam has shown unequal capacity for renewal. But renewal in Islam will always depend on the capacity of Muslims to think anew, keep on thinking and rethinking, and to never give up on keeping to think." —Ḥasan al-Turābī[1]

Certainty is up for grabs. With the paradigmatic crisis in the field of knowledge, Western modernism has come a full circle. The revolutions in industrialisation, science, theology and politics over the last 200 years were engineered to yield certainty and security. Today, modernity has entered a phase of uncertainty and insecurity. By engendering a historical moment of equivocation, ambivalence, contingency and indeterminacy, the paradigmatic crisis has created an opening for emancipation from the *logos* of logos, form, fixity, hierarchy and determinacy. In other words, this historical moment entails liberation from Eurocentrism, phallocentrism and ethnocentrism. Indeed, this opening for emancipation and decentering presents an opportunity, a space of contestation in which ideas are shut out. The available space of contestation permits a continuously self-critical and self-invalidating process. It is a space of contestation as much as it is a contested space. It is within this space and at this particular historical moment that the question of democracy in a non-Western setting can be considered more critically and more creatively than ever before. For, it is possible to discuss democracy without cementing it to a particular form, a *logos*, a master code, a grand narrative, a mastery of truth, an origin or a determined structure. In fact, the floundering of secure knowledge and the interrogation of Enlightenment discourses have opened up the momentous space of contestation.

[1] Author's interview with Ḥasan al-Turābī, 14 May 1994, Khartoum.

This very space of contestation has engendered a discursive dispersal. Just as secure anchors of knowledge-making produce insecurity and voicelessness of marginal voices, the insecurity of such anchors leads to security of the formerly peripheral voices. With the increasing undoing of binary oppositions, the "other" is no longer located in inferior anitheses to a centre or imaged as the inferior contrast of an Occident, Phallos, or *logos*. Hence the emerging politics of recognition and of identity through which identities are rebuilt, vocalness is restored, and the meanings of justice, participation, equality, democracy, community are recodified. Within and through these acts of rebuilding, recreation and recodification the capacity to be, do and think non-foundationally—outside foundations—is won. Like gays, blacks and women, the voices and struggles from within Islam can carve a terrain within the contested space of contestation. These voices and struggles from within Islam allow a rethink of Islam. Thus the rethinking of democracy becomes synchronous with a rethinking of Islam. This intersection of contestation and rethinking presents the Arabo-Islamic setting, as it is argued below, with a previously unavailable choice to realise good government.

The debate over democracy has concentrated on its concern for genuine political participation, pluralist social space, accountability, and the rule of law, amongst other criteria, as fundamental principles that need to be evident if democracy is to be anything other than the shallow rhetoric it has become in so many parts of the world. Another dimension to democracy that contemporary scholars, such as Claude Lefort, have emphasised is the absolutely fundamental condition of democracy's existence.[2] This is the proposition that, above all, democracy is a space of radical contingency. Democracy exists where there is an indeterminacy of power[3]—where power can never be owned by any particular individual, hereditary group, political party or organisation. Democracy is the space where power is an absence rather than a presence[4] and where politics actually takes place and political power is up for grabs. Democracy, in other words, is always a contingent space—a space where change is possible and

2 Claude Lefort, *Democracy and Political Theory*, trans. by David Macey (Cambridge: Polity Press, 1988). David Campbell is one of the first scholars to apply Lefort's work on democracy in his fine work, *National Deconstruction: Violence, Identity, and Justice in Bosnia* (Minneaolis: University of Minnesota Press, 1998), pp. 195–208.

3 Ibid., Lefort says democracy "preserves indeterminacy", p. 16. Also see p. 19.

4 Ibid., ch. 1, "The Question of Democracy", pp. 9–20.

where it takes place. If this criterion of democracy as an ethos can be met, then there can be optimism about the prospects for democratic governance in the Arab world as well as in other regions. This understanding of democracy as an ethos against fixity and foundations as well as space of indeterminacy goes beyond some Western structural model. Anyone can claim democracy on this modelled basis, by establishing a parliament and having elections from Mauritania to Kuwait. But refiguring and rethinking democracy as an anti-foundationalist ethos and a contingent space makes the issue of democracy more complex but more meaningful for a work on good government in an Arabo-Islamic setting. Thus rethought and reimagined, democracy cannot be claimed to be Western per se; nor can it be claimed to belong to any one culture or people. This chapter seeks to fit the empirical circumstances of the Arabo-Islamic setting into this kind of definitional thematic. But first, some unpacking of foundationalism is in order.

FOUNDATIONALISM

The evolution of democracy, its globalisation and widespread appeal and potential for adoption undermines the case of cementing its ideal and practice to fixed foundations. Democracy is, amongst other things, distinguishable for its tremendous ability to evolve, develop and change. Certainly, it has altered a great deal since the Greek *polis*. If democracy itself is congenial to change, it is then contradictory for foundationalists to keep on pressing the case for a fixed democracy. Democracy is no longer sacralised; at least, not unconditionally. This is as much true of discourses of democracy by Western theorists and intellectuals as of non-Western theorists and intellectuals. Many of the deep-rooted dogmas of democracy—secularism, capitalism, individualism, and nationalism—are being challenged. Hence the tendency of post-foundationalist and anti-foundationalist discourses to eschew understandings and interpretations of democracy in Western foundations, that is, the dogmas that have for so long underpinned most readings of democracy. Finding a middle path between the fixity and essentialism of foundationalism and the fluidity and relativism of anti-foundationalism, and between the claims of universalism and of particularism, is a challenge for political theorists. Certainly, it is no easy assignment for discourse formulators in many parts of the South, including the Arab world, where the urgency for entering the twenty-first century with revitalised political systems is most pressing.

As Gould puts it, foundationalism "take[s] human beings to have a fixed and innate essence" whereas anti-foundationalism allows for "the possibility of any normative and critical standpoint".[5] The approach favoured here dissents from outright foundationalism and outright relativism. No credible view of or quest for democracy in the Arab world or anywhere else can be taken seriously without some normative standpoint. However, a normative standpoint should not mean overlooking, for instance, cultural specificity. Whilst no democracy makes much sense without accepting freedom or rule of law, other democratic western standard categories, such as secularism, must be rethought in societies where pervasive religiosity contradicts with the privatisation of religion as in the West; where the "death of God" has no historically philosophical analogue; and where the onslaught of modernisation has riefied rather than displaced tradition.

Foundationalism refers to an ahistorical framework assuming certainty and incorrigibility in defining and justifying a "given", a "logos", an "essence", or a "basic premise". This is particularly so when it comes to distinguishing, for instance, the ethical from the unethical, the rational from irrational, the true from false; or when it comes to establishing what constitutes knowledge and what does not.[6] Foundationalism is derived from fifth-century Greek thinking posited on the idea that beyond the historical, political, cultural, and linguistic there is an essential principle which asserts an irreducible foundation for theory and practice. It emerged first in the Platonic discourse in which Plato asserts that the world needs to be understood in a duality

[5] Carol Gould, *Rethinking Democracy: Freedom and Social Cooperation in Politics, Economy and Society* (Cambridge University Press, 1988), p. 27.

[6] One useful definition states that "Foundationalist theories of knowledge have generally been taken to hold that if there is any knowledge at all, there is at least some knowledge with a special status. Generally, such knowledge may be called foundational." See Robert Audi, "Foundationalism and Epistemic Dependence", *Journal of Philosophy*, 77 (1980), p. 612. Another definition proposes that "Foundationalism is the view that there are epistemically privileged 'basic' propositions which confer justification upon all other empirical propositions which are justified for a person. The classical version of the theory maintains that these basic propositions are epistemically certain and are about what is given to a person through sensory experience." See Timm Triplett, "Rorty's Critique of Foundationalism", *Philosophical Studies*, 52 (1987), p. 115.

of forms—material and immaterial; unalterable objects of knowledge and alterable judgements about such objects. Plato's equation of knowledge with true judgement (reached in his *Theaetus*) resonates with the kind of logocentrism found today in many Western epistemological practices. The history of foundationalism, the belief that there is a "basic truth" which underpins, and is prior to, all knowledge, and upon which all other knowledge rests, can also be traced back to Aristotle in his *Posterior Analytics*.[7]

With regard to the present, foundationalism is understood as an essentially discursive principle upon which have been built contemporary perspectives like positivism (note how positivism replicates fifth-century Platonic dualisms). It has become increasingly dominant as Western philosophy became captured by modern science, framing modern science to be the sole arbiter of truth—foundational knowledge. Modern foundationalism in Western political thought has its origin in Descartes. Its assumptions hold that there is a "reality", or a realm of objective knowledge or truth, which exists externally to the observer. Furthermore, this reality can be made knowable to human beings by a process of rational observation. Descartes' foundationalist assumptions have become embedded in modernity. Bernstein, cited by George, outlines in *Beyond Objectivism and Relativism* that modern thought still resonates with "problems concerning the foundations of knowledge and the sciences, (the) mind–body dualism, our knowledge of the 'external' world, how the mind 'represents' this world, the nature of consciousness, thinking and will, whether physical reality is to be understood as a grand mechanism, and how this is compatible with human freedom".[8] In the assumption of foundational human knowledge lies the paradox of modern political thought, observes George. On the one hand, contemporary knowing and knowledge-making celebrates and exalts modernity for progressively liberating them from the shackles of tradition—e.g. "the primitive premodern world (and its idealism and metaphysics)". On the other,

[7] According to Siffler, "For Aristotle, scientific knowledge requires demonstration; but the premise of demonstrated knowledge must be primary…[emphasising the notion of an] 'appropriate basic truth'. A basic truth, Aristotle goes on to say, is an 'immediate proposition' or a proposition 'which has nothing prior to it'." See Eric Siffler, "A Definition of Foundationalism", *Metaphilosophy*, 15 (1984), p. 16.

[8] Richard Bernstein, *Beyond Objectivism and Relativism: Hermeneutics and Praxis* (Oxford: Basil Blackwell, 1983), quoted in Jim George, *Discourses of Global Politics: A Critical (Re) Introduction to International Relations* (Boulder, CO: Lynne Rienner, 1994), p. 49.

they remain captive to the past, operating within the foundationalist framework of fifth-century Greek thinking (*status quo ante*), namely, "the assumption that there *is* a foundation for human knowledge, prior to and beyond history, culture and language".[9]

Kantian philosophy contributed a great deal to the confidence and dogmatism of foundationalism. As Rorty puts it: "We owe the notion of philosophy as a tribunal of pure reason, upholding or denying the claims of the rest of the culture, to the eighteenth century and especially to Kant."[10] In the nineteenth century, Rorty further adds, neo-Kantian works consolidated Kant's kinship with the grounding of all knowledge claims in philosophy.[11] One of three influential discursive variants George accredits Kant with having contributed to social theory, directly or indirectly, is objectivism (the other two being what is called "positivist humanism" and Marxist political radicalism). Through this objectivism Kant dedicates part of his philosophy to the search "for a logical foundation for knowledge in a dualised world of sovereign subjects and 'things in themselves'".[12]

If foundationalism—Platonism, Descartes' rationalism, positivism or sciencism—grounds knowledge in universally valid, certain, non-referential, self-evident, self-validating and fixed sets of principles or assumptions, anti-foundationalism rejects such authorisation of knowledge as dogmatic. Anti-foundationalism challenges the notion of a fixed, certain and legitimate basis for knowledge. Thus deconstructed, foundationalism, in its Western contexts, has racist, ethnocentric, sexist and, generally, exclusivist connotations. Principally, the underlying core idea that describes anti-foundationalism is its promotion of relative, referential and, subsequently, non-fixed knowledge. Knowledge is authorised in reference to time, space, language and culture. This renders knowledge a lively organism, one which cannot be fixed or dependent on single or fixed foundations as time, space, language, history and culture are themselves variable. Blake stresses the notion of knowledge as being situational and contextual, relative to the history and society it is constructed within.[13] Rorty notes

[9] George, *Discourses of Global Politics*, p. 43.

[10] Richard Rorty, *Philosophy and the Mirror of Nature* (Princeton University Press, 1979), p. 4.

[11] Ibid., p. 4.

[12] See George, *Discourses of Global Politics*, pp. 55–6.

[13] N. Blake, "The Democracy We Need: Situation, Post-Foundationalism and Enlightenment", *Journal of the Philosophy of Education*, 30 (1996), p. 225.

that "nothing counts as justification unless by reference to what we already accept, and that there is no way to get outside our beliefs, and our language so as to find some test other than coherence".[14]

Perhaps one of the most appealing features of deconstructionist thought and of postmodernism is their advocacy of a knowledge that is, to paraphrase Derrida, centreless, undetermined, non-linear, discontinuous, and open to variable interpretations.[15] Postmodernism has a defoundationalising and pluralising value permeating it, namely, its promotion of respect for difference, which foundationalism, as an exclusivist project, does not permit, and its demotion of universal explanations, which gave the world Orientalism, racism and sexism, amongst other discursive formations used at some time or another to legitimate domination. So, the crisis of knowledge in late modernity is synonymous with a crisis of foundations; that is, the premises, assumptions, and justifications of human practices. This is evident in the writings of leading anti-foundationalists such as Quine, Rorty and Gadamer who are the inheritors of the anti-foundationalist tradition begun by Dewey, Wittgenstein and Heidegger. Drew Christie confirms the indebtedness of the former to the latter.[16] Others like Derrida have contributed greatly to the undermining of foundationalism. Blake observes that Derrida's strategy in this respect has been to demonstrate that "supposedly rational and thus logical uses of language are merely particular cases of the literary and rhetorical use of language".[17] Derrida denudes such a use of any special authority, considering it to be "another contingent linguistic practice". Blake notes that "[f]or Derrida since language does not *represent* reality, its references to it carry no special authority".[18]

But anti-foundationalism itself is not above reproach, nor is it without challenges. Steven Crowell sums up his reproach by using the notion of "dogmatic anti-foundationalism". This he uses to charge anti-foundationalism with the banalisation of inquiry and with foisting new foundations of thought, essentially becoming a neo-foundationalism: "If [it] is right to say that the 'concept of foundations

[14] Rorty, *Philosophy and the Mirror of Nature*, p. 178.

[15] J. Derrida, *Writing and Difference* (University of Chicago Press, 1978).

[16] Drew Christie, "Contemporary 'Foundationalism' and the Death of Epistemology", *Metaphilosophy*, 20 (1989), p. 114. Rorty himself acknowledges this link; see Rorty, *Philosophy and the Mirror of Nature*, p. 6.

[17] Blake, "The Democracy We Need", p. 222.

[18] Ibid., p. 222.

is at the base of all Western thought', and if anti-foundationalists not only question foundations but reject the very notion of foundations, then they find themselves in the situation of Descartes, namely, attempting to stand outside the tradition to think on the basis of... new foundations."[19] But in principle, at least, the opening of a contested space of contestation, being hospitable to self-criticism and inhospitable to singularity, fixity and dogmatism, should safeguard against anti-foundationalism being hijacked by any tendency to foundationalise. The most pressing challenge is how to transcend anti-foundationalism, going beyond the foundationalism–anti-foundationalism binary and the hermeneutics underpinning them. This is pertinent to the debate of defoundationalising democracy and how to go about it. The implications, therefore, of foundationalism and anti-foundationalism to democracy must be elaborated.

The challenge to foundationalism by anti-foundationalists revolves around the claim that knowledge does not need foundations. Transferred to the democratic debate, the question then becomes one of whether democracy needs foundations. This is no easy question as Seyla Benhabib and her co-authors of *Democracy and Difference* demonstrate, polarising the discussion amongst some 20 well-known scholars all of whom are clearly committed exponents of good government, justice, representation of difference, and active citizenship.[20] The arguments they all put forth are compelling. But all these excellent essays, including those accentuating anti-foundationalist tendencies, still propose democratic guarantees such as pluralism, individual or group rights, legality or constitutionalism. In other words, rejecting foundations for democracy is not a rejection of democracy. In explaining the implications of foundationalism and anti-foundationalism for democracy, Rorty distinguishes between "foundations" for and "idealizations" of practices. He writes:

> Idealizations answer the question "How can we make our present practices more coherent?" by downplaying some of the things we do and emphasizing others...Foundations, by contrast, are supposed to answer the question "Should we be engaging in our present practices at all?"[21]

[19] Steven Crowell, "Dogmatic Anti-Foundationalism", *Semiotica*, 110 (1996), p. 362. See also, Eric Stiffler, "A Definition of Foundationalism", p. 20.

[20] Seyla Benhabib (ed.), *Democracy and Difference: Contesting the Boundaries of the Political* (Princeton University Press, 1996).

[21] Richard Rorty, "Idealization, Foundations and Social Practices" in Benhabib (ed.), *Democracy and Difference*, pp. 333–4 (pp. 333–5).

Foundationalists, explains Rorty, believe that political practices must not only be coherent but must also have regard to "something that exists outside of those practices".[22] Rorty unpacks this "something" as being "human nature", "rationality", or "morality". Thus one major difference between idealisations and foundations is the latter's conceiving of an object as "without any special reference to what we are currently doing or hoping". Anti-foundationalism embodies the belief that political practices are not grounded in some objective truth but that they have evolved and may continue to evolve out of the "contingencies of culture and history".[23] As such, practices compete for survival for which the tool of competition is language, used both "to employ persuasion as well as force".[24] Thus, another difference is placing an object above criticism and commendation. For Rorty, to be anti-foundationalist is to understand that the only avenue for criticism or commendation of a social practice is in its "comparison with other actual and possible social practices".[25] Anti-foundationalists understand "human nature", "rationality", or "morality" not as incontrovertible truths that exist outside of actual practice against which the validity of that political practice can be judged, but only as aspects of the practices to be encouraged.[26] Hence Rorty explains that to say that a certain practice accords more with "human nature, or our moral sense or more rational, than another is just a fancy way of commending one's own sense of what is most worth preserving in our present practices".[27]

Whilst the question faced by foundationalists is how to introduce an ever-broadening range of moral and political concerns into the idea of a shared "human nature", the problem faced by anti-foundationalists is how to break with the conventional wisdom that the absence of shared premises enfeebles democracy.[28] One implication of insisting on a shared human nature or foundations is to revert to hegemonic and homogenising practices of universalising particularistic imaginings. The implication of conceiving of "shared premises"

[22] Ibid., p. 333.
[23] Ibid., p. 335.
[24] Ibid., p. 334.
[25] Ibid., p. 333.
[26] Ibid., p. 334.
[27] Ibid.
[28] Ibid., p. 335.

as vital for democratic politics defeats the gist of anti-foundationalism as a contested space of contestation. The idea is to share in continuously contesting and refiguring premises more than in sharing them. In this idea lies a negation of singularity and an affirmation of diversity.

Rorty's notion of "commending one's own sense of what is most worth preserving" or one's "utopian vision of…community" has resonance in Dahl's and Amy Gutman's essays. One interpretation by Dahl, affirming the necessity of democratic foundations is compelling: not having any foundations can play in the hands of non-democratic forces.[29] By foundations he means "a set of reasonable assumptions". These assumptions or criteria serve three purposes: "Providing grounds for believing that democracy is desirable…judging whether and to what extent a given system is democratic, and for judging what political practices and institutions" are essential to meet such criteria.[30] Dahl also stresses the importance of criteria for improving political practices. Gutman defends a two-fold position: democracy requires justifications not foundations and these justifications need be neither foundationalist nor anti-foundationalist.[31] Resting upon neither foundational truths about some notion of human nature, morality or self-evident rationality nor an anti-foundational dogma disregarding philosophical conceptions of human nature, needs or reason that do not accord with what a "democratic cultural community" believes to be democracy,[32] Gutman finds a solution in deliberative democracy. Deliberative democracy, argues Gutman, makes good sense for having advantages over alternative models of democratic politics. The main one is the "provisional nature of justification in politics" owing not only to changes in citizens' "empirical and moral understandings", but also to "deliberative interchange", a process involving both compromise and conflict.[33] Gutman points out how this feature makes deliberative democracy hospitable to difference. "Differences in practices and policies that result from deliberation among an inclusive citizenry are democratically legitimate, even if no one knows whether they are just in the strict

[29] Robert A. Dahl, "Democratic Theory and Democratic Experience" in Benhabib (ed.), *Democracy and Difference*, p. 338 (pp. 336–9).

[30] Ibid., p. 338.

[31] Amy Gutman, "Democracy, Philosophy, and Justification" in Benhabib (ed.), *Democracy and Difference*, p. 340 (pp. 340–7).

[32] Ibid., p. 345.

[33] Ibid., p. 344.

foundational sense."[34] Gutman narrows the scope of justification of deliberative democracy to a free and equal citizenry bound by it, noting that such a justification is defensible on account of the capacity of deliberative interchange to defuse conflicts even if provisionally.[35] Gutman is in effect defending a model of democracy that can be only "provisionally justified" and in which "provisional justifications" are never accorded the metaphysical stature of foundational axioms. Realising that the version of deliberative democracy she defends is itself contestable, like other models, Gutman stresses the urgency of transcending the foundationalism–anti-foundationalism conundrum and the directing of energies toward questions that occupy contemporary politics such as the contest over what kind of democratic politics is most defensible.[36]

Foundationalism through the Arabo-Islamic Prism

The implications for foundationalism and anti-foundationalism for the search for democracy in the Arabo-Islamic world are significant. Foundationalism articulates a rigidity which does not sit well with the globally plural and entrenched cultural differences and loyalties. This fixity on such a rigid position regards democracy to be self-evidently superior, singularly in possession of the kind of reason or morality other cultures are bereft of, leaves no room for a globally and cross-culturally deliberative interchange and exchange or for provisionality, relativity and contingency unique to a contested space of contestation. Anti-foundationalism, be it deconstructionist or pragmatist (e.g. Dewey's position that democracy "needs philosophical articulation" but not "philosophical back-up"),[37] is bold in its cultivation of dialogical interaction with diverse cultural practices and with difference. It declares a position of opposition to the claims of fixity, singularity and self-evidence of the kinds of foundational truths democracy is founded on. In so doing, it rejects ethnocentrism, Eurocentrism and Western cultural imperialism. By taking on the destabilisation of the foundationalist ideal of a presumably immutable

[34] Ibid.

[35] Ibid.

[36] Ibid., p. 347.

[37] Richard Rorty, "The Priority of Democracy to Philosophy" in Alan R. Malachowski (ed.), *Reading Rorty: Critical Responses to Philosophy and the Mirror of Nature (and Beyond)*, (Cambridge, MA, Basil Blackwell, 1990), p. 282.

human nature existing outside political practices or a universally axiomatic and applicable foundational truth, anti-foundationalists are opening possibilities for inclusive and alternative political practices. Their kind of critical reflection pertains to a moment in history in which the highest ideal intelligent democratic politics can hope to achieve is a shared space for contested contestation rather than "shared premises". Rorty quotes Rawls's idea about how conceptions of the good, such as justice, in a democratic community, and for that matter in the global community, "must allow for a diversity of doctrines and the plurality of conflicting, and indeed incommensurable conceptions of the good affirmed by the members of existing democratic societies".[38] The position defended by anti-foundationalists makes even the most foundationalist of Islamists in the Arab region feel very comfortable with sharing the world with the advocates of such views. For, they are views which propose no theses of civilisational "clashes", and have the potential of unhinging prevailing power relations informed by racism and supremacism.

When seen through Muslim or Arab spectacles, foundationalism in the main regards Western self-appointment as the legitimate source of norms of political practice—liberal democracy. This singularity of authorising norms is not uncoupled from the civilising history in which colonial power was cloaked. In Arab and Muslim eyes it bespeaks the plurality of cultural settings, loyalties and identities. This universalisation of Western particularism worries Arabs and Muslims more than any other aspect of Western power projection. But being inheritors of a civilisational heritage in the form of Islam with its own universalist claims, many Arabs and Muslims tend to be dismayed more by the singularity of Western-modelled cultural practices than by democratic foundationalism. There are strong currents that can be readily labelled foundationalist within the Islamic movement in the Arabo-Islamic setting. Knowledge authorising Islamist political practices are manifestly founded on transcendental morality and rationality which are not dissimilar from Western foundationalism. In both, there are assumptions of ahistoricity, atemporality and ordering of thought and practice by appeal to a superior and independent Truth. This links to a second objection against Western foundationalist democratic ideals that is raised in Islamist discourses, for instance. That is, the tendency to universalise with little or no

38 Rawls quoted in Rorty, see ibid., p. 283.

concern for specificity: diverse cultural settings must develop political practices that primarily reflect their locally-authorised and legitimated foundations. The inescapable irony is that whilst practising a form of knowledge and knowledge-making which has strong recourse to transcendence, which exists outside the realm of human experience, Islamists would readily, validate their opposition to Western democratic foundationalism by pointing out its origin in outside experiences, history, culture and language. As such, Western democratic foundational ideals are rejected as a shared premise for modelling political practice locally. Democratic "dogmas" resulting from such foundational ideals, for instance, presuppose secularism and individualism. The truth of the matter is that such dogmas cannot be defended on the basis of axiomatic human nature or superior rationality. As Rawls indicates, political not metaphysical dynamics condition practice and conception. Many of the practices or conceptions routinised and legitimated in the West as democratic "...have their origins in the Wars of Religion following the Reformation and the development of the principle of toleration, and the growth of constitutional government and the institutions of large market economies."[39] This is one significant reason why many Islamist conceptions of democratic government tend to stress proceduralism more than the foundations underpinning them.

THE ETHOS OF DEMOCRACY AND CONTESTATION IN THE ARABO-ISLAMIC SETTING

As mentioned earlier, the current historical juncture is unique in that there is a coincidence of contestation and rethinking within both democracy and Islam. Particularly interesting is the fact that both are being contested and rethought, and that discourses from within democracy are amongst those engaged in rethinking Islam and vice versa. Many voices within Islam are rethinking democracy to appropriate from it those fragments that can be identified as readily readable within tradition. Similarly, concerns from within democratic discourses are being expressed over the plight of Muslims living under authoritarian and Westernising rule and Western-led hegemony. This presents an ideal moment for cross-fertilisation, mutual

[39] Rawls quoted in Rorty, see ibid., p. 283.

understanding as well as self-reflection. In particular, the redefining of democracy in terms of *anti-foundationalist ethos* presents the Arabo-Islamic setting, as it is argued below, with a unique opportunity to realise good government. The question, however, is whether the contesting and rethinking within Islam are sufficiently defoundationalising to allow for a democratic breakthrough. Whilst still preliminary, it will be argued, that such contesting and rethinking provide a potentially coherent gestation that augurs well for good government.

Nothing helps the cause of democratisation in the non-Western world more than the current contesting and rethinking of democracy. Through them, democracy has emerged as an ethos. Here, then, this redefining of democracy interfaces with the global quest for good government in a way that is sensitive to cultural specificities. Democracy shorn of ethnocentricism is likely to be appropriated by those cultural forces that might have otherwise rejected it on the basis of rigid particularism. As an ethos, democracy rejects single foundations, opening possibilities and potentialities for culturally-plural alternatives or variations to Western forms of democracy. With such openings, the fluid space that the Anglo-American paradigm has frozen is reversed. These openings then mark a reversal of dogmatic foundationalism. Such foundationalism has reduced democracy to foundationalist premises, often "Americanising" or "Europeanising" its form and practice. Hence the essentialism of democracy: turning a putatively universalist system into a rigid particularism, making it unpalatable to cultural identities whose memories of the encounter with another form of Western universalism, colonialism, have not yet been put to rest, or at least not fully. Embedded in the redefining of democracy as an *ethos of anti-foundationalism* are the ideas of contingency and indeterminacy. Conceptualised as an ethos embodying principles of a democratic ethic, democracy denotes the opposite of fixity. That is, democracy becomes a space within which change can take place. Unlike other systems which preceded it, the ethos of democracy has no fixed loci of power. Most worthy about the redefining of democracy as an ethos is its capacity to flourish in all kinds of societies. However, there is an essential precondition. For such an ethos to work in any society, there has to be space for contingency, indeterminacy and fluid power relations.

Thus the ethos of democracy in Lefort's thesis stresses at least two significantly intertwined elements: absence of power and indeterminacy. He expresses the former in the notion of "the locus of power becom[ing] an empty place".[40] Absence of power does not entail absence of claimants to power; rather, it means absence of singular holders of power, be they political executors of raw political power, theological exegetes, or juridical experts. Lefort does not ignore democratic proceduralism and institutionalisation of power. He refers to these as the "mechanisms of the exercise of power"; that is, the apparatus that theoretically, at least, should prevent absolutism by political regimes—"incorporating [power] into themselves".[41] More importantly, Lefort reimagines democracy other than as a set of norms, institutions and apparatuses. He decentres the conventional wisdom, or what Connolly calls "congealed standards",[42] which conceptualises democracy as a fixed system of institutionalised principles. Lefort projects a revitalised notion of democratic politics defined as a concern to oppose this fixity of power. In other words, the democratic ethos equates with the concern for a fluidity of power so that no single claimant or contestant, human actors or the ideas, truths, and sets of knowledge from which they derive their hierarchical position in society, can monopolise power. Embedded within this reimagining of democratic ethos is a suspicion of fixed power relations whether they are based on theology, legalism, traditionalism or secular political conventions. To this end Lefort disentangles the sphere of power, the sphere of law and the sphere of knowledge. Through this disentanglement, power is prevented from being cemented to a single sphere, embodied within it and symbiotic with it. Here Lefort disembodies power, literally denuding it of a body as was the case under the medieval theologico-political matrix. Then "power was embodied in the prince, and it therefore gave society a body."[43] People, state and nation become empowered and serve as "the major poles by which social identity and social communality can be signified", presupposing one vital condition. That condition obtains when society, Lefort argues, ceases to be constructed as a "body" and stops being embodied in a single power figure: as is the case today in the AME.[44]

[40] Lefort, *Democracy and Political Theory*, p. 17.

[41] Ibid., p. 17.

[42] William E. Connolly, *The Ethos of Pluralization* (Minneapolis: University of Minnesota Press, 1995), p. xv.

[43] Lefort, *Democracy and Political Theory*, p. 17.

[44] Ibid., p. 232.

Accordingly disentanglement means disembodiment. A body politic without a body embodies the democratic ethos, that is one marked by fluidity not certainty, and by plurality rather than singularity. The corollary is a contested space for contestation:

> [T]he phenomenon of disincorporation…is accompanied by the disentangling of the sphere of power, the sphere of law and the sphere of knowledge. Once power ceases to manifest the principle which generates and organizes a social body, once it ceases to condense within it virtues deriving from transcendent reason and justice, law and knowledge assert themselves as separate from and irreducible to power. And just as the figure of power in its materiality and its substantiality disappears, just as the exercise of power proves to be bound up with the temporality of its reproduction and to be subordinated to the conflict of collective wills, so the autonomy of law is bound up with the impossibility of establishing its essence. The dimension of the development of right unfolds it its entirety, and it is always dependent upon a debate as to its foundations, and as to the legitimacy of what has been established and of what ought to be established. Similarly, recognition of the autonomy of knowledge goes hand in hand with a continual reshaping of the process of acquiring knowledge and with an investigation into the foundations of truth.[45]

Lefort's second notion of indeterminacy can be inferred from the above. The defoundationalising that accompanies his idea of disentanglement makes for a fluid space, one of contingency and indeterminacy. Only in such space can there be contestation and contesting of contestation. With the disembodiment of the body-politic of fixed and singular site of power, democracy is read as a project of continuously renewed provisionalism. Thus, for Lefort, democracy "is instituted and sustained by the *dissolution of the markers of certainty*. It inaugurates a history in which people experience a fundamental indeterminacy as to the basis of relations between *self* and *other*."[46] There is an element of risk in heralding a foundationless order. But the risk of a foundationless order pales when compared with the risk of a totalitarian order. Lefort reclaims a notion of democratic ethos in which power is absent rather than present and uncertainty prevails over certainty against a specific background. This background regards the history of modern totalitarianism under which the three

[45] Ibid., pp. 17–18.

[46] Ibid., p. 19. On "the dissolution of the markers of uncertainty", see p. 20.

spheres of power, law and knowledge are manifested in "condensation", rather than in disentanglement:

A condensation takes place between the sphere of power, the sphere of law and the sphere of knowledge. Knowledge of the ultimate goals of society and of the norms which regulate social practices becomes the property of power, and at the same time power itself claims to be the organ of a discourse which articulates the real as such. Power is embodied in a group and, at its highest level, in a single individual, and it merges with a knowledge which is also embodied, in such a way that nothing can split it apart.[47]

Lefort's explication of condensation is particularly potent. Although in the above quote he refers to a European brand of absolutist politics, the import of what he says applies fully to the Arab body politic. This is one important reason why reconceptualising the democratic ethos as absence of power and indeterminacy has strong application and relevance to the Arab context.

The democratic ethos in Connolly's work, *The Ethos of Pluralization*, is about a refiguring of the "pluralist imagination".[48] This enterprise of refiguring the pluralist imagination is generic to an original meaning of democracy which is being reclaimed by Lefort and Connolly, amongst others. Connolly's own refashioning of the pluralist imagination rejects closures. At the core of this rejection is the revitalisation of the democratic ethos or the "pluralisation of pluralism"—democratising democracy. Thus for Connolly such a revitalisation cannot happen without disturbing the naturalised relation between pluralism and pluralisation existing in conventionally democratic communities. Under the "paradoxical politics of pluralist enactment", pluralism is valued whereas pluralisation is suspect.[49] The former, for Connolly, points to the diversity of old identities and differences which, through processes of interactions and negotiations, give birth to new forms of positive identities as well as bargains for socially, politically and culturally pluralised co-existence. But this self-generating culture of pluralism carries within it dangers to renewed pluralisation. Connolly makes two very important connections to explicate the tension between pluralism and pluralisation under what he describes as "conventional pluralism". They regard

[47] Ibid., p. 13.
[48] Connolly, *The Ethos of Pluralization*, pp. xiii–xv.
[49] Ibid., p. xiv.

the misrecognition of the paradox of pluralism: curtailing pluralism entails limiting pluralisation. The reverse is just as true. He writes:

> [C]onventional pluralism...first misrecognizes the paradoxical relation between a dominant constellation of identities and the very differences through which the constellation is consolidated and, second, misrecognizes new possibilities of diversification by freezing moral standards of judgment condensed from past political struggles. These two patterns of misrecognition install an unconscious conservatism at the centre of the pluralist imagination.[50]

The refashioning of the pluralist imagination is integral to Connolly's own imagining of the democratic ethos. If conventional pluralism is a closure, a refashioned pluralism must, by contrast, be an opening. Closure begets marginalisation.[51] Conventional pluralism, Connolly argues, is bound by rigidly drawn boundaries of territoriality or morality, for instance.[52] Moreover, despite the putative resistance of an organic society founded on the oneness of a God or a rationality, conventional pluralism tends to manifest itself in a form of a quasi theologico-political system. The result is an unconscious captivation by Christian unitarianism: "When secularism is advanced as an alternative to monotheism in public life it often retains a unitarian conception of morality remarkably close in structure to that supported by the Christian faith."[53] Connolly therefore finds conventional pluralism, which thrives on exclusion and regulation, to produce abnormality, anarchy and cruelty. For, it is within the rigidly fixed boundaries of the "normal individual", nationalist territoriality, or of secular or religious morality, that the imaginings of self and other are ordered. It is according to these imaginings, and the presumptions resulting from them about a wide range of issues from national security to sexuality that normality and abnormality, right and wrong, good and bad, and familiar and alien, that conventional plurality becomes embodied in ambiguity as well as in tension between pluralism and pluralisation.[54]

Connolly proposes a way out of this ambiguity through his ethos of critical responsiveness. Through it he sets out to resolve the tension of conventional pluralism and the tension between pluralism and

50 Ibid.
51 Ibid., p. xiii.
52 Ibid.
53 Ibid., p. xiv.
54 Ibid.

pluralisation, hoping, by his own admission, for an ideally, and perhaps not entirely attainable, more generous pluralisation for the purpose of constructing a "new possibility of being".[55] At the core then of an ethos of critical responsiveness is a process of negotiation between dominant identities and newly-emerging ones striving to "cross the threshold of enactment", leading to "modified relations of co-existence".[56] Central to critical responsiveness to new movements of pluralisation is a rethinking of self-recognition for the sake of coming to terms with recognising difference. Hence Connolly's ethos of critical responsiveness makes recognition and, ultimately, toleration of alterity incumbent upon opening up "cultural space through which the other might consolidate itself into something that is unafflicted by negative cultural markings".[57] Again, an ethos of critical responsiveness must not be about recreating the world or otherness in one's own image. Such an ethos then "does not reduce the other to what some 'we' already is".[58]

While recognising that alterity defines identity,[59] Connolly insists that a democratic management of such a paradox must not lead to a conversion of difference into modes of otherness, often via exclusionary and regulative means as can be the case under conventional pluralism.[60] His notion of pluralisation of pluralism therefore sees possibilities in cross-cultural fertilisation away from rigidified claims and counterclaims to "intrinsic identity" or "exclusive morality".[61] He elaborates his democratic ethos, stressing multiplying lines of connection and intersecting constituencies. He notes that

> You do not need a wide universal "we" (a nation, a community, a singular practice of rationality, a particular monotheism) to foster democratic governance of a population. Numerous possibilities of intersection and collaboration between multiple, interdependent constituencies infused by a general ethos of critical responsiveness drawn from several sources suffice nicely.[62]

Further on, he captures the essential meaning of his ethos of critical responsiveness which is vital for democratic ethics which reject

55 Ibid., p. xv.
56 Ibid., p. xvi.
57 Ibid., p. xvii.
58 Ibid.
59 Ibid., p. xx.
60 Ibid., p. xxi.
61 Ibid., p. xx.
62 Ibid.

singularity and fixity. This meaning communicates, even if indirectly, a notion of contingency:

> It pursues an ethic of cultivation rather than a morality of contract or command; it judges the ethos it cultivates to exceed any fixed code of morality; and it cultivates critical responsiveness to difference in ways that disturb traditional virtues of community and the normal individual. It does not present *itself* as the single universal to which other ethical traditions must bow. Rather, it provides a prod and a counterpoint to them, pressing them to rethink the ethics of engagement and, crucially, to rework their relations to the diversity of ethical *sources* that mark a pluralistic culture. Such a Nietzschean ethic resists oligopolistic control over the currency of morality while affirming the indispensability of ethics.[63]

The kind of defoundationalising that Lefort and Connolly engage in intersects in decentring centrism, unhinging exclusivism and in guarding against essentialism. These three "isms" have been epitomised in absolutism, Eurocentrism, sexism, racism, colonialism, Orientalism and Occidentalism, all of which share the dubious distinction of their conversion of difference into modes of otherness. Otherness is produced via fixity in the pole of power; particularistic rationality in the pole of knowledge-making; and exclusivism in the pole of ethics. Fixity or exclusivism are guilty then of contempt for, if not outright hostility to, diversity. It is diversity that the works of Lefort and Connolly celebrate with passion. The result is an equally passionate ethos of democracy that cannot be intrinsically ethical without a newly-refigured politics of difference founded on recognition and toleration of otherness. Conceptualising the democratic ethos as a place of absence or demanding a critical responsiveness towards new movements of pluralisation, both of which are meant to democratise democracy, must begin with undoing fixity. Nothing is fixed except for renewed provisionalism, and a fluid space of contingency—continuously contested contestation. What is particularly refreshing and challenging about this refashioning and rethinking of democracy is not only the opening of new possibilities of being, thinking and doing, but also of rescuing democracy from banalisation and routinisation, the perilous routes treaded by conventional pluralism. Banalisation is noticeable in the way democratic practice in many countries has to a large extent been sapped of all creativity with democracy becoming reduced to proceduralism. This is particularly relevant to

[63] Ibid., p. xxiv.

the experiments with democracy in the AME. Routinisation is evidenced in the degeneration of what was meant to be an emancipatory project into a regulatory *modus operandi.* If Lefort finds it necessary to empty the locus of political power from single claimants or holders and Connolly insists on the introduction of otherness into it, it is because of their realisation that an ethos of democracy requires diversity not unity. Thus in their rethinking of democracy, Lefort and Connolly call into question notions of oneness, uniformity and unity to guard against otherness becoming reducible to a homogenising and hegemonising "us". Their ethos of democracy requires a degree of diffusion not fusion, plurality not uniformity and of non-conformism not conformism. For, democratic consensus is always forged through conflict, and conflict renews democracy, making it an endless process of periodically provisional bargains that are constantly negotiated in contexts of human diversity as well as of spatial and temporal variability.

A shallow reading of Islam and of Islamic history would, in light of the above, lead to misconceptions that are bound to translate the future partnership of Islam and democracy in disjunctive rather than conjunctive terms. The library of ahistorical scholarship that reduces Islam to an essence of sorts or to a totalitarian order has grown exponentially. But the pessimistic forecasting of a climate of inhospitality by Islam to democracy not only ignores history, but also misreads democracy. Because democracy has always been narrowly defined with emphasis on the procedural, Islam's democratic potential has largely been reduced to vague associations with *shūrā, ijmāʿ*, or *bayʿah* (oath of allegiance). Both Orientalists and Occidentalists are guilty of this essentialism. All three intellectual artefacts, which are respectively translated into equivalents for parliamentary power-sharing arrangements, a form of consensual order, and elections, do not on their own do justice to correlating Islam with democracy. The vital test is whether consultative or electoral processes are closed or open. The more closed they are, the less likely they are to enable good government. Openness opposes fixity and singularity of power which are synonymous with closure. It is a well-known fact that *shūrā* can be no more than an elite affair, an exclusive bastion of the learned scholars, and therefore not always demotic. Even autocrats engage in some form of consultation, albeit a limited and closed genre of it. Nor is its outcome always mindful of diversity. The artefact of *bay'ah* is only very partially convincing of Islam's compatibility with democracy. As a test of democratic rule, it can be no more convincing than elections. Active electoralisation throughout the Arab world represents no more than a procedural minimum. Therefore *shūrā, ijmā'* or *bay'ah* have to be regarded as the procedural minimum of an Islam-informed government. Similarly, the debate about the democratic potential of a government informed by Islam must not be driven too much by issues of secularism and religion. Neither can be assumed to be more compatible with democratic rule. Both can be oppressive, mitigating the chances of democratic maturity. The obverse is as true. The litmus test is the extent to which difference is tolerated, singularity and fixity of power are opposed, and a fluid space of contingency, allowing for the renewal and opening up new possibilities of being, doing and thinking, is permitted.

Contesting Islam: The Foundational and the Non-foundational

Accordingly, questions must be asked about the fashion in which a creed strongly rooted in religious foundationalism can cope with defoundationalisation; whether Islam's oft-assumed organic nature tolerates multipolarity; and what a defining of democracy as a place of absence means for the future partnership of Islam and good government. By raising these questions and developing lines of inquiry along them, more than providing answers to them, the intention is to show that there exists some congruence between Islamic societies and the most treasured Western possession, democracy. It is no easy or simple task to correlate Islam with democracy. The idea is to explore and affirm the possibilities for such a correlation in an age when Islam is in a state of flux. But as to what will become of those possibilities is a *quo vadis* question.

Generally, the scholarly discussion of Islam and democracy has been one-sided. Western linearity condemns religion to the margins and Enlightenment's singular practice of rationality denounces religious foundationalism. Fixity, singularity and determinacy have all been attributed to all religion, especially Islam, and cited as evidence of its non-demotic tendencies. On the contrary, secular foundationalism's compatibility with democratic government has been taken for granted. Very few anti-foundationalist trends have revised this position. For all their avant-gardism, most Western feminists, who are staunchly committed to values of tolerance of difference, remain hostile to religious "fundamentalism". Postmodernists are divided on this question.[64] Yet secular foundationalism has not always been demotic or difference friendly. With the advent of anti-foundationalism in many branches of Western knowledge, religious foundationalism, with its monotheistic determinacy and exclusive morality, has emerged as a stark opposite to plural practices of power, rationality and morality. This is one reason for so much millennial apocalypse about future relations between the West and Islam. In broad terms, anti-foundationalism is a contestation-based moment and movement provoking continuously provisional renewal of being/identity/self (recognition of difference/otherness); of thought/rationality/knowledge (questioning modernity and Enlightenment rationality); of morality (moving towards relativism and cultural pluralism); and of power (by undoing centricity and diffusing rather than fusing). In minimalist terms, it has been a ferment leading to the questioning of historically-accepted assumptions and dogmas justifying continuity of political or knowledge practices. But with all its profoundly destabilising tendencies, this ferment has not rejected the democratic heritage. Its quarrel is with the liberal and Marxist "grand narratives", which are seen as part of the problem rather than the solution in relation to the human quest for emancipation. Postmodernism implicates both narratives in oppression. It sees both as essentialist theories working on behalf of small groups and narrow interests. Postmodernism refigures emancipation in terms of what Foucault calls "sites of struggle", whereby people deploy their own knowledge resources in their local cultural and environmental contexts to emancipate themselves. That is, unaided by the grand theories of liberalism or Marxism. The democratic heritage therefore remains a relevant framework, an *esprit de corps*. Indeed it is this framework that inspires the ongoing reclaiming of what is seen to be Enlightenment's lost emancipatory spirit or ideals which are suspicious of fixed power relations and singularity. No matter how rethought and refigured, foundationalism always has degrees of itself.

If understood as a ferment of questioning and destabilising of age-old accepted assumptions for the purpose of renewal, then Islam can

[64] See Akbar S. Ahmed, *Postmodernism and Islam* (London: Routledge, 1992); also Ernest Gellner, *Postmodernism, Reason and Religion* (London and New York: Routledge, 1992).

be said to be experiencing its own form of anti-foundationalism. In fact *ijtihād* (independent reasoning) and *tajdīd* (renewal) are two powerfully entrenched Islamic artefacts. No dynamics are today more instrumental in setting in train a process of anti-foundationalism than the massification of education and the access to the "global village", both physically and ethereally, facilitated by migratory movements and modern communications technology. Higher literacy and increased availability of alternative non-Islamic frames of reference, as a result of what Anthony McGrew calls "the growing interconnectedness of national societies",[65] are undoing the fusion of the wider body of the *ummah* (Islamic community) with the opinion of the *'ulamā'* (the learned scholars). Just as print made the power of exegesis embodied in the *'ulamā'*, an elite privileged by its reading and writing skills, the keys to direct textual access, mass education and the empowering "penetration" of communications technologies,[66] has relatively disembodied the *'ulamā'* as an authoritative group, namely, the official expounders of religious orthodoxy. Dale Eickelman links his notion of "objectified" Islam to developments in the spheres of mass education and technological advancements in the global dissemination of information.[67] Objectification is in a sense the coincidence of religious soul-searching with discursive dispersion. Soul-searching proceeds from objective questions about the importance of religion to human existence and the kind of behaviour to be expected from it. Dispersion of discourse, which is helped by the explosion of information, is the process by which the objectification of religious imagining in the individual's consciousness takes place.[68] As self-knowing becomes increasingly independent and direct knowing via new ways of knowing, centrally controlled, interpreted, disseminated and applied knowledge becomes challenged, fragmenting

65 See "Preface" by Anthony McGrew in Anthony McGrew (ed.), *The Transformation of Democracy? Globalization and Territorial Democracy* (Cambridge: Polity Press, 1997), p. ix.

66 Based on a definition of globalisation by James Mittleman for whom it "is a coalescence of varied transnational processes and domestic structures, allowing the economy, politics, culture and ideology of one country to penetrate another". See James H. Mittleman, "The Dynamics of Globalization" in James H. Mittleman (ed.), *Globalization: Critical Reflections* (Boulder, CO: Lynne Rienner, 1997), p. 3.

67 Dale F. Eickelman, "Mass Higher Education and the Religious Imagination in Contemporary Arab Societies", *American Ethnologist*, 19 (1992), pp. 643–55.

68 Ibid., p. 643.

political and religious authority.[69] Levelling occurs through the decentering of knowledge. With the emergence of "communicative communities",[70] Connolly's new movements of pluralisation and new possibilities of being are nurtured. Eickelman and Anderson refer to this levelling or pluralisation as "civic pluralism", whereby state actors extend recognition of non-state actors, allowing them to share the public sphere. Thus a culture founded on values of mutual tolerance of difference gets entrenched.[71] Diffusion of power, whether in the realm of politics or knowledge, inhibits and prohibits fusion. Historically, it has been the insistence on state–society fusion and unity in the name of religious nationalism, unitary *ummaic* identity and, in the postcolonial state, in the name of secular nationalism, that is implicated in the deepening of singular and fixed power relations in most Arabo-Islamic societies. In both, the reconstruction of a collective identity was superimposed over pre-existing or marginalised religious, gender-based, tribal and ethnic identities. But the submerging and hiding of those identities, either in support of the antiquated dynastic state or the postcolonial state, did not entail their erasure. The modern Arab Middle East is currently the scene of a multiplicity of identity articulations, counter-articulations and disarticulations that the homogenising and hegemonising practices of the past and the present are ill-equipped to manage and resolve intelligently and tolerantly. The territorially-based monopoly over the loyalty of the homogenised and reformed national citizen, secured through distributive (pork-barrelling, welfare) but mostly via regulative (censorship, surveillance, coercion, cooption) and propagandist (indoctrination into nationalism via state-controlled schooling and media) mechanisms can only become more tenuous. For, the capacity to monopolise loyalty is being enfeebled by the deluge of multipolar flow of information made possible by the new information and communications technologies, such as the internet, that either defy official censorship or cannot be surveilled without imposing an unaffordable burden on the public purse. In either case, possibilities for new being and pluralisation within the AME, especially at a time of

[69] Dale F. Eickelman and Jon W. Anderson, "Print, Islam and the Prospects for Civic Pluralism: New Religious Writings and their Audiences", *Journal of Islamic Studies*, 8 (1997), pp. 43–62.

[70] Ibid., p. 47.

[71] Ibid., p. 43.

heightened objectification of Muslim consciousness and augmented discursive plurality must not be underrated.

> [N]ew forms of communicative communities...contribute significantly to a fragmentation of political and religious authority...multiplying the media through which messages can be transmitted diffuses political and religious authority. The state may continue to offer an "official transcript"...but it may not be considered authoritative and legitimate, even if it is seriously heeded. With the proliferation of media and weakened controls over many of them, "hidden" transcripts are now more likely to be "spoken directly and publicly in the teeth of power".[72]

Hence Islam becomes a variety of "islams," a multitude of interpretations of divine texts all of which will ultimately bear the imprint of divergent interests, and different socio-economic, political and historical contexts. There are the Occidental "islams" of the likes of Afro-American Malcolm X, of Salman Rushdie, and of French Roger Garaudy; and there are the Oriental "islams" in their many Sunni and Shīʿite brands. But plurality is not the same as pluralism or pluralisation. Not all "islams" are congruent with the kind of ethos of democracy that rejects singularity and fixity. (But even rejection of democracy must not justify state bans or violent oppression.) This great panoply of "islams" warrants a rethinking of reductionistic representations of Islam, namely, that it is a confessionally-centred collective identity, and of Orientalist essentialist constructions of it as bereft of multipolar voices and multilateralism. Similarly, exclusive essentialism has afflicted the Occidentalists' understanding of Islam as requiring holism and absolute uniformity demanded by the exigencies of solidarity against a Western civilizational "other" or by a moral rationality that is adverse to *tafriqah* (divisiveness) within the *ummah*. Orientalism and Occidentalism can be mutually reinforcing. Unsympathetic Orientalist constructions of Islam and Muslims lead many Occidentalists, especially those articulating political imaginings from the Qur'ān, to argue for a collective Muslim identity.

Perhaps nothing like singular command over the interpretation of divine texts by the learned scholars, especially as many of them became implicated in the underwriting of political power, congealed and fixed Islam. This might have been the biggest tragedy of Islam whose history is marked by dynamic contestation and provisional

[72] Ibid., p. 47.

renewal in theology, legalism and politics. Beyond *tawḥīd* (Unity of God/unitarianism) and the divine scriptures, namely the Qur'ān, nothing else was sanctified. The unity of God and the belief in God through holy scripture is the ultimate foundation. So, this is the non-negotiable element that is reproduced in any refigured religious foundationalism. But everything else is open. Under Islam, God alone is not looked upon as another site of power open for human contestability or contestation. Contestability and contestation were the standards by which Islam was reified as a religion, an imperium, and a multitude of ways of life. To a large extent, the history of early Islam, up to the times when the proverbial *bābu 'l-ijtihād* (gate of *ijtihad*) was supposed to have been closed, a position that Wael Hallaq questions,[73] in the late-ninth and early-tenth centuries,[74] was characterised by fluidity and contingency in the realms of legalism and politics. Both represented a space where power was not spoken for. They still continue to represent Muslims everywhere with a power vacuum for which competition is tense, divisive, conflictual and even violent. That fluidity permanently introduced an element of brokenness, as opposed to the putative unity within the *ummah*. That brokenness resulted from the tensely multipolar competition over the interpretation of religious texts and dogma in the bid to reify Islam into a religion as life. Notwithstanding the violence that punctuated Islamic history, that brokenness was healthy in that it prevented fixity and singularity of power.

Emblematic of this fluidity was the continuous struggle between foundationalist and anti-foundationalist currents throughout Muslim history. Whereas the former proceeds from a logic that attributes to Islam a fixed and singular essence and a collective identity recognising neither difference nor otherness only in exclusivist terms (such as *vis-à-vis* Christendom), the latter deploys a reasoning more congruent with fluidity, indeterminacy, provisionalism and diversity. Thus it neither locks Islam into a fixed and singular essence nor reduces differences into a collective Muslim identity. Muslim identity, being like any other, is context-bound with multiple layers, making it

[73] Wael B. Hallaq, "Uṣūl al-Fiqh: Beyond Tradition", *Journal of Islamic Studies*, 3 (July 1992), pp. 174–6. (pp. 172–202)

[74] W.M. Watt, "The Closing of the Door of *Ijtihad*", *Orientalia Hispanica*, 1 (1974): pp. 675–8. Compare with Wael B. Hallaq, "Was the Gate of *Ijtihad* closed?" *International Journal of Middle East Studies*, 16 (1984), pp. 3–41.

differentiated and therefore worthy of a degree of moral autonomy. Both logics, however, intersect in upholding God as an ultimate foundation with His divine text, the Qur'ān, being the ultimate reference for enacting His will—the ideal of *khayru ummah* (morally-sublime community). This "textual core" is widely claimed to be inextricably bound up with any imagining of a Muslim identity. But it is over this very textual core that dissonance has mostly prevailed since the end of the four rightly-guided Caliphs' rule. So, the 14 centuries of discord within the *ummah* has not been between apostates and believers; rather, it has mostly been between equally-believing members. The same goes for foundationalists and anti-foundationalists within Islam. Revelation was a given for both. In fact that discord was instrumental in revitalising the Islamic community. It was a communicative and discursively multipolar ensemble of epistemic communities scattered through Muslim chronology and dotted in the Islamic empire's vast geography, from Bukharah to Fez.

The question that these epistemic communities had to contend with was not over the sovereignty of God but over "ways of knowing" the divine texts and whether they should be assigned a spatially, temporally and socially contextual utility or whether they should be treated as transcendentally timeless Truth. "Rationalist" and "fundamentalist" are the clean labels invoked to refer to the reactions that represent these two hermeneutic ways of knowing the divine texts. If for the former knowing is by way of speculation, for the latter it is through God-given intuition. The rationalists' recourse to the rationalism of classical philosophy to defend Islam by fathoming the *bāṭin* (sub-textual and inner meaning), as opposed to the *ẓāhir* (literal meaning), is both futile and dangerous for the literalists. Its futility is put down to the inability of human intelligence to capture the essence of divine knowledge since God alone is the ultimate source of all ethical knowledge. Its danger lies in the risks of polluting, using, misusing and abusing revelation for worldly gains. Since Islam is believed to have a divine origin and Qur'ānic texts are claimed to be the word of God, Muslims are obliged, once they accepted them, to elaborate the religious sanctions contained within them for enacting the Islamic community. To engage the divine texts via speculative cognition is to rationalise revelation. Such a rationalisation could see a variety of unfixed and decentred interpretations of the texts and would be, established religionists fear, a defence of vested interests, in the name of defending the faith, and not a neutral and objective exercise. The jostling between revelation and reason, theosophy and philosophy, and between the hermeneutics of *ahlu 'l-ḥadīth* (the "traditionalists"/ the "literalists") and *ahlu 'l-ra'y* (the "rationalists"), were illustrative of the dynamism of contestation and contestability that went in tandem with the evolution of Islam and its contact with ideas and peoples from outside the original Meccan and Medinan precincts. The rationalist theology of the Muʿtazilah (Muʿtazalites), who were initially endorsed for nearly 40 years by the Abbasyds, especially al-Ma'mūn (813–33) in the ninth century, drew opposition from the literalist theology of the Ḥanbalī school. The Ashʿarites and the Sufis do not fit neatly into the rationalist or literalist categories. Although largely considered to be traditionalist, the Ashʿarites' theology was nonetheless noted for the overlap of reason and revelation within it. With its experience of religion through emotion, rather than reason or intuition, Sufi mysticism presented another facet of understanding the texts and reifying Islam's Godly-sanctioned moral community. Generally, the hermeneutics-based jostling pluralised and revitalised Islam.

Islam's formative history is fluid and diverse which have made Islamisation a process of provisional and multipolar renewal. Although by the time of the Prophet's death in the early-seventh century (d. 632) revelation was "completed", there remained a great deal of incompleteness with regard to elaborating, systematising or institutionalising it. The Qur'ān, claimed to be the literal word of God, was not assembled until the rule of the third rightly-guided khalīfah, ʿUthmān (d. 655). The compilation of *ḥadīth* (the Prophet's sayings and deeds) had to wait until the ninth century even though its juridical importance in supplementing the Qur'ān was recognised much earlier by the founding jurists, especially by al-Shāfiʿī (d. 820), of the four rites of Islamic jurisprudence. Here too, the wrestle with the texts, the foundational prerequisites of the inception of Islam's moral community, was tense. There have always been questions about the ways of knowing—whether in literalist or allegorical ways—these traditions regardless of the reliability of their *isnād* (chain of authority). Not even the most authoritative collections of Bukhārī and Muslim escape questioning. The schism within Islam over the question of succession produced a fifth *madhhab* (rite of jurisprudence)—Twelver Shīʿism—that represented Shīʿite difference, juridically setting it apart from the dominant Sunni order. But it would be a mistake to assume unity within either order. The question of who holds the *imāmah* (imamate/rulership), for instance, divided the Shīʿah. The brand of theology professed by the self-righteous and egalitarian Khawārij (seceders) proved to be too contemptuous of, and consequently irreconcilable with, the reigning wisdom within Shīʿite Islam. For the Khawārij, the just ruler does not have to be a lineal descendant of the Prophet, making the post equally open to all righteous Muslims. The Shīʿah insist on Prophetic lineage, infallibility and charisma, attributes which in their eyes made ʿAlī not only quasi-deified but also naturally deserving of the leadership of the *ummah* after Muḥammad's death. In the Maghrib, the jurist Ṣaḥnūn formulated a fairly distinctive *fiqh* (jurisprudence) drawn on the Sunni Mālikī school.[75] The Shīʿah, namely the Ismāʿīlis, challenged Sunni Abbasyd rule by establishing a rival seat of *khilāfah*, Fāṭimid, in North Africa.[76] Essentially, the jostling with the texts demystifies the Orientalist myth of a fixed and monolithic Islamic legal theory, even if the supposed closure of the doors of independent reasoning did not completely stop hermeneutical fluidity and diversity. Thus for Wael Hallaq, Islamic legal theory was neither single nor fixed. Differences, he rightly argues, represent interpretations ranging from uncompromisingly literalist to liberally pragmatist. In between these two ends of the spectrum, there exists a variety of theorists employing diverse exegetical tools to defend their theories. This is at the core of the controversial nature of Islamic legal theory and its diversity, to the point where theories even of a single century show wide-ranging difference in interpretations.[77]

The fluidity and multipolarity of Islam have for the greater part of Muslim history activated contestability and contestation, engendering many historical moments of provisional renewal. On the one hand, the polemical hermeneutics of literalism or rationalism represent a jostling between a conception of knowing and knowledge-making which returns the source of knowledge to God's ethical authority and another seeking not to demote man's moral autonomy. On the other, they have to be seen as part of a human vocation to

[75] P.M. Holt, Ann K.S. Lambton and Bernard Lewis (eds), *The Cambridge History of Islam*, vol. 2A (Cambridge University Press, 1977), p. 217.

[76] Ibid., pp. 217–20.

[77] Hallaq, "Uṣūl al-Fiqh: Beyond Tradition", p. 179.

search for certainty and truth in grappling with the uncertainty in many fragments of knowledge. God happens to be the only certain given in the Islamic realm of hermeneutics. This is one reason why Muslim history is replete with brokenness and polemics. Fixity, singularity and certainty could not have been possible within a religious community whose divine texts are noted for silence on so many issues that the ever-multiplying *ummah* confront and have to resolve by living up to the prescriptions of the faith as well as to the specificities and exigencies of variability of space and time. If medieval jurists such al-Ghazālī (d. 1111) and Ibn Taymiyyah (d. 1328) could not see eye to eye with regard to the existence or lack of an objectively moral knowledge within the grasp of human intelligence, Muslims separated from both men by several centuries cannot be frowned upon for refusing *taqlīd* (recourse to the authority of Muslim forebears) or differing on the ways of knowing and interpreting the texts. Ibn Taymiyyah's views on popular religion strikes a chord with many contemporary Muslims' calls for renewal.[78] Others find affinity with al-Ghazālī's preference for intuitive over philosophical knowledge.[79] Thus God is a unitarian, singular and fixed given. But the Muslim community is not and cannot be, perhaps only in its common submission to God's will and in its shared responsibility to enjoin the good. The divine texts which bind the *ummah* are ironically the very reason for its disunited nature. Equally ironic is the fact that this element of disunity is not necessarily negative. It diffuses rather than fuses the Islamic community with a singularly fixed centre, rendering power within it polycentric, unfixed and continuously fluid.

Islam's standards of polycentricity, unfixity and fluidity have mostly been congealed for fear of disunity, often misunderstood as abandonment of common responsibility, which is regarded to be offensive to religious purity. Yet religious purity can be diluted if not sacrificed in favour of political quietism over mutiny and rebellion in the face of unjust or unethical rule. Quietism has been rationalised

[78] Muhammad Umar Memon, *Ibn Taimiya's Struggle Against Popular Religion* (The Hague: Mouton, 1976).

[79] Richard M. Frank, *Al-Ghazali and the Asharite School* (Durham, NC: Duke University Press, 1994); Iysa A. Bello, *The Medieval Islamic Controversy Between Philosophy and Orthodoxy: Ijma and Tawil in the Conflict Between al-Ghazali and Ibn Rushd* (Leiden: E.J. Brill, 1989); and Eric L. Ormsby, *Theodicy in Islamic Thought: The Dispute over al-Ghazali's "Best of all Possible Worlds"* (Princeton University Press, 1984).

as a lesser evil than the prospect of rebellion and anarchy which are deemed perilous to the preservation of the Godly-appointed moral community. This is at least the reigning wisdom within Sunni Islam. This is a view common to traditionalists like al-Ghazālī as well as to rationalists such as the Muʿtazilah. With the exception of the Khawārij and the Azāriqah whose conceptions of the imamate commits their adherents to martial resistance against unjust rule, the bulk of opinion, especially in Sunni Islam, is more or less Machiavellian. Like in Machiavelli's *Prince*, such an opinion separates ethics and politics. This pragmatic stance unwittingly endorsed tyrannical rule. Twelver Shīʿism justifies quietism differently. It invokes the example of ʿAlī's elder son Ḥasan who boycotted temporal power by not disputing or resisting, as his younger brother Ḥusayn attempted in the battle of Karbala (680), the Umayyad's termination of his father's *khilāfah*. Ḥasan's quietism through spiritual inner knowledge meant putting salvation and redemption off to an eschatological time when *al-imāmu 'l-ghā'ib* (the Hidden Imam) makes a comeback from his occultation to restore justice and equality and ends the reign of oppression on earth. Whatever the rationale for quietist behaviour, it constitutes a historically-strong filament linking medieval with contemporary Arabo-Islamic order. The discourse of order and unity is prioritised by the postcolonial state and its brand of official Islam over that of political equality in the same way it was given precedence over just rule by medieval Muslim jurists.

Two major factors account for the congealing of medieval Islam's fluid, unfixed and polycentric standards: closing the door of interpretation and banning opposition to unjust rule. The closing of the gate of *ijtihād* meant effective freezing of dispersed discourse and diffused opinion in the interaction with the divine texts. Thus *ijmāʿ* ceased to be demotic. It became a monopoly of a high and insular "temple of wisdom" made up of learned scholars who were more intent on manufacturing consensus and safeguarding Muslim unity than on dealing with the anomic and anarchic potential of a multipolar religious field. Fusion of a particular brand of exegetes or legists with the state was to prove adverse for competing wisdom. While the sponsoring of al-Muʿtazilah by al-Ma'mūn produced free thought and fostered cross-fertilisation with classical philosophy, it also led to repression of traditionalists such as the Ḥanbalites. Eventually, al-Muʿtazilah themselves were to be the next victims when another

Abbasyd ruler, al-Mutawakkil (847–61), withdrew support for their *falsafah* (philosophy) which sought to use the tools of Greek philosophy in the service of revelation. The ban by Sunni Islam on opposition and resistance to political rule that may be interpreted to contradict with the Godly-sanctioned moral community produced contradictory effects. On the one hand, it disrupted the Godly command to enjoin the good and forbid evil. The evil of unjust rule became second to the greater evil of Muslim anarchy and disunity. Permitting the lesser of the two evils became the focal point of forbidding evil. On the other hand, enjoining the good was to become society-focused. If the unethical or unjust ruler was not qualified to uphold the moral standards of Islam, then the onus was on the Muslim public to do so. In such institutions as *waqf* (religious endowment) and brotherhoods, Muslim societies were to find the means of self-generation and preservation of the moral community. Nonetheless, political quietism entailed a degree of deference towards worldly rule at the expense of civic pluralism and power-sharing. Like *ijmāʿ*, *shūrā* stopped being demotic. Instead of evolving into a popularly-based institution of consultation for the enactment of civic responsibility, *shūrā* became a narrow-focused process between and within concentric circles of power. Thus except for the first 39 years of Islam, since the beginning of the Medinan period in 622 and up to the reign of the last rightly-guided khalīfah in 661, *shūrā* was absented from political rule. This is one reason why two of the most influential Islamist ideologues, Rāshid al-Ghannūshī and Ḥasan al-Turābī, insist that good government must begin with restoring *shūrā* to what Islam has always meant it to be, a demotic institution.[80]

Lefort's ethos of democracy as a place of absence provides an innovative and potent tool for rethinking the analytical approach of how to correlate Islam with good government. Its explanatory power resides in mapping out the democratic landscape within the boundaries of that space where power is not spoken for. Conventionally, democracy is understood as a place of presence of power interests and contestants. If democracy according to this conventional wisdom is a place of presence, then absence from its attendant power relations which are regulated, fixed and re-fixed periodically is, by inversion, autocracy. Lefort has in effect subverted the old paradigm of

80 Author's interviews with Ḥasan al Turābī, 12 May 1994, Khartoum; and Rāshid al-Ghannūshī, 15 April 1993, London.

democratic power relations by way of interest in the unoccupied space in which power is not competed for—the power vacuum, the power void, or the power gap. Such a vacuum is unmistakably available in Islam. It is through this gap that Islam can be said to be potentially equipped to negotiate the complexities of modernity, in general, and to harness *farāgh* (empty space)[81] within it in the bid to foster a more harmonious partnership with democracy. So, it is by way of revisiting and rethinking that *farāgh* that Muslims and competing "islams" can assign to Islam a democratic role.

The *farāgh* within Islam is ample. It concerns the space other than that site of power occupied by God, the ultimate foundation. Whilst such an ultimate foundation entails limitation by a zone of non-negotiability, such as in the realm of *sharī'ah* (Islamic law), human moral autonomy has its own arena of knowledge that capacitates it to reinvent itself and recreate the Godly-appointed ethical community according to context. If *sharī'ah* is the realm of the immutable, *fiqh* is that of the mutable. Intuition and submission guide the former; speculation and disputation the latter. Contestation is fierce when it comes to determining the scope, depth and breadth of speculative knowledge required to interpret revelation. Illustrative of the intensity of contestation over the place of reason in the rethinking of Islam is the wide spectrum of *ijtihādāt* (pl. of *ijtihād*, independent reasoning) from the time of Muḥammad 'Abduh at the turn of the century to Muḥammad Arkoun in the 1990s. Both reject *taqlīd*. For 'Abduh, the partnership of Islam and reason is irrefutable.[82] But 'Abduh's subscription to a notion of *ijtihād* tied to the *Shāfi'ī* tool of *ijmā'*, be it renewable and unbinding, is nowhere as radical as Arkoun's own notion of rethinking Islam. Not even the innovative al-Ghannūshī and al-Turābī would be remotely comfortable with Arkoun. Both accept the Qur'ān to be co-eternal with God, not a discourse created in time, that can be deconstructed like any other fragment of human history. Arkoun rejects textuality and the way it was deployed by traditionalist exegetes for political ends. He criticises both the state and the traditional expounders of Islamic orthodoxy for resisting a historical deconstruction of the divine texts. He puts their resistance

[81] For a similar use, see Azzam Tamimi, *Rachid Ghannouchi: Democrat within Islamism* (New York: Oxford University Press, 2001), p. 132.

[82] Muhammad Abduh, *The Theology of Unity*, trans. by Ishaq Musa'ad and Kenneth Cragg (London: Allen and Unwin, 1966).

down to the fact that they would be set to have their authority, which is partly derived from monopoly over the political manipulation of such texts, challenged.[83] He suggests a bold strategy of subjecting sacred texts to the test of historicity,[84] in the same fashion the holy books of the Jews and Christians came under the close scrutiny of historicism and philosophical criticism. This strategy stresses the relevance of extensive knowledge of historical context to comprehend the specificity of texts, which he does by deploying his *methode régressive* (regressive methodology).[85] Adopting a context-sensitive method to understand Islam in its politico-socio-historical past context would be, according to Arkoun, one way of reading in the divine texts new meanings for the contemporary context (progressive methodology), in which many Muslims are oppressed intellectually and politically. Emancipation then begins with unshackling the sacred texts from timeless and decontextualised renderings, and from politically motivated rationalisations which engender domination. For Arkoun, Robert Lee explains, "Rethinking Islam depends upon the freedom to think."[86] This is one reason why, for instance, ʿAbduh's reformism and deployment of reason is not sufficiently critical. Rather, Lee adds, Arkoun is dismissive of ʿAbduh's brand of reformism as apologetic owing to its dualistic framework which pits the Muslim "us" against the European "them". Hence the circularity of self-justifying and self-generating essentialism and counter-essentialism.

> Arkoun refers to these and other reformers as apologists...because they sought to prove that Islam had anticipated modern science...and liberal democracy. For Arkoun, such apologists misread history by reading it backwards; they sought to counter Europe-centeredness with Islam-centeredness, perpetuating the idea that there is a single Islam with a single, superior, exclusive capacity for generating truth.[87]

Since justice and liberation are the sub-texts of Arkoun's study of Islam, then ʿAbduh's reformism which revolves around legitimisation or delegitimisation of some form of power—Islamic epistemology—

[83] Mohammed Arkoun, *Rethinking Islam: Common Questions, Uncommon Answers* (Boulder, San Francisco and Oxford: Westview Press, 1994), pp. 35–6.

[84] Mohammed Arkoun and Louis Gardet, *L'Islam: Hier-Demain* (Paris: Editions Buchet/Chastel, 1978), esp. pp. 117–88.

[85] Ibid., p. 154.

[86] See the forward by Robert D. Lee in ibid., p. xi.

[87] Ibid., p. ix.

can only lead to domination.[88] If ʿAbduh can read science and democracy in the sacred texts, political power holders would demand rationalisations that perpetuate the status quo, something official Islam has performed without fail in the postcolonial state. But Arkoun's hermeneutics, which, if pushed too far can render the Qur'ān like any other human-created text, are bound to be read by devout Muslims not only as an attempt to de-divinise and desacralise their sacred texts but also downgrade the experience of intuition and of the past.

Naṣr Ḥāmid Abū Zayd's work on the nature of religious discourse and exegesis, which pushes the thesis of historicity further than some Muslim sensibilities can apparently bear, probes the techniques of *ta'wīl* (allegorical exegesis) in which religious discourse seeks to monopolise truth and manipulate meaning.[89] Abū Zayd shares Arkoun's concern for the tendency of the religious discourse to seek *imtilāku 'l-ḥaqīqah* (possession/monopoly of truth).[90] Common to both studies of the divine texts is the stress of historicity as an "objective" and "scientific" way of knowing the texts. Like Arkoun, Abū Zayd valorises the historical context of revelation. For him losing contextuality dilutes and humanises textuality. The practice of *ihdāru 'l-buʿdi 'l-tārīkhī* (invoking the historical context),[91] that is, leaving the historical context out, one of the tools he attributes to the religious discourse's manipulation of meaning, humanises the sacred texts. He considers this act of humanisation a self-interested and selective tool as it leads to a rationalised rendering of textuality.[92] As far as Abū Zayd is concerned such a practice is not specific to the Islamists; the state-funded "islam" is guilty of it too. Worse than humanisation of the rationalised renderings of the sacred texts is the sacralisation of those human meanings, readings and renderings attached to the originally metaphysical and pristine text. Thus *ijtihād*, the putatively human vocation of rendering provisional and fluid meaning, owing to the inevitability of fallibility and variability, becomes instead an

[88] For other related works by Mohammed Arkoun see *Essais sur la pensée islamique* (Paris: Maisonneuve et Larose, 1973); and *Pour une critique de la raison islamique* (Paris: Maisonneuve et Larose, 1984).

[89] Naṣr Ḥāmid Abū Zayd, *Naqdu 'l-khiṭābi 'l-dīnī*. [Deconstruction of Religious Discourse] (al-Qasr al-Ayni, Cairo: Sina li al-Nashr, 1994).

[90] Ibid., p. 79; see also a similar idea on p. 91.

[91] Ibid., pp. 94–9.

[92] Ibid., p. 87.

interpretation that is not only treated as singular and fixed, but also as one that can fathom and know God.[93] With the confusion with and elevation of human interpretation to a Godly status, the Godly attributes of fixity and singularity, and with them sanctity, become human attributes—which verges on polytheism.[94] The result of such a reversal is *sayṭarah* (domination) by the religious discourse of the discursive scene. Since the religious discourse assumes the place of God in becoming the final source of knowledge, especially as a result of the closing of distance between the object and subject of knowing,[95] a series of ruptures take place: between historical context and modern-day reading; and between *dalālah* (signifier) and *maghzā* (significance).[96] Pristine revelation as a teleological discourse is immutable. Abū Zayd calls this fixed element of revelation *dīn* (religion) which he distinguishes from *al-fikru 'l-dīnī* (religious rationality), the continuously changing by-product of human interpretations of the original sacred texts.[97] Abū Zayd displays utmost disdain towards this religious rationality as can be gleaned from his contempt for the discourse of the most prominent ideologues and spokespersons of political Islam from Sayyid Quṭb and to Fahmī Huwaydī down to the rationalisations of well-known figures of establishment Islam such Shaykh Mitwallī al-Shaʿrāwī.

What is at issue is not primarily Abū Zayd's irreverence for the religious discourse of Quṭb or Shaʿrāwī. Rather, it is his lack of appreciation of the *turāth* (cultural heritage), including the divine texts, and the past.[98] He represents both as a shackle. Thus, as he puts it, "The modern-day Muslim is made to live physically in the present by relying on Europe for the realization of his material requirements, and, [at the same time] to live spiritually, mentally and emotionally in the past by leaning on his religious heritage."[99] No human being can escape the shackles of the past or the present, the future past. There is much about identity and common memory and the cultural storage of the forebears that make yearnings for the past integral to being,

93 Ibid., pp. 94–5; p. 78.
94 Ibid., p. 197.
95 Ibid., p. 78.
96 Ibid., pp. 140–6.
97 Ibid., p. 197.
98 Ibid., pp. 84–94.
99 Ibid., p. 92.

thinking and doing. Abū Zayd tends to advance a thesis for the erasure of that past or, at least, a delinking from it, locking Muslims into the "here" and "now", to the exclusion of the "there" and "then". Here Abū Zayd is contradictory. On the one hand, he argues for the appreciation of socio-historical context, not for the purpose of extracting wisdom from but rather to discard the sacred texts as a frame of reference for moving forward in the present. On the other, he vilifies the past, completely writing off its relevance for the present. This smacks of linear rationalism in which the modern and the traditional are treated as opposites, and which assumes the rise of the former to precipitate the demise of the latter. This along with Abū Zayd's blind faith in reason, which throughout his work appears to be modelled on an Enlightenment-like rationality,[100] lead to underrating the power of faith as a rationality in its own right. Enlightenment rationality, even in the realm of scientific knowledge, is being relativised, creating space for other ways of knowing. Accordingly, Abū Zayd's quest for a "scientific" method of knowing the sacred texts may be a call for epistemological rigour and reflection but one that would sacrifice richness—intuition, faith.[101] But most importantly, what Abū Zayd is calling for would prohibit the ordinary Muslim's interaction and communication with his or her sacred texts. Knowing the texts will then have to be mediated by those who possess the necessary expertise. The result may well be more of the same alienation that Abū Zayd is trying to combat by way of outlining the anatomy of the religious discourse and its fixity and singularity in its claims to possessing truth. Fixity and singularity cannot be unhinged with new forms of fixity and singularity and by substituting one "temple of wisdom" with another.

Hence mapping out the terrain where power is still unclaimed within Islam may prove as controversial as debating the expediency of Islamic law for the good of people or disputing the relevance of the Caliphate in late modernity. What is certain is that contestation will be intense and reflect the diffused nature of the ideal of how to be Muslim. The site of *farāgh*, for enacting democratic power relations that oppose fixity, singularity and determinacy, can be expected to be as discursive and continuously contestable as that within which objectified "islams" intersect and interact. Being tensely discursive

100 Ibid. See, for instance, p. 103.
101 Ibid., p. 200.

and continuously contestable, the *farāgh* or gap mapped out for engendering the democratic ethos requires toleration of otherness and difference. In this respect, the positions by Arkoun and Abū Zayd, amongst others, which preclude the possibility of correlating Islam with democracy or freedom are self-enclosed. They are informed by a Western dogma that insists on secularism as a precondition of democratic politics. Abū Zayd, for instance, observes that secularism safeguards freedom of religion and thought, making it an essential prerequisite for civil society to flourish. Further, he makes the safeguarding of Islam itself incumbent on a secular reading of the sacred texts.[102] Secularism is not a non-prejudicial framework. It is a type of rationality in competition with religious rationality, amongst others. It occupies the locus of power in many a Western setting. Its decentring has become possible with the advent of postmodern emancipatory knowledge that makes the space of rationality fluid and multipolar, and as a consequence one that aims at inclusiveness not exclusiveness. Thus religious rationality with its attendant voices and identities cannot be excluded. In other words, the most important prerequisite for a dynamic civil society and freedom is the rejection of fixed, singular and determinate power relations. A secular order is not. To insist on the precondition of secularism is basically to ask religionists to forego the right to imagine freedom or democratic politics within a framework they value immensely and which they may hold to be inextricably linked to being. Rejection of fixity and singularity makes that gap or vacuum where power is not spoken for a site of intertexuality.

Similarly, the kind of *ghuluww* (religious extremism in the interpretation of the sacred texts) the Muslim world has become accustomed to in censoring different thinking or threatening, particularly secular readings of the divine texts with apostasy, may do more harm than good to the cause of a democratic ethos in the AME. Muslims live in a world of which they make up only one-fifth of the inhabitants. The implications of relegating the remaining four-fifths to the realm of unbelief can be very dangerous for an Islam shaped by those "islams" of *ghuluww*. A good example of this *ghuluww* is the saga of the former Cairo University professor of Arabic and Literature, Abū Zayd. His victimisation in the early 1990s by the legal system as well as many religious voices violates his right to think and engage in his

[102] Ibid., pp. 43–4.

academic research freely. Abū Zayd is not guilty of apostasy and nowhere in his work does he renounce his faith. Rather, he is guilty of essentialist dualism. For, he locates the whole religious experience within a Western framework positing faith against science or reason and religion against progress and freedom. This does not seem to be adequate justification for charging him with apostasy, on the basis of which the Court of Cassation had to submit in the late 1990s a ruling to force a divorce neither Abū Zayd nor his wife initiated.

Accordingly, an ethos of democracy worked out within an Arabo-Islamic setting must confront the problem of essentialism. In this setting, essentialism equates with the practice to reduce knowledge to a single or fixed reading of the sacred texts. Hence in the site of *farāgh*, the notion of incommensurability of different readings cedes to that of intertexuality. That is, that discursive practices are never independent of each other and that they can speak to each other, making dialogism possible. *Farāgh* then is the realm of continuously searching for provisional synthesis in an ongoing contestation between thesis and antithesis. Thus an ethos of democracy becomes embodied in power being permanently maintained as a place of absence—one without fixed and singular power holders. The notion of *ʿilm* (knowledge) assumes a wider meaning than hitherto has been the case within Islam. It is not an exclusive bastion of a single group of learned scholars, religious or secular. Rather, it becomes the variety of ways of knowing the texts that avail within the great panoply of "islams" that can be used for the good not only of Muslims but also of humanity. There is room in the site of *farāgh* for the knowledge practices of Abū Zayd and Arkoun as well as of Quṭb or Huwaydī. What is certain in this context is that power in Islam, the overarchingly contested ideal that a diversity of "islams" seeks to enact, is, except in its divine site, left fluid and indeterminate. With regard to the pole of political power, the Prophet Muḥammad did not appoint a successor and the Qur'ān provides no blueprint of government, leaving ample room for human moral autonomy, be it within Qur'ānically-ethical guidelines of oneness of God, humanity, piety, modesty, probity, justice, consultation and mutual compassion. In the pole of knowledge, contestation over meaning is fierce as can be gleaned from the foregoing. Whereas revelation is sanctified because of its divine provenance, the same has not been true of human additions and authorisations, including Prophetic ones which cannot be authenticated beyond reasonable doubt. Given the fierce contest over meaning, not even the conventional expounders of orthodoxy who are well versed in Islamic theology can singularly occupy this site of power. Historically, the learned scholars, especially Sunni, acted as a fixed and singular "temple of wisdom" because rulers enlisted their endorsement and rationalisations of the sacred texts not only in the service of faith but also, and most importantly, as collaborators in legitimising and reproducing profane power. Muḥammad occupied this site by virtue of Prophecy, mediation of revelation. Not even the rightly-guided Caliphs occupied that site singularly or claimed special knowledge, authority or power as receptacles of inner, secret or esoteric knowledge. Although at one level Shīʿite Islam gives much leeway to the *mujtahid's* (practitioner of *ijtihad*) reason and intuition in the validation of legal and theological knowledge, at another level it is elitist and hierarchical, making the authorisation of interpretations a site of power singularly occupied by the *ayatollahs* (literally proof of God), for instance. This practice is one of many human additions which attest to the continuous endeavour by Muslims to interpret the sacred texts in the bid to reify the Godly-sanctioned moral community, and live up to a particular understanding of the ideal of Islam. Therefore the fixity and singularity of power by the elitism and hierarchy of the Imami system can neither be completely blamed on Islam nor treated as specific to Islam. The reigning wisdom is that all power in Islam is spoken for whereas in Greek democracy it is not. The irony is that Greek democracy, the precursor of modern democracy on which the forms of democratic politics many Muslims are today seeking to emulate are modelled, may very well be the system in which fixity and singularity of power originated. Unless the intertextuality of Islam and Hellenic philosophy is to be denied, there can be no doubt that scholarly elitism in both is more than a mere coincidence:

> [N]on-Arab and non-Islamic traditions and institutions were instrumental in forming the direction of Islamic, particularly Shi'i, thought. Among such foreign influences was Greek philosophy, especially the neo-Platonic doctrine of emanation and the notion of universal intellect, which lent strong support to those *imamah* doctrines that attached divinity to the Shi'i imams and designated them as intermediary between man and God. The Greek philosophy exerted a similar influence on the post-*imamah* doctrines of leadership. The contemporary intellectual elitist approaches in Shi'ism resemble the neo-Platonic thought that envisions the ideal society as one in which the most knowledgeable rules.

> (…) In order to make neo-Platonic theory, which calls for the leadership of philosopher-king, applicable to the Islamic society, philosophy has to gain recognition by Muslims as a legitimate source of knowledge and perfect wisdom. To achieve this, philosophy needs to adapt to the fundamental principles of Islam. This requires the Islamization of philosophy, as long as this process does not jeopardize the truth as seen by philosophy. A host of Muslim scholars did indeed feel that such an adaptation is possible. In applying the Platonic theory to Islam, Farabi's philosophy substituted the prophet or the imam for the philosopher-king of Plato's Republic, and the *Shari'ah* for the laws…Similarly, a host of anti-democratic-pluralist Shi'i and Sunni reformers have rejected the idea of majority rule, and instead, have advocated the right of the learned few to rule.[103]

The question whether it is defensible to propose or to transpose to the Arab world a notion of democracy that was inaugurated in a different milieu, Athenian and feudal, founded on a structure in which there was slavery, sexism and discrimination, and where democracy itself was really a legitimating concept for those who conflated economic and political power is partly irrelevant. For, at an age when both democracy and Islam are in a state of flux, democratisation cannot be too inflexible to be adaptable globally. The same is true of the variety of emerging "islams", especially those which are serious about undoing authoritarian rule. This is an indispensable prerequisite for an approximation of the ideals of democracy and those of Islam. The contestability and contestation within both open up possibilities for mutual relativism as well as cultural pluralism. The defoundationalising occurring within democracy as well as Islam gives new impulse to imagining good government in a way that makes politics a fertile space for maximising options for cultural dialogism, pluralism and syncretism. Homogeny and consequent hegemony through fixity and singularity of democracy or of Islam would deprive the political imagination of that life and soul which belong to things that are syncretic.

Hence if it is morally questionable for Orientalists to insist on the universality of Western democracy as a fixed and singular cultural prerequisite for the realisation of the good society and polity in the Arab Middle East, it is then equally immoral for Muslim culturalists to fail to adopt a political system that they clearly know is a superior

103 Mehran Tamadonfar, *The Islamic Polity and Political Leadership* (Boulder, CO: Westview Press, 1989), pp. 103–104.

alternative to authoritarian rule. Similarly, Arab and Muslim culturalists cannot condemn Westerners for making a loud noise about abuses of power and violence in the Arab and Muslim world in the name of Western notions of human rights and democracy whilst they expect moral endorsement for their silence on such practices under the pretext of cultural imperialism or specificity.

The democratic moment in the Arab Middle East contains two aspects. One is the encounter between philosophical reasoning and revelation. It was the beginning of a jostling between Hellas and Mecca. This moment, which originated more than ten centuries ago, marked, above all else, the beginning of a defoundationalising moment within Islam, as can be gleaned from the above quote about the interaction, mutual inclusion and exchange and intertextuality of Islam and Greek philosophy. That was apparent in the space of unfixity, multipolarity, contestation and renewal that characterised the disputations between the *kalām* (dialectical theology) and *falsafah* (philosophy) medieval interlocutors. Deploying the reasoning tools of classical philosophy, both established a tradition that Islam can only be the variety of "islams" that jostle to fathom, defend or elaborate the ideal of Islam. Although in the intervening ten centuries between the tenth and the early-twentieth that tradition of multipolar intellectual disputation died, the jostle between the apodictic and the rhetorical, the foundational and the non-foundational, and between God and "Ceasar"—man—has survived. The ensuing chapters seek to capture the dialectical readings and renderings of democracy and its practice in the Arab Middle East from al-Fārābī down to the disputations of contemporary Orientalists and Occidentalists.

The second aspect of the democratic moment in the Arab Middle East has to do with a more recent encounter between Islam and European colonialism and then postcolonialism. The recent political ferment in the Arab streets and the demands for greater participation and inclusion have to be seen in this context. The medieval Arabo-Islamic encounter with Greek philosophy has a modern analogue but this time with Western modernity and democracy. There is a potent mirror-image in the contemporary discursive space in relation to democracy in the medieval argumentations and disputations on reason and revelation. Like their forebears, the contemporary Arabo-Islamic inheritors of such disputations are locked in the same dialectics of foundationalism versus non-foundationalism, Godly versus human morality, and teleology versus temporality. Proceeding on the basis of a refigured and refashioned notion of democracy as absence of fixed, singular and determinate power relations, it is proposed that the litmus test for democratising the Arab Middle East is not about a facile imagining of polity and citizenship in terms of mechanical uniformity or homogeny, both of which entail hegemony, around secular or religious nationalism. Rather, an indispensable requisite of that test is a fuller realisation of a democratic ethos that is not confined to procedurally performative acts that neither deepen nor widen citizenship. Vital to the democratic ethos is the processes of discursive and practical interaction and continuous contestation in the quest for dialogism and intertextuality with otherness and difference. God and man, state and society, revelation and reason, self and other, East and West, tradition and modernity become therefore refigured from antitheses to syntheses that make political imagination and remake the democratic ethos.

3

DEMOCRACY AS AN OCCIDENTALIST DISCOURSE

"It is hegemony, or rather the result of cultural hegemony at work, that gives Orientalism...durability and...strength. Orientalism is never far from what Denys Hay has called the idea of Europe, a collective notion identifying 'us' Europeans as against all 'those' non-Europeans, and indeed it can be argued that the major component in European culture is precisely what made that culture hegemonic both in and outside Europe: the idea of European identity as a superior one in comparison with all non-European peoples and cultures(...) In a quite constant way, Orientalism depends for its strategy on this flexible *positional* superiority, which puts the Westerner in a whole series of possible relationships with the Orient without ever losing him the relative upper hand."

"As a judge of the Orient, the modern Orientalist does not, as he believes and even says, stand apart from it objectively...His Orient is not the Orient as it is, but the Orient as it has been Orientalized. An unbroken arc of knowledge and power connects the European or Western statesman and the Western Orientalists; it forms the rim of the stage of containing the Orient." —Edward Said[1]

"A different sort of Occidentalism appears, and is of growing importance in anthropology, in studies of the ways that people outside the West imagine themselves, for their self-image often develops in contrast to their stylized image of the West." —James Carrier[2]

This chapter seeks to apply the Occidentalist paradigm to Islamist discourse on the "West" and "democracy". It begins by looking at the

[1] Edward Said, *Orientalism: Western Conceptions of the Orient* (London: Penguin Books, 1978), pp. 7, 104.

[2] James G. Carrier, "Introduction" in James G. Carrier (ed.), *Occidentalism: Images of the West* (Oxford: Clarendon Press, 1995), p. 6.

underpinnings of Carrier's Occidentalism, with a view to deploying this framework in understanding Occidentalism and Occidentalisation in the AME. It is against this background that Occidentalist modes of Islamist discourse and their attendant essentialisations are examined. This section mostly, but not exclusively, draws on interviews conducted by the author with Islamists from four Arab movements: Egypt's Muslim Brethren (hereafter al-ikhwān); the exiled Renaissance Party of Tunisia (hereafter al-nahḍah); the Islamic Action Front, Jordan's Muslim Brethren's political arm (hereafter al-ʿamal); and the Islamic National Front, the main opposition party led by Ḥasan al-Turābī, and active in Sudan between 1985 and 1989 (hereafter al-jabhah). The observations made in this section are important preliminary analyses which can only be understood in the context of a bifurcated discourse that exhibits both accommodation and rejection of Westerners and the "West". It is not surprising that many (though not all) Islamists, like many Orientalists, engage in their own essentialisations; specifically about a monolithic "West", disaggregated Westerners, and selected elements of Western modernity and culture. However, one caveat is in order: Islamists, like other anti-colonial secular nationalists, derive a great deal of their knowledge about the West from the West itself. In other words, Islamist representations of the West are not always derived from some Islamist discourse that constructs the West in the way Orientalism produced and continues to produce the Orient. Many of the essentialist "Occidentalist" views, analysed below, are based on self-constructions and self-representations of and by the "West" to the "non-West".

DEFINITIONS AND CONCEPTS

An understanding of the dynamics of language is crucial not only for understanding linguistic structure and semants but also the structure of political societies and ideological machinery or political thought. For culture is logocentric, i.e., the *logos*, either as a word, as a discourse, or as a fragment of a discourse mirrors the worldview of a cultural group. The way language takes hold is the way speakers of any language cut up the world, an idea which is already developed in the first chapter. Language is crucial to an analysis of specific cultures.

The Qur'ān, besides being considered by Muslims to be God's revealed word to Muḥammad, is a written discourse. For Quṭb, as well as other later Islamist ideologues, the Qur'ān canonises certain modes of reasoning that are uncongenial to, for instance, Western reasoning, such as on the question of the relation of politics and religion. Accordingly, even when discourses produced by Islamists tend to be diverse, they deploy linguistic elements, idioms and metaphors, which in their origin come from Qur'ānic Arabic; hence, their linguistic homogeneity.

Language and words are also political, as can be detected in the diglossia of any language. That the Islamists, for instance, prefer the language of *turāth* (cultural heritage) over the language of those influenced by European Enlightenment and humanism is indeed political. That the former speak a language that minimises the import of either direct calques or neologisms, from French or English, and the latter do, more or less, the opposite, is also very political. It is noteworthy that the political divide in Algeria is not simply one between religionists and secularists, but also one between the *Arabisants* and the *Francisants*. If tradition, religion and Arabic language are held by the *Arabisants* to be essential to nation-building, for the modernity they desire, and to Algerian identity, for the Francophones secularism and Western developmentalism are the cornerstones of their paradigm of state and nation-building. The inter-war period saw various academies (Cairo, Damascus, Baghdad) combat linguistic imperialism, a partner of political hegemony, which originated with the Napoleonic expedition into Egypt, and then gained momentum with the spread of colonialism over most of the Arab-speaking world.

Therefore, it is no coincidence that at the core of the Islamist project is the reclaiming not only of the Islamic cultural heritage and the Medinese paradigm but also of language. Indeed, linguistic science occupies an important place in the current effort of *ta'ṣīlu 'l-ma'rifah* (Islamisation of knowledge), and in Islamic sciences. *Ta'rīb* (Arabisation) is integral to *ta'ṣīlu 'l-ma'rifah*. Those who are familiar with the premium placed on language by Islamists or Islamic institutions and establishments, such as al-Azhar, appreciate the function of *tafsīr* (exegesis); again, an area with many implications for the political. In fact, as far as Islamists are concerned, no discourse can be impartial if Westernised language plays a large part in it; for Westernised language prejudices the outcome of any discourse on state–society relations, the place of religion or of women in it, and what is to be emphasised and de-emphasised—group versus individual rights, for instance.

Three terms call for explanation: Islamists, *istishrāq* (Orientalism), and *istighrāb* (the way "Occidentalism" would be rendered in Arabic). "Islamists" is a term widely used by Arab Islamists when they want to describe themselves. Between 1992 and 1994, I spoke to many Islamists from the movements mentioned above. Thus, the use of the term is justified on two grounds. First, instead of representing a group via a variety of Orientalist labels, it is a term which is self-referential. Second, the term "Arab Islamists" does succeed in picking out an intertextually-defined group. Thirdly, the term "Islamists" is used here in preference to the term "fundamentalists" as a matter of necessary epistemological caution. Although the terms "fundamentalists" or "fundamentalism" are still in currency, including by those who question their etymology and semantics,[3] they have largely been discredited by students of Islamic movements for various reasons. The terms have no analogues in Arabic, as pointed out by Barbara Stowasser and others;[4] and despite its ubiquity the Arabic word *uṣūlī* is no more than a borrowing of the term "fundamentalist". Bernard Lewis finds the notion of "fundamentalism" to be misleading for lack of clarity.[5] Besides, the notions of "fundamentalism" and "fundamentalists" are rejected by Islamists interviewed by the author on account of their Christian (Protestant) history and origin. Instead they use the self-descriptive term "*islāmiyyūn*", widely rendered as Islamists. Islamists interviewed by the author justify the use of this label by its Islamic history and origin. The term originated in the tenth-century work, *Maqālāt al-islāmiyyīn* [*The Islamists' Theses*], by Abū al-Ḥasan al-As'harī.[6]

Being self-referential, the term "Islamists" makes Islamist movements stand out in two ways: first, by being distinguishable from all adherents of Islam—all Islamists are Muslim but the reverse is not

[3] See, for instance, Yousef N. Choueiri, *Islamic Fundamentalism* (London: Pinter Publishers, 1990), p. 9.

[4] See Barbara F. Stowasser (ed.), *The Islamic Impulse* (Washington, DC: Centre for Contemporary Arab Studies, Georgetown University, 1987), p. 5.

[5] Bernard Lewis, *The Political Language of Islam* (Chicago University Press, 1988), p. 117.

[6] According to author's interview with Islamists from Egypt, Jordan, Sudan and Tunisia.

true; secondly, by being distinguishable from adherents of other creeds and ideologies, that is, from secularists, communists and socialists. Islam is as much an "ism" to Islamists as socialism is to socialists. Eickelman and Piscatori's notion of "objectification" is helpful in defining the term "Islamist".[7] Their "objectification" is understood as a process whereby Muslims seek answers to "objective" questions about their religion, its importance in life and its utility in guiding their lives.[8] Eickelman and Piscatori note that these questions represent "modern queries that increasingly shape the discourse and practice of Muslims in all social classes" and that through "objectification" "religion [becomes] a self-contained system that its believers can describe, characterize, and distinguish themselves from other belief systems".[9] Following from this, they succeed in bringing forth a more complete definition of the term "Islamists" as

> Muslims whose consciousness has been objectified...and who are committed to implementing their vision of Islam as a corrective to current "un-Islamic" practices. This commitment implies a certain measure of protest, demonstrated in a variety of ways, against the prevailing political and social status quo and establishments. The term "Islamists" (*al-islāmiyyūn*) is used by Muslim activists...for whom it contextually implies ideologically motivated Muslims.[10]

However, one caveat is in order. By and large, many analyses accept the idea of one Islamism. That there are variations, and that there is no monolith, does not mean that there are no common features of Islamism as a political tendency. The following features and positions are shared by most if not all Islamists:

1. Islamists tend to stress a moral/ethical approach to polity, society and economy.
2. Islamists tend to stress the relevance of Islam, Islamic scriptures and their otherworldly perspectives not only for expounding an alternative worldview for Muslims and non-Muslims but also for developing a holistic and harmonious framework for understanding

[7] Dale F. Eickelman and James Piscatori, *Muslim Politics* (Princeton University Press, 1996), pp. 37–45.

[8] Ibid., p. 38.

[9] Ibid., p. 38.

[10] Ibid., pp. 44–5.

the material and spiritual dimensions of human existence and for engineering visions and actions for political, social and economic correctness.

3. Islamists tend to believe in the righteousness of their programme of an Islamic-based political, social and economic order and in its possession of answers or solutions to the ills of secular and relativistic modern culture.
4. Islamists tend to reject the privatisation of religion, secularisation of knowledge and of life, and moral relativism.
5. Islamists tend to have a strong commitment to helping enact their models of political Islam which are rooted in a common memory shaped, on the one hand, by success of the Medinese example of seventh-century AD and, on the other, by colonial and post-colonial setbacks.

A superficial consideration of the roots and forms of *istishrāq* and *istighrāb* presents a neat semantic opposition. They are both estimative, tenth-form gerunds, one from "east" (sh-r-q), the other from "west" (gh-r-b). Closer analysis, however, particularly of the pragmatics of each word and its tenth-form cognates, shows this first conclusion to be wrong. In the pragmatics of Arabic, the derivatives of the theoretical *istashraqa* exists only as the gerund (*istishrāq*) and the active participle (*mustashriq*, i.e., Orientalist). This is in flat contradistinction to *istaghraba*, which is pragmatically exploited in all its derivatives. The semantic field of gh-r-b has to do with the west, alienation and foreigners, although the most immediate meaning *istighrāb* carries is that of "amazement" and "bewilderment". Occidentalism is rendered in Arabic as *istighrāb* as Ḥasan Hanafī does in his *Muqaddimah fī 'ilmi 'l-istighrāb* [*Introduction to Occidentalism*], which the analysis looks at below. Whereas *istishrāq*, in its estimative connotations of the root sh-r-q, is to consider something eastern; *istashraqa*, semantic field of the same root, has to do with seeking the East or to become Eastern in the sense of pretence. *Istashraqa*, being the tenth form of the actual verb *ashrāqa*, which refers to the sun's rising, carries an additional meaning: seeking illumination. Hidden in this latter meaning is the connotation that those who seek the East are presumed unilluminated and, by way of *istishrāq*, acquire illumination. Thus the term *istishrāq* can be said to be inherently Occidentalist.

REDISCOVERING THE WEST: FROM AL-AFGHĀNĪ TO AL-ṬAHṬĀWĪ

If harmony was characteristic of the early contact in Andalusia between Islam and the West, dichotomy, xenophobia, and bigotry were the themes of their re-encounter in the nineteenth century and beyond. The scene was set for discursive exchanges of Orientalisation and Occidentalisation. Both are attempts not only at self-recognition but also at recognition by the other. The following brief review of two important works is essential for understanding the context of such discursive exchanges.

Abu-Lughod's analysis of Arab writers and their reaction to European civilisation provides an infrastructure and a context for Keddie's study of Islamic response to the West through her analysis of al-Afghānī (especially with regard to his apparent inconsistencies).[11] The impact of Europe on Islamic society is shown to be both overwhelming and undermining. The immediate result was the acceptance of all that Europe had to offer, and of the Muslim community's lack of the essential ingredients for "progress". Abu-Lughod correctly notes that all reactions to Western progress were prescribed in the initial encounters between Arabs and Europeans in the late-eighteenth and early-nineteenth centuries.[12] Reactions moved from wholehearted acceptance of Western technologies to absolute rejection. These reactions occurred within the assumption that these technologies were not only desirable but also superior and progressive in comparison with contemporaneous Arab culture.

In studying al-Afghānī's "Refutation of the Materialists" and "Response to Renan", Keddie describes the kinds of contradictory debates occurring within the Muslim elites of the time. On the one hand, al-Afghānī defends Islam's role in the preservation of knowledge and the creation of a civilised society, and, on the other, he condemns all religions as being hostile to science and knowledge. He attributes Europe's ascendancy both to Islam's preservation of the knowledge upon which European society is founded, and to European secularisation, which enables the free pursuit of knowledge

[11] See Ibrahim Abu-Lughod, *Arab Rediscovery of Europe: Study in Cultural Encounters* (Princeton University Press, 1963) and Nikki R. Keddie, *An Islamic Response to Imperialism* (Berkeley and Los Angeles: University of California Press, 1968).

[12] Abu-Lughod, *Arab Rediscovery of Europe*, p. 137.

denied by the clerics. Similarly, al-Afghānī rails against the encroachments of the English and the slavishness of their Indian associates only to heap praise on the secularism and utility of European philosophy. Interestingly, he seems as enamoured of this facet of Europeanism as were those Indians he criticised.[13]

These encounters created an image of the "West" as progressive and materialistic, counterposing it to the spirituality of the "East". Europe's successful transformation from barbarity to civilisation occurred through bloodshed and without the benefit of Divine Revelation, a major flaw inherent in all European progress, including Reason. The most fascinating aspect of both Abu-Lughod and Keddie's studies is the inversion of Orientalism into a form of Occidentalism that, while it does not subordinate the "West", certainly "straitjackets" it within very narrow boundaries and stereotypes of utilitarianism and materialism. Arab writers of the nineteenth century described European society as utilitarian and lacking the spirituality inherent in Islam. While many Arabs were willing to acknowledge Europe's unassailable position of technological, scientific, institutional and philosophical superiority, they ranked such achievement as less valuable than the spirituality of Islam. The "West" became the mechanistic and "soulless" "other" to Islam; and this introduction of Occidentalism was the perfect foil to the Orientalism that had cast the "East" as the exotic, seductive "other" to the "West".

Abu-Lughod traces the relationship of Islam and the West through the excited travelogues of Arab writers, and through the translation of European texts into Arabic.[14] Through these encounters he is able to create a framework to map the unequivocal acceptance of Western influence on Islamic societies. He notes that there are three stages of interaction between Europe and Islam. These "stages" are not discrete entities, and they may even be more accurately described as "reactive cycles", of which Abu-Lughod describes three. They can be roughly broken down into a discursive-reactive cycle, relating to those who advocated wholehearted adoption of everything Western; another regarding those who advocated some caution in relation to Western philosophy, since it posed some threat to the beliefs of those not thoroughly familiar with the Qur'ān; and one concerning those who espoused, to varying degrees, the rejection of Westernisation for

[13] Keddie, *An Islamic Response to Imperialism*, pp. 53–73.

[14] Abu-Lughod, *Arab Rediscovery of Europe*, pp. 137–44.

the threat it posed to Islam and Muslim society. The common notion running through all accounts is the dependence of Europe upon Islam's previous pre-eminence for its current superiority. Islam provided for the preservation and development of the ancient Greek and Persian knowledges, which it then shared with a Europe newly emergent from a state of absolute barbarism. For Islam to emulate Europe, then, was not really an affirmation of European superiority but an acknowledgement that Islam had fallen from its own position and needed access to the products of European progress to regain its ascendancy.[15]

In the first stage,[16] Arabs came into contact with the West by travelling through Europe, writing enthusiastic accounts of the wonders of European technology and society and mourning the lack of similar achievements in their own society. Translation of French texts into Arabic also encouraged the growing Arab awareness of Europe and its achievements—literary, social, political, philosophical, scientific. Both forms of contact contributed to the mounting pressure by young intellectuals on the older, traditionally educated, elites to conform to the European examples. Particular attention was paid to perceived advances in the areas of administration; the creation of a political system that incorporated constitutionalism, freedom and justice; and the emphasis placed on the pursuit of knowledge as an end in itself. Europe's military success was acknowledged to have been built on the fundamental principles of education, free polities and efficient social organisation rather than on the means of achieving such a system. It was also acknowledged as a product of the system, rather than its precursor.[17]

The second stage involved non-Muslim actors,[18] such as missionaries and educators, who set up foreign schools within the Muslim communities, and commercial and financial agents, who created their own business empires and enclaves. The presence of foreign teachers, investors and business representatives had an immense effect upon Muslim society and accelerated both the rate of and the demand for change amongst the elites. The perceived benefits of such change included the construction of railway links and the Suez Canal, and

[15] Ibid., pp. 146–7.
[16] Ibid., pp. 156–9.
[17] Ibid., pp. 143, 158.
[18] Ibid., pp. 162–4.

the incorporation of Egyptian cotton into the international markets. Egyptian dependence upon the vagaries of the international market made it vulnerable to its fluctuations, encouraged the accrual of immense foreign debts, and opened the way for foreign interference in the Egyptian economy. Egypt became a valuable commodity for the West. The increase in contact with the West increased the demand for Westernisation, and Western-style reforms. This in turn led to an increased awareness of the West by Arabs—an awareness that expanded beyond France—and the emergence of a popular Arab press.

The increasing awareness of the West and the attendant Westernisation of Arab society also created hostility from within. There were many who felt threatened by the rapidity of the changes, and many felt the changes were imposed upon them. Awareness increased also of the actual and potential threats posed by modernisation to the Muslim community's social and cultural traditions. Some advocated "selective adoption" of Western reforms, others total rejection.

In the final stage, the chief proponents of reform again came from within the Muslim community. However, this time, they were members of the Western-educated elite, who brought with them values that had been instilled in them by exogamous forces, in foreign or foreign-run schools.[19] They were representative of the style of "Westernised Muslim" al-Afghānī had condemned in "Refutation of the Materialists", working as foreign agents against the interests of their own society. They advocated further political and social reforms, such as increased industrialisation and urbanisation, that is, economic and social transformation. For Abu-Lughod, this period was an intensified version of stage one; however, he seems to have discounted the impact of Western schooling on these individuals, when making that comparison. Whilst these agents of change were born a part of the society they acted within, they were also educated outside it, making their advocacy equivocal.

In the "Refutation of the Materialists", al-Afghānī represents himself as a defender of Islamic orthodoxy against the incursions of Westernised Muslims seeking to undermine the coherence of Muslim society. He is more than willing to embrace the benefits of Westernisation and promote modernisation, but not at the expense of the societies into which these reforms are introduced—al-Afghānī was

[19] Ibid., pp. 164–5.

himself strongly associated with the advocates of Westernisation he condemns in the "Refutation". He claimed that their advocacy of Westernisation was a thinly-disguised advocacy of British imperialism and, therefore, a threat to the Eastern cultures.[20] While he took care to be identified as a defender of orthodoxy during his attack on Sayyid Aḥmad Khān, al-Afghānī promoted the commonalities of linguistics, territory and shared history as a means of creating a unified resistance to imperialism in India.[21] He used the tactics that were so popular with his contemporaries—those of delving into the glories of the past—to prove a historical ascendancy that entrenched India as part of the source of Europe's current ascendancy. For al-Afghānī, nationalism was less about boundaries and more about common bonds of language and culture. He reserved his major criticisms for the followers of Khān who were British in attitude, and who appeared to have rejected their Muslim heritage in favour of absolute acceptance of Western superiority.

In contrast, his "Response to Renan" stated unequivocally that religion itself was the enemy of science and that Islam and Christianity were equally historically guilty of denying the pursuit of science and knowledge.[22] Al-Afghānī praised the West's utilitarian approach to learning and advocated similar secularist reforms for his own country. He believed that Europe and Muslim societies were on parallel social evolutionary courses. Christianity, of course, had had a head start on Islam by several hundred years that Islam was only now catching up, and this was why Islam was less modernised than the West.[23]

Al-Afghānī saw religion as an integral part of that evolution since it facilitated the acceptance of ideas by the masses who were unable, and unwilling, to embrace new knowledge.[24] He believed that the masses were incapable of accepting the higher truths, by their very faith, and therefore needed literalist revelation in order to learn.[25] Any deviation from revelation could result in splits and schisms within the community and a weakening of resistance to Westernisation. His

20 Keddie, *An Islamic Response to Imperialism*, pp. 55–6, 70.

21 Ibid., p. 57.

22 Ibid., p. 87.

23 Ibid.

24 Ibid., p. 63.

25 Ibid., pp. 86, 89.

ultimate aim was the secularisation of Muslim society in the same way that Christian society had been secularised. The masses would be placated with religious dogma, revelation and the promise of heavenly rewards while the educated elites would pursue knowledge.[26] Al-Afghānī held European society up as the example of civilisation that Muslims would attain once they broke free of religious dogma.

Al-Afghānī's other purpose in responding to Renan's comments was to refute his claim that Arabs were hostile to progress and that Islam opposed the pursuit of knowledge.[27] For al-Afghānī, all religions were hostile to the pursuit of knowledge, as Europe's own Christian history would show in relation to the many reformers who had been destroyed by the Christian churches. Such activities were a direct challenge to the churches' authority. As for Arab resistance to progress, he cited the rapid assimilation and continued development by early Arabs of the classical Greek and Persian philosophies and sciences whilst Europe was in its Dark Ages, and of their willingness to share such knowledge with the Europeans on their emergence from barbarism.[28]

Perhaps the most profound reaction to Europe, from the writers reviewed by both Keddie and Abu-Lughod, was the acknowledgement and acceptance of Western superiority in all things, since this acknowledgement had intrinsic to it the acceptance of Eastern inferiority and all the attached flurries of self-doubt, fear, rejection (of "self" and "other") and rationalisations which became the heart of their relations. Abu-Lughod notes that Arab writers of this period were particularly enthusiastic in their encouragement of emulation of the West and particularly scathing of their own society's ignorance and retardation. For example, al-Ṭahṭāwī alluded to the task of the educated to combat ignorance in Islamic society through teaching the masses to welcome and make use of Western advances.[29] He believed that ignorance bred inferiority and that emulation of Western achievements in the pursuit of all branches of knowledge was necessary in order to combat that ignorance. He urged caution in only one area of study, that of rationality in French philosophy,

[26] Ibid., p. 89.
[27] Ibid., p. 88.
[28] Ibid., p. 96.
[29] Abu-Lughod, *Arab Rediscovery of Europe*, pp. 137–40, 153.

claiming that the arguments contradicted "all Divine Books", were difficult to refute, and posed a danger to the understanding of those not well-versed in the Qur'ān. But he did not recommend that it not be studied.[30]

Al-Ṭahṭāwī romanticised the glories of historical Islam, of its superiority and perfection and emphasised its role in the current ascendancy of Europe. He also introduced the notion of Europe and Islam as polar opposites, in balance with each other—two separate worlds with complementary attributes. Islam possessed the *sharī'ah*, while Europe possessed science and other branches of knowledge; and unlike the Arabs, Europeans loved to pursue material things. Khayr al-Dīn urged adoption of the results of Western progress regardless of Muslim attitudes towards the West.[31] He claimed that if a thing was beneficial then the fact of its origin as European was immaterial, especially since Islamic literature and history showed that it was already part of Islam's past.

For Khayr al-Dīn, European civilisation was the result of its emulation of Islamic civilisation at the height of its wealth and military power. Emulation of Europe would have to be in accordance with the *sharī'ah*. According to him, the Islamic principles of consultation are the equivalent of European constitutionalism (see chapter 2), and were present in the Islamic states up until its split into Abbasid, Fāṭimid and Umayyad components. In other words, Europe did not possess any qualities which were not previously in the possession of Islamic states, before dissension caused splits in Islamic unity and its loss of ascendancy.

Al-Afghānī preached pan-Islamism to the masses as a means of resistance to the imperialism of the West; and the idea of Islam as open to progress to foreign and Muslim intellectual elites. He claimed that Islam was the closest of all religions to the sciences, and was more rational than Christianity because it lacked the inconsistencies contained in such Christian doctrines as the Trinity.[32] He attributed Islam's decline to the rejection of science by the Muslim countries' leadership and by the *'ulamā'*, legitimating his discourse of ascendancy through frequent references to historical figures of authority in Islam. The Islam to which he referred in his discourse was not an

30 Ibid., p. 148.
31 Ibid., pp. 141–4.
32 Keddie, *An Islamic Response to Imperialism*, pp. 96–7.

actually existing Islam but the idealised Islam of the (Golden Age of the) Caliphate, when the glories of Islam made it pre-eminent in the world and the repository of knowledges.[33] It was the "spirit" of Islam which was the basis of his discourse, the source of modern Christian excellence and the real defence against European encroachment. Actually existing Islam, the Islam embraced by the masses, was the barrier to modernisation and to science, and it was this Islam he denounced as hostile to science in his "Response to Renan".

The problem of potential conflicts between the new, rational European philosophies and the *sharī'ah* was side-stepped by writers like al-Ṭahṭāwī and al-Afghānī who argue that the modern European philosophies were derived from knowledge preserved and refined by the Arabs.[34] Hence, the adoption of these "new" philosophies was justified by the assertion that constitutionalism, political freedom and justice of the European system were the natural form of Islamic government, and that the spirit of *al-shūrā* was employed during the time of the Prophet and the Caliphate. They were essential for a return to Islam's earlier glory and for re-enacting the *ummah*'s bygone moment of ascendancy in the history of world civilisations.

Al-Afghānī was highly critical of Muslim philosophy in general. He claimed it was based on an uncritical acceptance of Greek philosophy as the absolute truth and that this acceptance had made Islam unquestioning and static, and dependent on traditional interpretations.[35] It was therefore necessary to introduce into Muslim society the questioning nature of European rationalism to combat problems of ignorance, poverty, and complacency amongst the *ulamā'* and some traditional elites. There was no threat to the Qur'ān from European rationalism since its infinite interpretations and meanings show that philosophy (including and especially European philosophy) was neither final nor perfect. He was a staunch proponent of the evolutionary theory of civilisation. Civilisation was an achievement that was not an inherent part of any one society, and it was not an indicator of status.

Common to both Abu-Lughod and Keddie is the strong contrast made between the "West" as a secular mechanistic, technological culture and the "East" as a culture dominated by "the spirit" of

[33] Ibid., pp. 80, 83.

[34] Abu-Lughod, *Arab Rediscovery of Europe*, pp. 152.

[35] Keddie, *An Islamic Response to Imperialism*, p. 64.

Islam. The depiction of the East as the spiritual contrast to Europe by these early Arab and Muslim writers created a dualist relationship that continues to permeate the attitudes of each to the other. Just as the "West" defines the "East" as the exotic, seductive, magical "other", the "East" has defined the "West" as the material, mechanistic "other", completely lacking the vital spirit of Divine Revelation. Each considers the other through these stereotypes and defines them by what they do not possess.

The depictions of the West as secular, materialistic and progressive in both Abu-Lughod's and Keddie's studies serve to underline the main point of the writers' arguments. The spirituality of Islam, be it actual or idealised, is what has made Islam great in the past and what will return it to that eminence. Europe attained its ascendancy through bloodshed and struggle, because it lacked Islam's spirituality. Al-Afghānī based his call to the masses on an idealised form of Islam to be used as a tool for facilitating change, and as a defence against the incursions of Westernisation. The inherent Occidentalism of Muslim and Arab writers made it possible for them to laud the achievements of Europe, whilst bemoaning the lack of achievements in their own communities and pitying Europe for its lack of a spiritual equivalent to Islam.

What transpires from Abu-Lughod's and Keddie's fine works is that the discursive parameters of Muslim and Arab self-imagining and defining as well as "worlding" and "othering" have been framed since the nineteenth-century rediscovery of the "West" by Arabs and Muslims. Abu-Lughod is right in concluding that "These early apologetics were in embryonic form but they foreshadowed a reaction which was to become a dominant response of Arabs to [W]estern culture."[36] In the same vein, Keddie correctly deduces from her study of al-Afghānī that

> [He] is in some sense the parent of various later trends that reject both pure traditionalism and pure Westernism...his style of thought [and of discourse] ha[ve] some affinity with numerous other trends in the modern Islamic world. These range from the Islamic liberalism associated particularly with...Muḥammad ʿAbduh, to the more conservative Islamic revivalism of the Egyptian Rashīd Riḍā and the Muslim Brethren, and include pan-Arabism and various other forms of Middle Eastern nationalism.[37]

[36] Abu-Lughod, *Arab Rediscovery of Europe*, p. 148.
[37] Keddie, *An Islamic Response to Imperialism*, p. 3.

Like their early counterparts, today's apologetics constitute a complex interplay in which boundaries of identities, cultures and epistemologies are engaged in processes of empowerment in the face of ominously disempowering forces of "otherness" and encounters with the "other". Moreover, they are engaged in processes of self-assuredness, or what is termed in Arabic *al-baḥth 'ani'l-dhāt* (self-defining), when tested by the insecurities and anxieties imposed by the outsider's real or imagined superiority; and of reclamation of the revered foundations, from the past, and their re-reinterpretation for the purpose of resisting fusion into the "other", or cultural and subjective dispossession in the present. Thus this dynamic interplay charts a discursive field that is fraught with many a risk, not only of generalisation and essentialisation, but also of contradiction. In this case, the early Occidentalist constructions of the "West" appear to be inconsistent, oscillating between acceptance and rejection, positiveness and defensiveness. Despite apparent inconsistencies, what is consistent in this discursive minefield is the contestation between a variety of voices to make, in the name of reason, their positions authoritative through religion. In this regard, one striking continuity from al-Afghānī to the more recent Islamist ideologues is the selective nature of discourse whereby Western political freedom, justice and institutions are cast as Islamic or read in Islam, even if with qualifications. In this contestation the "self" is not just posited against the "other" but also against the many forms of "otherness" within the realm of the "self", pitting Muslim against Muslim and Arab against Arab—religionists versus secularists; Westernisers versus non-Westernisers (e.g. the Shah versus Khomeini; Nasser versus al-Bannā; *Francisants* against *Arabisants* in the Maghrib).

ISLAMIST COUNTER-DISCOURSES AND THE POLITICS OF IDENTITY

The encounter with the "West" and the "modern" has had many enduring implications for the imaging and narrating of colonial and neocolonial subjectivity and identity in the AME. Neither the category "West" nor "modern" are taken here to mean a cartographical space. Most importantly, they are understood as a discursive space. The AME's encounter with the "West" and the "modern" was more than an encounter with a geography. Above all else, the encounter was with a mindset derived from an Enlightenment ethos. Accompanying this mindset are attitudes noted for their anthropocentrism as opposed to theocentrism, for man's self-assuredeness and self-confidence in the exactness and certainty of science and rationality-derived knowledge, and for man's ability to control his destiny and order human existence, aided by value-free and true knowledge, through mastery over nature. Just as the "West" is not defined spatially, the "modern" is not understood in temporal terms. The encounter with the "West" and with the "modern", which was almost invariably violent, engendered, at the conscious level, intellectual-ideological and cultural shock, and at the not so conscious level, a psychological-emotional impact.

This shock-impact still reverberates in the AME. It inheres in the insecurities of the ongoing search for an Arab identity or *huwiyyah*, which is neither fixed nor singular as shall be explained in the last chapter. In this respect, culture and cultural narratives come to play a major role in such a search. It is a site where the insecurities of both colonial and neocolonial identities and subjectivities find expression, that is, expression not only in the sense of resisting the hegemonic "other" and cultural otherness of the hegemon but also in the sense of self-defining and self-imaging, often via "counter-othering". Through counter-othering the threatened, the dispossessed, the marginalised and (neo-) colonised seek to dismantle the processes of othering initiated by the dominant "other". Counter-othering entails binding up one's language, narratives, and politics with an origin, with a logos or a foundational realm, and with a notion of authenticity. From this perspective, Occidentalism, as an Oriental discourse about the Occident, is not any less guilty of the logocentrism and ethnocentrism that characterise Orientalism. Counter-othering is about countering the logos of the "other" with one's own logos, speaking for oneself instead of being spoken for, and grounding one's agency in one's own cultural foundations. Nonetheless, counter-othering remains largely, but not solely, a resistance aimed at salvaging one's sense of self and autonomy, at asserting one's cultural belonging and meaning, and at securing recognition for them.

Here the Foucauldian anti-humanist critique, that is, interrogation of the Enlightenment project, what Lyotard calls the "grand narratives" of modernity[38] and the rational subject, are relevant.

[38] Jean-François Lyotard, *The Postmodern Condition: A Report on Knowledge* (Manchester University Press, 1984).

Foucault brings to the fore the colonising effect of humanism on knowledge. His notion of "epistemic shift" and that of "regimes of power/knowledge" testify to his rejection of Enlightenment's and modernity's arrogance in valorising the "modern" and devaluing the "traditional". This rejection extends to modernity's grand narratives, especially with regard to individualised human beings' supposed "emancipation through the progressive unfolding of reason". Thus, the French philosopher's anti-humanist framework is organised around three analytical trajectories—archeological (thinking), genealogical (doing) and ethical (being). The first, dating back to the 1960s, concerns forms of knowledge (*The Archeology of Knowledge*).[39] In the second, during the 1970s, Foucault turns to questions regarding the genealogy and disciplines of the body, i.e. power and modes of relations to others (e.g. *Discipline and Punish*).[40] Lastly, the 1980s Foucault (*The Use of Pleasure*; *The Care of the Self*) focuses on the historical constitution of individuals (self).[41]

Foucault's critique of the humanist framework, liberal and Marxist, is essentially about questioning humanist subjectivity. In fact, one tenor of Foucault's critique of modernity revolves around the degeneration of the Enlightenment's project of emancipation into domination. Thus the Foucault of the 1970s, in such works as *Discipline and Punish* and volume 1 of *History of Sexuality*, maps "power/knowledge regimes" through the institutionalisation of the disciplines of the body and the technologies of the self. He develops a conception of capillary power, by setting out to theorise the way power works in modern society outside the model of legal sovereignty. He uses his notion of discourse to describe the type of knowledge through which power operates.[42] To change the way subjectivity is conceived, Foucault

[39] Michel Foucault, *L'archeologie du savoir* (Paris: Gallimard, 1969) and Michel Foucault, *The Archeology of Knowledge*, trans. by Alan M. Sheridan Smith (London: Tavistock Publications, 1972).

[40] Michel Foucault, *Discipline and Punish* (New York: Vintage Books, 1979).

[41] Michel Foucault, *The Use of Pleasure, The History of Sexuality vol. 2*, trans. by Robert Harley (New York: Pantheon Books, 1985); Michel Foucault, *The Care of the Self, The History of Sexuality vol. 3*, trans. by Robert Harley (New York: Vintage Books, 1988).

[42] See Michel Foucault, *Power/Knowledge: Selected Interviews and other Writings, 1972–1977*, ed. by Colin Gordon (New York: Harvester, 1980); See also, Michel Foucault, "Truth and Power" in Paul Rabinow (ed.), *The Foucault Reader* (New York: Pantheon Books, 1984), pp. 51–75.

looks at how people's experiences of being subjects are produced. This he does by exploring the question of what kind of historical forces create experience of the self as a subject.

More specifically, the Foucauldian understanding of power and notion of discourse are invoked here for their relevance to how collective identity is constituted and produced, especially in a neocolonial setting such as the AME. Power can be aggregated into very large formations, e.g. "class" or "state". However, Foucault argues that "power is everywhere". That is, power is not localised or centred in one site, rather it resides in multiple sites. Only actual exercise begets power—power begotten is power exercised. Power, from this Foucauldian perspective, is the possibility to produce an effect. Social relations, for instance, have power at stake in them; and a social norm is a codified relationship of power. The relationship therefore between a subject and an institution, be it a carceral organisation, such as a prison or an educational one such as a school, is about power. Power does not only beget domination, it also entails resistance. The subordinated subject has the ability to get into the power relationship and modify it. In other words, there is the potential for reversal and resistance.

The Foucauldian power-knowledge strategem and the role played by any "discursive regime" to make and remake "real" meaning, construct reality, or constitute subjectivity informs Said's work, *Orientalism*. The indirect moral of *Orientalism* is that self-representation and the finding of one's own voice are very different from being represented or spoken for. But here lies the greatest paradox: self-representation and self-definition inevitably involve representing the "other" in juxtaposition to the "self". Thus, anyone who Orientalises must Occidentalise and vice versa. This is at the core of both Said's work, even if covertly, and Carrier's thesis, very overtly. Carrier notes that the kind of knowledge-making about non-Western cultures in which anthropologists engage breeds Occidentalism: "Occidentalism is the silent partner of their work and debate".[43] Unlike Said's Orientalism, Carrier's Occidentalism is dualistic: engaged in by the indigenous and the non-indigenous; hence, first:

> ... although "the Orient" may have appeared in Oriental studies to be a term with a concrete referent, a real region of the world with real attributes, in

[43] Carrier, "Introduction", p. 1.

practice it took meaning only in the context of another term, "the West". And in this process is the tendency to essentialize, to reduce the complex entities that are being compared to a set of core features that express the essence of each entity, but only as it stands in contrast to the other. In conventional anthropology, the Orientalisms that have attracted critical attention thus do not exist on their own. They are matched by anthropologists' Occidentalisms, essentializing simplifications of the West.[44]

Second:

> A different sort of Occidentalism appears, and is of growing importance in anthropology, in studies of the ways that people outside the West imagine themselves, for their self-image often develops in contrast to their stylized image of the West. The self-imagining that is known most widely in anthropology probably is the concept of *kastom*, the concern to preserve and perhaps recreate what people see as their traditional ways, reported originally in Melanesian ethnography.[45]

The rediscovery of the West by Arabs and Muslims, especially since the nineteenth century, has engendered a great deal of Occidentalisation and Occidentalism.[46] The earliest form of Occidentalism is summed up in the Muslim division of the world into *dār al-Islām* (abode of Islam)—the self, and *dār al-ḥarb* (abode of unbelief)—the other. *Dār al-amān* (abode of safety), however, is a kind of a synthesis, a space that believers of all faiths, subject to certain fiscal arrangements, share. Images of the rise of Christendom triggered reflections on the demise of *dār al-Islām* in the minds of those early reformers ranging from the Egyptian al-Ṭahṭāwī to the Tunisian statesman Khayr al-Dīn.[47] The institutions, constitutions, liberty and justice of Europe became images of the West—France—which for both men engendered what Carrier calls a "process of self-definition through opposition with the alien".[48] These stylised images of the West were set off against their own politically and administratively

[44] Ibid., p. 3.

[45] Ibid., p. 6.

[46] See, for instance, the work by David C. Gordon, *Images of the West: Third World Perspectives* (Totowa: Rowman and Littlefield, 1989), esp. pp. 61–86.

[47] See Rifā'ah Rāfi' al-Ṭahṭāwī, *Takhlīs al-ibrīz ila talkhīṣ bārīz* [*The Extraction of Gold from a Review of Paris*] (Tripoli, Libya: Al-Dar al'Arabiyyah lil-Kitab, 1991). See also Khayr al-Dīn al-Tūnisī, *Muqaddimat aqwām al-masālik fī ma'rifat aḥwāl al-mamlik* [*The Surest Path to Knowledge Concerning the Condition of Countries*] trans. by Leon Carl Brown (Cambridge, MA: Harvard University Press, 1967).

[48] Carrier, "Introduction", p. 3.

less developed systems. And these reduced "core features" became elements that they wanted for their own societies and wished to emulate. This was done through both identification and distancing. Like many other early reformers, they sought to appropriate such items by identifying with them, and by casting them either as "Islamic" or as congenial with the spirit of Islam. Thus emulation would be merely an act of re-borrowing and re-appropriating what Europeans had borrowed from Islam. Therefore, Europe's superior political systems were not seen as synonymous with the superiority of Christianity. From this perspective, the early Occidentalism was double-edged, operating concomitantly to highlight closeness and commonality as well as "dramatiz[e] the distance and difference".[49] But by casting the *ifranj*—as al-Ṭahṭāwī refers to Europeans—as "Islamic" in their justice and government, the intention was to make Europe palatable not repulsive, familiar not foreign, but, nonetheless, different.

Here Carrier is powerfully relevant as demonstrable by the example of a hierarchical India and an individualist West:

> ...[T]he Occidental and the Oriental define and justify each other, for the image of an individualist West makes non-individualistic elements in India noteworthy, just as the image of a hierarchical India makes individualistic elements in the West noteworthy.[50]

Following from the above, it can be said that the image of a justly, representatively, and accountably-ruled Europe made unjust and non-accountable elements in the then largely autonomous *ojaks* (provinces) of Egypt and Tunis noteworthy in the minds of al-Ṭahṭāwī and Khayr al-Dīn, just as the image of a non-accountable rule in either country made accountability and representativeness in France noteworthy. This, however, is different from taking either case to be absolute, at all times, and to be representative of all rule in Arab and Muslim lands, or even of nineteenth-century France itself. But the "asymmetry", which is induced by the presence of a "thesis" of a justly and accountably-ruled Europe and an "antithesis" of a less just or accountable order in Egypt or Tunis is "stylized" by Orientals Occidentalising, not Occidentals Orientalising.[51] Subsequent to this

[49] Said, *Orientalism*, p. 55. See also Ibid.

[50] See Carrier, "Introduction", p. 4.

[51] Here the author borrows the terms "asymmetry", "thesis" and "antithesis" and deploys them as done by Chris Fuller and cited in Carrier, "Introduction", p. 4.

"asymmetry" is a second one in which the "thesis" is the "Islamicity" of Egyptians or Tunisians as well as of justice, and the "un-Islamicity" of the Franks. The first "asymmetry" is a marker of fascination with the "other" and of "inferiority" of the "self" in a specific area—political and administrative organisation. The second is a marker of self-adulation and of the inferiority of the "other" in another area—religious identity.

The type of Occidentalism most observable in the AME, especially, though not exclusively, amongst many Islamist groups, is comparable in its inner dynamics and outward manifestations to its Melanesian and Pacific counterparts, as described by Carrier.[52] Its emblemata can be sketched comparatively

- It is a self-imagining or counter-imagining, that is, "in contrast to…stylized image[s] of the West".[53]
- Just as *kastom*, as anthropologists have discovered in the case of Melanesia, represents a reification of tradition, so do such notions as *turath* (cultural heritage), *aṣālah* (cultural authenticity), *'urūbah* (Arabness), and *ḥaḍārah islāmiyyah* (Islamic civilisation). And like *kastom*, these concepts are operationalised as markers of a separate identity, and the passwords for admission into the "us" membership—Arab life, Islamic way of life.
- Like *kastom*, these notions and concepts are what Carrier calls "reifications in context, and the context is…intruding colonial Western social forms".[54] It is in this context that the contrast with the "other" and the ways of the "other" is sharpened in order to reify or reinvent tradition. Resistance to colonialism either led by al-Mahdī in Sudan; al-Amīr 'Abd al-Qādir in Algeria; 'Abd al-Karīm al-Khaṭṭāb in Morocco; 'Umar al-Mukhṭār in Libya, amongst others, or by modernising nationalists (including Nasser; Bourguiba; Ben Bella) was explained, and legitimised through the operationalisation of religious metaphors and idioms, and couched in Qur'ānic language. Islam was seen as the defining boundary between the "us" and the "them". But what must not be forgotten here is that the "other" or the "them" happens to be the uninvited invader in this case. The claimers of the mantle of Islam in their

52 Carrier, "Introduction", pp. 6–9.
53 Ibid., p. 6.
54 Ibid., p. 7.

baḥth 'an'l-dhāt, are today the most vocal bearers of the banner of *turāth, aṣālah* and *al-shakṣiyyah al-islāmiyyah al-'arabiyyah* (Arabo-Islamic identity).

- Carrier's observation that "what began as image can be self-fulfilling and so become reality"[55] has confirmation in the AME as it has in Papua New Guinea. Chewing of the betel nut for the New Guineans is greater Islamic observance and *ṣaḥwah islāmiyyah* (Islamic resurgence/revival) for Muslims at large, and, Islamists, in particular. Eric Hirsch's research, as cited by Carrier, shows how the practice of chewing the betel nut was diffused, becoming very commonplace, after it was confined to coastal inhabitants. The reasons are that those who take up the chewing of the betel nut related to it on the basis of its Melanesian-ness versus European-ness; for "Europeans drink beer and disapprove of betel nut." Further, the diffusion of the practice, argues Carrier, was meant "to claim membership in Papua New Guinea centres of power". Finally, "in the process, the image of Melanesia as betel territory is reinforced and made more real".[56] The parallelism: by identifying themselves as distinctively Muslim versus non-Muslim, and Arab versus Western, Islamists have inwardly and outwardly sought to live up to the self-image they have of themselves, and the stylised image they constructed of the West. Inwardly, they have mostly modelled their lives on those of the so-called *al-salaf al-ṣāliḥ* (righteous forebears), achieving religiosity in their own personal realms and seeking to apply religion to the horizontal dimensions of life. Outwardly, the beard, the veil, the *jallābiyyah* (traditional garb), or the modest presentation even if in Western clothing, have become markers of an out-an-out rejection of *taghrīb* (Westernisation), commodification of life, of "Pierre Cardin" consumerism and materialism, and of "Coca Cola" accultural culture. To be Muslim is to live as one; hence, the endeavours to Islamise knowledge, science, polity, economy and society, and reclaim the Medinan model in a bottom-up fashion.

Occidentalist modes of discourse on the "West" or "democracy" must be understood as counter-discourses of resistance. The Islamist discourse on democracy or *'awlamah* (globalisation) grounds agency in Islamic foundations. Through it identity is constructed, "truth"

55 Ibid.
56 Ibid., pp. 7–8.

and "reality" are made and remade, and boundaries of solidarities and divisions are drawn within the parameters of Islamists' competing versions of rethought Islam. From this perspective, the resulting discursive representations are never neutral or value-free. They carry within them not only the justifications and assumptions of a rethought Islam but also the imprints of their authors and of their knowledge practices. Hence the power-knowledge strategem of any discourse that Foucault sets out to deconstruct.[57] Through their counter-discourses, Islamists make the "self" and the "other" distinguishable, real and knowable.

The difference between Islamists lies in determining the limits of the process of rethinking Islam. The fierce debates resulting from that process illustrate the divergences between Islamists. They concern such issues as the strategies of enacting their models of political Islam (e.g. via violent or peaceful means); the way in which Islamisation should proceed (bottom-up or top-down); the place of women in society and polity (whether women can lead a Muslim society or be judges); the Caliphate (its feasibility and desirability); and the appropriation of Western populist themes (e.g. is democracy in line with the spirit of Islam?).

Accordingly, deconstructing the "West" or "democracy" entails producing "otherness". This is not to say that Islamists are intolerant of all "otherness". The intention is, on one hand, to draw the line between "us" and "them"; on the other, it is for the purpose of not letting Western modernism be enthroned as the only legitimate framework for political and socio-economic engineering. It is therefore no surprise that for al-Ghannūshī and al-Turābī *'awlamah*, for instance, is read *kawkalah* (Coca Cola-isation).[58] Fahmī Huwaydī, the well-known Egyptian thinker and journalist, deploys the same term. His reflection on globalisation begs the question:

> Is the aim for Coca-Cola to become the human race's preferred drink, topping the list [of items] imposed on humans, from hamburgers to jeans and Madonna and Michael Jackson's songs? In other words, is this the meaning of globalization, [that is] to impose the West's taste and lifestyle on [the rest of] the world?[59]

[57] Foucault, *Power/Knowledge*.

[58] Author's interviews with al-Ghannūshī, 30 January 1998, London, and with al-Turābī, 14 May 1994, Khartoum.

[59] Fahmī Huwaydī, "ḍidd kawkaltu'l-'ālam" [Against "Coca Cola-isation" of the World], *Al-Ahram*, 10 October 1995, p. 11.

Deconstructing globalisation through the use of the term "Coca Cola-isation" is very potent. Such a reading deploys Western symbolism—Coca Cola—to describe globalisation for two chief reasons. One is to establish a link between Westernisation and globalisation, the latter being an extension of the former. Another is to deploy a Western symbol of economic, political and cultural hegemony not only in the Muslim world but also in the South. The Coca Cola metaphor is assigned the role of revealing the *who* of globalisation. That is, the globalisation not just of the West as a homogenised entity, but rather of a specific West, that of big business and of money markets, and, most importantly, that of the secularists and their allies in the South.[60]

The deconstructing of globalisation as "Coca Cola-isation" carries another significance. It has to do with the will and refusal to be purged as a *huwiyyah* (identity), cultural, historical, moral and linguistic. In a sense, this is an ontological preoccupation which is not specific to Islamists or Muslims. By way of counter-discourse, this preoccupation is confronted in a dualistic fashion, deconstructing "otherness" and constructing "selfhood", thereby opening new space for assertion of agency, as individual or collective action.[61] Agency, according to Giddens, is a "transformative capacity"[62] or a wilful power to act, that is, "to deploy a range of causal powers, including that of influencing those deployed by others". Moreover, it "depends upon the capability...to 'make a difference' to a pre-existing state of affairs or course of events".[63] Agency interpenetrates with discourse, as a form of knowledge-making and knowledge practice, to certify the reality of the constructed world and allocate and assign values to it. In doing so, Islamists are driven by the impulse to resist domination or the spectre of it, especially with the still-vivid memory of colonisation etched in the psyche of millions of Muslims. Through agency and counter-discourse, Islamists are striving not only to sabotage

60 Author's interviews with al-Ghannūshī, 30 January 1998, London, and with al-Turābī, 14 May 1994, Khartoum.

61 This distinction is clear in the literature on human agency and social structure. For Giddens, the agent is an individual actor: See Anthony Giddens, *The Constitution of Society: Outline of the Theory of Structuration* (Berkeley: University of California Press, 1984). Compare with Alaine Touraine for whom agency can be collective, See his *The Self-Production of Society* (Chicago University Press, 1971).

62 Giddens, *The Constitution of Society*, p. 15.

63 According to Giddens in ibid., p. 14.

dominant knowledge-power strategems—colonisation and Westernisation—and their attendant discourses but also to transmute marginality into identity. Spirituality and communitarianism are examples of the values the Islamists ascribe to this identity. In opposition is the materialism and individualism attributed to "otherness". From this perspective, the Islamist discourse is a counter-discourse and a form of resistance against forces of subjection—e.g. globalisation. It is a counter-discourse in that it remains framed by the dominant discourses of the past 150 years—from nationalism to democracy—and interlocked with "otherness" in battles, especially in the cultural sphere. It is nonetheless a discourse involving struggles and producing a collective agency that is, in the words of Touraine, "implementing one or more elements of the system of historical action and therefore intervening directly in the relations of [in this case, Western] domination".[64]

Through their counter-discourses of resistance, Islamists from Iran to Sudan have been aiming at breaking down the dominant forms of knowledge in order to change the existing power relations of domination, locally, regionally and globally. They have been seeking to accomplish this by integrating a different form of knowledge in their own knowledge practices and knowledge-making. From this perspective the "rules" by which the Islamist counter-discourse is seeking to break down the Western dominant discourse are two-fold: from within and from without. The former refers to the Islamist counter-discourses that sprang from within the dominant discourse in the Muslim world. In Iran, there is a counter-discourse by President Khatami and his allies springing from within "Khomeinism", the dominant discourse. This counter-discourse disowns the language of *mustakbirūn* (arrogant supremacists) and *mustaḍ'afūn* (the downtrodden), and of "satans". It stresses the language of "civil society" within Iran and "dialogue" with the West. In the AME, many Islamists, especially various Muslim Brotherhoods and off-shoot movements from within them such as in Sudan and Jordan, have since the 1980s and 1990s shunned Sayyid Quṭb's radicalism, replacing it with a Qur'ānic language that is moderate and conciliatory in its tone and, at the same time, appropriated the language of democracy, civil society. In a sense, this is akin to how liberalism sprang from within

64 Touraine, *The Self-Production of Society*, p. 459.

conservatism. The latter refers to how the Islamist counter-discourses have been responding to the dominant Western discourse, whether the subject matter is democracy or women. What is noticeable in this regard is the fact that Islamists, consciously or otherwise, realise that the Western discourse on democracy, which is over 2,000 years old, cannot be broken down overnight.

By having their own counter-discourses still framed by the dominant narrative, Islamists are making compromises with it and with the West. These compromises are positive in that they set Islamists and non-Islamists on a dialogical course and processes of mutual inclusion and exchange. The alternative is violence which neither can afford or win, especially the Muslim side. These compromises are evidenced in the Islamist counter-discourses acknowledging that the parameters of their own counter-discourses are Western in origin. But, as many Islamist seminal thinkers put it, difference of origin should not translate into difference in the ends. Many Islamists argue, for instance, the ends of *shūrā* and democracy are about deliberation, representation and consultation. In these compromises, there is some gain for the Islamists too: they get to legitimise their counter-discourses, the forms of knowledge they promote and the power structures they envision to result from them. Perhaps the biggest gain for Islamists and their counter-narratives in all of this is their ability to flourish in a world where, for instance, the Western democratic discourse is dominant. Through their counter-discourses, Islamists are beginning to appear in different forms and occupy different spaces. But this says a great deal not only about Islamists and their counter-discourses but also about the nature of discourse, in general. Discourse, such as the democratic one, is not a paradigm with fixed parameters. Its boundaries are fluid and its potential to shift varies according to the dynamics of history, culture and time.

These counter-discourses form part of an emerging counter-politics: of identity or identification, culture, rights, and moral protest against a superimposed "modern" identity. This modern and postcolonial identity has been most evident in the AME through its socialist variations up to the mid-1980s and is continuing through national-secularist states. It has been complicit in exclusion, subordination, oppression, misrepresentation and disidentification (negation of alternative identities, be they feminist, ethnic or religious). Like the colonial identity, the modern and postcolonial identity has been constructed as fixed and monolithic. Again, like its colonial predecessor, postcolonial identity owes its existence to force. It is therefore no surprise that in Islamist counter-discourses modern identity is deconstructed as akin to colonial identity and ruling elites as representatives of the ex-colonisers' identity. However, like colonial and postcolonial identities, the new identity is constructed in Islamist counter-discourses through contrast. That is, in the words of William Connolly, "[T]he consolidation of identity through the constitution of difference. The self-reassurance of identity through the construction of otherness."[65] The emphasis of contrast, coupled with the homogenisation of identity and culture as in some Islamist counter-discourses, has the potential of denying a share in public or opposition space for other identities, both individual and collective. This negation spells danger for the future of the democratic project in the AME; it certainly continues to do so under the postcolonial state. Thus Jonathan Friedman finds a correspondence between homogeny and hegemony, i.e. "a tendency toward assimilation to a dominant identity".[66] Both culture and identity have been minefields in the AME where states, along with other sub-systemic actors, and their discourses and counter-discourses have fallen in the trap of ignoring or simply not knowing

> ...their socially constructed (as opposed to primordially given) nature; their optional (opposed to deterministic) dimensions; their fragmenting/diversifying (as opposed to integrating/homogenizing) implications; and their multidimensional/dynamic (as opposed to unidimensional/static) features.[67]

The rise of the politics of identity and of culture is linked to the fragmentary nature of identity in late modernity. The stress of various homogenising and hegemonising modernist projects have led to the rise of counter politics, resulting in an explosion of formerly subordinated or marginalised voices, struggles and solidarities resurging to assert the distinctiveness of their identities and the languages, histories and cultures that underpin them. These struggles and solidarities

[65] William E. Connolly, *Identity/Difference: Democratic Negotiations of Political Paradox* (Ithaca and London: Cornell University Press, 1991), p. 9.

[66] Jonathan Friedman, "Order and Disorder in Global Systems: A Sketch", *Social Research*, 60 (summer 1993), pp. 205–34, p. 210.

[67] Yosef Lapid, "Culture's Ship: Returns and Departures in International Relations Theory" in Yosef Lapid and Friedrich Kratochwil (eds), *The Return of Culture and Identity in IR Theory* (Boulder, CO: Lynne Rienner, 1996), p. 7.

(new social movements—indigenous peoples, ethnic groups, environmentalists, gay groups, women, people of colour) positioning themselves in "the spaces of representation" intersect, argues Stanley Aronowitz, in displacement.[68] Displacement is both material (e.g. impoverishment, migration, etc.) and emotional (e.g. crisis, disillusionment, breakdown). These struggles also intersect in "the struggle for social justice" and "the space of opposition and alternative".[69] The semantics may vary but in essence these identities aim for "dealienation",[70] "dehomogenisation"[71] or, simply "recognition".[72] According to Nancy Fraser, as a new political imaginary displaces its socialist predecessor, class-based and interest-focused struggles defined by issues of socio-economic redistribution have ceded to gender or race-based struggles seeking cultural recognition. Accordingly, owing to "postsocialist" displacements, "cultural domination supplants exploitation as the fundamental injustice. [Similarly], cultural recognition displaces socioeconomic redistribution as the remedy for injustice and the goal of political struggle".[73]

Friedman captures the essence of displacement in a globalising world not too differently from Fraser, arguing that modernity as an identity-space is in crisis.[74] This crisis, embodied in the disillusionment with modernism, has awakened cultural leanings and collective identity attachments. Modernism, in the midst of an acute socio-economic crisis inhibiting its expansion, becomes unable to deliver such goods as development, mobility, self-realisation, and the very belief in the future itself; that is, certainty.[75] The result is two-fold. At one level, modernism's own crisis has led to crises of personhood. Hence individuals' search for refuge in social selfhood instead of individual selfhood: "The subject loses its self-project and becomes increasingly dependent on significant others".[76] This is almost a

[68] Stanley Aronowitz, *The Politics of Identity: Class, Culture, Social Movements* (New York: Routledge, 1992), p. 8.

[69] Ibid., p. 9.

[70] In R. Felix Geyer (ed.), *Alienation, Ethnicity, and Postmodernism* (Westport: Greenwood Press, 1996).

[71] Friedman, "Order and Disorder in Global Systems: A Sketch", p. 210.

[72] Nancy Fraser, *Justice Interruptus: Critical Reflections on the "Postsocialist" Condition* (New York and London: Routledge, 1997).

[73] Ibid., p. 11.

[74] Friedman, "Order and Disorder in Global Systems: A Sketch", esp. pp. 216–9.

[75] Ibid., p. 219.

[76] Ibid., p. 228.

quasi-reversal of or, at least, a challenge to, modernism's process of individualisation, which has been translated in many parts of the world, especially in the North, into "the separation of subject from socially determinate meaning".[77] At another level, this very search for a social meaning and sanctuary induced by modernism's crisis signals the onset of "a search for alternative identities".[78]

In the AME, this search for alternative identities has meant going back to forms of identification with rethought versions of traditionalism and with collective and particularistic identities. Hence politics of identity is inherently essentialist as can be gleaned from Islamist narratives, amongst others. This is true of most if not all identity narratives. Essentially, these narratives/counter-discourses by Islamists, for instance, engage in discursive duels with both the dominant identity within (engaging the Westernisers) and without (engaging the dominant West). In these duels, they give expression not only to essentialisms but also to shared interests and political emotions of disempowerment, subordination and marginalisation, all of which necessitate as well as legitimise political engagement and resistance. The experience of subordination and alienation by their authors helps to provide identity narratives and counter-discourses with emotional legitimacy because their inherent essentialism lends them psychological appeal.[79] Islamist identity narratives focus on the West or Western power apparatuses especially as a cultural hegemon. These narratives/counter-discourses therefore target this hegemony, which, according to Friedman, has meant homogeny, i.e. "a tendency toward assimilation to a dominant culture" and "a ranking of identities with respect to the dominant".[80] The aim of Islamist identity narratives and counter-discourses is to undo this hierarchy of identities and cultures and to gain primacy over, or at least parity with, the dominant cultural identity.

This is perhaps the most important context within which Islamist modes of Occidentalist discourse must be located. Their Occidentalism is mainly a counter-discourse. At the core of this counter-discourse is what Ḥasan Ḥanafī calls a "self–other continuous historical dialectic" in which the dominated seek to reassert their identity

[77] Ibid., pp. 218–9.
[78] Ibid., p. 219.
[79] See D.C. Martin, "The Choices of Identity", *Social Identities*, 1 (1995), pp. 5–20.
[80] Friedman, "Order and Disorder in Global Systems: A Sketch", esp. p. 210.

vis-à-vis the subjectification and the subjection of the dominant.[81] Ḥanafī puts the genesis of Occidentalism to resistance against *taghrīb*, or Westernisation.[82] The marks of this *taghrīb*, Ḥanafī notes, are everywhere—culture, lifestyles, architecture and language (through borrowing; hence the introduction of neologisms and calques). This process of *taghrīb* has then contributed a great deal to the hybridisation not only of postcolonial Arab cultures but also identities. The hybrid postcolonial identity is resisted by Islamist identity narratives as well as by scholars sympathetic to their narratives like Ḥanafī. These identity narratives are anchored in a fixed origin and in a specific and particularistic culture, i.e. within a cultural relativist framework. Thus Ḥanafī equates the marks of *taghrīb* with an identity crisis. In his words, the marks of Westernisation "threaten our civilizational autonomy".[83] He sees this identity crisis, for instance, in the hybridity of architectural styles of Arab cities, something that makes them void of a *huwiyyah* or bereft of any sense of belonging. Simply put, these identity-less Arab cities are neither of "then" or "now", nor of "there" and "here": "they are neither traditional…nor are they modern…and nor are they practical, resulting from environmental requirements".[84] Because of this lack of identity, *taghrīb*, being a strategy of subjectification and subjection, serves to intensify the struggle for civilisational autonomy and recognition. Islamist counter-discourses and identity narratives are integral to this struggle. Ḥanafī observes that:

> [As] the national costume became [almost] absent…reaction [to its absence] began with the Islamic dress, the beard and the *jilbāb* (long garment donned by males) as forms of reclaiming [Arabo-Islamic] identity…The more Westernization took hold in lifestyles, the more attachment to national or Islamic dress increased as a reaction [against it] as has happened in the Islamic revolution in Iran and in the contemporary Islamic groups in Egypt. So did attachment to the Prophet's [natural] medicine as a reaction against modern medicine, and to Quranic sciences in response to modern sciences.[85]

Westernisation as a central theme recurs through the identity narratives of Occidentalism. It interpenetrates with the question of identity,

[81] Ḥasan Ḥanafī, *Muqaddimah fī 'ilmi'l-istighrāb* [*Introduction to Occidentalism*] (Cairo: al-Dar al-Fanniyyah, n.d.), p. 24.

[82] Ibid., p. 22.

[83] Ibid.

[84] Ibid., p. 23.

[85] Ibid.

which Ḥanafī considers a *qaḍiyyah ḥaḍāriyyah* (civilisational question).[86] *Taghrīb* is seen as an extension to colonisation—colonisation-cum-Westernisation. Through it and the modernist discourses that sustain it, identity formation in the West as well as in its "others" takes place. Colonisation and Westernisation intersect in the attempt to "obliterate the markers of Arabo-Islamic identity", especially as epitomised by French colonialism in North Africa.[87] If cartographical spatialisation of Arab and Muslim lands is still the most prominent legacy of colonisation, then cultural spatialisation is that of Westernisation. For Ḥanafī, the latter is demonstrable in the ideological laboratory, owing to the deluge of Western "isms", and its fragmentary effects through the AME. As he puts it, "A considerable space of our contemporary culture has been turned into civilizational agencies [working] for the 'other', and into an extension of Western paradigms: socialism, Marxism, liberalism, nationalism, existentialism…"[88] The corollary is the loss of "national cultural unity;" hence, "the search for authenticity".[89] Like Islamist identity narratives, Ḥanafī's own narrative is correct in its bid to argue for the recognition of the specificity of Arabo-Islamic identity. But he is not correct in failing to recognise the plurality of cultural frames of reference available for Arabo-Islamic postcolonial identity. Like culture, identity is a lively organism. Both are caught in the "here" and "now" as much as in the "there" and "then"; they carry the imprints of ex-colonised and and ex-colonisers' cultures; and both are torn between forms and versions of primordialism and of modernism. Perhaps then the search for "authenticity" or a fixed, original Arabo-Islamic identity, as Ḥanafī and many Islamists label it, meaning an identity quarantined from the influences of the "other", will intensify rather than terminate the insecurities of postcolonial identity in the AME. The AME is no island; and the plurality of references as well as influences by the "other" must be recognised.

Accordingly, to consider cultural pluralism or the plurality of ideologies as a conduit for the culture of the "other" into the culture of the "self", as Ḥanafī puts it, is to revert to the totalising and homogenising projects of "imagined community" imposed on peoples

[86] Ibid., p. 26.
[87] Ibid., pp. 24–5.
[88] Ibid., p. 24.
[89] Ibid.

through the AME by postcolonial regimes in the name of national unity, Arab socialism, "Bourguibism" or Ba'athism. There is room for exposure to the culture of the "other" so long as it is adapted to cultural specificity (ideas) or environmental specificity (technology). It is untenable for any identity to borrow Western technology and fully quarantine itself from cultural influences from Europe or North America. Similarly, denial of intellectual or cultural pluralism, characteristic of some Islamist identity narratives and Ḥanafī's own argument but not peculiar to either, is no longer viable in a globalising world. The crossborder movement of ideas and people not only challenges territorial and cultural boundaries but also contributes to a form of cultural transnationalism. This cultural transnationalism is making possible the forging of global solidarities and movements of moral protest around issues of concern to all humanity. Nor is cultural or intellectual pluralism necessarily synonymous with *taghrīb thaqāfī* (cultural Westernisation) unless, for instance, religious or linguistic specificity is ignored. While "Westernisation is a form of alienation",[90] especially when it sustains a project of modernity that discards specificity, it must be recognised that some marks of Westernism are both inevitable and indelible. Ḥanafī recognises that falling into the trap of reflexivity, what he calls *inghilāq* (closure) by shunning influences from the "other" is dangerous.[91] But his identity narrative is clearly homogenising and, generally, fails to indicate how reclaiming what he constructs as a fixed and undifferentiated Arabo-Islamic *huwiyyah* is reconcilable with influences of the "other".

This kind of identity narrative spells danger for the future of a dynamic civil society as well as good government in the AME. For the insecurities of the postcolonial identity seem to forbid plurality and, by implication, pluralism. Ḥanafī shows disdain towards what he calls *bu'ar thaqāfiyyah* (cultural holes),[92] metaphorically suggesting that they puncture an organic whole of Arabo-Islamic culture. He associates the espousal of Western ideologies with *taba'iyyah* (dependence) and divisiveness. For these cultural holes, which manifest themselves in various groupings including political parties, not only fragment the organic whole but also lead to distanciation from *al-dhāt* (subject).[93] Here Ḥanafī's identity narrative can be faulted on

90 Ibid., p. 25.
91 Ibid., pp. 25–6.
92 Ibid., p. 24.
93 Ibid.

two grounds. It makes new exclusions whilst arguing for solidarity of the *ummah* and the unity of its culture and identity. It defeats his own argument for dealienation and emancipation by standing up against authoritarianism and oppression in order to earn fundamental freedoms—one of seven challenges confronting the *ummah* as he puts it.[94] Good government will not obtain unless freedoms of thought, association and organisation are available to all. Therefore to exclude these *bu'ar thaqāfiyyah* because they threaten the unity of culture or the nation is not consistent with the emancipatory goals of either democracy or Islam. The emancipatory goals of the politics of identity and of moral protest face the challenge of creating rather than closing spaces where partial identification with other "others", especially from the West, are taking place as well as building solidarities and negotiating commonalities with otherness within and without. This will remain the litmus test for the search for democracy and for the open society in the AME.

Nonetheless, Occidentalism as a counter-discourse is intended to be an emancipatory knowledge practice. For Ḥanafī, it seeks to resist Westernisation by casting away *murakkab al-naqṣ* (inferiority complex), the result of a long process of subjection to European colonisation, in order to assert agency, regain autonomy and reclaim identity. Therefore, *taḥarrur* (emancipation) from that complex, from alienation, colonisation and Westernisation involves an ongoing dialectic between the "self" and the "other"; between forces of domination and counter-forces of emancipation; between Orientalism and Occidentalism.[95] This emancipatory mission gives Occidentalism its moral appeal and validates it as a counter-discourse and a strategy of autonomy. Ḥanafī notes that at the core of the *ṣirā'* (struggle/clash) between the "self" and the "other" is the incompleteness of the emancipatory project of independence from colonialism. Little has therefore changed in the power relation between the ex-coloniser and the ex-colonised. The latter still seeks to emulate the former, while remaining the inferior partner in the power relation between the two. In this power relation, the former is dominant and the latter dependent, i.e. a "core-periphery" or a "master-servant" relation as Ḥanafī puts it. What ensues from the ideas of superiority and inferiority respective of this power relation, Ḥanafī

94 Ibid., p. 25.
95 Ibid., pp. 29–33.

argues, is what he calls *ʿuqdatun tārikhiyyatun fī ṣirāʿi'l-ḥaḍārāṭi* (historical complex in the clash of civilisations).[96] Accordingly, for Ḥanafī Occidentalism is a *ḍarūratun mulihḥatun* (urgent necessity), aiming at completing *taḥarrur* from colonialism and neo-colonialism.[97] This it does by "moving from military liberation to economic, political and cultural autonomy, and, above all else, to civilizational emancipation".[98]

Thus Ḥanafī considers Occidentalism to be an inversion of Orientalism.[99] Orientalism derived its authoritativeness from alliance with structures of power in the West, such as during the colonial period when it flourished immensely. Through Orientalism, as a knowledge practice and a discourse,

> ...the West assumed the role of the "self", becoming a subject, and assigned the non-West [the role of] its "others", making it an object. Classical Orientalism therefore refers to the imagining of the European "self" of the non-European "other", [that is] the [power] relation of the studying subject with the studied object. As a result, a superiority complex [*sic*] grew within the European "self"...and so did an inferiority complex within the non-European "other"...But in Occidentalism...[those] roles have changed; hence today the European "self", the observer of yesterday, has become the object of study [and] the non-European "other", yesterday's object of study, the studying subject.[100]

Ḥanafī, however, argues that Occidentalism aims at neither *sayṭarah* (domination) nor *haymanah* (hegemony), the way Orientalism has been deployed since the nineteenth century. Rather it seeks parity and equality.[101] This is so inspite of the chauvinistic and supremacist Occidentalisms of contemporary Islamists and the Islamic revolution in Iran. Ḥanafī puts down the chauvinism of Occidentalism to defensiveness against the very chauvinism and supremacy inherent in Western culture, noting that "counter-attack is the best form of defense".[102] Ḥanafī pushes this line of argument further. Because he sees Western culture as being explicitly and implicitly ethnocentric,[103]

[96] Ibid., p. 34.
[97] Ibid., p. 33.
[98] Ibid., p. 34.
[99] Ibid., p. 29.
[100] Ibid.
[101] Ibid., p. 31.
[102] Ibid., p. 30.
[103] Ibid.

he regards Occidentalism as a corrective to Orientalism and Eurocentrism. Thus non-European histories and civilisations are detached from those of Europe whose history and civilisation have been universalised as humanity's.[104] Therefore, "Occidentalism aims at debunking the myth that the West is representative of humanity...the world's history is the history of the West; humanity's history is [also] the history of the West; and the history of philosophy is that of Western philosophy."[105] In fact, "non-European history begins since the arrival of the coloniser, [that is] history is the history of the knowledge of the object not that of how the object knows itself."[106] Similarly, the Occidentalist strategy of emancipation and recognition decentres Eurocentrism by interrogating the uniqueness of Europe's model,[107] i.e. its monopoly over "truth".

For Ḥanafī, Eurocentrism is evidence that claims of neutral rationality and objectivity of human reason which have governed Western knowledge practices since the Enlightenment are hollow. Moreover, he argues that under the guise of neutrality and objectivity the European "self" was able to conceal bias and subjectivity.[108] Yet Ḥanafī's own claim that Occidentalism's rendering of the West is capable of greater neutrality and objectivity is biased: "the 'self' in Occidentalism disposes it to greater honesty, objectivity and neutrality than the 'self' in Orientalism".[109] Neutrality is difficult to obtain within value-laden and foundationalist knowledge practices. Despite incoherence and bias in his analysis of Occidentalism, Ḥanafī is essentially searching for a "new humanism"[110] that enables the non-West to rise from non-identity and subjection and fulfil its potential while making the West realise its limitations (e.g. via postmodernism and feminism). But a prerequisite for this post Occidentalism-Orientalism condition is parity of cultures and identities of the West and non-West, namely, that which is Arabo-Islamic.

What transpires from the above is that the elements of chauvinism, constitution of subjectivity and otherness (which are consistent

104 Ibid., p. 31.
105 Ibid., p. 42.
106 Ibid., p. 39.
107 Ibid., p. 38.
108 Ibid., p. 32.
109 Ibid., p. 32; also, see p. 76.
110 Ibid., p. 56.

with any inversion of Orientalism), of resistance, and of defensiveness are all characteristic of Islamist Occidentalist modes of discourse examined below. Nonetheless, these modes of discourse, notwithstanding their essentialism, represent a counter-discourse aimed at assertion of agency and acquisition of autonomy and recognition.

IMAGININGS OF THE "WEST" AND "DEMOCRACY" IN ISLAMIST DISCOURSES

Islamist critiques of democracy are not all original. In fact, some of them are more familiar than is commonly understood. Westerners of many political colours as well as Western scholars and philosphers have themselves produced the most comprehensive criticisms of democracy. What is new is perhaps the way Islamist criticisms have become constructions of *al-gharb* (the West). *Al-gharb*, as Mernissi remarks, "is the territory of the strange, the foreign (ghar[ī]b)... 'Foreigness' in Arabic has a very strong spatial connotation, for *gharb* is the place where the sun sets and where darkness awaits".[111] The crux of Said's *Orientalism* is how Orientalisations about the "Orient" and the "Oriental" constitute *al-gharb's* site of cultural hubris, discursive formations defining the self–other relation through images and stereotypes and caricatures of the "other", and contrasts of the essences of the "Occident" and the "Orient".[112] The result is not only a system of knowledge with consistent sets of essentialist and deterministic discourse defining the culturally and politically superior "self" against the culturally and politically "backward" "other" but also a strategy of "positional superiority" determining power relations of *al-gharb's* dominance over *al-sharq* (the East). Two ingredients present in Said's Orientalism have counterparts in Islamist renderings of *al-gharb*; insofar as they show inverted essentialising tendencies, these renderings amount to a form of "Occidentalism", or "reverse Orientalism".[113] The first regards the tendency to contrast favourably with the aim of highlighting difference and opposition: "For Orientalism was ultimately a political vision of reality

111 Fatima Mernissi, *Islam and Democracy: Fear of the Modern World*, trans. by Mary Jo Llakeland (London: Virago, 1991), p. 13.

112 Said, *Orientalism*.

113 See Lila Abu-Lughod, *Writing Women's Worlds: Bedouin Stories* (Berkeley: University of California Press, 1993), p. 10.

whose structure promoted the difference between the familiar (Europe, the West, 'us') and the strange (the Orient, the East, 'them')."[114] The second concerns the representing of the Orient as an atemporal essence: "a closed system, in which objects are what they are *because* they are what they are, for once, for all time, for ontological reasons that no empirical material can either dislodge or alter".[115]

Through their Occidentalist modes of discourse, Islamists aim not to establish the kind of hegemony Westerners realised through their more structured and institutionalised knowledge-making about the Orient, which was closely connected with various centres of political, military and financial power. That kind of hegemony, that is hegemony in the cultist sense: military, informational, economic and political, is outside the reach of Islamists, many of whom are on the margins of political power in their own countries, especially al-nahḍah and al-ikhwān. Those who are at the centre of power rather than on the periphery, like al-jabhah, have been marginalised by outside international forces through embargoes and media character assassination. Thus, while European Orientalism was the result of buoyancy of spirits, prowess and offensiveness, Islamist Occidentalist modes of discourse are the product of flagging spirits, weakness and defensiveness. Their aims are to: 1) Counter what they see as Western *ghazw fikrī* (cultural invasion) with their own *ghazw fikrī*. They view the Western *ghazw* as Orientalist, denigrating and aggressive.[116] Unlike the outward Western *ghazw*, their own is inward, taking the form of a *saḥwah* that hopes to liberate the Muslim mind and nation

[114] Said, *Orientalism*, p. 43.

[115] Ibid., p. 70.

[116] The idea of *ghazw fikrī* is closely tied with *istishrāq* (Orientalism). Islamists pay a great deal of attention to issues of knowledge, knowledge-making and epistemology. Related to their effort to Islamise their societies is the so-called *ta'ṣīlu 'l-ma'rifah* (Islamisation of knowledge), of which *ta'rīb* is an important component. The idea of Orientalism being denigrating and aggressive has been expressed by many Islamists I interviewed such as Ṣalāḥ Sulṭān, 30 March 1994, Cairo; Ma'mūn al-Huḍaybī, 4 April 1994, Cairo; Aḥmad Sayf al-Islām al-Bannā, 7 April 1994, Cairo; Ṣalāḥ Maqṣūd, 11 April 1994, Cairo; Ḥabīb Muknī, 5 April 1993, Paris; Rāshid al-Ghannūshī, 14 April 1993, London; 'Izz 'l-dīn 'Abd al-Mawla, 17 March 1994, London; Isḥāq Aḥmad al-Farḥān, 5 February 1992, Amman; Abu Bakr Jamīl, 19 June 1994, Amman; Bassām La'mūsh, 12 June 1994, Amman; 'Abd-Allaṭīf 'Arabiyyāt, 18 June 1994, Amman; Muḥammad 'Uwiḍah, 13 June 1994, Amman; Ḥasan al-Turābī, 12 May 1994, Khartoum; and Al-Tijānī 'Abd al-Qādir Ḥāmid, 28 May 1994, Khartoum.

from their *azamāt* (crises); to assert *al-dhāt* (the self) by rebuilding its links with the past—*aṣālah* and *turāth*—and to alert the *ummah* to flaws in categories of Western modernity: democracy, socialism, secularism and materialism. 2) Retort against those who detract from *al-manhaju 'l-Islāmī* (Islamic way and programme) by showing its strengths, relevance and moral superiority. 3) Sell (as Islamists are also politicians) the rightful claim of *al-mashrū'u 'l-Islāmī* (Islamist project) upon public affairs in its bid to reify the *ummah's* renaissance in an Islamic way, a task that demands exposing rival projects. 4) Reverse the hegemonic power relations with *al-gharb*, at least in the realm of ideas by showing *al-manhaju 'l-Islāmī* to be coherent, complete and potentially in possession of *al-ḥall* (solution) and the answers to Western democracy and developmentalism.

In order to establish the validity of the islamic programme niẓ*āmu 'l-shūrā* (Islamic consultative system) has to be shown to be able to do two things at the heart of the Islamist endeavour to operationalise *tajdīd* (innovation): *iḥtifāẓ* (preserving foundational or useful elements) and *tajāwuz* (discarding and surpassing that which is irrelevant).[117] This is in harmony with al-Turābī's formula defining *al-dīn* (religion) as being *thabāt* (permanence/fixity) plus *taṭawwur.*[118] Islamist *taṣawwur* of democracy is about being loyal to Islam's *uṣūl* and, at the same time, absorbing the positive values of Western democracy: hence *iḥtifāẓ*. It is also about discarding and surpassing those non-foundational religious-based dogmata that are hostile to borrowing as well as discarding those democratic elements that clash with Islam's *uṣūl* (such as secularism) and surpassing those that are uncongenial with *al-manhaju 'l-Islāmī*—owing to imbalances between the material and the spiritual in democracy.

Occidentalist modes of discourse deploy categories of tradition. Western Orientalism, in contrast, owes its dynamism to modernism and rationalism which make easy the demarcation between the essence of a sophisticated and advanced Europe and the essence of a backward Orient. Thus *akhlāq* (ethics) is the most predominant category in the Occidentalist genre. For Islamists no scheme of social,

117 The original formulation by al-Ghannūshī is that *taṭawwur* equals *iḥtifāẓ* plus *tajāwuz*. See Rāshid al-Ghannūshī, *Mina 'l-fikri 'l-Islāmī fī-tūnis* vol. 1 [*From Islamist Thought in Tunisia*] (Kuwait: Dar al-Qalam, 1992), pp. 33–48.

118 Al-Turābī, "*Al-Dīn thabāt wa-taṭawwur*" in al-Turābī, *Tajdīdu 'l-fikri 'l-Islāmī* [*Renewal of Islamic Thought*] (Jeddah: al-Dar-al-Saudiyyah Li al-Nashr, 1987), pp. 119–26.

economic and political correctness is complete without moral correctness. In their renderings of *al-gharb* and of its democracy, three dimensions related to *akhlāq* make the Western paradigm unworthy of emulation for the Islamists interviewed: *shudhūdh* (sexual perversity); colonial and imperialist tendencies; and materialism. First, the legislative initiatives in a few Western countries, namely, in the United Kingdom and the United States, with regard to issues of rights of gay and lesbian groups in society or in the armed forces feature repeatedly in comparisons of *shūrą̄* and democracy. Most Islamist interviewees mention them as an example of difference and distance between Western democracy and democracy in the Islamist perspective. Granting rights for these groups is invariably interpreted as defiance of *fiṭrah*. From an Islamist perspective such a democracy is anti-God as it breaches one of Allah's sanctions by committing an act of *taḥlīl* (permitting) of a matter that is *ḥarām* (forbidden). *Taḥlīl* and *taḥrīm* (forbidding) are outside the jurisdiction of humans in *niẓāmu 'l-shūrā*. As far as they are concerned *al-insān* (the human being) does not live up to the *takrīm* (ennobling) bestowed upon him by God by legislating for sexual perversity.

In the words of a young Sudanese Islamist from the student movement associated with the jabhah: "Al-gharb deludes itself for thinking it is superior with the bomb, with hitech and with its walk on the moon; morally it is inferior in spite of its democratic pretentions."[119] Naturally, Islamists would not conceive either of ethics outside a metaphysical frame or of a diversity of moral standards. For another Islamist:

> How there can be separation of democracy and *akhlāq*? How can leaders and the people's representatives take themselves seriously when they engage in extra-marital sexual activities, and have multiple lovers while at the same time they preach marital monogamy? And how can they be taken seriously by those who believe in God when they legislate for homosexuality?[120]

A jabhah veteran declares democracy's standards of *akhlāq* to be Godless, blaming it for the types of movies like "Jesus of Montreal" and the "Monty Python" variety of denigration of Jesus.[121] *Shūrā*,

[119] Author's interview with Walīd Fāyit, 27 April 1994, Khartoum.

[120] Author's interview with Abu Bakr Jamīl, 19 June 1994, Amman.

[121] Author's interview with Ibrāhīm Muḥammad al-Sanūsī, 28 May 1994, Khartoum.

argues al-Shāwī of the *ikhwān* and author of the most comprehensive work on *al-shūrā*, being in harmony with God's *manhaj*, is first and foremost *akhlāq* in the household, in the workplace and in the corridors of power.[122] This the Islamists relate not only to the harmonious integration of the cosmological and metaphysical in Islam but also to one of the overriding themes of *al-risālatu 'l-nabawiyyah* (Prophetic message), which is *itmāmu makārima 'l-akhlāq* (bringing to perfection noble traits).[123] In this respect the *shūrā*—democracy distinction is a reflection of the absence of *tawāzun* (equilibrium) between *al-manhaju 'l-ilāhī* (Godly path) and *al-manhaju 'l-waḍ'ī* (man-made path). Hence the universalist claims of *al-mashrū'u 'l-Islāmī* to work toward that *tawāzun*:

> Akhlāq knows no borders. Fighting injustice and corruption is a Muslim's duty everywhere in God's earth. America is part of God's earth. Is it not? Accordingly, I am, capacity permitting, required to obey God's call to enjoin *al-ma'rūf* (the good) even in America. Even a superpower like America with its democracy badly needs the *tawāzun* that *al-manhaju 'l-ilāhī* alone provides.[124]

Second, Islamists cannot separate democracy from *al-gharb's* colonial past and expansionist or hegemonic tendencies, real or imagined, in the present. In fact, colonialism and expansionism are both viewed by Islamists to be antithetical to *akhlāq*, and to be part of the pathology of *fardiyyah* (individualism) and scrambling for the phenomenal world's *shahawāt* (wants). Al-Ghannūshī, for instance, while recognising the positive potential of *fardiyyah* with regard to nurturing initiative and autonomous reasoning, warns against the inherent egoism and hedonism in considering it one of *taghrīb's* evils.[125]

122 Tawfīq al-Shāwī, *Fiqhu'l-shūrā wa'l-istishārah* [*Understanding* Shūrā *and Consultation*] (al-Mansurah: Dar'l-Wafa, 1992), pp. 15, 21.

123 See al-Ghannūshī, *Mina'l-fikri 'l-Islāmī fi-tūnis* vol. 1, pp. 119–20. Also author's interviews with Abu'l-'Alā Māḍī, 3 April 1994, Cairo; Ma'mūn al-Huḍaybī, 4 April 1994, Cairo; 'Iṣām al-'Iryān, 6 April 1994, Cairo; Isḥāq Aḥmad al-Farḥān, 5 February 1992, Amman; Ḥamzah Manṣūr, 4 June 1994, Amman; 'Abd-Allaṭīf 'Arabiyyāt, 18 June 1994, Amman; Al-Sayyid al-Firjānī, 14 March 1994, London; Lubābah al-Faḍl, 7 May 1994, Khartoum; Su'ād al-Fātiḥ, 10 May 1994, Khartoum; Ḥasan al-Turābī, 12 May 1994, Khartoum.

124 Author's interview with Ma'mūn al-Huḍaybī, 4 April 1994, Cairo.

125 See al-Ghannūshī, *Mina'l-fikri 'l-Islāmī fi-tūnis* vol. 1, p. 126.

The supreme guide of the *ikhwān* in Jordan, Khalīfah, sums up the overall feeling amongst Islamists when he observes:

> *Niẓāmu 'l-shūrā* is also *niẓām akhlāq*. Democracy's ideals are beautiful. But where is its humanist *akhlāq*? How could people with *akhlāq* commit what the French committed in Algeria in the past, and the Israelis do in Palestine today? How could the starving of Iraqi and Sudanese children and the slow death of Bosnians not happen without the democrats' order? Democrats have two modes of operation: a benign one for home and a malevolent one for abroad. The tragedy of the Arab world is that those Westerners who call themselves democrats have actively supported and imposed upon us their friends: Arab dictators! Muslim *futūḥāt* (conquests) were about spreading *akhlāq* and enjoining the good, and not about killing and pillaging. Muslim conquests were not colonial expeditions.[126]

Third, the Islamists interviewed associate democracy's imbalance with its materialism. And it is here that Islamists stress *al-manhaju 'l-ilāhī's* superiority over Western ideologies. Islamists believe such *manhaj* in both its social and political application to comply with human *fiṭrah* by balancing the material activity and needs with spiritual fulfilment. The association of democracy with materialism is expressed in terms such as *ahwā'* (whims), *ladhdhāt* (pleasures), *shahawāt* and *sa'adatu 'l-dunyā* (this-worldly happiness). Most Islamists find it necessary to emulate only what is positive in democracy. The forms and practice of democracy they observe in the "West" have impacted on them both positively and negatively. The positive makes democracy palatable and a borrowing that Islamists view to be compatible with Islam. The negative has become images of the "other" that help define the uniqueness of *niẓāmu 'l-shūrā*, and distinguish *al-manhaju 'l-ilāhī* as all-inclusive and superior to *al-manhaju 'l-waḍ'ī*. Among images cited are the use of financial power by the Italian media tycoon, Berlusconi, for political ends.[127] Al-Turābī argues that the influence of the very concentrated media and financial interests in many Western countries has compromised the values of democracy rendering them susceptible to *tazwīr* (fraud).[128] For al-Sanūsī,

126 Most Islamists express similar views. Author's interview with the supreme guide of the *ikhwān* in Jordan, Muḥammad 'Abd al-Raḥmān Khalīfah, 14 June 1994, Amman.

127 This example has been given by a number of interviewees from the four movements.

128 Al-Turābī, "*Murtakazātu 'l-ḥiwār ma'a'l-gharb*", p. 11.

"Democracy has been commodified with power going not to the competent and honest but to the financially well-off. This practice makes democracy the bastion of the rich; all this happens in the name of political equality! Money does not feature in Islam's democracy. The criteria of communal membership and political equality are *imān, taqwā* and *'amal.*"[129] Other images range from a prostitute's entry into the Italian parliament to Watergate. Even those most open to democracy like al-Ghannūshī criticise what some call *al-fasādu 'l-dīmuqrāṭi* (democratic decay).[130] Al-Ghannūshī, in Quṭbian fashion, remarks how man, driven by his endeavours to free himself, has renounced God and "has become enslaved by his wants and new idols that promise him an earthly paradise as do rationalism, secularism, nationalism, capitalism and communism."[131] This he refers to as *siyādatu mabda' 'l-ladhah* (hedonism).[132] From this perspective, he charges how "the gods of finance knew how to expunge democracy of its original meaning, turning it into a slogan to dupe the downtrodden and justify exploitation".[133]

The concepts and categories "Occident", "Orient", "East" and "West" are at the very least misleading. Similarly, the utility of Said's "Orientalism" and Carrier's "Occidentalism" hinges upon their use in conjunction not disjunction. The defining of the "self" and the "other" is a two-way flow involving processes of both "Orientalisation" and "Occidentalisation", even if the "positional superiority" of many "Westerners" makes for almost a one-way flow of information whereby Orientalists and Orientalisms reach much wider audiences than do the essentialisations about the "Occident" by many "Easterners".

Occident-Orient or East-West are homogenising, reductionistic and inflexible dichotomies. They are meant to account for the

129 Author's interview with Ibrāhīm Muḥammad al-Sanūsī, 28 May 1994, Khartoum.

130 Author's interviews with Mukhtār Nūḥ, 29 March 1994, Cairo; Usāmah al-Sayyid, 29 March 1994, Cairo; Maḥmūd 'Izzat Ibrāhim, 30 March 1994, Cairo; 'Iṣām al-'Iryān, 6 April 1994, Cairo; Aḥmad Sayf al-Islām al-Bannā, 7 April 1994, Cairo; Hammām Sa'īd, 4 June 1994, Amman; Yūsuf al-'Aẓm, 5 June 1994, Amman; Badrī Mukhtār, 17 March 1994, London; Luṭfī Zitūn, 18 March 1994, London; Sumayyah Abū Kashawwah, 5 May 1994, Khartoum; Lubābah al-Faḍl, 7 May 1994, Khartoum.

131 See al-Ghannūshī, *Mina'l-fikri 'l-Islāmī fi-tūnis* vol. 1, p. 100.

132 Ibid., p. 99.

133 Ibid., p. 100.

disconnections at the expense of the connections. Westerners such as Yusuf Islam (Cat Stevens), Roger Garaudy and Murad Hoffman defy categorisation: They are respectively American, French and German—"Occidental". And all three are Muslim—"Oriental". They constitute three faces of "Occidental Islam". So does European Bosnia today; and so did Andalusia a few centuries back. Also "Orientalists" ought to be disaggregated. Neat homogenising labels such as Muslim "fundamentalists" (a misnomer given its Christian and American history) have little utility. Al-jamā'ah al-islāmiyyah (the Islamic group) must not, for instance, be equated with al-ikhwān in Egypt. Al-Ghannūshī, Chairman of the Tunisian outlawed al-nahḍah (Renaissance) party, cannot entirely disown the "West"; he resides in London and travels with a British passport. Al-Turābī, the foremost Islamist ideologue, a polyglot (French, German and English), holds high degrees from London University (M.A.) and the Sorbonne (PhD). The Egyptian shaykh, 'Umar 'Abd al-Raḥmān, although opposed to Western powers and Muslim Westernisers, chose the United States—not Pakistan, Iran or Saudi Arabia—for political asylum. And like Westerners, Islamists are diffuse rather than unitary. Note how al-Ghannūshī defines the "West" in a letter he wrote to Lord Avebury in 1993:

> It is a grave mistake to simply judge a complex multi-lateral civilizational phenomenon such as the Western civilization. The West, as a civilizational phenomenon, is not monolithic, and neither is Islam. The term "the West" may be used to refer to the people, and these, just like any other people, comprise the good and the bad. Actually most of the people in the West strive to earn their daily living and secure a prosperous life, and they want nothing but peace for their countries and for the world. It is a mistake to hold these peoples responsible, partly or totally, for what has befallen our nations as a result of the mistakes and injustices of Western policies.
>
> The term "the West" may also be used to refer to the culture, thought and philosophy produced by Westerners to explain natural phenomena pertaining to man and life. Some of these aspects of knowledge conform with our own civilization while some disagree with it…The term may also be used to refer to technology and scientific progress. This aspect of civilization is predominantly neutral and is in itself a great bounty and the fruit of the human struggle that has been going on for thousands of years to discover nature and learn its secrets.
>
> The term "the West" on the other hand may refer to the policies of the superpowers that dominate the world, or to Western-based international organizations and financial institutions. It is this "West" which is the focus of

our blame because its policies have largely been stripped of the values of truth and justice, and because it has been dominated by interests and nationalist ambitions even if their accomplishment necessitated the destruction of other people's cultures and the shedding of their bloods.

The term "the West" may be used to refer to political economic thought and methods, such as liberalism and democracy. This field comprises some of the most important innovations of the West. Other peoples and nations may benefit tremendously by borrowing from these thoughts what they deem to be useful in rescuing them from oppressive and autocratic regimes.[134]

The bifurcation found in Islamist discourses of democracy and renderings of the "West" should serve to inhibit interpretations of Islamic culture, and for that matter any culture, in a reductionistic and deterministic way. Culture is neither static nor homogeneous. In its bid to cope and deal with change, accommodate or reject it, culture is bound to generate tensions that defy its rendering as a reified entity. It is therefore not surprising that Islamist discourses on "democracy" and on the "West" speak to a range of issues pointing to a clear bifurcation: they are at once the subject of hate and love, admiration and denunciation, and appropriation and rejection.

Both Said's Orientalist and Carrier's Occidentalist discourses are useful frameworks for understanding Occidental and Oriental peoples, cultures and politics. However, unless they temper their homogenising tendencies, they risk being inflexible in their renderings of Westerners and Easterners. Moreover, unless they are empathetic, both also can be inflexible ways of understanding Occidental and Oriental peoples. Diversity ought to be accounted for. The theoretical frameworks provided by Said's Orientalism and Carrier's Occidentalism are two sides of the same coin, both as regards dialectic imagining and defining of the "self" and the "other", and the political contingencies and power relations that shape and inform processes of Orientalisation and Occidentalisation. The analysis in chapter 4 turns to the question of democracy as an Orientalist discourse.

134 Letter from Rashīd al-Ghannūshī, Chairman of al-nahḍah, to Lord Avebury, Chairman of Parliamentary Human Rights Group (UK), 25 August 1993, p. 12.

4

DEMOCRACY AS AN ORIENTALIST DISCOURSE

"As regards the posing of the problem...[traditional Orientalists] consider the Orient and Orientals as an 'object' of study, marked by otherness, like everything which is other, be it 'subject' or 'object', but in this case by constitutive otherness, essentialist in character...This 'object' of study will be appropriately passive, non-participating, endowed with a 'historic' subjectivity, above all not active, not autonomous, not sovereign over itself; the only Orient or Oriental or 'subject' which one could accept at a pinch is the philosophically alienated being, that is, other than itself when considered as itself, postulated, understood, defined—and made to work—by another.

"As regards the thematics, [traditional Orientalists] adopt an essentialist concept of the countries, the nations and the peoples of the Orient in question, a concept which embodies itself in a strongly ethnist typology; it will not take much...to push the concept in the direction of racism.

"According to traditional Orientalists, there must exist an essence, which is sometimes even clearly described in metaphysical terms, which constitutes the inalienable and common basis of all the beings under consideration; this essence is at once 'historic', in that it arises out of the depths of history, and fundamentally ahistoric, in that it freezes the being, 'object' of study, in its inalienable and non-evolving specificity, instead of—as in the case of the other beings, states, nations, peoples, and cultures—turning it into a product, an outcome of the vector forces at work in the process of historic evolution." —Anouar Abdel-Malek[1]

This chapter looks at Orientalisations about Arabs, Islam and Islamists with regard to democracy. It explores the undercurrent of superiority in discourses of democracy and modernity by some Western

[1] Anouar Abdel-Malek, "L'Orientalisme en Crise", *Diogène*, 44 (1963), p. 113.

scholars in their relations with their Oriental objects. It analyses certain images (such as notions of "Oriental despotism") and the image formulators (from Weber to Huntington) and their discourses of power. The chapter revisits Orientalism and Orientalisation in the context of the quasi-global debate on Islamism and Islamists. Theorisations of political development and political culture are part of a discourse of power affirming the superiority of the Anglo-American developmental model. With dogmas like secularism and modernism, such theorisations reflect the ideals—the logos—of the European and American political "dream" which is grounded in an Enlightenment-based ethos and in modernist-humanist metanarratives and the "us"-"them" modes of discourse.

BACKGROUND

Orientalism lingers on. Twenty years after Said first published *Orientalism*, "Orientalisations" about Arabs, Islam and Muslims are pervasive.[2] Similarly, some 35 years since Anouar Abdel-Malek's *L'Orientalisme en Crise* [*Orientalism in Crisis*] appeared, Orientalism or neo-Orientalism cannot be said to have transcended its state of crisis.[3] Despite quantitative and qualitative accomplishments in Western scholarship on the society, history and civilisation of the Arab Middle East, many studies remain trapped within an ethnocentric and foundationalist discourse which takes the supremacy of Western models and cultures for granted, and assumes their yardsticks to be universally normative. This, however, does not warrant a non-nuanced treatment of Orientalism and Orientalists. It is a mistake to assume that all Orientalist scholarship distorts knowledge about Arabs, Islam, Muslims or the so-called Middle East. On the contrary, the field of Orientalism has furthered understanding of the region, its religions, languages, history and peoples. Some of these, in many instances, outclass anything produced by indigenous scholarship, for having deepened "native" knowledge about "local" subjects. Often this of course has more to do with political control and curbs on freedom of inquiry across the Arab and Muslim worlds than with some deficiency in the Arab or Muslim "mind". However, despite the many positive accomplishments

[2] See interview by Ken Shulman with Edward Said in *International Herald Tribune*, 11 March 1996, p. 6.

[3] Abdel-Malek, "L'Orientalisme en Crise", pp. 109–42.

of Orientalism and Orientalists, negative images and stereotypes constructed by many Western students of the "Orient" are still widely accepted as "truth". No discourses of "otherness" can be expected to be value-free especially when the boundaries of culture, history, geography, language and time have to be crossed.

Accordingly, Said's critique of Western discourses on the "Orient" is as relevant today as it used to be 20 years ago despite the fact that his seminal work has become subject to many criticisms. These criticisms fall into seven occasionally overlapping categories. First, there is the accusation that Said stretches his evidence. Victor Brombert, for example, cites Said's treatment of Bernard Lewis's *The Arabs in History*. He writes that Lewis is not as contemptuous of the Arabs as Said makes him out to be—i.e. Said exaggerates Lewis's view. To Fedwa Malti-Douglas, Said also exaggerates the Orientalist hold over Middle Eastern studies. Linked to this last point is the second major criticism, that of Said's selective reading. Here much of the criticism revolves around Said only reading British, French and, later, American Orientalism (because they had imperial contacts with the Middle East) and ignoring many other traditions, especially German Orientalism. This criticism also extends to a selective reading of authors within the traditions Said looks at.[4]

Another two closely linked criticisms are those of generalisation and reductionism, that is, Said has generalised the whole field of Orientalism into a field of study that is hostile to the Arab people. Malcolm Kerr observes that "In charging the entire tradition of European and American Oriental Studies with the sins of reductionism and caricature, he (Said) commits precisely the same error."[5] A fifth criticism is that Said is (or puts himself in the position of being) an Arab apologist in *Orientalism*. David Gordon charges that Said's "work is apologetic in that its unyielding attack on the sins of Orientalist analysis would seem to deflect criticism from the self unto others".[6] Another criticism, which is ironic considering Said's wish to support the Arab people, is that he perpetuates the view of their

[4] Malcom Kerr notes that Said, in his examination of American Orientalism, ignores a whole school of sympathetic American scholars produced at Princeton by Philip Hitti. See Malcom Kerr, "Orientalism", *International Journal of Middle Eastern Studies*, 12 (December 1980), p. 546.

[5] Ibid., p. 544.

[6] David Gordon, "Orientalism", *Antioch Review*, 40 (winter 1982), p. 111.

inferiority by rendering the Arabs as passive subjects.[7] One final challenge is that of theoretical confusion. This criticism is made primarily by James Clifford: "Frequently [Said] is led to argue that a text or tradition distorts, dominates, or ignores some real or authentic feature of the Orient. Elsewhere, however, he denies the existence of any 'real Orient', and in this he is more rigorously faithful to Foucault and the other radical critics of representation that he cites."[8]

Despite these criticisms, Said's critique of Occidental discourses of the Orient is useful. It is today validated by the continuous hegemony of Western logocentrism and foundationalism. Knowledge and knowledge-making are never neutral and, therefore, the imagining of the "other" is always filtered through a mindset whether the subject at hand is development, democracy, modernisation, religion, the woman-question, or human rights. By and large, logocentrism and foundationalism are deeply anchored in a humanist-modernist discourse from which they acquire their dogmas and yardsticks for determining what is "ideal" and "good" or not. This humanist-modernist discourse, which continues to inform Western knowledge practices and knowledge-making, despite recent challenges to its foundations and interrogation of its premises by feminists and postmodernists, is itself rooted in Europe's history—the Enlightenment, the Industrial Revolution, the French Revolution, and the Protestant Reformation.

The corollaries of this discourse were profound. The humanisation of life, i.e. ranking the individual's civil happiness at the top of all goals, and consecrating all institutions to the service of humanity and the attainment of such a happiness. The birth of modern science in the seventeenth century was celebrated with the rise of continental rationalism (e.g. scientific works like Copernicus' *On the Revolutions of Celestial Bodies*; Newton's *The Mathematical Principles of Natural Philosophy*; and Galileo's *Dialogue on the Two Greatest Systems, the Ptolemaic and the Copernican*, and his *Discourse and Mathematical Demonstrations Concerning two Branches of Science*. Also scientific academics like Descartes and Leibinz) and English empiricism (e.g.

[7] This criticism is made by Fedwa Malti-Douglas who writes that "Said, who sought to expose and combat the myths of ineradicable Oriental inferiority, has unwittingly perpetuated them." See Fedwa Malti-Douglas, "Re-Orienting Orientalism", *The Virginia Quarterly Review*, 55 (autumn 1979), p. 732.

[8] James Clifford, "Orientalism", *History and Theory*, 19 (May 1980), p. 208.

Francis Bacon's 1620 work, *Novum Organon* [*The New Tool*], on the theory of knowledge). Rationalism enshrined the sanctity of human reason as a source of knowledge and its instrumentality in the authorisation of knowledge. Empiricism defined prejudice-free methods for validating scientific knowledge and observation, stressing the primacy of fact over myth, objectivity over subjectivity, and rationality over emotion. This new faith in the importance of experience and reason in the validation of knowledge was bolstered by Locke's 1690 work, *Essay Concerning Human Understanding*. As a consequence to the humanisation of life, the secularisation of life, whereby religious principles ceased to exist in the organisation of society, was marked by the separation of the religious and the temporal. Thus not only was religion in the ecclesiastical and eschatological sense downgraded but was also ceded to a "modern religion"[9] based on reason and science.

On the whole, these innovations came to constitute not only the philosophical basis for science and reasoning but also for redefining man's place in the scheme of things in relation to nature, God, and authority. This faith in science and reason inaugurated the search for the "rational actor" (versus a deity), leading the march for inevitable and unilinear progress. Thus this new "European" man asserted himself master over nature, destiny, history, and, more importantly, over non-European fellow human beings who were deemed to be at a lower stage of "progress" or with an inferior civilisation, if any at all. The inevitability and unilinearity of the "march of progress" are no longer taken for granted. However, while the "march of progress" has been compromised by a record of militarism, reckless capitalism, social inequities, environmental degradation and androcentrism, its legacy of intellectual hegemony and cultural tutelage, amongst many Westerners and Westernisers, remains intact despite mounting questioning of its attendant conventional wisdom. More to the point, the logocentrism of this intellectual hegemony has had the interrelated effects of marginalising cultural and intellectual pluralism and absolutising and privileging the discursive singularity of Enlightenment practices. "Otherness" with its potentially diverse ways of doing, thinking and being is marginalised for its alleged conflict with either rationality, modernism or democracy. Yet in the name of harmony

[9] See Sidney Pollard, *The Ideal of Progress: History and Society* (London: Watts, 1968), pp. 3–4.

with democracy and with universal rationality, the humanist-modernist framework is foisted on all as the sole route to "progress" or "civil happiness". Thus Enlightenment discursive practices, by absolutising the logos of rationality or modernism, have subverted their very emancipatory project. Increasing interrogation is unmasking Enlightenment rationality as logocentric and ethnocentric. One observation about such a rationality is its inability to live up to two of the most important values of Enlightenment: "objectivity" and "neutrality".

Logocentrism, with its implications for Orientalism, ethnocentrism (in its many forms Eurocentrism, Westernism, etc.) and even (neo-) colonialism, has its foundation in this Western intellectual hegemony and cultural tutelage. Hence the charged semantic field of the linguistics of the culture of "reason" and of "progress". Lexical universals like "democratic", "developed", "modern", "rational", or "secular" go along with the presumed universals of progress and modernity, e.g. "democracy", "development", "modernism" or "secularism". This semantic field is charged in that the lexical symbols are not merely expressions with designata which are mutually inclusive with the discourse of progress, modernism or development. More strikingly, they are assigned to a subterranean field, to a quasi-subdiscourse or to a subtext of "othering" and exclusion. Terms like "rational" or "modern" no longer operate "neutrally" or "objectively" to designate a state of political or economic affairs; they are impregnated with value-laden meanings, and upon inversion can easily become subjective renderings of difference. When inversed, "rational" or "modern" are read "emotional" and "traditional". With their foundationalist dogmas, the logocentric assumptions in modernist discourse imply binary divides, dualities or dichotomies.

In this regard, Derrida's interrogation of logocentrism is insightful and helpful for understanding the inner working of essentialist modes of discourse. Western history can be said to be the history of logocentrism. Logocentrism is a matter of historical prejudice. This is one reason why Derrida questions the literary and linguistic prejudice against writing (phonocentricity), rejecting its subordination to speech.[10] For him, the logos has to do with claiming that the authority of the written word is as primal and as authoritative as the spoken word. History is littered with endless examples of logocentrism which

[10] Jacques Derrida, *Of Grammatology*, trans. by Gayatri Chakravorty Spivak (Baltimore and London: The Johns Hopkins University, 1976), p. 7.

over millennia have given idealised types of society or discourse their foundational premises and frameworks—philosophy, revelation, patriarchy, matriarchy, sedentariness, nomadism, orality, and literacy. His interrogation of logocentrism, which by way of deconstruction he seeks to dismantle, extends to ethnocentrism. For instance, in the opening of his *Of Grammatology*, Derrida finds a symbiosis between logocentrism and ethnocentrism in the tendency of some theorists, such as Rousseau and Hegel, to associate the highest forms of intelligence, conception of community or civility with writing.[11] Through deconstruction, the French textual philosopher sabotages logocentrism, by attacking the pretences of wholeness, originality or absoluteness of the logos. The logos, be it God, the self or truth, is valorised as the foundation for thinking, doing and being. However, the logos (or any transcendental signifier), textual or social, is never complete or meaningful in itself. For the inherent duplicity[12] in the signifier/text is not only signified by the presence of a contradiction but also by incompleteness or deferment of meaning. Contradiction results from the fact that signs are binary, consisting of signifier and signified,[13] and that the "signified always already functions as a signifier".[14] That is, the signifier is in itself "defective" as it has the "trace" of other signifiers. Hence the hierarchised binary oppositions and dichotomies—God-man; man-woman; self-other—which Derrida's deconstruction sets out to undo.[15] For Derrida, when meaning is incomplete or deferred it is *sous rature*, what Spivak renders as "under erasure".[16] This is what gives discourses their "provisional" status and "contortion". This has implications for all discourses from the standpoint of the objectivity–subjectivity binary. Subjectivity resides within objectivity. Furthermore, objectivity passes through the lenses of subjectivity (which is bound to a linguistic, cultural heritage). As Spivak puts it:

> ...Derrida suggests that what opens the possibility of thought is not merely the question of being, but also the never-annulled difference from the "completely other". Such is the strange "being" of the sign: half of it always "not

[11] Ibid., p. 3.
[12] See, for instance, "Translator's Preface" in ibid., pp. liii–liv.
[13] Derrida, *Of Grammatology*, p. 11.
[14] Ibid., p. 7.
[15] See "Translator's Preface" by Spivak in ibid., pp. lxxvii–lxxviii.
[16] Ibid., pp. xiv–xviii.

there" and the other half always "not that". The structure of the sign is determined by the trace or track of that other which is for ever absent.[17]

Spivak notes further, "For Derrida, however, a text…whether 'literary,' 'psychic,' 'anthropological,' or otherwise, is a play of presence and absence, a place of the effaced trace."[18] Like logocentrism, Orientalism resonates with this presence-absence structure. The "trace" of absence defines presence. The "trace" of traditionalism defines modernism; and of idealism rationalism. The "trace" of the Orient defines the Occident. For the Occident of today bore in its past sameness to the Orient, that is, it lacked rationality, secularity, and so on. In logocentrism, in any binary sign, the first term is valorised, and privileged as an authentic and original foundation—a logos—and the second term is, by virtue of its definitional relationship with the first, de-valorised, i.e. marginalised from the site assigned to the logos. In Orientalist binary representations, the site of the logos, from which the Orient is banished, is exclusive to the Occident. The Occident stands valorised, a metaphor for rationality, modernity or democracy. The Orient is its antithesis.

Derrida's deconstructive criticism of representation and indeterminacy of meaning is not without problems. A great deal of Derrida's literary criticism verges on semantic sophistry. For he is not just dealing with metalanguage (how to use language to talk about language) but also, and more particularly, about meta-metalanguage (how to use language to talk about metalanguage). Furthermore, although Said exhibits fondness of French deconstructionist social theory, especially the work of Derrida's compatriot, Michel Foucault, he and Derrida tend to radically differ over the question of meaning. Unlike Said, Derrida does not see cultural tradition as a relevant paradigm of analysis. In some civilisations with a tradition of a written script, writing takes on a high level of iconicity and authority. Said sets out to deconstruct meaning in culture into the underlying perceptions which are constructed by one culture's view of another. What Said is doing is looking at cultural relativism. Whereas Derrida deconstructs meaning in everything on the understanding that everything is open to any interpretation, depending on how you deconstruct it. The difference is whereas Said is providing a coherent worldview that he

[17] Ibid., p. xvii.
[18] Ibid., p. lvii.

then deconstructs to look at underlying values and norms, Derrida deconstructs language in value-free terms; he does not look at the values but simply at their constructs. Derrida's work becomes meta-linguistic philosophy, and Said's becomes cultural analysis because one cannot deconstruct a system in a value-free manner, especially if one is talking about culture. For culture by its nature is embedded in a value system.

In Orientalism, Said looks at Occidental perceptions of the Orient. Such perceptions of the Orient are not constructed on the basis of the norms and values of the Orient, but rather the cultural values of the Occident. What obtains is an oppositional perception which is reinforced by a deeply-embedded notion in Western culture of the adversarial nature of the argument. So when Orientalists construct a worldview, they are essentially saying "they" or the "other" is like "us"/"self" or unlike "us". This adversarial notion has its origins in Aristotle whose metaphysics is noted for its binary oppositions. The word "dichotomy" is derived from the Greek, meaning, things are separate entities that oppose each other. That tradition remains deeply embedded in Western thought, including the Christian religion. Derrida attempts to deconstruct the nature of language and philosophy. Such deconstruction may have value for the world of metaphysical philosophy but does it have value for culture? After all, for Derrida there is no such thing as a defined cultural construct. Rather, everything is related to the deconstruction of perceptions of metaphysics of language and philosophy. In some ways, Derrida is a hermeneutic philosopher.

For the purpose of the current discussion of Orientalism, the notion of logocentrism is invoked from the following standpoints:

- that there is an interplay between logocentrism, ethnocentrism, Orientalism and (neo-) colonialism;
- that Orientalist representations of the Orient are both logocentric and ethnocentric;
- that in these representations, the constitution of "otherness"—"Orient" and "Orientals"—is posited against an original or authentic logos or foundation;
- that this logos or foundation is hierarchically opposed and valorised;
- that the "Orient" as a sign presents some arbitrariness in that it is not necessarily a representation of an "Orient" "out there" as

much as it is a representation of a subjective discourse or an edited historical narrative about the "Orient".

ORIENTALISM IN MODERNIST DISCOURSES

Being logocentric and ethnocentric accounts of "otherness", Orientalism amounts to a divisive mode of discourse. For it accentuates opposition and contrast, as Bryan Turner has rightly established. Orientalist representations defeat the ideal of a multicultural world through a mode of being, thinking and doing that promotes tolerance and acceptance of cultural plurality, as opposed to cultural chauvinism, monism and cultural tutelage. Not even the so-called "globalisation of culture", be it wearing of blue jeans or idolising pop music, renders null yearnings for some form or another of local cultural identity and identification. By oversimplifying and deepening the contrast between Occident and Orient, Orientalism closes off the possibilities of indigenous "paths" or "routes" to state and nation-building. The story of democratic achievement in the modernist metanarrative is exclusively equated with its inception in parts of the Western world, especially, England, France and the United States. If those societies which are exemplars of democracy are, for instance, distinguished by rationalism, secularism, urbanism and individualism, then those societies which are characterised by the absence of these "universal laws" are condemned to continuous democratic impasse. In this manner, specificity is overlooked. The impasse of democracy cannot simply be ascribed to variables of nonindividualism or religion. Colonialism and capitalism cannot be absolved from the democratic impasse in the AME (see chapter 7). Nor can the possibility of a democracy or rationality informed by religion be precluded. Conventional explanations of democratic development are a good example of how the Orientalism, logocentrism and ethnocentrism of the modernist discourse have contributed to the closing off of indigenous alternatives to the much valorised Western model.

Political Development and Modernisation

Political development or political modernisation[19] are elusive concepts that occasion definitional nuances as well as circularity. Political

[19] For a discussion of the definitional nuances and usages of political development and political modernisation, with the latter being more open-ended and presupposing

modernisation is narrowly conceptualised here as being synonymous with democratic achievement. Accordingly, political modernisation and democratic development are used interchangeably. The criterion of democratisation is taken here to be axiomatically intrinsic to political modernisation.[20] There is no indigenous term for political modernisation/development.[21] *Al-Muqaddimah*[22] (*The Prolegomenon*) of Ibn Khaldūn, the fourteenth-century Arab[23] philosopher of history,[24] remains one of the earliest masterpieces on the study of the

---

a traditional order, see Clement H. Dodd, *Political Development* (London: Macmillan, 1972), pp. 9–15. See also C.E. Black, *The Dynamics of Modernization* (New York: Harper and Row, 1966), pp. 5–9.

[20] Lucian W. Pye, for instance, looks at how political development equated with the "building of democracy"—one of several criteria. See his *Aspects of Political Development* (Boston: Little, Brown and Co., 1966), pp. 40–1. For an excellent critique of various criteria of political development see Daya Krishna, *Political Development: A Critical Perspective* (Delhi: Oxford University Press, 1979).

[21] Such known focused case studies of Arab political development as by Khadduri and Aruri, on Libya and Jordan respectively, fail to address this problem. See Majid Khadduri, *Modern Libya: A Study in Political Development* (Baltimore: The Johns Hopkins Press, 1963) and Naseer H. Aruri, *Jordan: A Study in Political Development, 1921–1965* (The Hague: Marinus Nijhoff, 1972).

[22] Ibn Khaldūn, *Prolegomenon: An Introduction to History* (Princeton, New Jersey: Princeton University Press, 1967), in three volumes trans. by Frantz Rosenthal. In Arabic see, 'Abd al-Raḥmān Ibn Khaldūn, *Muqaddimatu Ibn Khaldūn* (Beirut: Dar al-Jeel, (n.d.)). On Ibn Khaldūn see Yves Lacoste, *Ibn Khaldun: The Birth of History and the Past of the Third World* (London: Verso, 1984); Muhsin Mahdi, *Ibn Khaldun's Philosophy of History* (London: Allen and Unwin, 1957); Bruce B, Lawrence (ed.), *Ibn Khaldun and Islamic Ideology* (Leiden: E.J. Brill, 1984); Aziz al-Azmeh, *Ibn Khaldun: An Essay in Reinterpretation* (London: Frank Cass, 1982); Aziz al-Azmeh, *Ibn Khaldun in Modern Scholarship: A Study in Orientalism* (London: Third World Centre for Research and Publishing, 1981).

[23] 'Abd al-Raḥmān Abū Zayd Ibn Muḥammad Ibn Muḥammad Ibn Khaldūn was born in Tunis on 27 May 1332. He is referred to here as Arab. His descriptions as Tunisian by Iliya Harik and Patricia Springborg or as Algerian by Edith Penrose are confusing to say the least. See Iliya Harik, "The Origins of the Arab State System" in Giacomo Luciani (ed.), *The Arab State* (London: Routledge, 1990), p. 4 and Patricia Springborg, *Western Republicanism and the Oriental Prince* (Cambridge: Polity Press, 1992), p. 272. See also, Edith Penrose, "From Economic Liberalization to International Integration: The Role of the Arab State" in Tim Niblock and Emma Murphy (eds), *Economic and Political Liberalization in the Middle East* (London: British Academic Press, 1993), p. 4.

[24] Ibn Khaldūn is claimed by some to be the precursor of modern social science, historical materialism and even economics. See for instance Ibrahim M. Oweiss, "Ibn Khaldun, the Father of Economics" in George N. Atiyeh and Ibrahim M. Oweiss

dynamics and dialectic of change. Ibn Khaldūn's analyses the medieval Maghribi *dawlah*'s (state) making and unmaking, rise and demise, expansion and retraction. He discusses governance and its leadership qualities. He employs the creative conceptual tool of *al-'aṣabiyyah* (tribal solidarity) as both integrative and divisive[25] in securing or losing royal authority and control. His awareness of the nexus between power and ideology (Islam), between *al-'aṣabiyyah* and Islam, between *al-'aṣabiyyah* and *ghulb*, between *ghulb* and *ri'āsah* (leadership), between the latter and *iltiḥām* (coalescence) and *mawālī* (clientelism),[26] and the interplay between all these variables provides an adequate foundation for the study and conceptualisation of Arab sociopolitical change.

Ibn Khaldūn calls attention to such earlier emerging systemic aspects of change as *tamaddun* (urbanisation), social organisation and an early form of "differentiation". He stresses the necessity of *ijtimā'* (association) and of *ta'āwun* (cooperation) viewing them as essential to human existence and to what he calls *'umrān* (civilisation).[27] Mahdi equates the Khaldūnian notion of "community of necessity" with division of labour.[28] If Ibn Khaldūn's *Muqaddimah* is a worthy place to search for an indigenous term for political modernization, his notion of *'umrān* is fitting for such a task. *'Umrān* is

---

(eds), *Arab Civilization: Challenges and Responses* (State University of New York Press, 1988), pp. 122–7.

25 Elbaki Hermassi convincingly disputes the received wisdom holding that *al-'aṣabiyyah* is solely integrative, making an original re-interpretative distinction that *al-'aṣabiyyah* is both cohesive and divisive. "First, *al-'aṣabiyyah* indicates tribal cohesion. By this, Ibn Khaldūn wants to illustrate that the establishment of central power within a culturally pluralistic and segmentary society is inconceivable without a minimum of cohesion among and within some tribal units… *Al-'aṣabiyyah* also indicates the propensity for segmentation. Thus, although Ibn Khaldun uses it when he speaks of the difficulties of establishing dynasties in heterogeneous societies, he is not referring to social cohesion." See Elbaki Hermassi, *Leadership and National Development in North Africa: A Comparative Study* (Berkeley: University of California Press, 1972), pp. 15–16.

26 For an excellent analysis of the dynamics of *ghulb, ri'āsah, iltiḥām, mawali* and *al-'aṣabiyyah* see Ghassan Salamé, "Strong and Weak States: A Qualified Return to the Muqaddimah" in Giacomo Luciani (ed.), *The Arab State* (London: Routledge, 1990), pp. 29–64.

27 'Abd al-Raḥmān Ibn Khaldūn, *Muqaddimatu Ibn Khaldūn* [*Ibn Khaldun's Prolegomenon*] (Beirut: Dar al-Jeel, n.d.), p. 47.

28 Mahdi, *Ibn Khaldun's Philosophy of History*, p. 188. See also the introduction in N.J. Dawood (ed.), *The Muqaddimah: An Introduction to History*, trans. by Franz Rosenthal (London and Henley: Routledge and Kegan Paul, 1967).

translated by Rosenthal as "civilisation". The root of *ʿumrān* in Arabic is *ʿammara*, which conveys the notions of "building up and developing".[29] Expressing dissatisfaction with Rosenthal's translation of *ʿumrān* as civilisation, Lacoste renders the term a wider meaning encompassing politics, culture and economics.[30] *ʿUmrān* is thus linguistically apt to denote development and modernisation. *ʿUmrān*, joined with the adjective *al-siyāsī* (political)—*al-ʿumrānu 'l-siyāsī*—is proposed here to refer to the Western notion of political modernisation.

In 1949 the Syrian strongman, Ḥusnī al-Zaʿīm, declared that given five years, he would emulate Switzerland's prosperity.[31] A few observations can be gleaned from this: 1) as an adaptive process, modernisation aims at assuming control[32] over polity, economy, society, and territory; 2) as a process, it is underpinned by optimism. Hence the "Switzerland syndrome"—increased independence, higher living standards, greater control over the future; 3) as a process, it is hasty and reactionary in that it seeks to catch up with the West. The AME encountered "modernity", as epitomised by the colonial powers' military, technological, administrative, economic and political superiority, through the colonial process. Those first instances of reactionary modernisation can be traced back to Egypt's Muḥammad ʿAlī[33] (1805–48) and Tunisia's Aḥmad Bey[34] (1837–65); 4) the Western model of modernisation is the paradigmatic example throughout the AME whether the professed legitimating creeds are religious dogma or secular nationalism. Lerner observes, "What the West is, in this

[29] Dawood, *The Muqaddimah*, p. xi.

[30] Lacoste, *Ibn Khaldun: The Birth of History and the Birth of the Third World*, p. 148.

[31] David Pryce-Jones, "Self-determination Arab Style", *Commentary*, 87 (January 1989), p. 40.

[32] For Black, "Modernization may be defined as the process by which historically evolved institutions are adapted to the rapidly changing functions that reflect the unprecedented increase in man's knowledge, permitting *control* over his environment, that accompanied the scientific revolution." See C.E. Black, *The Dynamics of Modernization*, (New York: Harper and Row, 1966), p. 7; see also, p. 13. In the same vein Rustow views modernisation as a "rapidly widening control over nature through closer cooperation among men". See Dankwart Rustow, *A World of Nations: Problems or Political Modernization* (Washington, DC: The Brookings Institution, 1967), p. 40.

[33] See P.J. Vatikiotis, *The History of Modern Egypt: From Muhammad Ali to Mubarak* (London: Weidenfeld and Nicolson, 1991), esp. ch. 4, "Muhammad Ali, the Modernizing Autocrat", pp. 49–69.

[34] L. Carl Brown, *The Tunisia of Ahmad Bey* (New Jersey: Princeton University Press, 1974).

sense, the Middle East seeks to become."[35] 5) Arab modernisation attempts to shortcut that European process the genesis of which Rustow dates back to the Renaissance[36] and Lerner estimates to have been a progression over three centuries.[37] The difficulties are enormous. The ex-colonisers, being today's standard bearers, can use the Arabs' rush for modernisation to reassert and perpetuate their political, economic and, if need be, military tutelage. The Arab quest for modernisation will always be circumvented by the West's own drive for sustained, superior, faster and hegemonic modernisation; the aims of Arab industrialisation and self-sufficiency will always be calibrated by the West's aims of keeping its industrial competitive edge, and hence its need for consumers (markets and recycling of petrodollars) rather than producers. The embargo on hi-tech items to Arabs, amongst others, is instructive. Economic development, for instance, depends, in large part, on oil, on Western investments or on foreign aid, prompting its description by a group of Arab scholars as misleading.[38] With the benefit of hindsight, Arab modernisation can, thus far, be said to have had the opposite results of its developmental goals. Instead of development, there has mostly been underdevelopment;[39] and instead of control and autonomy, there are varying degrees of dependence.

Al-ʿUmrānu 'l-siyāsī *and the Arab Setting*

Modernisation tends to describe at least two phenomena: first, the historical (temporal, post-medieval Europe), parochial (culturally Western) and linear process of change from traditional (premodern)

[35] It is through what Lerner calls "empathy" with the ex-colonisers or Westerners' modernity that the "transitionals" come to cultivate their own modernising aspirations in order to break with Lerner's "constrictive traditional universe". See Daniel Lerner, *The Passing of Traditional Society: Modernizing the Middle East* (New York: The Free Press, 1964), p. 47.

[36] Rustow, *A World of Nations*, p. 1.

[37] Lerner, *The Passing of Traditional Society*, p. 65.

[38] They observe: "Yesterday's enemy against whom the people had fought became the benefactor who would save them from under-development." See Ismail Sabri Abdalla *et al., Images of the Arab Future* (London: Frances Pinter, 1983), pp. 10–11.

[39] See for instance the fine work by Andre Gunder Frank, "The Development of Under-development" in Peter F. Klaren and Thomas J. Bossert (eds), *Promise of Development: Theories of Change in Latin America* (Boulder, CO: Westview Press, 1986), ch. 6.

to a modern (post-traditional) order; secondly, the global rush to replicate that modernisation owing to the impact[40] of the more modernised West (North) on the less-modernized world (South). Modernisation is generally viewed by functional liberal "developmentalists" with much optimism in so far as it is taken to embody universally sought after and compatible developmental goals that are conducive to the so-called "Good Society".[41] The "Good Society" is one that is "wealthy, just, democratic, orderly and in full control of its own affairs".[42] Some hold high hopes for a "world culture" based on a universal movement towards progress.[43] Countervailing this functional analysis are both structural (conflict theorists) and "synthetic" (reconciliation theorists) analyses.[44] If modernisation is the search for the "Good Society", political modernisation is similarly the search for what may be termed the "Good Polity". The image of the "Good Polity" has been depicted by multivariate operational values which at times appear to contradict one another. The omission or inclusion of the democratisation criterion or the prioritisation of order over equality are instructive in this regard.

Political modernisation pertains to the nature of a given system's[45] political structure (state-building) and political culture (nation-building). If differentiation, secularisation, rationalisation, institutionalisation, equality and capacity are taken to be the salient characteristics of the more modern political systems, does it follow that the reverse is true of the less modern ones? One scholar casts doubt on whether the attributes of the "pathology" of the more modernised

40 Black, *The Dynamics of Modernization*, p. 6.

41 Samuel P. Huntington, "The Goals of Development" in Myron Weiner and Samuel P. Huntington (eds), *Understanding Political Development* (Glenview, IL: Little, Brown and Co., 1987), p. 6.

42 Ibid., p. 6.

43 Pye, *Aspects of Political Development*, pp. 9–11 and 198–9.

44 The former dismisses the functionalist "compatibility assumption" highlighting the inherent contradictions between the five developmental goals (wealth/growth, justice, democracy, order and autonomy) as between growth and democracy or growth and equity. The latter concedes both to the possibility of materialising those goals and the tensions that rise in their pursuit and thus seeks to resolve them as through sequencing and structural innovations. For further details see, ibid., pp. 6–21.

45 For a comprehensive definition of political system see Gabriel A. Almond, "Introduction: A Functional Approach to Comparative Politics" in Gabriel A. Almond and James S. Coleman (eds), *The Politics of the Developing Areas* (Princeton University Press, 1960), pp. 5–9.

systems are always and invariably compatible with one reality, asserting at the same time that the opposite pathology of the less modernised systems is not necessarily reflective of their "underdevelopment" but rather of their "difference".[46] Another understands this notion of underdevelopment in terms of political and socioeconomic gaps.[47] The literature on political development abounds in definitions,[48] in criteria and in theoretical approaches (monodimensional, multidimensional and ideal-typical). This literature is not always uniform, either as regards the definitions or the features that are considered generic to political modernisation. It is pertinent to critique some of the unifying approaches and themes of political modernisation.

Assumption 1: *The ideal–typical continuum reflects the biased and misrepresentative proclivity in certain conceptualisations of political modernity that tradition is antithetical to change.*

Three ideas are subsumed under this assumption. One is the idea that modernity and tradition are polar opposites on one continuum. Gusfield disagrees.[49] Modernity and tradition are rather dimensions of two different continua. They are susceptible to both congruence and conflict. For him, tradition can furnish support for modernity, and modernity does not cancel tradition.[50] The roots of this assumption can be traced back to Weber and Parsons. In his discussion of types of authority, Weber posits a dichotomous relationship between legal/rational, on the one hand, and traditional, on the other.[51] Parson's

[46] See Gerald A. Heeger, *The Politics of Underdevelopment* (London: Macmillan, 1974), p. 2.

[47] See, Edward Shils, *Political Development in the New States* (New York: Humanities Press, 1962).

[48] Both Huntington and Pye survey some of the unifying themes and definitions of political modernisation. Pye identifies no less than ten ways of defining political development. See, Samuel P. Huntington, "Political Development and Political Decay", *World Politics*, 17 (April 1965), pp. 387–93; see also, Lucian W. Pye, *Aspects of Political Development* (Boston: Little, Brown and Co.), pp. 33–45.

[49] Joseph R. Gusfield, "Tradition and Modernity: Misplaced Polarities in the Study of Social Change", *The American Journal of Sociology*, 72 (January 1967), pp. 351–62.

[50] Ibid., p. 352.

[51] Max Weber, *The Theory of Social and Economic Organisation*, trans. by A.M. Henderson and Talcott Parsons (New York: Oxford University Press, 1947), see, "The Types of Authority and Imperative Co-ordination", pp. 324–57. See also Gusfield, *Tradition and Modernity*, p. 352 where he cites the example of Weber's "Conception of traditional versus rational economic behaviour". For further details consult Weber, *The Theory of Social and Economic Organization*, pp. 168–212.

multidimensional pattern variables of role-definition are posited on the same logic of a modern–traditional continuum.[52]

Another subsumed under the assumption is the fallacy, identified and refuted by Gusfield, that so-called "traditional societies" have been static societies.[53] The view he ascribes to India[54] as a product of eclectic change is applicable to many an Arab society. From the earliest recorded time, Arab societies have been exposed to multiple and multifarious winds and waves of change. Nor was civilisation coeval with the colonial's "*mission civilizatrice*".[55] The final idea implied in the assumption is that "traditional culture is a consistent body of norms and values".[56] As Gusfield shows, tradition is not a monolith.[57] In the same vein, Apter does not only distinguish between "traditionalism"[58] and "modernity", but also within traditionalism, between two operative value-types; instrumental and consummatory.[59] He regards

[52] Four of his five alternative-pairs dichotomise societies on the basis of relationships governing both social and non-social objects. The modern and traditional poles are differentiated in terms of neutral versus emotional polarity—affective neutrality versus affectivity. The former, being rational, places primacy on universalistic standards and norms. The latter, being emotional, accentuates particularistic ones. In the modern, achievement, measured by merit and performance, contrasts with ascription, as by inherited status, in the traditional. The first Orientation is towards diffuseness as versus the second's specificity. Parson's dichotomisation of societies along a modern–traditional continuum does not mirror the real world where the old and the new are usually fused. See Talcott Parsons, *The Social System* (London: Tavistock Publications Ltd, 1952). For a summary of all five pattern variables see "The Pattern-Alternatives of Value-Orientation as Definitions of Relational Role-expectations Patterns", pp. 58–67.

[53] Gusfield, *Tradition and Modernity*, p. 352.

[54] Ibid., p. 353.

[55] For a fine work on the breadth of historical changes throughout Arab peoples see Albert Hourani, *A History of the Arab Peoples* (London: Faber and Faber, 1991)

[56] Gusfield, *Tradition and Modernity*, p. 353.

[57] While the general traditional framework (Islam or Hinduism) is unifying, its actual manifestations and permutations are versatile. Islam's plurality, for instance, is not only a product of change but has itself also produced the framework, the legitimation and the substance for and against change.

[58] Apter defines traditionalism as: "Validation of current behaviour by reference to immemorial prescriptive norms. This is not to say that traditionalist systems do not change but rather that innovation—that is, extra systemic action—has to be mediated within the social system and linked with antecedent values." David E. Apter, *The Politics of Modernization* (University of Chicago Press, 1965), p. 83.

[59] Apter defines instrumental-hierarchical systems as "...those in which ultimate ends do not colour every concrete act... Such systems can innovate without appearing to alter their social institutions fundamentally. Rather innovation is made to save tradition." The consummatory-pyramidal system is one where "...society, the state,

the former to be more responsive and conducive to change than the latter. In an instrumental system, with its "hierarchical authority" (Apter explains it as a military type of system), an omnipotent and omnipresent leader, given the absence of competing centres of power, has ample space to modernise except politically. Apter cites Morocco as one such example. In a consummatory system with a pyramidal political structure, where religion pervades both the cultural and political structures, the ruling elite is relatively circumscribed by subordinate but semi-autonomous power clusters.

"Hybridity" is the most discernible feature of the present Arab macro body politic. Underpinning this macro body politic are two identifiable micro body politics—half-bred state and quasi-state systems.[60] First, a predominantly traditional order (still mostly ascriptive) exists where, despite higher literacy, modernisation and medium hydrocarbon industry, greater urbanisation and differentiation, centralised power structures, patriarchal rule by oil oligarchies[61] remains the norm. Second, is a predominantly authoritarian order where, in spite of mostly routinised single-party rule, greater nominal orientation towards secularisation, medium to low economic growth and a still fairly weak, although visibly growing, civil society, the impulse for democratisation has been the strongest since independence. The dualism of Arab systems is perhaps best described in Fred Riggs' notion of the "prismatic"[62] modernising society, a paradoxical blend

---

authority, and the like, are all part of an elaborately sustained, high-solidarity structure in which religion is pervasive as a cognitive guide. Such systems have been hostile to change. If change comes it produces fundamental social upheavals." See Apter, *Politics of Modernization*, pp. 85–6. See also illustrations of hierarchical and pyramidal authority, pp. 92–3.

[60] The idea of hybridity or crossbred systems as expressed here is indicated in other works where the term "dualistic" may be applied. Rustow captures the essence of this idea: "Modernization typically proceeds by degrees and stages and allows for wide margins of coexistence between traditional and modern cultural features...Modernization itself is a series of approximations...In society and politics, in art and religion, modernity remains at every stage linked to tradition." See Rustow, *A World of Nations*, p. 16.

[61] The term "oil oligarchy" is borrowed from Muhammad Muslih and Augustus Richard Norton. They present a typology of Arab political systems classifying them into: the leader state (Iraq, Syria); traditional monarchy (Gulf states); and quasi-liberal regimes (Egypt). For further details see their "The Need for Arab Democracy", *Foreign Policy*, 83 (summer 1991), pp. 3–19.

[62] Fred W. Riggs, *Administration in Developing Countries: The Theory of Prismatic Society* (Boston: Houghton Mifflin Company, 1964), pp. 3–49.

of tradition and modernity combining those features generic to what he calls "*industria*" and "*agraria*".[63] The surviving structures and features of the "fused" society (traditional) may be masked by those characteristics of the "diffracted"[64] (more differentiated) society.

Assumption 2: *Equality (participation/democracy) is antagonistic to order (capacity/authority) and, hence, to political modernisation*.

There is a propensity in the study of political modernisation to prioritise order over equality. This propensity presupposes either stages or sequences[65] whereby equality is delayed until state authority is strong enough to cope with societal inputs (demands), which are claimed to be disruptive to both state and nation-building. Contradiction is inescapable: participation is seen as both intrinsic and antagonistic to political modernisation. Capacity is held to be pivotal: Verba stresses "its centrality and importance in relation to political change".[66] Hence the clear tendency to define political development as being synonymous with capacity.[67]

[63] See also Fred W. Riggs, "Agraria and Industria" in William J. Siffin (ed.), *Toward the Comparative Study of Public Administration* (Bloomington: Indiana University Press, 1957), pp. 23–110.

[64] Riggs, *Administration in Developing Countries*, pp. 25–9.

[65] For a fine discussion of sequences and political development see Sydney Verba, "Sequences and Development" in Leonard Binder *et al., Crises and Sequences in Political Development* (Princeton University Press, 1971), pp. 283–316. See also Rustow, "The Problem of Sequence", *A World of Nations*, pp. 120–32. Huntington, "Reconciliation Policies" in Weiner and Huntington (eds), *Understanding Political Development*, pp. 18–21.

[66] Ibid., p. 292.

[67] Bill and Springborg justify this narrow perspective on the basis of "avoid(ing) a number of ethnocentric problems that have long haunted developmental studies". See James A. Bill and Robert Springborg, *Politics in the Middle East* (Glenview, IL: Scott, Furesman and Co., 1990), pp. 7–8. For Coleman this "special capacity" is *integrative:* "overcome…divisions and manage tensions created by increased differentiation"; *responsive*: "respond to or contain the participatory and distributive demands generated by the imperatives of equality"; *innovative*: "innovate and manage continuous change"; *adaptive-creative*: "create new and enhanced capacity to plan, implement and manipulate new change as part of the process of achieving new goals". James S. Coleman, "The Development Syndrome: Differentiation-Equality-Capacity," in Binder *et al., Crises and Sequences*, pp. 78–9. Coleman's "special capacity" is similar to Alfred Diamant's "increased capacity" which intimates sustainability, innovation and creativity. See Diamant's "The Nature of Political Development" in Jason L. Finkle and Richard W. Gable (eds), *Political Development and Social Change* (New York: John Wiley and Sons, 1966), p. 92.

Capacity is also referred to as either ability[68] or capability. Almond and Powell define capability in terms of regulative, extractive, distributive and responsive interrelated systemic functions.[69] With regard to the regulative capability most Arab states would be noted for their strong interventionist tendencies and high reliance on legitimate coercion to the point of illegitimacy. Extractive capabilities vary from rentier states to those relying on cash crops, expatriate remittances and foreign aid (Egypt, Tunisia and Morocco are examples). Extractive and distributive capabilities are linked. While the oil-rich states have plenty of largess to distribute, the poorer Arab states face a crisis of legitimacy in meeting ever increasing demands (jobs, houses, food) for ever-growing populations. The responsive and the distributive capabilities are equally linked. The bulk of Arab political systems can be characterised as having low responsive capabilities or highly selective responsiveness to certain interests (such as the army, bureaucracy or bourgeoisie). Distribution of power or its diffusion are largely limited. The low responsiveness of most Arab political systems can be associated with their inherently weak input functions: interest articulation, interest aggregation, political socialisation and recruitment, and political communication.[70]

In the more traditional Arab political systems, input and output functions remain largely undifferentiated. In the less traditional systems, interest articulation, aggregation and political socialisation and recruitment are the functions of the ruling mobilisational party. Interest articulation, for instance, is instrumental to the sustenance of equal and reciprocal state–society relations—a feature of polyarchies. "The particular structures which perform the articulation function and the style of their performance determine the character of the boundary between polity and society."[71] In most Arab political

[68] Talcott Parsons, "Evolutionary Universals in Society", *American Sociological Review*, 29 (June 1964), pp. 339–57. See also S.N. Eisenstadt, "Initial Institutional Patterns of Political Mobilization", *Civilizations*, 12 (1962), pp. 461–72.

[69] Gabriel A. Almond and G. Bingham Powell, Jr, *Comparative Politics: A Developmental Approach* (Boston: Little, Brown and Co., 1966), pp. 27–9, 190–212.

[70] Almond and Coleman consider "…the input functions rather than the output (rule-making, rule application and rule adjudication) [to] be most important in characterizing non-Western political systems, and in discriminating types and stages of political development among them". See Almond and Coleman, *The Politics of the Developing Areas*, pp. 16–17. See also, Almond and Powell, *Comparative Politics*, p. 26.

[71] Almond and Coleman, *The Politics of the Developing Areas*, p. 33.

systems, interest articulation is inhibited by weak, loyal (affiliated or controlled), marginalised or absent political parties and associations. In the absence of differentiated and autonomous political subsystems, a great deal of interest articulation is institutional (army), non-associational (power clusters within the ruling elite, kinship, family, status, and religious groups), and anomic (bread riots).[72]

The emphasis on capacity has almost invariably meant de-emphasis of equality (democracy). Bill and Springborg remark: "The proclivity to define political development in terms of a Western-Orientated view of democracy is one example of...ethnocentricity. Many 'democratic' systems may not succeed in political development because of their inability to effectively absorb the changes occurring in the contemporary world. In the Middle East, Lebanon is a tragic case in point."[73] Is it not equally ethnocentric to consider democracy as the West's reserve? Arabs cannot be excluded from democracy.[74] The view put forth by Bill and Springborg excludes simultaneous and multidimensional development. The prevalent assumption is that economic development must precede democratisation. The de-emphasis of democracy, being considered a prohibitive factor to order/authority is tantamount to its omission as development. Democracy is development.[75] Its omission is akin to legitimisation of an autocratic route to modernisation.[76] The pursuit of order at the expense

[72] This understanding is based on interpretative analysis by Almond and Coleman. See ibid., pp. 33–8.

[73] Bill and Springborg, *Politics in the Middle East*, p. 8.

[74] Were it not for the Arab translation and preservation of the Greek philosophical heritage the West would have had little of Plato and Aristotle. In a fine essay Patricia Springborg dispels the myths that "liberalism" is a one-way flow—from West to East—showing how the East (Egypt, Mesopotamia, and others) developed many prototypes of liberal institutions. See her "The Origins of Liberal Institutions in the Ancient Middle East" in Niblock and Murphy (eds) *Economic and Political Liberalization in the Middle East*, pp. 26–39. See also by the same author, *Western Republicanism and the Oriental Prince* (Cambridge: Polity Press, 1992).

[75] For a similar argument see Nicolas Ardito-Varletta, "Democracy and Development", *The Washington Quarterly*, 13 (summer 1990), pp. 165–75; Robert L. Rothstein, "Democracy, Conflict, and Development in the Third World", *The Washington Quarterly*, 14 (spring 1991), pp. 43–63; Jagdish Bhagwati, "Democracy and Development", *Journal of Democracy*, 3 (July 1992), pp. 37–44.

[76] Tim McDaniel advances the thesis that autocracy has been one route to modernisation in Russia and Iran, somewhat a challenge to Barrington Moore's classical work, *Social Origins of Dictatorship and Democracy: Lord and Peasant in the Making of the Modern World* (Boston: Beacon Press, 1966) where Moore identifies bourgeois,

of equality has reached an impasse. It has become apparent since the mid-1980s that many Arab polities have neither order nor democracy, and in Huntington's terminology, a few suffer, in varying degrees, from "political decay".[77]

One tendency views modernisation as multidimensional with democratisation being an inherently important component. Lerner views various aspects of modernisation as being "so highly associated...they went together so regularly because, in some historical sense, they had to go together".[78] Another is monodimensional. Huntington, for instance, does not only consider institutionalisation as the most salient characteristic of political development, but also "liberates" political development from modernisation. For he points out that institutionalisation "...as a concept, does not suggest that movement is likely to be in only one direction: institutions...decay and dissolve as well as grow and mature".[79] Deutsch's social mobilisation ushers in a revolution of expectations, attitudes and beliefs mediated by "new patterns of socialisation".[80] Only rarely is democracy cited as a correlate of political modernisation.[81]

---

conservative and peasant revolutions as routes to modernity. See McDaniel's *Autocracy, Modernization, and Revolution in Russia and Iran* (Princeton University Press, 1991).

[77] Samuel P. Huntington, "Political Development and Political Decay", *World Politics*, 17 (April 1965), pp. 386–430.

[78] Lerner, *The Passing of Traditional Society*, p. 438.

[79] Huntington, "Political Development and Political Decay", p. 393. He devises four criteria for measuring institutionalisation; adaptability, complexity, autonomy and cohesion. Compare with Samuel P. Huntington, *Political Order in Changing Societies* (New Haven: Yale University Press, 1968), pp. 12–24.

[80] Karl W. Deutsch, "Social Mobilization and Political Development", *American Political Science Review*, 55 (September 1961), p. 494. See also Karl W. Deutsch and William J. Foltz (eds), *Nation-Building* (New York: Atherton Press, 1963).

[81] This is so despite Frey's assertion that "the most common notion of political development in intellectual American circles is that of movement towards democracy". See Frederick W. Frey, "Political Development, Power, and Communications in Turkey" in Lucian W. Pye (ed.), *Communications and Political Development* (Princeton University Press, 1963), p. 301. In the light of his argument in Samuel P. Huntington, "The Democratic Distemper", *The Public Interest*, 41 (fall 1975), pp. 9–38 or too much participation, Frey's assertion looks doubtful. In the same vein, Rustow and Ward, who concede to the legitimacy and importance of scholarly exploration of the relationship between modernity and democracy, regress by noting: "democracy and representative government are not implied in our definition of modernization". See Dankwart A. Rustow and Robert E. Ward, "Introduction" in *Political Modernization in*

Assumption 3: *The nation-state is a positive framework for political modernisation.*

If "modernisation is a universal social solvent"[82] in the AME, then the nation-state has generally been its agent. It is, however, fallacious to take the positivity of the nation-state with regard to modernisation at face value. Arab nation-states and nationalist leaders can be claimed to have had a few modernising successes. Yet the ugly statism they spawned, with its chronicle of trial and error and its violence, cannot continue to be dealt with in the same unreflecting manner, especially in the age of globalisation. The nation-state has been accepted as axiomatic progression resulting from modernisation. Rustow accords national integration primacy over both authority and equality.[83] Rustow and Ward, and La Palombara[84] hold identification with the nation-state as an important dimension of political modernity. Shifting loyalty from parochial and primordial structures (tribe, clan, family) to the nation-state is identified as a developmental problem concerning nation-building—"the problem of groups identity and loyalty".[85] However, while the nation-state is a universalistic norm, it is also ethnic, linguistic, territorial and cultural, and, thus, embodies the particularism of many a national group.[86]

Japan and Turkey (Princeton University Press, 1964), p. 5. Nor do they include democracy in their eight-criteria scale of a modern polity (ibid., p. 7).

[82] Marion J. Levy, Jr, *Modernization: Latecomers and Survivors* (New York: Basil Books, 1972), p. 5. See also Marion J. Levy, Jr, *Modernization and the Structure of Societies* vol II (Princeton University Press, 1966), pp. 741–64.

[83] Rustow notes that "Among all possible sequences, there is little question that the most effective one would be unity–authority–equality" (pp. 126–7). The reason is that the formation of new nation-states is fairly rapid in comparison with the cumulative and generational growth of authority and equality (pp. 124–25). This sequence, he adds, "…tends to maximize the overall gains and hence the chances for success" (p. 132). See his *A World of Nations*, pp. 120–32.

[84] Rustow and Ward (eds), *Political Modernization in Japan and Turkey*, p. 7 (characteristic no. 5 reads: "widespread and effective sense of popular identification with the history, territory, and national identity of the state"). Lapalombara and Weiner talk of a "measure of identification with the nation-state as distinct from parochial groupings". See Joseph Lapalombara and Myron Weiner, "The Origin and Development of Political Parties" in Joseph Lapalombara and Myron Weiner (eds), *Political Parties and Political Development* (Princeton University Press, 1966), p. 4.

[85] Almond and Powell, *Comparative Politics*, p. 314.

[86] An enlightening exposé on the nature and origin of "nation-ners" and nationalism—"cultural artefacts"—can be found in Benedict Anderson, *Imagined Communities: Reflections on the Origin and Spread of Nationalism* (New York: Verso, 1987).

Seen from this perspective, the competing Arab particularisms between and within national units have neither allowed for a well-planned modernisation, nor for political modernisation which is democratic as versus autocratic, and sustainable rather than fluctuating. Under the banner of nationalism, various Arab modernising elites have mobilised their constituent masses to promote particularistic agendas. Hence as a mobilisational force for modernisation, nationalism has been both cohesive and divisive. Its congruence lies in the provision of rallying idioms and slogans, and an ideological framework to drum up patriotic sentiments. This, combined with the various welfarist initiatives (land reform and distribution in the 1950s and 1960s in Egypt and Algeria, free mass education and health care)[87] initially harnessed most loyalties towards the centre. In those Arab countries where the national-secular elites opted for a socialist mode of modernisation, the patterns of "statist, integrative programmes of national development and control"[88] were more pronounced.

Conflict lies in the very particularism of Arab brands of nationalist modernisation to the detriment of political modernisation. The nation-state has generally tended to pit the dominant particularisms against each other. The configurations of discord are legion: tribal versus national, secular versus religious, state versus society, and the military versus civilian polity. Modernisation increases conflict between and among "traditional" and "modern" groups—*Francisants* versus *Arabisants* in Algeria.[89] Moreover, under the aegis of nationalism,

---

On the dichotomy between the universalism and particularism of nation-states, Lucian W. Pye aptly observes "...how there is a basic tension in contemporary politics between the universal characteristics of the nation-state which arise from the functional requirements of being a member of the nation-state system and the particularistic character of each nation as it reflects its cultural and social history...Countries must follow the international styles if they are to be considered sovereign states. On the other hand, the essence of nationhood is also to give expression to the uniqueness of a people and to differentiate the self from all others." See Lucian W. Pye (ed.), "Introduction" in *Communications and Political Development* (Princeton University Press, 1963), pp. 16–17.

[87] For details of land reform see Roger Owen, *State, Power and Politics in the Making of the Modern Middle East* (London: Routledge, 1992), esp. ch. 2. "The Growth of State Power in the Arab World: The Single Party Regimes", pp. 32–54.

[88] Ibid., p. 38. An enlightening essay on the nature of Arab modernisation is Michael C. Hudson's "Modernization and its Consequences", in his *Arab Politics: The Search for Legitimacy* (New Haven: Yale University Press, 1977), ch. 6.

[89] Samuel P. Huntington, *Political Order in Changing Societies* (New Haven: Yale University Press, 1968), p. 39.

the modernising elites mask their particularism with universalistic objectives giving it wider appeal. Accordingly, modernisation does not only reflect the whims, choices, priorities and interests of nationalist leaders, but is also inextricably interwoven with the expediency of political survival. Modernisation of the military and security apparatus spheres is a case in point. Both had the benefit of huge financial outlays and probably the best human resources, to the detriment of more urgent socio-economic needs. The scenarios of a "chasm..., upheaval and political unrest"[90] are very real in some Arab countries.

The fulfillment of the demands stemming from the revolution of expectations has to be made through greater reliance on coercive capacity. The results in extreme instances are alienation and, to a lesser extent, anomie.[91] Also, socio-economic modernisation has always outpaced political modernisation. The absence, for instance, of autonomous associational subsystems had the twin effects of narrowing the margin of existence for rival particularisms, and of forcing many of them underground. Hence, two problems that Huntington identifies generally apply to Arab political modernisation and have been wrought by various nationalist modernisers: "the lag in the development of political institutions behind social and economic change";[92] and "change in and usually the disintegration of a traditional political system, [without] significant movement toward a modern political system".[93] Contemporary Saudi Arabia illustrates this point.

[90] Bill and Springborg, *Politics in the Middle East*, p. 5.

[91] Huntington uses alienation and anomie in connection with the clash between old and new. See his *Political Order in Changing Societies*, p. 37. Nationalism's bifurcated nature is superbly expressed by Black: "Modernization must be thought of, then, as a process that is simultaneously creative and destructive...Nationalism, a modernizing force in societies struggling for unity and independence, easily becomes a force for conservatism and oppression once nation-hood is achieved. Few political leaders have had the vision to place the human needs of their peoples above national aims." See Black, *The Dynamics of Modernization*, p. 27. In another instance Black states: "The most ruthless pillaging of wealth and the greatest excesses of violence and bloodshed to which the developing countries have been subjected have resulted from the efforts of their own modernizing leaders" (p. 125). The extent of this second statement is not totally applicable to the Arab world. The excesses of Russian and Chinese modernisation (Stalin's collectivisation, Mao's Great Leap Forward) are not known in the Arab world. Furthermore, the blood the French spilled in Algeria is nowhere near the oppression inflicted on Algerians by their own rulers.

[92] Huntington, *Political Order in Changing Societies*, p. 5.

[93] Ibid., p. 35.

In the wider Arab context, the nation-state and nationalism have pitted Arab against Arab. Beneath the veneer of pan-Arabism, various nationalist modernisers followed divergent aims. The ideologisation of the Arab macro body politic has often led to the establishment of competing means of connecting Arab with foreign particularisms. The great part of Arab post-independence history has been the history of the splits between "left" and "right", "radical" and "conservative" particularisms, and of intra-Arab wars.[94] Nationalism can be argued to have been a regressive force that impeded greater Arab integration.[95] The absence of democracy has also meant that Arabs lacked the democratic methods and procedures that facilitate such integration.

Assumption 4: *Secularisation of the political culture maximises the efficiency of the political system.*[96]

The explanatory power of this correlate of political development is simplistic because it does not account for cross-national, cultural and political differences. Higher levels of modernisation in the secularised West and the absence, thus far, of similar levels of modernisation should not automatically make the Western paradigm normative for the AME. Islam is not going to disappear. Islam, therefore, cannot be so confidently dismissed as anti-developmental or anti-change. Secularisation of politics is pertinent to systemic differentiation of structures and functions. A number of critics remain dubious about this received wisdom.[97] Pye, while considering differentiation as one

[94] Pryce-Jones writes: "Morocco and Algeria have fought, and for years Algeria has financed a proxy, the *Polisario* movement…Libya has raided across the Egyptian and Tunisian borders and interfered militarily in Sudan. Syria has twice invaded neighbouring Lebanon, and once neighbouring Jordan, and it has mobilized against neighbouring Iraq. Iraq has threatened (and invaded) neighbouring Kuwait and Syria and has twice sent forces into Jordan…Jordan, [before unification, the two] Yemen[s] North and South, and…(Lebanon) have experienced civil wars." See Pryce-Jones, "Self-determination Arab Style" p. 43.

[95] Rustow rightly observes how "Rival schemes for Arab unity have tended to exacerbate political conflict and to undermine loyalties in almost every one of the separate states." See his *A World of Nations*, p. 122.

[96] See, for instance, Almond and Powell, *Comparative Politics*, pp. 62–3; Pye, *Aspects of Political Development*, p. 47; Gabriel A. Almond and G. Bingham Powell, Jr, *Comparative Politics: System, Process and Policy* (Boston: Little, Brown and Co., 1978), pp. 49–50.

[97] See, for instance, Krishna, *Political Development*, esp ch. 2, pp. 41–65.

dimension of his "development syndrome", concedes to the possible contradiction—"acute tension"—between equality and differentiation: "Differentiation can reduce equality by stressing the importance of quality and specialised knowledge."[98] Differentiation is "an actual process of subdivision".[99] Subdivision refers to both structural and functional separation and specialisation—division of labour. Differentiation involves stratification of social structures and, most importantly, separation of the sacred and the secular—religion and politics, which is, at this historical juncture, of particular significance for the AME.

The rush for out-and-out secularisation has been ill-planned. It is doubtful whether in the Arab-Islamic setting, the ruling elites-led secularisation is achievable when Islamic religiosity and vocabulary permeate everyday language, and when Islamic slogans, symbols, idioms and metaphors pervade polity, society, economy and culture.[100] There is, at least, one invaluable caveat to consider, with particular relevance to the Arab context:

> Despite the apparent advantages of secularization for performance, one must be aware that there are important circumstances under which secularization is neither necessary nor sufficient to bring increased performance…

[98] Pye, *Aspects of Political Development*, p. 47.

[99] Krishna, *Political Development*, p. 42.

[100] Moshe Piamenta demonstrates this point via analysis of multiple lexical formulae and their Islam-derived semantics ranging from expressions of fear to thanking Allah, and so on. According to Piamenta these formulae "…are habits established and performed as a result of learning and training in social-emotional situations". See his *Islam in Everyday Arabic Speech* (Leiden: E.J. Brill, 1979). See also his *The Muslim Conception of God and Human Welfare as Reflected in Everyday Arabic Speech* (Leiden: E.J. Brill, 1983). Odette Petit, *Presence de L'Islam dans la langue Arabe* (Paris: Librarie d'Amerique et d'Orient, 1982) is also useful. On the question of Arabic language and change see Ami Ayalon, *Language and Change in the Arab Middle East* (Oxford University Press, 1987). On the question of Islamic symbolism, Donald Cole gives the example of Saudi Arabia's Second Development Plan for 1975–80 in which the first of seven developmental objectives states: "to maintain the religious and moral values of Islam". See his "Pastoral Nomads in a Rapidly Changing Economy: The Case of Saudi Arabia" in Tim Niblock (ed.), *Social and Economic Development in the Arab Gulf* (London: Croom Helm, 1980), pp. 106–21. Compare with James P. Piscatori, "The Roles of Islam in Saudi Arabia's Political Development" in John L. Esposito (ed.), *Islam and Development: Religion and Sociopolitical Change* (New York: Syracuse University Press, 1980), pp. 123–38. Michael C. Hudson shows how incumbent leaders of regimes and Islamic movements invoke Islamic symbolism for recruitment, mobilisation and empowerment with each "staking out" rival claims to Islamic legitimacy. See his "Islam and Political Development" in Esposito (ed.), *Islam and Development*, pp. 1–24.

> Secularization may also hinder performance when it becomes so pervasive that all values other than narrow self-interest break down…In addition, it seems that human beings very much need some sense of broader purpose in their lives … If a secular culture generates international discontent and erodes binding collective traditions and values, it may produce conflict and breakdown rather than effective development.[101]

The issue of sacralisation of development, politics and democracy and secularisation[102] has no consensus amongst Arabs[103] and non-Arabs. The same questions seem to rear with regard to Islam's interaction with change, its relevance in the age of hi-tech; its compatibility with nationalism, positivism and modernity. For instance, how could Islam with its preordained view of the world, of causation and of history be compatible with scientific methodology, rationalisation and the pragmatisation of modern life? Or, how could Islam's inherently organic nature correspond with modernisation's requirements for differentiation between *al-dīn* and *dawlah*; between *ʿibādāt* (worship) and *muʿāmalāt* (profane dealings); between the immutable divinely revealed scripts and constantly changing conditions and realities; between *sharīʿah* and the need for positive human law?

Dismissing what he labels as "millenarian dreamers", "neo-fundamentalist" and Islamist movements seeking "re-politicisation of Islam"—a process he describes as "counter-acculturation" or "cultural retrospection"—Bassam Tibi puts a strong case for secularisation, industrialisation and democratisation.[104] The main tenets of his thesis stress rejection of the repoliticisation of Islam; dichotomisation between the Western technological-scientific culture and the Muslim pre-industrial culture; "reformation of Islam" for the acquisition of a technological-scientific culture; rejection of the view that secularisation is antithetical to "cultural authenticity",[105] or that

[101] Almond and Powell, *Comparative Politics: System, Process, and Policy*, pp. 50–1.

[102] For an analysis of the polemics regarding separation of religion and politics see Rafiq Zakaria, *The Struggle Within Islam: The Conflict between Religion and Politics* (New York: Penguin, 1988).

[103] The divergence of Arab reflections on religion, politics and nationalism, modernity and social change can be found in Issa J. Boullata, *Trends and Issues in Contemporary Arab Thought* (Albany: State University of New York Press, 1990).

[104] Bassam Tibi, *The Crisis of Modern Islam: A Preindustrial Culture in the Scientific-Technological Age*, trans. by Judith and Peter Von Sivers (Salt Lake City: University of Utah Press, 1988). For Tibi's analysis of repoliticisation of Islam see pp. 43–54.

[105] Ibid., p. 147.

"secularisation portends the extinction of religion", defining it as "a diminution of the religious system to a subsystem of society",[106] or what he calls a "religious ethic"; "rationalisation and desacralization of the Arab Islamic culture",[107] for the development of an Islamic "technological-scientific culture".[108] Tibi's faith in a "technological-scientific culture" should not detract from the fact that it does not necessarily lead to the "Good Society" that ensures its members and non-members political, economic, spiritual, cultural and environmental relevance. It is doubtful whether Arab states will be allowed to pass the threshold of industrialisation and hi-tech under the current dismal state of affairs in the AME.[109]

[106] Ibid., p. 128. For a similar idea see p. 148.

[107] Bassan Tibi, *Islam and the Cultural Accommodation of Social Change*, trans. by Clare Krojzl (Boulder, CO: Westview Press, 1991), p. 69.

[108] Tibi points out that Muslims are historically equipped to achieve this task, showing how Avicenna and Averroes, for instance, "introduced Hellenized scientific terminology, alongside sacred terminology into Arabic" (ibid., pp. 68–69). For a similar view see also Tibi, *The Crisis of Modern Islam*, p. 148.

[109] Falk shows how Iraq has paid the price of attempting to subvert the "technology gap" paradigm through endeavouring to acquire delivery systems and weapons of mass destruction capabilities. The unwritten rule of the proclaimed new world order is posited on denial of such capabilities. He argues that "(i)n order to make the world safe for Nintendo war, the adversary must be denied the capacity to leap over the technology gap...The 'new world order' will attempt to deepen the vulnerability of the entire non-Western world to Nintendo war, both by widening the technological gap through a process of continuous innovation that improves the effectiveness of electronic warfare and by increasing the control and surveillance over Third World acquisitions of any weapons that threaten the invulnerability of the West." See Richard Falk, "Reflections on Democracy and the Gulf War", *Alternatives*, 16 (1991), pp. 270–1. Compare with Hudson who takes the political nature of Islam to be axiomatic. He even sketches what he views to be the salient characteristics of the "ideal developed Islamic polity", being membership of the *ummah* and *tawādud* and *tarāḥum* (co-operation) between its members; *'adl* (justice); legality and equality on the basis of the *sharī'ah*; *khilāfat* (Caliphate) or Imamat through *bay'ah* (popular confirmation); *al-shūrā* (consultation); *ijmā'* (consensus); and *'amal* (praxis) which is a clear negation of the "Orientalist myth of fatalism as an Islamic trait". See Hudson, "Islam and Political Development" in Esposito (ed.), *Islam and Development*, pp. 3–4. Hudson appreciates the dynamism of past Islamic political thought, asserting that Islam can still play a role in a modern political system. He observes: "It is far from self-evident that a polity informed by Islamic religious principles is incompatible with contemporary socioeconomic circumstances. The question to be asked is not the crude, falsely dichotomous 'Is Islam compatible with political development?' but rather 'How much and what kinds of Islam are compatible with (or necessary for) political development in the Muslim world?' One can envisage a range of roles for Islam in the modern political system, from fundamentalist theocratic models...to consensual, integrative, and normative

Islamic revivalism throughout the AME refutes the long-held assumption that the advent of modernisation spells the slow erosion of religion in public affairs. The resilience of Islam is a fact.[110] Secularist tendencies at the apex of power have not filtered down or affected the masses' religiosity.[111] In fact, modernisation can be said to reify the more traditional social forces. The resilience of Islam is not necessarily the result of incongruence with modernisation so much as it is of interaction with it. As Mernissi wrote, "Today university science departments and technological and scientific institutes are the breeding ground of fundamentalism."[112]

Culture

Cultural theses have historically been deployed to assert the rationalism of Occidental culture owing to its technical and scientific perfection and legal and formalistic calculability, conducive to practical rational conduct and capitalist activities. Its best expression is found in Weber's *Protestant Ethic and the Spirit of Capitalism*.[113] Oriental culture is largely viewed as despotic and lacking in rational calculability. Weber's Islam, interpreted by Turner, lacks in "asceticism", "rational, formal law, autonomous cities, an independent burgher class and political stability"; has a "warrior ethic preclud[ing] capitalism", and a "patrimonial domination which made political and economic and legal relations unstable and arbitrary, or irrational".[114] Some

advisory functions…", see ibid., p. 5. Compare with Tibi's position when he asks: "Could Muslims appropriate modernity while rejecting the world view related to it?" Further, "Recent events in Iran also serve to illustrate the problems inherent in the relationship between Islam and development." It is perhaps more accurate to state that such tension perhaps illustrates the relationship between a certain brand of Islam and Muslims with development. On the basis of the Iranian experience, Tibi concludes "It is not possible to achieve a solution to the conflict between Islam and development that has dominated the Islamic Middle East since the nineteenth century." See Tibi, *Islam and the Cultural Accommodation of Social Change*, pp. 43–4.

110 Ibid., p. 8.

111 Ibid., p. 9.

112 Fatima Mernissi, *Islam and Democracy: Fear of the Modern World*, trans. by Mary Jo Lakeland (London: Virago, 1993), p. 49.

113 Max Weber, *The Protestant Ethic and the Spirit of Capitalism*, 15th edn (London: Unwin Paperbacks, 1984).

114 Bryan S. Turner, *Weber and Islam: A Critical Study* (London and Boston: Routledge and Kegan Paul, 1974), pp. 12–15.

resonance of these outlines can also be found in Marx and Engel's "Asiatic mode of production thesis".[115] Gellner offers an opposing view of an Islam in possession of many "requirements of modernity".[116] The tradition of applying cultural theses trickled down to the practice and study of governance. In the context of Muslim societies, such theses do, in an unfailingly ethnocentric fashion, raise questions about the compatibility of Islam and democratic government. In this epistemology, knowledge and power conflate. For Said, Balfour's speech to the House of Commons in 1910, on British occupation of Egypt, captures the essence of a whole history of knowledge-assuming and -making by colonial masters dichotomising a despotic "other" with a good-governing "us":

> Western nations as soon as they emerge into history show the beginnings of those capacities for self-government...having merits of their own...You may look through the whole history of the Orientals in what is called, broadly speaking, the East, and you never find traces of self-government. All their great centuries—and they have been very great—have been passed under despotisms, under absolute government...But never in all the revolutions of fate and fortune have you seen one of those nations of its own motion establish what we, from a Western point of view, call self-government?[117]

Underlying cultural theses are the functionalist assumptions that culture is resistant to change and unitary. Their explanatory power, which peaked in the 1940s through the work of psychoanalysis and cultural anthropology, has been dismissed.[118] Shifts in the post-1970s in mainstream political science from the study of "political culture" to "dependency theory" approaches, on the left, and "rational choice" and "positive political theory", on the right, reflected similar doubts.[119]

[115] Ibid., p. 14.

[116] Gellner writes that "(T)raditional Islam possessed a high theology and organization, closer in many ways to the ideals and requirements of modernity than those of any other religion. A strict unitarianism, a (theoretical) absence of any clergy, hence, in principle, equidistance of all believers from the deity, a strict scripturalism and stress on law-observance, a sober religiosity, avoiding ecstasy and the audio-visual aids of religion—all these features seem highly congruent with an urban bourgeois lifestyle and with commercialism." See Ernest Gellner, *Plough, Sword and Book: The Structure of Human History* (London: Collins Harvill, 1988), p. 216.

[117] Said, *Orientalism*, pp. 32–3.

[118] See Gabriel A. Almond, "Foreword: the Return to Political Culture" in Larry Diamond (ed.), *Political Culture and Democracy in Developing Countries* (Boulder, CO and London: Lynne Rienner, 1993), pp. ix–xii.

[119] Ibid.

Almond, however, believes that, with retreats in Marxist and "public choice" theories, there is a "return" to political culture for the understanding of democratisation.[120] Political culture refers to "the particular distribution of patterns of Orientation toward political objects among the members of the nation".[121] Three patterns of Orientations are distinguishable: "a *cognitive* Orientation, involving knowledge of and beliefs about the political system; an *affective* Orientation, consisting of feelings about the political system; and an *evaluational* Orientation, including commitments to political values and judgements...about the performance of the political system relative to those values".[122]

There are many reasons for "cultural arguments not [to] be pushed too far".[123] One of these is to guard against ethnocentric and racist tendencies from permeating scholarship. Another is to resist the temptation to dismiss cultural relativism despite its inherent problems, especially, in this respect, how it has quite often been deployed by ruling elites to reject diversity, foster hierarchical relationships and nurture authoritarian practices. Cultural relativism must not equal "democratic relativism". Consequently, it is important to acknowledge the validity of other cultural values and knowledge practices throughout the South which no doubt have democratic potentialities even if they differ from Western values.[124] Like culture, political culture is not unitary. Accordingly, the cognitive, affective and evaluative Orientations of people towards their political systems are not uniform. Indeed, the politics of many countries in the South reflect only minimal congruity in the values, attitudes and behaviour of the ruling elites and of the masses. Thus it is not difficult to see that many elements of political culture in many regions, such as the Arab and

[120] Ibid., pp. xi–xii.

[121] Gabriel A. Almond and Sidney Verba, *The Civic Culture: Political Attitudes and Democracy in Five Nations* (Newbury Park: Sage Publications, 1989), p. 13.

[122] Larry Diamond, "Introduction: Political Culture and Democracy" in Diamond (ed.), *Political Culture and Democracy in Developing Countries*, p. 8.

[123] Gerald J. Schimtz and David Gillies, *The Challenge of Democratic Development: Sustaining Democratization in Developing Societies* (Ottowa: The North-South Institute, 1992), p. 52.

[124] Schmitz and Gillies give numerous examples of such indigenous democratic values and practices: ample village autonomy in imperial China; Botswana's village democracy via *kgotlas* (village meetings); Philippine *barangay* (village) elections of leaders; and the Malay village exercise of *'adāt* (customary law). See ibid., pp. 52–3.

Muslim worlds, contradict the authoritarianisms of their regimes.[125] Hence the limitations of the cultural determinism and psychological reductionism of political cultural approaches. The correlation between some expressive or cognitive Orientations of individuals and the structural-functional nature of their political systems is not easily measurable. In reassessing the value of the concept of political culture, which will be returned to in chapter 7, Diamond articulates three reasons for guarding against cultural determinism:

> One is theoretical…Three decades of research since the Civic Culture have shown the cognitive, attitudinal, and evaluational dimensions of political culture are fairly "plastic" and can change quite dramatically in response to regime performance, historical experience, and political socialization…A second reason…is empirical. Considerable evidence has accumulated…that although political culture affects the character and viability of democracy, it is shaped and reshaped by…broad changes in economic and social structure, international factors (including colonialism and cultural diffusion), and, of course, the functioning and habitual practice of the political system itself… A third reason…is normative, involving a "bias for hope." To argue that political culture is not at least somewhat "plastic" and open to evolution and change would be to condemn many countries to perpetual authoritarianism and praetorianism.[126]

No matter how "dense" or "subtle" the linkages are between political culture and democracy",[127] bias against Muslims in general, and Arabs in particular, is not uncommon.[128] An example of this tendency is Huntington's expression of an ambiguity of Islam which he finds to be both "congenial and uncongenial to democracy".[129]

[125] An example of this is the extensive popular support for democracy and participation in Mexico and Nicaragua, countries with a long history of authoritarian rulers. See the findings by John A. Booth and Mitchell A. Seligson, "Paths to Democracy and the Political Culture of Costa Rica, Mexico, and Nicaragua" in Diamond (ed.), *Political Culture and Democracy in Developing Countries*, pp. 107–38.

[126] Diamond, "Introduction: Political Culture and Democracy", pp. 9–10.

[127] Ibid., p. 26.

[128] Compare the excellent article by Lisa Anderson which cautions against applying the political culture thesis to Arab democratisation, and that by Michael C. Hudson which, in contrast, favours its careful application. See Lisa Anderson, "Democracy in the Arab World: A Critique of the Political Culture Approach", and Michael C. Hudson, "The Political Culture Approach to Arab Democratization: The Case for Bringing it back in, Carefully", both in Rex Brynen, Bahgat Korany and Paul Noble (eds), *Political Liberalization and Democratization in the Arab World*, volume 1: *Theoretical Perspectives* (Boulder, CO: Lynne Rienner, 1995), pp. 77–92 and 61–76 respectively.

[129] Samuel P. Huntington, *The Third Wave: Democratization in the Late Twentieth Century* (Norman and London: University of Oklahoma Press, 1991), p. 307.

In singling out Lebanon as unique amongst Arab countries for its consociational democracy he expresses pro-Christian and anti-Islamic biases: "Its democracy, however, really amounted to consociational oligarchy, and 40–50 percent of the population was Christian. Once Muslims became a majority in Lebanon and began to assert themselves, Lebanese democracy collapsed."[130] By contrast, Christianity and Judaism have often been seen to exemplify many democratic features: "The Christian and Hebrew faiths constitute a powerful matrix, a common denominator of the attitudes most essential to a flourishing democracy."[131] But if Christianity, or any other religion, displays any democratic characteristics, its millennial existence belies the very short history of democratic practice.[132] Even within Christianity itself, democratic characteristics have traditionally been denied to Catholicism. The changes of the 1980s have challenged the changeless thesis of non-democratic Catholicism.[133]

Snapshots of the objective and subjective political cultures[134] can be found in many treatments of various single Arab polities and,

130 Ibid., p. 308.

131 See Ernest S. Griffith, John Plamenatz and J. Roland Pennock, "Cultural Prerequisites to a successfully Functioning Democracy: A Symposium", *The American Political Science Review*, 50 (1956), p. 103.

132 Michael Levin, for instance, observes that "The current status of the term (democracy) is so overwhelmingly positive that it is easy to forget how comparatively recent such approval is." See his *The Spectre of Democracy: The Rise of Modern Democracy as Seen by its Critics* (London: Macmillan, 1992), p. 36.

133 According to Karl "As the church took an increasingly active role in opposing authoritarian rule, especially in Brazil, Chile, Peru, Central America and Panama, the argument about the so-called 'anti-democratic bias' of Catholicism became increasingly implausible." See Karl, "Dilemmas of Democratization in Latin America", p. 4. See also Paul E. Sigmund, "Christian Democracy, Liberation Theology, and Political Culture in Latin America" in Diamond (ed.), *Political Culture and Democracy in Developing Countries*, pp. 329–46.

134 Distinction between objective and subjective political cultures is provided by Chelkowski and Pranger: "Objective political culture involves those aspects of politics that demand attention from citizens and their leaders. Found in this culture are political actors, actions, settings (geographic boundaries, political vocabularies, economic systems, institutions, and the like). … Subjective political culture directs, rather than demands, the attention of citizens and leaders. This part of political culture involves 'insider' or 'member' status in a realm of shared experiences and meanings for citizens, and helps define 'us' as opposed to 'them'. What differentiates an 'American' from a 'Frenchman' or 'Russian' will be largely mediated by a subjective culture that comprises political communications, socialization and education, and role-playing, as well as feedback to objective political culture." See Robert J. Pranger, "Introduction:

especially, of elite politics.[135] Systematic studies of Arab mass political cultures still lag behind. A useful contribution to fill this lacuna is *Political Socialization in the Arab States*, with some ten case studies.[136] One of its many findings is the novelty in the Arab Gulf states of nationhood, civic culture, and political socialisation.[137] In describing elite political culture in Algeria, Entelis cites conflictual inter-elite relations, obsession with power, distrust of political opposition as well as tendencies towards collegiality and consultation amongst the ruling cliques.[138] These elements are not unknown to other Arab polities. Sharabi's "neopatriarchy" consists of four attributes that render the Arab sociopolitical structure uncongenial to modernity and, by implication, democracy:[139] "social fragmentation", "authoritarian organization", "absolutist paradigms" and "ritualistic practice".[140]

Arab political culture, argues al-M'Ghīribī, fosters authoritarian and hinders democratic rule.[141] This he blames on the patterns of

---

Ideology and Power in the Middle East" in Peter J. Chelkowski and Robert J. Pranger (eds), *Ideology and Power in the Middle East: Studies in Honour of George Lenczowski* (Durham, NC and London: Duke University Press, 1988), p. 21.

135 Michael C. Hudson's classic, *Arab Politics: The Search for Legitimacy* (New Haven: Yale University Press, 1977), is insightful in this respect. So are those works on Arab North Africa, John P. Entelis, *Algeria: The Revolution Institutionalized* (Boulder, CO: Westview Press, 1986) and *Comparative Politics of North Africa: Algeria, Morocco and Tunisia* (Syracuse University Press, 1980) and Jonathan Bearman *Qadhafi's Libya* (London: Zed Books, 1986).

136 See Tawfic E. Farah and Yasumasa Kuroda, *Political Socialization in the Arab States* (Boulder, CO: Lynne Rienner, 1987).

137 See Ahmad J. Dhaher, "Culture and Politics in the Arab Gulf States" in Farah and Kuroda (eds), *Political Socialization in the Arab States*, p. 75.

138 Entelis, *Algeria: The Revolution Institutionalized*, p. 157.

139 Hisham Sharabi, "Introduction: Patriarchy and Dependency and the Future of Arab Society" in Hisham Sharabi (ed.), *The Next Arab Decade: Alternative Futures* (Boulder, CO: Westview Press, 1988), pp. 2–3.

140 Sharabi describes these attributes as follows: "social fragmentation" whereby the "family, clan, religion, or ethnic group (rather than the nation or civic society) constitute the basis of social relations and…organization." Second, "authoritarian organization", marked by "domination, coercion and paternalism ([not] cooperation, mutual recognition, and equality)" in all relations—family and state based. Third, "absolutist paradigms" owing to "absolutist consciousness (…in politics, and everyday life) grounded in transcendence…and closure (rather than in difference, plurality, diffusion, openness…)." Fourth, "ritualistic practice" with behaviour being shaped by "custom and ritual" not "spontaneity, creativity, and innovation". See ibid., pp. 2–3.

141 Muḥammad Zāhī al-M'Ghīribī, "Al-thaqāfatu 'l-siyāsiyyah al-'Arabiyyah wa qaḍiyyatu 'l-dīmuqrāṭiyyah" [Arab Political Culture and the Question of Democracy] *Al-Dīmuqrāṭiyyah*, 3 (May 1991), pp. 6–11.

authority (domination, coercion and paternalism) mentioned by Sharabi, and the types of socialisation and its attendant "image-worlds" that inform political behaviours and attitudes in both the objective and subjective Arab political milieux. Al-M'Ghiribi finds *al-ʿajz* (impotence), *al-ittikāliyyah* (dependence), and *al-idhʿān* (conformity) to be the embodiments of Arab social and familial *tanshiʾah* (socialisation).[142] These ingredients find their most intensive expression in the Arab individual's relation to superiors. For, he argues, Arab social life represents an enduring system of interrelations based on *tasalluṭ* (domination) and *ruḍūkh* (subordination).[143] These relations of *tasalluṭ* and *ruḍūkh* prevail in the management of the household in a hierarchical fashion starting with the father down to the most junior family member, thus having a direct bearing on the functioning and organising of political power, itself comparably governed by relations of domination and subordination. The upshot is that the Arab individual accepts his or her place in the established order, usually devolving decision-making of personal and public affairs to superiors rather than actively participating, and accepting the pre-eminence of government, even when authoritarian, in complete indifference to his or her inner feelings of disapproval or passionate hatred towards it.[144]

In fact, the known phrase *nāqim ʿala al-waḍʿ* (disdainful of the situation) gives a clue to the vigour with which many Arabs oppose and disown their regimes. Yet, the frequency of conformity and compliance exceeds deviance. Because of embedded feelings of *ʿajz*, and tendencies toward *ittikāliyyah* and *idhʿān*, conscious of his or her own weakness to remove tyranny and, at the same time, concerned about salvation, the Arab individual looks up to *al-ṭabīʿah* (nature), *al-baṭal al-munqidh* (saviour), or some *baṭal usṭūrī* (legendary hero).[145] Hence the idolisation of the personal identity of the leader and dependence on the charismatic qualification of *al-baṭal al-munqidh* for deliverance from injustice.[146] Accordingly, al-M'Ghīribī calls for revolutionising Arab political culture, which tends to hinder creative and independent thinking, and foster *khawf* (fear) and *ṭāʿah* (obedience)

142 Ibid., p. 6.
143 Ibid.
144 Ibid.
145 Ibid., pp. 6–7.
146 Ibid., p. 7.

as well as a unitary mentality opposing diversity of opinion and dialogue.[147] Al-M'Ghiribi's insightful thesis somewhat de-emphasises the significance of the Arab history of protest.

SAID AND *ISTISHRĀQ*

Said's iconoclastic, and some might add controversial,[148] *Orientalism* is the seminal work which in its gist intelligently and powerfully alerts us not only to constructed and imagined myths, stereotypes and caricatures, but also to the devastating power wielded by intellectuals especially if their interests are cemented to those of structured power.

Neither Orientalism nor Orientalisation is new. Both *istishrāq* (Orientalism) and *mustashriqūn* (pl. of *mustashriq*, i.e., Orientalists) have, long before Said adverted to them, been the subject of study by Arab scholars. By giving wider audiences access to the Orientalisms about the "Orient", especially its Arab component, Said has opened vistas not only for critical evaluation of Orientalism as a practice and knowledge but also for the possibilities of anti-Orientalism. Said did what other disempowered Arab scholars before him could not do through Arabic, a disempowered language from the then and, largely still, disempowered Arab capitals. The great powers were and continue to be mostly either European and North American regions, the languages of which have, by dint of their military, economic, informational and political preponderance, been the *lingua franca* of international diplomacy, news and trade. Directly and indirectly Said expanded the debate about culture and "cultural imperialism",[149] inspiring the emergence, as Turner records, not only of "subaltern

[147] See ibid., pp. 7–11. However, contrary to al-M'Ghīribī, Hudson tends to be more cautious in backing the thesis that the authoritarian and patriarchal management of the household either directly or positively determines the nature of national politics. Excepted are those "…cases…in which a ruling family and the national government are virtually identical". See Hudson, *Arab Politics: The Search for Legitimacy*, pp. 85–6.

[148] For instance, see Bernard Lewis, *Islam and the West* (New York: Oxford University Press, 1993), esp. pp. 99–118. See also Fred Halliday, "Orientalism and its Critics", *British Journal of Middle Eastern Studies*, 20 (1993), pp. 145–63; Robert Young, *White Mythologies: Writing History and the West* (London: Routledge, 1995); S.J. al-Azm, "Orientalism and Orientalism in Reverse", *Khamsin*, 8 (1981), pp. 5–26.

[149] See Edward Said, *Culture and Imperialism* (London: Chatto and Windus, 1993).

studies" but also the rewriting of the history of formerly colonised cultures.[150] The corollary has been, on the one hand, a new-found confidence and new solidarities between previously silenced voices, leading to "Orientalist debate, subaltern studies and feminism",[151] and, on the other, the perception that the intellectual cannot render or represent the "other" "objectively".

The Orient of Balfour and Cromer is illustrative of the Orientalist attitude that constitutes "otherness", speaks for it, represents it, and dominates it under the guise of Occidental superior sociocultural dynamics—rationality and democracy. Not only are an Orientalist attitude and colonial hegemony mutually reinforcing, but also self-governance (democracy which is in conflict with expansionism and occupation) is in harmony with the ends of Britain's colonising of Egypt. The ethnocentric, logocentric and exclusionary ontological foundations of Orientalism are not specific to Balfour and Cromer's imperial era. They continue, as discussed below, to be replicated in Orientalist and neo-Orientalist texts whenever Arabs, Islam, Islamists are discussed in relation to democracy.

Self-governance in the Orient of Balfour and Cromer

Knowledge has to be power. This is true today of the postcolonial era as it was of the colonial era. The association is such that knowledge has sometimes to be invented for the purpose of power. One kind of knowledge that has been implicated in the service of imperial power is ethnography. Another is Orientalism. For Said the coincidence of Orientalism and colonialism is not accidental, but calculated: "To say that Orientalism was a rationalization of colonial rule is to ignore the extent to which colonial rule was justified in advance by Orientalism, rather than after the fact."[152] The most salient item in the list of characteristics of Orientalist discourses that Said brings to the fore and repeatedly interrogates is the power relationship of Occident and Orient. In that power relationship, the former's superiority over the latter is rendered absolute. In Orientalism, meaning comes from the Occident not from the Orient. Meaning comes from the agent writing or speaking rather than from that at the receiving end. Instructive

150 See Bryan S. Turner, *Orientalism, Postmodernism and Globalism* (London and New York: Routledge, 1994), p. 3.

151 Ibid.

152 Said, *Orientalism*, p. 39.

in this respect is the Orientalist mode of speaking and thinking in Balfour and Cromer's "us"-"them" mentality, especially in justifying the extension of dominion over Egypt. Their ethnocentrism takes for granted the righteousness of British occupation and the cultural and political preeminence of colonial rule over Egypt. An instance of this is Balfour's claim, in his speech in favour of occupation, to knowing Egypt. To which Said remarks:

> As Balfour justifies the necessity for British occupation of Egypt, supremacy in his mind is associated with "our" knowledge of Egypt and not principally with military or economic power. Knowledge to Balfour means surveying a civilization from its origins to its prime to its decline—and of course, it means *being able to do that*. Knowledge means rising above immediacy, beyond self, into the foreign and distant...To have such knowledge of such a thing is to dominate it, to have authority over it. And authority here means for "us" to deny autonomy to "it"—the Oriental country—since we know it and it exists, in a sense, *as* we know it. British knowledge of Egypt is Egypt for Balfour, and the burdens of knowledge make such questions as inferiority and superiority seem petty ones.[153]

Here the notion of the "white man's burden" is pushed to its most logical conclusion—occupation. By way of valorisation of British knowledge of Egypt over that of the Egyptians themselves, the privileging of the politics and culture of the "self" over those of the "other", a civilisational mission is invented: cultural and political tutelage. For the Egypt constituted by Balfour's speech is not versed in self-government, a preserve of the superior Occident. Said writes that the premise of Balfour's speech is "England knows that Egypt cannot have self-government; England confirms that by occupying Egypt; for the Egyptians, Egypt is what England has occupied and now governs; foreign occupation therefore becomes 'the very basis' of contemporary Egyptian civilization; Egypt requires, indeed insists upon, British occupation."[154] This mode of thinking is predicated on an Orientalist outlook which divides the world into the "West" and the "Orient". In it "the former dominate; the latter must be dominated".[155] This is because "[I]n Cromer's and Balfour's language the Oriental is depicted as something one judges (as in a court of law), something one studies and depicts (as in a curriculum), something

[153] Ibid., p. 32.
[154] Ibid., p. 34.
[155] Ibid., p. 36.

one disciplines (as in a school or prison), something one illustrates (as in a zoological manual)."[156]

More explicitly, from the claim of "knowing Egypt", Balfour and Cromer justify British colonial rule by way of patronage. That is, British rule over Egypt is for the sake of the Egyptians. The colonial power is foisted on the Egyptians as some kind of a saviour. Throughout Oriental history, Balfour claims, there have only been despots and absolutist rulers—whereas in Western nations the capacity for self-government has been present since they emerged into history.[157] Because the Egyptians are constituted as strange to self-government, Balfour couches occupation and British rule in moralism: "I think experience shows that they have got under it far better government than in the whole history of the world they ever had before."[158] Furthermore, Balfour intimates that sense of moral obligation, self-sacrifice and duty in Britain's self-assigned role of bringing self-government to the Egyptians, by describing British rule over Egypt as "dirty work, the inferior work, of carrying on the necessary labour".[159] In the same vein, and in the same ethnocentric and logocentric fashion, Cromer writes "It is essential that each special issue should be decided mainly with reference to what, by the light of Western knowledge and experience tempered by local considerations, we conscientiously think is best for the subject race, without reference to any real or supposed advantage which may accrue to England as a nation."[160]

Orientalism and colonialism work in tandem, the former finding political expression in the latter. Egypt had to be constituted as ontologically inferior, a receptacle as it were, necessitating Britain's role to teach her the rational ways of the Occidentals. Cromer displays complete contempt toward what he labels as "the Oriental mind". He mystifies it, cementing it to scientific and rational backwardness: "The mind of the Oriental…like his picturesque streets, is eminently without symmetry. His reasoning is of the most slipshod description." As to the opposition, the Occidental mind: "The European is a close reasoner; his statements of facts are devoid of any ambiguity;

[156] Ibid., p. 41.
[157] Ibid., pp. 32–3.
[158] Ibid., p. 33.
[159] Ibid.
[160] Ibid., p. 37.

he is a natural logician, albeit he may not have studied logic...his trained mind works like a piece of mechanism."[161] Through supremacist misrepresentation and edited history, colonialism is projected in a positive light—benign, respectable and altruistic. Because Egyptians know nothing of self-government, because their renascence is judged by Balfour as something of the past, and because of their deficient "logical faculty, English dominion is the only key to their future political and cultural rehabilitation".[162] To imperial figures like Balfour and Cromer, the governing of Egypt and her subsequent reform would thus benefit the prestige of both Great Britain and the civilised West. This is thought so because by this governing, this once great civilisation is shown not only to be incapable of self-rule, but also, the Egyptians under British dominion are claimed to have been ruled better than they had ever been. Thus Western colonial governing is far better than any Oriental nation is capable of. As Said puts it: "Egypt was not just another colony: it was the vindication of Western imperialism; it was, until its annexation by England, an almost academic example of Oriental backwardness; it was to become a triumph of English knowledge and power."[163]

Islam, Democracy, Orientalism and neo-Orientalism

If Orientalism is a shorthand for the creation or consumption of images of the "Orient" and the "Oriental", then questions about "Oriental Orientalists" deserve some attention. Is Ibn Khaldūn an Orientalist or is he engaging in civilisationalism, i.e., the study of systems and features of urbanism and civilisation? He essentialises about Arabs, imputing to them the propensity for destructive and disorderly behaviour.[164] His understanding of *'umrān* is dialectically defined: *badāwah* (nomadism; desert culture) is set off against *al-ḥaḍar* (sedentary culture); he essentialises the former to be lacking in

[161] Ibid., p. 38.

[162] Ibid., p. 35.

[163] Ibid.

[164] Ibn Khaldun states that "Places that succumb to the Arabs are quickly ruined". Why? "The reason for this is that (the Arabs) are a savage nation, fully accustomed to savagery and the things that cause it. Savagery has become their character and nature. They enjoy it, because it means freedom from authority and no subservience to leadership. Such a natural disposition is the negation and antithesis of civilization." See Ibn Khaldun, *The Muqaddimah: An Introduction to History*, vol. I, trans. by Franz Rosenthal (Princeton University Press, 1967), pp. 302–3.

those items of "civility", *'umrān*, on which he regards *al-ḥaḍar* to be specifically predicated. Great minds from Marx (European capitalism versus the Asiatic mode of production) to Weber (rational-traditional dichotomy)[165] are guilty of logocentric essentialisations. The dichotomies which involve accusations of Orientalism, and invite confusion with them, deploy metaphors based on oppositions (including rational/irrational; modern/traditional/; clear/obscure; "East"/"West"; male/female). The question about the metaphor (or synecdoche) and its valuation depends on its deployment by a given author, and the distance that author may be seen to be imagining between himself and the opposed term in the metaphor.

In the contemporary Arab Middle East, essentialism by intellectuals, politicians and ordinary citizens, is widespread, especially, in terms of stance towards Islamism and Islamists. The difference is that the Orientalists here are not Westerners but rather the avid cultural Westernisers. The columns of those writing in the state-owned Arab dailies are full of the kind of Orientalisms that "fundamentalist Islam" is "anti-democratic", "aggressive", "totalitarian", "extremist", and "anti-Western".[166] And nowhere is this more conspicuous than in those Arab capitals (Algiers, Cairo, Tunis) where Westernisers, existing regimes, are pitted against their own Islamists. Here the linkage between rule, the power of the purse and that of the pen is at play. The observation by Norman Cigar that "seldom in modern times has Orientalism had such a direct relationship to policy as it has to that of 'ethnic cleansing'...in Bosnia-Herzegovina"[167] rings true in many an Arab country where a form of "political cleansing" of Islamists is a declared and enforced policy. September 11 made this worse.

Oriental Orientalism underlies the links between modes of knowing, thinking, doing, and being in centres of power in parts of the

[165] See Bryan S. Turner, *Marx and the End of Orientalism* (London: Allen and Unwin, 1978); also by Turner, "Orientalism, Islam and Capitalism", *Social Compass*, 25 (1978), pp. 371–94; and by the same author, *Weber and Islam: A Critical Study*.

[166] These views are compatible with those expressed, for instance, by Daniel Pipes. See his "There are no Moderates: Dealing with Fundamentalist Islam", *The National Interest* (fall 1995), pp. 48–57. See also Mohammad Mohaddesin, "There is no such Thing as a Moderate Fundamentalist", *Middle East Quarterly*, 2 (September 1995), pp. 77–83.

[167] See Norman Cigar, "Serbia's Orientalists and Islam: Making Genocide Intellectually Respectable", *The Islamic Quarterly*, 38 (1994), pp. 147–70.

West and of the East. Thus Occidental Orientalist representations of the Orient trickle down to parts of the East. Whether the issue is development or women, democracy or Islamic movements, parallelism between Occidental and Oriental Orientalisms is striking. The quasi-debate contests in the early 1990s in Egypt brought face-to-face the propagators of the chief tenets of Orientalist modes of knowing and thinking (e.g. Farag Fūdā and Zakī), and those whose knowing and thinking were anchored in an Arabo-Islamic framework (e.g. Muḥammad al-Ghazālī and Muḥammad ʿUmārah). The former group valorised the dogmas of the modernist framework; the latter tended to strive to re-valorise venerable Arabo-Islamic traditions and institutions as the key to the impasse of democracy and development. Oriental Orientalism is evidence of the potency of Orientalism as a discourse of power. More than four decades after decolonisation in the AME, the battle for intellectual decolonisation is yet to be won. Orientals thinking of themselves within an Orientalist framework is not new. The past, as Timothy Mitchell demonstrates, gives a strong sense of dejà vu:

> The manner in which...Oriental self-conception was spread can be illustrated with the case of the writer Jurji Zaydan, a Lebanese Christian who lived in Egypt during the period of British occupation. Zaydan was commissioned to produce two textbooks for use in the new government secondary schools, *A Modern History of Egypt* (1889) and a *Universal History* (1890)... He was also the author of a five-volume *History of Islamic Civilization*, based on a wide reading of pre-modern Arab historians but also, by his own account, on half a dozen European studies of Islam...Describing the period of the first four caliphs as the highest phase of Islamic civilization, Zaydan represented every subsequent period, from the Umayyad and Abbasid caliphates onward, as a successive stage of decline...The view of history as a unilinear development in which Islam represented only a 'connecting link' in the medieval formation of an object called the West had direct political implications. Writing in the journal he had founded, *al-Hilal*, on the Indian uprisings of 1857 against the British, Zaydan warned Egyptians of the social disruption that faced them if they did not follow the steady course of development whose stages had been marked out by the West...
>
> The absolute opposition between the order of the modern West and the backwardness and disorder of the East was not only found in Europe, but began to repeat itself in Egyptian scholarship and popular literature, just as it was replicated in colonial cities. Through its textbooks, school teachers, universities, newspapers, novels and magazines, the colonial order was able to penetrate and colonize local discourse. This colonizing process never fully

succeeded, for there always remained regions of resistance and voices of rejection…[T]he power of colonialism was itself a power that sought to colonize…not only in the shape of cities and barracks, but in the form of classrooms, journals and works of scholarship. Colonialism—and modern politics generally—distinguished itself in this colonizing power. It was able at the most local level to reproduce theatres of its order and truth.[168]

Accordingly, just as Said describes his Orientalism as "an unbroken arc of knowledge and power connect[ing] the European or Western statesman and the Western Orientalists",[169] that metropolitan arc has been extended with a peripheral arc in which the representatives of the metropolitan power (military backers or political and financial sponsors of Arab Westernisers) adopt and routinise Orientalist discourses as befit political interest and expediency. French *laicisme* informs political behaviour in the Tunisian and Algerian centres of power. The debate on the veil in France[170] has had a spill-over effect in the Maghrib, the most clear-cut of which is Law 108, forbidding the veil in the work place (a negation of the earlier affirmative action policies in Tunisia), brought about in the 1980s by the Bourguiba regime, considered liberal by Paris and Washington. Likewise, the debate on terrorism has been globalised and Orientalised. Today a "terrorist" is most likely to be equated with a religious zealot, Islamist-affiliated rather than a secular activist. Two of the most recent successful cinematic productions in Egypt have been Adel Imam's *Al-Irhābi* (*The terrorist*), and the series *Al-'ā'ilah* (*The Family*), both of which deal with terrorism. Recent Hollywood movies such as *True Lies* and *Executive Decision* are other examples. The Islamists' terrorism and fanaticism are decried in Washington and in Cairo, in Algiers and in Paris, and in Tel Aviv and in Amman. The violence by a number of groups claiming the mantle of Islam has wrongly stigmatised Islam itself as violent, a theme explored in Esposito's work *The Islamic Threat*.[171] Halliday is right when he calls for delinking

168 Timothy Mitchell, *Colonising Egypt* (Berkeley and Oxford: University of California Press, 1991), pp. 169, 170.

169 Said, *Orientalism*, p. 104.

170 See, for instance, "Foulard, le complot: comment les islamistes nous infiltrent", (Veil, the Plot: How Islamists Infiltrate us) in *L'Express*, 17 November 1994, pp. 62–6.

171 See John Esposito, *Islamic Threat: Myth or Reality?* (New York: Oxford University Press, 1992). See also Leon T. Hadar, "What Green Peril?" *Foreign Affairs*, 72 (spring 1993), pp. 28–42.

Islam and terrorism.[172] That some Muslims are militant does not make Islam militant. Titles such as *Holy War, Militant Islam, The Dagger of Islam, The Islamic Bomb* and *The Crusade of Modern Islam* are not neutral; they are emotive and are, therefore, forms of Orientalisations.[173] They tend to either misrepresent or "demonise".

The new essentialisms are based on economic rationalism and profit-making. The new solidarities are likely to be power groups (for instance, political, military, economic or informational) cutting across nationality, race, religion, gender or colour, and forming not only comparable or compatible "worldviews" but also a form of cultural hegemony the markers of which are order, security and free trade. This is noted in a degree of overlap in the agendas of Arab and Muslim autocrats and Western democrats. These power congeries have a common interest in preserving the prevailing global order but nothing else politically and culturally. It is difficult to imagine Clinton and King Fahd or Bush and Mubarak having much in common. It seems that in the world of grand strategy, clientelism and interdependency, self-respected democrats bestow upon their friendly autocrats undeserved respectability. After 11 September 2001, "war against terror" has pitted Western foreign policy and its client regimes against political Islam. Political Islam has been caricatured into a monolith, a Caliphate, under centralised authority, sharing a univocal discourse and resources headed by Osama Bin Laden. This lack of sophistication not only serves to turn Huntington's "clash of civilisations" into a self-fulfilling prophecy, but also denies space to Islamist democrats. Many Islamist activists demand for their societies no less than those values the Burmese Aung San Suu Kyi wants for Burma: good government. The audiences the struggling Tibetan religious leader, the Dalai Lama, is deservedly given with secular Western heads of state would not have been possible had His Holiness been an Islamist.

This policy is not a random policy; it is a double-edged sword with positive (inclusion) and negative (exclusion) sanctions. Its yardstick

[172] See Fred Halliday, "International Relations: Is there a New Agenda?" *Millennium*, 20, 1 (1991), pp. 57–72.

[173] See, for instance, John Laffin, *Holy War: Islam Fights* (London: Grafton Books, 1988); John Laffin, *The Dagger of Islam* (London: Sphere Books Limited, 1979); G.H. Jansen, *Militant Islam* (London: Pan Books, 1979); Steve Weissman and Herbert Krosney, *The Islamic Bomb* (New Delhi: Vision Books, 1983); Robin Wright, *Sacred Rage: The Crusade of Modern Islam* (London: Andre Deutsh, 1986).

is the level of receptiveness, neutrality or hostility towards the prevailing world order. Neither is Aung San Suu Kyi a random international figure nor is the Dalai Lama. Both are engaged in particularistic struggles that are neither hospitable (although Aung San Suu Kyi is enmeshed in the global democratic narrative) nor hostile towards the prevailing order (the Dalai Lama is a self-professed pacifist). By contrast, Islamist leaders, although open to many democratic ideals and practices, are perceived to be hostile to the prevailing world order. They certainly espouse visions and revisions of epistemology, polity, society and economy that not only challenge the prevailing order but also constitute, as far as they are concerned, a boon to an alternative order.

Islamists are not self-professed pacifists even if many of them condemn violence as a political strategy. Islamist leaders like al-Ghannūshī (al-nahḍah of Tunisia), al-Farḥān (Jordan's Islamic Action Front or al-ʿamal) or al-Huḍaybī (Egypt's Muslim Brotherhood or al-ikhwān) have categorically declared their opposition to violence and abuse of the Islamic notion of *jihād* (martial struggle). These men and the movements they lead have ruled out deploying violence against the authoritarian regimes that have condemned them to political wilderness (the exception is al-ʿamal which until 1997 constituted the main opposition in the Jordanian parliament), thus refusing to take their countries on Algeria's bloody path.[174] This stance, however, is neither symbiotic with the kind of pacifism the Dalai Lama has professed for a long time nor with ruling out legitimate *jihād*, i.e. against outside aggression, big-power hegemony and injustice. In this respect, al-Turābī and al-Huḍaybī, for instance, concur that *jihād* is not divisible, i.e. greater and lesser or spiritual and physical, and that the Qurʿānic status, place and role of *jihād* as a divinely-ordained practice cannot be called something else such as lesser *jihād*, misrepresenting it, compromising it or relegating it to a lower status, a status of redundancy. In the words of al-Turābī, "let's call *jihād* nothing else but *jihād*, not something else like a lesser *jihād*..."[175] Al-Huḍaybī adds:

> Major powers of both the West and the East believe in and profess violence; they practise it; and, most importantly, when they don't practise it they

[174] According to interviews conducted by the author with the three leaders in 1992, 1993 and 1994.

[175] Author's interview with Ḥasan al-Turābī, 12 May 1994, Khartoum, Sudan.

commit great resources toward maintaining it as an option in international affairs. There is every evidence that they continuously prepare for violence. They couch their violence in the language of national interest, deterrence and international legal jargon all of which are man-made. Just as they have their notions of preparedness and of deterrence we have our own notion of jihād. And if they treat their earthly notions of violence in a very possessive, righteous and sacrosanct way, how can we be expected to treat jihād, a godly notion, less possessively or less seriously and give it up?[176]

Yet, the opposition to Islamists in some quarters appears to be based simply on the fact that they happen to be Islamist. The attitudes of commentators like Pipes are representative. He claims that "fundamentalist Islam [is]...a narrow, aggressive twentieth century ideological movement".[177] The reasons offered by Pipes are unconvincing, for example he states that "it is misguided policy to distinguish between moderate and extremist fundamentalists".[178] However, this is not the case. This example is a clear illustration of the bottom line of Said's work, that is, that generalising is generic to Orientalising. Islamists are not one and the same even if they share a common political *telos*. There is a diversity of democrats and a variety of Islamists. Al-Ghannūshī cannot, for instance, be equated with Egyptian ʿUmar ʿAbd al-Raḥmān. The former issues no *fatwahs* (religio-political counsel) for *jihād*.[179] Similarly, for obvious reasons the Islamists of Jordan's *al-ʿamal* are no Afghan Taliban.[180]

176 Author's interview with Ma'mūn al-Huḍaybī, 4 April 1994, Cairo, Egypt.

177 Pipes, "There are no Moderates", p. 55.

178 Ibid., p. 54.

179 One of the best references for explaining the different meanings of *jihād* can be found in M. Mazzahim Mohideen, "Islam, Nonviolence, and Interfaith Relations" in Glenn D. Paige, Chaiwat Satha-Anand and Sarah Gilliatt (eds), *Islam and Nonviolence* (Honolulu: Matsunaga Institute for Peace, University of Hawaii, 1993), pp. 137–43. Also see Fazlur Rahman, *Islam* (Chicago and London: University of Chicago Press, 1979), p. 37; John L. Esposito, *The Islamic Threat: Myth or Reality*? (New York and Oxford: Oxford University Press, 1992), pp. 32–3. Three types of *jihād*—personal, ummaic and martial—are listed by Mir Z. Husain, *Global Islamic Politics* (New York: Harper Collins, 1995), p. 37.

180 For useful analysis of American understandings and misunderstandings of Islam and the "Orient" see Fred von der Mehden, "American Perceptions of Islam" in John L. Esposito (ed.), *Voices of Resurgent Islam* (New York: Oxford University Press, 1983), pp. 18–31. Compare with another article by Dale Eickelman and Kamran Pasha, "Muslim Societies and Politics: Soviet and US Approaches: A Conference Report", *Middle East Journal*, 45 (1991), pp. 630–44.

Denial of any partnership between Islam and democracy is part and parcel of Orientalism and neo-Orientalism. Examples of this anti-Islam bias are numerous and only a handful can be sampled in this section. Lowrie's article "The Campaign Against Islam and American Foreign Policy", while not going into the detailed specifics or historical arguments or the neo-Orientalists, gives a contemporary context and reasoning for why they write with such hostility and one-sidedness towards Islam, or more specifically, Islamic forces in the Middle East. Most anti-Islamist writings fit into a Cold War and post-Cold War context. For example, to Amos Perlmutter, a professor of Political Science at the America University, the so-called "radical Islam" represents as much a threat now as Soviet-Style authoritarianism did in the 1930s. He equates one with the other because he considers "radical Islam" to be a "totalitarian, anti-Western and popular movement hoping to teach the modern-style Christian 'crusaders' some lessons in ultraviolence…The Western world… cannot permit the replacement of one form of totalitarianism with another; the [former] Soviet model with an Islamic one."[181] One can speak of Muslim extremists but not of "radical Islam".

Many writers, Lowrie's article shows, also portray Islam as a "fanatical", "intolerant" and "violent" movement. In some way, these adjectives are modern-day renditions of pejorative terms used in the nineteenth century—"barbaric", "primitive", "uncivilised", "patriarchal", and so on. Leslie Gelb of the *New York Times* writes that "Islam doesn't recognize coexistence as a basic doctrine. Coexistence goes against Islam's sense of world order."[182] In the same vein, Judith Miller, also with the *New York Times*, writes that "An Islamic state as espoused by most of its proponents is simply incompatible with values and truths that Americans and most Westerners today hold to be self-evident."[183] (Who doesn't recognise co-existence here?) Miller displays similar bias, contending that Arabs, in general, and the Islamists, in particular, do not have a complete understanding of democracy. To them, she notes, democracy is majority rule without any recognition of minority rights.[184] While Islam has been tolerant

[181] Arthur Lowrie, "The Campaign Against Islam and American Foreign Policy", *Middle East Policy*, 4 (September 1995), p. 212.

[182] Ibid., p. 214.

[183] Ibid., p. 214.

[184] Judith Miller, "The Challenge of Radical Islam", *Foreign Affairs*, 72 (1993), p. 51.

of minorities in history, under Islamic law minorities "are given protected, not equal, status".[185]

The premises of superiority, exclusion and ethnocentrism at the core of Orientalism permeate neo-Orientalist discourses. One difference stands out. In his article "The New Orientalism and the Democracy Debate", Yahya Sadowski argues that there has been a shift in the Orientalist view of Islamic politics.[186] Sadowski captures the essence of that difference by comparing both groups' Orientalisations which revolved around the question of democracy in reference to Islam and Muslims. While both traditional and new Orientalists hold that Islam is incompatible with liberal democracy, the way they argue this, or come to this conclusion, differ. To the traditional Orientalists, democracy cannot develop in Muslim countries because these countries currently have no civil societies, nor have they had one historically. Many political theorists, going back to Montesquieu and Thomas Paine, have argued that the organisations and associations which make up a civil society are necessary to resist the arbitrary use of state power, considering them a prerequisite to the development of democracy. The traditional Orientalists have utilised this claim as an explanation of why it is unlikely that Muslim countries, including the AME, would ever develop democracy. Those social organisations present in the Middle East, which could be seen as elements of a civil society, are generally seen as "informal, personalistic, and relatively inefficient as a means of winning support and extracting resources from the populace".[187]

Because of this fixation with a Eurocentric view of democratic transition and a fixed view of the function of civil society—a bulwark against the state—the traditional Orientalists argue that these groups are not aimed at challenging the ruler's authority. Rather, these "...groups in Islamic societies tended to be vehicles of supplication and collaboration. The most common form of political organisation was the clientage network whose members traded their loyalty for the patronage and protection of some notable."[188] For traditional

[185] Ibid., p. 50.

[186] Yahya Sadowski, "The New Orientalism and the Democracy Debate", *Middle East Report* (July–August 1993) pp. 14–21, 40.

[187] Quoted by Sadowski, from Robert Springborg, "Patterns of Association in the Egyptian Political Elite" in George Lenczowski (ed.), *Political Elites in the Middle East* (Washington, D.C.: American Enterprise Institute, 1975), p. 87.

[188] Sadowski, "The New Orientalism and the Democracy Debate", pp. 15–16.

Orientalists do not only see these types of groups as lacking in autonomy and unable to bring about democracy but also regard their political behaviour or disposition to be bound to Islam, an Islam in which "despotism [i]s implicit in [its] very core".[189] Despotism is implicit because, to the classical Orientalists, Islam is immune to democracy on account of its correspondence with totalitarianism: "The totalistic character of the faith seemed to imply that only a totalitarian state could put its dogmas into practice."[190] This totalistic character is taken to have engendered a culture of political quietism. The classical Orientalists notice the absence of autonomous groups and cities; record the history of quietism not of uprisings; misread values of societal mutual obligation as suppression of the individual by the group and the community by the ruler; highlight difference, editing out the fact that medieval despotism was not specific to Muslims alone; and decontextualise the predilection of Muslim jurists for "just despotism" over anarchy. Sadowski elaborates the last point:

> The classical Orientalists argued that Orthodox Islam promoted political quietism. Supposedly the great medieval Islamic thinkers, horrified by the periodic rebellions and civil wars that wrecked their community, decreed that obedience to any ruler—even an unworthy or despotic one—was a religious duty.[191]

Thinking along these lines was until recently the dominant intellectual "tradition" amongst Orientalists. That is, dominant until superseded by events in the mid-East region, forcing scholars into an acquaintance with new dynamics, and, Sadowski argues, leading to revisions of the traditional Orientalist view of Islamic history and politics. Sadowski identifies three new trends in Middle Eastern studies in the 1980s which have collectively undermined traditional Orientalism, especially after Iran's Islamic revolution. The first, studies on the phenomenon of political Islam, brought to light evidence tending to refute the early notion of political quietism in Islam as well as affirm Islam's support for opposition against unjust rule. The cliché generalisation of "strong states and weak societies" that was earlier on indiscriminately applied to Muslim lands, had to be reversed. The Islamic revolution concretised this new thinking, by

189 Ibid., p. 16.
190 Ibid.
191 Ibid.

demonstrating that an Islamic society was as capable as any other of creating a grassroots social movement capable of overthrowing a despotic government. The second trend was the demonstration that states in the Middle East were less powerful than were first theorised to be. Sadowski links this trend directly to the slump in oil prices; as these fell so did state revenue and, by implication, state capacity itself. The third trend was studies into anti-systemic forces or social forces, groups and organisations, working below and above the state, with the potential to perform the functions and tasks of a "civil society".[192]

All of these challenges meant that if the Orientalists wanted still to maintain that Islam and democracy were incompatible, they had to change tack. Thus the neo-Orientalists arose. Sadowski critiques works by the more prominent ones, including Patricia Crone and Daniel Pipes. Crone's main thesis is that in Islamic societies there has been a historical split between the state and the wider society which persists today. What accounted for this split in state–society relations, Sadowski argues, was the learned scholars' reluctance or outright opposition to underwrite political power, on the basis of their belief in the proneness of "secular rulers…to corruption and despotism".[193] The scholars' position found wide appeal and support amongst the mass of Muslims, with the corollary being that Muslim subjects "offered only tepid and intermittent support for their rulers".[194] Bias permeates Crone's *Slaves on Horses: The Evolution of the Islamic Polity*. It depicts Islamic polity as "clan-nic" and tribal; stresses imbalance and disjunction in state–society relations; and essentialises Muslim societies to be largely passive and polities to be more or less static, except in terms of dynastic change. As Sadowski argues, the crux of this bias revolves around the notion of an anti-state element in Islamic culture. Examples of this line of argument abound in Crone's work.[195] "Hence the political pattern that accompanied this disjuncture was one that oscillated between extremes of despotism

[192] Ibid.

[193] Ibid., p. 17.

[194] Ibid.

[195] Patricia Crone writes that "(B)y the 750s, Islam had acquired its classical shape as an all-embracing holy law characterised by a profound hostility to settled states." See her *Slaves on Horses: The Evolution of the Islamic Polity* (Cambridge University Press, 1980), p. 62.

and anarchy on the part of the state, and ritual avoidance and factionalism on the part of the notables."[196]

A manifestation of the disjunction in state–society relations, owing to society's withdrawal of support or refusal to lend it, was the state's recruiting of slaves, *mamluks*, for the army rather than of citizens. Crone notes how this phenomenon is unique to Islamic civilisation: "the systematic handing over of power to slaves (or for that matter to women) to the more or less complete exclusion of the free males of the community bespeaks a moral gap of such dimensions that within the great civilizations it has been found only in one."[197] Crone's other works, such as *God's Caliph*, are replete with notions about Islam's totalitarian polity. In this respect, Crone shows another type of disjunction, one between theory and practice. Islamic theory's exalting of a divinely-sanctioned good to be administered over and enacted through delegation of public affairs to a representative of God on earth verged, as illustrated by the Umayyads's rule, "…in practice [on] a total surrender of power to a ruler who was by definition always in the right".[198] In conclusion to her book, Crone writes:

> The fact that all aspects of life were rolled together in a single God-given package in the Islamic view of things was of crucial importance for the formation of a new civilization in an area in which civilization cannot be said to have been in short supply; the same fact lies behind the ideological intransigence *vis-à-vis* the Western world today. It is a fact which throughout history has given Islam extraordinary powers of survival; but at the same time it has always interfered with the capacity of Muslims to organize themselves.[199]

In deciphering the intellectual template of neo-Orientalism, Sadowski turns to the works of Daniel Pipes and John Hall. Sadowski finds that both scholars have taken cues from Crone's work, making their renditions of Islam, Islamic civilisation and Muslim polities mutually reinforcing with neo-Orientalist knowing and thinking. Pipes is found to agree with the gist of Crone's about the split between polity and society. One result of this was the refusal to serve in the armies—thus slaves had to be recruited to do this. Similarly, Pipes finds disjunction between the ideals of Islam as codified in the *sharīʿah* and

196 Ibid., p. 88.

197 Ibid., p. 81.

198 Patricia Crone, *God's Caliph: Religious Authority in the First Centuries of Islam* (Cambridge University Press, 1986), p. 106.

199 Ibid., p. 110.

political attitude and behaviour, between rigidity of a doctrinaire Islam and the medieval practice of government. Hence the failure of medieval polities to live up to those Islamic ideals, and the tendency of the mass of devouts not to support or confer legitimacy upon their rulers. On grounds of this medieval legacy of political instability, unruliness and imbalance in state–society relations, Pipes explicates the visible impasse of modernisation Muslims presently experience.[200] Thus contemporary Muslims are condemned, because of a past they neither are responsible for or are able to efface, to a future of little or no hope for positive change. This condemnation, which serves only to mystify Islam, is inherently Orientalist. As Said points out "The Orientalist attitude in general…shares with magic and with mythology the self-containing, self-reinforcing character of a closed system, in which objects are what they are *because* they are what they are, for once, for all time, for ontological reasons that no empirical material can either dislodge or alter."[201]

In his book *In the Path of God*, Pipes openly identifies himself as writing in the Orientalist tradition. His reason being that "Western academic study of Islam provides the only basis for an analysis of the religion in relation to public life."[202] His work does follow a (neo-) Orientalist line, as ably shown by Sadowski. A good example is his reference to the "Islam mentality" which is a dichotomous one where "things either conform to Islam or they oppose it."[203] Sadowski is accurate in his account of Pipes' neo-Orientalist mode of thinking—much of it can be clearly seen in *In the Path of God*. One finds no systematic attempt to explain nuances; hence Pipes generalises, suggesting that what he calls the "Islamicate pattern—customary withdrawal punctuated by bursts of activity—survived into the modern period.

[200] Sadowski, "The New Orientalism and the Democracy Debate", p. 18.

[201] Said, *Orientalism*, p. 70.

[202] Daniel Pipes, *In the Path of God: Islam and Political Power* (New York: Basic Books 1983), p. 24.

[203] Ibid., p. 39. Pipes' work contains many blinkered and apologetic views of events in the Middle East. One example of this is his explication of post-revolutionary hostility between Iran and the U.S. He writes that relations between the Shah's Iran and the U.S. were so cordial that this could not be the source of hostility; rather the hostility comes from a long history of Islamic-Christian hostility which the Ayatollah rekindled, see ibid., p. 13. This analysis ignores genuine grievances the Iranian people may have had, especially with regard to former U.S. support of the corrupt and brutal regime of the Shah.

Despite the adoption of Western ideologies which call for regular citizen participation, Muslims continued to avoid politics and warfare except when galvanised by issues relating to legalism or autonomism."[204] Thus the building blocs and values of democracy are typically comprehended as unfitting and Orientalised as alien. As Pipes puts it, the "concept of the citizen—an enfranchised, participating member of society who pays taxes, joins voluntary associations, elects government officials, and serves in the military—fitted awkwardly in Islamdom".[205]

Sadowski credits Hall with "drawing out the implications of Crone's work for contemporary Islamic societies".[206] Here, too, what is obviously conspicuous is the bias against Islam and Muslims. All analyses attempting to explain absence of democratic rule, political instability and lack of development lead to either indictment of Islamic civilisations and/or to invidious comparisons with Europe, something Hall does quite well. Five interrelated points sum up Sadowski's insight into Hall's view of Islamic history: First, it being a "story" of a "strong society" shunning cooperation with political authority; secondly, it being one of dynastic rulers tending to be only marginally rooted in society; thirdly, it being one where stability obtains only owing to societal solidaristic arrangements; fourthly, it being one where state instability demotes democracy; and, finally, it being one where the weak and dynastic state provides a stark contrast to the European "organic state", that is, strong, efficient, rooted in society and functional.[207]

What transpires from Sadowski's deconstructing of Orientalist thought, new and old, is that it is neither objective nor neutral, and, above all else, it is akin to any other discourse of power with binary oppositions, and with a logos—Western history, values and models. At least three recurring flaws are at the core of Orientalist knowing. The first regards the notion of a fixed Islamic essence, labouring under the duress of a history, conspiring against change or progress in the modern era—civil society, democracy.[208] The second relates to Orientalist reductionism in explicating the impasses of democratisation

[204] Ibid., p. 144.
[205] Ibid., p. 145.
[206] Sadowski, "The New Orientalism and the Democracy Debate", p. 18.
[207] Ibid., p. 18.
[208] Ibid., pp. 19–20.

or modernisation in Muslim countries. What is erased from the history of the Middle East is the importance and impact of external dynamics, e.g. European imperialism. Sadowski notes how a "fairly consistent refrain in Orientalist analysis is that 'in the Middle East the impact of European imperialism was late, brief, and for the most part indirect'".[209] Implicating European imperialism would undermine the Orientalist claim that "The obstacle to development are overwhelmingly internal and have not changed during the 1400 years of Islamic history. Essentialism and the dismissal of Western colonialism and imperialism are commonly paired together, since each makes the other more plausible."[210] The third flaw concerns the notion of a "balance" in state–society relations. Orientalist analyses tend to oversimplify or manipulate such a notion, that is, that such a balance is a prerequisite for democracy. Sadowski argues that the relationship is more complex than has thus far been accounted for by Orientalists; that it is not just a question of the state needing to be stronger than society or vice versa; and that power relations oscillate over time. Sadowski points out and savours the huge irony of the shift from traditional Orientalism to neo-Orientalism, noting that:

> When the consensus of social scientists held that democracy and development depended upon the actions of strong, assertive social groups, Orientalists held that such associations were absent in Islam. When the consensus evolved and social scientists thought a quiescent, undemanding society was essential to progress, the neo-Orientalist portrayed Islam as beaming with pushy, anarchic solidarities. Middle Eastern Muslims, it seems, were doomed to be eternally out of step with intellectual fashion.[211]

It is academically fashionable to compare Islam with the "West" in terms of their achievements in relation to "modernity", "democracy", and, more recently, to "postmodernity". The list of titles—"Islam and the West"; "Islam and democracy"; "Islam and modernity"; "Islam and postmodernity"—that exemplify this practice is fairly long. Waardenburg's *L'Islam dans le miroir de l'Occident* is one of the oldest.[212]

[209] Ibid., p. 20. The quote in Sadowski's comment comes from Bernard Lewis, *The Middle East and the West* (New York: Harper Torchbooks, 1964), p. 31.

[210] Ibid., p. 20.

[211] Ibid., p. 19.

[212] Jacques Waardenburg, *L'Islam dans le miroir de l'Occident* (The Hague: Mouton, 1963).

The newest is Esposito and Voll's work *Islam and Democracy*.[213] With very few exceptions, this academic practice, most evident in Orientalism and neo-Orientalism, is generally anchored in an essentialist form of knowing and of knowledge-making that more often than not preconceives the following:

- An unequal relationship between Islam and the "West", with the latter being exclusively and ethnocentrically associated with "modernity" or "democracy" and the former being assumed in a neo-Weberian fashion as bereft of the values or institutions congenial to either modernity or democracy.
- An irreversible zero-sum relationship between Islam and "modernity" or "democracy" with little or no room for exchange, dialogue or co-existence as if the notions of an "Islamic democracy" or "Islamic modernity" are no more than oxymorons.
- An epistemological bias that holds the dogmas of Western-style democracy and modernity to be universally normative.

Scholars like Pipes or Crone are hopefully representative of the "old guard" of blinkered Orientalists. However, there are some recent positions which bring to the fore more accurate representations of Islam, Islamists and democracy. The works of Eickelman, Piscatori, Voll and Esposito, to name only a few, represent the positive direction that discourse on Islamists and democracy can take. Their works share a concern with the roles of Orientalist and Eurocentric knowledge in the perpetuation of an anti-Islam bias. Generally, the non-discriminatory bias against Islamists cannot be separated from the bias against Islam. All four scholars have also challenged and reversed the freezing of Islamists into a homogenised category of Muslim activists: Islamists are not a monolith. From this perspective, the first-rate works, *Muslim Politics*, by Eickelman and Piscatori, and *Islam and Democracy*, by Esposito and Voll, contain within them a hidden discourse exposing the lacunae in some Orientalist knowledge and the ways in which it has shaped a non-discriminatory discursive bias against all Islamists. On how Islamists relate to democracy, Esposito and Voll's arguments are most illuminating.

Noting how Islam embodies values of consultation, egalitarianism and legal opposition which are not at odds with Western democracy,

213 John L. Esposito and John O. Voll, *Islam and Democracy* (New York and Oxford: Oxford University Press, 1996), p. 6.

Voll and Esposito stress how Islamist discourses resonate with the globalised "currencies" of democracy and democratisation. In this context, as they put it "the processes of democratization and Islamic resurgence have become complementary forces in many countries".[214] The endeavour by many Muslims and Islamists to read democracy in Islam and appropriate the language of democratisation seems to have elicited a kind of fear of Muslims and Islamists' own knowledge-as-power. This is due to the combination of an Islamic and democratic discourse appearing to go a long way in helping a number of Islamist political configurations carve out a space for themselves in the public domain. This has not been well received in either secular-nationalist or some scholarly circles. A good example of thc former is the banning of serious Islamist opposition in Algeria and Tunisia. A good example of the latter in parts of the Western world is that of "the concept of 'Islamic democracy' [as an] anathema".[215] The notion of an "Islamic democracy", which neither suggests a clearly and fully-developed conceptualisation nor a unitary one, intimates that understanding of democracy need no longer be grounded in Western foundations. Thus, as an enterprise to assert the Islamists' own knowledge-as-power, the notion of an "Islamic democracy" collides with those understandings which are grounded in Western ideal-typical definitions of democracy. And if the Western experience with democracy suggests contested conceptualisations and diffuse practices, then its Islamic counterpart cannot be expected to be "Athenian" or "Jeffersonian". Accordingly,

> Because democracy is in many profound ways an essentially contested concept, it is important to understand the perception of democracy within the movements of the current Islamic resurgence. This understanding is important even for those who view the Islamic resurgence as a threat, because it is important to understand the competing definitions of democracy. It may be even more important for this group because…advocates of democracy in the West might also be able to learn something about democracy from others. In the global environment of the present, narrow and parochial understandings of concepts as important as democracy are dangerous and limiting, even for long-established democratic systems.[216]

Indeed in practice and theory, the Islamist experience with democracy is one of hybridity and diversity. The claim that all those who are

[214] Ibid., p. 16.
[215] Ibid., p. 14.
[216] Ibid., p. 14.

called "fundamentalists" are against democracy cannot be corroborated by the conclusions of Voll and Esposito: "While some Muslim religious leaders and rulers, such as King Fahd of Saudi Arabia, and some Islamists have maintained that democracy is foreign to Islam and that Islam has its own specific traditions for political participation and governance, many others have embraced the rhetoric and politics of democratization."[217] Again they conclude that "the experiences and track records of Islamic movements with political participation and democratization have indeed varied".[218]

It has been pointed out that it is wrong to assume that Orientalists are always Western. There is a brand of "Oriental Orientalism" which is evidence of the discursive linkage and power relations between Westerners and Westernisers. Anti-Islamist bias is not uncommon amongst opponents of the forces of "radical" or "political" Islam in the AME. If anything at all, this conclusion should serve to caution against endorsing the kind of Orientalisms that are trapped in a single and homogenising way of understanding Islam, Islamism and Islamists as anti-"West" and anti-"democracy".

Orientalism is likely to creep into the twenty-first century. Hence the urgency for academic and journalistic vigilance against the search for "essential" features of Arab, Muslim or Middle Eastern societies. Questioning and interrogating Orientalism must guard against it becoming a stumbling block against forming more accurate and informed views of other cultures and against the world being what it has always been: a culturally plural place. Cultural plurality is essential for democracy, globally and locally. The dense discursive interconnections between ideas of the East and of the West suggest a middle-ground of hybridity—The "East in the West" and "West in the East". The ensuing chapters on conceptions of democracy by leading Arab intellectuals, leaders, feminists and Islamists illustrate this hybridity.

[217] Ibid., p. 193.
[218] Ibid., p. 195.

5

CONTEMPORARY ARAB CONCEPTIONS OF DEMOCRACY

"The problem of democracy in our homeland...is that all speak about it and yet all are far from it." —Muḥammad H. Haykal[1]

"Despite our civilizational heritage, of which... Islam is a component... the poor Arab has become one of the last peoples on earth to be denied a level of civil and political rights. Consequently, the cheapest commodity in our crisis-ridden Arab homeland is its people...[Man] is killed and nobody asks after him; he is jailed and his government and society forsake him...He is guilty until proven innocent...At the same time...the Arab mass media speak of Arab dignity, strength and of combating injustice, all of which belie reality...There is no [Arab] unity without excellence, and no excellence without democracy." —Muḥammad Al-Rumayḥī (soon after the restoration of Kuwaiti sovereignty)[2]

"Political discourse in the Arab world" has, as observed by an analyst, been "awash in ideology".[3] This has been exemplified by the various experiments to achieve Arab *ishtirākiyyah* (socialism),[4] *shuyū'iyyah*

[1] Muḥammad H. Haykal, *Al-Salāmu 'l-mustaḥīl wa 'l-dīmuqrāṭiyyatu 'l-ghā'ibah* [*The Impossible Peace and the Absent Democracy*] (Beirut: Sharikat al-Matbu'at li al-Tawzi' wa al-Nashr, 1988), p. 246.

[2] Muḥammad Al-Rumayḥī, "Suqūṭu 'l-awhām" [The Fall of Illusions], *Al-'Arabī*, no. 95 (October 1991), pp. 13–14.

[3] Michael C. Hudson, *Arab Politics: The Search for Legitimacy* (New Haven: Yale University Press, 1982), p. 20.

[4] Arab socialism calls for definition. As Albert Hourani points out, it draws its specific character from rejecting both Marxism's notion of class struggle and capitalism's emphasis of the individual. "In Arab socialism, the whole of society was thought to rally round a government which pursued the interests of all." Arab socialism had emancipatory objectives (liberation from international exploitation and oppression,

(communism), *qawmiyyah* (pan-nationalism), and, more recently, *al-unthawiyyah* (feminism).[5] Today the Arab world has become enmeshed in the global democratic discourse. While the Arab world's experience with democracy is not as rich as its experience with socialism (a theory which does not itself disown democracy), in theory, at least, there has been continuous discourse, mostly for, but also against, an Arab democracy. This chapter surveys examples of the many inputs into the Arab discourse on democracy, both past and present.

DEMOCRACY AND FREEDOM: A BACKGROUND

Whenever and wherever oppression is rife, the clamour for a fairer order sets the minds of the oppressed on an intellectual odyssey in search of the lexical and ideal opposites of oppression. Arabs have for a long time experienced oppression through non-indigenous and indigenous rule, through colonialism, and today through authoritarianism and varying forms of more subtle and dangerous neo-colonialism. *Al-ʿadl* (justice), for instance, one of many opposites of oppression, has historically been valued in the Arab world.[6] Equally valued is

---

and justice at home); economic objectives (progress and sufficiency); and unity of the Arab world. See Albert Hourani, *A History of the Arab Peoples* (London: Faber and Faber, 1991), pp. 406–7.

[5] The term "feminism" is shorthand for feminist ideology, and the various discourses that underpin them. It is also taken to denote the emancipatory activisms of Arab women (secular and religious, radical and conservative, past and present) aiming at resisting patriarchal, colonial and authoritarian orders and practices, improving their personal status and seeking political, social, economic and intellectual access and equality. Several articles deal with the linguistic, conceptual and historical aspects of Arab feminisms. See, for instance, Margot Badran, "Dual Liberation: Feminism and Nationalism in Egypt, 1870–1925", *Feminist Issues* (spring 1988), pp. 27–8. See also Leila Ahmed, "Feminism and Feminist Movements in the Middle East" in ʿAziz al-Hibri (ed.), *Women and Islam* (New York: Pergman, 1982), pp. 153–68; Mai Ghoussoub, "Feminism—or the Eternal Masculine—in the Arab World", *The New Left Review,* 161 (January/February 1987), pp. 3–18; ʿAfaf Lutfi al-Sayyid Marsot, "The Revolutionary Gentlewoman in Egypt" in Lois Beck and Nikki Keddie (eds), *Women in the Muslim World* (Cambridge, MA and London: Harvard University Press, 1978), pp. 261–76.

[6] Hence, according to Al-Husri, the Egyptian historian ʿAbd al-Raḥmān al-Jabarṭī (d. 1882), for all of his distrust and loathing of the Napoleonic invaders of his native Egypt in 1789, admired their 'justice'. Al-Husri also notes how al-Jabarṭī contrasts the French trial of Sulaymān Al-Ḥalabī, for his assassination of General Kléber, with the lawlessness of the soldiers of co-religionist Mamluk rulers under the pretence of Islam

ḥurriyyah (freedom). The Tunisian poet, Abū al-Qāsim al-Shābbī, equates *ḥurriyyah* with *al-ḥayāt* (life) itself.[7] The Arab novel has been a medium of allegorical commentary on political oppression. *Al-Karnak* by the Egyptian Nobel laureate, Najīb Maḥfūẓ and *'Awdatu 'l-wa'y* by Tawfīq al-Ḥakīm are excellent examples. Both are an indictment of Nasser's politics.[8, 9]

Four important Arab historical landmarks are relevant for the issues of freedom and justice, associates of democracy. The first is the advent of Islam in Mecca and Madīnah in the seventh century, which remains—at least in Muslim eyes—a humanist revolution of the first order. Islam was, in a sense, a revolution against *al-jāhiliyyah* (pagan ignorance) and the patriarchal political order in Arabia where a minority of Meccan tribal and merchant *a'yān* (notables) had a free hand to exploit and enslave. Islam introduced an *ansinah* (humanism) preaching new values like *al-musāwāt* (equality), and *al-'adl*, fought female infanticide and trade in *'abīd* (slaves), and introduced new *ḥuqūq* (rights) for women to inherit and learn. It established *al-shūrā* (consultation) as the basis for decision-making, and *al-bay'ah* (oath of allegiance) by the populace, a *prima facie* recognition of the right of the ruled to a say in choosing *ūlū 'l-amr* (those in charge). Hence many Muslims spurn the reductionistic Eurocentric view of history that links the genesis of good government with the

---

and *jihād*. See Khaldun S. Al-Husri, *Three Reformers: A Study in Modern Arabic Political Thought* (Beirut: Khayats, 1966), pp. 8–9.

[7] In the widely-known poem written in the 1940s, "*Irādatu 'l-ḥayāt*" (The Will to Live, i.e. to be free), al-Shābbī, although seeming to defy the divine, in fact intimates *ḥurriyyah* to be so sacred that *al-qadar* (destiny/God) grants it for whomever seeks it: "When the people will to live some day, destiny will have to obey." See Abū Al-Qāsim Al-Shābbī, *Aghānī 'l-ḥayāt* [*Life Songs*] (n.p.: Dar al-Kutub al-Sharqiyyah, 1955), pp. 167–70. Al-Shābbī's poetry is a cry against colonisation of Tunisia and the Arab world. Thus, in another poem, "*ila ṭughāt al-'ālam*" (To the World's Oppressors/Tyrants), he employs the metaphor "*'aduwwa al-ḥayāt*" (enemies of life) to describe oppressors (p. 185).

[8] See the fine article by Menahem Milson, "Najīb Maḥfūz and Jamāl 'Abd al-Nāṣir: The Writer as Political Critic", *Asian and African Studies*, 23 (1989), pp. 1–22.

[9] *Kalīlah wa dimnah*, written more than eight centuries ago, remains the ultimate allegorical political text, and a classic work that reflects the historical concern with justice and freedom. Written in the form of fictitious and clever scenarios depicting interrelationships between various animals of the jungle, it is a satirical statement about the rulers and the ruled. See 'Abd Allah Ibn al-Muqaffa, *Kalīlah wa dimnah* (Beirut: Dar al-Fikr al-'Arabi, 1990).

French Revolution, but not with Islam.[10] *Al-khulafā'u 'l-rāshidūn* (rightly-guided Caliphs), whose combined rule lasted for nearly 30 years after the Prophet's death, generally sought consensus in their rule, which was not hereditary.[11] The *fitnah*[12] (conflict and schism) after the assassination of the fourth Caliph ended in the Umayyad dynasty. The Umayyads' political style differed from that of *al-khulafā'u 'l-rāshidūn*, with rule becoming hereditary and less consultative, and tending toward *de facto* secularisation. The total number of years of good rule under the Prophet and the rightly-guided Caliphs did not exceed 40. Yet so deep are the virtues of this period carved in Muslim common memory that they continue to inspire a return to the forebears' exemplary politics of consultation and justice. Consultation and justice may since the advent of the Umayyad order have lost their practical eminence. But their discursive eminence continues well into the present.

Another historical landmark is the nineteenth century intellectual and political ferment known as *al-nahḍah* (Renaissance). *'Aṣru 'l-nahḍah*, or "the liberal age of Arabic thought" as Albert Hourani calls it,[13] covers a time span of nearly 140 years, from 1798—a date coinciding with Napoleon's invasion of Egypt—until more or less the beginning of the Second World War.[14] *Al-nahḍah* is a shock, an

[10] The known French revolutionary line that people are born equal has a precedent in seventh-century Arabia. The second Caliph 'Umar Ibn al-Khaṭṭāb is accredited with the saying: "*Matā ista 'badtum al-nās wa qad waladt-hum ummahātu-hum aḥrār?*" (when was it permitted for you to enslave free-born human beings?). See Elias 'Abbūd, *Judhūru 'l-dīmuqrāṭiyyah fī ˉ'l-mashriqi 'l-'Arabī* [*The Roots of Democracy in the Arab East*] (Tripoli, Libya: Al-Markiz al-'Alami Li 'l-Dirasat wa Abhath al-Kitab al-Akhdar, 1990).

[11] Elias 'Abbūd's *Judhūru 'l-dīmuqrāṭiyyah fī 'l-mashriq al-'Arabī*, defends Islam's democratic record. 'Abbūd does not only defend Islam and al-Qadhāfī's *Green Book* democracy, but also puts forth the view that many "democratic" institutions had their roots in (what is, at least, today) the Arab East. He shows how the first *jumhūriyyah* (republic), for instance, appeared between the sixth and fifth centuries BC in Tyre almost 200 years before it did in either Athens or Rome. See *Judhūru 'l-dīmuqrāṭiyyah fī 'l-mashriqi 'l-'Arabī*, p. 122.

[12] See the fine work by Hishām J'ayiṭ, *Al-Fitnatu 'l-kubrā: jadaliyyatu 'l-dīn wa 'l-siyāsah fī 'l-islāmi 'l-mubakkiri* [*The Great Discord: The Dialectics of Religion and Politics in Early Islam*] (Beirut: Dar al-Tali'ah, n.d.). See also the earlier work by Ṭāhā Ḥussayn, *Al-Fitnah al-kubrā* [*The Great Discord*] (Cairo: Dar al-Ma'arif, 1958).

[13] Albert Hourani, *Arabic Thought in the Liberal Age, 1798–1939* (London: Oxford University Press, 1962).

[14] For a brief discussion of the lack of consensus on the dates when *al-nahḍah* actually began or ended see Aḥmad Al-Samāwī, *Al-Istibdād wa 'l-ḥurriyyah fī fikri 'l-nahḍah*

awakening, and a soul searching. Napoleon's invasion was a shock to the Ottoman-Mamluk-ruled Arabs. It awakened them to the fact that they lagged behind the lands of Christendom in the arts, sciences, technology and warfare. It forced a soul searching amongst statesmen,[15] intellectuals[16] and religious leaders,[17] the corollary of which was the reopening of the gates of *ijtihād* or independent reasoning. While the scope of *ijtihād* was far-reaching, encompassing every sphere of human knowledge, it primarily concentrated on the question of governance, and the need for political *iṣlāḥ* (reform). It was here that the key to *iqlāʿ* (take-off)[18] and catching up with Europe was seen to reside. If Napoleon's invasion "was to set the modern Arab mind on its course of political thinking",[19] then the institution of an infrastructure of good governance, and the "rejection of oppression and the clamour for freedom"[20] were the crux of *al-nahḍah*.

Al-nahḍah's relevance for political reform is embodied in a number of developments regarding the earliest experiments with constitutional and representative government, innovations in political vocabulary, and the influx of nationalist ideas. The earliest Arab experiments with, or notions of, constitutional and representative government date back to the nineteenth century. The general diagnosis of the causes of Arabo-Muslim scientific-technological inferiority *vis-à-vis* Christendom highlighted one factor: Europe's superior political institutions and constitutional representative systems. Like their co-religionist Turkish reformers in the much weakened Ottoman Empire, many members of the first generation of *nahḍāwiyyūn* (*nahḍah* advocates),

> ...set high value on the social morality of Islam, and tried to justify the adoption of Western institutions in Islamic terms, as being not the introduction of

---

[*Despotism and Freedom in the Thought of* al-Nahḍah] (Syria: Dar al-Hiwar, 1989), pp. 15–18.

[15] Such as Muḥammad ʿAlī, Aḥmed Bey, Khayr al-Dīn al-Tūnisī and Bashīr al-Shihābī.

[16] Such as ʿAbd al-Raḥmān al-Kawākibī, Fāris al-Shidyāq, Buṭrus al-Bustāni, Qāsim Amīn, al-Ṭāhir al-Ḥaddād and Ṭāhā Ḥussayn.

[17] Rifāʿah Rāfiʿ al-Ṭahṭāwī, al-Shaykh Maḥmūd Qabādu and Muḥammad ʿAbduh. Muḥammad ʿAbduh's (1849–1905) promotion of *ijtihād* and *tajdīd*, as against *taqlīd*, has a wide and lasting influence on the learned. Amongst those he influenced was Qāsim Amīn. ʿAbdu himself was influenced by Jamāl al-Dīn al-Afghānī (1839–97).

[18] Ibid., p. 15.

[19] Al-Husrī, *Three Reformers*, p. 9.

[20] Al-Samāwī, *Al-Istibdād wa 'l-ḥurriyyah*, p. 8.

something new but a return to the true spirit of Islam. In political matters they were democrats, believing that the modern parliamentary system was a restatement of the system of consultation which had existed in early Islam and was the sole guarantee of freedom.[21]

Aḥmad Bey's Tunisia of the 1860s remains a prime example of political *iṣlāḥ* in which an ephemeral emulation of European political notions and institutions was attempted. The Bey's *'ahdu 'l-amān* (Covenant of Social Peace) stressed *maṣlaḥah* (public interest), liberty, and equality before the law between Muslims and non-Muslims, and Tunisians and foreigners. A key reform of *'ahdu 'l-amān* was the introduction in 1860 of the Muslim world's first ever constitution.[22] But the effectiveness of these early *iṣlāḥāt* (reforms) was limited. Amongst statesmen, including the most ardent advocates of reform, there rarely existed genuine belief—much less political will and courage—to share power through restraining parliaments and constitutions. Thus the tendency to reform remained mostly a figment of the political imagination and of the desire for renewal and regeneration. Hourani notes how Khayr al-Dīn, for instance, while supporting the Young Ottomans' "demand for an elected Assembly…in principle…thought it dangerous in fact".[23] Likewise, during his prime ministership in the 1870s, he resisted calls to "restore the constitutional laws". Khayr al-Dīn's justification of his unwillingness to have these laws restored was the lack of will on the part of ruling elites to promulgate them, and on the part of those ruled to understand them, much less accept them.[24]

Moreover, the early *nahḍāwiyyūn* considered reform within an Islamic frame of reference. They faced the onerous task of seeking a balance between *aṣālah* (cultural authenticity), or *turāth* (cultural heritage) on the one hand, and *ḥadāthah* (modernity) on the other.[25] For them there was no discord between Islam and modernity. There

[21] Hourani, *Arabic Thought in the Liberal Age*, p. 68.

[22] Ibid., pp. 64–5.

[23] Ibid., p. 93.

[24] Ibid., p. 94. The resemblance between yesteryear and present-day politics is striking. Contemporary Arab elites have adopted liberal constitutions that have mostly remained ink on paper. The idea of elected parliaments being dangerous has equivalents in many an Arab polity. And the masses' ignorance has often been invoked to delay democratisation.

[25] Al-Samāwī, *Al-Istibdād wa 'l-ḥurriyyah*, p. 25. See also the work by Ḥasan Ḥanafī, *Al-Turāthu wa 'l-tajdīd* [*Cultural Heritage and Regeneration*] (Cairo: n.p., 1980).

was therefore no imagining of a modernity project outside the Islamic framework. Accordingly, there was never a question politically of a self-governing *ummah*; the question was about how to restrain the power of *ūlū 'l-amr*.[26] That era's debates about "better" government belonged to a mindset that strongly linked the scope and nature of authority to identity. That mindset equated the political divestiture of Islam in favour of secular European systems with an assault against Muslim identity. More recent *nahḍāwiyyūn*, especially in the 1930s, were to become more courageous and, as a consequence, quite controversial in addressing issues of *huwiyyah* (ipseity) and *ḥadāthah*. 'Alī 'Abd al-Rāziq and Ṭāhā Ḥusayn were among them. The former's book, *al-Islām wa Uṣūlu' l-ḥukm* [*Islam and the Principles of Governance*],[27] questioned the Caliphate, and the widely accepted idea of the existence of an Islamic State during the Prophet's life.[28] The latter's work, *Mustaqbalu 'l-thaqāfah fi Miṣr* [*The Future of Culture in Egypt*], accepted Europe's cultural superiority, called for its emulation, and stood for its "humane culture…civic virtues [and] democracy".[29] Not less important were the European designs on the Arab Ottoman provinces, indebtedness to foreign powers, incursion of foreign interests, and looming colonisation which posed added limitations on the reform movement.

Al-nahdah's drive for renewal spawned a more lasting linguistic modernisation of political vocabulary. That modernisation overtook the Islamic conceptual approximations that 'Abduh, a prominent religious *mujaddid* (renewer) and *mujtahid* (who applies *ijtihād*), applied to respond to European political concepts. As Hourani remarks, in doing so, 'Abduh, driven by his greater aim to counter secularisation, perhaps unknowingly compromised the uniqueness of Islam and its concepts, and, more importantly, the "distinguish[ing] [of] Islam from other religions and even from non-religious humanism".[30]

[26] Hourani, *Arabic Thought in the Liberal Age*, pp. 94–5.

[27] See Muḥammad 'Umārah, *Qāsim Amīn: taḥrīru 'l-Mar'ah wa 'l-tamaddun al-Islāmī* [*Qāsim Amīn: The Liberation of Women and Islamic Urbanism*] (Beirut: Dar al-Wihdah, 1985). Amongst those who responded to 'Abd al-Rāziq's controversial book were Muḥammad al-Ṭāhir Ibn 'Ashūr, *Naqd 'ilmī li kitābi 'l-islām wa uṣūli 'l-ḥukm* [*A Scientific Critique of the Book Islam and the Principles of Government*] (Cairo: n.p., 1925); and Muḥammad Bakhīt, *Haqīqatu 'l-Islām wa uṣūlu 'l-ḥukm* [*Islam's Truth and the Principles of Governance*] (Cairo: n.p., 1926).

[28] Hourani, *Arabic Thought in the Liberal Age*, pp. 183–92.

[29] Ibid., p. 328.

[30] Ibid., p. 144. See also similar commentary on p. 344.

> In this line of thought, *maslahah*...gradually turns into utility, *shura* into parliamentary democracy, *ijma'*...into public opinion; Islam itself becomes identical with civilization and activity, the norms of nineteenth century social thought.[31]

Ami Ayalon shows that *dīmuqrāṭiyyah* and *barlamān* (parliament) are among a number of permanent loan words adopted in the nineteenth century.[32] Ayalon identifies 17 permanently assimilated terms—new derivations as distinct from borrowings like the first two—that linguistic purists allowed into the Arab political vocabulary. Examples of these are *aghlabiyyah* (parliamentary majority), *aqalliyyah* (minority of votes), *jinsiyyah* (nationality/citizenship), *jumhūriyyah* (republic), *mu'tamar* (conference/congress), *muwāṭin* (compatriot/citizen), *'uḍwiyyah* (membership), and *waṭaniyyah* (patriotism).[33] He further identifies a third group of lexical adaptations, comprising 45 terms (see examples in Table 5.1), the original meanings of which have been permanently modified by Arab philologists[34] to respond to the spirit of renewal and the influx of European political ideas. This process of modernisation of political vocabulary is intrinsic to the overall process of *iṣlāḥ*. Also, it was during *'aṣru 'l-nahḍah* that the embryo of *waṭaniyyah*, a precursor of nationalism, was transplanted. While the term *waṭan* (*patrie*, homeland) found its way into the literary works of many *nahḍāwiyyūn*, it was not semantically applied with the same consistency. Both al-Ṭahṭāwī and Amīn employed it in a sense approximating its European usage, that of nationalism. Thus in 1894 the idea of *waṭaniyyah* was for Amīn synonymous with 'Egyptianness', as the title of his book *al-Miṣriyyūn* indicates. Al-Ṭaḥṭāwī's *waṭan* was specifically Egypt, for which he preached *ḥubbu 'l-waṭan* (love of country).[35] Al-Bustānī's *waṭaniyyah* was comparable to that

[31] Ibid., p. 144.

[32] See the fine article by Ami Ayalon, "*Dimuqrāṭiyyah, Ḥurriyyah, Jumhūriyyah*: The Modernization of the Arabic Political Vocabulary", *Asian and African Studies*, 23 (1989), p. 27, (Table 1). See also Jamīl M. Minayminā, "Namādhij min taṭawwuri 'l-muṣṭalihị 'l-siyāsī 'l-'Arabī: Al-sulṭān, al-shūrā, al-ummah" [Samples from the Modernisation of Arab Political Terminology: *Al-sulṭān, al-shūrā, al-ummah*], *Al-Fikr al-'Arabī*, 71 (March 1993) pp. 91–104.

[33] Ayalon, "*Dīmuqrāṭiyyah, Ḥurriyyah, Jumhūriyyah*", p. 29, (Table 2).

[34] Ibid., pp. 32–4, (Table 3).

[35] Hourani, *Arabic Thought in the Liberal Age*, pp. 78–9. See also al-Husri who elaborates on al-Ṭaḥṭāwī's patriotism. Like Hourani he reproduces the known phrase "*Ḥubb al-waṭan mina 'l-'imān*" [love of one's country is part, or an article of faith].

Table 5.1 POLITICAL LANGUAGE: SEMANTICALLY-MODIFIED TERMS

Term	*Original Meaning*	*19th-century Meaning*
aḥrār	free people (not slaves)	members of the liberal party
dustūr	set of regulations	constitution
ḥizb	faction, group (negative)	political party
ḥukūmah	jurisdiction, dominion	government, cabinet
ḥurriyyah	individual freedom	political freedoms and rights
inqilāb	inversion, rotation	revolt, *coup d'état*
iqtirā'	casting lots, choosing	voting by ballot
istiqlāl	personal independence	national independence
jalsah	sitting, gathering	session of an institutional forum
kursī	chair	seat in parliament
majlis	sitting place	chamber, assembly, parliament
muḥāfiẓ	attendant, guardian	member of the conservative party
murashshaḥ	one designated for a post	candidate in elections
nā'ib	official deputy	representative of the people
ṣawt	voice	vote
sha'b	tribe, a people	the people (not the government)
shimāl	left-hand side	political left
thawrah	excitement, agitation	revolution
'uḍw	organ of the human body	member of society or institution
waṭan	place of residence	national homeland
za'īm	spokesperson, pretender	leader

Source: Adapted from Ami Ayalon (see notes 33–5).

of al-Ṭaḥṭāwī. For al-Bustānī, the national homeland—Syria—had to be the focus of one's first loyalty and love.[36] Elsewhere, in the Ottoman-dominated Arab world of the nineteenth century, *waṭan* and *waṭaniyyah* were understood in the broader framework of the *ummah*, and hence in a pan-Islamic sense. According to Hourani this latter tendency was clear, for instance, in Khayr al-Dīn's usage which imparted the idea of "political community" and "public spirit".[37] However, no matter how rudimentary or blurred the notion of nationalism might have been in the thought of *nahḍāwiyyūn*, it was significant in that it harnessed thinking about sovereignty, self-determination

This appears to be a harmonisation of the concept of the Islamic *ummah* and the new more parochial notion of *waṭan*, national homeland. For Al-Husri's analysis of al-Ṭaḥṭāwī's patriotism refer to *Three Reformers*, pp. 29–31.

[36] Ibid., p. 101.

[37] Ibid., p. 89.

and co-existence. 'National' sovereignty had, as it does today, relevance for political institutionalisation, political freedoms and thus democracy. Co-existence in a common *waṭan*, a national homeland, had relevance for equality and tolerance.[38]

The third landmark is more contemporary. Decolonisation in the 1960s, and the concomitant "republicanisation" of many Arab political realms, raised expectations of greater popular sovereignty to match the hard-won and newly-acquired national sovereignty. Yet the new structures, flags, anthems and indigenous elites at the helm were to be a disappointment, at least where political and civil liberties were concerned. The imperative of hanging onto the new-found independence Arabs had lacked for centuries overrode all other imperatives (including those espoused by the new liberally worded and Western-modelled constitutions). The final landmark is more recent, relating to reforms in the 1980s and the 1990s—by any measure the most significant with regard to the scope of Arab political liberalisation, and the prospects of democracy. Both endogenous and exogenous catalysts lay at the core of this transformative phase.[39] Among endogenous catalysts was Iraq's invasion of Kuwait. It has once again driven home the realisation that one-man/one-party rule and mummified parliaments have been at the root of political miscalculation, and caused many disasters. Naseer Aruri observes:

> Iraq and its protagonists suffer from a common problem: the absence of democratic legitimacy as a means to govern. Had the Iraqi decision-making process been the beneficiary of the normal inputs and critiques of civil society, the chances of miscalculation…might have been significantly reduced.[40]

[38] Hence, al-Bustānī's 'sophisticated' *waṭaniyyah* calls for "religious freedom and equality, and mutual respect between those of different faith" (ibid., p. 101). His *waṭaniyyah* also embraced his vision of a "civilised" Syria built on "just and equal laws", and his favouring of a secular order—a prerequisite, at least, of Western democracy (p. 102).

[39] Pertinent to the former are Egypt and Morocco's political liberalisations; the accession to power of a coalition of opposition forces in the free and fair multiparty elections of 1986 in Sudan; the bread riots of 1988 and 1989 in Jordan and Algeria, which have precipitated political liberalisations in both countries; and both continuous and aborted electoral success stories as in Algeria, Jordan and Yemen which have either placed opposition forces (Jordan) in parliaments, or brought them to the verge of power (Algeria).

[40] Naseer Aruri, "The Recolonization of the Arab World", *Middle East International*, 385 (12 October 1990), p. 19. In the same vein, Samir al-Khalil equates the Iraqi invasion of Kuwait with an Arab crisis of legitimacy and democracy: "[T]he Arab world…is congenitally hostile to liberal democracy. The Iraqi pillage of Kuwait, for

Among the exogenous factors, mention must be made of the dissolution of the former Soviet Union, the collapse of 'securitate' states in Eastern Europe, and the subsequent political reforms that have taken place—which raised hopes for a new era of politics of renewal based on respect for human rights, legality and democratisation. This latest phase of both cosmetic and genuine Arab political liberalisations has resonance in the first *iṣlāḥāt* of the nineteenth century. They are both reactionary responses to crisis and despair, external and internal.

AL-FĀRĀBĪ'S VIRTUOUS CITY

If the Greeks invented democracy, Arabs and Muslims did more than just preserve and transmit it. Of the Arabophones,[41] those who either received the bulk of their education in Baghdad or Damascus or wrote in the ecumenical Arabic of the time, al-Fārābī (870–950)[42] is certain to have known Greek democracy and the politics of the Greek *polis*. Al-Fārābī devoted close to 50 years of his life to the study of Greek philosophy in which he was initiated by his Arab mentors—Syrian Christians—from the Alexandrian philosophical school. He read more works by Aristotle and Plato, amongst other Greek philosophers, than any other Muslim student of the encyclopedic Hellenic

---

example, has lifted the lid on the historic failure of Arab political culture to deal with questions of democracy, citizenship, ethnic minorities and…the right of individuals, communities and states to be separate and different." Samir al-Khalil, "In the Middle East, does Democracy have a Chance?" *New York Times Magazine* (14 October 1990), p. 54.

41 Al-Fārābī's full name is Abu Naṣr Muḥammad Ibn Muḥammad Ibn Tarhkān al-Fārābī. According to Ian Richard Netton "any description of al-Fārābī's life is problematic" (p. 4). Netton, like other students of al-Fārābī, takes the year 870 to be his birthdate, which cannot be verified in the absence of an autobiography by al-Fārābī (Ibid.). Al-Fārābī, widely considered to have founded a philosophical school of his own that Netton refers to using the term Fārābism (p. 1), was born at Wasij, near the village of Fārāb, in Turkestān (p. 5). He received his scholarly training mostly in Baghdad, and lived for the greater part of his life in the Arab world, travelling in Egypt, Aleppo and Damascus where he died in 950. See Netton's *Al-Farabi and His School* (London: Routledge, 1992).

42 Al-Fārābī is also referred to as the "Second Teacher" (*Al-Mu'allim al-Thānī*), with Aristotle being known as the "First Teacher" (*Al-Mu'allim al-Awwal*). See the article by Seyyed Hossein Nasr, "Why was Al-Fārābī called the Second Teacher?", *Islamic Culture*, 59 (October 1985) pp. 357–64.

curriculum. Nowhere in his works does he mention democracy by name. However, al-Fārābī's notion of *al-madīnatu 'l-jamā'iyyah* (democracy) points to his familiarity with this originally Hellenic concept. Greek-Hellenistic philosophy (Aristotelian, Platonic and neo-Platonic—Porphyry, Plotinus and others whose aim was to harmonise Aristotle's and Plato's philosophies) forms the departure point of Arabo-Islamic *falsafah*.[43] Drawing mostly on works by Plato and Aristotle, Arabo-Islamic *falāsifah* (philosophers) contemplate the abstruse relationships between the real, the ideal and the transcendental (God).[44] Being rooted in Islam, their *falsafah* seeks answers to cryptic questions regarding this life and the hereafter through *tawfīq* (harmonisation):[45] harmonisation of Greek-Hellenistic and Arabo-Islamic civilisations; of revelation (religion) with reason (philosophy);[46] of "prophetic revealed law" with "human law" (such as the Greek *nomos*);[47] and of worldly and heavenly happiness. But

[43] For a comprehensive analysis of this background see Erwin I.J. Rosenthal, *Political Thought in Medieval Islam: An Introductory Outline* (Cambridge University Press, 1962). See also the translation by Muhsin Mahdi, *Alfarabi's Philosophy of Plato and Aristotle* (Ithaca: Cornell University Press, 1969).

[44] See Leo Strauss, "Farabi's Plato" in Arthur Hyman (ed.), *Essays in Medieval Jewish and Islamic Philosophy* (New York: KTAV Publishing House, 1977), pp. 391–427. See also, Yusuf K. 'Umar, "Farabi and Greek Political Philosophy" in Anthony J. Parcel and Ronald C. Keith (eds), *Comparative Political Philosophy* (New Delhi: Sage Publications, 1992), pp. 185–216.

[45] Yūḥannā Qumayr explains how al-Fārābī's political thought is essentially one of *wifāq*. See his *Falāsifatu 'l-'Arab: Al-Fārābī* [*The Arabs' Philosophers: Al-Fārābī*] (Beirut: Dar al-Mashriq, 1986), p. 42.

[46] As Rosenthal observes the Mu'tazilites applied considerable intellect to the revelation-reason question: "They sought to defend revelation against Aristotle by discarding anthropomorphism and opposing the concept of the God of revelation to the god bound to the eternity of matter of Aristotle. They devised a figurative interpretation of scripture to demonstrate that scripture did not contradict reason. This inner meaning of scripture could be ascertained by reason only; it was additional to the literal, external meaning. Al-Ash'arī, in his opposition to the Mu'tazilites from whom he stemmed, had to admit reason as a source of religious knowledge. *Kalām*, or dialectic theology, was the result, and this was Islam's official answer to the challenge of Greek-Hellenistic philosophy." See *Political Thought in Medieval Islam*, pp. 114–15. On the question of revelation and reason see ch. 1. The Mu'tazilites are considered to have, through their "philosophising" on religion, created the first foundation of an Islamic scientific thought that, alas, was not allowed to develop. For a standard work on the subject see Muḥammad 'Umārah, *Al-mu'tazilah wa mushkilatu 'l-ḥurriyyatu 'l-Insāniyyah* [*The Mu'tazilite and the Problematic of Human Freedom*] (Cairo: Dar al-Shuruq, 1988).

[47] The Greek word *nomos*, as Rosenthal explains, refers to "the man-made law of Greek philosophy". See *Political Thought in Medieval Islam*, p. 116. The term *nāmūs*

harmonising revelation and reason can be a very difficult task. This difficulty is, for instance, apparent in the positions towards the relationship of revelation and philosophy of al-Fārābī (Pharabius), Ibn Sīnā (Avicenna), and Ibn Bājja (Avempace) on the one hand, and al-Ghazālī on the other, argues Rosenthal.[48] Al-Ghazālī doubts the capacity of human reasoning to fathom divine revelation. The gist of his well-known work, *Tahāfutu' l-falāsifah* [*The Incoherence of Philosophers*], is that there can be no harmony between Islam and philosophy. Whereas al-Fārābī and those later Muslim philosophers he influenced, such as Ibn Sīnā (d. 1037) and Ibn Rushd (d. 1198), find no contradiction between philosophy and revelation. They reconcile the two: that is, Islam and philosophy can be in harmony. Philosophy (which is for any philosopher who is enough of a Muslim, such as al-Kindī, a God-given faculty) can be of service to revelation. One distinctive imprint of Hellenic rationality on al-Fārābī is his ranking of philosophy above theology. The first thrives on intellectual perception; the latter on imagination.

Al-Fārābī finds an analogue for the Greek notion of philosopher-king in the ruler-philosopher and ruler-prophet, that is, the *ra'īs* (ruler/leader), Imām or first chief. As a philosopher, the *ra'īs* is endowed with the faculty and virtue of superior intellect enabling him to engage in a demonstrative form of reasoning for the purpose of esoteric understanding. As a prophet-ruler, the *ra'īs* can deploy dialectical and rhetorical types of reasoning in which emotional appeal is the key to making the masses understand religion and flock to it. By using allegorical exegesis, or the Muʿtazilites' twofold device *al-ẓāhir* (external, superficial) and *al-bāṭin* (hidden) to the Qur'ānic scriptures, *falāsifah* could explicate and expound those *bāṭin* (as distinct from *ẓāhir*—the literal meanings as imparted by parables) in the *Qur'ān*.[49] Thus *falāsifah* could pursue both philosophical and religious perfection. Influenced by Plato and Aristotle before them, Muslim philosophers such as al-Fārābī, Ibn Sīnā and Ibn Rushd, hierarchised society and knowledge by making philosophy an elite vocation, the bastion of those who have a superior intellect, and religion a public one, for those lacking in philosophical rationality and wisdom. Noteworthy,

(plural *nawāmīs*), meaning law, occurs in al-Fārābī's treatises as is obvious from Mahdi's translation and Rosenthal's analysis of al-Fārābī's philosophy (ch. 6).

48 Ibid., esp. ch. 5.

49 Ibid., p. 115.

however, is that the "Platonised Aristotelism" of Muslim philosophers was recast in an unmistakably Islamic framework. It accorded divinity a great deal of importance, making no separation between this life and the hereafter, between God and man, or religion and politics. Thus the attainment of happiness for a Muslim *failasūf* (s. of *falāsifah*) like al-Fārābī obtains not only in a Greek-like philosopher-king-led polity, but also in a divinely-sanctioned state and society where the ideals of revelation and philosophy become mutually reinforcing and inclusive. The teleological attainment of perfection, which in its Platonic sense resides in a philosophical kingdom, would be incomplete for al-Fārābī without a philosopher-Imām or philosopher-prophet as the source of both intellectual power (e.g. speculative wisdom) and political/temporal/practical power (e.g. practical wisdom). From this perspective, al-Fārābī represents two contradictory phenomena. His philosophy is a meeting point of Islamic and Western civilisations, representing the ideal early paradigm attempting a kind of a synthesis of the two civilisations. It is one of the earliest attempts of syncretism between the claims of Hellenic rationalism and those of Islam. At the same time, al-Fārābī's work is witness to the early tension between Islamic and Western notions of political theory. Plato's or Aristotle's law-giver or philosopher-king is free of all religion. In contrast, al-Fārābī's *failasūf* is not:

> He should be pious, yield easily to goodness and justice, and be stubborn in yielding to evil and injustice. And he should be strongly determined in favour of the right thing...He should have sound conviction about the opinions of the religion in which he is reared, [and] hold fast to the virtuous acts in his religion.[50]

Nonetheless, it is in political philosophy that Rosenthal claims that a common ground is found between revelation and philosophy with law being the lynchpin between the two:

> This means that the study of the *Republic*, the *Laws* and the *Nicomachean Ethics* led the Muslim philosophers to grasp more fully the political character implied in the *shari'a* of Islam...Hence revelation is for them, not only a transmission of right beliefs and convictions, a dialogue between a personal God of love, of justice and of mercy and man whom he has created in his image; it is also and above all a valid and binding code for man, who must live in society and be politically organized in a state in order to fulfil his destiny. In short, it is the law of the ideal state...Greek and Muslim philosophers are

[50] In "The Attainment of Happiness", Mahdi, *Al-Farabi's Philosophy*, p. 48.

agreed that without law there can be no state and that unlawful behaviour is damaging to the state...In the state under the *shari'a* such deviations will cause error, heresy and schism, and prove the undoing of the state.[51]

The above forms a part of the backdrop against which al-Fārābī's politics, reflections on Greek democracy and his own response must be understood. His theorising is rooted in a process of dialectic between his Islamic faith and Greek philosophy. Like Aristotle he conceives of a person as a *zoon politikon*, a political being, and of politics as "the royal political art".[52] He, however, parts company with Aristotle and Plato. Mahdi points out that al-Fārābī makes the attainment of happiness the function of political science;[53] political science inquires, *inter alia*, into the "right actions" that help perfect people's ways of life. It is quite natural for a believer (and al-Fārābī is one) not only to distinguish between the transient happiness of this world and the hereafter, but also to consider the latter more important. This is concordant with al-Fārābī's position which sees happiness in the hereafter to be "supreme".[54] The key point, however, is al-Fārābī's positive disposition towards the pursuit of happiness as an intrinsically human endeavour. Thus his investigation into politics, being "those actions and volitional ways of life",[55] is an investigation into the variegated forms of happiness, and the frameworks within which they are striven for, and approximated.[56] One condition, however, is indispensable for happiness: human association. Al-Fārābī, like Aristotle, sees human association to be *fiṭriyyah* (natural and intuitive),[57] for it is the site of maximising happiness. The state is the ideal site of human association. Accordingly, as Rosenthal explains, for al-Fārābī, "individuals living in isolation forfeit their chance of true happiness, which they can attain only as citizens performing their civic duties".[58] In the same vein, al-Fārābī holds that decay befalls people upon their "abandoning political society".[59]

51 Ibid., pp. 116–17.

52 Ibid., p. 119.

53 Mahdi, *Al-Farabi's Philosophy*, pp. xi–xii.

54 See "The Attainment of Happiness", in ibid., p. 13.

55 Rosenthal, *Political Thought in Medieval Islam*, p. 119.

56 See "The Attainment of Happiness" in Mahdi, *Al-Farabi's Philosophy*, p. 14.

57 ʿAbdah Al-Ḥuluw, *Al-Fārābī: Al-muʿallimu 'l-thānī* [*Al-Fārābī: The Second Master*] (Beirut: Bayt al-Hikmah, 1980), p. 74.

58 Rosenthal, *Political Thought in Medieval Islam*, p. 138.

59 Ibid., p. 165.

If the state is al-Fārābī's ideal site for *taḥṣīlu 'l-sa'ādah* (attaining happiness), what then is his ideal state? Al-Fārābī's ideal state can be analysed in terms of thesis, antithesis and dialectic. The thesis is specifically the Greek *polis*, al-Fārābī's departure point. It is one foundation upon which he builds his political treatises on various forms of political society or polity. The polis is *al-madīnah* (city). This is the Greek-Hellenistic foundation bequeathed by his masters, Aristotle and Plato. The Greek *polis* is the incubational milieu of democracy. Hence al-Fārābī's concept of *al-madīnatu 'l-jamā'iyyah* (democracy):[60]

> The democratic city is the one in which each one of the citizens is given free rein and left alone to do whatever he likes. Its citizens are equal and their laws say that no man is in any way at all better than any other man…And no one…has any claim to authority unless he works to enhance their freedom… Those who rule them do so by the will of the ruled, and the rulers follow the wishes of the ruled.[61]

Al-Fārābī both praises and depreciates *al-madīnatu 'l-jamā'iyyah*. His praise and criticism of its values are in tune with his "Islamicity". Thus he praises the legal freedom and equality of its citizens. Al-Fārābī perhaps sees in them equivalents to the Islamic concepts of *musāwāt*, *'itq* (emancipation of slaves) and *al-lā ikrāh* (non-compulsion) which are associates of freedom. It is worth noting here that the reading of al-Fārābī's political thought needs to be contextualised in its political milieu—the beginning of Abbasyd decline and increased despotism in the 950s. 'Abd al-'Āli's remark that *iṣlāḥu 'l-khilāfah* (reform of the Caliphate) shadows al-Fārābī's political thought is valid.[62] His highlighting of the values of freedom and equality might have been intended to show the increasingly militarised class of rulers in Baghdad, the seat of the Caliphate, and the universality of freedom and equality even in the non-Muslim Greek *polis*. The best index of al-Fārābī's approval of the democratic city is his distinction of *al-madīnatu 'l-jamā'iyyah*,

60 *Al-madīnatu 'l-jamā'iyyah* is widely considered (for instance, by Mahdi, Rosenthal and others) to correspond with democracy in the Greek *polis*. One Arab scholar, however, seems to challenge this accepted wisdom. See 'Abd al-Salām Ibn 'Abd al-'Āalī, *Al-Falsafatu 'l-siyāsiyyah 'inda 'l-Fārābī* [*Al-Fārābī's Political Philosophy*] (Beirut: Dar al-Tali'ah, 1986), p. 73.

61 Al-Fārābī in the translation by Muhsin Mahdi, "Al-Farabi: The Political Regime" in Ralph Lerner and Muhsin Mahdi (eds), *Medieval Political Philosophy: A Sourcebook* (New York: The Free Press of Glencoe, 1963), p. 50.

62 Ibn 'Abd al-'Āali, *Al-Falsafatu 'l-siyāsiyyah 'inda 'l-Fārābī*, pp. 62, 73.

of all the ignorant cities, to be "the most admirable and happy city".[63] Accordingly, he further singles it and its literati out for special praise. Only it, besides *al-madīnatu 'l-ḍarūriyyah* (city of necessity or indispensable city)[64] has a foundation from which his *al-madīnatu 'l-fāḍilah* (virtuous city) can develop.[65] Out of its literati can arise virtuous rulers.[66]

Nonetheless, al-Fārābī finds imperfections in *al-madīnatu 'l-jamā'iyyah*. He classifies it among the cluster of *al-mudunu 'l-jāhilah* (ignorant states),[67] the antithesis of his virtuous city, albeit the least imperfect of the imperfect. *Al-madīnatu 'l-jamā'iyyah* is *jāhilah* (ignorant). Here al-Fārābī can be easily misinterpreted as being ethnocentric, especially if *jāhiliyyah* is to be seen in its relation to Islam, i.e. pagan ignorance. But al-Fārābī's reservations are not unique; Plato, amongst other Hellenes, had reservations about democracy. In fact, it is not until fairly recently that democracy has stopped being a derogatory concept. The Islamic paradigm stands out as al-Fārābī's yardstick for what is and is not *fāḍil* (virtuous); for what is and is not *kāmil* (perfect); and for what is and is not closest to *al-sa'ādatu 'l-haqīqiyyah* (supreme happiness). Both Rosenthal and 'Abd al-'Ālī point to the possibility that al-Fārābī's usage of *jāhiliyyah* has Islamic overtones.[68] His disapproval of *al-madīnatu 'l-jamā'iyyah* can be put down to three main possible reasons. The first is its earthly and sensual materialism which contradicts Islam's spiritualism, and al-Fārābī's own life of *zuhd* (asceticism). As in all ignorant cities, the democratic city's rulership "aims at having its fill of bare necessities",[69] including domination and freedom. What can be presumed is al-Fārābī's aversion to the kind of material freedom that is deleterious to supreme happiness. For those who are materially freer can buy power:

> Rulerships are actually bought for a price, especially the positions of authority in the democratic city…Therefore, when someone finally holds a position

[63] Ibid., p. 51.

[64] *Al-madīnatu 'l-ḍarūriyyah* is translated as the 'state of necessity' by Rosenthal, and 'the indispensable city' by Mahdi.

[65] Al-Fārābī in Mahdi (trans.), Lerner and Mahdi (eds), *Medieval Political Philosophy*, pp. 51–2.

[66] Ibid., p. 51.

[67] See Al-Ḥuluw, *Al-Fārābī: Al-mu'allimu 'l-thānī*, pp. 101–5; see also Ibn 'Abd al-'Āali, *Al-Falsafatu 'l-siyāsiyyah 'inda 'l-Fārābī*, pp. 61–73.

[68] Rosenthal, *Political Thought in Medieval Islam*, p. 135; Ibn 'Abd al-'Āali, *Al-Falsafatu 'l-siyāsiyyah 'inda 'l-Fārābī*, p. 63.

[69] Al-Fārābī in Mahdi (trans.), Lerner and Mahdi (eds), *Medieval Political Philosophy*, p. 51. See also 'Umar, "Farabi and Greek Political Philosophy", p. 186.

of authority, it is either because the citizens have favoured him with it, or else because they have received from him money or something else in return.[70]

Again ʿAbd al-ʿĀlī's contention that al-Fārābī's political thought is perhaps an indirect commentary on the state of *fasād* (decay and corruption) in the declining Abbasyd Caliphate, holds here as well. The new non-Arab ruling class—the Turkic military class—was literally "bought" through the allocation of vast land holdings to guard the much weakened Abbasyd rulers.[71] Accordingly, in this context al-Fārābī's commentary on *al-madīnatu 'l-jamāʿiyyah* is double-edged. The second reason is *al-madīnatu 'l-jamāʿiyyah's* alienation of virtuous people of learning which perhaps offends al-Fārābī's own high esteem of like-minded literati, and the Islamic tenet of the *ʿulamā'* being amongst *ūlū' l-amr.* Thus he laments:

As for the truly virtuous man—namely the man, who, if he were to rule them, would determine and direct their actions toward happiness—they do not make him a ruler. If by chance he comes to rule them, he will soon find himself either deposed or killed or in an unstable and challenged position.[72]

This can easily be taken as al-Fārābī's expression of displeasure at the embattled and dying Abbasyd dynasty as well as a criticism against desacralisation of rulership in the Abbasyd dynasty. The third explanation is *al-madīnatu 'l-jamāʿiyyah*'s diversity and "contesting interests", which perhaps for al-Fārābī represents a deviation from the Islamic concept of *tawḥīd* (unity of God) and the one *ummah*. For he appears to deride the democratic city's citizenry in whose "eyes the virtuous ruler is he who has the ability to judge well and to contrive well what enables them to attain their diverse and variegated desires and wishes…"[73] This rather sophisticated view of the democratic city in terms of vying "desires and wishes" somewhat contradicts his functional approach in the crafting of his *al-madīnatu 'l-fāḍilah*, in which he presents a view of a society bound by a common interest.

States antithetical to al-Fārābī's virtuous city include *madinatu 'l-karāmah* (timocracy), *madīnatu 'l-khissah* (plutocracy), and *madīnatu*

70 Al-Fārābī in Mahdi (trans.), Lerner and Mahdi (eds), *Medieval Political Philosophy*, p. 51.

71 Ibn ʿAbd al-ʿĀali, *Al-Falsafatu 'l-siyāsiyyah ʿinda 'l-Fārābī*, p. 39–41.

72 Al-Fārābī in Mahdi (trans.), Lerner and Mahdi (eds), *Medieval Political Philosophy*, p. 51.

73 Ibid.

'l-taghallub (tyranny).[74] Relevant to this analysis is al-Fārābī's opposition to tyranny and despotism. His repetitive highlighting of domination, subjugation and humiliation—the ways of tyrannical states and despots which he describes as "the enemies of all men"[75]—divulge al-Fārābī's strong belief in human dignity. Tyranny is dualistic:[76] domestic, involving abuses of power and travesties of justice; and external, akin to modern-day colonialism and hegemony. He seems to be aware that tyranny is most likely to result from military rulers and thus, according to ʿAbd al-ʿĀlī, al-Fārābī overlooks those who hold military positions in his virtuous city,[77] and furthermore, lists no martial qualities in the essential requirements of the virtuous *al-ra'īsu 'l-awwal* (the first ruler). Martial qualities are considered inferior to scholarship, knowledge, insight, truthfulness, justice, magnanimity and eloquence. Al-Fārābī lists—last—only one martial requirement out of six qualities for the second ruler. That this is indicative of al-Fārābī's opposition to the increasingly praetorian nature of the declining Abbasyd rulership is a fairly safe assumption.

Al-Fārābī's virtuous state constitutes the process of dialectic or, more aptly, the process of its resolution. It is *mithāliyyah* (ideal). It approximates divinity, for *al-kamāl* (perfection), an Islamic quality reserved to Allah, is obtainable in the virtuous city. In this dialectic, "Islamisation" of Greek-Hellenistic borrowings and "Hellenisation" of Islamic tenets occur. That al-Fārābī expects perfection from mortals in an earthly *madīnatu 'l-fāḍilah* would seem to verge on *ishrāk* (polytheism). For it is an Islamic axiom that *al-kamāl li-llāh* (perfection is only for God). The Fārābian notion of human perfection indicates a dialectic between Hellenistic and Islamic tenets. The Qur'ānic notion of *al-qawmu 'l-ṣāliḥūn* (the righteous people) is in concordance with al-Fārābī's idea of virtuosity. The notion of human perfection appears to derive from the Platonic influence on al-Fārābī's own philosophy.

Al-[Fārābī] realized the importance of politics in the philosopher's search for truth about God, the universe, reality and man. Philosophy aims at the

[74] For further details on the various types of ignorant cities see Al-Ḥuluw, *Al-Fārābī: Al-muʿallimu 'l-thānī*, pp. 65–72; Qumayr, *Falāsifatu 'l-ʿArab: Al-Fārābī*, pp. 76–8.

[75] Al-Fārābī in Mahdi (trans.), Lerner and Mahdi (eds), *Medieval Political Philosophy*, p. 47.

[76] See Rosenthal, *Political Thought in Medieval Islam*, p. 136.

[77] Ibn ʿAbd al-ʿĀali, *Al-Falsafatu 'l-siyāsiyyah ʿinda 'l-Fārābī*, p. 41.

perception of the Creator, and the philosopher must strive "to become in his actions like God" as far as this is humanly possible. For man, the way to this end is first to improve himself and then to improve others in his house or state.[78]

Al-Fārābī realises the impossibility of the twelve Platonic virtues (physical, spiritual and intellectual) of the first ruler being combined in one human being.[79] He perhaps also recognises the fallibility of one-man rule. He therefore appears, as al-Ḥuluw points out, to advocate a form of collegial rulership, and "rule through councils" in *al-ri'āsatu 'l-thālithah* (the third rulership).[80] This can be interpreted as a form of harmonising institutions of the democratic and virtuous cities. Al-Fārābī stresses the virtues of loving justice and loathing injustice, and the strong sense of community and cooperation for the common good—supreme happiness. Al-Fārābī's virtuous city is i) differentiated: "There will be certain ranks of order."[81] ii) But it is also integrated: "The function of the city's governor…is to manage the cities in such a way that all the city's parts become linked and fitted together [like the human body]."[82] iii) It is also civic and participant where "the citizens…cooperate to eliminate the evils and acquire the goods;"[83] and where "the supreme ruler [can] enjoin the citizens [to be active on] certain matters."[84] iv) It is universal: "There may be a number of virtuous nations and virtuous cities whose religions are different, even though they all pursue the very same kind of happiness. For religion is but the impressions of these things or the impressions of their images, imprinted in the soul."[85]

Whether al-Fārābī's syncretism bears witness to the difficulty of harmonising the speculative wisdom of philosophy and the imagination of religion is beside the point. What is at issue is that tradition of

[78] Rosenthal, *Political Thought in Medieval Islam*, p. 122.

[79] The first must, for instance, be physically able, perceptive and imaginative, have a retentive memory, be intelligent, eloquent, scholarly, not gluttonous, truthful, magnanimous, not avaricious, just, and strong-willed. See al-Ḥuluw, *Al-Fārābī: Al-mu'allimu 'l-thānī*, pp. 52–64.

[80] Ibid., p. 63.

[81] Al-Fārābī in Mahdi (trans.), Lerner and Mahdi (eds), *Medieval Political Philosophy*, p. 39.

[82] Ibid., p. 40. The emphasis (like the human body) is a Fārābian notion used in *al-madīnah al-fāḍilah*.

[83] Ibid., p. 40.

[84] Ibid., p. 39.

[85] Ibid., p. 41.

syncretism has been handed down from the times of Arabo-Islamic medieval antiquity by the likes of al-Fārābī to later generations of intellectuals and practitioners of politics, as can be gleaned from the discussion below. Modern attempts at syncretism have yet to conclude with a happy ending. In both cases the search for a syncretism in which the attainment of earthly and otherworldly happiness stems from the silence of Islam on the model polity. For neither the Qur'ān nor the Sunnah elaborate a blueprint of statecraft. In old and newer attempts of syncretism, the difficulty resides in constructing a polity that is loyal to the Arabo-Islamic heritage, morality and identity and yet bold enough to tap into the Western tradition of political philosophy and practical instrumentality to forge an ethic of government for achieving human and Islamic felicity.

NAHḌĀWIYYŪN: *IṢLĀḤ* WITHOUT *DĪMUQRĀṬIYYAH*

Harmonisation seems to be the common thread running from al-Fārābī to such *nahḍāwiyyūn*[86] as al-Ṭahṭāwī, Khayr al-Dīn and al-Kawākibī. Like al-Fārābī, they seek, in varying degrees, harmonisation between reason and revelation. In doing so they find themselves torn between *taqlīd* and *tajdīd*; between *aṣālah* and *ḥadāthah*; and between *iṣlāḥ* and *dīmuqrāṭiyyah*. Their strong Islamic conviction leads them to dressing certain European institutions in an Islamic garb. The result is *iṣlāḥ* within Islamic bounds. While their *iṣlāḥ* seems to reject wholesale "democratisation" (not that it considers it in the first place), it reflects the attraction of European democratic institutions.

Iṣlāḥ is the common denominator for these three reformers. They seem to be motivated by the danger facing *dāru 'l-Islām* from *dāru 'l-ḥarb*. The danger is none other than Muslim backwardness, especially in comparison with the progress within Christendom. They are also motivated by their own parochial loyalties. Al-Ṭahṭāwī (1801–73) leaves no doubt that his first loyalty lies with his native Egypt. His *Manāhiju 'l-'albābi 'l-miṣriyyah fi mabāhiji 'l-adābi 'l-'aṣriyyah* (*The Paths for Egyptian Hearts into the Joys of the Contemporary Arts*)[87] is a

[86] For good articles on the luminaries of *al-nahḍah* (al-Ṭahṭāwī, al-Afghānī, 'Abduh, al-Tūnisī, and Arsalān) see the special issue of *Al-Muntalaq*, 58 (Aylul 1989).

[87] This translation is adopted from Hourani, *Arabic Thought in the Liberal Age*, p. 72. Al-Husri's translation reads "The Programmes or Paths for Egyptian Minds into the Joys of the Contemporary Arts" in *Three Reformers*, p. 23.

kind of *iṣlāḥ*-ist manifesto for Egypt (although he might very well have realised that reforming Egypt,[88] "the heart of the Arab world", would have a beneficial spill-over effect in the rest of the "body"). The *iṣlāḥ* of Khayr al-Dīn (1810–89), a most devoted member of the non-indigenous *mamluk* ruling class in the Ottoman province of Tunis, has in its sight the woes of both the Ottoman realm and nineteenth-century Tunisia. Brown contends that Khayr al-Dīn's "ultimate loyalty was to an Ottoman ruling-class of state service".[89] Al-Kawākibī (1848–1902) is both anti-Ottoman and relatively pan-Islamic. More importantly, however, he is pan-Arabist. His *Ṭabā'i'u 'l-istibdād wa maṣāri'u 'l-isti'bād* (*The Nature of Despotism*)[90] addresses *al-sharq* (the East), in general, and Arabs, in particular. In his introduction, al-Kawākibī calls on Arab political editors to enlighten their "Eastern brethren, especially Arabs, about those matters they do not know".[91] In *Ummu 'l-qurā* (*The Mother of Cities: Mecca*),[92] he expresses Arab pride. He ascribes a number of qualities and values to Arabs and to the inhabitants of the Arab peninsula, assigning them the role of being the natural custodians of Islam. He also stresses the importance of Arabic to all Muslims.[93] It is *iṣlāḥ* without *dīmuqrāṭiyyah* that all three reformers advocate. This cannot be understood without looking at the nature of their *iṣlāḥ*. The dimensions of religion and politics, in particular, call for special attention.

[88] In fact, there is no consensus on Khayr al-Dīn's date of birth. The date of 1810, which is no doubt an approximation, is the most widely quoted, as by Hourani. For further details on this point see the introduction by Leon Carl Brown in his translation of Khayr al-Dīn's *Muqaddimat Aqwām al-Masālik fi Ma'rifat Aḥwāl al-Mamālik* [*The Surest Path to Knowledge Concerning the Condition of Countries*] (Cambridge, MA: Harvard University Press, 1967), p. 29, esp. fn. 31. Khayr al-Dīn died in Constantinople in 1889. We presume that Al-Husri's date of 1899 is a printing error. See *Three Reformers*, p. 36.

[89] Brown, 'Introduction', *Muqaddimat Aqwām al-Masālik*, p. 35. Although as Brown notes, "no one in nineteenth century Tunisia worked harder to strengthen Tunisian government and society", p. 35.

[90] Al-Husri's translation in *Three Reformers*.

[91] 'Abd al-Raḥmān al-Kawākibī, *Ṭabā'i'u 'l-istibdād wa maṣāriu' 'l-isti'bād* [*The Nature of Despotism*], with an introduction by As'ad al-Saḥmarānī (Beirut: Dar al-Nafa'is, 1986), p. 28.

[92] Another adopted translation from Al-Husri's *Three Reformers*.

[93] 'Abd al-Raḥmān al-Kawākibī, *Ummu 'l-qurā* [*The Mother of Cities: Mecca*] (Beirut: Dar al-Ra'id al-'Arabi, 1982), see (*Qarār 6*) pp. 217–22.

Religion

The three reformers' thought is anchored in Islam. All three had a grounding in Islamic teachings. Al-Ṭahṭāwī, in particular, stands out. He was a graduate of al-Azhar mosque-university, and an Imam (prayer leader) by profession. For all three, Islam must have meant *dīn wa-dunyā* (a religion and a regulative system of life), and, in line with this belief, it must have also meant the answer to *sa'ādatu 'l-dārayni* (happiness in this world and the hereafter). Accordingly, while both al-Ṭahṭāwī and Khayr al-Dīn concede to the superiority of Christian France, admire the Europeans' advancement, there is no question of them equating European superiority with the superiority of Christianity over Islam. In the account of his Parisian sojourn, *Takhlīṣu 'l-ibrīz ilā talkhīṣ bārīz* (*The Extraction of Gold from a Review of Paris*),[94] al-Ṭahṭāwī harks back to religion and reproaches the French for being only nominally Christian.[95] Further still, he describes France as *diyār kufr* (the realm of unbelief),[96] which like "other lands of *ifranj* (the French) is fraught with vice, innovations and deviations".[97] Nor does he hold priests and their ways in high esteem. In one passage he speaks of their *fisq* (impiousness).[98]

Al-Ṭahṭāwī praises the Parisians' "unique intelligence and perceptiveness", but disassociates those qualities from Christianity. His proof seems to be the ignorance of the Copts (a reference to those in Egypt).[99] In the same vein, Khayr al-Dīn suggests, as Brown points out, how the "Papal states were amongst the most backward in Europe".[100] That Christianity, as al-Ṭahṭāwī and Khayr al-Dīn contend, has nothing to do with European advancement is indeed interesting. Does it then follow that religion contributes nothing to worldly advancement? If the answer is in the affirmative, then can Islam be expected to play a role in reversing the *ummah's* material misfortunes? Neither systematically considers this question. They do,

[94] The title as translated by Al-Husri in *Three Reformers*.

[95] Rifā'ah Rāfi' Al-Ṭahṭāwī, *Takhlīṣu 'l-ibrīz ilā talkhīṣ bārīz* (Tripoli: Al-Dar al-'Arabiyyah li 'l-Kitab, 1991), esp. "On the Religion of Parisians", pp. 185–7. See also p. 34.

[96] Ibid., p. 17.

[97] Ibid., p. 95.

[98] Ibid., p. 186.

[99] Ibid., p. 89.

[100] Brown, 'Introduction', *Muqaddimat Aqwām al-Masālik*, p. 38.

however, advocate a number of *iṣlāḥāt* the departure point of which is religion. Thus not only do they look into Islam for justification of reform, but also the *iṣlāḥ* they look for justifies reforming Islam itself. From this perspective no aspect of social organisation that requires *tadbīr* (governing/managing) is separable from religion.

Islam's relevance to all facets of life has resonance in al-Kawākibī's thought. If his *Ummu 'l-qurā* stresses religion, *inter alia*, as being at the core root of Islam's decline,[101] *Ṭabā'i'u 'l-istibdād* searches for salvation and solution in none other than Islam. The former attacks many of those heretic and/or polytheistic practices[102] that leading modernising reformers like 'Abduh and al-Afghānī set out to eradicate in order to purify, renew and recuperate Muslim vigour. It is in a way a statement about al-Kawākibī's own reformist tendency along *salafī* lines.[103] The latter, for instance, attacks secularists, in general, and detractors of Islam, in particular.[104] He rejects the Western suggestion that "all political despotism stems from religious despotism".[105] He denies that such a proposition is applicable to Islam, and retorts by asserting that religious reform effects political reform. His evidence is the Protestant Reformation.[106] Hence he opts for religious reform both as an end in itself, and as a means to political *iṣlāḥ*.[107] Khayr al-Dīn, for instance, associates the *ummah's* past status "at the peak of wealth and power" with its adherence to the straight path of Islam.[108] For both men religious difference should not stand in the way of learning from non-Muslims. The kind of Islam they preach is an ideologically rich repertoire of positive answers and solutions to worldly matters, and not the Islam of dervishes and ignorant *'ulamā'* that pull the *ummah* back rather than push it forward.[109]

101 Al-Kawākibī, *Ummu 'l-qurā, passim*; see, for instance, the religious causes of the *ummah's futūr* (weakness or lethargy), pp. 158–60.

102 Such as *al-ṣufiyyah* (Sufism), *al-maqābiriyyah* (cemetery cults) Dervish orders, Maraboutism like *al-qādiriyyah*. See ibid., for instance, p. 159; see also the Congress proceedings (*al-ijtimā' al-rābi'*), pp. 75–104.

103 Al-Kawākibī, *Ummu 'l-qurā*, p. 199.

104 Al-Kawākibī, *Ṭabā'i 'u 'l-istibdād*, p. 35; pp. 35–49.

105 Ibid., p. 35.

106 Ibid., p. 38.

107 Ibid.

108 Khayr al-Dīn al-Tūnisī, *muqaddimat aqwāmu 'l-masālik*, p. 97.

109 Al-Ṭahṭāwī views learning from the West not only in terms of re-learning from it what the *ifranj* were themselves taught by Muslims in the past, but also in terms of an Islamic *farīḍah* (duty). He adduces the Prophet's saying: "Seek learning even onto

Politics

Not surprisingly, all three reformers are as concerned with politics as they are with religion.[110] The crux of the three reformers' political reform is good government. Good government must conform with the *sharī'ah*; must lead to *maṣlaḥah*; and must provide justice. In fact there is no clear-cut separation between these aims and guidelines. For *sharī'ah* in itself is presented as *maṣlaḥah*, as is justice. No justice is conceived of outside the bounds of *sharī'ah*. Al-Ṭahṭāwī exhibits this thinking when he equates French liberty with *al-'adl wa 'l-inṣāf* (justice and fairness) of Muslims.[111] The notion of good government each man proposes in his political project differs from Western *dīmuqrāṭiyyah* even if all are impressed by its dispensation of justice, separation of powers, and freedoms of press, assembly and organisation. Some of the ideas they espouse about good government need to be briefly considered.

Rulership The reform the three men attempt does not aim at transferring power from the centre to the periphery, i.e., from the Pasha or the Bey to the people. In fact their *iṣlāḥ* is an approximation of

---

China" (Al-Ṭahṭāwī, *Takhlīṣu 'l-ibrīz*, pp. 17–22). Khayr al-Dīn upholds al-Ṭahṭāwī's position noting that all learning from non-Muslims that does not contradict the *sharī'ah* and benefits the *ummah* is permitted by many of Islam's great *'ulamā'* like al-Ghazzālī and Shaykh Muḥammad ibn 'Ābidin al-Ḥanafī Al-Tunisī. See *Muqaddimat aqwām al-masālik*, pp. 74–81. Selective learning from the more advanced is an attitude that al-Kawākibī shares with both reformers who preceded him. Although he attacks *al-tafarnaj* (Westernisation) (Al-Kawākibī, *Ummu 'l-qurā*, pp. 184–6), he sees value in the West's press, and associational and organisational practices (ibid., pp. 62–4).

110 While in Paris, al-Ṭahṭāwī was witness to the revolution of 1830, he closely learned about the French political, administrative and legal systems, and his own career waxed and waned with the change of rulers. 'Abbās I, for instance, more or less banished al-Ṭahṭāwī to Khartoum, Sudan, where he headed a high school for four years (1850–4). This was a demotion for al-Ṭahṭāwī. Khayr al-Dīn served in various ministerial positions, and as Prime Minister from 1873 to 1877 in the Regency of Tunis, and, for less than a year, he was Grand Vezir of the Ottoman Empire in 1878. His career too fluctuated owing to absolutist superiors and palace intrigue. Al-Kawākibī was not as close to the rulers of his day, especially the Ottomans and the Hamidians, whom he criticised. As a result he suffered both imprisonment and censorship. In the preface to *Ṭabā'iu' 'l-istibdād*, al-Saḥmarānī mentions the banning of al-Kawākibī's newspapers, *Al-Shahbā'* in 1878 and *Al-I'tidāl* in 1879. He also mentions al-Kawākibī's persecution brought about by the hostility of 'Ārif Bāsha and the "Turks' man" Abu al-Hudah al-Ṣayyādi, see pp. 19–22.

111 Al-Ṭahṭāwī, *Takhlīṣu 'l-ibrīz*, p. 125.

"just despotism" (a contradiction in terms) checked by what may be termed *al-wāzi'u 'l-dīnī* (religious deterrent or restrainer) as in the form of *sharī'ah* and the *'ulamā'*. The ruler remains *waliyyu 'l-amr* (first in charge).[112] Thus his authority must confer obedience. Al-Ṭahṭāwī, for instance, does not question Muḥammad 'Alī's autocracy as can be judged from the praise he heaps on him.[113] As Hourani points out, al-Ṭahṭāwī deems it necessary for the autocrat to "use his powers properly" for the sake of reform.[114] Neither Khayr al-Dīn nor al-Kawākibī question the "centrality of the centre". Khayr al-Dīn discusses the importance of sound ministerial advice and responsibility, noting that they do not only enhance the ruler's authority "to attain the public interest", but also "facilitate the maintenance of the monarchy in the King's family".[115]

The People All three reformers recognise a certain margin of public interest. Thus *maṣlaḥah*, implicit and explicit, of the *ummah*, the empire or the homeland appears as the guiding principle of good government. However, the people are *ra'āyā* (better in status than subjects and less than citizens) and while they are accorded certain *ḥuqūq*, foremost amongst their *wājibāt* (duties) are to obey, to work diligently and to "pay taxes".[116] Al-Ṭahṭāwī extols civic virtues in Parisians.[117] He also relates it to the consultative procedures in the French Chamber of Deputies, seeing it as not different from Islamic *mashūrah* (consultation), and welcomes his country's own chamber.[118] While Khayr al-Dīn supports the principle of a Grand council, he "is completely mute on the question of representative government".[119] Al-Kawākibī appears elitist in his allocation of responsibility: "Those charged with *tadbīr* are the wise, the devoted leaders and the *'ulamā'* amongst the *ummah*."[120] His predilection for the rulers' consultation with the

[112] See Al-Ḥusrī, *Three Reformers*, p. 25.

[113] See, for instance, the *al-khuṭbah* (the sermon) in *Takhlīṣu 'l-ibrīz*, pp. 9–13.

[114] Hourani, *Arabic Thought in the Liberal Age*, p. 73.

[115] Al-Tūnisī, *Muqaddimat Aqwām al-Masālik*, p. 86.

[116] Al-Ṭahṭāwī, *Manāhiju 'l-albābi 'l-miṣriyyah fī mabāhiji 'l-adābi 'l-'aṣriyyah* [*The Paths for Egyptian Hearts into the Joys of the Contemporary Arts*] (Cairo: n.p., 1912), p. 350.

[117] Al-Ṭahṭāwī, *Takhlīṣu 'l-ibrīz*, p. 91.

[118] Al-Ṭahṭāwī seems to be taken by the French *mashūrah* in the country's Chamber of Deputies. See *Takhlīṣu 'l-ibrīz*, pp. 113–30, 241–3. See also his *Manāhiju 'l-albāb*, p. 323.

[119] Brown, 'Introduction', *Muqaddimat aqwām al-masālik*, p. 32.

[120] Al-Kawākibī, *Ummu 'l-qurā*, p. 192.

subjects' *ashrāf* (noblemen)[121] is another example of al-Kawākibī's elitist tendency. He identifies this type of *mashūrā* as intrinsic to his *islāmiyyah* (an Islamic-derived system for dealing with all facets of Muslim life according to *ijtihād*),[122] which he translates into what he calls *al-idāratu 'l-dīmuqrāṭiyyah* (democratic administration). He defines this as being *al-shūrā 'l-aristuqrāṭiyyah* (aristocratic *shūrā*).[123] Education, however, forms part of the three men's reformist projects. So if they appear not to stress strongly enough a participatory role for *al-ra'iyyah* (populace), it is perhaps because of the prevalence of illiteracy. For them participation is latently a function of education.[124]

Checks and Balances In general the contours of authority are delimited by the "Public Good". It is the ultimate yardstick against which wielded power is checked. The "Public Good" itself is regulated by the concepts of *al-ma'rūf* (the good) and *al-munkar* (the reprehensible). *Al-ma'rūf* is all that is *ḥalāl* (permitted). *Al-munkar* is all that is *ḥarām* (forbidden). Thus the "Public Good" must meet with these laws of Islam, and respond to the needs of a Muslim public. Therefore it has to be administered by "good" Muslim rulers. The notions of *al-ma'rūf* and *al-munkar* are implicitly and explicitly expressed in the three reformers' political thought. While all three men seem to restate many of the tenets of traditional Islamic political thought, they nonetheless apply a new and bold independent reasoning, but without undermining faith. For instance, while they believe in a strong but just *waliyyu 'l-amr*, they do not do so unconditionally. Hence they provide for checks and balances through such mechanisms as the

121 Al-Kawākibī, *Ṭabā'i 'u 'l-istibdād*, p. 41.

122 See Muḥammad Jamāl Ṭaḥḥān, "Al-Kawākibī bayna 'l-Islāmiyyah wa 'l-dīmuqrāṭiyyah" [Al-Kawākibī Between al-Islāmiyyah and Democracy], *dirāsāt 'Arabiyyah*, 10–12, (August/September/October 1992), pp. 34–55.

123 Al-Kawākibī, *Ṭabā'i 'u 'l-istibdād*, p. 42.

124 Al-Ṭahṭāwī mentions the advisory utility of technocrats; he stresses the importance of an educated people for obeying laws they comprehend, and for being politically aware; and in a way he makes these conditions for 'open government'. Khayr al-Dīn's role in reforming education for the purpose of *al-nahḍah* is well known: his founding of the European-modelled *ṣādiqiyyah* college; his reforming of the Zaytouna mosque-university; and his opening of libraries. Al-Kawākibī realises that educating men and women is essential for Arab and Muslim renaissance. In *Ummu 'l-qurā* he identifies ignorance as the *ummah*'s main ailment, and he launches the *Muwaḥḥidīn* (united on the basis of *tawḥīd*) educational project. See al-Kawākibī, *Ummu 'l-qurā*, pp. 191–2.

Rule of Law without which no justice or liberty are attainable, accountability, and the inputs of the *'ulamā'*. All men associate the Rule of Law with the *sharī'ah*. But their conceptualisation of *sharī'ah* is not one of a rigid corpus of laws. Hence the relevance of *ijtihād* to make *sharī'ah* amenable to happiness in this life and the hereafter. All three do not view the *sharī'ah* as an obstacle to *al-nahḍah* especially if the *'ulamā'* are enlightened about the worldly matters of the day, and if *ijtihād* is applied. Furthermore, al-Ṭahṭāwī[125] along with al-Kawākibī[126] find an additional bonus in the diversity of *al-madhāhibu 'l-fiqhiyyah* (Islamic rites of jurisprudence). With such diversity, modernising Muslims can take recourse to any of the four rites to solve and resolve arising problems. This process is known as *al-talfiq* as referred to by al-Kawākibī.[127]

Both men envisage active political roles for the enlightened amongst the *'ulamā'* as sources of counsel to the rulers, and possible watchers over them. Hourani makes the valid point that if al-Ṭahṭāwī stresses the importance of the *'ulamā'*, it may be owing to his realisation that they form the only Egyptian ruling stratum.[128] Al-Kawākibī does not tire from pointing out the importance of Arabs as the natural guardians of Islam. With the same fervour Khayr al-Dīn advocates an "association of the *'ulamā'* with the statesmen". This association, he argues, has two interrelated functions. It enhances the "cognisance" of the *'ulamā'* with the real and this-worldly milieu for better "administration" of the *sharī'ah*; to stop rulers from "act[ing] without restraint".[129] As Brown observes, in advocating a participatory role for the *'ulamā'*, Khayr al-Dīn breaks with the orthodoxy that the *'ulamā'* stay out of the business of governing for fear of contamination.[130] Brown further notes that Khayr al-Dīn in fact equates *ahlu 'l-ḥall wa 'l-'aqd* (the *'ulamā'* who loosen and bind) with the deputies in European parliaments.[131] Al-Ṭahṭāwī and Khayr al-Dīn appear to be more open to some adoption and adaptation of rational laws than al-Kawākibī. Khayr al-Dīn, for instance, makes the function of "restraining the restrainer" of "either…heavenly *sharī'ah* or a policy

125 Al-Ṭahṭāwi, *Manāhiju 'l-albāb*, pp. 388–9.

126 Al-Kawākibī, *Ummu 'l-qurā*, pp. 147–56.

127 Ibid., see, for instance, p. 151.

128 Hourani, *Arabic Thought in the Liberal Age*, p. 75.

129 Al-Tunisī, *Muqaddimat aqwāmu 'l-masālik*, p. 124.

130 Brown, 'Introduction', *Muqaddimat aqwāmu 'l-masālik*, p. 61.

131 Ibid., p. 61. See also al-Tūnisī, *Muqaddimat aqwāmu 'l-masālik*, p. 113.

based on reason".[132] This notion of *al-wāzi'* (restraint)[133] which is in this case religious and non-religious, ministerial responsibility, *al-qānūn* (the law),[134] and the role of *ahlu 'l-ḥall wa 'l-'aqd* all allow for an effective *iḥtisāb* (accountability).

Relevant to the restraint of the law and of the *'ulamā'* are the notions of justice and of liberty. Here again all three adhere to the established bounds of Islamic orthodoxy by presenting such concepts, especially when relating them to European institutions, as intrinsically Islamic. It has been mentioned above that al-Ṭahṭāwī has a grasp of *al-ḥurriyyah* as practised by the French; he equates it with *al-'adl wa 'l-inṣāf* and stresses its importance for *al-musāwāt* before the law. Khayr al-Dīn makes happiness incumbent upon the acquisition of "political *tanẓīmāt* (institutions/systems) based on justice".[135] In other instances he links the prosperity of countries with the attainment of "the roots of liberty and the constitution, synonymous with political *tanẓīmāt*".[136] He emphasises the importance of such institutionalisation for the administration of justice and liberty with the full realisation of their potential to ward off, or at least limit, the abuses of office. Khayr al-Dīn distinguishes between personal and political liberty. He acknowledges the discomfort, poverty, high prices, and insecurity that befall people in the absence of liberty.[137] In extolling the virtues of these liberties he appears to acknowledge the value of *al-ḥurriyyah* in its Western sense. As al-Husrī notes, "its untraditional usage [by Khayr al-Dīn]...cannot be easily made to harmonize with traditional Arab political theory".[138] According to this theory there is no "concept of individual liberty *vis-à-vis* the state...The state is...absolute...[and] all rights belong to [it]".[139]

Al-Kawākibī's commitment to justice and liberty is unequivocal. For him *al-ḥurriyyah* is multidimensional. It is freedom from materialism, from ignorance and backwardness, from *taqlīd*, from disunity, from despotism and from militarism.[140] It is, however, *al-istibdād*

[132] Al-Tunisī, *Muqaddimat aqwāmu 'l-masālik*, p. 84.

[133] For further details see fn. 152 by Brown on p. 121 in *Muqaddimat aqwāmu 'l-masālik*.

[134] Al-Tūnisī, *Muqaddimat aqwāmu 'l-masālik*, p. 112.

[135] Ibid., p. 159.

[136] Ibid., p. 164.

[137] Ibid., p. 165

[138] Al-Husri, *Three Reformers*, pp. 42–3.

[139] Ibid., p. 42.

[140] Al-Kawākibī, *Ṭabā'i'u 'l-istibdād*, pp. 32, 39. See also Al-Husri's analysis of al-Kawākibī's aversion to militarism in *Three Reformers*, pp. 70–3.

(despotism) that forms the crux of al-Kawākibī's reflections on the issues of justice and liberty. They are essential bulwarks against despotism. Despotism is multifaceted as attested to by the multiple definitions that al-Kawākibī produces. As argued by al-Husri, from a religious angle al-Kawākibī sees *al-istibdād* as a form of polytheism. For it contradicts with *tawḥīd*, the indivisible sovereignty of the one God.[141] Al-Kawākibī stresses the anti-majoritarian character of *al-istibdād*. It is "the management of common affairs according to one's whim";[142] and "the reliance on the view of one person in matters that require wide consultation".[143] From this perspective a despot is, al-Kawākibī argues, the "absolutist ruler and tyrant".[144] He, however, shows particular distrust in the state. Accordingly he stresses despotism by the state, for in his view "it is the strongest factor that has rendered man the unhappiest of living creatures".[145] Thus he contrasts the despotic state with that which is "just, responsible, restrained and constitutional".[146] However, despotism, he argues, is not alien to those constitutional and elected governments that are neither accountable to legislatures, nor are restrained by mechanisms of checks and balances.[147] Al-Kawākibī presupposes the existence of a "*sharī'ah*", such as a constitution, "principles and rules", or a "general will" that govern the governors, and regulate their behaviour. Despotic governments are the exception to these norms.[148] Although al-Kawākibī's aversion to despotism and emphasis on justice and liberty have religious overtones, they also mirror a sophisticated vision for a code of human, social, political and civil rights. These are the only protection against states and against latently despotic rulers. In this respect al-Kawākibī's cynicism is somewhat Hobbesian—hence his trust is in the one God, the *sharī'ah*, and in *al-qānūn*. For he warns that the oath of office is no protection against latent despotism.[149]

Procedures The reflections of all three reformers on the complexities of good government reveal a maturity of Arab political thought

141 Al-Husri, *Three Reformers*, p. 63.
142 Al-Kawākibī, *Ṭabā'i 'u l-istibdād*, p. 29.
143 Ibid., p. 30.
144 Ibid., p. 31.
145 Ibid., p. 30.
146 Ibid., p. 31.
147 Ibid., pp. 31–2.
148 Ibid., p. 31.
149 Ibid., p. 134.

in the nineteenth century, as well as familiarity with the modalities, functions and preconditions of good government. Their combined political treatises also mark a linguistic leap for Arabic, with the recurrence of neologisms such as assemblies, deputies, opposition elections, free press, parties, liberty, justice, consultation, accountability and democracy. They collectively index those governmental procedures instrumental for their ideal polities. Those procedures can be summarised as follows.

First, all three reformers stand for incremental *iṣlāḥ* as against revolutionary change. Change through education is a lengthy process. Al-Kawākibī advocates that emancipation from despotism be through *al-tadrīj* (gradualism).[150] They do not seek desacralisation of polity or society. On the contrary, they build on the Islamic legacy, activating and rehabilitating what they firmly believe to be relevant and venerable concepts, institutions and practices. In so doing they retrospectively seek to emulate European political achievements. Al-Kawākibī appears to be the more traditionalist *muṣliḥ* (reformer) of the three. His suggestion that the deeds of the *al-salafu 'l-ṣāliḥ* (pious ancestors) bear lessons for his contemporaries is not matched by al-Ṭahṭāwī nor Khayr al-Dīn. Secondly, all three countenance peaceful change. Al-Kawākibī is not only staunchly anti-militarist, but he also advocates peaceful resistance to despotism.[151] Al-Ṭahṭāwī and Khayr al-Dīn value the political method. Thirdly, and this is related to the political method, their support for a consultative mode of *tadbīr* through *al-shūrā* tempers (especially for al-Ṭahṭāwī and Khayr al-Dīn) their preference for effective rule by a just but strong ruler or imām. All three dislike one-man rule. Khayr al-Dīn counsels:

> It is never permissible that the affairs of the kingdom should be given over to a single man with both [its] happiness and [its] difficulties in his hands, even if he be the most perfect of men, the most balanced in intelligence, the widest in knowledge.[152]

Al-Ṭahṭāwī's *waliyyu 'l-amr* is restrained by such means as *al-qānūn* and a parliamentary structure.[153] Al-Kawākibī asserts that consultation is not new to Arabs whom he considers "one of the oldest nations to be steeped in the principles of *al-shūrā* and their practice

150 Ibid., p. 140.

151 Ibid.

152 Al-Tūnisī, *Muqaddimat aqwām al-masālik*, p. 94.

153 Al-Ṭahṭāwi, *Manāhiju 'l-albāb*, pp. 323–56.

in common affairs".[154] His vision of an Arab Caliph in *Ummu 'l-qurā* is one with reduced powers limited by laws, and by a consultative body that also elects him.[155] Fourthly, like al-Fārābī before them, all three perceive of society as constituted by a common *maṣlaḥah*. As a result they tend toward fostering a propensity for unity. For instance, while all three are familiar with political parties, there is not enough evidence in their treatises of commitment to them. In fact, al-Kawākibī adopts many of the democratic tools including the secret ballot and the principle of majority rule,[156] but not political parties. The Meccan Congress in *Ummu 'l-qurā* finds that one of the political causes of Muslim stagnation is the "*ummah*'s division into *'aṣabiyyāt* (pl. of *'aṣabiyyah*, i.e. various group loyalties) and political parties".[157] Political parties obviously would not form part of his understanding of "Islam's political liberty which is somewhere between democracy and aristocracy".[158]

DĪMUQRĀṬIYYAH: A CONTEMPORARY KALEIDOSCOPE

The contemporary rich panoply of reflections and eclectic inputs on Arab *dīmuqrāṭiyyah* can only be sampled here. The theme of *azmah* (crisis) is common to the study of Arab *dīmuqrāṭiyyah*. Muḥammad Mazāli associates Arab crises with *azmatu 'l-ḥurriyyah* (crisis of freedom).[159] Democracy is problematic. The Arab world generally lacks it, and yet, with it, it is contended by many Arabs, a few problems (war, disunity, developmental problems, dependence, corruption...) could be solved.[160] *Azmatu 'l-dīmuqrāṭiyyah fi 'l-'ālami 'l-'Arabī* (*The Crisis of Democracy in the Arab World*) is, for instance, both the

154 Al-Kawākibī, *Ummu 'l-qurā*, p. 221.

155 Ibid., pp. 234–6.

156 Both mechanisms form part of the rules guiding al-Kawākibī's fictitious Society of al-Muwaḥḥidīn; see ibid., p. 195.

157 Ibid., p. 160.

158 Al-Kawākibī, *Ṭabā'i'u 'l-istibdād*, p. 40.

159 Muḥammad Mazālī, "*Al-Azmatu 'l-'Arabiyyah hiya azmatu ḥurriyyah*" [The Arab Crisis is a Crisis of Freedom] in Ibrāhīm Nāfi' (ed.), *Mādhā ba'da 'āṣifatu 'l-khalīj: ru'yā 'ālamiyyah li mustaqbali 'l-sharq al-awsaṭ* [*What After the Gulf Storm: An International Vision for the Future of the Middle East*] (Cairo: Markiz al-Ahram li al-Tarjamah wa al-Nashr, 1992), pp. 137–49.

160 One of the earliest arguments extolling democratic values was made by Egyptian Ṭāhā Ḥusayn. See his *Mustaqbalu 'l-thaqāfah fi miṣr* [*The Future of Culture in Egypt*], vols 1 and 2 (Cairo: Al-Hay'ah al-Misriyyah al-'Ammah li 'l-Kitab, 1993).

theme and the title of two fine works.[161] The wide discourse on democracy from the perspective of an *azmah* mirrors the fact that it is an issue that has long occupied Arab intellectuals.[162] Fu'ād Bīṭār sums up the crisis of Arab *dīmuqrāṭiyyah* by asking:

> Why this contradiction between [the discourse of] democracy and [the reality of] autocracy? Why hasn't democracy been realized in our lands despite everybody's belief in it? Why does the military still rule over us, and why do royalties still inherit crowns within narrow groups and lineages? Why do the representatives in the national or consultation assemblies still move in the orbit of the rulers not of the ruled? Why have a few Arab countries rejected and banned political parties, while others have turned them into one single party, or into one dominant over other parties? And, in other words, why this absence of democracy?[163]

Leaders

The inputs of Arab leaders on democracy have mostly been grand proclamations, few of which have been put into practice. Even those leaders who enjoy a high standing in Western capitals because they supposedly rule over so-called "*pays pilote*", making possible "a brilliant showcase of development"[164] have usually been disappointing in both their practice and view of democracy. Bourguiba, one of the leading figures of Tunisia's liberation from French colonialism, expresses a derogatory view of democracy: "Democracy, the return

[161] Fu'ād Bīṭār, *Azmatu 'l-dīmuqrāṭiyyah fi 'l-'ālami 'l-'arabī* [*The Crisis of Democracy in the Arab World*] (Beirut: Dar Birayt li 'l-Nashr, 1984) and Sa'ad al-dīn Ibrāhīm (ed.), *Azmatu 'l-dīmuqrāṭiyyah fi 'l-'ālami 'l-'arabī* [*The Crisis of Democracy in the Arab World*] (Beirut: Markaz Dirasat al-Wihdah al-'Arabiyyah, 1987). See also, Ṣālah Ḥasan Sumay', *Azmatu 'l-ḥurriyyatu 'l-siyāsiyyah fi 'l-waṭani 'l-'Arabī* [*The Crisis of Political Freedom in the Arab Homeland*] (Cairo: Al-Zahra' li 'l-I'lām al-'Arabi, 1988).

[162] Some of the oldest titles on democracy are: Khālid Muḥammad Khālid, *Al-Dīmuqrāṭiyyah abadan* [*Democracy Ever*] (Baghdad: Maktabatu 'l-Muthannah, 1958), which first appeared in 1953 and his *Min hunā nabda'* [*Here we Begin*] (Cairo: n.p., 1966) published in 1950, and *Muwāṭinūn lā ra'āyā* [*Citizens not Subjects*] (Cairo: n.p., 1951) which was published a year later. Others include Ibrāhīm Ḥaddād's *Al-Shuyū'iyyah wa 'l-dīmuqrāṭiyyah bayna 'l-sharqi wa 'l-gharbi* [*Communism and Democracy Between East and West*] (Beirut: Dar al-Thaqafah, 1958) and, also by Ḥaddād, *Al-Dīmuqrāṭiyyah 'inda 'l-'arab* [*Democracy Amongst Arabs*] (Beirut: Dar al-Thaqafah, 1960). See also Al-'Adawī 'Abd al-Fattāḥ Ḥasan, *Al-Dīmuqrāṭiyyah wa fikratu 'l-dawlah* [*Democracy and the Concept of the State*] (Cairo, Mu'assasatu sijill al-'Arab, 1964).

[163] Fu'ād Bīṭār, *Azmatu 'l-dīmuqrāṭiyyah*, p. 14.

[164] See Dirk Vandewalle, "From the New State to the New Era: Toward a Second Republic in Tunisia", *Middle East Journal*, 42 (autumn 1988), p. 602.

of power to the people, is a dangerous undertaking, an adventure filled with risks."[165] Nasser seems to have had a bifurcated approach towards democracy.[166] Al-Sadat deemed him "mad" for voting alone for democracy and against dictatorship in the first meeting of the eight-member Revolutionary Command Council (RCC), in July 1952.[167] Nasser's stance seems to have been based on his dislike for absolutism, as al-Sadat explains it:

> It would be senseless, he said, to rid the country of a dictatorship exercised by the old political parties only to plunge it in our brand of dictatorship. Indeed, this would be worse, as the old factions feared the king and the British, but we had absolute power and feared nobody.[168]

If Nasser was genuine about democracy there is little evidence to substantiate it. As al-Sadat himself shows, all political parties, for instance, were banned by an RCC decree in January 1953.[169] Nasser was no doubt disillusioned with, if not totally antagonistic toward, liberal democracy. He referred to it as a sham, referring to Egypt's experience with democracy under the patronage of colonial Britain as "constitutional façades", "the great masquerade of phoney democracy", "the façade of false democracy", "the democracy of the reactionaries", "reactionary democracy", "the artificiality of this façade", and "the mockery of reactionary democracy".[170] The fact that Egypt, like most Arab countries, has suffered colonialism at the hands of the leading European democracies has for a while weakened the case for an Arab democracy, and the position of its

[165] As quoted from his Bizerte Congress speech of 1964 in ibid., p. 602.

[166] See the details of a conversation on the question of democracy between the Egyptian Islamic thinker Khālid Muḥammad Khālid and Nasser in Khālid Muḥammad Khālid, *Difā'un 'ani 'l-dīmuqrāṭiyyah* [*In Defence of Democracy*] (Cairo: Dar Thabit, 1985), pp. 279–330.

[167] Nasser called that meeting to discuss the new mode of governance. Al-Sadat, who acknowledges having argued in that meeting ardently in favour of dictatorship "for what may be achieved 'democratically' in a year can be accomplished 'dictatorially' in a day", was flabbergasted by Nasser's single stand for democracy. The reason, according to al-Sadat, was the wide disenchantment, even of Nasser himself, with the discredited and then newly-defunct British-sponsored democracy "played" by the King and the landed aristocracy. See Anwar al-Sadat, *In Search of Identity: An Autobiography* (New York: Fontana, 1978), p. 146.

[168] Ibid., p. 146.

[169] Ibid., p. 153.

[170] Jamal Abd al-Nasser, "The Morrow of Independence" in Abdel-Malek, *Contemporary Arab Political Thought*, pp. 76–7.

advocates. Nasser's "character assassination" of liberal democracy stemmed from his firm ideological standpoint of Arab socialism. In it resided his solution to "false democracy". Accordingly, he associated socialism with "justice", "social freedom", "a revolutionary march towards progress" and "an unavoidable fact of history".[171] He contrasted socialism's "social freedom" with false democracy's long association with exploitative capitalism and imperialism.[172] For Nasser: "Political democracy and political freedom alone are seen to be meaningless without economic democracy and social freedom."[173] The panacea was socialism, "the path of democracy, in all its political and social forms."[174] The rhetoric of Nasser, an autocrat by any standards, won him the admiration of a measurable segment of the Arab intelligentsia.

Kamāl Junblāṭ, the late Lebanese Druze leader and admirer of Nasser,[175] subscribes, more or less, to a similar theorisation of democracy. He, for instance, criticises the Universal Declaration of Human Rights (UDHR) for not being "synthetic" enough, and thus not adequately representative of various cultures and diverse peoples.[176] He sees it as being fundamentally particularistic, reflecting, in the first instance, the "dominant ideology", the will of its founding fathers.[177] He scorns the UDHR as not being too different from other "documents of bourgeois democracy…in which the individualist spirit supersedes that of the group".[178] Junblāṭ seeks a harmonisation between "authority and equality, morality and legality, individualism and communitarianism…between East and West, and tradition and modernity"[179] to constitute the essence of what he calls *al-dīmuqrāṭiyyatu 'l-sha'biyyah* (popular democracy). He does not reject all of the Western democratic heritage; especially not the institutional and procedural instruments of governance.[180]

171 Ibid., p. 77.
172 Ibid.
173 Ibid.
174 Ibid., p. 79.
175 See Kamāl Junblāṭ, *Aḥādīth 'ani 'l-ḥrriyyah: mukhtārāt* [*Speeches on Freedom: Selections*] (Al-Mukhtarah, Lebanon: Al-Dar al-Taqaddumiyyah, 1987), pp. 167–84.
176 Ibid., pp. 56–7.
177 Ibid., p. 56.
178 Ibid., p. 58.
179 Ibid., p. 56.
180 Ibid., p. 83.

However, he definitely rejects the Western bourgeois and liberal democracy in which the freedoms accorded to the individual are meaningless if, for instance, "millions of unemployed people cannot find work",[181] which he equates with security. Thus Junblāṭ argues that combining liberty with security is the answer to *al-dīmuqrāṭiyyatu 'l-ṣaḥīḥah* (genuine democracy).[182] He regards unfettered liberty as *fawḍah* (disorder). Therefore the individual's liberty must be delimited by the group's (whether Junblāṭ's feudal background has anything to do with this formulation is another matter).[183] He, for instance, values the role of the mass media for the working of a democracy. But he criticises concentration of media outlets, and their domination by commercial and capitalist interests. For him the bias that results from such concentration corrupts democracy. For manipulation of information leads to the concentration of power in an economic or political minority, a situation he likens to Lebanon's (which is a reference to the then-dominant Maronite interests).[184] The route to his *al-dīmuqrāṭiyyatu 'l-ṣaḥīḥah*, which is participatory, lies in the wedding of democracy to socialism.[185]

In his *Al-Kitābu 'l-Akhḍar* (*The Green Book*), Libya's Muʿammar al-Qadhāfī elaborates his so-called Third Universal Theory. Al-Qadhāfī applies one set of negative assumptions to examine the problem of democracy, and another of positive assumptions to solve that problem. Underlying his negative assumptions is that genuine democracy is nowhere extant, asserting that all political systems of the world are in fact dictatorships. He attacks parliamentary structures as "legal barrier[s] between the peoples and the exercise of authority";[186] "[r]epresentation [as] a denial of participation";[187] and periodic elections as "false external appearance[s]".[188] Why does al-Qadhāfī

181 Ibid., p. 84.

182 Ibid., p. 85.

183 Ibid., p. 122.

184 Ibid., pp. 122–3.

185 See how he remarks, "[N]o doubt democracy is in need of a true revolution through which we can achieve effective popular participation at all levels; and socialism itself needs to open up to a political system that completely guarantees such participation." Ibid., p. 126.

186 Muʿammar al-Qadhāfī, *The Green Book* (Tripoli: World Centre for Researches and Studies of the Green Book, n.d.), p. 7.

187 Ibid.

188 Ibid.

consider parliaments as "legal barriers" to direct self-government? First, he deems representatives to be "isolated from the people" given the large size of most electorates, and considers that parliamentary immunity turns parliaments into "means of plundering and usurping the people's authority".[189] Second, party politics means that parliaments are about representation of parties, not of peoples.

He dismisses political parties as "overt" instruments of dictatorship of the "part over the whole". For they are made up of interest groups with "a common outlook or a common culture",[190] and who are motivated by the common aim of empowerment. Thus democracy is the hegemony of the electorally-victorious interests. Al-Qadhāfī enumerates the drawbacks of the party system. First, the arbitrariness of such a system allows for the "domination" of a given set of party members over non-members, and even the people as a whole.[191] Second, multipartyism is divisive owing to the squabbling between those in power and those in opposition.[192] This is not only "stultifying", but is also inimical to the "higher and vital interests of society".[193] He dispels the notion of parliamentary opposition fulfilling the supervisory role of checks and balances, for it is primarily preoccupied with replacing the ruling party in office.[194] Here al-Qadhāfī indirectly invokes the Islamic notion of *fitnah* to discredit multipartyism. Third, parties, like votes, "can be bought".[195] Fourth, party politics makes both ruling and checking conflate in the hands of the majority party.[196] Fifth, partyism is similar to sectarianism: "The society governed by one party is exactly like that which is governed by one tribe or one sect."[197] The solution[198] resides in the institutions and the instruments of al-Qadhāfī's democracy—*al-jamāhiriyyah* (the state

[189] Ibid., pp. 7–8.
[190] Ibid., p. 11.
[191] Ibid., p. 12.
[192] Ibid.
[193] Ibid., p. 13.
[194] Ibid., p. 14.
[195] Ibid., p. 13.
[196] Ibid., pp. 14–15.
[197] Ibid., p. 15.
[198] Al-Qadhāfī writes: "*The Green Book* announces to the people the happy discovery of the way to direct democracy, in a practical form…Since no intelligent people can dispute the fact that direct democracy is the ideal—and since this Third Universal Theory provides us with a realistic experiment in direct democracy, the problem of democracy in the world is finally solved"(ibid., p. 26).

of the masses)[199]—are *al-mu'tamarātu' l-sha'biyyah* (popular congresses); *al-lijānu' l-sha'biyyah* (people's committees); and syndicates, professional associations, and unions. If al-Qadhāfī has discovered the way to genuine democracy, his *modus operandi* as a ruler cannot be said to reflect his implementation of that democracy.

In a 1992 speech before the democratically-elected National Assembly, the late King Ḥusayn of Jordan defined the constitution and its supplement, *al-mithāq al-waṭanī* (the National Charter) of 1992, as the legal frame of reference for the country's parties. He likened Jordan to an *usrah* (family) bound by what is akin to a "General Will"—*maṣlaḥatu 'l-waṭan* (the homeland's higher interest). He related *al-ḥiwāru 'l-'aqlānī* (the rational dialogue) in Jordan to the country's incipient democracy, warning against extremism, violence and fanaticism. He also insisted on majoritarian principles.[200] His speech stressed a number of democratic values and institutions that clearly underpinned his understanding of the form of pluralist polity he envisaged for his country.

> Our country has gone some way towards the consolidation of democratization, of institutionalization, and of building a state of laws wherein the citizen enjoys liberty, equality, justice and security. We have issued the law of political parties which will open the way for citizens to participate in politics via nationally-oriented parties with local objectives, instruments and funds.[201]

Morocco's late monarch, al-Ḥasan al-thānī (Hasan II), gave a vision of a crossbred democracy as an amalgam of paternalism, autocracy and

[199] In this system, the most basic structure is the popular congress. At the grassroots level *al-jamāhir* (the masses) form multiple basic popular congresses with each one having its own secretariat. The ensemble of these secretariats "form popular congresses, which are other than the basic ones". The people's committees which administer over government are directly chosen by the basic popular congresses, and are answerable to them. In al-Qadhāfī's participant democracy citizenship is fulfilled through the membership of popular congresses, the people's committees and workers' unions and associations. The General People's Congress (GPC) is the forum where the masses' concerns and the interests are finalised and aggregated only to be passed on to the people's committees for implementation. The GPC differs from a parliament in that it is claimed to be "a gathering of the basic popular congresses, the people's committees, the unions, the syndicates and all professional associations". See ibid., pp. 27–8.

[200] Al-Ḥusayn Ibn Ṭalāl Al-Hāshimī, *Khiṭābu 'l-'arsh fī iftitāḥi 'l-dawrati 'l-'adiyyati 'l-rābi'ah li-majlisi 'l-ummati 'l-urdunī 'l-ḥādī 'ashar* [*Crown's Speech: Opening of the Fourth Session of the Jordanian National Assembly, 1992*] (Amman, Jordan: 1 January 1992), p. 2.

[201] Ibid., pp. 2–3.

pluralism. He invoked the Islamic principle of *al-bay'ah* as a *'aqd ma'nawī* (spiritual contract) and a *ribāṭ khāṣṣ* (special bond) between the monarch and his *ra'āyā* (subjects).[202] He defined both in religious and paternalistic terms, a reciprocal family relationship with his *ra'āya*. *Al-bay'ah* makes every citizen a member of his *'ā'ilah* (family).[203] And being *amīru 'l-mu'minīn* (the commander of the faithful), it was his religious duty to consider himself an essential member of every Moroccan family.[204] He was his people's *khādim* (servant) and *malik* (king).[205] His personal "responsibility for the *maṣīr* (destiny) of every family is the best *ḍamānah* (guarantee) against injustice and despotism".[206] After all as the "commander of the faithful" he saw himself as a "shadow" and a "sword"[207] which are referents to his roles as protector and distributor of justice. He based these roles on the role of *amīru 'l-mu'minīn* "to uphold the *sharī'ah* and administer over temporal affairs",[208] rejecting the European medieval notion of divine right to rule.[209] He again invoked Islam in defining his brand of democracy, stressing Morocco's Islamic values and identity,[210] and arguing that democracy cannot trespass the boundaries of what is considered *ḥarām* in Islam. Since *ḥarām* relates mostly to moral issues, and with divine injunctions on political matters being rare, there was scope for democracy in Morocco.[211] He recognised the constitutionality of *al-ta'addudiyyatu 'l-ḥizbiyyah* (multipartyism), considering political parties as agents fostering socialisation. He saw it as fitting with Morocco's heterogeneous society.[212] King Ḥasan's democracy was a guided democracy:

> Democracy is granted in Morocco because I am the first to demand it… The word "grant" means "offer", and this carries no condescension for my

[202] Al-Ḥasan al-Thānī, *Dhākiratu malik* [*Memoirs of a King*], interviews by Eric Le Ran (n.p.: Kitab al-Sharq al-Awsat, 1993), p. 55.

[203] Ibid., p. 55. See also p. 60 where he refers to himself and his people as one family.

[204] Ibid.

[205] Ibid., p. 56.

[206] Ibid.

[207] Ibid.

[208] Ibid.

[209] Ibid.

[210] He banned the Communist Party because of its godlessness in the 1960s. See ibid., pp. 56–8.

[211] Ibid., p. 57.

[212] 'Irfan Niẓām al-Dīn, *Ḥiwārātun 'alā mustawā 'l-qimmhah* [*Interviews at the Leadership Level*] (London: Manshurat al-Mu'assassah al-'Arabiyyah al-urubiyyah li 'l-Nashr, 1988), p. 136.

people. Shouldn't my granting of democracy to my people be considered a noble deed?[213]

Other Arab leaders' usage of democracy copies Western conceptions. Egypt's Mubarak speaks of *siyādatu 'l-qānūn* (the Rule of Law) in his state.[214] He states that given the sovereignty of the law, he does not fear democracy.[215] Mubarak appreciates freedom of the press.[216] He concedes to the supervisory role of the opposition in parliament.[217] However, while he approves of multipartyism, and is open to the principle of an opposition, he clearly states: "If I find [the opposition] to act against the people I will oppose it".[218] He considers his role as president to be facilitated by *mu'assasāt dustūriyyah* (constitutional institutions).[219] In Tunisia, the post-Bourguiba ruling elite's rhetoric on political reform is similar to that found in Egypt. President Bin Ali speaks of his objective of *al-taṣāluḥu 'l-waṭanī* (national reconciliation), capitalising on the tolerance and homogeneity of Tunisians.[220] He declares the cornerstones of his democratisation to be *al-infirāj al-siyāsī* (political détente) and the building of *dīmuqrāṭiyyah ḥaqīqiyyah* (genuine democracy),[221] rejecting presidency-for-life as

[213] Ibid., p. 58. Compare with the approach of Saudi monarch King Fahd, who sees no scope for Western democracy in his country. He regards democracy to be contradictory to the Islamic *sharī'ah*. As to free elections he describes them not only "as not good for Saudi Arabia", but also as alien to Islam (see *al-'Ālam*, 425 [4 April 1992], p. 6). He points out that the fact that democracy works in the West does not necessarily make it meet with the same success elsewhere. He, however, notes that "there is no harm in learning from what is good over there providing that it is not against the tenets of our religion" (ibid.). *Al-majlis* (council), which is considered 'democratic' (see Niẓām al-Dīn, *Ḥiwārātun*, p. 237), remains a medium of contact between the rulers and the ruled. King Fahd has, according to Niẓām al-Dīn, encouraged his officials to use it in order to sound out the public on their concerns. He refers to it as *siyāsatu 'l-bābi 'l-maftūḥ* (open-door politics) (ibid.).

[214] Ibid., pp. 166, 197.

[215] Ibid., p. 197.

[216] Ibid., p. 166.

[217] Ibid., p. 175.

[218] Ibid., p. 197.

[219] He favourably compares himself to Syria's Ḥāfiẓ al-Asad noting that the existence of such institutions makes his pursuit of foreign policy objectives, especially with regard to the signing and honouring of international treaties, much more difficult. Cancelling the Camp David Accord with Israel, for instance, requires him to refer the matter to the people. Al-Asad, Mubarak implies, being the ruler of a personalist regime, "has absolute freedom" (ibid., p. 207).

[220] Ibid., p. 433.

[221] Ibid.

was his predecessor's tenure, and emphasising freedom of the press and multipartyism.[222] He envisages to build *dawlatu 'l-qānūn* (a state of law); *al-ta'addudiyyah, al-shar'iyyatu 'l-dustūriyyah* (constitutional legitimacy), and *al-tanāfusu 'l-ḥurr wa 'l-nazīh* (free and fair contestation) all crop up in his rhetoric.[223] The practice tells a different story.

Religionists

Religionists stand for an Islamic state. On the question of how Islam and democracy relate to one another, the theses set forth by religionists can broadly be divided into rejectionist and adaptationist. Here lies the clearest evidence of how Islam lends itself to variable interpretations. While both groups assent to the supremacy of Islam, they differ when it comes to reasoning on the relevance and adaptability of Islam to democracy. The former deny democratic principles and Islamic tenets to be compatible. The latter refer to Islam as being democratic, and/or see some grounds for reconciliation between the two.[224]

The position of the rejectionists is that Islam and democracy are incompatible.[225] They are usually seen to hold diametrically opposed ideological sources, sets of values, methods of political, economic, social and moral means of control, emphases and aims. Their presuppositions lead them to dismiss democracy as *kufr* (blasphemy). One religionist describes democracy as sacrilege since it violates the essence of deity: *al-ḥākimiyyah* (God's sovereignty).[226] *Al-ḥākimiyyah* thus contradicts democracy's popular sovereignty. He puts forth a number of points to illustrate his thesis. First, to divest God of His *ḥākimiyyah* and disregard *shar'* (Islamic law) and invest authority in

222 Ibid., p. 434.

223 Ibid., p. 436.

224 For an insight into some of the religionists' views see, for instance, details of a debate between them and secularists on the question of the secular state and the Islamic state in *Miṣr bayna 'l-dawlatu 'l-Islāmiyyah wa 'l-dawlatu 'l-'almāniyyah* [*Egypt Between the Islamic State and the Secular State*] (Cairo: Markaz al-I'lam al-'Arabi, 1992).

225 See the comparison between democracy and the Islamic principles of government by Salīm Al-Bahansāwī, *Al-Khilāfah wa 'l-khulafāu' 'l-rāshidūn bayna 'l-shūrā wa 'l-dīmuqrāṭiyyah* [*The Caliphate and the Rightly Guided Caliphs Between* al-Shūrah *and Democracy*] (Cairo: Al-Zahra lil-I'lam al-'Arabi, 1991), esp. pp. 63–70.

226 See "Al-dīmuqrāṭiyyah wasīlatun li iḥtiwā' 'l-ṭayyāri 'l-Islāmī" [Democracy: A Method to Contain the Islamic Current], *Al-'Ālam*, 357 (December 1990), p. 34.

people who are fallible goes against true *ijtihād*. Second, democracy and elections are a game that is calculated to contain the Islamic tide. Third, Islamic parties cannot contest elections with secular and unbelieving parties; in an Islamic state, contestation is permissible only between Islamic parties, with those winning office assigned with the administration of the *sharīʿah*. Fourth, non-use of violence to gain power is a repudiation of *jihād* and therefore is unacceptable.[227]

In a booklet entitled *Al-Dīmuqrāṭiyyah niẓāmu kufr* (*Democracy: A System of Unbelief*) ʿAbd al-Qādir Zallūm argues that democracy, in being *kufr*, is *ḥarām* for Muslims to practise or propagate it.[228] Zallūm argues that popular sovereignty and separation of politics and religion as in democracy are anti-Islamic.[229] He attributes moral decay (promiscuity, homosexuality, etc.) to democracy's personal freedom;[230] he finds freedom of religion, opinion, property and personal freedom to be contrary to Islam.[231] He shows how apostasy is forbidden in Islam; how freedom of opinion is regulated by the *sharīʿah* and what is *ḥarām* and *ḥalāl*;[232] how freedom of opinion as understood in democracy does not exist in Islam—there is instead compliance with *aḥkām al-sharʿ* (the rules of the *sharīʿah*);[233] and how in Islam freedom of property according to the liberal ethos is non-existent—enrichment through colonisation, exploitation of other peoples' resources, speculation, interest, gambling, the making and selling of wine, and through prostitution are *ḥarām*.[234] Zallūm contends that what is held to be the "General Will" in a democracy is nothing but the capitalists' will.[235] He rejects multipartyism, especially in that in the absence of an absolute majority either instability or dictatorship of coalesced minor parties prevails.[236] He concludes:

It is out of ignorance and distortion that one says that democracy comes from Islam, and that it is *al-shūrā* itself, the enjoining for what is good and

[227] For further details on these arguments, see ibid., p. 35.

[228] ʿAbd al-Qādir Zallūm, *Al-dīmuqrāṭiyyah niẓāmu kufr: yaḥrumu akhdhuhā aw taṭbīquhā aw al-daʿwah ilayhā* [*Democracy is a System of Unbelief: It is Forbidden to Adopt, Practice or Propagate*] (n.p.: n.p., 1990).

[229] Ibid., pp. 42–3.

[230] Ibid., pp. 20–4.

[231] Ibid., pp. 54–5.

[232] Ibid., pp. 55–6.

[233] Ibid., pp. 56–7.

[234] Ibid., pp. 58–9.

[235] Ibid., pp. 16–18.

[236] Ibid., pp. 18–19.

preventing what is reprehensible, and that it is holding rulers accountable. These are the rules of the *sharīʿah* that God sanctioned. Democracy is man-made, and it is not the same as *al-shūrā*…It is therefore forbidden on Muslims.[237]

Muḥammad Quṭb lauds such rights as of work and education, and the political freedoms that democracy have made possible, although asserting that these rights have been earned not granted.[238] However, he opposes democracy, considering its two facets (political liberalism and capitalism) to be part of one *luʿbah* (game) that causes *inḥirāf* (deviation) from God's path and His *sharīʿah*.[239] For Quṭb, capitalism with its profit motive, individualism, materialism and principles of "*laissez faire*" and "*laissez passez*" leads to many forms of *inḥirāf* ranging from exploitation of workers to social disintegration.[240] Hence, "Capitalism is the economic façade of liberal democracy which is itself the political façade of capitalism."[241] Quṭb implies that capitalism hides behind the gloss of political democracy, asserting that parliaments and parliamentarians and their laws are the very instruments which give capitalism free reign. Hence the real legislators are the capitalists themselves.[242] Accordingly, Quṭb appears to be convinced that it is impossible to adopt democracy without capitalism.[243] He believes that capitalists, being the owners of the mass media, are the real manufacturers of public opinion, and all other ideas that are amenable to their interests.[244] His critique sounds Marxist.

Quṭb takes his opposition to democracy a step further by describing it as both a *luʿbah* and a *masraḥiyyah* (play),[245] considering it a modern-day *jāhiliyyah*.[246] Under the guise of freedom this *jāhiliyyah* has, for instance, led to moral decadence. Democracy, Quṭb argues, is equally the game of *al-yahūdiyyatu 'l-ʿālamiyyah* (international Jewry).[247]

[237] Ibid., pp. 60–1.

[238] Muḥammad Quṭb, *Madhāhib fikriyyah muʿāṣirah* [*Contemporary Ideological Trends*] (Cairo: Dar al-Shuruq, 1987), p. 205.

[239] Ibid., pp. 203–205.

[240] Ibid., pp. 202–204.

[241] Ibid., p. 203.

[242] Ibid., pp. 203–205.

[243] Ibid., p. 204.

[244] Ibid., pp. 206–207.

[245] Ibid., p. 219, 224.

[246] Ibid., p. 218.

[247] Ibid., p. 218; Quṭb observes (p. 218, n. 2) that the Jews have also employed communism to achieve their own goals.

The Jews lead this *jāhiliyyah*.[248] And "Jewish capitalist interests mobilize political parties, parliaments, people's deputies, and the mass media" to achieve their own ends, such as the accumulation of gold which increases their domination over all people, and "the spoiling of people's faiths and morals" in such a way that their exploitation becomes easier.[249] This is done "through the slogan of freedom,"[250] and through the idea that "the further humankind is from religion, the more advanced they are".[251] Quṭb divides people in the democratic-capitalist *jāhiliyyah* into *sādah* (masters) and *'abīd* making *al-ẓulm* (injustice) its salient feature.[252] In this *jāhiliyyah* flourishes *shirk*, undermining God's *ḥākimiyyah* and consequently the Islamic principle of *al-tawḥīd*: "The dollar is a god; production is another... reason is a god...What is worshipped in liberal democracy is not Allah."[253]

Khālid al-Ḥasan[254] compares Islam, liberalism and communism concluding that Islam is *al-badīl* (the alternative).[255] The prominent *shi'ite* scholar, Faḍl-Allah,[256] observes that "when it comes to democracy and dictatorship, the latter is much worse; when it is a question of democracy and Islam, Islam is the only choice".[257] Although he

[248] Ibid., p. 221.
[249] Ibid., p. 220.
[250] Ibid.
[251] Ibid., p. 221.
[252] Ibid., pp. 225–6.
[253] Ibid., p. 230.
[254] Khālid al-Ḥasan is a prominent PLO member, and co-founder of *Fateh*. He is known for his Islamic tendencies.
[255] Khālid al-Ḥasan, *Ishkāliyyatu 'l-dīmuqrāṭiyyah wa l'-badīlu 'l-islāmī fi 'l-waṭani 'l-'arabī* [*The Problematic of Democracy and the Islamic Alternative in the Arab Homeland*] (Jerusalem: Wakalat Abu 'Arfah li al-Sahafah wa al-Nashr, 1988). See the table that compares Islam, liberal democracy and communism using 41 criteria, pp. 232–41.
[256] Muḥammad Ḥusayn Faḍl-Allah is the Lebanese Shi'ite spiritual leader of Ḥizbu'llah. For more insights into his views on whether democracy relates to Islam see, "Qirā'atun Islāmiyyah sarī'ah li-mafhūmayi 'l-ḥurriyyah wa 'l-dīmuqrāṭiyyah" [A Brief Islamic Reading of the Concepts of Freedom and Democracy], *Al-Munṭalaq*, 65 (Nisan 1990), pp. 4–21. Compare with al-Shaykh Muḥammad Mahdī Shams al-Dīn, Vice-president of the Supreme Shi'ite Islamic Council. His views on democracy are expounded in a booklet entitled, *Al-Malāmiḥu 'l-'ammah li lubnān fi 'l-nizāmi 'l-ṭā'ifi 'l-ḥālī wa niẓāmu 'l-dīmuqrāṭiyyah al-'adadiyyah al-qā'imah 'ala mabda'i 'l-shūrā* [*General Features of the Lebanon's Political System Under Sectarianism and Pluralistic Democracy on the Basis of* al-Shūrā] (Lebanon: n.p., 1985).
[257] Muḥammad Ḥusayn Faḍl-Allah, "Al-Islām wa 'l-dīmuqrāṭiyyah" [Islam and Democracy], *Al-Bilād*, 23 (January 1991), p. 54. See similar reflections by the same author

rejects democracy on the basis of popular sovereignty, he states that "*al-shūrā* is a point of reconciliation with democracy".[258] This reconciliation is not, he adds, with the ideological underpinnings of democracy, but rather with the democratic method. The democratic method, however, does not yield legitimacy. Legitimacy, for him, stems from the Islamic framework.[259] He contends that "the *imām* permits freedom to criticize the government".[260] Faḍl-Allah regresses on the question of multipartyism intimating that any "committed ideology does not give another the opportunity to overthrow it".[261] His reflections on democracy also smack of pragmatism. In a non-Muslim pluralist society, Islamists should support freedom regardless of its negative aspects. Here, he argues, the pros outweigh the cons.

> It is possible for us to win government through the democratic method, and adopting a few of democracy's elements is not necessarily symbiotic with recognizing their legitimacy. The question is to reach people and muster their support through them. As to the question of legitimacy, we...move through these channels to obtain legitimacy.[262]

The inputs of those religionists who reconcile democracy with Islam suggest that Islam has many foundations agreeable with democracy. Nonetheless the adaptationists' style is not highlighting so much the failings of democracy as the points where it intersects with Islam.[263] Their inputs constitute repudiations of the rejectionists' premises.

---

where he has occasion to comment on democracy, in "Awlawiyyatunā 'l-dukhūl ila 'l-'aṣr" [Our Priority is to Enter the Modern Age], *Al-'Ālam*, 425 (April 1992), pp. 36–7.

258 Ibid., p. 54.

259 Ibid.

260 Ibid.

261 Ibid. This view is very comparable to the one expressed by another Muslim scholar Muḥammad Ḥassan al-Amīn. He argues that the demand for democracy is reasonable in a Muslim society where Islam is not the source of law and government. But it is not in an Islamist state, for *al-shūrā* then takes precedence over democracy. See his article "Bayna 'l-shūrā wa 'l-dīmuqrāṭiyyah" [Between *al-shūrā* and Democracy], *Al-Munṭalaq*, 98 (Rajab 1993), pp. 39–49.

262 Ibid., pp. 39–40.

263 Adaptationists have no qualms whatsoever about applying the Western notion of democracy to Islamic concepts, practices or happenings. Thus 'Abd al-Salām al-Sukkarī describes as "history's greatest democratic debate" the public debate between the second Caliph 'Umar and Khālid Ibn al-Walīd, upon the latter's sacking as *wālī* (provincial leader) of al-Shām. Al-Sukkarī also criticises those Muslims and non-Muslims who see no compatibility between Islam and democracy, calling them "Islam's enemies". See 'Abd al-Salām al-Sukkarī, *A'ḍam ḥiwār dīmuqrāṭī fi 'l-tārīkh:*

Khālid Muḥammad Khālid equates Islam with being the pristine source of democracy, and *al-shūrā* with democracy.[264] He defines democracy as "that political system that establishes state-society relations on the basis of *al-ḥurriyyah* and *al-'adl*",[265] noting that democracy does not contradict the *sharī'ah*.[266] Khālid's earliest books on democracy such as *Min hunā nabda'* (*Here We Begin*), and *al-Dīmuqrāṭiyyah abadan* (*Democracy for Ever*) clearly distinguish between the religious and the non-religious state, making the latter a precondition for *al-madaniyyah* (civility). At the time, separation of religion and politics was a natural matter for Khālid. In *Here We Begin*, first published in 1950, he considers the concept of *al-waḥdāniyyatu 'l-muṭlaqah* (absolute oneness) to be incompatible with the principles of opposition and expression of opinion.[267] In *al-Dīmuqrāṭiyyah abadan*, Khālid goes as far as stating that "we can consider natural law as revealed law in that it aims at the same goals that revelation so desires and strives for",[268] observing how some 90 per cent of Islamic jurisprudence is man-made.[269]

He criticises those who reject democracy because it is an alien word and concept.[270] For Allah has not forbidden democracy, parliaments, free press, parties, or opposition as there are no Qur'ānic injunctions to that effect.[271] No authority can forbid what God has not forbidden.[272] Khālid finds no difference between borrowing the

---

'Umar Ibn al-Khaṭṭāb ma'a Khālid Ibn al-Walīd [*History's Greatest Democratic Debate*: *'Umar Ibn al-Khaṭṭāb with Khālid Ibn al-Walīd*] (Cairo: Al-Dar al-Misriyyah li 'l-Nashr, 1992). The late Muḥammad al-Ghazālī, one of the leading *'ulamā'* of Egypt, was open to learning and borrowing from democracy in order to "protect society" and fend off despotism See Muḥammad al-Ghazālī, *Azmatu 'l-shūrā fi 'l-mujtama'āti 'l-'arabiyyah wa 'l-Islāmiyyah* [*The Crisis of* al-Shūrā *in Arab and Islamic Societies*] (Cairo: Dar al-Sharq li al-Nashr, 1990), pp. 69–78. He views democracy as a synonym of *shūrah*. He is also open to democratic institutions, such as constitutions, and elections—the rigging of which he considers "high treason".

[264] Khālid, *difā'un 'ani 'l-dīmuqrāṭiyyah*, p. 191.

[265] Ibid.

[266] Ibid.

[267] See Khālid's own reflections on *Min hunā nabda'* in the introduction of one of his more recent books, *Al-Dawlah fi 'l-Islām* [*The State in Islam*] (Cairo: Dar Thabit, 1989), pp. 10–11.

[268] Khālid, *Al-Dīmuqrāṭiyyah abadan*, p. 145.

[269] Ibid.

[270] Khālid, *Difā'un 'ani 'l-dīmuqrāṭiyyah*, p. 191.

[271] Ibid., pp. 228–9.

[272] Ibid., p. 229.

Western-made airplane and Western democracy. The practice of democracy, he argues in a manner resonant of the early *nahḍāwiyyūn*, is a return to *al-shūrā*.[273] Although God has not specifically permitted democracy and there is no scriptural text on it, Khālid argues that through *ijtihād* it is not difficult to see that democracy is one with *al-shūrā*. He relates freedom of religion to the Qur'ānic injunction "*lā ikrāha fi 'l-dīn*" (there is no compulsion in religion).[274]

Others have found grounds to affirm how *al-shūrā*, both as a concept and as an institution, is compatible with democracy.[275] Fahmī al-Shannāwī uses the term *al-shūraqrāṭiyyah* (*al-shūrā*-cracy) instead of democracy.[276] The assumption that the *ummah* is the source of the ruler's authority leads al-Shannāwī to establish a parallel between ideal democracy and Islam: in both "the people stand above the ruler".[277] This implies that there is a form of popular sovereignty in Islam. The difference, however, is that in Islam God's law stands above both the *ummah* and the ruler.[278] Others have found grounds in the Qur'ān to show that multipartyism is permissible in Islam,[279] or that "it serves the cause of Islam better than the single-party system".[280] As Muḥammad Salīm al-ʿAwwā demonstrates, *ḥizb*, the Arabic term for party, recurs in the Qur'ān where there is mention of *ḥizbu Allah* (the party of God, i.e. of the faithful), and *ḥizbu 'l-shayṭān* (Satan's party, i.e. the unbelievers).[281] Al-ʿAwwā regards multipartyism to be

273 Ibid.

274 Ibid., p. 193.

275 See, for instance, Aḥmad Kamāl Abū al-Majd, *Ḥiwāru 'l-muwājahah* [*The Debate of Confrontation*] (Cairo: Dar al-Shuruq, 1988), esp. "Al-Shūrā wa 'l-dīmuqrāṭiyyah" [*Al-Shūrā* and Democracy], pp. 120–32.

276 Fahmī Al-Shannāwī, "Al-dīmuqrāṭiyyah wa 'l-shūraqrāṭiyyah" [Democracy and Shuracracy], *Al-ʿĀlam*, 380 (May 1991), pp. 36–7.

277 Ibid., p. 37.

278 Ibid.

279 A useful source is by Ṣalāḥ Al-Ṣāwī, *Al-taʿaddudiyyah al-siyāsiyyah fi 'l-dawlati 'l-Islāmiyyah* [*Political Pluralism in the Islamic State*] (Cairo: Dar al-Iʿlam al-Duwali, 1992).

280 See the argument made in favour of multipartyism by Fārūq ʿAbd al-Salām, *Azmatu 'l-ḥukmi fi l-ʿālami 'l-Islāmī* [*The Crisis of Governance in the Islamic World*] (Qalyub, Egypt: Maktab Qalyub li-Altabʿ wa 'l-Tawziʿ, 1981), esp. pp. 126–37.

281 Mention in the *Qur'ān* of *ḥizb* is both in a positive and negative sense. The *Qur'ān*'s silence on multipartyism, or for that matter on democracy, is according to the Islamic rule open to *ijtihād*, as silence means that it is neither permitted nor forbidden. See Muḥammad Salīm Al-ʿAwwā, "Al-taʿaddudiyyatu 'l-siyāsiyyah min manzūr Islāmī" [Multipartyism from an Islamic Perspective], *Al-ʿArabī*, 395 (October 1991), pp. 30–6.

permissible since it is in the Muslims' *maṣlaḥah*. Pluralism as al-ʿAwwā observes does not negate *al-tawhīd* or the unity of the *ummah*,[282] as there is scope for diversity within unity.

Mālik Bin Nabīy[283] begins his probing of democracy in Islam using a framework based on three-criteria: "(i) democracy as a *shuʿūr* (a feeling) towards the self; (ii) as a *shuʿūr* towards society; and (iii) as an ensemble of necessary social and political conditions to cultivate those attitudes in the individual".[284] Bin Nabīy's *al-insānu 'l-ḥurr* (the free person) is one who forsakes the attitude of domination, and the slave's attitude of submission.[285] These two *nāfiyatān* (negations) are essential *qiyam* (values) and *iltizāmāt* (commitments/obligations) for Bin Nabīy's democratic person.[286] The democratic person must, therefore, first be liberated from the legacy of submission and the *nazʿah* (instinct) of domination. For submission and domination are antithetical to democracy. He argues that democracy is not a mechanical political operation of "passing power to the people in accordance with the constitution".[287] For him *al-insān* has been ennobled to be God's representative on earth. *Al-Dīmuqrāṭiyyah fi 'l-Islām* (Democracy in Islam)[288] by ʿAbbās Maḥmūd al-ʿAqqād, a prominent Arab writer, speaks of *al-dīmuqrāṭiyyatu 'l-insāniyyah* (humanist democracy). Al-ʿAqqād distinguishes four principles that characterise Islamic democracy: (i) individual responsibility; (ii) equality; (iii) *al-shūrā*; and (iv) unity of the *ummah*.[289]

See also Muḥammad ʿUmārah, *Al-Islām wa Al-taʿaddudiyyatu 'l-ḥizbiyyah* [Islam and Multipartyism], *Al-ʿArabī*, 403 (June 1992), pp. 97–9.

[282] Al-ʿAwwā, "Al-taʿaddudiyyatu 'l-siyāsiyyah min-manḍūr Islāmī", p. 35.

[283] Mālik Bin Nabīy (1905–73) was an Algerian intellectual who received his tertiary education in France where he obtained an electric engineering degree in 1935. He was a prolific writer and strong defender of cultural relativism. He also had a strong humanist tendency that led him to advocate wider co-operation between Afro-Asian peoples.

[284] Mālik Bin Nabīy, "Al-dīmuqrāṭiyyah fi 'l-Islām" [Democracy in Islam], *Taʾammulāt* [*Reflections*] (Beirut: Dar al-Fikr al-Muʿasir, 1991), p. 68.

[285] Ibid., p. 70.

[286] Ibid.

[287] Bin Nabīy's analysis fits with the Islamic concept of God's oneness: all patronage is from God; and all submission is to God; and obedience to rulers is conditional on their distribution of justice according to the teachings of Islam. See *ibid.*

[288] ʿAbbas Maḥmūd Al-ʿĀqqād, *Al-Dīmuqrāṭiyyah fi 'l-Islām* [*Democracy in Islam*] (Beirut: Manshurat al-Maktabah al-ʿAsriyyah, n.d.).

[289] Ibid., p. 29. He shows how individual responsibility is implied in a number of Qur'ānic verses, asserting that the individual is accountable for both his/her own

Secularists

It is perhaps an exaggeration to refer to advocates of the separation of religion and politics in Arab polities as secularists. Their political rhetoric mixes the language of Marx, Mill or Rousseau with Qur'ānic parables and injunctions. It is worth noting that *al-'almāniyyūn al-'Arab* (Arab secularists) recurrently insist on the importance of separating politics and religion as a prerequisite for democracy.[290] Many activists who appear to be predominantly secular advocate the accommodation of religious forces in politics.[291]

Activists, both inside and outside the party system, have in the course of political wilderness, opposition, crises, and even persecution, developed a view of democracy that reflects learning from these experiences. The case of Egypt is instructive.[292] For Sayyid Mar'a, a veteran politician, democracy requires fair laws for political parties as parliamentarians do need channels of expression to reach the

---

"good" and "bad" deeds. Equality refers to equality of rights, of duties, and before the *sharī'ah*. The fact that Islam is for all humankind, he argues, is evidence of Islam's insistence on the relevance of racial equality (p. 31). *Al-shūrā* is consistent with the widely-held view that it approximates consultation in democracy. The *ummah*'s unity is a function of the individual's civic responsibility that facilitates and fosters cooperation, which is the *ummah*'s "general responsibility" (p. 31). Popular sovereignty, which is subsumed by God's (pp. 39–46); the mutual obligation between the ruler and the ruled and the latter's right to choose the former (pp. 47–51); political responsibility and consultation (pp. 52–60); social justice; moral responsibility; and a humanist law (pp. 83–86) are all ingredients that lead al-'Āqqād to call Islam's democracy *dīmuqrāṭiyyah khāṣṣah* (specific democracy), entailing political, social and economic equality, as well as *akhlāq dīmuqrāṭiyyah* (democratic standards of morality) (pp. 73–6).

290 'Abd-Allah Nu'mān, *Al-ittijāhātu 'l-'almāniyyah fi l-'ālami 'l-'arabī* [*Secular Trends in the Arab World*] (Junih, Lebanon: Dar Nu'man li al-Thaqafah, 1990), p. 15.

291 Munṣif al-Marzūqī, a Tunisian human rights activist, has repeatedly done so stressing the importance of dynamic associational life and pluralism. See Ḥasan Zīne Al-Dīn, "Ra'īsu 'l-rābiṭatu 'l-tūnisiyyah li 'l-difā' 'an ḥuqūqi 'l-Insān: Al-dīmuqrāṭiyyatu' l-ḥaqīqiyyah ghā'ibah wa nuṭālib bi ḥaqqi 'l-Islāmiyyīn ka ghayrihim fi 'l-tanẓīm" [The Tunisian Human Rights League President: Genuine Democracy is Absent and We Call for the Islamists' Right to Organize like Other Groups], *Al-Diyār* (12 February 1991), p. 12. Compare with the official stance expressed by al-Ḥabīb Boula'rās; see Usāmah 'Ajjāj, "Al-mustashāru 'l-Ḥabīb Boula'rās: Lā-majāla li ḥizb dīnī fi tūnis" [Presidential Adviser al-Ḥabīb Boula'rās: A Religious Party in Tunisia is out of the Question] *Al-Ḥawādith*, 23 March 1992, pp. 28–9.

292 See Ṭāriq Al-Basharī, *Dirāsāt fi 'l-dīmuqrāṭiyyati 'l-miṣriyyah* [*Studies in Egyptian Democracy*] (Cairo: Dar al-Shuruq, 1987); see also Aḥmad Ḥamrūsh, *Qiṣṣatu thawrat 23 yūlyū: Al-baḥthu 'ani 'l-dīmuqrāṭiyyah* [*The Story of the 23 July Revolution: The Search for Democracy*] (Cairo: Dar Ibn Khaldun, 1982).

populace; noting that rigging elections is non-democratic.[293] The President of *ḥizbu 'l-wafd* (the Wafd Party), Fu'ād Sirāj al-Dīn, associates democracy with the limiting of the ruler's powers and the legalisation and inclusion of all tendencies in the political game if they so desire.[294] He, along with others such as Muḥammad Turk, President of *al-ḥizbu 'l-ittiḥādī 'l-dīmuqrāṭī* (the Unionist Democratic Party),[295] insists that the head of state be non-partisan, and the ruling party and the state separate. Ḥāfiẓ, a former Free Officer (briefly) and a veteran member of the People's Assembly, recognises that democracy is best served by a freely-elected parliament and a democratic constitution.[296] Another, Ṣalāḥ Ḥāfiẓ, a prominent journalist, regards participation as one of the essential keys to genuine democracy.[297] He criticises, for instance, the grabbing for votes whereby the landed aristocracy receives those of the *fallāḥūn* (peasant-farmers), and the practice by candidates who seek support not directly from the people but from their patrons: the notables and the *al-'umad* (shire leaders).[298] Similarly, he sees "Egyptian society as not differentiated on the basis of interests but rather on the basis of clans, of tribes and of municipalities".[299] All these reflections sum up the Egyptian civil society's concern with what one activist calls *al-dīmuqrāṭiyyatu 'l-kāsiḥah* (sterile democracy).[300]

Experiences elsewhere revolve around similar issues. Al-Jāsim, who has served on the Kuwaiti National Assembly, quite strongly spelt out the idea that democracy is not a mode of governance that is open to manipulation. From his reading of the local political reality of democratic breakdowns he deduced that "democracy is a system of government…for the administration of state affairs", that must be sustainable.[301] Naqd of Sudan values democracy as pertinent to the

[293] Muḥammad Musṭafa, *Al-Dīmuqrāṭiyyah wa 'l-intikhābāt* [*Democracy and Elections*] (Cairo: Dar al-Ma'arif, 1990), pp. 7–23.

[294] Ibid., pp. 35–47.

[295] Ibid., pp. 195–204.

[296] Ibid., pp. 129–54.

[297] Ibid., pp. 161–75.

[298] Ibid.

[299] Ibid.

[300] Ismā'īl Ṣabrī 'Abd-Allah, *Miṣr allatī nurīduhā: Taqrīr siyāssī wa barnāmaj marḥalī* [*The Kind of Egypt We Want: A Political Report and a Gradual Programme*] (Cairo: Dar al-Shuruq, 1992), pp. 72–5.

[301] Muḥammad 'Abd al-Qādir al-Jāsim, *Al kuwait…muthallathu 'l-dīmuqrāṭiyyah* [*Kuwait…the Triangle of Democracy*] (Cairo: Matabi' 'l-Shuruq, 1992), p. 15.

consciousness of the working class, their organisation and protection.[302] Naqd, a communist, thus indirectly argues for the inseparability of democracy and socialism.[303] The socialists' search for such a balance has historically underlined the prevalent belief amongst Arab socialists that liberal democracy has little or no significance for the workers' freedom of choice and genuine political participation.[304] Arab leftists' definition of democracy gives precedence to the elimination of exploitation and the satisfaction of workers' needs,[305] whereby democracy becomes the route to socialism, not *vice versa*.[306] Arab secularists not only tend to treat democracy as a kind of universal religion but also give descriptions and definitions that are very closely modelled on the Western paradigm.[307]

Although nuanced, the notions and conceptions of Arab democracy point in one direction: the search for *al-dīmuqrāṭiyyatu 'l-ṣaḥīhah*. Today, while democracy along with religious nationalism suffuse Arab political discourses, socialism and pan-Arabism seem to have faded from such discourses. It is, however, both hazardous and premature to write the latter two off. Perhaps the fullest flowering of pan-Arabism, in particular, will emerge with the attainment of Arab democracy. Could future Arab democrats achieve the goal of Arab unity that has for so long eluded Arab autocrats? This vision, which is shared by many Arabs, was expressed by Kuwaiti lawyer Ḥamed

302 Muḥammad Ibrāhīm Naqd, *Qaḍāyā 'l-dīmuqrāṭiyyah fi 'l-Sudān* [*Issues of Democracy in Sudan*] (Cairo: Dar al-Thaqafah al-Jadidah, 1992), p. 17.

303 In the same vein, one Arab socialist views democracy in terms of an intersection that creates the necessary balance for coexistence between the forces of production, and those who own their means. See ʿAbd al-Razzāq ʿAid, *Naḥnu wa 'l-bīrūstūrīkah* [*We and Perestroika*] (Ladhikiah, Syria: Dar al-Hiwar li al-Nashr, 1991), pp. 70–1.

304 See Samīr Amīn's reflections on democracy, *Baʿḍu qaḍāyā li 'l-mustaqbil: Taʾammulāt ḥawla 'l-ʿālam al-muʿāṣir* [*A Few Questions for the Future: Reflections on the Challenges of the Contemporary World*] (Cairo: Maktabat Madbuli, 1991), esp. ch. 2, "Qaḍiyyatu 'l-dīmuqrāṭiyyah fi 'l-ʿālam al-thālith" [The Question of Democracy in the Third World], pp. 36–63.

305 ʿAziz al-Hajji, "Arab Nationalitarianism, Democracy and Socialism" in Abdel-Malek (ed.), *Contemporary Arab Political Thought*, pp. 166–8.

306 Ibid., p. 168.

307 ʿAbd al-Raḥmān Manīf, *Al-dīmuqrāṭiyyah awwalan, al-dīmuqrāṭiyyah dāʾiman* [*Democracy First, Democracy Always*] (Beirut: Al-Muʾassassah al-ʿArabiyyah li 'l-Dirasat wa 'l-Nashr, 1992), p. 26.

Juwān in 1991, at the height of the Iraqi-Kuwaiti crisis: "We believe in a united Arab world. But not unless it is a democratic Arab world. We will never accept unity under a dictatorship."[308] Al-Jābirī views democracy as a *ḍarūrah qawmiyyah* (pan-Arab necessity) as much as a national one.[309]

At least four conclusive remarks emerge from the above. First, the search for good government from the time of al-Fārābī to the present has constituted an endless series of efforts to harmonise *falsafah* with the Qur'ān, the *nomos* with the *sharī'ah*, the Greek *polis* with the Muslim *madīnah*, the philosopher with the *Imam, tajdīd* with *taqlīd*, *'aql* with *naql, ḥadāthah* with *aṣālah*, the individual with society, the will of the people with the Divine Will, the political with the economic, and the national with the pan-Arab. The result is a mélange of tension, failure and success. It is the ingredient of tension between so far seemingly irreconcilable historical and modern trends of thought and highly foundationalised knowledge traditions by which democratic narrative and political identities are shaped and constrained. Nonetheless, in the main in the *telos* (ultimate end) of happiness the ancient Greeks and Muslims had a common theme in their philosophies. The difference lay in the type of wisdom and the means for its translation into action they imagined and ordered toward its attainment. For the former, the conception of *eudaemonia* (happiness) centred around the cultivation of philosophical knowing and of wisdom. For the latter, as exemplified by al-Fārābī's philosophy, *sa'ādah* is dualistic: philosophical/theoretical/rational and religious/practical/imaginary. Philosophical midwifery alone cannot deliver the Muslim from either *jāhiliyyah* or tyranny. What is *eudaemonia* for the Greeks is *sa'ādah-sa'ādah* (happiness-happiness) for the Muslims, happiness in this world and the next, aided by the wedding of philosophy and prophecy, the virtues of the *polis* and of the philosopher-king with those of the philosopher-prophet in a Fārābian ideal state. Today, very few in the Arab and Muslim worlds, if any, can match al-Fārābī's success in producing a synthesis out of the dialectics of Muslim and non-Muslim brands of rationality.

[308] See Ḥamed Juwān, "Democracy, Not Dictatorship", *Washington Post*, 10 April 1991, p. A23.

[309] Muḥammad 'Ābid al-Jābirī, "Al-mas'alatu 'l-dīmuqrāṭiyyah wa 'l-'awḍā'u 'l-rāhinah fi 'l-waṭani 'l-'arabī" [The Democratic Issue and the Present Conditions in the Arab Homeland] *Al-Mustaqbal al-'Arabī*, 157 (March 1992), p. 13.

Second, and subsequently, the dialectics of the search for democracy, which began since the earliest encounter between Greek and Muslim philosophers with al-Fārābī's own search for the ideal or virtuous state, continue unabated in the AME. These dialectics were superbly documented by Malcolm Kerr in his 1963 essay, "Arab Radical Notions of Democracy".[310] The early 1960s, when Kerr wrote his treatise, coincided with the rise of revolutionary legitimacy. Pivotal to that revolutionary ideology was the promotion of a "radical concept of democracy" with constitutional liberalism being eclipsed from the Arab political landscape.[311] At the time, "revolutionary government [was] looked upon by its enthusiasts not as a path back to liberalism but on to a radically different form of democracy".[312] With the benefit of hindsight, revolutionary government has been nothing less than disastrous in the AME. Then the crux of the Arab radicals' conception of democracy, on the one hand, negated individualism, private interests and minimalist government, and, on the other, affirmed sociability, national interests and maximalist government.[313] It was a project of a hegemonic and homogenising state and nation-building. Arab radicals worked to a plan that gave democracy little or no chance to flourish in the AME:

> ...the Arab radical rejects the familiar Western assumption that the division of power and initiative in society among competing groups is inherently desirable, and that too much concentration of power in the hands of the state is a national threat to private right. For him, the essence of democracy is found not in the existence of a parliamentary opposition but in the creation of a socialist programme and the enlistment of mass support in implementing it.[314]

In the 1990s, it is Arab radicals and their conception of democracy which have "receded into the background", with liberal democracy presenting a relatively greater symbolic appeal. Third, the arguments mobilised in the past in favour of social and economic democracy at the expense of political democracy have been invalidated. There will be no return to "*khubz* (bread) now, the vote later", or what Nasser

310 See Malcolm Kerr, "Arab Radical Notions of Democracy", *Middle Eastern Affairs*, 3 (1963), pp. 9–40.

311 Ibid., p. 10.

312 Ibid.

313 Ibid., p. 11.

314 Ibid.

once called *dīmuqrāṭiyyatu 'l-khubz* (the democracy of bread).[315] As argued by al-Jābirī, Arab experience, one of authoritarianism, over-bureaucratisation, intellectual inertia and relative pauperisation, has proved the fallacy of such arguments. He shows enthusiasm for the Scandinavian model where political democracy has, according to him, led to a social democracy.[316] The idea of political democracy not only as a prerequisite for enacting all other reforms or for realising any *taḥawwulāt thawriyyah* (revolutionary transitions), but also as a prerequisite which no reform, no matter how profound, can succeed without, is today promoted by a large segment of the Arab intelligentsia.[317]

Finally, since the return of the discourses on the question and viability of Arab democracy corresponds with the Islamic *ṣaḥwah* (revivalism), the search for competing versions of *al-dīmuqrāṭiyyatu 'l-ṣaḥīhah* will further divide rather than unite secular and religious visionaries and polarise their polities and societies. Hence, the greatest challenge facing Arab democrats is not so much to enter into analytical and hermeneutic forays to prove themselves and delegitimise other versions as to open spaces in which power is neither fixed not singular in order to bring the Arab democratic project closer to fruition. For, the various Arab narratives of democracy share the characteristic of being quasi-"grand narratives" that over the past forty years have been implicated in doing a great deal of oppressing. From this perspective, these narratives continue to be locked into an imagining of politics that is teleological in its ideals and hegemonic and homogenising in its praxis. In the final analysis, these narratives may only reproduce the existing political praxis, one which is characterised by fixity and singularity rather than by fluidity and multipolarity.

Neither the opening of fluid and multipolar spaces in political practice nor the discursive advancing of the cause of good government everywhere in the AME can happen without women. Man and

315 From author's interview with Professor Aḥmad Shalabī, Dar al-ʿUlūm, Cairo University, 30 March 1993.

316 Al-Jābirī, "Al-mas 'alatu 'l-dīmuqrāṭiyyah wa 'l-'awḍāʿu 'l-rāhinah fi 'l-waṭani 'l-ʿArabī", p. 12.

317 Khidhr Zakariyā, "Ghābat ʿani 'l-maqālāt mas'alatu 'l-dīmuqrāṭiyyah" [The Absence of Democracy in Writings] in Marwah Karam *et al., Ḥiwārāt: mufakkirūn ʿArab yuḥāwirūn Karam Marwah fi 'l-qawmiyyah, wa 'l-ishtirākiyyah, wa 'l-dīmuqrāṭiyyah, wa 'l-dīn, wa 'l-thawrah* [*Arab Intellectuals Debate Karam Marwah on Pan-Arabism, Socialism, Democracy, Religion and Revolution*] (Beirut: Dar al-Farabi, 1990), p. 357.

woman remain an insoluble polarity in Arab and non-Arab societies. Harmonising man and woman in either a Godly-appointed system or a secular one is as challenging as harmonising reason and revelation. It is a challenge that democracy from Aristotle and Plato down to Rousseau and Hobbes has failed to rise to. But women everywhere are rising to the challenge of democratisation in the late 1990s. Arab women are no exception. The following chapter looks at how Arab women, regardless of their religious or national identities, are increasingly joining the formulators of a democratic narrative.

6

ARAB WOMEN AND DEMOCRACY

BREAKING OUT

> "To deprive woman of her civil rights constitutes not only an injustice towards her, but also a harmful obstacle in the path of the development and evolution of the people, a lacuna in the country's democratic process…It is frankly ridiculous to assert that the participation of women in parliament or other political offices would lead her to neglect her home… the enemies of woman are the fiercest enemies of democracy." —Injī Aflāṭūn, 1949[1]

> "We know that *dīmuqrāṭiyyat al-gharb* (the West's democracy) is a very recent phenomenon even if it dates back to the time of Plato. We know also that its practice has not historically been informed by its many positive and sound ideals; nor have such ideals been always informed by the practice. We know that non-Western cultures and peoples have not generally fared well with *dīmuqrāṭiyyat al-gharb*; nor have women. We in the Muslim world set to benefit from democracy if we are to defeat despotic rule, roll back mal-development, and all the perils that threaten our very existence. Our understanding of democracy does not ignore the fact that there are lessons to be learned from democratic experiences elsewhere. However, our understanding of democracy cannot also ignore our religion, culture, and other types of specificity."—Zakiyyah ʿAwaḍ Sātī, 1994[2]

Orientalist renderings of the woman question in the Arab and Muslim worlds have been like a baton with which to first hit Arab and Muslim cultures. For Muslim women are often depicted as counted

[1] Injī Aflāṭūn, "We Egyptian Women" in Margot Badran and Miriam Cooke (eds) *Opening the Gates: A Century of Arab Feminist Writing* (Bloomington: Indiana University Press, 1990), pp. 347–8.

[2] Author's interview with Zakiyyah ʿAwaḍ Sātī, 3 May 1994, Khartoum, Sudan.

out, veiled, suppressed, nameless, invisible, silent and disenfranchised. This chapter instead shows Arab and Muslim women as powerful agents of change, increasingly presenting intellectual, social, political and religious models in the AME. This refutes the conventional constructions of them as lesser entities lacking agency. The present focus on women's understandings of democracy is guided by the belief that political renewal in the AME will be incomplete without the inputs of women. Arab women's increasing visibility is contributing a great deal to the undermining of authoritarian rule. They have been part of a spreading grassroots resistance not only to Arab authoritarianisms but also to the dominant discourses, ideologies, knowledge practices and power politics that underlie them.

Scholarly treatment of the question of democracy in the AME tends to be limited when it comes to considering the contribution of Arab women to its discourse. Much of the current discourse on democracy and democratisation in the AME tends to be influenced by a state-centred approach. The impact of the resulting knowledge has been two-fold. First, alternative understandings are often marginalised with the very few exceptions on Islamic movements and women. Second, within this marginalisation, a prejudicial inclination caused by the ideological biases of secularism and liberalism tends to exclude Islamist women's knowledge of issues related to polity and society. The present chapter examines conceptions of democracy by Arab women, both secular feminists and partisan Islamists, with a special reference to the activism of Islamist women. Three issues arise: the theoretical background to the question of gender; the rise of "male feminism" in the AME; and the achievements of "Islamist feminists" in creating both political and discursive space within Islamic movements. Contrary to widespread scholarly and popular belief, it is argued that these achievements have brought harmony to the relationships between the processes and goals of Islamisation, feminisation and democratisation. Islamist women's own narratives support this position. The chapter draws on interviews with a number of female members from four Islamist movements: al-jabhah of Sudan; al-ʿamal of Jordan; Egypt's al-ikhwān; and al-nahḍah of Tunisia. The analysis, however, draws mostly on interviews with Islamist women from the first two movements.

One caveat is in order. The terms *nisā'iyyah* and *unthawiyyah* (feminism) and *nisā'ī* (feminist/of woman) pose philological problems in that they are not perfectly compatible with Euro-American paradigms. The meanings of these Arabic terms do not readily correspond to their approximated English counterparts. The epithet *nisā'ī*, for instance, while is used to refer to "feminist" is more readily understood to mean "of woman". In fact as many Arab women activists are from the middle-class, and are often polyglot, a number of them tend to use the French terms "*feministe*" or the English "feminist" as self-description. Margot Badran's term "gender activism" is indeed more applicable to the AME than "feminism".[3] Badran observes that women activists very often reject the feminist label for its imprecision, for its Western associations, for being considered "superfluous" or "heretical" by Islamist women, and ideologically unsound by socialist activists.[4]

Similarly, the term "Islamist feminists" is used here to describe female members of Islamic movements. It will be used interchangeably with the Arabic term "*islāmiyyāt*", literally meaning "Islamist women". This latter term is rendered here as "Islamist feminists" not because Islamist women profess to being feminists or anchor themselves in feminist thought, but rather because of the feminising effects of their politics. The term "Islamist feminists" is problematic for being made up of two words, neither of them easily definable. What qualifies as either "Islamist" or "feminist" is subject to competing interpretations and may therefore take more than one form. That which qualifies as "Islamist" can be polymorphous and is widely confused with negative ideas towards women. If both terms are sufficiently controversial as single words, they become even more so when joined. Accordingly, any treatment of the term "Islamist feminists" with disdain or caution should come as no surprise. The *islāmiyyāt* as a category of women stands out in more than one way: most have at least one university degree; they are not a class of battered or subordinated women and oppose such practices within the Muslim family; many are married to Islamist men who are equally active and educated; and they are committed to a rethinking of Islam. Because of who they are and what they represent, activism by the *islāmiyyāt* draws opposition from traditional Islamists.

[3] See Margot Badran, "Gender Activism: Feminists and Islamists in Egypt" in Valentine M. Moghadam (ed.), *Identity Politics and Women: Cultural Reassertions and Feminisms in International Perspective* (Boulder, CO: Westview Press, 1994), pp. 202–27.

[4] Ibid., p. 203.

THEORETICAL BACKGROUND

The feminist movement and theories emerged in the West around the same time as did movements for democracy. Women activists pointed out the limitations of existing democracies in the United States and several European countries. By the 1970s, most significant battles, especially in the legal sphere, were won, though equality was still some way off. The mid-twentieth century witnessed a period of crisis for Western feminism when there was a retreat. Since then, however, the movement regrouped itself and began to interrogate patriarchy more closely. It found links between power and masculinity, masculinity and war-making, sexuality and domination, and masculinity and episteme-making. This enquiry opened up new spaces for the women's struggle in the West and extended to critiques of conservative disciplines like International Relations (IR) in which women have been absent.[5] So effective has been the movement that it has forced gender and sexuality issues into the mainstream and made political correctness contingent on the recognition of these issues.

Since the exercise of patriarchal power in the West was evident in decentred locales, in advertising and other hidden places, its questioning had to be equally sophisticated. Correspondingly, the various projects of feminist scholarship have been both deconstructionist and reconstructionist. They challenge the logocentrism and androcentrism of the conceptual frameworks of many disciplines and their epistemological, ethical and political grids. They equally interrogate sex, class, cultural imperialism and race, amongst other forms of subjugation, inherent in Western social structures as well as methodologies of knowledge-making. These challenges are essentially consonant with deconstructing the supportive and reinforcing cultures and values of many branches of Western knowledge that have for so long not only helped construct exclusionary processes but also define "otherness". From this perspective, these challenges amount to concerted efforts to revise the history of, as well as discredit, the Western "phallocentric" modernity project. At the core of reconstructionism is the development of alternative and progressive forms of knowledge-making and emancipatory epistemological, moral, social and political meanings and practices.

[5] See Fred Halliday, "Hidden from International Relations: Women and the International Arena" in R. Grant and K. Newland (eds), *Gender and International Relations* (London: Open University Press, 1991).

Since these feminist theories originated in the West, they reflected the social and cultural background of the writers and activists and the nature of the specificities in which they found themselves. The same historical condition (nuclear family, separation of church and state, advanced capitalism, marriage patterns) did not obtain in the developing world, including the AME. Western feminist ideas could not be generalised without modification or elaboration elsewhere. They were found lacking in the context of the Middle East and met with open hostility even by Islamist women activists. Western feminism was deemed to be informed by value-laden epistemological programmes, guided by inadequate concepts and conceptualisations that defied transplantation, and marred by a misunderstandings of Islam, Arab cultures and traditions. For interviewee Islamist women, a number of Western feminist critiques employing gender as an analytic category were simply engaged in their own patriarchal-like knowledge-making, exclusion, racism and cultural imperialism. This is certainly true of the early homogenising and hegemonic Western feminism. It was clear that the gender question ought to be culturally situated, which it was not in the Western discourse. Further, oversimplification of gender relations between Arabs in the context of a globalising world and predatory international political economy gave rise to new forms of power relations that created additional conditions of subjugation and disempowerment.

Women activists and thinkers in the AME, have, like their sisters in the rest of the developing world, retained a critical relationship with Western feminism. Though, within the international women's movement this recognition of divergent goals has meant a setback to the notion of universal sisterhood, efforts to reconcile differences are evident in global fora. However, even overtly, there is acknowledgment that women unite in oppression, even though the form of oppression may vary. Feminists converge when it comes to the processes that shape gendered societies. Hence social life is construed in logocentric terms dichotomising between what is perceived to be superior man/masculinity and inferior woman/femininity. This logocentric symbolism influences the allocation of roles and values in society. Feminist critiques evoke these processes when explaining the status of women in the AME. Here the problematisation of the gender question tends to eschew all notion of relativism.[6] With their

[6] See, for instance, Melville J. Herskovits, "Cultural Relativism and Cultural Values" in John Ladd (ed.), *Ethical Relativism* (Belmont: Wadsworth, 1973); see also Bimal

Western value-frameworks many critiques have often engaged in unchecked Orientalisation. Leila Abu-Lughod critiqued a number of those prejudiced accounts of the gender question in the AME.[7] The gender question in such works is too often reduced to what Abu Lughod calls "harem theory",[8] or to a synonym for the profanation of Islam. For the contrast is, for instance, stark between how andro-centrism in the West is attributed to no religious factors and how those in the AME are imperfectly correlated with Islam. Thus Algerian scholar Marnia Lazreg, while recognising the role played by Islam in gender relations, doubts the explanatory power of the religious paradigm:

> With few exceptions gender inequality is attributed to Islam's presumed influence upon the lives of women and men in North Africa and the Middle East. The unstated assumption is that religion is at once the cause of and the solution to gender inequality. Somehow, if religion is done away with, equality between men and women will ensue. Yet it is hardly necessary to point out that in societies where religion has been forcibly suppressed from the political and social spheres gender equality has not ensued.[9]

Inconsistencies of this kind engender stereotypical Orientalisms of an imagined Orient which is static and where the oppression of women is taken to be universal and unchanged. Lazreg again observes that "western gynocentrism has led to an essentialism of otherhood". Everywhere women have been both oppressors and oppressed. The woman question needs to be disaggregated. Class, region, family, education and affiliation would in all probability show women in the AME, to be as disparate as anywhere else. Women are not a unitary category. More men are indeed in positions of power than women. But even if numerically inferior, there are many women who are far more empowered than both most men and most women. The male–female dichotomy does not always account for the full gamut of power relations in any society. Society is more heterogeneous than sex differences would imply.

Krishna Matilal, "Ethical Relativism and Confrontation of Cultures" in Michael Kraus (ed.), *Relativism: Interpretation and Confrontation* (Nortre Dame University Press, 1989).

[7] Leila Abu-Lughod, "Zones of Theory in the Anthropology of the Arab World", *Annual Review of Anthropology*, 18 (1989), pp. 267–306.

[8] Ibid.

[9] Marnia Lazreg, "Gender and Politics in Algeria: Unraveling the Religious Paradigm", *Journal of Women and Culture and Society*, 15 (summer 1990), p. 756.

Research is yet to venture into the extent to which women who are co-opted in a power-holding elite, political or epistemological, lend support to the reproduction of patriarchy and concomitant forms of oppression over both men and women, and the marking of otherness. No matter how implicated patriarchal structures are in processes of oppression, they could not have sustained themselves for so long without some backing from at least a small fraction of the female population in societies with oppressive regimes. Male domination must have been partly reproduced by enlisting the support not only of fellow men but also compatriot women—"state feminism" in the words of Hatem. The various national women's associations that were cemented to the state and its authoritarian structures cannot be absolved of lending legitimacy and paying deference to autocrats in the AME. The members of those associations, who identified with the national-secular postcolonial order, swore allegiance to its ideals and became integrated into its power structures. They could not have done so without the full knowledge that the systems they were part of were engaged in suppressing many of their compatriots, including those women their associations meant to represent and protect. Strongmen like those in Libya and Iraq, oppressors by any standards, are referred to as "women's liberators". Wherever there is violence or oppression, there are degrees of complicity with the oppressors. Feminists may and do justifiably decry patriarchy and its disempowerment of women. Women, through connections with authoritarianism, are not completely neutral as far as the history of oppression is concerned even if prime responsibility rests with male-dominated power structures, and male-oriented practices and discourses of power. These links, though covert, further oppression.

At the discursive level, the woman question has noted the silence of many disciplines on it, such as in IR. Nor has it figured much in discourses on democracy and citizenship until fairly recently. Women were also hidden in classic notions of democracy as they were marginalised in the Greek *polis* where the prototype form of *demokratia* was conceived. Neither Enlightenment nor the generation of post-Enlightenment philosophers and political theorists that shaped Western political tradition concerned themselves with the woman question. John Stuart Mill's *The Subjection of Women*,[10] which remained

[10] John Stuart Mill, *The Subjection of Women*, ed. by Susan Moller Okin (Indianapolis: Hackett Publishing Company, 1988).

neglected until the "rebirth of feminism" in the 1960s,[11] stands as the only significant work of feminist theory written by a major male philosopher—his wife is known to have influenced the work.[12] Generally, however, the silence of Enlightenment political thought on women represents a form of knowledge production that has for so long reduced women to non-entities, objects without moral or intellectual worthiness. Implicit in this is the binary epistemology evident in the narrative of Enlightenment. In this narrative, Western man, his values, thought and rationality, are placed at the centre of the universe and all that contradicted it at the periphery. As knowledge production and as practice, Enlightenment is another sequel in the ontology of domination of woman by man. The result has been a man-centred modernity continuously recreated in the image of Western man who has arrogated to himself a higher status. The rest—women, Orientals or blacks—is simply the "other", "objects" of lesser being, thinking and doing. The notion of women as the "other" finds its most eloquent expression in *The Second Sex* by Simone de Beauvoir. In questioning androcentrism and its "othering" of women, de Beauvoir also interrogated socialist feminists' class reductionism which implicated capitalist economics in the subordination of women. For her, multiple dimensions ranging from social to cultural, account for women's subjection.[13]

However, the silence on women that has pervaded Western political theory for so long is being rolled back. Feminists of all political and intellectual shades have forced a questioning of man-centred binary epistemologies and practices. Feminism and postmodernism, however defined, are useful paradigms of contemporary critical thought on democratic theory and polity. Like postmodernists, feminists have for some time interrogated Western democracy, and with it modernity, from which they have been erased. Feminists have sought to do this by highlighting the gendered content and practice of politics, namely, citizenship in democratic states. Anne Phillips foresees the end of gendered politics and gendered democracy, with their inherent inequalities between the sexes, in the redefining of citizenship and in the revamping of representativeness so as to equalise between men and women.[14] Iris Young, acknowledging and

[11] See editor's introduction in ibid., p. v.

[12] Ibid., p. v.

[13] Simone de Beauvoir, *Le Deuxième Sexe* [*The Second Sex*] (Paris: Gallimard, 1949).

[14] Anne Phillips, *Engendering Democracy* (Cambridge: Polity Press, 1991).

challenging the exclusiveness of politics to dominant groups and the limits of the "common good" given the compound of group identities, differences and interests in society, makes a case for a cosmopolitan democracy in which the partiality of representation and justice, and the cultural oppression of the disempowered and the invisible, such as women, cease.[15] In fact, most feminist/postmodernist scholars find a symbiosis between patriarchy and democracy. Hence, for instance, Carole Pateman's critique of the male-structured social contract theory. She deconstructs contract theory by highlighting the links between employment and conjugal contracts, with the former presupposing the domination and possession of women in the latter.[16] These contractual relations of domination render the public–private dichotomy no more than an unnatural and arbitrary convenience for a male-oriented society that marginalises women economically and politically. Thus:

> Without the sexual contract there is no indication that the "worker" is a masculine figure or that the "working class" is the class of men. The civil, public sphere does not come into being on its own, and the "worker," his "work" and "working class" cannot be understood independently of the private sphere and his conjugal rights as a husband. The attributes and activities of the "worker" are constructed together with, and as the other side of, those of his feminine counterpart, the "housewife."[17]

Furthermore, Pateman argues that not only is capitalism male-structured, so is the whole sphere of civil society.[18] If civil society is patriarchal, the type of democracy that is conceived within it cannot but be male-oriented. The achievement of political equality ends up being the bastion of men, leading to a form of citizenship in which men are more equal than women; and this inequality is the antithesis of democracy:

> The idea of universal citizenship is especially modern, and necessarily depends on the emergence of the view that all individuals are born free and equal to each other. No individual is naturally subordinate to another, and all must thus have public standing as citizens that upholds their self-governing status. Individual freedom and equality also entail that government

[15] Iris M. Young, *Justice and the Politics of Difference* (Princeton University Press, 1990).

[16] Carole Pateman, *The Sexual Contract* (Cambridge: Polity Press, 1988), p. 131.

[17] Ibid., p. 135.

[18] Ibid., p. 38.

can arise only through agreement or consent. We are all taught that the "individual" is a universal category that applies to anyone or everyone, but this is not the case. "The individual" is a man.[19]

If democracy and political rights are male-oriented, it is because the texts of its theories belonged to a pantheon of thinkers for whom man was the only referent and woman was always absent. Almost a decade before Pateman, Susan Okin hit at the woman-blindness of Western political thought:

"Human nature," we realize, as described and discovered by philosophers such as Aristotle, Aquinas, Machiavelli, Locke, Rousseau, Hegel and many others, is intended to refer only to male human nature. Consequently, all the rights and needs that they have considered humanness to entail have not been perceived as applicable to the female half of the human race. Thus there has been, and continues to be, within the tradition of political philosophy and political culture, a persuasive tendency to make allegedly general statements as if the human race were not divided into two sexes, and then either to ignore the female sex altogether, or to proceed to discuss it in terms not at all considered with the assertions that have been made about "man" and "humanity".[20]

Pateman finds women in contract theory to be "civilly dead"; in fact, all that is "civil", pertains to "civility" or to the realm of "civil society", women are excluded from or are constructed as its opposite. Furthermore, the conception of civil society presupposes domination and control of women.[21] Women' biology becomes a marker of difference, a device of exclusion from citizenship, rationality or individuality, and a mechanism for male monopoly of civic activities, as Okin puts it.[22] Hence the public/private dichotomy which serves to perpetuate male-structured and oriented polity and economy. Thus directly and indirectly Okin and Pateman cast doubt on the universality of rights, citizenship and the whole project of Western liberalism and democracy. It is a project by men and for men. This has been possible through a series of oppositions premised on male constructs of who qualifies for the label "citizen" or "individual". Pateman argues

[19] Pateman quoted in Chantal Mouffe, "Radical Democracy: Modern or Postmodern" in Andrew Ross (ed.), *The Politics of Postmodernism* (Minneapolis: University of Minnesota Press, 1988), p. 35.

[20] Susan M. Okin, *Women in Western Political Thought* (London: Virago, 1980), pp. 6–7.

[21] Pateman, *The Sexual Contract*, p. 102.

[22] Okin, *Women in Western Political Thought*, pp. 274–5.

that the very meaning attached to the term "individual", a shorthand for "man", would collapse should the oppositions—natural/civic/, private/public, women/individual, and sex/gender—that sustain civil society in contract theory disappear.[23] Other universals like liberty and equality are themselves premised on the subjection of women in the marriage contract. The universality of liberty and equality as civil rights is doubtful because they are attributes of the males who create the social order in their own image; fraternity is no more than a charade, in reality a brotherhood of males, not a community of equals.[24]

Classic theorists, with the exception of Mill, bequeathed to the Western world contradictory theories of civil society and democracy. On the one hand, they place high value on liberty, equality, rule of law and citizenship. On the other, the authors of these theories understand women in a functional way which make them unable to enjoy fully the rights bestowed upon men by membership of political community. This exclusion from the entitlements of membership of the legal community is based on one factor, being of the female sex. This implies that women, Okin argues, are deficient and inferior in rationality.[25] This is as true of Aristotle as it is of Rousseau. The former's political philosophy is one of functionalism, explains Okin, whereby political equality for free males requires inequality for women, amongst others. The disenfranchised groups "exist in order to perform their respective functions for the few free males who participate fully in citizenship".[26] Rousseau founds his republicanism on the necessity of civic participation. But this self-evident right that is so internal to Rousseau's republic turns out not to be all that self-evident or universal. For, "the private sphere of family life is crucial for him…as a highly important aspect of affective life".[27] The existence of a private sphere as a realm for women enables male monopoly of the public sphere. The flaws in political community and civil society lie in the prism through which the male icons of Western political philosophy configured their theories. Pateman writes:

> The story of the original contract tells a modern story of masculine political birth. The story is an example of the appropriation by men of the awesome

[23] Pateman, *The Sexual Contract*, p. 225.
[24] Ibid., p. 114.
[25] Okin, *Women in Western Political Thought*, pp. 276–7.
[26] Ibid., p. 276.
[27] Ibid., p. 277.

> gift that nature has denied them and its transmutation into masculine political creativity. Men gave birth to an "artificial" body, the body politic of civil society; they create Hobbes' "artificial Man, we call a Commonwealth", or Rousseau's "artificial and collective body", or the "one body" of Locke's "Body Politic". However, the creation of the civil body politic is an act of reason rather than an analogue to a bodily act of procreation...The birth of a human child can produce a new male or female, whereas the creation of civil society produces a social body fashioned after the image of only one of the two bodies of humankind.[28]

Muslim women have never subjected Qur'ānic scriptures to the kind of gender-based re-examination of classic theory and political philosophy undertaken by Western feminists. Generally, Muslim women tend to revere these orthodox texts even when their notions of political community are founded on liberal dogmas like secularism and individualism. Whereas Western feminists interrogate classic theories of political community for being hidden from them or subsumed under a humanist discourse of citizenship or civil society imaged by men and for men, Muslim women and feminists can only question that fragment of Islam which is man-made, namely, *fiqh*. Their problem is not with Islam but with those learned male scholars whose interpretations of the texts exclude women from polity and determine their place in society. The kind of questioning, much less apostasy, Westerners tend generally to show towards Enlightenment-based knowledge and narratives is not possible within Muslim societies. Westerners do not cease to be democratic by re-examining or destabilising classic theories. By contrast, Muslims who attempt to destabilise the divine texts risk apostasy or accusations of apostasy, an act of *khrūj* (secession) from the community of believers.[29] This can destabilise identity itself, especially in Muslim societies where religion remains one of its strongest markers. The example of Bangladeshi writer Taslima Nasreen, accused of putting forth ideas about revising the Qur'ān, is a case in point.[30] Muslim women's quarrels are therefore with the expounders of the divine texts and the *ta'wīl* many male learned scholars fall into. It is through this tool that the world of women is constructed and organised, inevitably engendering a

[28] Pateman, *The Sexual Contract*, p. 102.

[29] But the accusations are first made by interpreters of the Qur'ān; also, such pronouncements may be more politically than religiously based.

[30] See Bruno Philip, "Taslima Nasreen, romanicere maudite du Bangladesh", *Le Monde* (30 December 1993), pp. 1, 4.

gendered subjectivity. This kind of misinterpreting of the orthodox texts rests on hiding women and on "veiling" their rights in Islam. Three generations of Arab female activists have since the turn of the twentieth century attempted to deconstruct and destabilise that part of *tafsīr* (exegesis) that has tended to privatise and marginalise women.

The *mufassirūn* (jurists/expounders of orthodoxy) is one of three types of masculinity that Muslim women have quarrelled with. The second is nationalist masculinity which hijacked the project of national liberation. In so doing, it corrupted it through exclusive politics and totalising discourses. The third type is Western masculinity—the colonial man. This masculinity revealed itself under civilisational and universalising guises. Here too the nobility of the mission of universalising Western civilisation seemed self-evident only to the Western man. The political arrangements in the colonies mirrored those of the metropoles. The fraternities of contractarians had analogues in the power congeries of *colons* and local aristocrats. Formerly colonised societies may be likened to disenfranchised women in England, or France under the sexual contract. In a word, the political orders that the colonisers set up epitomised the dominative and exclusive practices characteristic of the metropoles' civil societies. If humankind represented a society, then under colonialism the metropoles were its free males—synonyms of civilisation, rationality and attributes of liberty and equality, a realm of civility; the colonies were its females—realms of barbarity. The domination and exploitation of the latter were required to sustain the former just as contractual theory or Aristotle's ideas on women presupposed female "denizenship" to maintain male citizenship. Whereas Arab and Muslim women's contempt for or caution *vis-à-vis* Western liberty and equality are inextricably linked to colonialism, those of Western women are directly related to sexism. Neither, however, has given up on liberty or equality. Both endeavour to refashion them into their own images, taking into account their histories of subjection, personal and communal sensitivities, and ideological preferences.

There is an overlap in women's politics of protest against exclusion and subjection all over the world. Although many *islāmiyyāt*, for instance, can be disdainful of Western feminisms, they still recognise that women's protests and struggles form common platforms around which transnational and transcultural solidarities resist discrimination and oppression everywhere. Not even the octogenarian Zaynab al-Ghazālī, whose activism in the ranks of Egypt's Muslim Brethren spans some 50 years, denies a form of a singular space of shared positions, morals, protests and struggles binding women everywhere:

> We share God's Earth as the children of Adam and Eve. Western women may not be Muslim; they speak tongues different from Arabic; and the colours of their skins may look different from ours. But they are no less moral than Muslim women. Like us, many of them did in the past oppose colonialism and the *ghaṭrasah* (arrogance) of Western colonial men. Today many of them engage in resistance against war, prostitution and exploitation in the Third World...These women are our sisters in humanity but not in Islam.[31]

Zaynab al-Ghazālī's view is shared by many other *islāmiyyāt*. Uṣāl al-Mahdī, the great-granddaughter of Imām al-Mahdī of Sudan, the man who fought the British and once defeated them in the late-nineteenth century, observes that her knowledge of many Western women confirms their strong moral opposition to colonialism and neocolonialism. She notes that hundreds of thousands of them stand in solidarity with Arab women on questions ranging from the Israeli occupation of Palestine to the politics of hegemony and interventionism in the Arab world.[32] Rubā al-Farkh, an Islamist from Jordan, records that the voices of Western women against violence and destruction in the Middle East in 1991 were amongst the loudest. She posits Western women's humane solidarity with the region and its peoples against the inhumanity of the European man whose illiberal history in the region tells a story of subjection and exploitation.[33] The focus on *al-rajulu' l-urūbbī* (the European man) or *al-musta 'mir* (the *colon*) in both male and female discourses is more than a strategy for keeping alive the history of the encounter with colonialism. It is a strategy for exposing the contradictions embedded within the European man's thought and practices. Thus prominent Sudanese Islamist and parliamentarian Zakiyyah 'Awaḍ Sātī identifies four attributes of European masculinity which contradict its lofty ideals of democracy, equality and liberty: colonialism; racism; Orientalism; and sexism. She tests the European man's claim to *'aqlāniyyah* (rationality) against his practices of colonialism and genocide, neither of which she finds to be compatible with democracy or liberty. She also

31 Author's interview with Zaynab al-Ghazālī, 11 April 1994, Cairo.

32 Author's interview with Uṣāl al-Mahdī, 3 May 1994, Khartoum.

33 Author's interview with Rubā al-Farkh, 11 June 1994, Amman.

describes the European man's rationality as Orientalist because it rests on holding non-European peoples to be culturally inferior. Artistic and literary representations of Muslim women reducing them to Harem artefacts and objects are some of its products which do injury to Islam and Muslims, she argues. For her these practices exemplify the outward symptoms of *tamyīz ʿunṣurī* (racism).[34] The colonial syndrome intertwines with gender, religion and nationalism, contributing to women's understandings of democracy in the AME.

The "woman question" has a practical side. A great deal is being done about gender equity, especially in the political sphere. Women's solidarities forged across borders of states, bureaucracies, cultures, languages and masculinities are setting the agenda for eroding male monopolistic decision-making. Since the United Nations General Assembly adopted the Declaration on the Elimination of all Forms of Discrimination Against Women (CEDAW) in 1967, women have increasingly gained visibility and agency. Instruments for making women's participation real are today too numerous to list. Worthy of mention are avant-garde NGOs such as the New York-based Women's Environment and Development Organization (WEDO) and the International Women's Tribune Centre (IWTC). WEDO's 1991 conference "World Women's Congress for a Healthy Planet", held in preparation for the 1992 Rio UN Conference on Environment and Development, produced a visionary document for the future, *Women's Action Agenda 21*. Such activism demonstrates that the women's agenda encompasses issues of the sustainability of development and the environment. Nonetheless, its main item is women's participation in decision-making, nationally and internationally. For women to introduce a humane voice into world governance, they have to be able to represent their differences and bring their "otherness" out of the margins of exclusion. From Cairo (the 1994 International Conference on Population and Development) through to Beijing (the September 1995 Fourth World Conference on Women and NGO Forum on women) and Rome (the November 1996 World Food Summit), the larger international women's movement has forced a rethinking of gender relations, female participation and justice. The UN policy process has been most responsive to this trend. The final communiqué of its Fourth World Conference on Women addresses gender

[34] Author's interview with Zakiyyah ʿAwaḍ Sātī, 3 May 1994, Khartoum.

equity, insisting on equal political participation for women. World parliaments are called upon to raise the number of female deputies by implementing a 30 per cent quota system. Similar demands for equal political participation are also made in the Beijing Declaration of Indigenous Women.

The achievements of the larger international women's movement have influenced many nations and regions, including the AME. Initiatives have come from both state and society. Others, like the founding in 1997 of the Arab Permanent Court Against Violence Against Women, are forged within a pan-Arab framework, attesting to an emerging pan-Arab civil society. Women's groups, working with the Arab League, the Centre for Arab Women for Training and Research and with Jordan's National Committee for Women's Affairs which is chaired by Princess Basma, held a regional conference in November 1994 in preparation for the Beijing Fourth World Conference on Women. The result was the adoption of an "Arab Plan of Action for the Advancement of Women to the Year 2000". This document shows that Arab women have a clear vision of how to think and act locally and globally in order to improve their lot. If implemented, the document's recommendations should set the scene for more equal gender relations in the AME.[35] To this end, the Arab Parliamentary Union promoted the cause of gender equality by sponsoring and organising the first symposium for Arab female members of parliament in February 2001 in Damascus.[36]

Society-based initiatives have given rise to a number of organisations and conferences. These have been instruments and fora for Arab women and men to engage in politics of coalition-building and degendered struggles against authoritarianism. Examples of these dynamic NGOs struggling for equal political participation for Arab women are the Tunisian Association of Democratic Women and the Lebanese Women's Rights Committee. Mushrooming NGOs representing women's interests in the AME supplement the struggle for citizenship rights waged by the Arab Women Solidarity Association (AWSA). Before it was banned the Cairo-based Ibn Khaldūn Centre for Development Studies, and the Amman-based Al-Urdun al-Jadīd Research Centre have organised conferences on women's political

35 The full text of the *Arab Plan of Action* can be found on the web: [gopher://gopher.un.org:70/00/esc/cn6/1995/1995—5.en5]

36 See, *Asharq al-Awsat* (2 February 2001), p. 1.

participation. As early as mid-June 1994, the former held a two-day conference on "Egyptian Women and Democratic Transformation". One of the important symposia the latter organised was held in March 1996 on "Jordanian Woman and Electoral Law". This particular conference canvassed the recommendation by the Beijing Fourth World Conference on Women of a 30 per cent quota aiming to close the huge gap between female and male parliamentary representation.[37] State initiatives are numerous with Tunisia and Egypt taking a clear lead in the undertaking of initiatives and the allocation of resources aimed at improving the status of women. Like Jihan al-Sadat before her, Egypt's current first lady Suzan Mubarak has been very active in women's issues, hosting a three-day conference in early June 1994 on "Egyptian Women and the Challenges of the Twenty-first Century". Women's equal political participation was the chief item of the agenda's conference. Tunisia is a unique case in both the Arab and Muslim worlds where gender equity is pushed vigorously in the policy sphere, often in response to the powerful women's lobby. In 1993, a Ministry of Women and the Family and a National Observatory for Women were created. Two years earlier, councils for women and development and for women and the family were established to advise various government departments on policy formulation addressing gender equity. The work done by the Centre for Research, Documentation and Information on Women, set up in 1991, has been vital for realising gender equity.

These state initiatives in the AME build not only on the international momentum which is pushing issues of gender equity to new frontiers, but also respond to society-based women's activism and struggles. Arab regimes are keen not to lose their female power bases which they have, since independence, taken for granted. As in Egypt and Jordan, women's a struggles for equal political participation draw opposition, especially from some ultra-orthodox religious groups in the AME. Opposition can be expected in societies where the forces of patriarchy, religion and tribalism are still powerful though not all men, religion or tribalism are inhospitable to the "woman question" in the AME. In fact, versions of political Islam have promoted within them greater female participation, and many men spearheaded the call for female equality.

[37] See Ḥusayn Abu Ramān (ed.), *Al-mar'atu 'l-urduniyyah wa qānunu 'l-intikhāb* [*Jordanian Woman and Electoral Law*] (Amman: Sinbad Publishing House, 1997).

"MALE FEMINISM"

Arab "male feminism" originated with the nineteenth-century intellectual and political ferment resulting from *al-nahḍah*. The early attempt to regenerate Arab political thought extended to another "taboo" area: gender relations and women's liberation. *Al-nahḍah*, it was reasoned, could not be complete without the inclusion of Arab women. A few enlightened men (not women because women rarely received education or travelled to Europe at the time) took it upon themselves to articulate their vision of a "new" society. In that "new" society, "new" women partake, liberated from the shackles of male domination and social disenfranchisement—shackles which were historically facilitated by the misinterpretation of the *sharīʿah* and by the denial of women's rights in Islam. Male feminists differ in the approach to the woman question. For instance, Qāsim Amīn and Ṭāhir al-Ḥaddād were more systematic in the treatment of the woman question than the iconoclast Aḥmad Fāris al-Shidyāq. Al-Shidyāq is without a doubt one of the pioneering defenders of women's rights in the Arab World.[38] But his defence of women was part of a commentary on his travels in the West—England, France and Malta. From this perspective, his representations of the West are Occidentalist, containing elements of generalisation, fascination and denunciation. His representations of French or English women reflected his own movement in the capitals of Europe and its urban centres. In many instances his depictions of women, the upbringing of children or family life are sweeping generalisations that do not account for any diversity on the basis of class, income, rural–urban divide or level of religiosity. The misery that his Western contemporaries, such as Victor Hugo or Emile Zola, so ably capture in their depictions of their own societies was absent in al-Shidyāq's writings. He praised women's visibility in public places and salons, their promenades in public gardens, the non-segregation of the sexes,[39] premarital acquainting and friendship,[40] flexibility and choice in marriage and divorce,[41] and freedom from domestic violence. But what was true of Paris or London could not have been true of rural areas and smaller cities in France and England. These areas were more conservative and religion still

[38] Aḥmad Fāris al-Shidyāq, *Al-sāq ʿala al-sāq* (Beirut: Dar al-Hayat, 1966).
[39] Ibid., p. 470.
[40] Ibid., p. 415.
[41] Ibid., p. 420.

informed matters regarding segregation of the sexes, marriage and divorce very strongly. Al-Shidyāq is right in using his encounter with fragments of the Occident, French or English, to have reflected on how his own society measured up to various women-related indices. It is from such encounter that he derived his reformism. He opposed domestic violence against children and women, one of the very few Arab and Muslim defenders of women's rights to do so.[42] He denounced over-protectiveness of women, leading to their hiding indoors, which isolated them and contributed to their ignorance of what goes around them,[43] or veiling.[44] On the one hand, he was unwavering in the support of women's education and equality, as one way of reversing the position of women in Arab society as an object of pleasure for man.[45] On the other, al-Shidyāq's writing about women paid too much attention to their looks, clothing and sex appeal.[46] Al-Shidyāq's work, *Al-sāq 'ala al-sāq*, confirmed his defence of a better status for Arab women. He may not be as well-known as those male feminists who came after him. But there is no doubt that he paved the way for them. This is perhaps one factor that al-Shidyāq's critics ignore. Ibrahim Abu-Lughod tends to detract from al-Shidyāq's defence of women's rights, noting that he adds nothing new to the debate beyond the contributions of al-Ṭahtāwī and other early reformers.[47]

Egyptian Qāsim Amīn stands out as the first male feminist to have, even if marginally at the time, advanced the cause of Arab women. His ideas are present in two books. The first, *Taḥrīru 'l-mar'ah* (*The Liberation of Woman*), appeared in Cairo in 1899. The second, *Al-mar'atu 'l-jadīdah* (*The New Woman*), was published two years later. Qāsim Amīn was not always a "feminist". According to Muḥammad 'Umārah, *Taḥrīru 'l-mar'ah* was a departure from his earlier work, *Al-miṣriyyūn* (*The Egyptians*).[48] In *al-miṣriyyūn*, Amīn held conservative views in support, for instance, of *al-ḥijāb* (the veil) and of *al-*

[42] Ibid., pp. 89–101.

[43] Ibid., pp. 458–80.

[44] Ibid., 457.

[45] Ibid., pp. 457–8.

[46] Ibid., pp. 392, 469, 499.

[47] Ibrahim Abu-Lughod, *Arab Discovery of Europe* (Princeton University Press, 1963), p. 126.

[48] Muḥammad 'Umārah, *Qāsim Amīn: Taḥrīru 'l-mar'ah wa 'l tamaddunu 'l-islāmī* [*Qāsim Amīn: The Liberation of Women and Islamic Modernism*] (Beirut: Dar al-Wihdah, 1985), pp. 65–90.

infiṣāl (segregation) of the sexes. *Taḥrīru 'l-mar'ah* is innovative. Here, as ʿUmārah explains, he questioned polygamy, saw no wrong in desegregation of the sexes, called for curbs on the husband's unfettered discretion to divorce which has been deleterious to both women and society, and found nothing in the *sharīʿah* that sanctions the *ḥijāb* describing it as *ʿādah* (a custom) that is not peculiar to the Arab East.[49] The *ḥijāb* is thought to have preceded Islam. Amīn's intellectual maturity resided in establishing a linkage between the political system and the household system, between political freedoms and women's liberation, and between women's economic independence and education and their social and political enfranchisement.[50] He observed:

> A political regime which is based on despotic authority cannot be expected to accord woman her rights and freedom…For in every country there is an interconnectedness between the state of politics and that of the household. Everywhere where man degrades and enslaves the woman, he degrades and deprives himself of freedom. In those countries where men enjoy political liberties, women enjoy greater personal freedom…The nature of government influences the "politics" of the household, which in turn influence society…Consider the lands of the East, you will find that the woman is at the mercy of man, and man at the mercy of government; he is oppressor in his house and oppressed outside it…[51]

From the above, women's freedom seems instrumental to men's. Tunisian al-Ṭāhir al-Ḥaddād[52] followed in the footsteps of Amīn. His book published in 1929, *Imra'atunā fi 'l-sharīʿah wa 'l-mujtamaʿ* [*Our Woman in the [Eyes of] the* Sharīʿah *and Society*), echoed many of Amīn's concerns over issues such as polygamy, divorce and *ḥijāb*. In one section of his book, al-Ḥaddād daringly raised 12 questions some of which pertain to women's consent in marriage, their own right to call for divorce if unhappy, to manage their own business independently

49 Ibid., pp. 65–90.

50 For further details refer to ibid., pp. 91–114.

51 In ibid., pp. 97–8.

52 Al-Ṭāhir al-Ḥaddād was an active member of the first generation of Tunisian nationalists. Al-Ḥaddād's tendencies were clearly socialist and influenced by the Bolshevik Revolution of 1917. He was ardently opposed to French colonialism. Besides standing for women's rights, he also fought for workers' rights. One can thus argue that al-nahḍah saw the flourishing of the earliest Arab Union movement. Al-Ḥaddād supported the movement through writing and in 1927 published *Al-ʿummālu 'l-tunisiyyūn* (*The Tunisian Workers*).

of their husbands, and to their state as equals to men in marriage. Women were then at a disadvantage in these areas because Tunisian men, being the law-makers, judges, and husbands, often either misinterpreted the *sharī'ah* or were silent on them. In question three, al-Ḥaddād confronted the *'ulamā'* (expounders of Islamic orthodoxy) of the time with another taboo area—sexuality:

> Does long absence [by the husband] that neglects *al-mut'ah al-zawjiyyah* (marital sex) accord the wife the right of choice [primacy before the judge] in a divorce case, or is that impossible so long as maintenance continues, and, in such a case, are both partners equal [before the judge]?[53]

He intimated that the liberation of women in the East was conditional on liberation from misinterpretation of Islam, and from those oppressive elements of tradition such as fatalism; asserted that their liberation is integral to true *nahḍah*; and foresees a role for women in liberation from colonialism, and in nation-building.[54] While well-intentioned, it is not difficult to see why this early male feminism has been interpreted by some feminist writers as a "male affair", something which can be decoded as a discourse to keep women in their place. That is, to perpetuate the status quo.

ARAB WOMEN'S CONCEPTIONS OF DEMOCRACY

Secular Feminists

Arab women have since the turn of the twentieth century been at the forefront of both the discourse on and the struggle for democratising polity, economy and society. In antiquity, both pre- and post-Islam, women were prominent in the lands that presently cover the AME—Bilqīs (Queen of Sheba—tenth century BC/modern-day Yemen), Cleopatra (Queen of Egypt 193–176 BC), or Elissa (also called Dido—founder of Carthage 814 BC/modern-day Tunisia). Mernissi's *Forgotten Queens of Islam* documents Arab and Muslim Women's participation and visibility since the advent of Islam.[55] The precursors of

53 Al-Ṭāhir al-Ḥaddād, *Imra'atunā fī 'l-sharī'ah wa 'l-mujtama'* [*Our Woman in the Islamic Law and in Society*] (Tunis: Dar Busalama li al-Tiba'ah wa al-Nashr wa al-Tawzi', 1989), p. 70.

54 Ibid., pp. 193–5.

55 Fatima Mernissi, *The Forgotten Queens of Islam*, trans. by Mary Jo Lakeland (Cambridge: Polity Press, 1993).

those Arab women still struggling today originated in the Arab Mashriq, especially nineteenth[56] and early-twentieth century Egypt. The women of this first wave of Arab feminism struggled to terminate intellectual, social and political invisibility.[57] Through their struggles, they became visible and heard. They linked national liberation to personal emancipation. They saw compatibility between Islam and democratic governance. They demanded equality by reinterpreting Islam and stressing the immunities it accorded them, in which they saw no contradiction with the rights enjoyed by citizens in a democracy. They organised and mobilised themselves via associations; they deployed the power of the pen; and struggled in many contexts—nationalist or pan-Arabist. They also employed both conservative and radical paradigmatic approaches that suited their struggle for securing political, educational and workers' rights. Their struggles continue over *al-aḥwāl al-shakhṣiyyah* (personal status) rights. They have made gains but not enough to claim victory yet. Generally, however, fruition of their struggles is more visible in minds than in institutions.

Egyptian journalist Malāk Ḥifnī Nāṣif was one of the pioneering Arab feminist voices at the turn of the twentieth century. Bāḥithat al-Bādiyah, her pen-name, became associated with women's efforts to lift many restrictions that were either wrongly sanctioned by conservative religious authorities or embedded in social custom. She distinguished herself by her 1911 address to the Egyptian Legislative Assembly in which she directly lobbied for education and personal status rights.[58] Unlike Bāḥithat al-Bādiyah, Munīrah Thābit was one of the first Arab feminists to direct attention to political disempowerment of women. Early in the twentieth century she raised the question of female suffrage. Her criticism of the 1923 Egyptian constitution was centered on that omission as well as its denial of women's right to run for public office.[59] The activism of the first generation of Arab feminists was indeed daring. These pioneer activists faced the risk of

56 Judith E. Tucker, *Women in Nineteenth-century Egypt* (Cambridge University Press, 1985).

57 See the introduction by Badran and Cooke in *Opening the Gates*, pp. i–xxxvi.

58 See Juan Ricardo Cole, "Feminism, Class and Islam in Turn-of-the-Century Egypt", *International Journal of Middle Eastern Studies*, 13 (November 1981), pp. 387–405.

59 See Mervat F. Hatem, "The Paradoxes of State Feminism in Egypt" in Barbara J. Nelson and Najma Chowdhury (eds), *Women and Politics Worldwide* (New Haven and London: Yale University Press, 1994), p. 233.

being seen as threatening to nationalists and the religionists, both of whom were popular. The popularity of these two forces coincided with and intertwined in the struggles for national liberation from colonialism, struggles that women themselves were very active in. Though women were active in anti-colonial struggles, by engaging in a struggle for their own rights, they risked being discredited for working against national and religious unity, i.e. anti-country and anti-God.[60] Activism by latter waves and generations of feminists still runs similar risks, not to mention those of imprisonment and torture. However, more recent women's activism has one advantage which pioneer activists lacked: relatively more open Arab societies with wider sympathies for women's struggles. In practice, these sympathies translate into interested and aware audiences, and into resources for communicating, publicising and representing their preferences, demands and differences. Thanks to this resourcefulness, the latter waves of Arab feminists have shown boldness in the challenge of authoritarianism and the expression of political demands for rights and greater inclusiveness.

The first wave of Arab feminists' struggle for political rights in the 1940s was carefully presented. Factored into it were dutifulness towards country, reverence of Islam and complementarity with men. Two elements come to the fore with this regard. First, early feminists were influenced by the ferment of *iṣlāḥ* and *tajdīd* that *ʿaṣr al-nahḍah* brought about. Second, and as a consequence, they felt encouraged to respond to it. Thus early Arab feminism was not an imported fad. It was neither anti-man nor anti-religion. It was partly nurtured by the *fikr* (thought) of the likes of ʿAbduh, Amīn and al-Ṭahṭāwī. Like them, Arab feminists presented their inferior status as un-Islamic and inimical to the *nahḍah* of country and society. Hudā al-Sha ʿrāwī  opened up her address to the Arab Feminist Conference in 1944 by averring the equality of woman to man in both "duties and obligations".[61] Al-Sha ʿrāwī, then President of the Egyptian Feminist Union (EFU), in a style reminiscent of al-Ṭahṭāwī, amongst others, used the "West" as her point of reference highlighting its "equality of the sexes in all rights".[62] Like al-Ṭahṭāwī who never attributed the superiority of the French to Christianity, she had to qualify her praise of

60 See the introduction by Badran and Cooke, *Opening the Gates*, p. xxiii.

61 See her translated speech in ibid., pp. 338–40.

62 Ibid., p. 338.

Western equality of the sexes so as not to be misconstrued as putting Islam in a trial in which Christendom is favoured:

> Their religious and secular laws have not reached the level Islam has reached in terms of justice towards the woman. Islam has given her the right to vote for the ruler and has allowed her to give opinions on questions of jurisprudence and religion. The woman, given by the Creator the right to vote for the successor of the Prophet, is deprived of the right to vote for a deputy in a circuit or district election by a (male) being created by God.[63]

The difference, however, between al-Shaʿrāwī's feminism and the variety of male feminisms was confronting men with their contradictory politics in order to mobilise their sense of empathy for the sake of a more just and equal society. Hence al-Shaʿrāwī addressed the equality between Arab men and women in that they were both victims of European colonialism. But men made themselves more equal than women for they monopolised whatever limited power was invested in them. Al-Shaʿrāwī demanded equality observing that "The Arab man who demand[ed] that the others [i.e. European colonisers] give him back his usurped rights would be avaricious and not give the woman back her own lawful rights."[64] Another difference that al-Shaʿrāwī employed forcefully was her rejection of paternalism and the assumption of women's inadequacy. She rejected the protectiveness—such as "spar[ing] the woman the perils of election battles"[65]—presented by male chauvinists as an alibi for excluding women from public affairs. Her retort was that women, being powerless, had a natural inclination, "more than men" to endorse and support participatory and democratic politics through "the election of deputies".[66] For they lose more than men do under authoritarian rule. By implication, representative and constitutional government held hope for women's enfranchisement and emancipation. Al-Shaʿrāwī put it that "If man [was] sincere in what he [said; i.e. sparing her perils…] let him prove this by first giving the woman her political rights without her having to go through cruel political battles."[67] Finally, there is a difference that transcends the particularistic demands for equal rights for women. The battle for women's rights

63 Ibid.
64 Ibid., p. 339.
65 Ibid.
66 Ibid.
67 Ibid.

as seen by al-Sha'rāwī was about the welfare of society as a whole. A society that excludes half of its ensemble cannot but produce an oppressive second half which is antithetical to the causes of open society, good rule and equal citizenship.[68]

In her treatise "We Egyptian Women" written in 1949,[69] Injī Aflāṭūn reproduced many of the arguments deployed by her predecessors to press for women's equal political rights. Aflāṭūn, however, who like al-Sha'rāwī belonged to Egypt's aristocracy, developed a clearer notion of democracy than earlier feminists. The irony was that despite her leftist leanings—in the early 1940s she was a member of the communist organisation "al-Sharārah" (the sparkle)[70]—she projected a conception of democracy that was participatory and representative, one which is closer to the liberal paradigm than is the socialist. Her conception neither challenged economic discrepancies nor called for economic equality. In her own life, Aflāṭūn was not only ideologically sound but was also practically committed to her ideological position. Her work with destitute women in Cairo, through the EFU's youth organisation, is evidence of her concerns with issues of equality in an evidently class-based society.[71] All that can be speculated here is perhaps her conception of democracy was a reflection of her upper-class background as well as of her concern with the inferior status of women more than that of the poor. Her conception of democracy was premised on representation and participation:

> Democracy recognizes the political rights of every member of society, without distinction between rich and poor, influential or otherwise, and advocates the participation of the people in the power structure through the mediation of representatives elected by them through universal suffrage. If we deprive half the members of the nation of the right to enjoy political rights, if we deprive half of the Egyptian people of the right to elect its representatives to parliamentary organization through universal suffrage, we are going against the fundamental principles of a democratic regime, and we will thus find ourselves faced with a demi-democracy instead of a total one... Woman's participation in the political life of society constitutes an important element in a healthy democratic regime and a prime factor in the evolution and development of this society.[72]

68 Ibid., pp. 339–40.

69 See the translation in Badran and Cooke, *Opening the Gates*, pp. 345–51.

70 See the editors' biographical note on Aflāṭūn in ibid., pp. 343–4.

71 Ibid., p. 343.

72 Ibid., p. 347.

However, unlike many aristocratic feminists including al-Shaʿrāwī, Aflāṭun's conception of a non-gendered democratic order is far more egalitarian. She rejected the feminist elitism that called for according equal political rights to "the educated woman…[who] deserve[d] them more than illiterate men".[73] Aflāṭūn rejected this elitism as destructive not only because it contradicted with her notion of representative and participatory democracy but also because it made women who adopted it prepared to engage in the same exclusionary politics and capable of the same patriarchal subordination of both men and women. Two interconnected notions of democracy were the corollary. There was affinity in the enfranchisement and empowerment of women: "The struggle of Egyptian women for their political rights is part of the struggle for the strengthening of democracy in Egypt."[74] The other notion affirmed the principle of equality in a non-gendered democracy: "Democracy is not the exclusive prerogative of men, nor of educated men or women only; it is the power of the whole people, men and women together."[75] Aflāṭun's counsel to those feminists and aristocrats, men and women, who preferred a democracy only for the literati was to spare no effort in ridding society of illiteracy and in spreading mass education.[76]

Independence has brought both progress and reverses to women in Arab societies. Their conditions have irrevocably been improved by the revolution in state-subsidised mass education. Nonetheless, nationalism in the AME remains a gendered discourse and practice. Most nationalist governments, keen to control all activities of their citizens and widen their power bases, have created their own women's organisations, giving the partisans a medium for mobility. This is a kind of state-guided "feminism", which Mervat Hatem equates with a new patriarchy—"state patriarchy".[77] The non-partisans have mostly found themselves with a limited scope for expression and

[73] Ibid., p. 350.
[74] Ibid.
[75] Ibid.
[76] Ibid.
[77] According to Mervat F. Hatem, in "state feminism" the state acts as a purveyor and dispenser of welfare benefits, legal, political and civil rights leading to the cooptation of feminist elites in the state corporatist structure and winning women's allegiance to the system. Hence the dividends of increased "national and international legitimacy" (p. 230). However, as Hatem points out, state feminism, as the case of Egypt (and indirectly the Arab world) amply demonstrates, suffers from at least two drawbacks: the artificial nature of political inclusiveness of women as they are the last

organisation.[78] This is regressive. Equally reactionary, however, is the narrowing of the margin of activities for women soon after independence. The role played by Algerian women during the liberation war is well-known. Independence has not been generous to them in the sense that the equality they fought for, as demonstrated by the *mujāhidāt* (combatant women) sharing in the liberation effort, has been slow in coming.[79] From this perspective the questions of power and of gender relations increasingly underpin the discourse on Arab democratisation, and on the viability of an emancipatory project that is gendered.[80]

Tunisian feminist ʿAzza Ghānmī, an editorial member of the former magazine *Nisā'* (*Women*), links to democracy women's activism through their independent organisation in the late 1980s:

> Everything turned on the notion of democracy: the question of what language to use was based on our idea of democracy, our rules of order were based on democracy, the fact that we rejected all kinds of hierarchy was based on democracy...Given the domination by the PSD [the then ruling *Parti Socialiste Déstourien*] over public institutions and the domination by the extreme left in other arenas, the women's club Tahir al-Haddad was really the only democratic place in all Tunisia, the only place where people could actually get up and express different ideas, and still meet the following week to continue the discussion.[81]

Arab women's struggle to widen their public margin of existence involves fighting all forms of repression from the household up

---

to gain political and civil rights, and the failure of the state to dismantle anti-women patriarchal practices in areas, more or less, outside its jurisdiction such as the private sector and the family (p. 230). Moreover, she argues that state feminism constitutes "a new form of patriarchy originating in state control—state patriarchy" (p. 230). See her article, "The Paradoxes of State Feminism in Egypt", pp. 227–42.

[78] The struggle of women's non-governmental organisations in Egypt continues against all odds, namely, increased restrictions imposed by the state to prevent them from reaching wider audiences. Examples of such women's NGOs are Jamʿiyyat Bint al-Arḍ (Daughter of the Land Association), and Nawāl al-Saʿdāwī's taḍāmun al-mar'ah al-ʿarabiyyah (Solidarity of Arab Woman's Association), ibid., pp. 237–41.

[79] For further details on this point see Valentine M. Moghadam, *Modernizing Women: Gender and Social Change in the Middle East* (Boulder, CO and London: Lynne Rienner: 1993), pp. 83–5.

[80] See, for instance, Earl L. Sullivan, "Democratization and Changing Gender Roles in Egypt", *American-Arab Affairs*, 36 (spring 1991) pp. 16–18.

[81] Kevin Dwyer, *Arab Voices: The Human Rights Debate in the Middle East* (Berkeley: University of California Press, 1991), p. 195.

to what Fatima Mernissi calls "the masculine circuits of power".[82] Women's lower status in Morocco, for instance, has politicised a small proportion of women.[83] Although critical of this "power-hunger" which render women just as manipulative and money-seeking as men, Mernissi notes how Moroccan men are discovering women in their new roles: "It is only recently that men here, and men on the left, began to realise that women are progressive and willing to challenge authority even more so than the men are."[84] In her book *Islam and Democracy: Fear of the Modern Age*, Mernissi somewhat philosophically contemplates the fears and hopes that democracy inspires in the modern Arab world. She observes that democracy is not alien to the Muslim East arguing that the age-long conflict between the leader's authority and the individual's sovereignty has historically suppressed the latter.[85] She proffers a partly unconventional definition of democracy:

> The term covers an impressive array of freedoms and privileges, of rights to exercise and taxes to pay, from the right to eat pork or drink wine or read censored works; to the right to fall in love, have a platonic friendship or embark on an affair, marry one's partner or not, have children or not; to the right to demand a wage at least equal to the legal minimum wage, and appeal to a union if unjustly treated; to the right to elect a prime minister, and then to protest when the government-run television station gives him prime airtime at taxpayers' expense.[86]

For Egyptian Nawāl al-Sa'dāwī, one of the leading Arab feminists who suffered in many ways because of her feminism, women have been politically and economically disempowered even under 'Abd Nasser's regime despite efforts to ameliorate their conditions. This al-Sa'dāwī, who for so many years presided over AWSA, puts down to the absence of real freedom, and the persistence of the class system.[87] In the 1980s, al-Sadat's *infitāḥ* (open-door) has pushed women further to the periphery of the liberalised economy, and

[82] Ibid., p. 183.

[83] See Aicha Afifi and Rajae Msefer, "Women in Morocco: Gender Issues and Politics" in Nelson and Chowdhury (eds), *Women and Politics Worldwide*, pp. 463–77.

[84] In Dwyer, *Arab Voices*, pp. 183–4.

[85] Fatima Mernissi, *Islam and Democracy: Fear of the Modern World*, trans. by Mary Jo Lakeland (London: Virago Press, 1993), p. 16.

[86] Ibid., pp. 50–51.

[87] Dwyer, *Arab Voices*, p. 187.

subsequently to that of polity and society.[88] Accordingly, al-Saʿdāwī sees a democratic imperative in the link between economic and political fairness:

> The real distinction is between capitalist democracy and socialist democracy. You cannot have real freedom in a capitalist society, it is impossible. And you cannot have real freedom for women in a capitalist society. The problem in capitalism is that you are supposed to have freedom in the economic sphere, but what you actually have is domination by the people who have money. And this is tied to the domination by men in the family.[89]

Al-Saʿdāwī's above notion of democracy is informed by her socialist convictions as well as by a different kind of feminism, one that is more female-centered than that of the first wave. As a result she incurred the wrath of both political and religious orthodoxies. Most of her writings, while enjoying a wide Arab readership, remain banned. She was imprisoned in the 1980s for her vociferous and unorthodox political and non-political views.

Al-Saʿdāwi gives a narrow conceptualisation of power, insisting there are only two kinds, military and political.[90] For her, since women are excluded from military power, they should organise politically in order to transcend mere awareness of rights to actual exercise and enjoyment.[91] Her concept of emancipation requires confronting politics, that bastion of man that is highly disregarded and suspected in the Arab world. Her notion of politics is one that connotes treachery, perfidy, trickery, manipulation and dishonesty.

Palestininan Hanan Awwad spells a two-fold conceptualisation of democracy: conventional and revolutionary.[92] The conventional sees democracy in terms of equality and freedom.[93] The revolutionary

[88] Ibid.

[89] Ibid.

[90] Ibid.

[91] Ibid., pp. 187–8.

[92] Debating democracy in Palestinian circles is not new. In March 1970, Palestinians representing various organisations, including the PLO, discussed in Beirut the idea of a Palestinian state. Details can be found in *Al-Anwar*, 8–15 March 1970. See also Said Zidani, "*Iṭlālah ʿala al-dīmuqrāṭiyyah al-lībirāliyyah*" [Introduction to Liberal Democracy], *Al-Mustaqbil al-ʿArabī*, 135 (May 1990): pp. 4–21. See also a series of papers published by the Palestinian Academic Society for the Study of International Affairs (PASSIA) under the title *Naḥnu wa 'l-dīmuqrāṭiyyah* [Democracy and Us]; see those by Mahdī ʿAbd al-Hādī, by Riyāḍ al-Mālikī, and by Muḥammad Jād-Allah.

[93] Hanan Awwad, "Gender Issues in Democracy: The Palestinian Woman and the Revolution" in Elise Boulding (ed.), *Building Peace in the Middle East: Challenges for*

contextualises democracy in the wider Palestinian milieu of ineluctable occupation, and the broader struggle for freedom from occupation. Awwad isolates the central issue: genuine freedom, for both the occupied society and the individual, is banished under occupation which is clouded by the "hues of liberty".[94] Freedom of the former equals and entails freedom of the latter: "national freedom is the combination of all types of freedom".[95] Palestinian men and women are inextricably linked in occupation and in liberation, and in inequality and equality. Accordingly, liberation is very much her responsibility as much as it is his. Hence the Palestinian woman's participatory role is liberational—against the occupier—as well as democratising—against patriarchal despotism. By participating in national liberation she "gains her own freedom";[96] and by assuming wide-ranging "revolutionary responsibilities", she helps erode "gender stereotypes" and lift "traditional reservations".[97]

Awwad widely interprets freedom not only by insisting on ending occupation and of lifting traditional reservations, but also by heeding attention to "sociopolitical dimensions…institutionalized monopolies, and the forces of hunger and poverty".[98] Like al-Saʿdāwī, she rejects the notion of bourgeois freedom that dwells on individualism. If freedom is so broadly defined it is because of the multifarious "forms of oppression and tyranny",[99] liberation from which necessitates "readjustment from the personal to the collective".[100] Such a readjustment involves "achievement of a qualitative change for the better; and…the creation of both the moral and humanitarian framework within which to achieve this goal".[101] The *intifāḍah* (uprising) has been for Palestinian women a medium of reifying conceptualisations of freedom and democracy into the practicalities of struggle

---

States and Civil Society (Boulder, CO: Lynne Rienner, 1994), p. 91. For a wider Middle Eastern feminist perspective of democracy see in this book the article by Simona Sharoni, "Gender Issues in Democracy: Rethinking Middle East Peace and Security from a Feminist Perspective", pp. 99–110.

94 Awwad, "Gender Issues in Democracy", p. 92.

95 Ibid.

96 Ibid., p. 91.

97 Ibid.

98 Ibid., p. 92.

99 Ibid.

100 Ibid., p. 93.

101 Ibid.

for statehood. Thus Awwad explains the visibility of Palestinian women through the *intifāḍah* to their high involvement at many levels, both inside and outside the home. They have done so by committing themselves to activism in the civil society (membership of organisations and associations, public disobedience, rioting); in the economy (integration into the Palestinian economy and labour, acquisition of skills, boycott of Israeli products); and in the household (leadership, sustenance).[102]

The Islāmiyyāt

Here there are two discourses: a male Islamist discourse, and a female Islamist discourse. The male discourse, which by no means is universal amongst male Islamists, is increasingly liberating itself from its discourse of morality, i.e. dealing with women as *fitnah* (a form of temptation)[103] that legitimates discourses on their code of dress, the necessity of covering their body and their *zīnah* (make-up), and of *iḥtishām* (modesty) as versus *tabarruj* (flaunting). The silence over women's rights and freedoms as citizens, not just good mothers and wives, is being addressed within the four movements. The approaches are different. Al-jabhah and al-nahḍah, in that order, are pace-setters in the sphere of women's freedoms. Specificity such as of nationality (e.g., communist influence), local traditions (e.g., overall visibility of women), and even of schools of jurisprudence (e.g., Mālikī lenity) is important. Female Islamists in Sudan possess more latitude than their counterparts in the other movements to mingle with fellow male Islamists, form relations that end in marriages, shake hands with males, and generally be proactive and visible. In fact "Rā'idatu 'l-Nahḍah", a social and welfare Islamist women's group, was one of the jabhah's successful affiliate organisations that was dynamic in the 1980s not only in the Islamic *da'wah* (call), but also politically (recruiting women for the jabhah, especially at universities), politically (holding demonstrations, joining professional unions, running for office in professional, municipal, local and national councils, holding seminars), and socially (charity services).

The far-sightedness of al-Turābī (al-jabhah's leader) is mentioned as one reason for the dynamism and visibility of female Islamists

[102] Ibid., pp. 94–5.

[103] This is a term that is very difficult to translate into English. *Fitnah* refers to social discord that emanates from women walking uncovered in the community.

interviewed. His treatise on women, *Al-ittijāhu 'l-Islāmī yuqaddimu 'l-mar'ah: bayna ta'ālīmi' l-dīn wa taqālīdi 'l-mujtama'* [*Islamism and Women: Between Religious Dogma and Social Traditions*],[104] which he wrote in the 1970s, was criticised in many Islamist circles for its *tajdīd* and creative *ijtihād*.[105] Men like himself and al-Ghannūshī, whose own book on women, *Al-mara'tu 'l-muslimah fī tūnis: bayna tawjīhāti 'l-qur'ān wa wāqi'i 'l-mujtama'i 'l-tūnisī* [*The Muslim Woman in Tunisia: Between the Instructions of the Qur'ān and the Reality of Tunisian Society*] is positive,[106] have opened up new possibilities for non-gendered Islamism. In both movements, the thinking is that there is more to women than just *mas'alat al-hijāb* (the question of the veil). Women's participation in both movements and contribution to the thought of both leaders is worth separate study. Suffice it to say that their influence has come to fruition with the International Islamist Movement's adoption in 1994 of a motion which was eventually approved due to the wide influence and weight of al-Turābī and al-Ghannūshī, amongst few others. The motion clarifies and defines the Islamist position on women's political participation.

The document, resulting from the motion, is entitled, *Al-mar'atu 'l-muslimah fī al-mujtama'i 'l-muslimi wa 'l-mawqif min mushārākatihā* [*The Muslim Woman in Muslim Society and the Position on her Participation*]. Four areas articulate the Islamist position, which according to one source was subject to long debate. Many amendments were made before the final print was adopted. The document's introduction produces familiar ideas about woman being "half of society"; *shaqā'iqu 'l-rijāl* (equal to as well as codependent with men); mothers and sisters; and the role of women in Islamic history either in the battlefield or in the Prophet's life; and ideas about women's rights in the Qur'ān.[107] Although the document is progressive the rights it grants women are qualified. It, for example, gives the husband, by

[104] See Ḥasan al-Turābī, *Al-ittijāhu 'l-Islāmī yuqaddimu 'l-mar'ah: bayna ta'ālīmi 'l-dīn wa taqālīdi 'l-mujtama'* [*Islamism and Women: Between Religious Dogma and Social Traditions*] (Jeddah: al-Dar al-Sa'udiyyah li al-Nashr wa al-Tawzi', 1984).

[105] Author's interview with Ḥasan al-Turābī, 12 May 1994, Khartoum.

[106] See Rashīd al-Ghannūshī, *Al-mara' al-muslimah fī tūnis: bayna tawjīhāti al-qur'ān wa wāqi' al-mujtama' al-tūnisī* [*The Muslim Woman in Tunisia: Between the Instructions of the Qur'ān and the Reality of Tunisian Society*] (Kuwait: Dar al-Qalam li al-Nashr wa al-Tawzi', 1993).

[107] See *Al-mar'atu 'l-muslimah fī al-mujtama'i 'l-muslim wa al-mawqif min mushārākatihā* [*The Muslim Woman in Muslim Society and the Position on her Participation*], (n.p.: n.p., 1994), pp. 1–6.

dint of his *ḥuqūq shar'iyyah* (legitimate rights), the right to veto his wife's activities outside the household. Interviewee Islamist women confirm such legitimate rights but argue that the husband's right to have a say in his wife's activities outside the household is often the outcome of mutual negotiation not forcible decision by the male spouse. It emphasises the Muslim woman's significance for the preservation of the family and, subsequently, society. That is, the Muslim woman's family obligations are a priority. But that is not to say that she is unsuited or unavailable for work or political participation. Availability often increases with diminished family obligations, sharing of those obligations between spouses, and negotiation. The document notes that no authority can interfere in the private affairs between a husband and his wife, leaving the matter of women's participation in the hands of men—a form of *wiṣāyah* (guardianship).[108] Nonetheless, the document goes some way in defining women's political rights in the following areas.

First in the area of *al-intikhabāt* (elections); woman is found to be equal to man in the duty of *al-amr bi al-ma'rūf wa al-nahy 'an al-munkar* (enjoining the good and preventing the reprehensible). Therefore nothing can stop her from voting or being elected to office, especially that no hindrance is found in the *sharī'ah* for her participatory role in society. Second, *ikhtiyāruhā fī al-majālisi 'l-muntakhabah* (her participation in parliaments and elected bodies) is regulated by similar criteria regulating participation of men, namely, knowledge and competence. But naturally, a Muslim woman's activities apart from being regulated by her husband's approval are also subject to her modest attire and presentation. The Islamic dress is promoted for the main reason that it promotes woman's participation. In the words of an Islamist from Jordan's al-'amal al-islāmī, "Woman is not required to don the veil so that she stays at home; the whole point behind the veil is women's mobility and participation."[109] This point is made clear: women are permitted parliamentary participation so long as the rules of *iḥtishām* are applied, i.e., no *tabarruj*, and minimum mixing with men or only when necessary in the course of duty.[110] The veil, and by extention women, are integral to Islamist discourses on morality and cultural identity and authenticity. When seen from the

108 Ibid., p. 6.

109 Author's interview with Bassām La'mūsh, 12 June 1994, Amman.

110 See *Al-mar'atu 'l-muslimah fī al-mujtama'i 'l-muslim wa al-mawqif min mushārākatihā*, p. 6.

outside, Islamist moralising and theorising about the place of women and the rules of chastity expected of them are represented as male dominative practices over passive females. For the *islāmiyyāt*, being Muslim entails accepting responsibilities, Godly and earthly. In fact, many of those interviewed point out that chastity rules apply to Muslim men too. But more importantly, as a member of Jordan's al-ʿamal puts it, power-sharing involves responsibilities and commitments that Muslim women choose to take up and rules they are happy to abide by. In her opinion, no rights of participation and citizenship come without responsibilities and duties.[111] Therefore it is within this Islamic framework of obligations and entitlements that the *islāmiyyāt* find it easiest to satisfy deity and community, without necessarily sacrificing deep existential needs for self-fulfilment or personhood.

Third in *tawallī 'l-waẓā'ifi 'l-ʿāmmah wa 'l-ḥukūmah* (holding public and high office), Muslim women can have a career in public life, subject to the aforementioned conditions. The one area that is to remain the bastion of men is *al-imāratu 'l-kubrā* (greater governance), whatever the highest office means. Traditionally this position refers to the office of the khalīfah. *Ijtihād* in the future could move to argue for women's occupying the highest office in the political hierarchy of their countries since this office no longer exists. For what is *al-imāratu 'l-kubrā* nowadays? It cannot be kept alive, when it does not physically exist, unless it is intended to be a convenient device of exclusion. Last regarding *al-ʿamal ʿumūman* (employment in general), woman is stressed to have rights to equal employment. Rights to women are God-given but so are the sanctions to what she is and is not supposed to be able to do.

The discourse amongst female Islamists is not one that challenges the male position at all. In fact, it supports it. These women who choose to be Islamist and to live by the rules set out in the Qur'ān see in it the key to their emancipation and their *saʿādat al-dārayn* (happiness in this life and the hereafter), even if in the eyes of outside observers it is patronisingly interpreted to routinise and legitimise their subjection and invisibility. Islamist women invariably find the deepest meaning of democracy in the Qur'ānic term "*al-insān*" (the human being).[112]

[111] Author's interview with Arwā al-Kilānī, 13 June 1994, Amman.

[112] A view expressed in interviews with Rubā al-Farkh, 11 June 1994, Amman; Arwā al-Kilānī, 13 June 1994, Amman; Nawāl al-Fāʿūrī, 13 June 1994, Amman; Fadwā Abū

Zaynab al-Ghazālī, the very well-known activist from the ikhwān in Egypt, sees the existence of such a term as evidence of God's wisdom as His ennobling is not the reserve of one sex; of the dignity of humankind and their God-given freedom; and of the existence of an Islamic philosophy and of an Islamic framework within which freedoms and restrictions, and duties and responsibilities, whether in struggle or in establishing religion and *iqāmat al-dawlah* (founding the state), are addressed to *al-insān*, applying equally for man and woman. For her, the history of Islam is the history of great men and great women, even if men outnumbered women in that history. Her views on the position of women in Islam is that:

- there has largely been *taqṣīr* (limitation) on the part of men in understating the rights of women, not *taqṣīr* on thc part of thc Qur'ān;
- a genuine Muslim woman can balance between her duties at home and outside home, but not at the expense of raising the model Muslim family. She holds woman to be the most important social agent that, since she is the one who raises the family, can both resist and defeat *taghrīb*, and, if she succumbs to it, imperil the Muslim *huwiyyah*;
- Woman can hold all positions of government and in the judiciary but must be excluded from *al-imāratu 'l-kubrā*;
- Woman's political rights are equal to men in the areas of freedom of expression, *al-bay'ah* (oath of allegiance), elections, the right to deny her oath of allegiance to rulers she does not consent to, the right to withdraw her confidence from rulers, and in the duty of *raqābah* (keeping rulers in check and accountable). But since *raqābah* can entail candidature for and tenure in parliament, al-Ghazālī believes that the Muslim woman, with *taghrīb* being heightened and Muslims facing an onslaught from an aggressive and dangerous cultural imperialism and the *ummah* divided, can for some

---

Ghaydā', 14 June 1994, Amman; Ḥayāt al-Misīmī, 15 June 1994, Amman; Asmā' al-Farḥān, 14 June 1994, Amman (women from al-'amalu al-Islāmī, Jordan). Sumayyah Ja'far 'Uthmān, 27 April 1994, Khartoum; Zakiyyah 'Awaḍ Sātī, 3 May 1994, Khartoum; Uṣāl al-Mahdī, 3 May 1994, Khartoum; Sumayyah Abū Kashawwah, 5 May 1994, Khartoum; Lubābah al-Faḍl, 7 May 1994, Khartoum; Su'ād al-Fātiḥ, 10 May 1994, Khartoum (this group from al-jabhah, Sudan). Also, Sumayyah Ghannūshī, 7 May 1996, London; Rashīdah 'Abd al-Mawlā, 7 May 1996, London (both from al-nahḍah, Tunisia).

time forego holding positions in parliament until such a time as the *ummah* puts its house in order, and that could be indefinite.[113]

For her, women are a kind of a "last line of defence" against *taghrīb*, that is the last rampart against assimilation. It is in the household that the rising generations of Muslims get their cultural and religious identities shaped, reinforced and protected only to be passed by them to future generations. This role of *tarbiyah* (education), since Muslim men spend a great deal of their time outside the home, falls on the shoulders of Muslim women. Thus for al-Ghazālī, the Muslim woman is not just a kind of *madrasah* (moral and educational beacon or lighthouse) but also a *ḥalaqah* (a link) in the inter-generational *tathqīf* (acculturation) and *aslamah* (Islamisation).

Although Zaynab al-Ghazālī enjoys high popularity amongst female Islamists for her role in helping revive the ikhwān, her views on parliamentary participation do not meet with the same approval from other female Islamists in the other movements. For Su'ād al-Fātiḥ, another Arab woman with a history of activism spanning more than four decades, delaying women's parliamentary participation would be a retrograde step for women in Sudan. Al-Fātiḥ who along with Ḥikmat Aḥmad Sayyid Aḥmad, also from the jabhah, were the only women candidates voted into parliament in the 1986 multiparty elections believes that *shūrā* is a duty and a *taklīf* (responsibility) that cannot be left to men alone, and active Muslim men need active Muslim women. For al-Fātiḥ, *shumūliyyah* (all-inclusiveness) is Godly and therefore cannot be made incomplete by presenting arguments against women's parliamentary participation at a time when the Arab world is defying authoritarian rule.[114] This view by al-Fātiḥ is representative of most Islamist women's thinking on women standing for parliament. The difference between al-Fātiḥ and al-Ghazālī is rooted in the history of the movements they belong to. The jabhah has accommodated women and recognised their contribution by giving equal responsibility and leadership positions in the movement, such as in its *majlis al-shūrā* (consultative council). Article 23 of its constitution

113 Author's interview with Zaynab al-Ghazālī, 11 April 1994, Cairo. See also her views on women and their participation in Ibn al-Hāshimī, *Humūmu al-mar'ah al-mulsimah wa al-dā'iyah Zaynab al-Ghazālī* [*The Muslim Woman's Concerns and Preacher Zaynab al-Ghazālī*] (Cairo: Dar al-I'tisam, 1990), pp. 242–3.

114 Author's interview with Su'ād al-Fātiḥ, 10 May 1994, Khartoum.

stresses commitment to "eradicating social injustice" against woman and paying special attention to her role in nation-building.[115] The ikhwān, mostly owing to a history of confrontation with the regime, lacked the environment to be open about its membership, especially that of its consultative council, the conduct of its internal elections and the leadership of the various specialised bodies within it.[116] Not even al-Ghazālī's prison experience and her leadership of al-sayyidāt al-muslimāt (Muslim Women) in the 1940s–50s qualified her for inclusion in the all-male *majlis al-shūrā* of the ihkwān. The idea of more open elections and the inclusion of women in this *majlis* appeals to al-Ghazālī who believes that it will be introduced in the future.[117] The same view is popular among the younger generation of Islamist leaders who have, within their own professional unions, shared power of the executive boards with women colleagues in their professions.[118]

Lubābah al-Faḍl of the jabhah explains that her Islamicity and commitment to a struggle against all types of injustice within an Islamic framework is symbiotic with freedom. Because she is Muslim as well as Islamist, she is free. She can be free of apathy, injustice and despotism due to Islam and to the opportunities to be active that Islamism opens up for her. She takes this to be no more than an activating of Islamic principles that have for so long been deviated from, singling out more traditional interpretations of Islam for criticism. Thus she agrees with her fellow *islāmiyyāt* that any claim that democracy gives women more rights has to be viewed with caution for so long as Islam's emancipatory potential remains unfulfilled exegetically and, most notably, practically. The problems therefore of despotism and lack of accountability in the Arab world have little to do with Islam and democracy being ontologially the products of distinct frameworks, religious and secular. These problems are therefore not a reflection of a knowable Islam as much as they are of given social, historical, economic and political forces. The challenge for Muslims

115 See *Dustūru al-jabhah al-Islāmiyyah al-qawmiyyah* [*Jabha's Constitution*] (1985).

116 Author's interview with Ma'mūn al-Huḍaybī, 4 April 1994, Cairo.

117 Author's interview with Zaynab al-Ghazālī, 11 April 1994, Cairo.

118 In interviews with Abū al-'Alā Māḍī, 3 April 1994, Cairo; 'Abd al-Mun'im Abū al-Futūḥ, 27 March 1994, Cairo; Aḥmad 'Abd-Allah, 28 March 1994, Cairo; Ibrāhīm Za'farānī, 1 April 1994, Alexandria; Hishām Nabīh, 30 March, 1994, Cairo; 'Iṣām al-'Iryān, 6 April 1994, Cairo.

is to tap into Islam and operationalise many of its emancipatory principles and institutions. For al-Faḍl, Islam has much to offer to men and women of the world in the realm of rights, justice and good government. One example she cites is the non-sexist notion of *insān*. She understands it to embody *shūrā* and democracy because as a term it suggests a person with God-given rights that positive laws cannot interfere with. This suggests duties and responsibilities not only *vis-à-vis* fellow compatriots but also humanity. The political meanings she attaches to the term are indeed creative:

> As an *insān* my subjectivity is continuously constituted and reconstituted by thinking and acting out my rights in a manner that is consistent with the way revelation means them to be, nothing less and nothing more. As an *insān*, who happens to be a woman, I have a right to reject the manipulative exegeses of our *sharīʿah* that threaten my existence in a way that is not consistent with the Godly way, and to apply my own *ijtihād* to rectify erroneous tendencies by some *shuyūkh* (Muslim elders). What we have been able to do in Sudan is tap into the *sharīʿah* to think, be and do like an *insān* and nothing less. I have participatory rights as an *insān* and these I alone choose to assert or forego as befits my situation, my family and my agreement with my husband. But as an *insān* I am ennobled by God by being part of the human race. As an Islamist I have a *huwiyyah* (ipseity), I have a mission to stand up to injustice everywhere, and my being an *insān* is part of this *huwiyyah*. My faith is part of my *huwiyyah*. My veil is part of this *huwiyyah*. I feel empowered to control those who try to control me and my environment, my *thaqāfah* (culture), my space, my consumption habits, my reading habits and even my weight.[119]

Nawāl al-Fāʿūrī, the Western tendency to define relations between men and women in terms of dichotomies, is pre-empted by the term *insān*, which for her also embodies Godly rights and the potential and disposition for Muslims to have *shūrā* and democracy. Al-Fāʿūrī, the first female voted to the *majlis al-shūrā* of al-ʿamal, observes that God's address to both men and women as *insān* is an affirmation of the equality of the Godly *manhaj* (way). She is critical of some tendencies (a reference to a dozen powerful members who also double up as members of the Muslim Brotherhood) within the movement to limit women's participation. Generally, however, she is of the view that although women's participation is strongly promoted by more liberal voices within the movement, it still has a long way to go.

119 Author's interview with Lubābah al-Faḍl, 7 May 1994, Khartoum.

She does not agree with the criticism levelled by some women, including from within the movement, that her election in the *majlis al-shūrā* of al-ʿamal al-Islāmī, is a token. It is, she points out, a positive step from a newly-created party that will grow and see similar initiatives at the parliamentary level. The lack of consensus over the participation of women in the Islamic Action Front reflects the tension within the strategic alliance between the country's ikhwān, many of whose affiliates are also members of al-ʿamal al-Islāmī, and the non-ikhwān members, especially female Islamists amongst others. Whereas many members of the Muslim Brotherhood are not favourable to women's political participation or, at least, their unrestricted political participation, non-Brotherhood members tend to stand for full-fledged and equal participatory role for women. The question of women's participation could not have been without controversy in a society like Jordan that is very religious and still tribal. Even liberal voices like al-Farḥān, the former leader of al-ʿamal al-Islāmī, have to calibrate their positive messages advocating greater participation of women to these specificities and sensitivities. In his work entitled *Mushkilātu 'l-shabāb fi ḍaw'i 'l-Islām* [*The Youth Problem in the Light of Islam*], al-Farḥān balances these views with those holding that women have a duty to be fulfilled as mothers, wives and makers of generations of Muslims.[120] From a Westerner's perspective, these notions probably do not go far enough in challenging gender relations or de-emphasising the importance of the private space.

FEMINISATION, ISLAMISATION AND DEMOCRATISATION

The relationships between feminisation, Islamisation and democratisation are fairly complex. Three sets of relationships—that of feminisation and Islamisation, of feminisation and Islamisation and of democratisation and Islamisation—of concern to this section's analysis have generally been oversimplified. Islamisation, itself a process with more than one model throughout the AME, is often assumed to be antithetical to the goals of either feminisation (minimally defined here as greater participation and representation by women) or political liberalisation (minimally defined here as the process of greater local, national and global participation and

[120] See Isḥāq al-Farḥān, *Mushkilātu al-shabāb fi ḍaw'i al-Islām* [*Problems of Youth in the Light of Islam*] (Amman: Dar al-Furqan, 1984), pp. 52–3.

representation). Repudiating this long-held prejudiced view is the ongoing rethinking of Islam and of Islamic activism. The corollary of this rethinking is that women are increasingly being included in the four models of political Islam in which the interviewees are involved. The counting in of women is a step towards the feminisation and democratisation of Islamic movements and of Islamisation itself. This feminisation and democratisation from within work in tandem with the overall goals of democratisation from without, that is, at the levels of the state in the AME. From this perspective, feminisation serves democratisation either in terms of degendering Islamisation or in terms of degendering the predominantly gendered Arab politics, especially at the level of the state and below it.

Feminisation and Islamisation

Islamist women, especially in al-jabhah and al-ʿamal, take their visibility and activism along with fellow male Islamists as proof that as a *dīn nayyir wa mustanīr* (rethought religion), Islam is a uniquely emancipatory force. In this vein, Islamist women baulk at any suggestion that Islamic movements or Islamic resurgence—like all so-called religious fundamentalisms—are retrograde phenomena, mostly noted for retarding the visibility of women in Arab societies. The *islāmiyyāt* find their rights as laid down in the Qur'ān, ḥadīth and the Sunnah to be evidence of God-given equality. These cover the rights to life (abolition of female infanticide), employment, property, inheritance, divorce, education, wilful marriage and remarriage. A saying attributed to the Prophet Muḥammad, "*Innama al-nisā' shaqā'iqu 'l-rijāl*" (women are the twin halves of men) is a popular reference amongst Islamist women from al-jabhah and al-ʿamal. They find this particular saying along with numerous Qur'ānic verses to be evidence that inequality between men and women is not sanctioned by Islam but rather by Muslims. Further, the *islāmiyyāt* agree that Islamic-based knowing does not posit women against men. Rather, antagonism between women and men is instigated by sociocultural influences, especially those of customs. An interviewee from al-ʿamal makes the point that nowhere in the Qur'ān is there a reference that God's vicegerency is the exclusive bastion of Muslim men.[121] Reflecting on her own experience, Zaynab al-Ghazālī argues that the political influences

[121] Author's interview with Arwā al-Kilānī, 13 June 1994, Amman.

of authoritarianism must not be discounted when accounting for Muslim women's low level of participation:

> I have been active in public life for nearly fifty years. My religiosity had lots to do with my activism. It has been an impetus and never an obstacle, something the secular and authoritarian ʿAbd al-Nāṣir imprisoned and tortured me for as he did thousands of committed Muslim men and women like myself. It is authoritarianism not Islam or al-ikhwān that placed and continue to place restrictions on the participation of women and men almost everywhere in the Arab world.[122]

True, points out al-ʿamal's Nawāl al-Fāʿūrī, that the status of Muslim women in the AME still leaves much to be desired as can be confirmed by indicators of literacy, tenure of political, judicial and professional seats of power. But it is not true, she adds, that women's lower status is a correlate of Islam. It should not therefore be confused with Islam, noting that "Islam is a religion many confuse with all that is wrong with Arab and Muslim societies."[123] Like her, Islamist women in all four movements rather lay the blame on Muslims themselves for either misinterpreting Islam, misunderstanding it or for manipulating the Qur'ān and the Sunnah for earthly ends. This misinterpreting and manipulating have, according to Uṣāl al-Mahdī, been translated into social customs and practices that contradict the essence of Islam and its accent on the dignity of human beings and their deserving of the God-given favours of justice and equality. That is the reason, she observes, why for so long Muslims themselves have been under the false impression that the "household is the only place for the good Muslim woman or that pheroahic circumcision is sanctioned by Islam".[124]

For many Islamists, men and women, the fact that Islamic movements or the Islamic resurgence are singled out for criticism ignores other dynamics, national (introduction of secularism) and supranational (imposition of predatory capitalism and new forms of colonialism). Thus a great many of them tend to suggest that thorough emancipation for both men and women cannot be attained at a time when the AME never fully severed its ties of political and economic dependence with the former colonial metropoles. In fact, it is quite

122 Author's interview with Zaynab al-Ghazālī, 11 April 1994, Cairo.
123 Author's interview with Nawāl al-Fāʿūrī, 13 June 1994, Amman.
124 Author's interview with Uṣāl al-Mahdī, 3 May 1994, Khartoum.

vexatious for Islamists that academics and journalists have a tendency to oversimplify the problems of the AME. For instance, with regard to democracy, many Islamists charge that Orientalist research is almost obsessed with either looking for democratic deficiency in Islam or else by explaining such a deficiency in the Arab and Muslim worlds by pointing the finger at Islam. Hence,

> It is neither objective not fair to blame on Islam or Islamists the injustices and inequalities experienced by Arab women. We have to ask about the role incompetent and intrusive governments play in all of this. We have to ask about the roles played by the international economy, capitalism or by economic liberalization. We have to ask about the roles of reckless development, the content of education in our school systems...The lack of gender equality and participation in Muslim societies does not make the problem inherently Islamic.[125]

Contrary to popular belief, Islamist women are of the view that the Islamic resurgence of the 1980s with its strong emphasis on inclusiveness has yielded a unique brand of rethought Islam that is woman-friendly. The upshot has been an openness within and without. The openness within has meant a revolutionisation of the way many male Islamists and leaders perceive women, namely, as an element whose representativeness in the ranks of Islamist movements is taken far more seriously than ever before. These movements want not just to appear representative to the wider Muslim community; they want to discard traditionalist thought and practice that tended to subordinate women. Islamist movements cannot expect to look consistent and credible if they criticised Arab regimes for excluding them whilst themselves excluding and marginalising women. Uṣāl al-Mahdī, Ḥasan al-Turābī's wife, says of the seminal Islamist ideologue's push for more inclusiveness of women in the jabhah as an imaginative response to a desire of thousands of religious Sudanese women for a platform. Al-Turābī picked the cue for his reforms from women themselves.[126] This to Zakiyyah ʿAwaḍ Sātī has meant restoring a much revered Islamic ethos, that of power-sharing whereby women's God-given worthiness as an ennobled human being—which entitles her to be man's equal in shouldering responsibility, fulfilling duties, and enjoying rights—is fully recognised and appreciated. According

[125] Author's interview with Lubābah al-Faḍl, 7 May 1994, Khartoum.
[126] Author's interview with Uṣāl al-Mahdī, 3 May 1994, Khartoum.

to her, women's worthiness and rights are sanctioned by God; that is, man cannot take them away.[127]

In the context of the National Islamic Front, the main opposition party in parliament between 1986 and 1989 in Sudan, this meant active recruitment of women throughout the country's university campuses, workplaces and other women's networks. The intention was not solely to equalise women but also to widen the arena for recruitment. This was not difficult in a country where women had less social restrictions placed on them than elsewhere in the AME. This national specificity was an already existing foundation that the jabhah capitalised on, making the recruitment of thousands of female members quite easy, especially in the predominantly Arab and Muslim north where religiosity is strongly deep-rooted. This recruitment effort is unprecedented in Islamist movements, namely, the ikhwān in neighbouring Egypt where the population is more than twice the size of Sudan's. This expanding of political space to women within an Islamist political party has had effect on other Islamist movements in the AME. This new development in the late 1980s and early 1990s, for example, influenced Jordan's Muslim Brethren and more specifically, its political arm, al-ʿamal, al-nahḍah of Tunisia and, to an extent, the ikhwān of Egypt. The successful mobilisation of Islamist women in Sudan through the jabhah remains so far unprecedented amongst Islamist movements in the AME. In Jordan, explains Rubā al-Farkh, the handicaps are: strong tribal structures, religious conservatism and and incipient democratisation. While tribalism has paradoxically allowed women a margin of space in the countryside such as in the fields where they are quite active, it has entrenched patriarchy and hierarchy. Religious conservatism has generally been slow in adopting independent reasoning to interpret anew the Qur'ān and the Sunnah which accord women many rights to inclusiveness. The third factor relates to the fact that democracy and political parties have been absent for the greater part of Jordan's history. Relative to the reality of Jordan, what the jabhah has achieved in terms of recruiting women is positive indeed. As al-Farkh puts it:

> May be the small number of female members look mediocre by outside standards. By Jordan's standards they represent a very positive achievement that women find very encouraging. We are still getting used to the idea of

[127] Author's interview with Zakiyyah ʿAwaḍ Sātī, 3 May 1994, Khartoum.

democracy which is still new and fragile. In our case we are getting used to democracy and shūrā within the Islamic Action Front where the number of female members is higher than in the other weak and small Jordanian parties.[128]

Special circumstances have prevented both al-nahḍah and al-ikhwān from fully developing into licensed political parties in Tunisia and Egypt respectively. The former has been in a state of exile in Europe since the early 1990s. The latter has been in a quasi-state of siege which has not permitted it to operate openly. Whilst many of its leaders and members are well-known, there is a lot about al-ikhwān which is not known. It can be said that the bitter experience of confrontation and persecution by successive regimes in Egypt since the 1950s has taught al-ikhwān not to disclose all its activities or all its members, especially its female members and its fifth generation of young activists, making it a unique example of a movement which is semi-underground. This is a strategy of survival as al-ikhwān's spokeserson, al-Huḍaybī, describes it. However, al-ikhwān has thousands of female members and sympathisers who are very active in hundreds of voluntary associations, NGOs, clinics, hospitals, charity organisations, and schools. Operating below state politics offer them many advantages. They gain protection from state intrusiveness and heavy-handedness as well as a space within which their silent struggles are carried out with a great deal of benefit for society. These struggles are unadvertised forms of defiance against authoritarian rule. The faithful, al-Ghazālī stresses, need not be in parliament or in a political party to effect change and carry out Islam's obligations of communal help, of cooperation and of *al-amr bi''l-ma'rūf* (enjoining the good). For her, and this is a view all Islamist women share, participation and visibility do not equate with public authority.[129]

This relatively gradual rise to prominence below the state is at odds with the conventional wisdom that religion or so-called religious fundamentalism has been a regressive and restrictive force, acting to disempower and disenfranchise women globally.[130] The projecting of religion as a force indissolubly intertwined with women's

128 Author's interview with Rubā al-Farkh, 11 June 1994, Amman.

129 Author's interview with Zaynab al-Ghazālī, 11 April 1994, Cairo.

130 See, for instance, Kate Clark *et al., Women Against Fundamentalism*, Journal 7 (November 1995).

disempowerment is for Islamist women a bias that stems from a Western modernist discourse in which religion is assumed to be its polar opposite—an associate of traditionalism. Part of this bias is the assumed progressive trajectory of the humanism-based modernism of the West and positivist politics. Linked to this reasoning is the assumption that veiled women are subjugated in conjugal, professional and political relations. Interviewee Islamist women find the scholarly obsession with the veil not only insulting and patronising but, more importantly, reductionistic. The veil, as al-Ghazālī notes, "is not just a head-dress; it is a way of thinking, being and doing; it is linked to the Muslim woman's faith, convictions, struggle, and personhood".[131] For all of these women the veil is about values of community, responsibility and humanity with no actual or potential harm to any society. They all agree that as an emblem of their mode of thinking and doing, the veil fosters the Muslim woman's physical, social, intellectual and professional mobility. The veil is not meant to be restrictive. Rather, it is meant to link woman to her community not marginalise her, making her a participatory agent with much profit to the community as a whole. Implicit in this is the idea of being assigned with a good share of moral, professional, social and personal and communal responsibility. Accordingly, the *islāmiyyāt* view the veil to be about a broader meaning of identity and belonging, those of a human brotherhood and sisterhood of people committed to the enjoining of good and the forbidding of evil globally. As eloquently put by al-Fāʿūrī of al-ʿamal, "Good anywhere in God's earth benefits all human beings everywhere; and evil inflicted on human beings anywhere on God's earth is evil against people wherever they may be."[132]

The aforementioned ideology underpinned by religiosity explains the following positions (most of which separate Islamist women from secular feminisms which are informed by humanism and modernism) shared by all Islamist women:

- commitment to religion and religious ethics;
- belief in the relevance of religion as an emancipatory force for the modern world;
- belief that the marginalisation of women has historically been the result of the misinterpreting of divine scriptures;

[131] Author's interview with Zaynab al-Ghazālī, 11 April 1994, Cairo.
[132] Author's interview with Nawāl al-Fāʿūrī, 13 June 1994, Amman.

- belief that Islam offers a superior alternative framework for reconciling men and women, earthly with heavenly needs in the fulfillment of people's obligations toward each other, toward God and toward nature; and for conducting political struggles within it;
- necessity of moral struggles, voices, platforms and approaches to knowing, thinking, being and doing;
- Islamic values are in harmony with the values of equality, justice, the worthiness of human beings, and good government;
- good government must reflect Islamic values not ape imported ideologies.

Feminisation and Democratisation

Islamist women have been actively translating the prominence they gained via the Islamic resurgence of the 1980s into effective presence in the fledgling democratisation experiments in the AME in the 1990s. Interviewees from both al-ʿamal and al-jabhah felt that being present and active in the current politics of renewal is important for the following reasons:

- taking an active role in promoting good government and ridding the AME of authoritarian rule presents Muslim women just as it does Muslim men with an opportunity to live up to the divine command to enjoin the good and prevent the reprehensible;
- women's intellectual, social and political participation and presence promote good government;
- failure to do so would lead to the marginalisation not only of women as has been the case since independence but also to the marginalisation of Islam and cultural identity;
- failure to do so would leave the task of bringing about good government in the AME to authoritarian ruling elites whose politics aim at survival in office.

However, Islamist women take a critical position on the globalisation of democratic discourses on three grounds. Most secular democratic discourses display a patent bias against religion, especially Islam and Islamic movements. Islamism is generally constructed as the antithesis of republican values and as a "threat" to the West. This bias, points out Nawāl al-Fāʿūrī, has had enough influence locally, making democratisation experiments in many Arab countries exclusionary and violent. She says "If the opinion on Islamism in the West has been favourable, it would have been as favourable amongst Arab rulers and secular intellectuals and, ultimately, democratic experiments would have been smoother in the larger states like Algeria or Egypt."[133] Moreover, and as a consequence of the embedded anti-Islamist bias in the West, Islamist women tend to think of the global democratic discourses as contradictory, i.e. they do not serve democratic diffusion. Rather, they serve no more than the global diffusion of Western modes of thinking and doing about how to go about democratisation in disregard of whether such modes actually suit non-Euro-American peoples. However, the adversarial discourse on Islamists in many parts of the West has more to do with constructing public opinion and local identities than just with being about hostility against Islam or Islamists. Nothing brings in sharper focus the contrast between Western democracy and Arab non-democracy or so-called "Islamic fundamentalism" than television footage of warring Algerians and their bloodied victims or massacred tourists in Egypt. Islamists tend to think of themselves as the only targets of adversarial discourses. In fact, the following view expressed by Zakiyyah ʿAwaḍ Sātī is fairly widespread amongst Islamists:

> The fact that we are Islamists has not prevented us from trying to understand the West or engage in finding out about Western democracy and modernity. We have prejudicial ways of thinking of our own. Not even these have prevented us from discovering whatever we can about the West. Yet our detractors in the West are not disposed to accept what we believe in except on their own terms, meaning they do not wish us to occupy any space in the realms of politics or of ideas. These are people who talk about pluralism and equality but they do not seem to be prepared to treat us in a democratic or equal fashion.[134]

Many *islāmiyyāt* level a more serious criticism at the global democratic discourse: that its language of women's liberation and rights bespeaks its derision of veiled women. The issue here is not one of donning the veil or not. It is more of a question of being or not being Muslim as far as Islamist women are concerned. Being is about obeisance of Islamic teachings as enunciated in the Qur'ān and the Sunnah. According to these two sources, human beings neither possess their own bodies nor the outside physical world. God alone does. Human beings own them only in so far as these Godly favours are consecrated

[133] Ibid.
[134] Author's interview with Zakiyyah ʿAwaḍ Sātī, 3 May 1994, Khartoum.

for enjoining the good which entails submission to God's commandments. For Islamists, with every act of submission, they translate God's commandments into an act of being. This is the perfect symbiosis: they protect God's laws to be protected by them; and they enact the divine commandments and in the process have their own being enacted. Thus Islamist women do not think of their bodies as their own but rather as Godly favours that must be respected and maintained according to His laws. This teleological worldview stands in contrast to that internal to anthropocentrism, namely, that people own their bodies and everything on Earth, animals and materials. Zakiyyah 'Awaḍ Sātī notes that Islam stresses modesty, care and moderation in treating one's body and one's environment. For her, the excesses of the Western way have wrecked havoc on human beings, their morals and their environment.[135] The view amongst the *islāmiyyāt* is that donning the veil is an act of faith and submission to God not to man. Interviewees mention how headscarves continue to spark controversies in Europe, namely France, as well as in Muslim countries. In the case of France, these controversies raged over Maghribi schoolgirls wearing scarves in breach of deeply entrenched rules of secular education. What is so intriguing about these controversies in the eyes of Islamist women is their authors' doublespeak. Zaynab al-Ghazālī observes:

> Many Western men and women tend to think of veiled women as submissive and without a will of their own to resist donning the veil. At the same time, others, as happened in France, claim that these very submissive veiled women can challenge French values and the French system. Here you have two images, one of weakness and another of strength. If veiled women are weak, as many Westerners think, how could a few of them pose a threat to the might of republican France?[136]

Furthermore, she adds:

> In the name of freedom, women in some Western countries may choose to have abortions. But Islamist women are continuously told that veils suppress them. There are of course those who go further than that by saying that Muslim women must not wear the veil altogether. What choice are these women given? Are they supposed to disobey God's law and obey man's law?[137]

135 Ibid.
136 Author's interview with Zaynab al-Ghazālī, 11 April 1994, Cairo.
137 Ibid.

Islamist women regard concern in some Western quarters for the welfare of Arab women because of oppressive patriarchal practices, culture or customs to be phoney. They agree that colonial experiences in the Arab world have set a lasting negative precedent, noting that the European powers of the time suppressed men and women and considered both as belonging to barbaric cultures. The neocolonial experiences do not fare any better as far as they are concerned. The political and economic policies Western interests pursue in the Arab world hurt Arab women. Politically, the close ties with authoritarian ruling elites in the AME are singled out for criticism. Economically, so is the Western promoting of *laissez faire* and free market economies. From this perspective, Islamist women from al-ʿamal and al-jabhah are of the view that their activism is more in harmony with the ends of realising good government than is either state-led democratisations in the AME or the global democratic discourse. Both are regarded as hindrances to the inclusion of Islamist women. That discourse, according to a member of al-ʿamal, has biased the prevailing thinking of what type of democracy must be diffused and who must be counted in and counted out in the global process of democratisation.[138]

Democratisation and Islamisation

Two widely prevalent ideas stand out in explaining the linkage between the two global processes of democratisation and of Islamisation. The first is that the *islāmiyyāt* do not consider the goals of Islamisation and democratisation to be in conflict. They understand the resurgence begun in the 1980s to be intimately bound up with the struggle for justice and good government. If democratisation is about wide consultation, participation, and laws that protect freedoms of worship, speech and organisation, as many *islāmiyyāt* tend to understand this transformative process, their own struggles support it. Whether below the state or at the level of the state, these women contend that Islamist activism has opened up new possibilities for accommodating Muslim women and men in the struggles throughout the AME to bring about good government. Similarly, they believe that the forces of Islamic resurgence have been able to pluralise the political scene in the AME. This pluralisation has allowed for the reconfiguring of the political map in many Arab countries like Jordan, Yemen, Sudan,

[138] Author's interview with Fadwā Abū Ghaydā', 14 June 1994, Amman.

Algeria and Egypt, both spatially and discursively. Although the forces of secular-nationalism are still dominant and monopolise the reins of state power, Islamists have been successful in carving out, primarily, a discursive space, and, secondarily, a political space, making Islamism and the project of Islamisation the most formidable forces challenging the status quo in the AME. For Islamist women, for so long as Islamists are denied political space, Arab democratic experiments will remain meaningless. Simply put,

> Arab regimes cannot pretend that their peoples or the rest of the world lend any credence to their political reforms so long as they continue to ban Islamists and make elections cosmetic affairs amongst like-minded secularists. Democracy is not meant to be about exclusion by law or by force of those who hold different views and philosophies from the rulers. European countries did not ban communists, not even in the height of the Cold War. Had they done so, they would have made mockery of democracy.[139]

The second idea is that the global processes of democratisation and Islamisation have a number of irreconcilable differences. These differences have more to do with the perception amongst Islamist women of the contradictions within democratic practices in the West than with the principles of representative, accountable and legal government. At the core of the imperfections they perceive is democracy's routinisation of contractual politics to the point of complacence *vis-à-vis* the flaws inherent in its practice. Democracy in the West, these women charge, has meant living with cultural arrogance and expansionism; with inequality between the rich and the poor; with many types of exclusion; and with economic exploitation at home and abroad. These charges are not unlike those levelled by Westerners—postmodernist deconstructionism/feminism—themselves against their democratic systems. By contrast, Islamist women represent Islamisation to be about rethinking Islam. They understand it as an intergenerationally and slowly evolving process of knowing, being and doing, geared towards challenging the imperfections of Muslim polities and societies. For the *islāmiyyāt*, Islamisation is therefore evolving in many corners of the Muslim world as the devouts' vote of confidence in the divinely-sanctioned forms of power, authority, morality and legitimacy. In spite of pressure from within and without, Islamisation coheres by virtue of its goals of sustaining the Islamic community's

139 Author's interview with Ḥayāt al-Misīmī, 15 June 1994, Amman.

drive for *nahḍah*; of renewing and rethinking Islam and regenerating its moral, political, social and economic substance to fit the spirit of the age; and of reasserting a high sense of collective and cultural identity.

Accordingly, for the *islāmiyyāt* Islamisation is not just about dealing with the "other" but is about dealing with the "self". Important is the creation of the Muslim person, the key to the realisation of the democratically-minded individual. It is the sum of this individual that creates the Muslim society and the democratic society. Many Islamist women agree that the Muslim who is morally sound (incorruptible, does not cheat or lie), socially conscious (committed to justice; helps the needy; questions injustice and wrong-doing), fair-minded (respects rules even when unfavourable—as in elections; accepts responsibility for own faults instead of passing the buck); and is consultative is more likely to help the cause of democracy than not. Hence the creation of the Muslim and by extension democratic Muslim is a bottom-up approach. It begins inside the family, perhaps the most important social unit in Islam and one in which women's roles are of paramount importance. This role is never belittled by Islamist women; nor is it made to be distinct from the public sphere. According to the former Sudanese parliamentarian, Suʿād al-Fātiḥ, the Muslim woman is involved in politics indirectly by cultuvating into children Islamic and civil values. This politically and religiously didactic role within the family unit does not mean, she argues, that Muslim women are not available for political participation outside the household.[140] Ideally, as many Islamist women point out, inducting children into Islam aims at socialising them not only into beliefs and rituals but also into the morals of consultation, participation and the virtues of equality and communal mutual obligations.

Because Islam, Islamists and Islamisation remain widely misunderstood, suspect or demonised, presenting a more favourable "face" of Islam and Muslims to the rest of the Arab and international publics is a tough assignment. It is tough because of the widely entrenched anti-Islamism bias amongst these publics, especially amongst the highly educated and empowered. This is one reason why many *islāmiyyāt*, like most Islamist men, express consternation at the collusion between many Westerners and Arab avid cultural Westernisers

140 Author's interview with Suʿād al-Fātiḥ, 10 May 1994, Khartoum.

to construct Islamists or Islamisation as anti-democracy, anti-West and anti-women. They take this collusion to stem from fear of Islamism's interrogation of corruption, immorality, dominative practices, materialism, cultural arrogance and neocolonialism. This collusion is viewed as a signifier of a relationship of *maṣāliḥ* (political interests/expedience) and *'amālah* (subservience).

Regardless, Islamist women are optimistic that bias against their belief will not impede either Islamism or efforts to reconstruct in Islam. Islamist women have carved out a discursive space. This space they occupy in their own professional fields, syndicates, charity organisations, newspapers, national and international conferences, in party meetings, and in the *ḥalaqāt* (discussion groups) of debates with both Islamist and non-Islamist women. Al-jabhah's Su'ād al-Fātiḥ frequently hosts dozens of Islamist women in her own house which is equipped with a seminar room for holding *ḥalaqāt*. She is the most prominent and longest serving female Islamist but certainly not the only one with such facilities. Many prominent women of al-jabhah such as Uṣāl al-Mahdī, Zakiyyah 'Awaḍ Sātī, and Sumayyah Abū Kashawwah are as committed to these *ḥalaqāt* and possess similar resources for hosting them. Zaynab al-Ghazālī is another Islamist activist whose contribution to the creation of a discursive space by Islamists, in general, and Islamist women, in particular, is second to none. Her home acts as a headquarters from which she speaks out against Westernisation, authoritarianism, corruption, injustice, poverty and cultural imperialism. Her prominence as the leading Arab Islamist woman gave her in the past access to palaces of Saudi monarchs (e.g. the late King Fayṣal of Saudi Arabia) and of presidents (e.g. the late Zia ul-Haq of Pakistan), amongst others.

As part of renewing and reconstructing, Islamist women's discourse appears to be charged with asserting subjectivity and grounding agency in an Islamic framework. Thus their exploring of the differences of democracy and of Islam is not about transforming the "foreignness" and "otherness" of democracy into religiously and culturally familiar signifiers of Islamic morality, justice, equality and consultation as much as it is about reconceptualising several democratic dogmas. In so doing, the chief element of this discursive exercise is always to subject all reconceptualisation to the test of being in harmony with the Islamic framework. Here the Islamic is primary; the democratic secondary. That is not to say that the democratic is unimportant.

Rather it is important only in so far as it is co-extensive with the Islamic, actually or potentially. It is this idea that provides coherence to Islamist discourses on democracy, whether their authors are male or female.

When the *islāmiyyāt* question Western democracy, they do not query the ideal of good government and due process. Rather, they question aspects of it that impinge on those which are taken to be normative in Islam or Muslim societies. Their questioning of democracy therefore vacillates between criticism and identification. Identification relates to the fact that they recognise that the democratic system opens for Muslims unfettered space for free worship without which *muwāṭanah* (citizenship) itself is meaningless. Only Muslims free from the encroachments of an authoritarian state can fulfil their obligations toward God and community thoroughly. Freedom from autocracy is the organising principle of both the Islamic and democratic political communities. Autocracy is a threat to that freedom in Islam and in a democracy. Here the *islāmiyyāt* identify with democratic rule. But when it comes to religion, notions of political community in Islam and in a democracy part company. Democracy guarantees freedom of religion, relegating it to the personal sphere. In Islam there is freedom of religion but not freedom from religion. In fact, for Islamist women religion-less freedom can be subjugating. The religious realm as understood by Islamists interpenetrates with every sphere of Muslim daily life. Thus the kind of political identity that sustains political community in Islam knows no distinction between the public and the private (even though in practice, centuries of unlimited authority by Muslim men over women tells a different story). Hence country or community is a public matter; and so is God. Accordingly, the idea that the "personal is political", made popular by Western feminists a few decades ago, is not new for the *islāmiyyāt*.

The political identity that the *islāmiyyāt* have in mind is wedded to a religious identity. Citizenship rights—participating in consultation, voting or standing for office—are not disassociated from enacting religious obligations toward God, community, family and the self. Whereas democratic political identity focuses attention on the individual; that in Islam places premium on the group. The former limits its activities to the here and now; the latter has the hereafter in its sight. What issues from this is a hierarchisation of rights. God's rights, that is, obligations towards God, supersede those owed to the community, the family and the self. Thus the space the *islāmiyyāt* endeavour to carve out in Muslim society is bound up with obligations towards God, community and family. God is the ultimate norm-sender; Islamicity, submission to God's law, is the highest form of civility; and *ummah* is the ideal community. What is therefore good for God, community and family is good for the self. Characteristic of civility is then selflessness.

It is this selflessness that the *islāmiyyāt* find to be inexorable and missing in Western democracy. Political identity and activity are not about self-advancement; they are rather about being constantly engaged in negotiating an interface in which to merge the personal with the Godly and with the communal. As a result, success is not measured by office tenure or winning parliamentary seats. It is, more importantly, a function of how office tenure or parliamentary membership do not take place at the expense of one's obligations towards God, community and family. Moreover, when these rewards are realised, they are utilised to enjoin the good as enunciated in the Qur'ān. For Islamist women, other criteria of success include inducting one's progeny into Islam, raising family and fostering communal coherence. All of these, argue many *islāmiyyāt*, are political.

Political vocation in Western democracy, point out many interviewees, places too much emphasis on the individual. Hence the familiar criticisms of self-centred individuals whose interests can at times override communal interests. This tension between communitarian/holistic and individualistic/atomistic notions of political identity disappears under an Islamic order according to all interviewees. For instance, Uṣāl al-Mahdī points out that this friction is seen historically through a variety of political communities and identities patterned on the Western model. Under colonialism, the colonisers' interests were at odds with those of the colonised who were transformed into a sub-class of human beings. Under neo-colonialism, nationalism, the ideological heir of the Western model, pitted the state against society, subjecting the religious, women and others. This was and is still possible, she points out, because of the wide use of violence.[141] In fact, the element of violence is regarded by many *islāmiyyāt* to sustain Western democracy, especially at the global level. Again, this is an aspect that Islamist women ascribe to the

141 Author's interview with Uṣāl al-Mahdī, 3 May 1994, Khartoum.

nature of the Western worldview which killed God only to elevate the individual or the state to its level of transcendence. Thus, sacralisation of the individual or the system the Western man creates in his image celebrates man's self-createdness. God is the point of anchorage in the Islamic worldview. Hence, at least in theory, political identity is not hierarchised and paired into opposites: masculine/feminine or national/non-national. Likewise, political community is not reduced to territoriality. Political activity and *muwāṭanah* become expressions of a Godly morality that sees humankind as ennobled creatures whose promise of happiness is neither self-centred nor limited to the here and now. Political vocation impoverishes humankind when what is meant to be a criterion of civility and citizenship is converted into competition and domination of humans and nature. As Suʿād al-Fātiḥ puts it, Islamists have doubts about a system in which the compulsions of naked political power, competition and domination can justify expansionism, racism, cultural imperialism and the threat of total annihilation: "When men and women, God's creatures, are held ransom to nuclear weapons by so-called peoples' democracies and liberal democracies, then as Muslims we are obligated to challenge such arrogance and such egoism and the wisdom of their systems of thought and politics."[142]

WOMEN AND POLITICS IN THE AME

Arab women's gains from recent political liberalisations are both discursive and practical. Despite the fact they may disagree on the kind of modernity that must be promoted in the AME, these women activists agree on the necessity of democratic rule. At the discursive and epistemological levels, women in many parts of the Arab world are engaged in debating and deconstructing democracy, a system they recognize as important for their own struggles for gender equality as well as for the overall struggle against authoritarian rule. Their engagement with democracy aims at degendering political thought and practice in the AME. But their deconstruction and redefinement of democracy is never focused on gender alone.

Locally, both secular and Islamist women understand democracy in ways that do not bypass Islam or challenge its place in Arab societies. The difference between secular and Islamist women is not over the

[142] Author's interview with Suʿād al-Fātiḥ, 10 May 1994, Khartoum.

place of Islam but rather over whose Islam, how much Islam and what type of Islam best serve the visions of modernity and society espoused by these two groups. Islamist women's ideas are rooted in a more teleological or God-centred than a man-centred framework unlike their secular counterparts' debating of democracy. Nonetheless, both groups call into question the existing systems oppression and inequality in the AME. Both sides of the debate unite against authoritarian orders. Implicit in their politics of protest is the endeavour to assert the place of women in the political process, and the choices and contributions their political inclusion can bring to them and to the various Arab communities they live in.

Globalisation both promotes and demotes women's, and for that matter men's, opportunities for inclusion and empowerment. In theory at least, the enabling role of communications technologies creates openings for self-expression, mobilisation and organisation for people everywhere. In practice, it is the well-endowed who dispose of access for such media. In fact, not all globalisation is good. Globalisation has, for instance, in the economic sphere created new types of inequality and injustices that count women out rather than in. The spokesperson for women's affairs in Egypt's leftist Tagammuʿ Party, Farīdah al-Naqqāsh, is critical of globalisation's disempowering effects on Arab women.[143] She points out to the fact that the neo-liberal agenda, especially its element of *khaṣkhaṣah* (privatisation), has been detrimental to working women in the AME, namely, Egypt. For her, Arab states' rush to embrace *khaṣkhaṣah*, under the auspices of the IMF and the World Bank, are hurting women who are seen as the first expendable fraction of the labour force in the job cuts executed by the managers of newly-privatised public assets. This she finds to be detrimental to gender empowerment. Gender empowerment is aided by the availability of opportunities for women to disengage from exclusively domestic labor and by entering into salaried activities, even if on a part-time basis.

This is not happening in the AME. Al-Naqqāsh points to the deterioration of working conditions and loss of benefits (maternity leave, sick leave, social insurance and superannuation) in increasingly privatised industries such as the textile sector, the oldest state-owned industry in Egypt and traditionally the biggest employer of women. Al-Naqqāsh doubts whether the free market can offer prospects of

143 Author's interview with Farīdah al-Naqqāsh, 18 February 1998, Cairo.

growth and rising living standards for women in the AME especially when globalisation's dismantling of the public sector opens up the way for the kind of exploitative sweatshops found in Asia. For her, any talk of political democracy that excludes economic democracy is futile; she considers them two sides of the same coin. Moreover, local small business and industries are feeling the pinch of globalisation, finding themselves squeezed out of any type of government assistance or subsidy with many forced out of the market. Those that survive thrive on the exploitation of poor women's cheap labour. Women who are employed by this sector work in appalling conditions and accrue little or no benefits, something al-Naqqāsh likens to medieval slavery—feminisation of poverty. Pregnant women are automatically sacked. Several women do not announce their pregnancy for many months for fear of retrenchment, exposing themselves to occupational health hazards; these small industries and businesses do not have even minimum occupational health and safety standards or safeguards. Compounding this, she argues, is the immaturity of state-led democratisation. For instance, government laws require a minimum of 250 workers for the forming of a trade union. This figure is far below the number of employees of most small industries and businesses in Egypt. Hence women find themselves doubly disempowered with economic exploitation conflating with political exclusion.[144] These very conditions which undermine gender empowerment and equality have mobilised new democratic forces who are taking on government, bureaucracy and the legal sector in Egypt and other Arab countries in order to empower the voiceless and give them legal and political representation and rights. An example of these new democratic forces are Marākizu 'l-musā'datu 'l-qānūnniyah li-ḥuqūqi 'l-insān (Centres of Legal Aid for Human Rights), a few of them operate in Egypt and similar ones already exist in Tunisia and Morocco, countries where privatisation is proceeding apace.

Al-Naqqāsh's own reflection on political Islam in Egypt and the rest of the Arab world is one of a medieval force that is hostile to women's emancipation. Her position contradicts that held by the *islāmiyyāt* for whom Islamic revivalism has had a feminising effect on Islamic movements where women are increasingly being accommodated despite traditionalist disapproval. Al-Naqqāsh associates both

[144] Ibid.

market forces and forces of political Islam with women's disempowerment and exclusion.[145] But her account is not atypical of the left in the AME. Noteworthy, however, is that national-secularism and Islamic revivalism, the two forces currently at loggerheads in the AME, are both selective in their inclusiveness of women. National-secularism is inclusive of secular women and exclusive of Islamist women. The inverse is true of Islamic movements. In Egypt and Tunisia, veiled women are the subject of systematic discrimination by the public sector. Tunisia's Article 108 of the mid-1980s, as noted before, illustrates how the state deploys the legal process to coerce women to shun the veil in return for employment. It is a form of an arbitrarily blatant and flagrant disregard for personal privacy and choice. It is akin to traditionalists' insistence upon the veil; that is, another extremism. This kind of negative discrimination is the opposite of affirmative action used in the West to empower women. The Islamists' own constructions of secular women exhibit derision, disdain and misunderstanding. If the veiled woman is constructed as the opposite of "progress" and "modernity" in secular nationalist rhetoric; her unveiled counterpart is represented in Islamist discourse as an agent of Westernisation who is incompatible with the *ummah's nahḍah*. But views on globalisation tend to converge with both secularists and Islamists agreeing on its disempowering effects on women and the AME in general. Islamists raise their own suspicions of the market and market-based democracy because of its links with colonialism in the past, and with commodification effects, cultural plundering, and the militarism of Western democracies in the present.

Globalisation as epitomised by extensive cross-border travel of the ideas of democracy and democratisation is not seen to be gender-neutral by many *islāmiyyāt*. The veiled woman is constructed in many narratives as "oppressed" or "backward". This image is contrasted with that of the unveiled, liberated, sophisticated, assertive and secular woman, Westerner or Westerniser. Thus the veiled woman is mystified into a medieval relic whose hidden womanhood does not fit with the notion of open society, an essential component of democracy. Western feminists express a different type of doubt about the universality of democracy and equality: its male-structured and male-oriented character. Men are citizens; women are denizens. They locate the ontology of domination not only in the silence of classic democratic

145 Ibid.

texts on women but also in the practices of exclusion within civil societies as well as the work forces of most nation-states that perpetuate the status quo. The male–female dichotomy in classic theories of democracy is replaced in counter-narratives by postmodern feminists, amongst others, by a female–male antagonism. Such an antagonism is rarely mirrored in deconstructions of democracy by female activists in the AME. Islamist women, in particular, shun ideas that posit them as adversaries of men. Rather, they venerate the orthodox texts' position that men and women are equally ennobled and equally assigned with enacting God's vicegerency on earth. Men and women are not only interdependent but also united by the oneness of origin. From this perspective, neither the ontology of women's domination is put down to divinity nor to masculinity in general. Antagonism is confined to specific masculinities, colonial, nationalist and traditionalist. They find both to strip them of Godly-given worthiness and rights. Arab secular women have their own quarrels with these three masculinities whose discourses and practices they find to be subversive of gender equality and gender-sensitive citizenship. Like their Islamist counterparts, secularist women probing the question of democracy do not find the origins of inequality in Islam but rather in Muslim customs, social, political and economic conditions that vary in context and nature.

Generally, Arab women do revere the divine texts even if they hold in contempt those traditionalist religious establishments, official and unofficial, whose "islams" (with a lower case "i") have been gender-blind. Islamist women's understandings of democracy discard these "islams", a task consistent with the aim of regenerating Islam (with an upper case "I"). But these understandings are nonetheless anchored in an Islamic framework. This is true of secularist women. The difference is whereas for the *islāmiyyāt* Islam is inextricable from every facet of life, for the secularists it is a private matter. Nonetheless, the new generation of female activists are not complacent *vis-à-vis* exegesis. Being learned themselves, they are in a position to re-interpret the scriptures and rethink the whole corpus of tradition in order to reclaim rights they claim to be enshrined in the Qur'ān, the ḥadīth and the Sunnah. Whereas women are able to read gender equality and economic, legal and political rights in the scriptures, traditionalists may not do so and/or they do so only grudgingly and in a token fashion.

In parts, the divine texts speak of equality and yet in others seem to suggest men's superiority over women. Gender equality is beyond doubt in the verse: "I will deny no man or woman among you the reward of their labours. You are the offspring of one another."[146] In another interdependence and oneness of origin of males and females are read clearly: "Men, have fear of your lord, who created you from a single soul [*min nafsin wāḥidah*]. From that soul He created its mate, and through them He bestrewed the earth with countless men and women. Fear Allah, in whose name you plead with one another, and honour the mothers who bore you. Allah is watching over you."[147] Other verses signify male superiority, specifically with regard to the issue of *qiwāmah* (economic providence): "Men have authority over women [or are in charge of women—*al-rijālu qawwāmuna 'ala 'l-nisā'i bimā faḍḍala 'lāhu ba'ḍahum 'alā ba'ḍin*] because Allah has made the one superior to the others, and because they spend their wealth to maintain them. Good women are obedient."[148] One verse speaks of both equality of rights between the sexes only to suggest what seems to be unequal status between the two: "...Women shall with justice have rights similar to those exercised against them, although men have a status [*darajah*, also a ranking] above women."[149] Exegetical talent of women themselves as well as of men throughout the Muslim world faces the challenge of fleshing out what may appear to the inquisitive non-Muslim inconsistency in the texts. More importantly, it is only through an exegesis of the texts in line with Islam's *istiḥsān* and *istisḷāḥ* (public utility) can traditionalist opposition to women's equality be stopped. For, it is the traditionalists' decontextualised readings of verses like the last two that can be misused to perpetuate the status quo.

Arab political reforms are still hampered by exclusion despite markedly higher participation and contestation and, in some instances, broader recruitment into the political process of formerly silenced or invisible social forces. The centre's intent on minimalist democracy continues to handicap unfettered inclusion and formidable opposition seriously. By and large, the dynamics of exclusion and inclusion

146 Qur'ān, 3, p. 195 *The Koran*, trans. by N.J. Dawood (Harmondsworth: Penguin, 1975).

147 Qur'ān, 4: 1 (ibid.)

148 Qur'ān, 4: 34 (ibid.)

149 Qur'ān, 2: 228 (ibid.)

in most Arab polities remain those of gender, family, class, ethnic group, religious and political affiliations, networking and patronage, and education. One or a combination of these dynamics explicate exclusion in most Arab democratising countries. Status and empowerment can be a function of influential family and class background, high education and, definitely, the right political connections and patronage networks. These dynamics make a huge difference in the lives of men and women endowed with them. In many Arab countries the *ʿāʾilāt* (families) in whose hands conflate political and economic power have not changed much from what they used to be in the colonial era.

It is therefore no coincidence that the three women sitting in Lebanon's Legislative Council are well-endowed politically, economically and socially. One female deputy is a prime minister's sister (Bahiyyah al-Ḥarīrī for Sidon); another (Nāʾilah Muʿawwaḍ representing Zgharta) is the widow of the late President Muʿawwaḍ; and the third (Nuhād Saʿīd) comes from a political family—her late husband, Antoine Said, was himself a deputy for Jubayl, the same constituency represented by his wife. The first two were first elected in 1992 and were re-elected in 1996. Before her election, Muʿawwaḍ was one of 40 deputies appointed to parliament in 1991. Pointing to these women's backgrounds of influence must not detract from their skills and abilities which no doubt have a bearing on why they get to succeed in a predominantly men's world for leadership roles where other women with similar backgrounds fail.

The dynamic of gender-based exclusion is common to most Arab polities, especially to the more conservative oildoms of the Gulf.[150] In all six monarchies women are visibly excluded from the political process. The profile of gender issues was raised during the deployment of the multinational forces following Iraq's invasion of Kuwait. The sight of female American soldiers did not go unnoticed. The 1990 symbolic procession in the Saudi capital by some 47 women behind the steering wheel demanding driving rights openly challenged the monarchy's androcentric discriminatory policies. Also, it indirectly

[150] For a general discussion of the questions of gender and democracy in the Middle East see Simona Sharoni, "Gender Issues in Democracy: Rethinking Middle East Peace and Security from a Feminist Perspective" in Boulding (ed.), *Building Peace in the Middle East: Challenges for States and Civil Society.*

flouted the whole creed of puritanical Wahhabism and its interpretations and legalisms which accord rights to men that women cannot enjoy.[151] Not a single woman sits in the newly expanded Consultative Council whose members are handpicked by the Royal House.

Kuwait has held four elections (1992, 1996, 1999 and 2003) since its "liberation" in 1991 by the US-led multi-national forces. In all elections women, who already vote in professional and council elections, were not extended the franchise. Kuwaiti women, who widely participate in society, remain politically disenfranchised. Women, however, are not the only disenfranchised social forces—naturalised citizens and segments of the country's decreasing Bedun (stateless nomads) population. Kuwaiti Philosophy professor, Aḥmad al-Rabʿī, describes the Emirate's exclusionary system as a "two-tier system" in which citizenship is effectively divided into first and second classes.[152] Pro-democracy activists[153] have been pressing the ruling al-Sabahs for universal suffrage arguing that exclusive voting rights for some 70,000 males (who possess proof of forebear residence prior to 1920) do not make for genuine pluralism. According to Salih, Electoral Law No. 35 (1962), which also disenfranchises members of the armed and police forces, contradicts Article 29 of the Constitution[154] "…which grants women the right to vote and to stand for election. It contend[s] that it is unfair to disenfranchise a social force that represents half its citizens of voting. Especially since women ha[ve] proven themselves in all fields and ha[ve] an important role to play in the state."[155] This very line of argument has been advanced by leading

151 Said K. Aburish writes that most of these protesting women, the majority of whom held Ph.Ds, were punished by being retrenched from their university jobs while others were jailed. See *The Rise, Corruption and Coming Fall of the House of Saud* (London: Bloomsbury, 1994), pp. 73–4. See also, W. Dowell, "Life in the Slow Lane", *Time* (26 November 1990), p. 35.

152 See "Kuwait: Pro-democracy Reformer Demands Abolition of Two-Tier Citizenship", *Reuters Textline* (Reuters News Service), 24 January 1992.

153 Support for the female franchise has existed for some time within the five pro-democracy and Islamic opposition groups that contested the October 1992 elections. Pro-democracy figures such as Aḥmad al-Khaṭīb, Jāsim al-Qaṭamī and ʿAbd-Allah al-Nibārī of the Kuwait Democratic Forum, are unequivocal in their support.

154 Article 29 reads: "People are equal in dignity and before the law in rights and duties and there is no discrimination among them because of sex, race, language and religion."

155 Salih, "Kuwait's Parliamentary Elections", p. 22.

women's rights activist and legal expert Badria al-ʿAwadī.[156] Kuwaiti women expressed disappointment and outrage for being yet again discriminated against in the October 1992 elections despite Amiri promises to the contrary during the Jeddah Kuwait Popular Congress of October 1990.[157]

However, women's political exclusion in the Arab Gulf should not be overstated at the expense of understating their disadvantaged status in the Arab Maghrib and Mashriq. In both regions, women remain politically under-represented despite much progress. The allocation of low-key portfolios for female ministers in governments should not mask the ineptitude of state and male-led "women's liberation" to empower Arab women. Although women are politically absent in the Arab Gulf states, recent United Nations *Human Development Reports* show them to be out-performing traditionally less gender-blind countries in the AME in relation to the gender-related development index (GDI) which measures annual percentages of female–male disparity using indices such as life expectancy, adult literacy, school enrolment and share of earned income. Both in GDI ranking and value, Kuwait, Bahrain and the U.A.E. are placed ahead of Algeria, Egypt, Lebanon, Morocco and Tunisia. Low GDI value corresponds with high levels of gender inequality (see Table 6.1). This latter class of Arab countries is more populous as well as materially less endowed than the Gulf states whose smaller populations and economic largesse allows greater investment in gender-related development.

By comparison, when it comes to Gender Empowerment Measure (GEM), which looks at female-male disparity in economic and political decision-making, the Arab Gulf states, barring Kuwait and the U.A.E., do not fare as well as the populous and poorer Arab states. GEM measurements are based on a different set of indices looking at female percentages of total seats held in parliament, of administrators and managers, of professional and technical workers, and of share of earned income. Again, higher levels of GEM value indicate lower levels of inequality (see Table 6.1). A single index measuring the female percentage of total seats in parliament yields a zero result

156 See "Kuwait: Election Law Unconstitutional", *Reuters Textline* (Reuters News Service), 5 December 1991.

157 See "Amir Upholds Women's Right", *Kuwait Times*, 16 February 1992, p. 1; see also, the Crown Prince's assurances of the Emirate's return to democracy in *Al-Siyasah*, 26 February 1992, p. 1.

Table 6.1. GENDER INEQUALITY IN THE AME

Country	*GDI*		*GEM*		*%Female seats in parliament 1996*
	Rank	*Value*	*Rank*	*Value*	
Algeria	92	0.614	74	0.282	7
Bahrain	56	0.742	–	–	–
Egypt	100	0.555	75	0.278	2
Iraq	117	0.433			–
Jordan	–	–	–	–	3
Kuwait	51	0.769	66	0.333	0
Lebanon	66	0.708	–	–	2
Libya	77	0.655	–	–	–
Mauritania	127	0.341	94	0.177	1
Morocco	105	0.515	72	0.303	1
Saudi Arabia	95	0.581	–	–	–
Sudan	135	0.306	87	0.225	5
Syria	84	0.646	–	–	10
Tunisia	74	0.668	78	0.260	7
Qatar	64	0.713	–	–	–
U.A.E.	61	0.727	84	0.237	0
Yemen	–	–	–	–	1

Source: United Nations Development Program, *Human Development Report 1997* (New York and Oxford: Oxford University Press, 1997), pp. 149–54, 57–8.

or a blank in relation to women's political decision-making in the Arab Gulf where Kuwait alone has an elected assembly and Saudi Arabia an appointed Consultative Council. Women sit in neither.

However, scepticism toward empirical evaluations must be maintained. Egypt, with a population approximating 70 million, has a larger pool of educated and highly-trained women than Arab countries with smaller populations. More Egyptian women are active in the labour force, acquiring the means for self-sustenance and autonomy, than the combined population of active workers in the Gulf states where voluntary unemployment is widespread. The same goes for other populous states such as Morocco, Algeria and Sudan. Many women in these populous countries have progressively moved into top managerial and technical positions, sharing with men both the rewards of power as well as the responsibility of decision-making. But the reverse is equally true. Populous countries have also more underemployed or unemployed women than Kuwait or the UAE whose combined indigenous populations do not surpass four million. There is pressure on limited material and human resources to provide adequate social services. Hence comparative readings of GDI values are useful but somewhat partial guides to the state of gender equality. Similarly, GEM values do not provide entirely accurate accounts of gender empowerment. Again, the example of Egypt is instructive. It is the Arab country where more women have for decades sat in parliament through election and appointment than anywhere else in the AME (see Table 6.2).

Table 6.2. FEMALE PARLIAMENTARY MEMBERSHIP EGYPT 1957–90

Year	*Number*
1957	3
1960	6
1964	8
1969	3
1971	9
1976	6
1979	35
1984	36
1987	19
1990	10

Source: Nādiah Ḥāmid Qūrah, *Tārīkhu 'l-mar'ah fi 'l-Ḥayāti 'l-Niyābiyah fi Miṣr Min 1957 ilā 1995* [*History of Woman in Parliamentary Life in Egypt, 1957–1995*] (Cairo: al-Hay'ah al-Misriyyah al-'Ammah Li al-Kitab, 1996), p. 528.

The combined number of Arab female parliamentarians falls short of that of Sweden or Norway, countries distinguished for gender equality in decision-making. But the standard set by Nordic countries is too high even for consolidated democracies like France and Italy. Another point is whether sheer numbers mean anything at all. The fact that in the late 1970s and up to the mid-1980s, there were more Egyptian than French women in parliament is no indicator that gender equality in political decision-making in Cairo was higher than in Paris. Because of all sorts of political restraints, most Arab deputies just "sit" in parliament; the majority of their European or Nordic counterparts do more than just "sitting". The sitting arrangements in most Arab parliaments resemble those of a classroom; deputies face a portrait of the leader just like students face their teacher whose authority reigns supreme. Whatever the standards, female parliamentary membership, although on the rise, still pales into insignificance when compared with figures for males. Figures for female-membership of the Egyptian People's Assembly (Table 6.3) and the Consultative Council illustrate this point (Table 6.4). Female participation in political decision-making is also uneven in the AME. The 1997 elections in Jordan and Yemen saw the single female members in both countries lose their seats. Elsewhere, such as in Algeria, Lebanon, Morocco, Sudan and Tunisia, women deputies are increasingly becoming a staying factor in parliamentary life. These represent benchmark beginnings in countries whose experiments with electoral politics and parliamentary life are still very new.

Table 6.3. FEMALE-MALE PARLIAMENTARY MEMBERSHIP IN THE EGYPTIAN PEOPLE'S ASSEMBLY 1971–90

Year	*Members*	*Females*			*Female %*
		Elected	*Appointed*	*Total*	
1971	360	7	2	9	2.2
1979	392	33	2	35	7.9
1984	457	35	1	36	7.9
1987	457	14	5	19	3.9
1990	453	7	3	10	2.2

Source: *Rafiqah Salīm Ḥammūd, Al-Mar'atu 'l-Miṣriyyah: Mushkilātu 'l-Ḥāḍir wa Taḥiddiyātu 'l-Mustaqbal* [*The Egyptian Woman: Present Problems and Future Challenges*] (Cairo: Dar al-Ameen, 1997), p. 203.

Table 6.4. FEMALE-MALE PARLIAMENTARY MEMBERSHIP IN THE EGYPTIAN CONSULTATIVE COUNCIL 1980–92

Year	*Females*	*Males*	*Female %*
1980	7	203	3.3
1986	4	206	1.9
1992	12	246	4.7

Source: *Rafiqah Salīm Ḥammūd, Al-Mar'atu 'l-Miṣriyyah: Mushkilātu 'l-Ḥāḍir wa Taḥiddiyātu 'l-Mustaqbal* [*The Egyptian Woman: Present Problems and Future Challenges*] (Cairo: Dar al-Ameen, 1997), p. 204.

Much has been achieved since the early male feminisms of Amīn and ʿAbduh. The legacy of those who dared to ponder the woman question in the late-nineteenth century to the feminists of the twentieth century was to initiate rethinking social custom and religious obscurantism in order to restore women to their rightful position in Islam and Muslim societies. They made nationalist liberation and religious regeneration contingent upon raising the social and political profile of women. Their feminisms were the by-product of an awakening to the shackles of religious dogmatism and of European colonialism. Thus the rights they were prepared to voice for women and on their behalf were themselves calibrated not to offend religious purity or detract from the struggle for national liberation as a top priority. Two generations have passed since al-Shaʿrāwī and Munīrah Thābit, amongst others, began the struggle for women's rights. These rights continue to rally female activists from al-Saʿdāwī (an avowed secularist and socialist) to al-Ghazālī (a staunch Islamist). In theory, the ideological stances of these two women are irreconcilable and inform their understanding of democracy differently. Also, they set apart their visions for women's equal participation, freedoms and rights. In practice, however, both have suffered under the authoritarianism of secular nationalist rule. Moreover, the two stand as symbols of how women's activism for equality in the AME, whether informed by Islam or by a secular ideology, has become so enmeshed in the struggle against autocracy. This legacy of women's struggles against autocracy has been bequeathed to their heirs in the twenty-first century. That is encouraging for the struggles for gender equality and for challenging the fixity and singularity of political and patriarchal structures.

Unlike the woman question and gender empowerment, international politics has not been made a vital site for the erosion of autocracy in the AME. The next chapter turns to this site where debate is heated, surveying discourses and counter-discourses on the West, Islam and democracy by Islamist leaders. No debate on the potentialities of democratic openings in Arab states can be complete without considering the external connection.

7

THE WEST AND THE SPONSORING OF ARAB AUTHORITARIANISMS

ISLAMIST NARRATIVES

"Democracy can mean different things to different political groups. It is unlikely that there is a single model that will be applicable in every setting. American attempts to engender democracy should be perceived as attempts by the United States to expand its own influence, a perfectly legitimate pursuit, and not to establish democracy in a value-free or politically neutral fashion." —Jerrold Green[1]

"A few international actors ranging from nation-states to financial institutions can be implicated, directly and indirectly, in the survival of a variety of Arab authoritarian regimes. We are not asking the West to export and impose democracy on the Arab and Muslim peoples. Democracy is not for export; whole-sale exportation of democracy entails imposing a whole host of values and practices that could endanger indigenous values. Learning from Western democratic achievements and adopting those values most congenial with deepening just, legal and consultative government in the Arab world must be compatible with our Arab and Islamic values. Indeed we are questioning the close associations of Western democrats with Arab autocrats. We are not telling the West what to do or not to do. However, for the West the inescapable question is whether it can indefinitely live with its economic and moral support for violators of human rights and regimes that stand in the way of fostering and promoting genuine good rule, constitutionalism and legality in the Arab world." —Rāshid al-Ghannūshī[2]

[1] Jerrold Green, "Challenges to Democratization in the Middle East", *American-Arab Affairs*, 36 (spring 1991), p. 12.

[2] Author's interview with Rāshid al-Ghannūshī, 15 April 1993, London.

Whether external powers have historically made a difference to the Arab world's embrace of good government remains unanswered. Two lines of investigation form the analytical agenda of this chapter. The first assesses the history of involvement by a number of Western powers and interests in the AME, showing its subversive effects on democratisation. The second looks at Islamist treatments of questions pertinent to culture, democracy and the specific role to be played by the West (i.e. governments and interests from both the United States and Europe) with regard to the Arab quest for good government and improved human rights practices. This line of investigation is warranted by the explosion of interest in the 1990s in linking issues of democracy, human rights and culture. This explosion has not spared the AME. The chapter draws on interviews with four leading Islamists—Rāshid al-Ghannūshī, the exiled leader of the outlawed al-nahḍah of Tunisia; Ma'mūn al-Huḍaybī, spokesperson of the Muslim Brethren in Egypt; Muḥammad 'Abd al-Raḥmān Khalīfah, former supreme guide of the Muslim Brethren in Jordan, and Isḥāq Aḥmad al-Farḥān, former education minister and former leader of the Islamic Action Front (IAF), the political arm of the Brotherhood in Jordan. What transpires from this section is that while Islamists generally are enmeshed in the discourse of and struggle for democracy, the type of democracy they have in mind revises and challenges Western foundations such as individualism and secularism. In other words, Islamists see no route to democracy without Islam. Before turning to these questions, the article briefly considers the broad contours of the discourse on Arab democracy, notably the issue of Eurocentrism and the politics of culture.

Democracy remains pending in the Arab world. Two contradictions confirm this state of affairs. First, democracy and human rights represent no more than a vogue: in the key Arab political liberalisers (Egypt, Lebanon, Tunisia, Jordan, Algeria, Yemen, Morocco and Kuwait) varying degrees of inconsistency persist between rising electoral activities, on the one hand, and genuinely accountable and representative rule, and human rights practices, on the other. Neither the current "electoralisation" or "parliamentarisation" of the Arab world is yet to presage substantive as against the present cosmetic democratic order. Nor the holding of elections, the results of which are sometimes preordained, is likely to serve as a harbinger for deepening rule of law, representative government, and authentic and durable democratic rule.

Second, if democracy and human rights matter for the democracies of Europe and North America, then greater Arab association with them through commercial, financial, strategic and diplomatic links should presumably translate into more "Arab democracy" or, at least, lead to a kind of "trickle down effect", advancing the cause of good government throughout the AME. The historical track record of that association, colonial and postcolonial, however, points to the fallacy of such reasoning. It seems that Euro-American policy-makers prioritise cultivating "friendly" or "pliant" over "democratic" regimes in the AME. There have been many cases in which the Western bloc had lectured "tough" international actors, who are usually not easily swayed, about democracy and human rights. This includes the former Soviet Union, and currently, China and Cuba. The near silence on those issues *vis-à-vis* the AME is a clear case of inconsistency on the part of Euro-American foreign policy-makers. Although in 2002 the US looked poised to overthrow Saddam Hussein citing his dictatorial rule.

ISLAMISTS AGAINST EUROCENTRISM AND ORIENTALISM

Islamists are enmeshed in the two most important processes in the Arab and Muslim worlds: Islamisation and democratisation. As Esposito and Voll point out "The dual aspirations of Islamisation and democratisation set the framework for most of the critical issues in the contemporary Muslim world."[3] If democratisation implies the endeavour to carve out a margin of existence in the public space or what Esposito and Voll define as the global "demand for empowerment in government and politics",[4] then Islamists from Yemen to Jordan are indeed active participants in the process of Arab democratisation. However, the point has to be made more forcefully that Islamisation and democratisation are not just "dual aspirations" but also mutually reinforcing processes, at least, as far as many Islamists are concerned. For many Islamists democratising Arab polities by claiming greater space in the public domain is not enough. Democratisation is understood as claiming greater space in the sphere of knowledge; hence the necessity of Islamisation. Through democratisation, Islamists hope to reclaim legally many revered institutions for

[3] John L. Esposito and John O. Voll, *Islam and Democracy* (New York and Oxford: Oxford University Press, 1996), p. 6.

[4] Ibid., p. 13.

enacting just, accountable and Islamic rule. Through Islamisation they hope to reclaim and operationalise concepts of justice, consultation, legality, accountability and probity in the management of economy, polity and society. In fact, the process of democratisation many Islamists have in mind is one that eventually and gradually serves their quest for Islamising knowledge and, subsequently, many spheres of public life. For Islamists, therefore, democratisation and democracy cannot be said to be "democratic" if they thwart their bid for Islamisation. Islamisation, especially of knowledge, a project that is being developed in Muslim countries, ranging from Sudan to Malaysia, is about cultural reassertion and self-determination. Through it Islamists do not aim at thwarting the democratic project but rather use it to enact their own imaginings of Islamic identity and of political and epistemological space.

These imaginings and the new possibilities they open up for reordering Muslim societies and approximating the ideal Islamic society have been spawned by what Eickelman and Piscatori call the "objectification of Muslim consciousness",[5] of which Islamists are a prominent configuration. These imaginings are anchored in the "objective" questioning Eickelman and Piscatori's "objectification" triggers, a theme invoked in this book more than once.

> Objectification is the process by which basic questions come to the fore in the consciousness of large numbers of believers: "What is my religion?" "Why is it important to my life?" and "How do my beliefs guide my conduct?"...These explicit, widely shared, and "objective" questions are modern queries that increasingly shape the discourse and practice of Muslims in all social classes, even as some legitimize their actions and beliefs by asserting that they advocate a return to purportedly authentic traditions.[6]

With objectification comes commitment. Islamists are committed activists, "committed to implementing their vision of Islam as a corrective to current "un-Islamic" practices".[7] With commitment comes a "certain measure of protest, demonstrated in a variety of ways, against the prevailing political and social status quo and establishments".[8] Protest is not only moral and political but also epistemological. The remaking of the world they live in starts with reshaping meanings,

[5] Dale F. Eickelman and James Piscatori, *Muslim Politics* (Princeton University Press, 1996), pp. 37–45.

[6] Ibid., p. 38.

[7] Ibid., p. 44.

[8] Ibid.

languages, symbols, that is, discourse. Their discourse is one that is formulated by tapping into the Qur'ān and the Prophet's sayings. The Islamists' imaginings, despite their polysemantic register, look for and find therefore their expression, meaningfulness and legitimacy within these sacred resources. Accordingly, these imaginings tend to challenge existing and dominant forms of knowledge-making, identity and political space.

Grounding human agency in foundations has often and everywhere precipitated crises and hubristic contestations between the opposed ideas, paradigms and understandings of universalists and particularists, transculturalists, cultural determinists and cultural relativists on social change, governance, development and nation and state-building. The crises of universalism and foundationalism are intertwined. As a knowledge practice, whether dressed in the garb of developmentalism in the past or democratisation as in the present, universalism has been nothing less than a concerted effort to both "objectify" and homogenise foundations of scholarship. Thus the language, concepts, methodologies and paradigms of Euro-American scholarship have been cast as explanatory universals in many a discipline. Juxtaposed to this scholarly foundationalism has been a second one, the essence of which is the supremacy of the foundations on the basis of which American and European models of economic and political prowess have been built: scientific reason and methodology versus magic and superstition; science and technology; secular deism which aims at privatising religion; and private enterprise.

Although culture is not a concept that is easy to unpack,[9] it has occupied degrees of prominence in the works of many known names from this century and the last. Its meaning, particularly in ethnographic and anthropological works, has from the eighteenth century up to now undergone a number of changes, gradually tempering the ethnocentrism of the early cultural determinists. This early cultural determinism eventually ceded to cultural relativism; anthropology

[9] For good and critical accounts of the concept of culture see the articles in Herbert Applebaum (ed.), *Perspectives in Cultural Anthropology* (Albany: State University of New York, 1987); the articles in Eliot Deutsch (ed.), *Culture and Modernity: East-West Philosophic Perspectives* (Honolulu: University of Hawaii Press, 1991); see also, Raymond Williams, *Keywords: A Vocabulary of Culture and Society* (London: Fontana, 1983); and James Clifford and George E. Marcus (eds), *Writing Culture: The Poetics and Politics of Ethnography* (Berkeley: University of California Press, 1986).

and ethnography almost reversed roles from the service of colonialism to that of emancipation, namely through respect of difference and sensitivity to cultural particularities. Hence anthropologists and ethnographists whose theses of European superiority, informed by the universality of Enlightenment, presented colonialism with its "civilising" rationale *vis-à-vis* "native populations", today show and practice sensitivity to the cultural context of "indigenous peoples". The evolutionary history of the concept of culture is manifest in its more imaginative usage going beyond dichotomous classifications of culture into "barbaric" and "civilised", and increasingly less constrained by a Eurocentric and ethnocentric worldview. Herder, Boas and Geertz are prime examples, tending toward a more relativistic approach, i.e. one stressing the relative value of culture.[10]

Sociology has not been spared the pitfalls of Eurocentrism and ethnocentrism. Weber, Marx, and Wittfogel's works, for instance, particularly with reference to non-European societies, resonate with dialectical definitions, i.e. self-definitions developed in contrast to stylised images of the "other". The "dynastic", "Sultanic" or "patrimonial" "Orient", in general, and Islam, in particular, as understood by Weber and the "Asiatic mode of production", a formulation epitomising Marx's (mis)understanding of non-European economies, are uncongenial with modernity.[11] Wittfogel renders the "Orient" with its "hydraulic" societies as lacking in civility, essentialising it into a simple and homogenised case of "strong" states and "weak" societies.[12] Generally, these renderings are based on racialised conceptions of non-European societies and cultures. In contemporary renderings, and past, the Euro-American model is the rule, the standard bearer from which the rest of the world's peoples are assumed to reap benefits; converge toward and strive to copy, politically (democratisation), economically (marketisation), socially (individualisation), and culturally (secularisation). If Europe and America are the rule and the model, the AME, like many other areas, is the exception to the rule. So exceptionalism can be understood as an exceptional position of multidimensional advantage that leads many of its holders—

[10] For more details on Herder see Williams, *Keywords*, p. 89.

[11] Bryan S. Turner, *Weber and Islam: A Critical Study* (London: Routledge and Kegan Paul, 1974); Bryan S. Turner, *Marx and the End of Orientalism* (London: Allen and Unwin, 1978).

[12] Karl A. Wittfogel, *Oriental Despotism: A Comparative Study of Total Power* (New Haven: Yale University Press, 1957).

the "us"—to arrogantly interpret economic, technological, military and political disadvantage of the "other" to be an exception and an inequality, and to further interpret the root problem as "outmoded"—not different—and consequently dispensable cultural traditions and teachings, and knowledge practices inspired by them.

Culture is the basis upon which peoples are being "worlded". Culture, like colour (black/white), has not only become political but often also signifies a political position, ranking or standing of dominance or leadership or of subservience and following. This is increasingly so in the age of communication and its technologies—the internet, satellites, cable television—which represent systems of power and empowerment, nationally, and most importantly, globally. While problematic for its reductionism, the term "Western culture" is shorthand for "Western" (itself a homogenising adjective) cultural dominance. If knowledge is power, technology is its delivery system. Equally, if knowledge is power, then those equipped with the technology to disseminate their systems of meanings and systems of knowledge informed by their cultures are no doubt poised to be doubly powerful, i.e. to dominate and lead culturally and technologically. For the disempowered technologically, countering against what Gramsci calls hegemony, a reference to "cultural domination", with their own brand of hegemony, will prove less possible. In a sense, the danger of "cultural imperialism" is now more real than ever before, especially when monopoly of communication technologies makes for a one-way information flow—North to South but not *vice versa*. This continues despite the proliferation of some of these technologies (e.g. the internet) to the AME. The nexus of culture and imperialism is either explained or hinted at in many works, especially those concerned with the subaltern and the formerly colonised.[13] But even Said, whose anti-Orientalism exposes cultural determinism and hegemony, cannot escape incoherence. A case in point is his criticism of the United States for not being historically supportive, *inter alia*, of the struggle for secularism in the Middle East.[14] To what extent does secularism represent a fragment of Western systems of knowledge, history, terminology and developmentalism? How congruent is secularism with the Middle East with its Muslim majority

[13] See, for instance, Edward Said, *Culture and Imperialism* (London: Chatto and Windus, 1993).

[14] Ibid., p. 363.

and where duality of power (state and church) is not the norm? Does not secularism qualify as one form of asserting cultural dominance if it can be established as alien to the Middle Eastern setting? Struggles by secular groups are as authentic as religious struggles and being Muslim and secular should never be considered a binary. But to suggest that secularism holds the key to democratising the AME and is alone worthy of moral and political support, to the exclusion of religious or other forms of non-theistic struggles is potentially prejudicial to the search for democracy and democratization. Ideally, theistic and non-theistic struggles should combine to defeat authoritarian rule.

The fusion of politics and culture is equally challenging.[15] The long-standing faith in and quest for "objectivity" and "science" explain the incorporation of culture in political science and comparative government. The concept of "political culture" was invented by scholars who were serious about establishing political science as a "science" and reasserting the utility of comparative government as a relevant and powerful paradigm.[16] This "invention", however, did not take place in a vacuum. It was informed and inspired by behaviouralism in political analysis, itself an outgrowth of the combined innovative methodologies of psychology and sociology in the study of the political behaviour of collective and individual actors. As a paradigm, political culture is not only about the challenge of living up to the requirements of "objectivity", as a standard of scholarly rigour, and the quest for "scientific" certainty, but also about meeting the standards of a new scholarly "ism", relativism.[17] There is an inescapable paradox inherent in the paradigm of political culture. On the one hand, being concerned with cultural variety, i.e. the political outcomes of particularity in each culture, as manifested in the modal sets of public and private attitudes, values and feelings, the history of the political system and the histories of its members which govern political behaviour and influence political outcomes, political culture can be said to have won some claim to universalism. This is a move away from turning the experiences and values of Europeans

[15] See Maurice Cranston and Lea Campos Boralevi (eds), *Culture and Politics* (Berlin: Walter de Gruyter, 1988).

[16] See Gabriel A. Almond and Sidney Verba, *The Civic Culture: Political Attitudes and Democracy in Five Nations* (Newbury: Sage Publications, 1965).

[17] See Stephen Welch, *The Concept of Political Culture* (New York: St Martin's Press, 1993), esp. p. 74.

and Americans into explanatory universals. On the other, by essentialising "civic culture" and "democracy" to be the norms of the "good polity" which represent some "high point" in Western political development and social organisation and assumed to be worthy of universalisation, political culture is inescapably particularistic and ethnocentric.

Thus debates about the applicability and theoretical merits of the concept of political culture, which is experiencing a revival,[18] are an extension of the universalist–relativist dichotomous discourse in the postmodern era.[19] This revival has happened despite the many criticisms levelled at political culture[20] as a paradigm for examining the links between various stages of political and cultural socialisation and the attitudes and values therein that reproduce coherent political culture susceptible to sustaining different types of polities. Amongst the most commonly identified pitfalls in the political culture paradigm is the heterogeneity of political culture. That is, the notion of an undifferentiated "mass" political culture approximates a myth that ought to be treated more cautiously than has so far been the case. So sub-cultures exist both at the mass and elite levels. It is also worthwhile mentioning that it is quite common to encounter, especially in the South, little congruence between the elite political sub-cultures and those of the masses. In fact the many imports—ideology, language, etiquette, ideals—in elite political sub-cultures make them more congruent with the attitudes, values and sentiments of elites from the North than those produced locally. While reference to cultural variables sheds some light on types of political systems and outcomes, and socialisation processes, other variables cannot be overlooked: such as class, gender, ethnicity, and identity. Nonetheless, the inconclusiveness of the debate about the utility of political culture in the study of polities has extended into the study of political systems in the AME.

Apart from the obvious observation that Arab political culture is diffuse rather than unitary, political culture anywhere is not immutable.

[18] For renewed debate on the utility of political culture see Larry Diamond (ed.), *Political Culture and Democracy in Developing Countries* (Boulder, CO and London: Lynne Rienner, 1994).

[19] See John R. Gibbins (ed.), *Contemporary Political Culture: Politics in a Postmodern Age* (London: Sage Publication, 1988).

[20] See, for instance, Richard W. Wilson, *Compliance Ideologies: Rethinking Political Culture* (Cambridge University Press, 1992).

It is also the case that elements that favour democratic rule exist in varying degrees in any political culture. Their promotion or demotion are intertwined with other dynamics, some of which are external, international, fiscal, historical, structural, and sometimes even strategic, to the service or disservice of good government. Accordingly, interpretations of the absence or presence of democratic rule in exclusively and culturally relative terms verge on ethnocentrism, racism and a form of intellectual "apartheid". Neither democracy nor despotism are exclusive to one culture or one political culture. Both are acquired; therefore, both can be disowned. Also, if political values, norms and Orientations of the elites and the masses are to be disaggregated, then what power does the concept of political culture have as an explanatory variable? Mostly, in the hands of culturalists, this concept has served to produce self-other-type polarities and debates whipsawed by essentialisations contrasting familiarity with alienness, civility with barbarity, tolerance with intolerance, and good governance with misgovernance, and by all sorts of reductionism.

The utility and disutility of the political culture variable continues to be hotly debated amongst students of Middle Eastern politics.[21] Lisa Anderson and Michael Hudson, for instance, take opposite stances. The former cautions against its application to Arab democratisation. The latter favours deploying it carefully. Hudson's position has merits in that it makes the utility of the political culture approach contingent upon such "epistemological lessons" as "avoid[ing] reductionist concepts and essentialist assumptions"; "disaggregat[ing] political culture: [by] Look[ing] at subcultures (vertical and horizontal)...[and]...at elite cultures and mass cultures"; "focus[ing] on group identities, Orientations toward authority, and principles of equity and justice"; and "[being] methodologically multifaceted".[22] If Hudson's propositions warrant reconsidering the case for a careful incorporation of the political culture variable in the future, the

[21] For a summary of this debate, see Rex Brynen, Bahgat Korany and Paul Noble, "Introduction: Theoretical Perspectives on Arab Liberalization and Democratization" in Rex Brynen, Bahgat Korany, and Paul Noble (eds), *Political Liberalization and Democratization in the Arab World*, vol. 1: *Theoretical Perspectives* (Boulder, CO and London: Lynne Rienner, 1995), esp. pp. 6–10.

[22] Michael C. Hudson, "The Political Culture Approach to Arab Democratization: The Case for Bringing it Back in, Carefully" in Brynen, Korany and Noble (eds), *Political Liberalization and Democratization*, p. 73.

practice thus far weakens the case for its adoption, as Anderson shows convincingly:

> [T]here are logical and epistemological flaws in most of the cultural analyses…[R]ather than simply survey the attitudes and behaviour of the population in question, most analysts begin with an effort to explain the absence of something desirable—democracy—by the presence of something undesirable—in this instance, "bad attitudes". Perhaps, however, this lacuna is more appropriately attributable to the absence of other desirable traits—full national sovereignty, for example, or greater economic prosperity—rather than the presence of some kind of congenital defect. There are two mistakes here and together they compound the problems they separately create. First…accounting for what is absent, while not impossible, is extremely difficult and requires very rigorous specification of the feature whose absence is to be explained. Second, when the feature is something so simultaneously intricate and value-laden as democracy, that requirement for rigour is almost guaranteed to be relaxed in the face of the complexity and desirability of the phenomenon itself.[23]

Today, culture has become a site within which all sorts of claims and counter-claims are being advanced in one of the fiercest phases of hubristic contestations between supposedly clear-cut macro-cultural and civilisational units, themselves sometimes essentialised ahistorically and reductionistically. Huntington, for instance, declares that the "great divisions among human kind and the dominating source of conflict will be cultural".[24] The manifold expressions of cultural-civilisational or ideological triumphalism[25] or cultural authenticity belie the ever-shifting, transforming and intersecting boundaries between civilisations and cultures. Transculturalism does not in anyway negate cultural pluralism or multiculturalism in our world. For instance, at least at the most basic level, the idea of the desirability of and quest for good government represents an area where there is some compatibility between many non-European and European cultural-civilisational units and their attendant knowledge practices.

23 Lisa Anderson, "Democracy in the Arab World: A Critique of the Political Culture Approach" in Brynen, Korany, and Noble (eds), *Political Liberalization and Democratization*, p. 89.

24 Samuel P. Huntington, "The Clash of Civilizations", *Foreign Affairs*, 72 (summer 1993), pp. 22–49.

25 Francis Fukuyama, *The End of History and the Last Man* (London: Penguin, 1992).

Hence, despite the cultural specificities, different historical contexts, and the verities that underpin Greek-derived Western democracy,[26] Islamic *shūrā* is a linguistic expression that underlies the basic idea of the desirability of good government. Certainly, within Muslim political thought, the need for government has been valued even if the government is corrupt or evil.[27] Despite the diversity of Islamists' stances on democracy and their still inchoate thought and practice of good government, Islam and Islamic theology present them with many potentialities for realising legal and just rule. As mentioned before, Esposito and Voll confirm this view. They observe that "Islam has a full spectrum of potential symbols and concepts for support of absolutism and hierarchy, as well as foundations for liberty and equality."[28] They add that "egalitarian participation and concepts of legitimate opposition" form important "conceptual resources within Islam for democratisation".[29]

It is not at all surprising that currently democracy is the most commonly-shared slogan in a near-universal quest for good government. However, germane to this commonality is the contestability of democracy. Neither cultural exclusivity nor cultural particularity have stood in the way of democracy captivating the minds and imaginations of millions of human beings everywhere. Yet both have persistently stood in the way of a "fixed" understanding and practising of democracy. Interpretations of democracy are often grounded in notions of cultural particularity. Non-European cultures and non-Enlightenment epistemologies cannot be expected not to ground their interpretations of democracy in their heritages. In a multicultural world democracy will not be able to satisfy the needs of diverse peoples nor meet their aspirations unless it is adapted when adopted. That is, unless, for instance, interpretations of democracy are manipulated under the guise of some notion of an "Arab democracy", or "Islamic democracy" to disown inclusive, just, legal, accountable and representative government, a practice that has many analogues in the Pacific as Lawson ably shows in her study of government in island states

26 See, for instance, Bhikhu Parekh, "The Cultural Particularity of Liberal Democracy" in David Held (ed.), *Prospects for Democracy* (Cambridge: Polity Press, 1993), pp. 156–75.

27 Ann K.S. Lambton, *State and Government in Medieval Islam* (Oxford University Press, 1981).

28 Esposito and Voll, *Islam and Democracy*, p. 7.

29 Ibid.

such as Fiji.[30] Rejecting some form of democratic government on the grounds of prioritising culture over democracy is no longer a defence in a world where so many peoples and transforming cultures are enmeshed in the discourse of and clamour for good government.

The point that has so often been driven home in interdisciplinary scholarship is that of the irreconcilability of tradition and modernity, and of certain cultures and of democracy. A new point of departure can be that both cultures and democracy are set to win if they serve one another. No matter how antiquated, many cultures have foundations that have relevance for helping democratic transition and government happen. Democracy presents many groups with the opportunity for a number of its ideals, norms, institutions to validate not negate the relevance of many values and variables in their cultures. Discourse on democracy, especially in reference to the AME, can then be reconstructed critically with due sensitivity paid to cultures, but without the excesses of exclusivity. Confidence in democracy must not read singularity of truth or deterministic exceptionalism.

FOREIGN POWERS IN THE AME AND DEMOCRACY

Democracy and human rights have been victims in both the theory and practice of international politics. Both the mainstream (realist school) and alternative (liberal) modes of thinking on these issues fail these two causes, albeit in different ways. Realism, being the dominant paradigm, regards democracy and human rights as illusory concepts in a world of sovereign and anarchical states. The alternative paradigm, while recognising the importance of democracy and human rights, is caught in its Western ethnocentricity. Hence it takes a serious Lockean notion of human rights and an American notion of pluralism. Thus Gilbert states that ideas of human rights and democracy not only fail to make "some difference in the foreign policy of contemporary democratic regimes [and] fall outside prevailing paradigms", but also "the international sphere appears not as a constraint on democracy but as its denial".[31] The United Nations is

30 Stephanie Lawson, *Tradition Versus Democracy in the South Pacific: Fiji, Tonga and Western Samoa* (New York: Cambridge University Press, 1996); Stephanie Lawson, "The Politics of Tradition: Problems for Political Legitimacy and Democracy in the South Pacific", *Pacific Studies*, 16 (June 1993), pp. 1–29.

31 Alan Gilbert, "Must Global Politics Constrain Democracy? Realism, Regimes, and Democratic Internationalism", *Political Theory*, 20 (February 1992), p. 9.

no less guilty of retarding democracy and human rights than are democratic state actors.[32]

The United States is by far the most active advocate of democracy in the world. This is one reason why it is singled out for criticism. For despite the sheer supremacy of the human and material resources it harnesses to promote good government, its democracy-promotion programmes in the AME remain inferior to those conducted in other regions. This failure to get serious about promoting democracy in the AME is a kind of moral deficiency on the part of a global actor that not only will for some time depend on Middle Eastern oil for its economic welfare, but who will also continue to try to retain its influence in the region. The American government uses three primary agencies, the US Agency for International Development (USAID), US Information Agency (USIA) and the non-governmental National Endowment for Democracy (NED). USAID is primarily responsible for economic development but has some democracy-promoting activities which stem from the belief in the intimate connection between market economics, wealth, democracy and peace. The USIA participates in promoting democracy by spreading information about the benefits of freedom and wealth to the oppressed peoples of the world through outlets such as Radio Free Europe (or Radio Liberty) and Asia, Voice of America, radio and TV Marti, and libraries. They also facilitate exchange programmes to bring people to the United States to get first-hand experience of democracy in action. The USIA also has an Eastern Europe Initiative where it participates in Support for Eastern Europe Democracies (SEED) programme. There are no similar programmes or specific radio or TV broadcasts for the Middle East.[33] NED is the primary agency for spreading democracy. It was set up in 1983 by the Reagan administration for precisely this reason. It supports four constituent institutes through which it distributes the grants. These are the Centre for International Private

[32] Its membership is open to all states, a number of which have in the past 50 years been guilty of crimes (including environmental and cultural) against humanity, and many more have had regimes ruling in total disregard of Article 21 of the UN Universal Declaration of Human Rights—"Everyone has the right to take part in the government of his country, directly or through freely chosen representatives." This is a point that is well documented by Elie Kedourie, *Democracy and Arab Political Culture* (Washington, DC: The Washington Institute for Near East Policy, 1992). The UN's complacency no doubt reflects the dominant members' outlook on these questions.

[33] See USIA's homepage [http://www.usi.gov/usis.html].

Enterprise (CIPE), the Free Trade Union Institute (FTUI), the International Republic Institute (IRI), and the National Democratic Institute for International Affairs (NDI).

However, and as far as state actors are concerned, especially the United States, it is important to realise that its endeavours to promote democracy will be quite likely to run into serious problems in many parts of the South. In this respect, three interrelated issues are worth considering: the first, as mentioned, concerns the fact that the type of democracy the United States wants to promote suffers from ethnocentric overtones; the second relates to the self-interest motive at the core of promoting American pluralism; and the third is the track record of foreign powers in the AME, leaving lingering suspicions about Western motivations behind democracy and human rights-speak.

Rarely do notions of American pluralism accent social justice or on economic fairness which make them mono-dimensional in many parts of the world where immediate concerns over issues of bread and butter are no less important than the vote. The definitions below give some important clues to the type of democracy promoted by the United States. Diamond wrote that a democracy must consist of three elements:

1) open competition for all places of government power;
2) inclusive political participation in the selection of candidates for positions of power and their election by free and fair voting;
3) civil and political liberties which include freedom of expression, press and organisation.[34]

Goldman notes that a democratic system has nine attributes none of which is about economic justice: individualism, popular sovereignty, civil liberties, majority rule, rule of law, natural law (the equality of all mankind, "it applies the same moral constraints upon the conduct of all governments and individuals"), constitutionalism, accountability and civil–military relations (where the military is subordinate to civilian rule).[35] The American promotion of democracy is premised

[34] Larry Diamond, "Beyond Authoritarianism and Totalitarianism: Strategies for Democratisation" in Brad Roberts (ed.), *The New Democracies: Global Change and US Policy* (Cambridge, MA: The MIT Press, 1990), pp. 228–9.

[35] Ralph Goldman, "Assessing Political Aid for the Endless Campaign" in Ralph Goldman and William Douglas (eds), *Promoting Democracy: Opportunities and Issues* (New York: Praeger, 1988), p. 261.

on these conceptualisations of democracy. American and Western aid disbursement is being increasingly linked to some degree of respect of these democratic values by recipient states. Conditionality of aid reception is, at least in theory, geared towards lending support to the freeing of the press, women and minority rights, the forming of volunteer and political organisations, promoting legal systems and constitutions, holding free and fair elections, and the observing of human rights. This emphasis on the conditionality of foreign aid has become noticeable in the policies of major international financial institutions (IFIS), namely, the World Bank and the IMF.[36]

However, this whole notion of conditionality of foreign aid disbursement is ostensibly political. Hence the inevitable juggling of double standards. Accordingly the idea that foreign aid to the developing world is increasingly being tied to political reform in recipient countries must be qualified in the case of the AME where commercial and geo-strategic dynamics are at work. These dynamics, Gorm Olsen argues, explain why the West has approached the question of conditionality more rigorously in Kenya than in Algeria.[37] The former's position in the global economy, like many African countries, is shown to be more reliant on aid and less integrated into world commercial activities. The latter, being a hydrocarbon state with substantial vital gas reserves, is by comparison more relatively articulated with the international economy, which is the case of other Middle Eastern petroleum exporting states. Keeping these relative positions in mind, Olsen proposes that Malawi or Kenya's marginal value, both commercially and geo-strategically, to the West is the root cause of the shift in conditionality of foreign aid. Kenya, he shows, is coming under tremendous pressure from Western aid donors to move towards political liberalisation. By contrast, in Algeria, most Western governments supported a crackdown on the popularly-elected FIS (Front Islamique du Salut, Islamic Salvation Front) which was poised to gain control of the National Assembly after the 1991 first

[36] See, for instance, Ibrahim F.I. Shihata, "The World Bank and Human Rights" in Franziska Tschofen and Antonio R. Parra (eds), *The World Bank in a Changing World: Selected Essays* (Dordrecht, Boston and London: Martinus Nijhoff Publishers, 1991), pp. 97–134; Daniel D. Bradlow and Claudio Grossman, "Limited Mandates and Intertwined Problems: A New Challenge for the World Bank and the IMF", *Human Rights Quarterly*, 17 (1995), pp. 411–42.

[37] See Gorm Rye Olsen, "Africa and the Middle East in the New International System: Democracy, Aid and Security", *Journal of Developing Societies*, 10 (1994), pp. 125–47.

round of elections. Algeria, for reasons of politics, geography and commerce, is much more geo-politically important to the West. Despite a bloody record, the military-backed regime in Algeria continues to be sponsored to the tune of five billion francs a year by France as well as hundreds of million of dollars, not to mention technical and military assistance, from various sources such as Spain, Italy and Japan.[38] This example illustrates the contingent geo-political nature of demands for political reform.

With regard to the Gulf states, Olsen sees Western dependence on regional oil production as a barrier to Western demands for political reform in exchange for technical or military aid. Oil revenues decrease reliance on aid, while the threat of oil embargoes (or perhaps more correctly higher oil prices given that embargoes are very unlikely) precludes stronger Western pressure. In addition, Olsen maintains that Western pressure for political reform in recipient nations complements both older-style conditionality as well as domestic democratisation demands. With regard to the former, good administrative skills in recipient nations, increasingly a precondition of foreign aid, are seen to be complemented by a system of accountable government: thus democratisation is an extension of donor demands for administrative efficiency. In the latter, Olsen deems foreign requirements for political reform as often just another force acting on a regime already pressured from within.

Given the political nature of foreign aid, contradictions are inevitable in the behaviour of donor states. Withholding of aid or withdrawing it in protest against human rights violations or lack of democratic achievements is decided by taking into account the possible costs and benefits of such a policy outcome. If the outcome is likely to be inimical to the donor state's interests, then no negative sanctions will be threatened much less implemented to the persistent detriment of good government. Democracy or human rights are not ends in themselves regardless of the declaratory policies even of the most democratic states. They are ends only in so far as they serve the "national interest" or as the "national interest" may at times dictate. In its dealing with the mid-East region, in general, and key client regimes or states, in particular, the contradictions at the heart of

[38] Author's interview with al-'Arabī Zaytūt, former senior consul in the Algerian Embassy in Libya and currently living in exile in London, 14 March 1998, London.

American foreign aid policies illustrate this point. Major recipients of aid continue to perpetrate human rights abuses upon their citizens (such as Egypt, Morocco, Tunisia, and Turkey) or upon conquered peoples (Israel).

Egypt is a good example of a key American ally which receives substantial aid, second only to Israel's, while commonly resorting to authoritarian behaviour. Hicks, for instance, cites its government's hardline policies against Islamists and other non-democratic practices which undermine the rule of law and the flourishing of civil society and asks whether such activities actually exacerbate the problem of militancy. His answer is that the United States should adjust its aid programme to support the establishment of a freer and fairer form of governance within Egypt. Similarly, he criticises Israel's continued abuse of Palestinian human rights. Hicks exposes the contradictions inherent in Western policy-making when he points out how United States officials, while demanding the Palestinian National Authority (PNA) crack down on Islamic militants, seem to ignore the continual abuse of Palestinian rights by Israeli defence and police forces.[39] Given its interest motive, the United States' Mid-East foreign policy will for the foreseeable future continue to aid Israel unconditionally and commit itself to helping keep Egypt's friendly but pseudo-democratic regime in power. The loss of close to three billion dollars of foreign aid for the Arab world's most populous state could mean uncertain future for the rulers. This scenario will be unacceptable for the US and the EU alike. It is therefore difficult to envisage how democracy and human rights will, at least in the short term, form key concerns of the US and their European allies' foreign aid policies in the AME. Accordingly, Egyptians will have to do without free and fair elections for some time, especially if their most probable outcome would be an Islamist-led government whose foreign policy orientations could be harmful to US and Israeli interests. Accordingly, Hicks' suggestion that the United States modify her aid budget to be more attuned to the promotion of democracy can be expected to fall on deaf ears in Washington. In 2002, the US withheld additional aid in protest against the jailing of Professor Saad Eddin Ibrahim. US pressure partly explains why he was surprisingly freed by the Egyptian regime in 2003.

[39] Neil Hicks, "US Aid and Human Rights in the Middle East", *Middle East International*, 17 March 1995, pp. 17–18.

There is another side to the use of foreign aid in pursuit of foreign policy objectives. The utilisation of aid packages as an instrument of foreign policy in the Middle East enabled the United States to secure bilateral peace treaties between Israel and its neighbours—the former PLO and Israel (funds for the PNA and more aid for Israel) in 1993 and between Jordan and Israel in 1994 (writing off of Jordan's debt).[40] Similarly, the foreign aid slated for the PNA after the Oslo Accords has been diverted. By demanding certain reforms, namely financial managerial transparency and accountability, from the PNA, which they have not received, aid donors have legitimised the bypassing of the PNA's development plans in favour of programmes run by previously-established NGOs and UN organisations.

In a word, foreign aid is a potent and discretionary tool with many an application, both positive and negative. How aid is utilised cannot be expected to be subject to a clearly definable logic. The international system is still very much an "anarchical society" in which the exigencies that are mostly applied are those of the "national interest" or "national security". Authoritarian regimes in the AME invoke them or the so-called "national unity" to crack down on formidable opposition, especially Islamist. It is on the basis of the logic of "high" politics that their democratic foreign sponsors allow them leeway through silence, financial and military sponsoring or both. But this is a major weakness: in 2002 President Bush sought to get Arafat removed from power. Failing that, the US forced the weakened Palestinian 'President' to share power with a Prime Minister acceptable to several Western governments as well as Israel.

The United States' idea of democracy is also embedded in an economic understanding of what fosters a good democracy, i.e. the dependence of the survival of a democracy on a thriving market economy. In a paper entitled "From Containment to Enlargement", Anthony Lake, former Assistant to the President for National Security Affairs, lists four components for a United States' strategy of enlargement. In all four components, he weds democracy to market economy; democracy is "market democracy":

> First, we should strengthen the community of major market democracies... Second, we should help foster and consolidate new democracies...Third, we

[40] Hashim F. Abu Sido and Mona Ghali, "Aid and International Organisations in Palestine: Instruments of Development of Foreign Policy?" *Middle East International*, 28 April 1995, pp. 16–17.

must counter the aggression—and support the liberalization—of states hostile to democracy and markets...Fourth,...work...to help democracy and market economics take root in regions of greatest humanitarian concern.[41]

The usage of "democracy" and "markets" or "market economies" in conjunction aims at stressing the correlation between democracy and capitalism. But more importantly, the stress is more on the preconditionality of the former on the latter. To John Sullivan, amongst many others, there is evidence that market systems are an "economic precondition of democracy".[42] Sullivan argues that market economics suit democracy because, first, democracies need financial wealth (which the market economy is the best system to provide) in order to set up the mechanisms of an election (such as an up-to-date civil registry and employing polling staff) and to support an educated middle class (however defined) who will be in a position to support and sustain democracy. Furthermore, economic wealth is seen as providing some certainty and security especially in the face of uncertain political results from elections. Also market economics is a system assumed to promote decentralisation, and the freedoms of association, movement and information. In this sense, according to Samuel Huntington, "A market economy is more likely to give rise to the economic wealth and the resulting more equitable distribution of income that provide the infrastructure of democracy."[43]

It could be said that the assumption that democracy and capitalism are intimately linked is based upon the simple observation that the most successful democracies exist in the rich industrialised market-based societies and not in the formerly communist world or in the mostly poor South, with a few qualified exceptions. Accordingly, the promotion of democracy is heavily tied to the promotion of capitalism. For instance, this is evident in USAID's strategy for promoting democracy. This linkage of the market and democracy is highlighted in a document entitled "USAID's Strategies for Sustainable Development: Building Democracy", especially where it states:

USAID's strategic objective is the transition to and consolidation of democratic regimes throughout the world—as an end in itself and because it is a

[41] Anthony Lake, "From Containment to Enlargement", (US State Department) *Dispatch*, 4, 39, 27 September 1993, p. 5.

[42] John Sullivan, "A Market-Orientated Approach to Democratic Development: The Linkages" in Goldman and Douglas, *Promoting Democracy*, p. 156.

[43] Quoted in Sullivan, "A Market-Orientated Approach to Democratic Development: The Linkages" in ibid., p. 143

critical element for promoting sustainable development. This objective is achieved through the establishment of democratic institutions, *free and open markets*, an informed and educated populace, a vibrant civic society, and a relationship between state and society that encourages pluralism, inclusion, and peaceful conflict resolution (emphasis added).[44]

The United States' promotion of democracy can to an extent be self-defeating especially given that the motivatations of American foreign policy-makers are not just about spreading democracy. The reasons for the promotion of democracy range from genuine altruism to pragmatic national security and economic calculations, and from ideas of historical missions to tinges of imperialism. On the altruistic side, there is the belief that everyone wants and deserves to be free from government oppression and that it is America's duty as both a democracy and as a wealthy country to help other peoples to achieve this freedom. In this vein, democracy is seen as "America's great gift to the world".[45] USAID's statement of strategies starts with the claim that "People throughout the world have demonstrated by their own actions that freedom is a universal concept."[46] Linked to this is the view expressed by Diamond that it "…is the legitimate business of all nations to be concerned about the status of human rights in any of them".[47] Concerns over sovereignty are dispelled by the notion that "[T]rue sovereignty resides not with the regime in control of the state but with its people."[48] It is perhaps from this that the whole basis of promoting democracy—i.e. that democracy is a universal system and hence transferable—is derived.

On the pragmatic national security side there is the (un-self-reflective) belief that because it is a historical *fact* that democracies do not go to war against each other,[49] the more democracies there

[44] USAID, "USAID's Strategies for Sustainable Development: Building Democracy", [http://info.usaid.gov/democracy/strategy.html].

[45] Statement by Josh Muravchik in House of Representatives (1992) "Foreign Assistance Legislation for Fiscal Years 1992–93", p. 414, US Information service code 1992 H381–68.

[46] USAID "USAID's Strategies for Sustainable Development: Building Democracy", [http://info.usaid.gov/democracy/strategy.html].

[47] Diamond, "Beyond Authoritarianism and Totalitarianism", p. 241.

[48] Ibid.

[49] This belief is commonplace. One example is in Lisa Anderson's statement in the U.S. House of Representatives that "as a rule democracies do not go to war with one another…" In House of Representatives, Committee on Foreign Affairs (11 August 1992) "Promoting Pluralism and Democracy in the Middle East", p. 6, US Information service code 1993 H381–40.

are in the world, the more peaceful it will be and the safer the United States will be. Furthermore, there is the assumption that "the more democracies there is (*sic*) the more pro-American the world will be"[50] (a claim analysed below). There is also a "historical mission" aspect to the American promotion of democracy whereby from the early years of their republican system, "Americans have believed that their model of governance was the natural, rational solution for every country and that all societies would eventually copy it."[51] John Schoff notes that America's "political heritage calls for" the United States to "encourage actively and forth rightly the growth of democratic institutions and attitudes in Third World countries".[52] American scholarship resonates with this inflated sense of missionary zeal and historicism when it comes to the promotion of democracy. The claim by Josh Muravchik that the United States has been the sole "engine" for the spread of democracy, including to France and England, around the world for the past 200 years is neither single nor unfamiliar.[53] Whilst to an extent true, claims like Muravchik's would be very difficult to defend when it comes to the Middle East.

Perhaps the most negative aspect of the American promotion of democracy and human rights lies in its veiled imperialist motivation, both in the past during the height of the ideological standoff between communism and now as the United States further asserts its sole superpower status. A hint of this veiled imperialism can be found in Ralph Goldman's revision of the Monroe Doctrine. To most other writers the Monroe Doctrine is seen as the American marking off Latin America as its sole preserve in terms of wielding power and influence. To Goldman, however, the doctrine is designed to promote democracy in the region. He observes that the "Monroe Doctrine reflected the national commitment to the advancement of democratic institutions wherever possible and the protection of the democratic way of life in the United States as the example for others. The haste with which the new Latin American republics adopted

[50] Statement by Josh Muravchik in House of Representatives (1992) "Foreign Assistance Legislation for Fiscal Years 1992–93", p. 413.

[51] Raymond Gastil, "Aspects of a US Campaign for Democracy" in Goldman and Douglas (eds), *Promoting Democracy*, p. 25.

[52] John Schott, "Promoting Democracy in Authoritarian Countries: Problems and Prospects," in Goldman and Douglas (eds), *Promoting Democracy*, p. 95.

[53] Statement by Josh Muravchik in House of Representatives, "Foreign Assistance Legislation for Fiscal Years 1992–93", pp. 414–15.

large components of the US constitution...is testimony that the Monroe Doctrine was a democracy-promoting as well as a national security policy."[54] Richard Falk finds hegemonic motivation is at the heart of America's declaratory policies of human rights, noting that "When the United States explicitly proclaims a human rights diplomacy that it will implement as a general element of its foreign policy, this entails an explicitly hegemonial attitude toward the internal affairs of certain countries."[55]

This begs the obvious question that if the Monroe Doctrine is seen as a democracy-promoting policy, then what lies behind current policies for democratic expansion? Part of the answer lies in the belief that democracies are inherently pro-American (this point will be returned to below), and in the encouragement of "the development of private-sector American business relations"[56] with the emerging private sector in countries where democracy is being promoted.

At least partially, foreign aid has humanitarian and developmental goals. If and when the recipient countries' use of it fail these goals, then it should become morally incumbent upon the donor community to make continuity of aid flow conditional on positive achievements in governance. In theory, at least, the Bretton Woods system has made a qualitative shift in this respect. Nearly ten years have passed since the World Bank introduced the word "governance" into discussions about development,[57] blurring the boundaries between the political and the economic. According to this reconceptualisation, governance partakes of two interrelated dimensions, political and economic, deemed indispensable for achieving "good governance". The first accords primacy to democratic institutionalisation and reform. The second accentuates the necessity of organisational and administrative transparency. This new thinking has not only influenced the policy discourse, especially in terms of the conditionality of foreign aid, but also brought a revision of the meanings of development and democracy. Indirectly, democracy may be considered

54 Ralph Goldman, "The Democratic Mission: A Brief History" in Goldman and Douglas (eds), *Promoting Democracy*, p. 5.

55 Richard Falk, "Theoretical Foundations of Human Rights" in Paula Newberg (ed.), *The Politics of Human Rights* (New York University Press, 1980), p. 72.

56 Comment by Lisa Anderson in House of Representatives, Committee on Foreign Affairs, "Promoting Pluralism and Democracy in the Middle East", p. 66.

57 See World Bank Report, *Sub-Saharan Africa: From Crisis to Sustainable Growth* (Washington, DC: World Bank, 1989).

development and *vice versa*. Directly, democracy does not have to be a sequel to economic development.[58]

In practice, the way the United States, or the European Union, should go about promoting democracy is a delicate matter. For democracy-promoting activities are always likely to invite accusations of cultural insensitivity (on the basis of tension between universal principles of good governance and national particularities) or imperialism or meddling in domestic affairs from one party or another. From this perspective, strategies for promoting democracy will therefore be acceptable to some but objectionable to others. Diamond provides a good outline of some of the democracy-promoting strategies. For him, the most important point is that "Aid efforts should focus on fostering pluralism and autonomy in organizational life and the flow of information. This is particularly important because it builds the social and cultural foundations for democracy without dictating to a country what its constitutional structure should look like."[59] Diamond's second point is that external democratic actors need to promote the rule of law in authoritarian regimes. To do this, he recommends the supporting of human rights organisations which will expose regime abuses of human rights and help the victims, as well as educate people of their rights. A third strategy is that once a regime opens sufficiently to allow the emergence of opposition parties, the United States should provide financial and technical assistance to allow these parties to develop and mobilise mass support. Methods of getting the authoritarian regime to open up include diplomatic pressure, economic sanctions, linking aid to liberalisation and, in some cases, the threat or use of military force.[60] Diamond's last strategy recommendation is the use of economic means, either sanctions against an authoritarian government or assistance, such as debt relief, for new, struggling democracies.

The United States makes extensive use of non-government organisations and private groups to promote democracy. The reason, as

[58] A. Leftwich who points out that "democracy is a necessary *prior or parallel* condition of development, not an outcome of it". See his "Governance, Democracy and Development in the Third World", *Third World Quarterly*, 14 (1993), pp. 605–24.

[59] These four points come from Larry Diamond, "Beyond Authoritarianism and Totalitarianism", pp. 242–5.

[60] This last action, the threat or use of military force, is mentioned by Marilyn Anne Zak in "Assisting Elections in the Third World" in Roberts (ed.), *The New Democracies* p. 185.

William Douglas explains, is due to the fact that in some countries official American contact with opposition groups may be disapproved of by the regime in power and so the country uses private groups to do this.[61] This of course causes problems when the opposition groups see the United States still enjoying diplomatic relations with the regime while unofficially providing aid to them. The suspicion of America's double standards or hypocrisy arises. Contact with opposition groups can be problematic, especially in the Mid-East region. Diamond points out that for the United States, in promoting democracy, this could be counter-productive. He notes that outside assistance in the formation of democracy may be ineffective. Outside aid may delegitimise pro-democracy groups and activists for democratic rule because they risk being tainted with receiving foreign (and hence suspect, e.g. American assistance in Latin America because of fears of imperialism) help. Furthermore, the dependence upon aid by these groups has the potential of "undermin[ing] the necessary process of citizens empowering themselves and defining and waging their own struggle for democracy".[62] The United States seeks to overcome many countries' suspicion of its assistance by trying to make democracy-promoting efforts multilateral, i.e. in concert with other wealthy democracies.

The Western track record in the AME presents the promotion of democracy with difficulties. In the past, European colonial powers manipulated Arab domestic politics in favour of conservative and usually undemocratic forces. Colonial Britain and France's roles in the rise of Arab monarchical rule is well documented by Lisa Anderson.[63] The British meddled in fragile Iraqi[64] and Egyptian parliaments, although not always as directly as the French in Syria.[65] Lesch observes that the British garrison, beside the landed aristocracy, lent

[61] William Douglas, "Democracy Promotion and Government-to-Government Diplomacy" in Goldman and Douglas (eds), *Promoting Democracy*, p. 246.

[62] Diamond, "Beyond Authoritarianism and Totalitarianism", pp. 239–40.

[63] See Lisa Anderson, "Absolutism and the Resilience of Monarchy in the Middle East", *Political Science Quarterly*, 106 (spring 1991), pp. 1–15.

[64] For British support of the Iraqi monarchy see Phebe Marr, *The Modern History of Iraq* (Boulder, CO: Westview Press, 1985).

[65] Khaldoun Hasan al-Naqeeb, "Social Origins of the Authoritarian State in the Arab East" in Eric Davis and Nicolas Gavrielides (eds), *Statecraft in the Middle East: Oil, Historical Memory, and Popular Culture* (Miami: Florida International University Press, 1991), pp. 44–5.

support to the palace to sabotage Egypt's incipient parli institutions.[66] The record of the new post-Second World W powers, the United States and the Soviet Union, of advancing the cause of democracy in the Arab world was not any less dismal. Four years before its masterminding of the 1953 overthrow of Iranian Prime Minister Mossadegh's democratically elected government,[67] the CIA orchestrated the coup that placed in power Syria's first military dictator, Ḥusnī al-Za'īm.[68]

Perry indicts American anti-democratic foreign policy in Egypt, stating that Washington's hostility towards Nasser had more to do with the latter's "refusal to be an American proxy", than the former's "dislike for authoritarianism".[69] In fact, when Nasser and his Free Officers toyed with the idea of restoring democracy, the American response was discouraging, with its Ambassador, Jefferson Caffrey, warning that "elections at the present time would be disastrous".[70] Enormous evidence supports Perry's idea that the West has "stood in the way of democracy",[71] in the Middle East. Since the 1992 coup, investments and loans from Italy, Japan, Spain and France have ensured survival of the military-led regime in Algeria. The Islamists there decry how France's preference for secularism has been translated into full backing for an increasingly discredited and bloody

[66] Ann M. Lesch, "Democracy in Doses: Mubarak Launches His Second Term as President", *Arab Studies Quarterly*, 11 (fall 1989), p. 88.

[67] William Blum, *The CIA: A Forgotten History: US Global Interventions Since World War 2* (London and New Jersey: Zed Books, 1986), pp. 67–76.

[68] Glenn E. Perry, "Democracy and Human Rights in the Shadow of the West", paper presented at the Champaign, Illinois, YMCA's Friday Forum series on "Peace, Justice and Human Rights in the Middle East", p. 9. See also, Douglas Little, "Cold War and Covert Action: The United States and Syria, 1945–1958", *The Middle East Journal*, 44 (winter 1990), pp. 51–75. Perry explains how American oil interests led to act against what was at the time an approximation of democracy in Syria: "The Syrian parliament refused to approve the concession to ARAMCO allowing the Trans-Arabian Pipe Line (better known as Tapline) to be constructed. CIA operative Stephen Meade met regularly with al-Za'īm for months to push the idea of an 'army supported dictatorship'. The two men planned the coup. The United States provided funds to [al-]Za'īm and apparently complied with his request that its agents 'provoke and abet internal disturbances'. Washington quickly recognized its new dictator and committed itself to military and economic aid. Tapline was approved." See Perry, "Democracy and Human Rights in the Shadow of the West", p. 9.

[69] Ibid., p. 13.

[70] Ibid., pp. 13–14.

[71] Ibid., p. 1.

regime.[72] The fall of Eastern European Stalinist regimes was partly precipitated by the former Soviet Union's withdrawal of financial and political sponsorship in the late 1980s. The prospect of history repeating itself in the Middle East and North Africa should similar Western financial, moral and military sponsoring of Arab authoritarianisms cease must not be underestimated.

Sudan presents a precedent for this scenario. Brown links the overthrow of al-Numayrī regime in March 1985 to the donor community's refusal to bankroll Sudan's "$60 million projected balance of payments deficit, thereby stalling the final agreement on the crucial 1984/5 Standby Loan Arrangement, soon thereafter freezing parts of their 1984 aid monies, and postponing indefinitely the all-important Paris Club and Consultative Group meetings".[73] This along with the IMF austerity package imposed on Sudan in March 1985 precipitated the regime's fall. A key question Brown raises is over the US change of heart *vis-à-vis* the regime: what motivated the Reagan administration which lobbied the IMF for easier terms to be given to the Sudan to insist later on austerity measures as the *quid pro quo* for "releasing US $67 million of aid monies frozen under its 1983/4 programme"?[74] Brown's conclusion is "either that this was a big mistake, or that it was a deliberate move to topple the regime".[75]

The implications of the above for the Arab state, or perhaps more precisely for those in charge of it, are potentially quite serious. The partial autonomy that has characterised their rule in the postcolonial era is not without its vulnerabilities. Today, the dynamics conspiring to weaken it are legion. As Arab states and societies become increasingly more interconnected with a complex web of globally political, economic, social, cultural and informational relations, the greater the potential of the external to wield influence and power internally and help shape domestic events, both positively (slow but certain

72 The FIS spokesperson in Germany, Rabeh Kebir, observes that "it is France's ammunition, helicopters and money that are further embroiling Algeria in its killing fields". See Larbi Sadiki, "The Battle for Algeria and the French Connection", *Pacific Research*, 8 (February 1995), p. 12.

73 Richard Brown, "A Background Note on the Final Round of Economic Austerity Measures Imposed by the Numeiry Regime: June 1984 to March 1985", in Tony Barnett and Abbas Abdelkarim (eds), *Sudan: State, Capital and Transformation* (London, New York, and Sydney, Croom Helm: 1988), p. 81.

74 Ibid.

75 Ibid.

diffusion of the global democratic revolution) and negatively (a share of economic hardship and marginalisation).

On the fiscal side, Arab states either rely on petrodollars or on supplements to their income from IFIs and aid donors from North America and Europe. Taxation as a source of state income is still weak in most Arab states, especially as its implications for political representation are well-known ("no taxation without representation"). On the political side, for some 40 years, ruling elites in the AME have relied on outside moral and political (through diplomatic or protégé status) legitimacy as a substitute for electorally-based legitimacy. Certainly the Cold War fostered a political culture in world politics whereby membership in the former Soviet or American camps qualified client regimes for unfettered assistance, often in disregard of their appalling records of human rights violations, autocratic politics and mismanagement of resources. If and when this outside financial and political power becomes subjected to rigorously moral standards, assuming more responsibility than it has so far done, the likely victims will be autocratic rulers and the bases of their autonomy. Pressure from within in the form of increased democratic habituation, awareness, struggle could coalesce with supranational pressures to erode Arab authoritarianisms. This pressure can only intensify as the AME is itself becoming more linked socially (through Arab expatriates and migrants), culturally (globalisation of democratic values), and informationally (internet, satellite TV, etc.) with the "global village". Paradoxically, while supranational pressures and globalisation effects have some capacity to undermine the autonomy of autocratic power holders, democratically-based legitimacy inside is the best protection for national rulers and their sovereignty in limiting the impingement from outside.

Algeria is a good example of a state under increasing supranational pressures to explain appalling massacres and deaths that took place between 1992 and 1999. Potentially, it is not immune to supranational pressures and actions taken by the international market, capital or foreign political patronage. The February 1998 visits to Algeria by European Union ministerial and parliamentary delegations keen to garner more facts about the killings met with little cooperation from the regime. The regime and its partners in the National Assembly, namely, the Movement of Society for Peace (SMPP), formerly Hamas, naively rejected such visits or outside calls for international inquiries into the massacres as unacceptable meddling into domestic affairs. This stance ignores the reciprocal relationships between IFIs and the international political economy with national politics and the whole notion of national sovereignty. With a staggering debt (from 26 in 1986 to more than USD 30 billion in 1997), Algeria has in so many ways to be accountable to the international political economy and IFIs, especially with regard to either servicing, renegotiating and rescheduling. As a developing country, it cannot do without technical and financial assistance from international lenders. As a rentier state, it depends on the international oil and gas market for the bulk of its national income. Accordingly, to reject outside meddling on the grounds of national sovereignty is somewhat absurd. Sovereignty does not seem to matter much when it comes to seeking financial assistance from Western aid donors and lenders, the IMF or the World Bank. For the regime it is political not economic sovereignty that seems to be more at stake. Although the Zeroual regime expressed concern over "international terrorism" and asked for international help, it was hostile to demands for an international inquiry. For now, at least, the state-holders will continue to take comfort in the knowledge that its international sponsors will not take any drastic measures to hurt its chances of survival and enhance those of an Islamist take-over, a scenario the European Union dreads. A fine work by Fawaz Gerges illustrates how similar fears of Islamist threat grip American administrations to the detriment of good government and human rights in the AME. Cultural bias towards "secular" and rational politics, absence of dialogue with "moderate" Islamists and fear of Islamic movements unseating pro-Western regimes combined with an overriding concern with economic and strategic interests rather than democracy explain hostility, ambiguity and passivity *vis-à-vis* Islamists by American foreign policy makers under successive presidents from Carter to Clinton.[76]

Financial, military and political sponsoring of Arab authoritarianism by a number of Western governments amounts to a demotion of democracy. Direct and indirect demotion of democracy will continue to enmesh them with Arab authoritarianism. While the West is not required to impose democracy on the Arab world, it is in a position to delink itself from authoritarian regimes. NED, founded in the

[76] See Fawaz A. Gerges, *America and Political Islam: Clash of Cultures or Clash of Interests?* (Cambridge University Press, 1999), esp. chs 1 and 4.

mid-1980s[77] elicited little or no interest in the Arab world. Although in its September 1989 hearing, before the Subcommittee on International Operation of the Committee on Foreign Affairs, Algeria's joining of "Tunisia in moving toward a more liberalized government and economy"[78] was welcomed, actual NED programmes existed in neither country. The hearing, however, gave no details of NED's "important programme"[79] in Sudan, the Arab exception in the mid-1980s. Testimony by NED's then President, Carl Gershman, indicated that NED's programmes were underdeveloped in both Africa and the Islamic world.[80] Such overlooking of that part of humanity which happens to be Middle Eastern has led Quandt to observe: "I find it almost a racist notion that everybody else in the world is up to the game of democracy...but somehow the Middle East is...unqualified for it."[81] His remark that in the Middle East "the United States has felt quite at ease with regimes that are authoritarian",[82] has also meant that Arab authoritarian rulers have confidence and reassurance in their dealing with the West.

A case in point is al-Sadat's reply to Saʿad Eddin Ibrahim who in August 1981 quizzed the late Egyptian President about his human rights record, and its negative implications for his regime's image in the West. Al-Sadat retorted:

> Your talk of the West surprises me, especially that you studied and lived over there for many years...Don't you know that what concerns the West is primarily its interests? And don't you know that the West uses the issue of human rights only to embarrass the Soviets and regimes hostile to it? And if you don't know that, then how do you justify the West's silence on what used to happen in Iran during the days of the Shah, and in Korea, and in Pakistan, and in the Philippines? Don't human rights get violated there without Western disapproval?[83]

[77] NED was to "build democratic institutions in countries with dictatorships" through "supporting such programs as election monitoring, voter registration...[and] party infrastructure development", *The National Endowment for Democracy in 1990: Hearing Before the Subcommittee on International Operation of the Committee on Foreign Affairs*, US House of Representatives, 28 September, 1989, p. 2.

[78] Ibid., p. 43.

[79] Ibid., p. 31.

[80] Ibid.

[81] William B. Quandt, "After the Gulf Crisis: Challenges for American Policy", *American-Arab Affairs*, 35 (winter 1990–91), p. 18.

[82] Ibid.

[83] Sa'ad Eddin Ibrahim, *I'adat al-i'tibar li-ra'īs al-sādāt* [*Restoring Esteem to President al-Sadat*] (Cairo, Dar al-Shuruq, 1992), p. 43.

USAID spends the most money on promoting democracy. According to its fiscal year 1995 budget report, it spent USD2,853 million (this is made up of USD1,430 million provided by US Information Agency and USD1,423 million by the State Department) on "Building Democracy" out of its total budget of USD20,861 million. Of this USD2,853 million spent on building democracy, USD900 million is spent on the states of the former Soviet Union and USD380 million is spent in Eastern Europe. Furthermore, the USD1,430 million provided by the USIA is spent upon "Information and Exchange" which include programmes such as Radio Free Europe and Asia; of this money very little is specifically targeted at the Middle East. This leaves USD143 million spent on "Countries in Transition" which include countries in Latin America, Africa and the Middle East.[84] The NED budget is far smaller than USAID. In its annual report for 1995, the total moneys spent by NED in the Middle East came to approximately USD3.5 million, compared with a bit over USD4.5 million in Eastern Europe and USD3.6 million in the former Soviet Union.[85]

Specific country by country programmes by USAID in the Middle East include:

Algeria Here the focus is on pressuring the regime to restore the electoral process which was aborted in 1992. However, the United States does not want the elections to lead to an "extremist, anti-democratic regime" coming to power, that is an Islamist-led regime. This stance is more or less a recipe for an exclusionary democracy which is hardly compatible with the democratic values of inclusion and equal participation.

Egypt In 1997 USAID gave a total of USD815 million to Egypt of which USD33.3 million was spent on democracy programmes. This included USD3.3 million for "increased use of information services by the legislature in decision making", USD25 million for "increased civil society organisations' participation in public decision-making" and USD5 million for improving the civil legal system. The programme

[84] This is from the House of Representatives Report, "Foreign Operations, Export Financing, and Related Programs Appropriations for 1995", p. 346.

[85] Information on NED programmes and funding are taken from National Endowment for Democracy; see *Middle East Report*, [http://www.ned.org/page_6/96annual/mideast96.html].

to help Civil Society Organization (CSO) is designed to help them challenge the Egyptian government's restriction upon their activities.[86] The US is also speaking out against the Egyptian government's use of torture.[87] What vitiates this effort is the close ties between the United States and the Egyptian government, an indispensable regional ally. Here too the United States prefers the status quo to an Islamist-led Egypt. Furthermore USAID's emphasis is on economic not political reforms.

Jordan The American government offers its "strong support and encouragement" for Jordan's democratisation process. The financial assistance for democracy programmes is less than 20 per cent of that earmarked for Egypt's.

Lebanon USAID gave USD1 million to help the Lebanese government and parliament recover after the civil war. The money was spent on information technologies and the training of staff to use it.[88]

Palestine The United States government pressed the Palestinian Authority to commit itself to democratisation in the 1993 Declaration of Principles. A fair deal of work has been done in conjunction with NGOs to help build Palestine's election system, the monitoring of elections, and the foundations of a civil society and the rule of law.[89] Specifically, USAID has earmarked USD10.3 million for 1998 to help in voter training, election observation, technical assistance to the Election Commission and the drafting of the Palestinian Basic Law.[90] The American government has also been seeking to promote democracy but with limited or no funding in Tunisia, Iraq, Kuwait, Morocco and Yemen. Because of the limited funding and the government's desire not to alienate its friends in the region, United States efforts to promote democracy have been small and relatively ineffective.

[86] See "USAID Congressional Presentation FY 1997", [http://www.info.usaid.gov/pubs/cp97/countries/eg.html].

[87] See House of Representatives Report: "Foreign Operations, Export Financing, and Related Programs Appropriations for 1995", p. 350.

[88] See "USAID FY 1998 Budget", [http://www.info.usaid.gov/pubs/cp98/ane/countries/lb.html].

[89] Refer to the "Foreign Operations, Export Financing, and Related Programs Appropriations for 1995 Report", p. 350.

[90] From "USAID FY 1998 Budget", [http://www.info.usaid.gov/pubs/cp98/ane/countries/wb-gaza.html].

While a recent Congressional report states that the Gulf states, such as Saudi Arabia, Oman and Bahrain, are making progress because they have consultative councils,[91] it can hardly be said that there is progress towards democratisation in these states while there is still torture, disenfranchisement of women and so on.

When compared to moneys and programmes in Eastern Europe and the former Soviet Union it becomes clear that the focus of United State's democracy promotion is not on the Middle East. Furthermore, until the early 1990s issues of democracy and human rights in the region elicited little or no academic research interest. This academic disinterest fed into the policy-making sphere and *vice versa*. Books such as *The New Democracies* and *Promoting Democracy*, both of which were concerned more with the 1980s, show by virtue of their silence on the AME that American interest in promoting democracy in the Mid-East region is a very recent phenomenon, be it a very timid one. Neither book makes much mention of any such programmes, except an abortive one in Lebanon. There was more of an emphasis on democratic programmes and prospects in Asia, Latin America, Africa, and on the then "Communist World".

Hearings in 1992 in the House of Representatives Subcommittee on Europe and the Middle East dealing with the promotion of democracy in the Mid-East region provide testimony to current United States' disinterest in this domain. Witnesses admitted to American double standards when it came to promoting democracy in Eastern Europe, Russia and Latin America, on the one hand, and the Middle East, on the other. Lee Hamilton, the chairman of the proceedings, asked "Does the United States have a double standard with regard to democracy? Do we push it in Latin America and push it in Eastern Europe and Russia and don't push it very hard in the Middle East and North Africa?" Lisa Anderson, Director of the Middle East Institute at Columbia University, and Michael Hudson, Professor of Middle East politics at Georgetown University, replied in the positive, confirming that the country maintained double standards. Augustus Richard Norton, Professor of Political Science at the US Military Academy at West Point, preferred not to comment on US policy. Anderson elaborated by saying: "I don't think there was any justification for not making as much of an issue about the

[91] See House of Representatives Report: "Foreign Operations, Export Financing, and Related Programs Appropriations for 1995", p. 351.

suspension of elections in Algeria as we made about a similar event in Peru. And we didn't make an issue about the suspension of elections in Algeria to nearly the same extent." Her reason for why this is so is that there is a fear of Islamic fundamentalism which prevents the United States from pushing too hard for democracy. Hudson concurs.[92] Another reason why America may not be too keen to promote democracy in the Middle East is because Islamist governments might not be friendly to America. In this regard, Anderson refers to a strong correlation "in the Arab world between the extent of domestic political liberalization and the level of opposition to American policy in the recent Gulf War".[93]

The persistence of Western direct and indirect support of authoritarianism in the Arab Middle East betrays the democratic claims and practices of the guardians of the new world order. It is worth considering the question of democracy in the context of the Gulf war. The Gulf war was not fought under the banner of democracy. Yet the Bush administration (1988–1992) was quick to demonise Saddam Husayn and the authoritarian practices of his *mukhābarāt* state.[94] Saddam certainly was a leader with megalomaniac instincts, and a dictator whom the West originally supported against a "bigger evil"—Iran—conveniently choosing to overlook his regime's human rights violations. And again, in 1990, it was only for the sake of convenience that the West chose to take notice of Halbaja and the gassing of Kurds and other atrocities against the Iraqi people.[95]

[92] House of Representatives, Committee on Foreign Affairs "Promoting Pluralism and Democracy in the Middle East", 11 August 1992, pp. 49–50.

[93] See Comment by Lisa Anderson to House of Representatives Committee on Foreign Affairs "Promoting Pluralism and Democracy in the Middle East", 11 August 1992, p. 5.

[94] Eden changed his mind and "wrote to Eisenhower that he [did] not think Nasser a Hitler, but that the parallel with Mussolini [was] close". See Ritchie Ovendale, *The Middle East Since 1914* (London: Longman, 1992), p. 75. Note how like Nasser during the 1956 Suez crisis, Saddam was likened to a Hitler. Saddam's technologically-dependent Iraq cannot be compared to Hitler's industrialised Germany. See Robert Springborg's criticism of the Hitler thesis, "Selling War in the Gulf" in St. John Kettle and Stephanie Dowrick (eds), *After the Gulf War: For Peace in the Middle East* (Sydney: Pluto Press, 1991), pp. 26–43. And his murderous record is no match for Hitler's calculated genocide.

[95] This point has not been missed by Noam Chomsky: "...[T]he US is one of the major violators of the principles now grandly proclaimed...George Bush warns of appeasing aggressors and clutches to his heart the Amnesty International (AI) report

The West's "triumph" in the Gulf is meaningless as far as human rights and democratisation are concerned. The Western response to Arab democratisation has been less than enthusiastic. A number of crucial points explain why the West would rather put the question of Arab democratisation on the backburner. First, the West will not tolerate the fall or overthrow of friendly Arab regimes, especially those sitting on vast oil reserves. One Shah's fall is one too many. The West will, in accordance with its interests, guarantee the survival of friendly and pliant regimes even when they are unelected and autocratic. Such protégé regimes, being almost invariably representatives of international capitalism and ruling without the inputs of democratic opposition and virtually free from societal and constitutional restraints, engage unhindered in concessionary (military facilities and low oil prices) and beneficial deals with the West (subsidisation of the Western military industrial complex and petrodollars recycling).[96] The West is no beacon of democracy in the Middle East. The nonchalance towards democracy, which besmirched the United States' messianic role and international reputation, led many Arabs to conclude that the country's commitment is not to democracy or human rights but to the status quo. Pro-Western authoritarian Arab regimes permit the United States far more leverage and patronage than would be possible through Arab democratic regimes.[97] The Arab members

on Iraqi atrocities (after 2 August), but not AI reports on El Salvador, Turkey, Indonesia, and the Israeli Occupied territories." See Noam Chomsky, "The US and the Gulf Crisis" in Haim Bresheeth and Nira Yuval-Davis (eds), *The Gulf War and the New World Order* (London and New Jersey: Zed Books, 1991), p. 19.

[96] Saudi Arabia is a classic example. The stationing of the Coalition troops on her soil contrasts with the kingdom's longstanding reluctance to grant such concessions. In the mid-1950s and the early-1960s the US deployed strategic bombers at Dahran to deter Soviet and Egyptian aggression scenarios. See C. Madison, "Mastering the Game", *National Journal* (3 November 1990), p. 251. The US had no problem securing funds from the Saudis for "Desert Shield", with King Fahd reported to have told visiting James Baker that "his government [would] pay all the monthly in-country costs of the US troops..." See details in W. Mossberg and P. Truell, "Arab Allies of the US Promise Billions to Help Cover Pentagon's Expenses", *The Wall Street Journal* (10 September 1990), p. A5. The pliancy of the Saudis encouraged American legislators to make further requests through George Bush—namely, the reduction of oil prices (whatever happened to market forces?). See "Senators' Call on Saudis to Reduce Oil Prices", *East Asia/Pacific Wireless File 193*, US Information Service (4 October 1990), p. 19.

[97] For instance, Jordan suffered greatly, with her US aid suspended, as a result of her anti-US-led forces' deployment stance, and her favouring of a diplomatic

of the US-led Coalition were no paradigms of democracy, and were motivated by self-interest.[98]

Second, the execution of a financially, environmentally,[99] and humanly devastating[100] war which restored a Kuwaiti autocratic oligarchy stands in sharp contrast with the West's tough stance against despots elsewhere (such as Haiti). A sense of dejà vu is strong with regard to this bifurcation, expressed in Jeane Kirkpatrick's distinction between "bad" and "good" dictators.[101] The 1999 elections excluded women and Bedun. The Emir promised a women's delegation that visited him that year the franchise in the 2003 election. But in 2000 the vote on the proposal to give women the franchise was defeated in the National Assembly, 32 against 30. Thus, another promise was broken since the Kuwait Popular Congress in Jeddah, Saudi Arabia.[102] The human rights violations that took place after

---

solution to the crisis. These stances were, in great measure, influenced by a democratically-elected Low House and an anti-war public opinion. Tim Niblock observes that Arab states which opposed the coalition forces' deployment were those in which democratic initiatives were being taken (Jordan, Yemen, Algeria). See his "The Need for a New Western Arab Order", *Middle East International*, 385 (12 October 1990), p. 17.

[98] Dina Haseeb and Malak S. Rouchdy illustrate this, pointing out the pecuniary motives of Egypt (which also applied to Syria). See "Egypt's Speculations in the Gulf Crisis: The Government's Policies and the Opposition movements" in Bresheeth and Yuval-Davis (eds), *The Gulf War*, pp. 70–9.

[99] For a detailed report on environmental damage associated with the Gulf War, particularly concerning the use of chemical weapons, see Sue Mayer and Paul Johnston, *Chemical Weapons and their Effects on the Environment*, Greenpeace Environment Briefing (London: Greenpeace, 1991). See also Andrew R.G. Price, *Possible Environmental Threats from the Current Gulf War* (University of York Press, 1991).

[100] See, for instance, Ramsey Clark, *The Fire this Time: US War Crimes in the Gulf* (New York: Thunder's Mouth Press, 1992). See also *Needless Deaths in the Gulf War: Civilian Casualties During the Air Campaign and Violations of the Laws of War* (New York: Human Rights Watch, 1991).

[101] Noam Chomsky, referring to a similar convenient distinction, notes: "It is fashionable to distinguish between 'authoritarian' and 'totalitarian' regimes…A regime is 'totalitarian', hence the essence of evil, if it restricts 'economic freedom', a term that does not refer to the freedom of workers or communities to control production, but rather to the freedom for private business…to conduct its affairs without constraint. If it does not restrict the freedom to invest and exploit, a state is at worst 'authoritarian'. This distinction has little relation to the concern of the regime for the welfare of the population." See his *Towards A New Cold War* (London: Sinclair Browne Ltd, 1982), p. 6.

[102] A popular joke underscores the rulers' slowness to respond to Kuwaiti women's demands for enfranchisement. It states that the quickest decision the Amir has ever made was to escape Kuwait on the eve of the Iraqi invasion.

Kuwaiti independence was restored went almost unnoticed in the corridors of power in Western capitals. Similarly, human rights violations by key Western allies (Egypt, Jordan Tunisia, Morocco) draw little criticism except for the perfunctory treatment given in the US State Department's annual country reports.[103]

A classic case of Western confusion and disinterest over Arab democratisation is the response of the United States to the cancellation in January 1992 of the results of Algeria's first multiparty parliamentary elections. The initial response, read on January 13 by White House spokesperson Margaret Tutwiler, was clearly supportive of the coup, describing it as "constitutional". The following day, seeking to alleviate the damage and embarrassment caused by the previous statement, Tutwiler announced to a startled media that the United States would not comment further on the constitutionality, or lack thereof, of the Algerian military takeover.[104] According to one Western commentator, "by neither criticizing nor approving the Algerian army's action, Western countries cloak their real attitude—that democracy is fine up to a certain point".[105] The idea is that "sovereign" Algerians cannot be allowed to elect Islamists (supposedly anti-democratic) who appeared on the verge of winning a majority. It is, however, quite acceptable for Western citizens to vote into office leaders (supposedly democratic) who, if need be, are prepared to go to war and bomb cities in the name of the national interest.

Muḥammad al-'Arabī Zaytūt, the former First Secretary in Algeria's Embassy in Tripoli who was granted political asylum in the United Kingdom in 1997, claims that outside nonchalance partly explains the current Algerian miasma. He even blames Nelson Mandela personally for what he describes as "his failure to empathize with the Algerian people's tragedy", saying that defence joint venture deals and the sale of "instruments of terror" to a regime that does not meet

[103] For details of human rights violations in these countries, see country reports in *Huquq al-insan fi al-watan al-arabi* [*Human Rights in the Arab Homeland*] (Cairo: Arab Human Rights Organization, 1992, 1993, 1994, 1995).

[104] *East Asia/Pacific Wireless File 009* (14 January 1992), pp. 14–15.

[105] Jim Hoagland, "Washington's Algerian Dilemma", *The Washington Post* (6 February 1992), p. A27. Another excellent article is by David Ignatius, "Islam in the West's Sights: The Wrong Crusade?" *The Washington Post* (8 March 1992), pp. c1–c2. For the United States' response with regard to the restoration of democracy in Haiti see "Restoring Democracy in Haiti: Persistence and Patience", *State Dispatch*, 3 and 8 (24 February 1992), pp. 132–3.

the "minimum standards of civilized rule and political behaviour" towards its people and its opponents is morally questionable.[106] Zaytūt, however, lashes at France, another bastion of democracy and republican values. He claims the Algerian regime would have collapsed in 1993 had not been for unfettered French support, saying that the exact volume of France's financial aid to Algeria is more than the declared five billion francs which does not cover the costly arms transfers. Whilst he praises the conditions and standards the United Kingdom is to impose on prospective arms buyers, he is critical of a number of Western governments' indifference to human rights violations and authoritarian rule throughout the Arab world.

While European powers are closely linked with the sponsoring of authoritarian rule in the AME, it is the United States that more often than not takes a greater share of the blame. One reason for this is that America has replaced the former leading colonial powers, the United Kingdom and France, as the major influential force in the mid-East region in the post-war period. Another is that the United States, owing to the power it projects and the influence it commands, is often hoped and expected to provide moral leadership more so than the French and the British whose involvement in the region is still tainted by colonialism. It is perhaps owing to this fact that the Europeans are, wrongly of course, more absolved of authoritarianism in the AME than the Americans. The more the country fails to live up to this moral standard, the more it is implicated in authoritarianism in the AME, not only for what it does but also for what it can do and yet does not do. The rise of America in the post-war period presented Arabs, amongst other peoples, with a new moral force to look up to for assistance and support against injustice and colonisation. To an extent and up to the Suez crisis, the Americans succeeded in impressing on Arabs a relatively positive image of a moral and neutral force worthy of superpower status. Perhaps it is the obsession with what America *ought* to be or *should* stand for that still colour views about *what is* flawed or imperfect in its global role and leadership. As Edward Said puts it: "[F]or two generations the

106 These deals refer to an arms transfer worth more than $US 16 million already been approved by South Africa's National Convention of Arms Control Council in late 1997. The centrepiece of the transfer is the Seeker remote-piloted vehicle that the Algerian army wants to deploy to monitor the hideouts and movements of rebels from the Islamic Armed Group (GIA).

United States has sided in the Middle East mostly with tyranny and injustice. No struggle for democracy, or women's rights... and the rights of minorities has the United States officially supported."[107]

Arab Cynicism

The equation that America's democracy-promoting initiatives help create governments friendly to it must, on the basis of its dismal track record, look anything but convincing in the AME. The United States is projected within oppositional circles as having committed little of its political, moral or material weight to induce its Arab allies into genuine democratisation or greater observance of human rights. What seems to escape foreign policy-makers in the United States, and for that matter their counterparts in the European Union, is that if democracy promotion wins Western governments friends, the obverse is sadly as true. The sponsoring of authoritarian rule in the AME creates foes whose suspicion and distrust of Western policies and presence in the mid-East region will not be easily shaken. Hence Arab cynicism, amongst both secularists and Islamists as briefly sampled below, is not unwarranted with regard to Western proclamations about democracy and human rights.

Arab cynicism toward the role of Western governments in the AME is characterised by lack of neutrality and outright contradiction. These themes recur in both Islamist and secularist criticisms against the West despite their difference of political platforms and positions towards the West in general. The views aired by opposition groups and activists throughout the AME, privately and publicly, reflect frustration and anger at Western silence on human rights abuses or, worse still, continuous assistance of nominally democratic regimes and unrepresentative and unaccountable regimes. The damage is immense: alienation of democratically-minded forces in the AME, amongst Islamists and secularists, Western and non-Western educated. America's image of itself as a democratic missionary has no substance in this part of the world. It remains to be substantiated. Two Egyptian opposition leaders, Musṭafa Mashhūr, the Grand Master of al-ikhwān in Egypt, and Rif'at al-Sayyid, the Chairman of the leftist Unionist Socialist Progressive Party, represent two diametrically opposed forces of the largest Arab country's political spectrum and

107 Edward Said, *Culture and Imperialism*, p. 363.

yet concur that the West has a case to answer for its complicitous silence on misrule in the AME. They respectively doubt Western neutrality:

I doubt that American and European silence on abuses of power and political corruption is based on *ḥiyād* (neutrality) in domestic politics in the Arab world. We are not accustomed to such a neutrality in the way the West has over an extended historical period dealt with the region, its governments and its peoples. Silence does not equal neutrality. Most Western powers have interests in our region; that does not make them neutral. They maintain certain friendships in the Middle East; that too does not make them neutral. They openly oppose certain forces they call *uṣūliyyah* (fundamentalism) which is not neutral either. Were they neutral, the political landscape in the Arab region would have been very different from what it is today, a landscape of authoritarian regimes of the worst kind.[108]

Rif'at al-Sayyid more or less concurs:

I do not wish to point the finger at any Western government in particular. However, the record of many governments from the West is one of meddling in foreign countries' politics. The list of examples in this region alone is a long one and so is the history of such meddling. Had there been no history of meddling, one would be inclined to favour an argument that silence towards human rights violations and lack of democratic rule is motivated by a scrupulous foreign policy. Meaning, that the West wishes to have no part in influencing local politics. Unfortunately, direct and indirect meddling exists and influences the shape of some regimes we have in this region. This meddling has often served the regimes not the democratic movements and political parties in our Arab region.[109]

The above verdict that most Western powers are not neutral is not an isolated one. It engenders a great deal of cynicism about any future positive role for the West, in general, and the United States, in particular, in the AME. Compounding this cynicism, especially towards the United States, is the American-Israeli alliance. This is a factor that Islamists and secularists deploy quite effectively in their diatribes against America. The lack of neutrality links the United States to the impasses of peace and democracy. The United States is at once Israel's staunchest ally and the chief sponsor of the peace process to the detriment of carrying out its role as an honest peace broker. Likewise, its close ties with a number of Arab non-representative

[108] Author's interview with Musṭafa Mashhūr, 18 February 1998, Cairo.

[109] Author's interview with Rif'at al-Sayyid, 14 February 1998, Cairo.

and unaccountable regimes has been at the expense of promoting democracy in a non-interventionist or coercive manner. Both instances illustrate clashes of interest. Current conventional wisdom within Western policy-making communities is to place neither economic and business interests nor the actors and states that facilitate their continuity in a vulnerable position. This pragmatism should come as no surprise. What is rather surprising is the lack of insistence on minimum standards of civilised behaviour by ruling elites in client regimes. This is an important point another prominent secularist activist, Farūq Abū 'Isā, President of the Arab Lawyers' Union, seizes upon:

> Some Western governments are guilty by association. They seem to have no criteria of how they come to befriend at once elites whose hostility to democratic rule is religion-based and others, who though are secular, behave dictatorially. Western governments must not be blamed for pursuing interests which all countries do. They must be blamed for having no moral principles to guide how they go about achieving their legitimate interests. These interests can be achieved in a way that does not compromise people's rights to self-determination and to democratic rule. These are rights that should at least elicit moral support.[110]

In line with this view, Abū 'Isā reckons that one of the biggest challenges facing the West in the AME is how to harmonise principles of human rights and democratic government with pragmatism. Continuity of the status quo means not only tension between principles and interests but also, on the one hand, between Western governments and important segments of Arab civil societies, and, on the other, between the latter and their own governments. This is a situation that brings with it heavy penalties for all concerned. Hence *ḥiwār* (dialogue) within and without is high on the agenda of oppositional forces in the AME. This is one reason why Islamist leaders—for instance, 'Abd al-Majīd Dhnibāt, the current General Master of Jordan's Muslim Brotherhood; 'Abd al-Laṭīf 'Arabiyyāt, former Speaker of Jordan's Parliament and the current leader of al-'amal; Musṭafa Mashhūr—insist upon it. All three share the view that having good relations with Europe and America is a necessity. They are of the view that dialogue dispels mutual mistrust; helps create bridges with powerful countries with whom they wish greater mutual understanding; and aids work towards tolerating and managing differences

110 Author's interview with Farūq Abū 'Isā, 17 February 1998, Cairo.

amicably. For instance, Dhnibāt addresses the question of mistrust, by noting:

As Muslims we do not shy away from sitting with the "other" and establishing dialogue with. This is a Prophetic sunnah we intend to live up to. Dialogue in good faith with Europeans or with the US would show that we wish no harm on any one and that Islamists are not terrorists or enemies of just and good rule. It would be useful for both parties to dispel myths and clear misunderstandings. Perhaps we sometimes do not read Western governments and non-government organizations as much as we should and would like to learn more about how they see a range of issues and learn about our similarities and dissimilarities.[111]

But dialogue is more than just didactic argues ʿAbd al-Laṭīf ʾArabiyyāt. He sees in it a key to reworking relations between Islamists and the West as well as between Islamists and their governments at home. Where there is breakdown or outright absence of dialogue in the second set of relations, precariousness characterises the first set of relations with Western governments either cutting off channels of communication with Islamists for fear of upsetting friendly regimes or relegating them a low-key status. The reverse is true. A number of Islamist groups (e.g. in Yemen and Jordan) have an ongoing dialogue with Western governments as well as with NGOs from the West. The crackdown on al-ikhwān in Egypt deprived its Islamists of important channels of communication with the West. North African Islamists active in Europe have extended their ties with Western parliamentarians, human rights activists, academics, and NGOs. This is as true of al-Ghannūshī's al-nahḍah as it is of the FIS. Through these contacts a whole set of cross-identifications and cross-cultural exchanges take place around moral causes (democracy; human rights). What ensues is a set of transnational solidarities around these issues. ʿArabiyyāt recognises the vital role of these transnational solidarities in today's world which for him can happen only through contact and dialogue:

Had the Prophet not sought contact and dialogue with the [other], Islam would not have enjoyed its present global reach uniting peoples of many colours, lands, languages and geographies. There is no escape from dialogue and contact with Westerners, Chinese, Russians and others, all of whom are our brothers in humanity. We need each other. Through dialogue we will together be more capable of maintaining hope, hope that we will be able to

[111] Author's interview with ʿAbd al-Majīd Dhnibāt, 7 February 1998, Amman.

generate respect for our differences, to generate *khayr* (good) for all human beings and fend off *sharr* (harm). We consider consultative and democratic government to be an example of *khayr*; and tyranny an example of *sharr*.[112]

Like Dhnibāt, he attaches religious significance to dialogue. This is a recurring theme in Islamist discourses. Al-Ghannūshī and al-Turābī strongly argue that Muslims are compelled to conduct dialogue within and without the Islamic community, i.e. with co-religionists as well as non-Muslims.[113] In fact, al-Turābī says a global dialogue is a God-sanctioned duty on Muslims. For him this dialogue alone can ensure global partnership in terms of both obligations and entitlements. He particularly rejects the notion of a *ṣirā'u'l-ḥaḍārāt* (clash of civilisations), noting that Islam throughout its history has been engaged in *ḥiwāru'l-ḥaḍārāt* (inter-civilisational dialogue).[114] For 'Arabiyyāt dialogue takes another significance; it helps understand, manage and represent *ikhtilāf* (difference). He puts polarisation in all its forms down to the failure of understanding, managing and representing difference. He exonerates neither Islamists nor secularists from this failure. This is one reason why he champions dialogue in the Arab world between Islamists and other oppositional forces with their governments. Similarly, he emphasises dialogue between the forces of Islam and the West. He deems both to be essential for confidence-building and for the future of good government in the AME, adding that:

One tragedy for democratic and consultative government in the Arab world is that sometimes some Western governments haste into adopting the regimes' stance towards Islamists as their own. Therefore whatever measures are taken by these regimes against Islamists including banishment, internment, torture, killings, harassment, and exclusion go unnoticed…When tyranny elicits no condemnation and tyrants draw no opposition from the outside world, the public and civil societies everywhere in the Arab world [draw lines] between those who care and those who do not care and pass their own judgements about those who do not care for democracy and human rights and other issues like why the international community is unable to find a just solution for the Palestinian cause or is not doing enough to relieve the suffering of innocent children dying of malnutrition in Iraq because of the sanctions.[115]

112 Author's interview with 'Abd al-Laṭīf 'Arabiyyāt, 5 February 1998, Amman.

113 Author's interviews with Rāshid al-Ghannūshī, 29 January 1998, London; and with Ḥasan al Turābī, 14 May 1994, Khartoum.

114 Author's interview with Ḥasan al Turābī, 14 May 1994, Khartoum.

115 Author's interview with 'Abd al-Laṭīf 'Arabiyyāt, 5 February 1998, Amman.

Indeed the questions the different Arab publics raise about the nature of ties between Western and Arab governments and the kind of judgements and linkages made must not be undermined. The longer unfavourable judgements and negative linkages become entrenched, the harder it is for the West to repair the damage and restore trust. Although on the surface there seem to be no catalytic forces that can overthrow the political status quo in the AME, the forces of change or the potential for change must not be underestimated. The fall of the Shah in Iran in 1979 and the dissolution of the former Soviet Union a decade later took political practitioners and academics by surprise. More notice must be taken of the sobering lessons of both events. A number of Arab countries are good candidates for change in the twenty-first century. When and if democratic change comes about, whether goodwill towards Western governments is exhausted will depend on whether these governments will continue to soft-pedal values and principles of democracy and human rights. Concern for democracy and human rights must not be equated with imposition or coercive intervention. Similarly, pragmatic pursuit of business interests in the AME should not mean neglect of democratic and human rights principles. For now at least, it is doubtful whether foreign policy-makers in the United States and EU are serious enough about harnessing their economic and political weight in support of higher standards of democracy and human rights in various countries in the AME. There is no clear winner in the pulls of pragmatism and principle. Ambivalence, as can be gathered from the quote below from a US State Department document, persists:

> Our strategy must be pragmatic. Our interests in democracy and markets do not stand alone. Other American interests at times will require us to befriend and even defend nondemocratic states for mutually beneficial reasons.[116]

Lake's plan for the world and the United States' role as argued in his paper "From Containment to Enlargement" suffers from too much strategic-box thinking and scheming. Similar strategic-box thinking characterises Martin Indyk's understanding of foreign policy in the Middle East.[117] Indyk, the originator of dual containment, defines dangers and specifies challenges facing the Mid-East region. The

[116] Lake, "From Containment to Enlargement", p. 5.

[117] Indyk Martin, "The Clinton Administration's Approach to the Middle East", keynote address, Washington Institute on Near East Policy, 5 August 1993.

dangers, although meant to deal with a post-Cold War Middle East, are rooted in a Cold War mentality. He prescribes dual containment of Iran and Iraq, a recipe for further militarisation of the region; and vigilance against religious extremism, one reason for unfettered support for United States' allies faced with such a threat. Containment against Iran has all but failed and religious extremism has anything but vanished. Neither non-democracy and brutality against religious extremists nor Western complacency towards them are likely to cure extremism. On the positive side, Indyk's challenges for American foreign policy under Clinton are peace promotion and what he calls a "vision of a more democratic and prosperous" Middle East.[118] The flaw here is that he does not argue for peace for the sake of peace or because of the righteousness of the Palestinian cause but rather as one way of making containment against Iran and Iraq stick and work.[119] His conception of peace, no matter how genuine, intertwines with his scheme for containment. Nonetheless, he has more to say about peace than about democracy for the Middle East. His vision for more democracy is vague and brief. This stands in a staggering contrast to his details about the military agenda and the strategic alliances for containing Iran and Iraq as well as stopping the danger of religious extremism by states (e.g. Sudan, Iran) and organisations (e.g. Hamas, Hizbullah).[120]

EXPORTING DEMOCRACY: THE ISLAMIST DIMENSION

Fascination and frustration characterise the AME's relationship with the West. The discovery of the West by the AME, in the past via expeditions and colonialism and now through multidimensional links in which the Arab side has little comparative advantage, continues to be a source of frustration. Fascination with the military and technical superiority of Europe was a major stimulus for emulating its advancement. Muḥammad 'Alī's Egypt was a trailblazer in this domain, sending some 100 students to France between 1826 and 1835, to be inducted in the secrets of the European "miracle" and receiving technicians to help with the drive to modernise. Under Aḥmed Bey, the Beylicate of Tunis followed suit. Fascination was not

118 Ibid., p. 4.
119 Ibid., p. 3.
120 Ibid., pp. 1–6.

confined to mechanisation; it extended into the machinery of government and society. There were mixed feelings and reactions by Muslim modernists to nineteenth-century liberalism and humanism but many found a number of their ideals to be compatible with the general purpose of Islam.

The dialectic of fascination and frustration with the West continues unabated amongst Islamists. Islamists view the West as a paradox: On the one hand, it is *progressive* with its high-tech, economic growth, and political institutions; on the other, it is *unprogressive* in the way it utilises its high-tech to subjugate and dominate, disseminate its values, and achieve economic development at the expense of other peoples and cultures. A standardising characteristic of the Islamist discourse on the West is its distinction between *al-ḥaḍārah al-gharbiyyah* (Western civilisation) and *al-thaqāfah al-gharbiyyah* (Western culture). The former is the subject of exaltation; the latter of denigration. *Al-ḥaḍārah al-gharbiyyah* is exalted for putting man on the moon, superior institutions and organisation, its high-tech and science, and even warfare know-how. *Al-thaqāfah al-gharbiyyah* is denigrated for nurturing profanity and sexual promiscuity, legalising homosexuality, for being comfortable with greed and prioritising the interests of the individual over those of the community.[121] Although contemporary Islamists are fond of the "progressive" side of Europe, they have historically opposed all forms of Western political engineering in the AME, regardless of the labels (socialism, democracy, development), strategies and motivations. The chief frustration of Islamists over democracy is the "unprogressiveness" of many Western governments in that they choose democracy for themselves and their peoples while actively supporting non-democratic rule elsewhere, especially in the AME.

Agreement is complete between the four interviewee leaders as to American or European political engineering aimed at imposing democracy on the Arab world. Four reasons they produce explicate their opposition to such a political engineering. First, although they all stand for emulation of some of the democratic achievements enacted in Europe and North America, their chief reservation

[121] This analysis is consistent with the views expressed by the four leaders in author's interviews with Isḥāq Aḥmad al-Farḥān, 5 February 1992, Amman; Rāshid al-Ghannūshī, 14 April 1993, London; Ma'mūn al-Huḍaybī, 4 April 1994, Cairo; Muḥammad 'Abd al-Raḥmān Khalīfah, 1 June 1994, Amman.

against Western exporting of democracy is the promoting of what they regard as "alien values" that accompany it. Secondly, they express disdain of any active exporting of democracy to the AME, regarding it as interference in domestic affairs. The encounter of the West via colonialism has impacted negatively on Islamists. Thus Khalīfah warns of any complacency towards yesteryear's colonisers: "How can we trust *ghuzat al-ihtilal* (conquering colonisers) when not in the too distant past they divided our lands, dispossessed our brethren in Palestine, and very recently destroyed Iraq. They will keep coming under different guises, like progress, that have rarely led to the *khayr* (welfare) of Muslims."[122] Thirdly, they insist that for good government to take root and be sustainable and successful it has to not only be home-grown but also sensitive to local conditions and cultures, according Islam a special role in the nurturing and informing of such a government. Finally, the best way Western countries can foment good government in the AME is by not actively supporting authoritarian regimes. Islamists blame diplomatic support for according a few Arab regimes undeserved respectability and legitimacy internationally; and they blame material and financial support for prolonging Arab misrule domestically. On the whole, Islamists reject active support of Western democracy for being not morally neutral, and active maintenance of non-democratic regimes for being counter to the very ethics of democracy. As put by al-Farḥān, "Democrats letting down democracy is a contradiction obvious to all observers of the Algerian scene. How can France, for instance, pretend that its siding with the *junta* and against the people's verdict of the cancelled polls in Algeria serve human rights or conform to the ideals of its own revolution?"[123]

More specifically, Islamists oppose Westerners directly fomenting democracy in the Arab world for one main reason: cultural-civilisational specificity. In fact, all four leaders express a similar idea the crux of which is that as Muslims they are obligated to benefit from whatever good values and useful knowledge there exist anywhere whatever their provenance. This obligation is a function of the Muslim endeavour to enjoin *al-maruf* (the good), a Godly command, not only of the *ummah* but also of humankind. The interviewed

[122] Author's interview with Muḥammad 'Abd al-Raḥmān Khalīfah, 14 June 1994, Amman.

[123] Author's interview with Isḥāq Aḥmad al-Farḥān, 5 February 1992, Amman.

leaders recognize that there is some *maṣlaḥah* in democracy that ought to be adopted for being congenial with enjoining the good. Despite their diverse backgrounds—al-Farḥān and Khalīfah (Jordan); al-Ghannūshī (Tunisia) and al-Huḍaybī (Egypt)—all share the belief that Muslims can benefit from the experiences and achievements of old and consolidated democracies; that a number of democratic values are congenial with enjoining the good; and that therefore Islam's alleged incompatibility with democracy is a myth.

A few qualifications are in order. When these Islamists approve of a number of democratic values and principles for being congenial with the good they do so convinced that copying Western democracy—elections, parliaments, parties—is not going to make the AME really democratic. Al-Ghannūshī observes that the "superficial copying of democratic procedures and having the façades of democracy by Bin Ali has not turned Tunisia into a democracy".[124] Similarly, al-Huḍaybī remarks:

> The quantity of elections, of parties and the sham of democracy have not duped aware Egyptians. What counts is *rūḥ al-dīmuqrātiyyah* (ethos of democracy) which effectively remains absent. The quantity of irregularities in elections, the quantity of arbitrary arrests of those opposing injustice and corruption, and the quantity of those whose rights are violated everyday in Egypt do not reflect *rūḥ al-dīmuqrātiyyah*. Democracy equals *al-shakl* (form) plus *al-rūḥ* (spirit). Accordingly, *al-shakl* without *al-rūḥ* is not but *tazyīf* (a forgery) of democracy.[125]

However, common to all four is the fact that the spirit of democracy, exemplified, amongst other things, by *tasāmuḥ* (tolerance) and *nazāhah* (probity), does not operate in a vacuum. The spirit of Western democracy, points al-Ghannūshī, is the by-product of cultural-civilisational histories, experiences and events, ranging from the rise of capitalism and the Industrial Revolution to the Reformation and the French and American Revolutions. The brand of democracy born out of these developments, he adds, engendered values that continue to be specific to the Western cultural-civilisational heritage. Two of these values, namely, secularism and individualism, have no analogues in the Muslims' cultural-civilisational heritage.[126] For al-Farḥān, the challenges facing Muslims today is to transcend superficially copying

[124] Author's interview with Rāshid al-Ghannūshī, 14 April 1993, London.
[125] Author's interview with Ma'mūn al-Huḍaybī, 4 April 1994, Cairo.
[126] Author's interview with Rāshid al-Ghannūshī, 14 April 1993, London.

the procedures of Western democracy, like voting and parties, and create a democratic *namūthaj* (model) with an Islamic spirit in which *shūrā* (consultation), *tarāḥum* (mutuality), *ta'āwun* (cooperation), *musāwāt* (equality), *'adālah* (justice) and *al-mas'ūliyyatu'l-jamā'iyyah* (mutual obligation) between *jamā'atu'l-muslimīn* (Muslim community) inform political ideals, norms and behaviour.[127]

Indeed, as far as Islamists are concerned, Western democracy has historical, economic and cultural-civilisational specificities that render any expectation or ambition of its "wholesale" exportation unrealistic. Compounding this is the Arabo-Islamic world's own *khuṣūṣiyāt* (specificities/particularities). Accordingly, Khalīfah notes that priority ought to be given to the local *khuṣūṣiyāt*:

> We oppose the label "democracy" because it reflects Western histories and *khuṣūṣiyāt*. We believe in *al-niẓām al-shūrī* (consultative government). However, if practised properly by Muslims, this Godly *niẓām* can perform many of the functions of democracy and even achieve more than it in terms of social justice and rights for the *ra'iyyah* (populace).[128]

For al-Farḥān, al-Ghannūshī and al-Huḍaybī individualism and secularism represent major stumbling blocks to any outside attempt to foment Western democracy, with its own cultural-civilisational specificity, in the Arab world. Al-Farḥān notes that as a Muslim he sees many *ḥasanāt* (merits/virtues) in Western democracy that he would like to see emulated by Arab governments. The rule of law, free and fair elections, the non-continuing tenure of office, the separation of powers, checks and balances, organised labour unions, free press and demilitarised polity are examples of the virtues of Western democracies he cites. Yet for him what detracts from Western democracy is the unfettered individualism that makes narrow interests supersede public interests and gives unelected rich individuals or companies the power to get concessions from elected office-holders and lawmakers. On the basis of this alone he declares that neither in Jordan nor in the Arab world will democratic government when it matures resemble, for instance, either French or Italian democracy. He observes that "Although the individual has a share of responsibilities as well as a place in a Muslim society the *jamā 'ah* (the group) is in the Islamic

[127] Author's interview with Isḥāq Aḥmad al-Farḥān, 5 February 1992, Amman.

[128] Author's interview with Muḥammad 'Abd al-Raḥmān Khalīfah, 14 June 1994, Amman.

scheme of things the highest ideal of *ummah* as shown to us by the example of the Prophet."[129]

Al-Huḍaybī is equally troubled by individualism. But it is Western secularism that he finds particularly problematic and unsuited to Arab and Islamic societies. Defending the right of Arabs to political self-determination according to their cultural and civilisational heritage, he denounces the drive to universalise secularisation as a precondition for attaining democracy. As he puts it "Those who are lecturing us that secularization is a principal condition for achieving democratic government are numerous in Egypt; they are in government, in the universities, in the newspapers, and in radio and television. If secularization is a key to democracy, then why its advocates in Egypt and the Arab world are mostly not democratic?"[130] Al-Huḍaybī records that Islam is expanding not shrinking, both in terms of greater observance by individual Muslims, and as a force of organisation and mobilisation occupying a special place in public affairs even when not licensed by delegitimised and threatened regimes in the AME. Being a staying force, Islam has to be part of any plan to achieve legality, representativeness, accountability, constitutionalism, justice, human rights, equal opportunity in the AME. For al-Huḍaybī, being an Islamist does not contradict with goals like these. The contradiction, he observes, would be if Arabs sought to "be Muslim but anti *shūrā* or anti-democracy or to adopt democracy but without Islam and its principles". Being Muslim and being consultative and democratic are mutually inclusive and reinforcing. The bottom line for him is:

> Secularism is a concept rooted in specific history, the history of Europe and Christianity, the history of the state and the church. Such a history has no parallel in Islamic history, culture or civilization. It is therefore wrong to use secularism as a *miqyās* (criterion) in Arab and Islamic settings. Islam, especially for Sunnis, has no theocratic past or any basis upon which a *thiyūqratiyyah* (theocracy) can ever be legitimated. Islamic government is not rule by religious authorities. However, in it reference must be made by legislators and rulers to Allah's *sharī'ah* (God's Law). Islam knows no absolute government by man, for man and to man. There is a Godly side that Western democracy overlooks; here we differ.[131]

129 Author's interview with Isḥāq Aḥmad al-Farḥān, 5 February 1992, Amman.
130 Author's interview with Ma'mūn al-Huḍaybī, 4 April 1994, Cairo.
131 Ibid.

Al-Ghannūshī remarks that the obligation to consult with others on all matters of public nature concerning the entirety of the community is an Islamic *khuluq* (ethic).[132] Therefore whereas for Westerners and many Westernisers it seems difficult to conceive of Muslims as being open to democracy, for Muslims it is a simple matter of religiosity and Islamic ethics to practice *shūra* and behave democratically. Al-Ghannūshī holds that democracy is a moral issue, questioning the morality of those Western governments that either directly or indirectly support nondemocratic regimes. He expresses a similar view to al-Huḍaybī with regard to the Muslims' right to political self-determination according to their cultural-civilisational heritage. In this respect, two important ideas expressed by al-Ghannūshī are relevant to any debate on the subject of the exportability of democracy to the AME. First, al-Ghannūshī reminds some Westerners not to be hasty or arrogant in assuming that military and economic preponderance are the only items of relevance and self-assertion; that unipolarity of the world order must not be taken to mean paradigmatic singularity (the liberal model); and that the items of creating justly and popularly-governed societies are not specific to the liberal model. Second, he notes that with its moral force, the cultural-civilisational heritage bequeathed to Arabs has the potential not only to emulate the democratic and other material achievements of the West but also to avoid their shortcomings, particularly in terms of total focus on earthly ends and of excessive emphasis on individualism. For al-Ghannūshī, the Muslims' struggle for the right to develop political systems that consider their cultural particularities has wider implications not only for international order but also for a democratic international order:

> Today we hear so many voices championing democracy. All the while many of these very voices are calling for the combating of Islam and Islamists who are accused of hostility against democracy. If democracy is about pluralism, then why the bias against other cultures, systems and peoples? It is no good talking about a world order. It is better working to achieve a democratic world order. And a democratic world order must promote toleration of differences. Furthermore, it must promote not only partnership between cultures, religions, and peoples but it must also reflect the diversity of cultures, religions, and peoples.[133]

132 Author's interview with Rāshid al-Ghannūshī, 14 April 1993, London.
133 Ibid.

Many problems and imponderables inhere in the debate about the exportability of democracy to the AME. One particular problem that will continue to divide Arabs well into the third millennium is how to be democratic without being insensitive to the Arabo-Islamic *turāth*, i.e. how to be simultaneously genuinely democratic, genuinely Arab and genuinely Muslim. This is not only a question of how to be Arab, Muslim and democratic but also one of how to be modern and traditional as well as *what* and *how much* modernity and tradition help that hybridisation of identity—i.e. one in which Arabness, Islamicity and democracy intertwine—happen. The debate over question of exportability of democracy will also continue to draw lines between those (e.g. Islamists) who oppose direct fomenting of Western forms of democracy which is neither value-free nor neutral and those (secularist oppositions; human rights activists) who advocate a more active role and tougher stance (on say the freeze on military and police equipment) against violators of human rights and democratic waverers. Both groups, however, implicate Western governments in the survival of authoritarianism in the AME.

Coincident with cultural-civilisational narratives, the current debate will also divide Arab and non-Arab. Noticed for their own cultural-civilisational narrative, Islamists represent one formidable political configuration for which the questions of *what* and *how much* modernity and tradition is a real issue in respect to both the Islamisation and democratisation of Arab societies and polities. The notions of cultural specificity and exceptionalism encountered in certain Western discourses have resonance in the Islamist perspective. In both, specificity is a site where the difference between the "self" and the "other" becomes the essence of identity and therefore a non-negotiable given. In both, specificity spells exclusion. Certain Western discourses claim democracy to be a Western cultural-civilisational by-product unsuited to the "other" while others claim it to be a universal *telos*. Advancing discourses of cultural particularity and universalism of their own, Islamists reject the first by reading democracy in Islamic sources and retort to the second by upholding their right to borrow *what* democracy and *how much* democracy as befits culture, history and local values.

Consequently, contemporary Islamists tend to follow the same itinerary of earlier Islamist reformers, rejecting all Western political engineering in the AME. One obvious reason for this stance is the suspicion and the bias harboured by many Western governments against Islamists. Other reasons range from reciprocated suspicion against Western intentions. The colonial experience; the fear that outside fomenting of democracy could serve foreign interests and disseminate alien values; the view that such fomenting will be undemocratic if it is not home-grown or if it is dismissive of the indigenous values, cultures and histories and, in particular, of Islam.

The colonial experience was antithetical to democracy at more than one level. In particular, democracy was confined to European citizens in the various former colonial metropoles with the colonised, bar the co-opted elites, enjoying no citizenship rights whatsoever. The Western historic record in the AME was evidently subversive of democratic rule. Little has changed. Today the mesh of connections between Arab autocrats and Western democrats is stronger rather than weaker. "Political correctness" has ceded to "economic correctness" (marketisation and privatization) geared to preparing the AME for another phase of scrambling for profits by plunder machines made up of congeries of indigenous and non-indigenous "power-crats" in the name of peace and the so-called Middle Eastern economic market. In this new chapter of Arabo-Western relations, democracy is simply a footnote. The uncritically continuous support of authoritarian regimes in the AME by some Western governments is immoral and irresponsible. The West can ill-afford to close down its eyes to human rights violations and misrule in Egypt, Morocco or Tunisia and highlight them in Cuba or China.

Culturally, as hinted at by the four Islamist leaders, democracy needs reconstructing if it is to co-exist with Islamic values. Its individualism has to be balanced with Islam's emphasis on the community, and its secularism has to yield to radically opposed precepts of temporal and spiritual oneness and an imagining of political legitimacy in which the will of man is subordinate to the will of God.

The question of whether Western democracy travels is fundamentally a question about the limits of Western foundations. Hence the necessity of a post-foundational democracy. Post-foundational democracy is one that is not based on Western criteria—individualism, secularism or market economics. A condition for this is a reconstructing of political science, amongst other social sciences, in such a way that post-foundationalism becomes an attack upon knowledge forms that claim that they are irreducible bases of social life, singular truth and reality in the world, i.e. bases independent of social, cultural, historical and linguistic interpretations. In many ways democratic thinking and democratic politics, being symbiotic with questioning, are in themselves threats to the foundationalist ethic. Such an ethic has for so long embedded conservative status quoism and rigid ideologies that until recently, especially owing to the advent of postmodernism, could not be challenged. The political implications of the foundationalist ethic have been some four hundred years of Western and Christian disasters everywhere around the world.

Transcending Western foundations, in particular, and the foundationalist ethic with its fixed and singular power relations, in general, is an awesome challenge. This is even more so in the AME. While warranted for challenging Western foundations and standards of democracy such as individualism and secularism, the Islamist endeavour to transpose the foundational individual with the foundational believer is for many as problematic as Western foundationalism. It seems that, at least, in part, the failure so far for a *modus vivendi* to emerge in the AME between Islamists and secularists, is due to the latter's suspicion of religious foundationalism's long-term commitment to democracy. Rather, there is only one tacit *modus vivendi* between a number of indifferent Western powers and deligitimised ruling elites currently operating in the AME. Through it, the pretext of protecting democracy has become rubber-stamped as an acceptable justification for excluding, cracking down on Islamists and reversing democratic initiatives. Hence despite many modest democratic gains in key Arab liberalisers, political reforms in the AME have neither gone beyond proceduralism, nor have they allowed for the emergence of a genuine site of contestation or unfixed and multipolar power relations. With the continuing depredations of authoritarian rule, "electoralisation" and "parliamentarisation" of the AME cannot be said, at this historical juncture, to augur well for engendering an ethos of democracy that can open up possibilities for new movements of pluralisation and of being.

8

DISCOURSING ISLAM AND DEMOCRACY

TESTS AND CONTESTS, TEXTS AND CONTEXTS

"...The claim to liberty permeates all the existential planes of Arab consciousness, because the absence of freedom is experienced as a lack, then as an oppression and it [its insistent demand] has provoked the violent responses of the powers-that-be."

"Though state violence can be a result of state necessity...what makes it perverse and evil is that such violence is not exercised only in the name of nation-building, development, or modernization. State violence targets all those who question the [ruling] elite or those who seek to replace it."

"Arab democracy is thus postponed to an indeterminate future. For its birth would require a new autonomous and self-determining individual in a society which would offer real possibilities for freedom and dignity. Genuine democracy has two bases: firstly, the experience of freedom and, secondly, the feeling that the national community embodies humane values that condition social discipline and solidarity. For this to obtain, it is important to agree on stable but progressively social and civilizational projects. Only then can you establish institutions which would translate such projects into a political reality. Before this can be done we will experience the chasms, aborted revolutions and turmoil of a difficult maturation." —Hichem Djaït, 1974[1]

Maturation of democracy, like any other evolutionary process, does not easily lend itself to conclusion. This book narrates only one episode of that story, that of the maturation of the discourse of

[1] Hichem Djaït, *La personnalité et le devenir arabo-islamiques* (Paris: Éditions du Seuil, 1974), pp. 272–3, 276.

democracy in the Arab World, or *al-dīmuqrāṭiyyatu 'l-ḥaqīqiyyah* (genuine democracy). But what is unmistakable about the variety of renderings of *al-dīmuqrāṭiyyatu 'l-ḥaqīqiyyah* is that it is locked in a straight-line, centric and elitist imagining of polity. This imagining may not square with the notion of anti-foundationalist ethos of democracy or ethos of pluralisation, which oppose fixed and singular power relations. The story of democratic maturation will no doubt have many sequels as well as many tellers. There is no Arab *dīmuqrāṭiyyah* as yet; and *ḥurriyyah, shūrā*, *'adl* and *musāwāt* are all still great intangibles. What is maturing, rather, is the plethora of competing discourses about the extent and the quality, the form and the substance of democratic reform.

Working with difficult questions cutting across issues of religion, identity, culture and philosophy, the preceding chapters have sought to throw up a number of questions for debate. Some are dealt with in the book; others are open for further studies. The Anglo-American approach which seems to have a beginning, a middle and an end—the question–answer approach—is not found here. The gist here is to raise questions that need to be confronted rather than to conclude with set answers. The answers in this book throw up several questions. A conclusion is perhaps an end of a beginning, not in any way a totalising agenda that closes off the debate started here.

But essentially the preceding chapters attempt to unpack the search for democracy in the Arab World by seizing on a specially historical moment. It is a moment of global fluidity and contestability. How to be a *democrat* and how to be a *Muslim* are both the subject of ongoing contests. In the Arab World there is a contest within a contest. The discursive contests over *which, whose* and *how much* democracy take place within an existing contest over *which, whose* and *how much* Islam must be given eminence in the political and cultural sphere. There is *Democracy* (with an upper case D) and there are *democracies*. There is *Islam* (with an upper case I) and there are *islams*. The diversity of attempts at living up to the ideal of each continues to give rise to variable interpretations of both Democracy and Islam. What is particularly special about this historical moment is how the mutuality of denial, monologism and exclusivity that used to obtain from the certainty and order of singularity and fixity is ceding to the mutuality of recognition, dialogism and exchange that stem from the uncertainty and disorder of plurality and indeterminacy. When plural and indeterminate *Democracy* and *Islam* intersect they should generate opportunity not "clash" or oddity. Opportunity is the antithesis of the zero-sum game that yields from the hubris of fixed *Democracy* and fixed *Islam*. Thus the refashioning of Democracy as an anti-foundationalist ethos opens up possibilities for Muslims to partake in its global contesting and interpreting. Similarly, the rethinking of Islam as a communicative tradition should bode well for adopting democratic forms of government. The opening of such possibilities hinges on transcending the complexes of righteousness underpinned by fixity and singularity. To this end the discoursing and interpreting of Democracy and Islam must go beyond the search for a universally applicable "Truth" that tests correctness of the "self" and the "other". Test must cede to contest. The accent ought to be on partnership and humility towards learning from and with the other. Thus "Truth" translates into truths that share not only in co-learning in a plurally dispersed discourse, but also in expanding the boundaries of toleration and interpretation that are essential for breaking with the fixity, singularity and univocality of foundationalism. Text must therefore yield to context. Both Democracy and Islam are well-equipped to deal with these challenges.

FROM TEST TO CONTEST

The move from test to contest is legitimised by a historical moment in which certainty is up for grabs and knowing everywhere is relinquishing its mooring in singular and fixed foundationalist postulates, whether these are set in theistic or nontheistic rationality. The discourse of Democracy is being conducted against the backdrop of hubristic contestations engendering many "endisms" (end of history,[2] communism, civilisation, pan-Arabism) and giving rise to a host of hybrid democracies (e.g., Arab democracy, African democracy, Islamic democracy). The latter are renewed attempts at formulating notions and understandings of Democracy by grounding them in a specific culture. There is a kind of revisionism not only with regard to Western concepts and institutions of republicanism[3] but also *vis-à-vis* the

[2] Francis Fukuyama, "The End of History", *National Interest*, 16 (summer 1989), pp. 3–18; see also his *The End of History and the Last Man* (New York: Free Press, 1992).

[3] Patricia Springborg, *Western Republicanism and the Oriental Prince* (Cambridge: Polity Press, 1992).

whole history and origin of Western civilisation.[4] In his *Black Athena*, Bernal revises Greek history, proposing instead of the dominant "Aryan model" his "Revised Ancient Model". Bernal argues that to begin with, the Aryan model originated in the mid-1800s coinciding with racist and anti-Semitic currents in the 1890s, 1920s and 1930s;[5] and, secondly, Greek civilisation was Europeanised only in recent history: "For 18th- and 19th-century Romantics and racists it was simply intolerable for Greece, which was seen not merely as the epitome of Europe but also as its pure childhood, to have been the result of the mixture of native Europeans and colonizing Africans and Semites."[6] Accordingly, on the basis of new archaeological evidence, his Revised Ancient Model restores what he sees to be the missing truths about the many influences and inputs into Greek civilisation through colonisations and borrowings from Egyptians, Phoenicians and other cultures across the East Mediterranean.[7] Islam, too, is today subject to increasing revision and rethinking, a point to be elaborated below. The moment heralded by revised and rethought Democracy and Islam provides a unique opportunity for renewed and confident self-recognition and recognition of the other, a new movement of pluralisation. Pivotal to this new movement is to eschew reference to timeless, ahistorical, universal, fixed and singular tests of correctness, that become tools for the trial of otherness, grounds of inclusion and exclusion of alterity, and markers for the essentialisation of difference. To eschew reference to fixed and singular tests is to give up claims to the mantle of moral superiority or leadership which place a particular worldview, perspective, particularity and their attendant representations as the final arbiters of what is and is not right.

The global discourse and appropriation of Democracy will enmesh it with a multitude of cultures, political priorities, histories, ethical paradigms which will lead to further additions and subtractions, refiguring the democratic ideal in its millennia-long journey from Hellenic Greece. Never before has the terrain of Democracy been

[4] See the illuminating and controversial work by Martin Bernal, *Black Athena: The Afroasiatic Roots of Classical Civilization*, vols 1 and 2 (London: Free Association Books, 1987, 1991).

[5] See Bernal's introduction to vol. 1, *The Fabrication of Ancient Greece, 1785–1985*, pp. 1–2.

[6] Ibid., p. 2.

[7] Ibid.

traversed so plurally nor the space for imagining it so discursively crowded as at the current historical moment. With its global appropriation, Democracy has become a ground where "East" meets "West" and North encounters South. As multivocality augments so do the terms of the global democratic discourse, thus stretching the boundaries of imagining and interpreting the democratic ideal. But what is novel is that through the "East"–"West"/"North"–"South" encounters, intensified by the intermingling of deterritorialised subjectivities, goods and concepts, including Islam and Democracy, cultural prejudices, knowledge practices, political programmes, theistic and non-theistic convictions and the representations that underpin them get habituated with difference and otherness. It is subsequently through this habituation that the potential for dialogism across difference is augmented and with it the opportunity for opening toward a new being. Increasingly, Islam and Democracy are enmeshed in discourses that are attempting to fashion reciprocally rethought strategies to undo the thesis–antithesis dyad typical of the standoff between theistic and nontheistic forms of rationality and belief. The answer does not reside in a synthesis of the ideals of Islam and Democracy. For syntheses lead to closure that does not sit well with the notion of an open future. An open future is premised on the idea that change in time and context becomes the history through which change of ideas and cultures necessitate refashioning of the sensibilities and the perspectives, which are inevitably subjective, deployed to interpret theistic and non-theistic ideals of the "good". Hence a process of dialectic, as against a synthesis, is a necessity between Islam and Democracy and the provisional systems their interpreters produce at various times and places in the form of islams and democracies. In the quest for good government in the Arab World, the dispersed discourse of Democracy and Islam should ideally stimulate interlocutors representing indigenous forms of explanation and European-based frameworks in which knowledge practices from "East" and "West" engage in what Cantori calls a "cross-cultural dialogue".[8] Here lies one way of shifting emphasis from test to contest. If fixed and singular power relations form the matrix within which tests are incubated, contests tend to harbour suspicion toward fixed power relations whether they are based on theology, secular politics or legalism.

[8] Louis J. Cantori, "The Old Orthodoxy and the New Orthodoxy in the Study of Middle Eastern Politics", *Political Science & Politics*, 27 (September 1994), p. 516.

The challenge facing the Arab search for democracy is for it to continue to be a *munāẓarah* and remain close to the dialectic referred to above. Dialectical interaction lends itself to widening references more so than does synthesis. Synthesis assumes a finished point where answers are finalised. A dialectic process ensures interaction across difference between the past and the present, and the old and the new. Above all else, a dialectical process means that intellectual life, discourse, and knowledge practices and acts are in flux. If Arabo-Islamic history does not furnish us with many bright stretches of history, precedents or antecedents of enlightened, just and good rule,[9] the *munāẓarah* (s. of *munāẓarāt*), epitomises the dynamism of medieval Islam and its confidence to interact with the "other" (with *kalām* being the answer to Hellenic philosophy), and concretises the Prophetic tradition bidding the *ummah* to seek knowledge relentlessly even if in remote China. The *munāẓarah*, being the medieval Arabo-Islamic forum for logicians, grammarians, philosophers, theologians, jurists and "lovers of wisdom" to debate one another on all sorts of controversies and disputed matters, and being the "exemplification of the process of dialectic",[10] constitutes Muslim enlightenment. Through these *munāẓarāt, al-munāẓirūn* (the contestants of a *munāẓarah*), impervious to the risks a *munāẓarah* posed to their intellectual standing and keen to subject their minds to the rigours of dialectics and debate and to engage other minds, kept alive not only the tradition and practice of knowing and learning but also of *ḥurriyatu*

[9] Apart from the Madinan state-community founded by the Prophet in 622 (the beginning of the Muslim Calendar, the year of the *hijrah*), and the rule of *al-khulafā'u 'l-rāshidūn* (Abū Bakr: 632–4; 'Umar: 634–44; 'Uthmān: 644–56; 'Alī: 656–61), especially that of the second *khalīfah*, 'Umar, the rule of successive dynastic rulers degenerated into varying forms of despotism. This despotism, however, was punctuated by enlightened and just rule, such as that by the Umayyad *khalīfah*, 'Umar Ibn 'Abd al-'Azīz, also often referred to as 'Umar II (717–20).

[10] Peter Riddell and Tony Street, *Islam: Essays on Scripture, Thought, and Society. A Festschrift in Honour of Anthony H. Johns* (Leiden: E.J. Brill, 1997). *Munāẓarah* is understood to refer to the idea of disputation. According to George Makdisi, disputation is "the more frequent use of the term *munāẓarah*". Other meanings associated with the term are *munāqashah* (argument), *munāza'ah* (struggle), and *muḥāwarah* (dialogue). Makdisi further remarks that "with the development of dialectic it came to be used scholastically in the sense of disputation…in ordinary language, [it] had the meanings of confrontation, altercation and consultation". See his *The Rise of Colleges: Institutions of Learning in Islam and the West* (Edinburgh University Press, 1981), p. 110.

'l-fikr (freedom of inquiry), intellectual *shūrā*, and intellectual *ta'addudiyyah* (pluralism). Hence the adage, *al-ra'y wa 'l-ra'yu 'l-ākhar* (the opinion of the "self" and the "other"). Usually, even political despotism did not interfere with these *munāẓarāt*. If at its simplest *munāẓarah* means *the response to a challenge* as well as *the resulting dialectical discourses and debates* that such a response elicits, stimulates or simulates, then no other metaphor equals this one in capturing the significance of the search for Arab democracy through plurally cross-cultural contests, and not on the basis of fixed and singular tests.

Only when bereft of universally applicable, singular and fixed tests, Islam and Democracy truly become conducive to the forming of a fluid space of indeterminacy and an ethos of anti-foundationalism. But the irony in all of this is that as the *munāẓarāt* and contests open up cross-cultural dialogues across difference, with their respective exegetes grappling with time and place to particularise islams and democracies, Islam and Democracy are universalised. Islam and Democracy are thus rendered a common human heritage whose ideals are available to all to appropriate, interpret and reify. Islam and Democracy are universal; islams and democracies are specific. Islam is no longer just "Oriental"; and Democracy ceases to be only "Occidental". As places of presence, in which they are represented as final judges according to transcendentalised tests, Democracy and Islam generate hubris and demarcate divides. As places of absence, where their ideals are subject to renewed provisionalism and contestability according to temporal and spatial exigencies, Democracy and Islam create opportunity for mutual recognition, toleration, and communication. Tests exist only within a system of oppositions, and oppositions curtail or completely deny intersection, much less collaboration or communication across difference. Both Orientalism and Occidentalism are guilty of this. Furthermore, tests are congealed standards that do not speak to change of time and place.

Two historical moments, pertinent to the inquiry in this book, problematise the search for good government in the Arab World. The first concerns the increasing contestability of both Democracy and Islam. Their ideals are truly global goods that continue to travel further afield around the world. As a consequence, Muslims and democrats are increasingly being turned into hybrid citizens who defy precise or simple definition. Their identities are neither singular nor fixed. They are protean with multiple layers of identity or containing sub-identities within them. To describe them as hyphenated citizens in a globalising world is no exaggeration. Muslims can be Arab, African, Asian, European or American, practising and non-practising, educated and lay, political and non-political, and belong to a wide range of socio-economic strata. Roger Garaudy, Malcolm X, two very good examples referred to in the second chapter, and Osama Bin Laden illustrate the endless hyphens of Muslim identity. Garaudy is a European-French-former communist-Muslim. Malcolm X was an African-American-Muslim. Bin Laden is a Saudi-Yemeni-Wahhābī-Muslim. The layers of identity in each informs their vision of Islam and their disposition for being, thinking and acting. Their islams converge and diverge and their responses to themes regarding the status of women, democracy, political strategies, and relations with foreign powers can be expected to differ. Many Muslims consume alcohol and are guided by the belief that only a state of inebriation is forbidden by the divine scriptures and not the actual act of consumption of wine. Others adopt a ceremonial Islam that is limited to the Friday and Feast prayers. Many others exalt the aerobic or meditative benefits of the daily five prayers. Millions of Muslims may be seen to be zealous in their adherence to the rituals of Islam going above the prescribed daily prayers in imitation of the Prophet, and modelling the manner of simple acts such as drinking water, eating, sleeping and dressing according to His Sunnah. Similarly, Arab identity is no longer a given. Arab identity overlaps with layers of identity shaped by region, class, gender, economic status, history, politics, religion and religious sect or particular school of jurisprudence. The imprints of these will be evident in the determining of how society and polity are organised and the shape, substance and manner in which Arab democracies shall evolve.

Similarly, democrats are hyphenated citizens of this world, belonging to a multitude of backgrounds, classes, ethnic groups, nationalities, politics, and faiths (theistic and nontheistic). This illustrates strongly how Democracy, like Islam, is being increasingly problematised in relation to time and place. There is nothing stopping the democratic game, its standards, procedures and rules from changing. Hundred years hence the very democratic foundational principle of "one person one vote" may itself be destabilised. The hypothesis of hyphenated citizens being accorded a vote for each identity may not seem far-fetched in hundred years time. The preceding chapters have established how Democracy continues to evolve with many scholars calling for group-specific rights in democratic states with multicultural societies. Others have argued for positive discrimination for the sake of greater inclusion of women in the political process. The Arab World has been shown to be no exception in this regard.

The second moment emerges with the intersection of Islam and Democracy. It is within this intersection that a new possibility of being is presented. If in the first moment Islam ceases to be "Oriental", in the second moment Democracy ceases to be "Occidental". Thus both cease to be exclusivist. Contending islams and democracies in a newly crafted space may diverge and converge, both supporting and undermining the opening toward a new being. In so doing, islams and democracies can be expected to intensify mutual exclusion and inclusion, depending on who is doing the interpreting of Islam and of Democracy. Most importantly, however, it is within this intersection that many interpreters may create shared space and with it the opportunity for the Muslim-democrat or democrat-Muslim. But this eventuality hinges on an important premise on the basis of which Islam and Democracy are rethought as provisionalism. Since the opportunity for a new being, as far as this book is concerned, regards the opening of a new avenue of communication between Islam and Democracy, then the domain of neither ideal should be delimited by the second. The challenge resides in the two ideals engaging each other in conjunction and not in disjunction. Neither Islam nor Democracy is going to cease to have adherents or appeal at a global scale; and neither is going to fade away. If each of these two ideals is to be rethought as an ethos of indeterminacy, there has to be a parallel ethos of dialogue across difference. An ethos of dialogue presupposes engagement with not disengagement from difference. This is essential for stretching the parameters of the Islamic-Democratic discourse which requires continuous negotiation for the reconciling of religious faith with secular belief. Enlightenment-based thought insists on "post-conventional rationality". But even the authoritative Habermas, the inventor of the concepts of "postconventional" rationality and "postmetaphysical thinking", recognises the durability of religion. Neither the 'march of progress' nor his own preference for a post-metaphysical thinking seem to be able to render religion redundant. Thus Habermas offers the admission that

> ...[E]ven postmetaphysical thinking continues to coexist with religious practice...This ongoing coexistence even throws light on a curious dependence

> of a philosophy that forfeits its contact with the extraordinary. Philosophy, even in its postmetaphysical form, will be able neither to replace nor to repress religion so long as religious language is the bearer of a semantic content that is inspiring or even indispensable.[11]

This position is empirically sustainable not only in the Arab World but also elsewhere around the globe as the passions of theistic belief continue to arouse billions of human beings. Similarly, amongst the proponents of expanding the public realm to incorporate the ideals of Islam, there is no escape from commitment to the ideals of Democracy. The ideals of Islam already intrude into the public domain with diverse interpreters deploying it for causes of justice, liberation, opposition or pan-Islamic solidarity. It is in the secular world that a variety of islams mete out punishment against Muslim and non-Muslim, visit colossal destruction upon supposedly arrogant foreign powers (e.g. the 11 September 2001 crashing of planes on the New York World Trade Centre Twin Towers), use lethal and non-lethal technology, and take advantage of liberal secular politics in many Western countries to reticulate and propagate their islams. Consequently, the brands of Islam that are to flourish democratically and embrace the ideals of Democracy very openly call for a reconfiguring of the way modernity itself is understood. The opening up of possibilities for islams and democracies require modernities, rather than a single paradigm of modernity understood in a linear fashion or premised on notions of Habermasian post-metaphysical rationality. If Islam and Democracy are to revolve around indeterminacy, i.e. temporally and spatially determined series of reconfiguration and correction, the non-theistic tests that delimit religion (read counter-modernity) and the theistic tests that delimit democratic ideals (read incompatible with Godly sovereignty) call for reconfiguration. Modernity is as contestable as Islam and Democracy. Neither can claim singular authority or superiority or justify tests that exist apart of time and place.

FROM TEXT TO CONTEXT

There are no tests but contests of meaning. Increasingly, extrication of meaning is being subjected to the scrutiny of context. To move

[11] Jurgen Habermas, *Postmetaphysical Thinking*, trans. by William M. Hohengarten (Cambridge: Polity Press and Blackwell, 1992), p. 51.

from text to context is not about effacing the past or purging its voice. Rather, it is about hearing the voice of the past so that the present can speak. Thus contexts allow for the re-reading of old and revered texts in order to situate meaning in relation to time and place. This condition is essential for reconfiguring modernities, and refashioning the ideals of Islam and Democracy into relevant islams and democracies that promote good government, sustain communication across difference and remain open to continuous correction. Here difference assumes more than one form. Besides otherness, it refers to difference as of time and place as well as discursive representations. The fierce contesting of the ideals of Democracy is today without doubt an exciting moment in which determinacy is being replaced with indeterminacy. Feminists and postmodernists continue to persevere with the interrogation of Democracy's quasi-transcendentalised foundations upon which the imaging, ordering, meaning, wording and "worlding" of the so-called "West" have been built. The opening chapters of this book have argued the case for defoundationalising Democracy, defining it as an ethos of indeterminacy and a place of absence, as Lefort puts it, or an ethos of pluralisation, as Connolly proposes. Fixed and singular Democracy is no more than a specific value system unable to speak to diversity and difference. Thus conceived or defined it delimits its ability to speak to issues of cultural pluralism and to Islam, the predominant religion in the Arab World. The book has argued that a defoundationalised Democracy creates openings and possibilities for a globally democratic diffusion. But Islam itself has to be part of that diffusion if the Arab World is to secure good government. To this end, speaking of Islam as an ethos of indeterminacy is not out of place today as contending islams increasingly prove not only its contested nature but also its potentialities for renewal and dialogue with Democracy. Even if incipient and timid, the move from text to context holds the key to the opening in the future of a shared space with Democracy and dialogue with systems and ideologies based on non-transcendental morality.

The opening chapters of this book suggest that as Democracy has travelled over time it has evolved into an essentially contested concept. Its texts are interrogated, rethought and re-read in ways that relativise them to time and place but without diluting the relevance of the democratic ideal itself. Re-reading Islam in the light of changing contexts cannot be expected to mean or lead to the adoption of an abridged version of the Qur'ān. It ought to be noted that Muslims read the Qur'ān not only in search of deep meaning. Many Muslims read or recite it in obeisance of a Godly command to read, memorise and teach the Holy Book; others do so to seek solace, soul-searching, piety and peace. These are additional reasons why many Muslims revere the Qur'ān. Americans revere their constitution and the English the Magna Carta. But neither reads those documents with a view to seeking solace or peace from them. The US Constitution is quasi-transcendentalised but that does not stop law-makers and legislators from amending it if need be. Re-reading the Qur'ān is not about amending it. Rather, it is an exegetical exercise aiming to shed new light on the divine texts by accounting for context and amending and even setting aside the huge corpus of laws and interpretations, which cannot escape scrutiny and correction.

This is essential if islams are to be made congenial to the needs of Muslims, which are temporally and locationally variable, and evolving challenges, for good government, advancement, equity, gender equality, integration in the world economy, establishing sound relations with non-Muslim countries in a world that is not of Muslim making or ordering, settling and working in non-Muslim countries as minorities, and for being citizens of non-Muslim countries, which sometimes entail conscription and even combat along compatriots against fellow Muslims. Muslim needs include not only how to be a good Muslim, but also how to be a good citizen, a successful businessperson or industrialist and a universal citizen. Such an exercise would have to involve an abridgement of the documents bequeathed to Muslims by their learned forebears and which contain within them the meanings they extricated from the Qur'ān at various times and places. Reverence of the Qur'ān does not therefore equate with unqualified reverence of the voluminous works of interpretation accumulated over hundreds of years. But re-reading the Qur'ān may at times mean moving from text to context, involving additional exegetical talent via tools that highlight public utility, as some new interpretations have been attempting. Others are trying to take interpretation further by by-passing text when need be. But both claim that their interpretations are in accordance with the ideals of Islam. Generally, the gist of these exercises is not to discard the divine texts. No Muslim is seeking to renounce daily prayer or alms giving, for instance. But the *how, when* and *where* of how context may determine public utility more than text is no longer beyond the realm of possibility, a point that shall be elaborated below. What is noteworthy is that moving from text to context, even if rare in Muslim history, has precedents. The most referred to example is that of the second of the four rightly-guided Caliphs suspending alms giving owing to severe drought conditions that brought about financial ruin to those obligated to pay the *zakāt* (the mandatory tax). If anything, this example attests to the fact that Islam is neither fixed nor singular and that either by silence on many issues (e.g. AIDS, cloning, conquering space, In Vitro Fertilisation), diversity of Muslims (e.g. hyphenated identities), and changing contexts (time, place, ideas) there is a fluid space and a place of absence in Islam around which there is much indeterminacy.

It is this area of indeterminacy that this book holds to be the key to Islam's ability and potential for opening an avenue of communication across difference with Democracy. The questioning and deconstructing of the "sacred" texts and foundations of Democracy in the light of new and multiple contexts enables this ideal to travel, be adopted and adapted globally. But its travel to the Muslim world, including Arab countries, is incumbent on Islam being re-read contextually when and where there is a need, such as ending authoritarian rule. The point is that dialogism entails that the possibility of new being requires the expounders of Islam and Democracy meeting each other half-way. Communication across difference has to be a genuinely two-way flow. Historically, renewal and reform have been dictated by Muslim defeat or retreat. The reformist movement and discourse initiated by al-Afghānī and ʿAbduh in the nineteenth century illustrate this point. In between defeat and retreat the space available for epistemic dynamism, multivocality and re-reading the divine texts was curtailed in the name of religious unity, order or heresy, resulting in absolutist political and religious orders with power becoming embodied in small groups, single individuals, and dominant discourses. Moving from text to context need not be inspired by defeat and retreat. It ought to be motivated by sustaining the appeal of Islam's ideals so that it shares with those of Democracy adherents and a wide margin of existence in the public space in Europe and North America, the centres of political, economic, technological and informational power in the world. Perhaps no single factor accounts for the defeat and retreat of the ideals of Islam from Andalusia

(Spain) than the congealing of medieval islams. Had the ideals of Islam maintained their presence in Europe and spread to North America, the world's political and geostrategic map would have been different today. Islam would have opened up an avenue of communication with Democracy at some time or another, and today there could possibly have been one or two largely Muslim and democratic states in the heart of the EU, which might have facilitated the diffusion of Democracy to the contemporary and largely authoritarian Arab World. All of this is hypothetical.

But what is not hypothetical is the fact that at some point in their early history the ideals of Islam stopped to spread northward. With their exit from Europe, the ideals of Islam ceased to be re-read creatively and in a socio-historical fashion owing to the loss of a shared space with difference which the early islams and Muslims opened dialogues and *munāẓarāt* across difference with. This they did with confidence and humility towards learning from and in partnership with the other. It is not surprising then that it was through encounters with the other (e.g. Hellenic Greece, India, China, Persia and Europe) that at an earlier time islams and Muslims contributed to human knowledge, excelling in the practical and theoretical sciences. Only when congealed, being Muslim becomes a synonym for a fixed and singular identity. In the height of its fluidity and plurality, being Muslim is a multi-hyphenated identity—transcultural and transterritorial. Recognising difference within the house of Islam is essential for recognising, respecting and living with otherness. More importantly, this is vital for a plural Islam that has relevance for non-Muslims so that they may live with its ideals just as they live with the Arabic numerals or Chinese alternative medicine. What ought to be noted is that the fine notion of "objectification of Muslim consciousness" expounded by Eickelman and Piscatori begs a few "objective" questions such as "What is my religion?" "Why is it important to my life?" and "How do beliefs guide my conduct?"[12] They convincingly argue that underlying objectification is the diffuse, as opposite unitary, nature of Islam. But what they do not mention is that "objectification" has an outside dimension, leading non-Muslims to ask another equally "objective" and relevant question: "What kind of Islam can the world live with?" But this is not specific to Islam. The postmodern

[12] Dale F. Eickelman and James Piscatori, *Muslim Politics* (Princeton University Press, 1996), p. 38.

moment has imposed on the human consciousness as series of "objective" questions: "What kind of environment the world can live with?" "What kind of gender relations can humanity live with?" and "What kind of Democracy can the world have?" These questions do not exhaust the list but do underscore the point that plural Islam is vital for Muslims and non-Muslims just as is plural Democracy.

The confidence and humility mentioned above did once serve Muslims well by furnishing the needs of their specific historical moments. Al-Fārābī's search for virtuous rule, at a time when the Abbasyds were engulfed in decay and corruption, led him to open up an avenue of communication with Aristotle and his "pagan" philosophy. The same quest put Averroes (1126–98), a European-Andalusian-Arab-Muslim, on a similar course of knowledge-making. Neither man's religiosity abated as they dialectically engaged Hellenic philosophy, seeking clues to good rule. As explained in chapter 5, al-Fārābī's virtuous city is premised on a dualistic notion of happiness pertaining to the herenow and the hereafter. Nor did Muslims refrain from looking into the texts of Greek philosophy, as opposite the canonical sources of monotheistic belief in Islam, or employing philosophy's methods of questioning and research, thus widening the frame of reference and with it the Muslim search for virtuous rule and penultimate aim of earthly and otherworldly happiness. In attempting to comment on Plato's *Republic*, Averroes did not take the supposed completeness or supremacy of Islamic law for granted or that it was beyond correction;[13] nor did he assume that there was nothing to be gained from non-Muslim and Greek philosophers. But like al-Fārābī, Averroes is critical of Greek philosophy. It is true that Ralph Lerner regards Averroes to be a "faithful companion of Plato".[14] Furthermore, he suggests that "In deciding to paraphrase the *Republic*, Averroes is asserting that his world—the world defined and governed by the Koran—can profit from Plato's instruction."[15] But Averroes has a mind of his own and there are instances throughout his commentary when he projects a voice that may disagree with Plato, though not necessarily by siding with Islamic law. Just as he critically quarrelled with many fragments of Plato's *Republic*, he modestly adopted others. An example of the latter is Averroes'

[13] Ralph Lerner, "Introduction" in *Averroes on Plato's Republic* (Ithaca and London: Cornell University Press, 1974), p. xiii.

[14] Lerner, "Introduction", p. xxviii.

[15] Ibid., p. xxvii.

unequivocal feminism, relative to his time, on the status of women in the virtuous city. In this regard, he surpasses his contemporaries, going beyond anything the various brands of Islamic law and Muslim practitioners of jurisprudence had to offer on the position of women. Moreover, with his strong advocacy of women's equality with men politically and intellectually he surpasses anything written by the variety of Arab male feminists discussed in chapter 6. Text is set aside in support of women's fitness for rule, which remains till this day in most exegetical texts the exclusive bastion of Muslim men.

> This is therefore the place for an investigation whether women possess natures similar to the natures of every single class of citizens—and in particular the Guardians—or whether the feminine natures are different from masculine.
>
> If the former is the case, then women are essentially on the same level with men in respect of civic activities in the same classes, so that there are among them warriors, philosophers, rulers and the like. Otherwise, women are fitted for such activities in the State as the whole male population is not qualified to discharge, such as upbringing, procreation and the like.
>
> We say that women, in so far as they are of one kind with men in respect of the ultimate human aim, necessarily share in it and only differ in degree. This means: man is in most human activities more efficient than woman; though it is not impossible that women are in some activities more efficient, as is thought in respect of the art of practical music....
>
> As this is so, the nature of women and men being of one kind—and the nature that is one in kind turns in the State to one and the same activity—it is obvious that women will practice in this State the same activities as men, except that they are weaker at it...
>
> As for their participating in the art of war and the like, this is clearly observable among the inhabitants of deserts and frontier villages. Similarly, since some women are formed who have a distinction and a praiseworthy disposition, it is not impossible that there may be among them philosophers and rulers. But because it was thought that this type rarely exists among them, some laws refused to admit women to priesthood, that is, the High Priesthood. Other laws, however, refrained from this, since the existence of such women among them was not impossible.[16]

Philosophy might have been "pagan", as Democracy could also be in the minds of many Muslims. What is edifying in Averroes' example is, the fact that Greek philosophy might have been "pagan" did not

16 Averroes, "The First Treatise" in *Averroes' Commentary on Plato's Republic*, ed. and trans. by E.I.J. Rosenthal (Cambridge University Press, 1966), pp. 164–5. For a similar idea, see Tariq Ali, *The Clash of Fundamentalisms: Crusaders, Jihads and Modernity* (London & New York: Verso, 2002), p. 66.

stop devout and learned Muslims from seeking enlightenment from it, that is, outside the narrow boundaries of Islamic law. Averroes' confidence to engage the "other" and humility to learn from and with non-Muslim ways of knowing, traits found in Muslim *falāsifah* and literati, led them to open an avenue of communication with Greek philosophy, thus broadening their frame of reference and knowledge. That history should serve as a source of inspiration to contemporary Muslims to engage Democracy, be it critically, in the same fashion their forebears deployed philosophy to improve and enrich the experience of being Muslim, whether in the pursuit of virtue in civic duties or the rearing of children. What is certain is that the correcting and improving of the experience of being Muslim may require questioning and even "upsetting" certain texts. Thus Averroes disapproves of the literalism and lack of questioning practised by Muslim theologians, whose exegesis produces sophistry and misreading of Islam.

> As for the people of our [nation] known as Mutakallimūn, their legal inquiry led them to the position that what God wills has no definite nature and merely turns on what the will—i.e., the will of God (may He be exalted!)—lays down for it. According to this, there is nothing beautiful or base other than by fiat. Furthermore, there is no end of man other than by fiat. What brought them to this was their thinking of defending the attributes with which God (may He be exalted!) is described in the Law, to the effect that He is capable of doing whatever He wills, and that it is possible for the [divine] will to extend to all things, including particulars as well. Hence all things are possible. What happened to them happens often in legal inquiry. That is, God (may He be exalted!) is first described by [certain] attributes. Then one seeks to make what exists agree [with the teaching without [upsetting] whatever of those attributes has been laid down. But these [people] are distressed in [trying] to discover the explanation of this question if these things that they consider clearly evident in the Law are as they believe. As a result this leads them to an opinion close to sophistry, very far from the nature of man, and far from being the content of a Law.[17]

Upsetting what has been laid down through revelation is no easy matter, especially when claims to identity and myths are grounded within its texts. Challenging any theistic or non-theistic text that is so defining of a particular identity or the collective imagination explains why even amending secular constitutions can draw obdurate

[17] Averroes, "The Second Treatise", in *Averroes on Plato's Republic*, trans. by Lerner, pp. 81–2.

resistance and opposition. Resistance and opposition to re-reading divine scriptures, as the history of all religion shows, can even be life-threatening. Recent events in the Muslim world are replete with examples of cruelty, carnage, derision, ostracism, and Manichaen symbols reserved for those who are judged to be in contempt of a particular brand or reading of Islam or insensitive to Muslim sensibilities in general. These range from the death *fatwah* on Salman Rushdie and Ḥāmid Naṣr Abū Zayd to the stabbing of the Nobel laureate Najīb Maḥfūẓ. These acts, which in effect only serve to obliterate the Muslim history of communicative tradition and practice of *munāẓarāt*, have not deterred many other Muslims from persevering with re-reading Islam. The trend to re-read the Qur'ān in the quest of islams equipped with that condition of questioning essential for any type of modernity is set to gain momentum in a world of intensified cross-cultural exchange and increased literacy. One constant dynamic, however, Hallaq notes, has been the "literal grip of the hermeneutic" that is historically characteristic of Muslim jurisprudence.[18] He explains how as a result of the firm grip of the positive legal doctrines, historical attempts to stretch the parameters of juristic thinking, through restatement of the law, were marginalised.[19] Hallaq puts down this legal conservatism to preservation of the status quo by the legal profession as well the underlying power structures that underpin it, making juristic thinking no more than a superstructure reflective of such structures. But Hallaq's main assertion is that such a grip accounts for the timidity of all reform from the early master jurists of Islam down to the reformism of the Wahhābī and Sanūsī movements, both of which invoked the right to invoke *ijtihād* but with the chief purpose of claiming back a notion of pristine Islam.[20] Hallaq points out the legal paradox within the history of Islam, noting how law moved from a progressive to a regressive force.

In fact, law has been so successfully developed that it would not be an exaggeration to characterize Islamic culture as a legal culture. But this very blessing of the pre-modern culture turned out to be an obstacle in the face of modernization. The system that had served Muslims so well in the past now

[18] Wael B. Hallaq, *A History of Islamic Legal Theories* (Cambridge University Press, 1997), p. 207.

[19] Ibid., p. 208.

[20] Ibid., p. 213.

stood in the way of change—a change that proved to be so needed in a twentieth-century culture vulnerable to an endless variety of Western influences and pressures.[21]

Apart from the use of terms like "Islamic culture", which suggests the presence of a unitary or monolithic culture, Hallaq is right. Elsewhere he indicates how the historical insistence that Muslim legal practitioners work within the established juristic wisdom of the founding fathers, that is, the main schools of jurisprudence, engendered a form of authoritative hierarchy.[22] To an extent, the congealing of standards by insisting on the righteousness of the tests and texts bequeathed by the juristic masters congealed the very ideals of Islam. This state of affairs warrants revisiting one of the points from which this book departed: suspicion of hierarchy and logocentrism, both of which entrench fixity and singularity. For the ideals of Islam to present Muslims with a space of radical contingency, just as is the case with the ideals of Democracy, there has to be a corresponding indeterminacy of power (legal, political and religious). Where power is defined by any particular juristic thinking and delimited by particular tests and texts, the potential for pluralisation and even creativity is sabotaged.

But the conundrums of Islamic jurisprudence may find answers in the innovations of two movements, religious utilitarianism and religious liberalism, according to Hallaq. Surely, slowly, creatively, but not always cohesively, many thinkers are working on managing the text-context tension, even if not yet to a widespread influence or observable effect. These thinkers share a brand of reasoning that ventures outside the narrow boundaries of historically practised *ijtihād*. In so doing, they depart from superficial juristic tinkering by going beyond the use of legal tools such as *takhayyur* ("amalgamated [legal] selection from several traditional schools") or *talfiq* (mixing of doctrines from two legal schools).[23] These dual trends have two meeting points. The first over their belief that the literalist interpretations of medieval jurists were fallible as well as incapable of adapting law to new contexts.[24] The second is that they are both inspired by the nineteenth-century Egyptian reformer, ʿAbduh, whose reform

21 Ibid., p. 209.
22 Ibid., p. 209.
23 Ibid., p. 210.
24 Ibid., p. 231.

did not invent a new legal methodology, observes Hallaq. Rather, in seeking to put into place a theology that was equipped to restructure and rehabilitate legal ideas, ʿAbduh sought to harmonise reason and revelation, blaming misinterpretation for their disharmony.[25] ʿAbduh is motivated by the urgency of responding to change. The context of his ideas was the nineteenth century, which it must be remembered, was a period of Muslim retreat. Hallaq maps the terrain traversed by these two trends in greater detail. The key problems the two trends address and the legal reformulations they provide in support of their positions point to a space of indeterminacy within Islam. Questions are for instance raised about the relevance of conventional legal theory, which Ḥasan al-Turābī completely dismisses as incapable of responding to contemporary problems, going as far as stating that both Islamic communal life and jurisprudence deviated from the "dictates of the divine law".[26] For others, namely Rashīd Riḍā (d. 1935), whom Hallaq situates within religious utilitarianism, *qiyās* is obsolete. Riḍā takes the Qur'ān to be the key foundation of Islam, pointing out, like al-Turābī, that in worldly affairs the Prophet was known to have made mistakes. Thus he qualifies his reverence of the Sunnah by limiting it to matters of worship.[27] Riḍā thus holds matters of worship to be immutable and not in need of change unlike worldly matters which should be regulated contextually. The implication, Hallaq adds, is that "The concrete legal status of these mundane matters remain within the province of man's discretion."[28] In general, a few points distinguish the utilitarians from religious liberalism. The former base their juristic thinking on the concept of *maṣlaḥah*, which had limited application for medieval jurists. Another concept that is heavily relied upon by them is that of *ḍarūrah* (necessity). Hallaq criticises the reliance on these two concepts for the subjectivism they produce as they are not based on a cohesive legal methodology, making legal reasoning on their basis "a highly relativistic venture".[29] Religious liberalism refrains from borrowing medieval legal principles.[30] Hallaq is optimistic about the prospects of this trend to disclose a

25 Ibid., p. 212.

26 Ibid., pp. 226–7. For more details on this see pp. 226–30.

27 Ibid., p. 216.

28 Ibid., p. 216.

29 Ibid., p. 231.

30 Ibid., p. 214.

credible legal methodology able "to bring into a dialectical relationship the imperatives of the revealed texts and the realities of the modern world".[31] Its main intent, as he puts it, is to understand revelation as both text and context. For Hallaq, the soundness of this trend resides in the fact that the "connection between the revealed text and modern society does not turn upon a literalist hermeneutic, but rather upon an interpretation of the spirit and broad intention behind the language of the texts".[32]

One representative of religious liberalism deserves a special mention: the Syrian Muḥammad Shaḥrūr. In his work *al-Kitāb wa'l-Qur'ān: Qirā'ah Mu'āṣirah* (*The Book and the Qur'ān: A Re-reading*), Shaḥrūr elaborates what Hallaq considers to be a "new holistic and contextual approach to legal language and legal interpretation".[33] It is not surprising then that Shaḥrūr's boldly innovative approach is amongst the most controversial in the entire Middle East.[34] From the outset Shaḥrūr defines the key problems that beset Arabo-Islamic knowledge-making. He singles out the failure of Muslim scholars to develop an objective and neutral scientific research methodology in their interpretations of Islam; hence they are unable to demolish preconceptions. He gives the example of many Muslim scholars' preconception that Islam's position on the woman question is fair. He deprecates this lack of scientific objectivity, likening it to the Orientalism of non-Muslim scholars who assume exactly the opposite without recourse to thorough investigation. In particular, he reproaches the inability of Arabo-Islamic knowledge-making to interact confidently and creatively with and benefit from non-Muslim knowledge practices. It is impossible, he correctly points out, that all human knowing, from Hellenic Greece up to now, to discard as incompatible with the ideals of Islam. More importantly, and as far as the task of rethinking Islam contextually, Shaḥrūr states that contemporary Muslims are in the midst of an acute crisis of jurisprudence. He boldly calls for a re-reading of the *Sunnah* in order to stretch the parameters of juristic thinking outside the boundaries of the five schools of Islamic Law if an alternative set of legal doctrines and principles serving the evolving and diverse contexts in which Muslims

31 Ibid., p. 231.
32 Ibid., p. 231.
33 Ibid., p. 261.
34 Ibid., p. 246.

live are to be elaborated.[35] There is ample evidence that Shaḥrūr's ideas on Islamic government do live up to his rigorous search for an alternative methodology and epistemology for understanding and reifying the ideals of Islam contextually. The principles he outlines as constitutive of Islamic government are compatible with democratic rule since, according to him, they are mandated by broad consensus, multipartyism and freedom of expression.[36] What is new in this reformulation of Islamic government is Shaḥrūr's rejection of the *sharī'ah* as the source of legislation in an Islamic state. He justifies this position by stressing the changing nature of the *sharī'ah*, which is produced by people in specific contexts making its constitutive laws relative to time and place. Thus such laws can be repealed or abrogated. Also, he deploys a device which he calls *ḥudūdu Allāh* (Allah's sanctioned limits), which may be evaluative and regulative.[37] The Godly sanctioned limits constitute an immutably and absolutely foundational framework setting the boundaries that Muslims cannot trespass. But the interpreting and rendering of that framework into a living Islam is assigned to people and is therefore mutable. Hallaq renders Shaḥrūr's notion of Godly-sanctioned limits as the "Theory of Limits" and explains its legal implications.

> It is the divine decree, expressed in the Book and the Sunna, which sets a Lower and Upper limit for all human actions; the Lower Limit represents the minimum required by the law in a particular case, and the Upper Limit the maximum. Just as nothing short of the minimum is legally admissible, so nothing above the maximum may be deemed lawful. Once these Limits are transcended, penalties become warrantable, in proportion to the violation committed.[38]

Shaḥrūr, who as mentioned above rejects Islamic jurisprudence as obsolete, radically alters the conventional understanding of the very term Qur'ān, which is variably referred to by other names as the Book (hence peoples of the Book in reference to the three Abrahamic monotheistic religions—Judaism, Christianity and Islam). His understanding of the term casts the ideals of Islam and its openness to

[35] Muḥammad Shaḥrūr, *Al-Kitāb wa'l-Qur'ān: Qirā'ah Mu'āṣirah* [*The Book and the Qur'ān: A Re-reading*] (Beirut: Sharikat al-Matbu'at li-al-tawzi wa' al-Nashr, 1992), pp. 30–2; also see p. 585.

[36] Ibid., p. 725.

[37] Ibid., pp. 224–5.

[38] Hallaq, *A History of Islamic Legal Theories*, p. 248.

interpretation and human rendering in a new light. For Shaḥrūr the two terms are not to be treated as synonyms, which he contends not to exist in Arabic.[39] On the basis of this linguistic assumption, Shaḥrūr divides the Muslim Holy Book into four segments,[40] the main ones being the Qur'ān as *nubuwwah* (prophecy) and the *Ummu'l-kitāb* (the Book) as *risālah* (message).[41] The exegetical possibilities that emerge from this rendering of language are far-reaching. On the basis of this distinction, the Holy Book is neither single nor fixed. It is not single since it contains parts which do not share the sanctity reserved for the Limits. Some parts simply elaborate previous revelation or add information or explain the context of revelation and therefore may not be as binding. Others contain Godly commandments setting the limits and their sanctity and binding content leave little or no room for human interference. Again, Hallaq fleshes out the legal implications of Shaḥrūr's methodology:

> This distinction [is]...between the function of Muhammad as Messenger (*rasūl*) and as a Prophet (*nabī*). As Prophet, Muhammad received a body of information having to do with prophecy, religion and the like. As Messenger, he was recipient of a corpus of legal instructions, in addition to that information he received as a Prophet. The function of the Prophet, then is religious, whereas that of messenger is legal. Now, prophetic information is textually ambiguous, capable of varying interpretations. This is the Quran. On the other hand, the legal subject matter is univocal, but nevertheless capable of being subjected to *ijtihād*. This is the Book.[42]

Thus with this distinction, Shaḥrūr opens possibilities for greater human agency for rendering text in relation to context but without renouncing fragments of the Holy Book or valorising prophecy over message. Each has implications for the reifying the kind of islams this book deems essential for a democratic as well as Islamic ethos of anti-foundationalism, communication with difference and pluralisation within and without. His work goes some way, even if it remains unknown not to mention opposed as Hallaq notes, in loosening the firm grip traditional legal theory has had on Muslims. It is one approach that displays unprecedented suspicion towards exegetical fixity and singularity. Shaḥrūr declares his reverence of the Prophet

[39] Shaḥrūr, *Al-Kitāb wa'l-Qur'ān*, p. 583.
[40] Ibid., pp. 39–42.
[41] Ibid., pp. 37–8.
[42] Hallaq, *A History of Islamic Legal Theories*, pp. 246–7.

Muḥammad but he treats ḥadīth with less reverence, stressing that by refusing to document or transcendentalise His own sayings, the Prophet did succeed in relativising the absolute, leaving the door open for human interpretation of the ideals of Islam.[43] With this Shaḥrūr accords pre-eminence to a dispersed discourse of the ideals of Islam. That is, islams that are contextually, variably and continuously interpreted. The endeavours by Shaḥrūr, Arkoun, Abū Zayd, and other Muslim scholars, to re-read the divine texts call for intelligent engagement, by both those who agree and disagree with their scholarship. Their efforts are attempts to reassert the preeminence of *ijtihād*, a tradition which has been more vigorously practised in Shi'ite than in Sunni Islam. Despite the limitations of their re-readings, their efforts encourage self-examination, a practice Muslims are today most in need of. If Muslims free themselves from the urgent obligation to engage in self-examination, they will fail God (Islam) and fellow citizens (democracy).

Islam and Democracy may never be realised. But islams and democracies may be. Islam and Democracy may individually be treated as possessing their own repository of ideals that give cogency to the idea of ennoblement and worthiness of human beings. Their histories have been about reinventing commitment to those ideals and their actualisation. Thus their attempts to deploy those ideals politically have continuously locked them in processes of mutual exclusion. The origins of islams and democracies have been messy, punctuated by mutual violence (conquests and colonisations) and tainted by reciprocal essentialism (Orientalism and Occidentalism). Bright origins remain largely obscured: the partial revival and transmission of the Greek heritage to humanity by Muslim and Arab philosophers and the Arab Renaissance that resulted from such a revival. In order to refashion how islams and democracies may reinvent commitment to the ideals that seem to separate them, they have to renew commitment to the bright origins that once united them: cross-cultural dialogue via Hellenic philosophy.

The search for Democracy in the Arab World brings a renewed urgency to such a dialogue, especially since Islam and Democracy

[43] Shaḥrūr, *Al-Kitāb wa'l-Qur'ān*, p. 39.

are today being contested in conjunction not in disjunction. They are enmeshed in discourses in a moment of paradigmatic transition, fluidity, hybridity and contestability. The discursive contests of Islam by a variety of configurations of different social agencies (rulers, secularists, Islamists, learned scholars, secular and Islamist feminists) have historically been conducted to manage many a dyad: reason versus revelation; politics versus religion; nationalism versus Arabism and Pan-Islamism; innovation versus imitation; man versus woman; and Occident versus Orient. These polarities were conditioned by myriad contexts. The influx of Greek philosophy and the subsequent Renaissance was a context in which the ideals of Islam formed part of the dominant discourse. Islam was still rising. Colonisation, modernisation and Westernisation were contexts in which the ideals of Islam did not inform the dominant discourse. Islam stagnated and its ideals were not vigorously interpreted. The current context is one of intensified cross-cultural exchange in which the ideals of Islam have no choice but to share the discursive space with other ideals, namely, those of Democracy.

The current historical situation has potentialities for supporting co-learning, sharing and dialogism. It is the way forward for defeating opprobrium, extremism, othering, worlding and essentialising. Humanity has entered a stage of "liminality", to use Homi Bhabha's concept.[44] Liminality is Janus-faced: a blend of "self" and "other"; and an interface of "here" and "there". The enmeshment brought about by an intensification of globalisation fosters liminality. The deterrotorialised Islamic community with its endless hyphens exemplifies liminality, or the "in-between-ness" that I refer to in the preface. The search for Arab democracy cannot be complete without an investigation of the hybrid realm Arab-Muslims find themselves in at this historical moment. It is within this hybrid realm and liminal space that binary knowledge, which posits the "self" against the "other", can be sabotaged. Perhaps it is within the expanding space of liminality occupied by American, French and British Arab-Muslims that lie some of the answers to the prospects for democratising and pluralising the Arab world. Academic research can no longer afford to ignore this liminal space. The exilic identities in the diaspora can be agents of dialogism, positive change and mutual accommodation

[44] Homi K. Bhabha, *The Location of Culture* (London: Routledge, 1994).

with "otherness". Thus they may hold the key to a peaceful renegotiation of difference and dialogical collaboration between Democracy, Islam and "Arabness". This should revive hope that these liminal identities may also be a conduit of a re-thought Islam and agents for the diffusion of a radically critical notion of democracy to the rest of the Arab World. My own search for Arab democracy continues, refocusing attention on what I call *liminal Islam* and *liminal Islamism*.[45] The emerging new Europe and post-11 September America will continue to provide the discursive space and the cultural interface for liminal Islam and Liminal Islamism or *liminal political Islam*. The "exilic predicaments" of millions of Arab-Muslims living in the EU or America defy not only fixity and singularity. They have the potential to refigure and refashion a liminal political Islam that is open to dialogical collaboration with the ideals of Democracy. In so doing, they also remake Arab-Muslim identity, away from fear and repugnance with regard to difference. The "liminal Islam" of Averroes and al-Fārābī, amongst other Muslim and Arab luminaries, is most inspiring. They confidently and brilliantly negotiated in-betweenness between philosophy and revelation, between science and spirituality, and between Europe and the house of Islam. The knowledge they produced and bequeathed today benefits all humanity. This is not a history to just glory in. Its lessons command attention by Arabs and Muslims alike. There is no reason today why the liminality of the American-Arab or the French-Arab should not be brought into play, fusing the ideals of Islam and Democracy. As they both continue to travel on their millennial journeys, Islam and Democracy will increasingly be enmeshed in liminality. Liminality becomes a site for *munāẓarāt*, continuous discourses and counter-discourses, and contests in search for democratic 'islams' and Muslim 'democracies'. In these democratic 'islams' and Muslim 'democracies' one good to cherish is diversity; one evil to repulse is singularity; and one ethos to cleave to is indeterminacy. God is the only determinate that Islam transcendentalises.

Democracy has joined Islam in jostling to inform the political process in many Arab societies as a normative standard. Their struggle is against a brand of secular-nationalism embodied today in decaying

[45] Larbi Sadiki, *Re-thinking Arab Democratisation: The Making of Liminal Islam, Hyphenated Citizenship and Salon Democracy* (forthcoming).

authoritarianism, clan or family-based politics, delegitimised rule, failed states and bankrupt revolutions. Over forty years, the pan-Arabists, the revolutionaries, the monarchists, the republicans, the Islamists have all inflated expectations everywhere in the AME. Their promises of delivering the goods—autonomy, Arab socialism, security, development, good government, an Arab common market and a free Palestine—after independence are unfilled. Their governance is today as questionable as the logic of linearity, which was employed to legitimate the ruling elites' political preferences and narrow interests and prove the value of their policies. In some cases, the logical outcome of linearity has been tragic. A number of Arab states have gained no peace, security or territorial dividends from the ruling elite's policies of belligerence, armament and, in one or two cases, involvement in international terrorism. To the contrary, in two cases, the state's security has been undermined via a combination of UN sanctions and United States hostility against the rulers. When politics operates without reference to a wider plane of contest, contestation, inclusiveness, consultation and legality, the end result can be catastrophic. The postcolonial Arab state is, to borrow an idea by Elbaki Hermassi, "privatised". A notion that is so absurd yet sadly true. Almost always and everywhere in the AME a minority of families or clans have 'colonised' the postcolonial state. In at least three Arab republics, the rulers have in their wisdom begun grooming heirs from within their own progeny. Caesar's and God's realms are both rendered unto single rulers who hold political, economic and, indirectly, religious power.

Democratisation is one of two objectives defined for the Anglo-American coalition's mission in Iraq, which in early 2003 looked poised to strike Baghdad and oust Saddam Hussein by force. In the short term, at least, this will no doubt precipitate a flurry of electoral activities in the AME, including in Saudi Arabia, when the guns fall silent. The Anglo-American coalition has got the firepower to oust Saddam Hussein, a ruler who should have relinquished power given the colossal human and material losses he caused his people in the Iran-Iraq war. However, when the Anglo-coalition sacks Baghdad it cannot superimpose or "teach" democracy. Not only because democracy is a contested and value-laden concept, but because democracy is a process. It was precisely through the international reaction to the "selective and convenient" monitoring of "democracy" in Iraq, that

Saddam the tyrant was transformed into Saddam the hero who stood up against imperial might. So while most democracy lovers in the Arab World may rejoice at the fall of Saddam, they may not rejoice at what ensues, at least not publicly, since here nationalism also comes into play. Arab regimes such as those in Libya, where one man's demagogy, adventurism and nepotism have weakened both state and society, can be expected to fear a similar fate. Libya's strongman has rejected democracy in his Green Book, as shown in chapter 5. His decaying revolution today calls for serious revision. Such a revision would be hollow without a programme of renewal that re-admits democracy into the public sphere. But that re-admission could delegitimise al-Qadhāfi's own status as Libya's single and fixed mentor and ideologue. Re-admission of democracy's utility would amount to an admission of failure of the indigenous fixed and singular "democracy" he devised for his country. On the evidence of the past thirty years his particular brand of "democracy" can be said to have empowered his own clan and region. The United States and the EU need to assess their close ties with non-representative regimes in the AME, including the oil-rich Arab Gulf states. America's passivity vis-à-vis democratisation in the AME, as elaborated in chapter 7, must be revised. At least the United States has been historically presenting itself as the custodian of the state of democracy in the world, even while it has itself been systematically favouring patently undemocratic regimes. Thus far the case for expecting anything positive coming from the United States in actually aiding fledgling democratic forces anywhere in the world, with the exception of very few states such as Germany and Japan, is yet to be made very convincingly. Whether post-Saddam Iraq would be a trial-run for the United States democracy promotion in the Arab World remains to be seen. Arabs themselves must earn democracy inclusively, sensitively and preferably through negotiated transitions that allow incumbent regimes to hand over power to democratic forces within consensual legal and time frameworks.

Distinction must be made between pooling Arab and Western efforts for the cause of Arab democracy, and a notion of an Anglo-American democratic tutelage, particularly if this tutelage is aided by a military strategy in support of a capitalist agenda aiming at reversing the processes of nationalisation, especially of oil wealth, of the 1970s. Such tutelage would most certainly revive memories of colonial excesses. At best, outside tutelage can do no more than instituting elections. Important as they may be, elections may pass the test of proceduralism but not necessarily that of democracy. They may simply produce "elected autocracy" not democracy. Elections can be open to manipulation. Dispersion of political power requires decentralisation of economic power. In the Arab Gulf, for instance, elections would not lead to democratisation as long as the rulers' siphoning off of unknown shares from the oil rent goes unchallenged. Elections in Bahrain or Qatar may legitimise rule without empowering society. Elections in Saudi Arabia would rubber-stamp the status quo in the absence of serious "de-privatisation" of the state and "de-personalisation" of public wealth. When the oil barons own the media, hire and fire, determine the content of knowledge and educational syllabi, provide patronage to the religious establishment, and have control over the military and civil bureaucracies, elections would amount to no more than a farce to select, rather than elect, regime clients. Without democratic substance, elections become the means for a return to fixity and singularity. Then there would be the question of whether universal suffrage would be adopted or whether Saudi women would be counted out. Generally, the indeterminate space needed for enacting equal state–society relations in the AME remains absent. Power-holders continue to intervene, making their presence felt at every site of informational, social, economic or political activity. Even graffiti is the exclusive bastion of the state in some Arab countries, especially in those regimes that articulate themselves through slogans and symbols than substantive policies.

Elsewhere in the AME, elections cannot be expected to deliver democratic "miracles" when cellular telephones, the Internet, printers and dissident media are banned in some states; and when in most Arab countries universities continue to be policed: note the hostility of many Arab regimes to the al-Jazeerah satellite TV, which has given dissidents a voice but without excluding officialdom. At this historical juncture, as most democratisation experiments stagnate, with very few qualified exceptions, the search for good government has many challenges to rise to. Continuous corruption, human rights violations, exclusion of minorities, gendered political and social practices, hegemonic ruling parties and unlimited executive power in statecraft weaken the case for Arab democracy. Democracy cannot obtain when Arabs are caught between the extremes of the arbitrariness of political decrees and the obscurantism of religious *fatwahs*. The former intrudes into intellectual expression, freedom of academic inquiry and research, in general, and the Friday sermon with non-establishment preachers often banned or jailed. The latter threatens any kind of creativity, such as musical composition or poetry. It is no surprise then that the luminaries of the Arab verse for the past fifty years have chosen exile over political or religious persecution in Arab countries. Thus the well-known Arab poet Adonis deprecates the haste and ease with which one Saudi magazine relegates a fellow poet to the realm of the "infidel"—apostasy. In seeking to defuse the tension between religion and poetry he defends the imaginary and imagery in poetry against accusations of heresy by unimaginative religious scholars. He notes that poetry uses language figuratively and metaphorically, which is characteristic of poetic writing.

> Poetic language is metaphoric. Thus what [meaning] it communicates does not delve into the realm of what is "right" or "wrong". It is suppositional, pertaining to [the realm of] imagination and symbolism. It [delves not] in that which is non-imaginary, [that which] relates to beliefs and creeds, as we observe in the language of science, philosophy and logic. So when the poet, for instance, states that "Allah has turned into ash", what is signified is not the obvious, direct and literary meaning. That is, it is not meant that Allah that the Muslim believes in has Himself become ash. Just as the [Qur'ānic] verse, as an example, "The Beneficent is firmly established on the throne", cannot be taken literally, i.e. that Allah sits physically on a palpable throne as do [mortal] power-holders.
>
> The poet in this case symbolically comments on a general trend of regression in the notion of the oneness of God, and the values subsumed under such a notion and the behaviour it entails. To the contrary, he [the poet] criticises this trend manifest in the prevalent religious practice, which vulgarises the ideal idea of God and taints it. As such [the ideal idea of] Allah looks, through this practice, as though He became ash. [In fact], the poet's faith in Allah is as wholesome as [faith] can be.[46]

It is no wonder then that Adonis's own reflections on *ḥadāthah*, or modernism, put him at odds with both the religious and political establishments in the AME. Adonis articulates a notion of modernism that demands interrogation and rejects determinacy, fixity and

46 Adonis ('Alī Aḥmad Sa'īd), *Al-Naṣṣu 'l-Qur'ānī wa Afāqu 'l-Kitābah* [*The Qur'ānic Text and the Horizons of Writing*] (Beirut: Dar al-Adab, 1993), p. 184.

singularity. The overall tenor of his belief sits well with the stress in the *Search for Arab Democracy* on a notion of defoundationalised Islam and democracy.

But whilst the gist of his thinking is correct, Adonis can be faulted for using dichotomous categories (the secular versus the religious)[47] and for sweeping generalisations (e.g. use of terms such the "Arab mind")[48] Although Adonis's focus on modernism is concerned with "liberating" the Arab verse from classical formalism and conventions, he assigns his *ḥadāthah* a holistic meaning that has implications for the Arab quest for development and contributes to human knowledge. Adonis blames what he calls *thaqāfatu'l-waḥy* (culture of revelation/religious culture) for overall Arab stagnation given the indelible mark of religious rationality on what he considers to be an ossified "Arab modernism". That culture of revelation continues, he argues, to be the yardstick for evaluating the arts, literature, politics and daily life. He understands why within such a culture, revelation is treated as immutable. However, he opposes the tendency to apply revelation's immutable quality to the arts, literature or politics, for instance.[49] In other words, religious faith should not preclude a form of apostasy in the realm of knowledge or politics. Adonis treats what he labels in a totalising fashion "Western" and "Arab" modernisms as contrasts, that is, two mutually exclusive mindsets. The former favours the individual, originality as a frame of reference, desacralisation, interrogation, indeterminacy, critique, plurality, relativism, anthropocentrism and fluidity. The latter clings to the group, imitation of tradition as a frame of reference, sacralisation, blind faith, determinacy, conformism, singularity, absolutism, theocentrism and fixity.[50]

Adonis leaves no doubt that his sympathies lie with Western modernism. He oversimplifies the role of revelation, essentialising it to be averse to change. Revelation did not once prevent the likes of Averroes to speak to philosophy, dialectically and dialogically (Adonis is aware of this, as can be gleaned from his work *Al-Thābitu*

[47] Adonis presents sacralisation and desacralisation as polar opposites, taking the latter to be a pre-requisite of modernism, something he gleans by citing the Western example. See ibid., p. 115.

[48] He expresses this by use of terms such as *al-fikru 'l-'arabī*, and *al-dhihnu 'l-'arabī*. In so doing he fails to account for diversity, see ibid., pp. 107–8.

[49] Ibid., p. 104.

[50] Ibid., pp. 105–7.

'l wa'l-mutaḥḥawwil, vol. 3). Equally, his bias in favour of religion assumes that modernism is incompatible with religion, a clearly contested position. Adonis, though, by no means belittles the religious experience. All of these criticisms aside, Adonis has got a point. Labouring with a notion of cultural heritage weighted down by the duress of determinacy, fixity, singularity and faith can be damaging for politics or artistic creativity, but not obviously for belief in a unitary, fixed and determinate notion of deity. Thus Adonis calls for total rupture with the heritage if it ossifies thought and blocks creativity. Essentially, for him modernism will remain elusive unless absolutism is renounced, current epistemology is deconstructed, destroyed in order to be reconstructed. He notes that "Arab thought" relies on rhetoric and determinacy, in poetry as well as in politics. The existing epistemological system, Adonis argues, cannot then energise Arab modernism because it is devoid of such building blocks as desacralisation, relativism, indeterminacy, interrogation, fluidity and plurality.[51] Deconstruction and destruction of Arab modernism is akin to a process of opening up myths for scrutiny and taboos for debate:

> Simply put, modernism is a move towards stating what is not voiced in [Arab] society, [and] envisioning spheres free of all the theoretical and practical obstacles, [that is,] in complete freedom of imagination and expression. This will not be possible without surpassing the existing epistemological system, which is, and I reiterate, [one of] sacralisation of life.[52]

Adonis takes creative destruction, which he describes as the "second face of reconstruction", and rupture as means of creating an epistemological system more geared towards a new notion of Arab modernism. Such a modernism valorises innovation and even "rebellion", as against conformism, and rejects immutable foundations and what he calls *al-ma 'āyīru 'l-thābitah* (fixed criteria).[53] From this perspective, Adonis provides an important link with the deconstructivist ideas of LeFort and Connolly. In fact, Adonis's notion of *al-ma'āyīru 'l-thābitah* is similar to Connolly's idea of "congealed standards" elaborated in chapter 2. From this perspective, Adonis's project, even if it is primarily concerned with modernising Arab poetry, has broader implications. When translated politically, the flaws Adonis

51 Ibid., pp. 107–8.
52 Ibid., p. 108–9.
53 Ibid., p. 115.

identifies within Arab modernism—e.g. imitation of tradition as a frame of reference, blind faith, determinacy, acceptance, singularity, absolutism and fixity—can be read as demoted agency, hegemony, homogeny, domineering authority, non-participatory polity, "denizenship", as opposed to citizenship. One element that Adonis reproaches Arab modernism for is the deification of tribe, political party or ideology, a practice without an equal in Western modernism.[54] His opposition to sacralisation must not be read as rejection of religion. Sacralisation colours and creeps into politics, turning political rulers into demi-gods, their ideologies into "gospel", and political parties into quasi-sects. Adonis is in all of this an iconoclast. His predilection is for fluidity, plurality and provisionalism. The bias towards a framework of secular eschatology is no guarantee against fixity, singularity or autocracy. Secular eschatology is part and parcel of the now discredited modernist linearity that is cemented to notions of nationality, territoriality and rationality.

Students of Arab politics may not help but side with Adonis, even if they may not accept desacralisation as the only route to modernism. The icons of Arab politics (from Qadhāfī to Saddam Hussein), its gospels, such as the Green Book, and its sect-like ideologies like Ba'athism have all cultivated and entrenched political iconolatry, weakening the case for citizenship, interrogation, debate, pluralism, contestation and, subsequently, good government. Thus Adonis's iconoclasm is justified. In fact, decaying affairs in the AME, described above, demand democratic change—perhaps rebellion but not conformism, Adonis would argue. Adonis's quarrel as far as the questions of Arab identity, modernism and heritage go is with conformism—literary or political (and for him there is a connection between the two). Both in *Al-Naṣṣu 'l-Qur'ānī* and his earlier work *Al-Thābitu 'l wa'l-Mutaḥḥawwil* Adonis depicts the religious establishment as a regressive force that is too possessive of the past and the heritage of the forebears. Thus his call for rupture with the past is to invent a new Arab modernism that goes further than just re-adopting and reworking the traditional canons bequeathed by the *salafiyyah* of the ninth and tenth centuries.[55]

54 Ibid., p. 105.

55 Ibid., p. 115. See also by Adonis, *Al-Thābitu 'l wa'l-Mutaḥḥawwil: Baḥth fī 'l-Ibdā' 'inda 'l-'Arab* [*The Mutable and the Immutable: A Study of Arab Originality and Conformity*] (Beirut: Dar al-'Awdah, 1983).

In this environment, democratic vociferousness must intensify. Arabs can ill-afford to be complacent towards the democratic deficit that is conspicuous almost invariably in all Arab states. That deficit accounts for the ills that continue to beset them both as individuals and collectivities. Such a deficit has eroded the Arabs' ability to have a voice and to act decisively both nationally and internationally. The Arab League, supposedly the "Arab House", has hit the nadir of incapacity and lack of democracy visible at the level of individual member-states. The result is diminished confidence and consensus-building, decreased capacity to realise pan-Arab projects as well as heightened tension within the League. The member-states have lacked the creativity to experiment with democratic forms as a collective, as did the EU parliament for example, and have failed to fulfil a historical mission that was within their grasp. Since innovative forms of democracy were not given space within the region, the Western imported notion of "democracy" of one-person-one-vote has established itself as the ideal. Nationalism, pan-nationalism, competing imprints of political Islam and secular struggles cannot ignore substantive democracy. While democracy does not have to be a Western category, neither should it be a permanent *azmah*, crisis. Some representations of democracy tend to locate it between these two poles. The flourishing discourses and counter-discourses of democracy are cause for optimism. The emerging politico-cultural "salons" in Beirut, Cairo, Rabat and Tunis are bound to cultivate dialogism and democratic habituation, thus promoting values (respect and tolerance of difference, equality) and skills (participation, association) necessary for democratic citizenship. This is one line of investigation I follow in exploring the question of how Arab countries democratise, elaborating what I call "salon democracy", in a forthcoming title.

There is a discursive tradition that Arabs must mobilise and build on. In this tradition, Islam itself, as Talal Asad has discovered long time ago, "should be approached as a discursive tradition that connects variously with the formation of moral selves, the manipulation of populations (or resistance to it), and the production of appropriate knowledges".[56] Furthermore, he adds, that "there clearly is not, nor can be, such a thing as a universally acceptable account of a living

[56] Talal Asad, "The Idea of an Anthropology of Islam", Occasional Papers Series (Centre for Contemporary Arab Studies, Georgetown University, 1986), p. 13.

tradition. Any representation of tradition is contestable. What shape that contestation takes, if it occurs, will be determined not only by the powers and knowledges each side deploys, but by the collective life they aspire to—or to whose survival that are quite indifferent."[57] This matches the overall tenor of the argument contained within this book in favour of discovery of meaning through discourse and counter-discourse, taking account of time and space, over fixed and singular understanding of either Islam or democracy. Only in a discursive context will Muslims and Arabs grasp the lesson of Asad's notion of Islam as a discursive tradition. Only then can they today negotiate the relationship of Islam to democracy by rediscovering both as discursive human traditions. This task demands ample capacity for reflexivity on the part of Arabs: if they cannot engage with the tradition they revere discursively, they will not be equipped to meaningfully interact with democracy as indeterminate, plural and non-fixed. Equally important, this task requires reflexive meaningful interaction of self and other: neither can afford to adopt a monocular view of the good—e.g. an Arab exceptionalism ("Islam is the solution" as in some narratives) or Western triumphalism (secular democracy is the end as once argued by Fukuyama).

The capacity for self-criticism and for assimilation of notions of Islam and democracy as discursive traditions raise questions about the role of society in the AME. Indeed, the state is indelibly tainted in most analyses of political power in the AME. No state can democratise without an empowered society that can share in substantive political reform as well as present initiatives of its own to spur democratisation. The various projects of Arab socialism and pan-Arabism, for example, failed for being exclusively state-led. A democratic project without a participatory society or without the partnership of its various and diverse forces is doomed to failure. In this context, decentring requires moving away from state-centric academic inquiries. The notion of democracy as an *azmah* in the AME echoes ideas of an *azmah* of government and of the state. The wide body of scholarship shows that the state in the Arab world has been assigned many labels denoting failure, hegemony or autocracy—"*mukhābarāt* state", "failed state", "over-stated state", and, very recently, a "bunker state".[58] The search for Arab democracy should be located in social struggles,

[57] Ibid., p. 17.

[58] For details of this label and others coined by Clement Moore Henry and Robert Springborg see their *Globalisation and the Politics of Development in the Middle East* (Cambridge University Press, 2001).

continuously shifting practices of power, political activism, agency, knowledge, morality, language and of identity, as well as discourses and counter-discourses of these to further the inquiry of how Arab countries might democratise. Without an approach that decentres the state, students of Arab politics would themselves be implicated in entrenching the Orientalist caricatures of Middle Eastern societies as incapable of self-government. The previous chapters contribute only marginally to this approach, mostly attempting to foreground Arab discourses about democracy and Islam while at the same time contextualising them in a broader Western political theory framework. Students of Arab politics have hardly begun probing hundreds of questions awaiting serious investigation. Little is known about the accumulation of democratic knowledge, if any, past and present, in the AME. In this context, the role of the *muthaqqaf* (member of the literati or intelligentsia), for instance, remains under-researched. Conventionally, he or she is identified as the power-holders' instrument for privileging centralised authority's practices and narratives as the register of truth, thus legitimating hegemonic political discourse and practice. Dissident literary works and poetry, as forms of emancipatory knowledge practices, could correct this impression if explored. As far as agency and political activism are concerned, there are questions to be asked about quietist and conformist tendencies, if any. There are very few clues as to why dictators are toppled through public disobedience and peaceful rebellion in Manila, Jakarta and even Moscow but not in Algiers, Tripoli or Baghdad. These questions do not lend themselves to easy answers. But engaging with them may facilitate critical assessment of the prospects for transition from autocracy to good government, i.e. from subjection to citizenship.

This book has argued the case for a new possibility of representing Democracy and Islam individually and together as an ethos of anti-foundationalism. The contested nature of the ideals of each gives space for fluidity and contingency. The move from test to contest favours the growth of a shared space for nurturing a culture of cross-cultural dialogue, pluralisation, mutual tolerance and co-learning. To this end, the Arab tradition of *munāẓarāt* is worthy of revival. The move from text to context facilitates the relativisation of the ideals of Islam and Democracy so that islams and democracies may be realised away from ahistorical interpretations, hegemonic meanings and rigid literalism of theistic or non-theistic foundationalism.

BIBLIOGRAPHY

ENGLISH

Abduh, Muhammad. *The Theology of Unity*, trans. by Ishaq Musa'ad and Kenneth Cragg. London: Allen and Unwin, 1966.

Abu-Lughod, Ibrahim. *Arab Rediscovery of Europe: Study in Cultural Encounters*. Princeton University Press, 1963.

Abu-Lughod, Lila. "Zones of Theory in the Anthropology of the Arab World". *Annual Review of Anthropology*, 18 (1989). pp. 267–306.

——. *Writing Women's Worlds: Bedouin Stories*. Berkeley: University of California Press, 1993.

Accad, Evelyne. *Sexuality and War: Literary Masks of the Middle East*. New York University Press, 1990.

Afifi, Aicha and Rajae Msefer. "Women in Morocco: Gender Issues and Politics". In *Women and Politics Worldwide*, ed. by Barbara J. Nelson and Najma Chowdhury. New Haven and London: Yale University Press, 1994. pp. 463–77.

Aflāṭūn, Injī. "We Egyptian Women". In *Opening the Gates: A Century of Arab Feminist Writing*, ed. by Margot Badran and Miriam Cooke. Bloomington: Indiana University Press, 1990. pp. 347–8.

Ahmad, Khurshid. *Political Islam: Religion and Politics in the Arab World*. London: Routledge, 1993.

Ahmed, Akbar S. *Postmodernism and Islam*. London: Routledge, 1992.

Ahmed, Leila. "Feminism and Feminist Movements in the Middle East". In *Women and Islam*, ed. by Aziz al-Hibri. New York: Pergman, 1982. pp. 153–68.

Al Tunisi, Khayr al-Din. *The Surest Path to Knowledge Concerning the Condition of Countries*, trans. by Leon Carl Brown. Cambridge, MA: Harvard University Press, 1967.

Al-Azm, S. J. "Orientalism and Orientalism in Reverse". *Khamsin*, 8 (1981). pp. 5–26.

Al-Azmeh, Aziz. *Ibn Khaldun in Modern Scholarship: A Study in Orientalism*. London: Third World Centre for Research and Publishing, 1981.

——. *Ibn Khaldun: An Essay in Reinterpretation*. London: Frank Cass, 1982.

Al-Gahnnushi, Rashid. “Islam and the West: Realities and Prospects”, trans. by Azzam Tamimi, unpublished paper delivered at the Westminster University, London, 1993.

Al-Hajji, Aziz. “Arab Nationalitarianism, Democracy and Socialism”. In *Contemporary Arab Political Thought*, ed. by Anouar Abdel-Malek. London: Zed Books, 1983. pp. 167–8.

Al-Husri, Khaldun S. *Three Reformers: A Study in Modern Arabic Political Thought*. Beirut: Khayats, 1966.

Al-Khalil, Samir. “In the Middle East, does *Democracy* have a Chance?” *New York Times Magazine* (14 October 1990). p. 54.

Almond, Gabriel A. “Introduction: A Functional Approach to Comparative Politics”. In *The Politics of the Developing Areas*, ed. by Gabriel A. Almond and James S. Coleman. Princeton University Press, 1960. pp. 5–9.

——. “Foreword: The Return to Political Culture”. In *Political Culture and Democracy in Developing Countries*, ed. by Larry Diamond. Boulder, CO and London: Lynne Rienner, 1993. pp. ix–xii.

Almond, Gabriel A. and G. Bingham Powell, Jr. *Comparative Politics: A Developmental Approach*. Boston: Little, Brown and Company, 1966.

——. *Comparative Politics: System, Process and Policy*. Boston: Little, Brown and Company, 1978.

—— and James S. Coleman, eds. *The Politics of the Developing Areas*. Princeton University Press, 1960.

—— and Sidney Verba. *The Civic Culture: Political Attitudes and Democracy in Five Nations*. Newbury Park: Sage, 1965.

Al-Sadawi, Nawal. “The Political Challenges Facing Arab Women at the End of the 20th Century”, trans. by Nahed El-Gamal. In *Women of the Arab World: The Coming Challenge*, ed. by Nahid Toubia. London: Zed Books, 1988. pp. 8–26.

Al-Sadat, Anwar. *In Search of Identity: An Autobiography*. New York: Fontana, 1978.

Al-Sayyid, Mustapha Kamal. “A Civil Society in Egypt”. In *Civil Society in the Middle East*, ed. by Augustus Richard Norton. Leiden: E. J. Brill, 1995. pp. 269–93.

Anderson, Benedict. *Imagined Communities: Reflections on the Origin and Spread of Nationalism*. New York: Verso, 1987.

Anderson, Lisa. “Democracy in the Arab World: A Critique of the Political Culture Approach”. In *Political Liberalization and Democratization in the Arab World*, vol. 1: *Theoretical Perspectives*, ed. by Rex Brynen, Bahgat Korany and Paul Noble. Boulder, CO: Lynne Rienner, 1995. pp. 77–92.

Applebaum, Herbert, ed. *Perspectives in Cultural Anthropology*. Albany: State University of New York, 1987.

Apter, David E. *The Politics of Modernization*. University of Chicago Press, 1965.

Archigubi, Daniele. "Principles of Cosmopolitan Democracy". In *Re-imagining Political Community: Studies in Cosmopolitan Democracy*, ed. by Daniele Archibugi, David Held and Martin Köhler. Cambridge: Polity Press, 1998. pp. 209–12.

—— and David Held, eds. *Cosmopolitan Democracy: An Agenda for a New World Order.* Cambridge: Polity Press, 1995.

——, David Held and Martin Köhler, eds. *Re-imagining Political Community: Studies in Cosmopolitan Democracy.* Cambridge: Polity Press, 1998.

Arendt, Hanna. *The Human Condition*. University of Chicago Press, 1958.

Aristotle. *The Politics*, ed. by Stephen Everson. Cambridge University Press, 1988.

Arkoun, Mohammed. *Rethinking Islam: Common Questions, Uncommon Answers*. Boulder, CO, San Francisco and Oxford: Westview Press, 1994.

Aronowitz, Stanley. *The Politics of Identity: Class, Culture, Social Movements*. New York: Routledge, 1992.

Averroes. *Averroes on Plato's Republic*. trans. by Ralph Lerner. Ithaca: Cornell University Press, 1974.

——. *Averroes' Commentary on Plato's Republic*, ed. and trans. by E. I. J. Rosenthal. Cambridge University Press, 1966.

Awwad, Hanan. "Gender Issues in Democracy: The Palestinian Woman and the Revolution". In *Building Peace in the Middle East: Challenges for States and Civil Society*, ed. by Elise Boulding. Boulder, CO: Lynne Rienner, 1994. pp. 91–7.

Ayalon, Ami. *Language and Change in the Arab Middle East*. Oxford University Press, 1987.

——. "The Modernization of the Arabic Political Vocabulary". *Asian and African Studies*, 23 (1989) pp. 23–42.

Badran, Margot. "Dual Liberation: Feminism and Nationalism in Egypt, 1870–1925". *Feminist Issues* (spring 1988). pp. 27–8.

——. "Gender Activism: Feminists and Islamists in Egypt". In *Identity Politics and Women: Cultural Reassertions and Feminisms in International Perspective*, ed. by Valentine M. Moghadam. Boulder, CO: Westview Press, 1994. pp. 202–27.

Bannerman, Patrick. *Islam in Perspective*. London: Routledge, 1988.

Barbalet, J. M. *Citizenship: Rights, Struggle and Class Inequality.* Milton Keynes: Open University Press, 1988.

Barzun, Jacques. "Is Democratic Theory for Export?" In *Ethics and International Affairs: A Reader,* ed. by Joel H. Rosenthal. Washington, DC: Georgetown University Press, 1995. pp. 39–57.

Bello, Iysa A. *The Medieval Islamic Controversy Between Philosophy and Orthodoxy:* Ijma *and* Tawil *in the Conflict Between al-Ghazali and Ibn Rushd*. Leiden: E. J. Brill, 1989.

Bhagwati, Jagdish. "Democracy and Development". *Journal of Democracy*, 3 (July 1992). pp. 37–44.

Bill, James A. "Comparative Middle East Politics: Still in Search of Theory." *Political Science and Politics*, 27 (September 1994). pp. 518–9.

—— and Robert Springborg. *Politics in the Middle East*. Glenview, Illinois: Scott, Furesman and Company, 1990.

Binder, Leonard. *Islamic Liberalism: A Critique of Development Ideologies*. University of Chicago Press, 1988.

—— *et al.*, eds. *Crises and Sequences in Political Development*. Princeton University Press, 1971.

Black, C. E. *The Dynamics of Modernization*. New York: Harper and Row, 1966.

Bromley, Simon. *Rethinking Middle East Politics*. Cambridge: Polity Press, 1994.

Brown, L. Carl. *The Tunisia of Ahmad Bey*. Princeton University Press, 1974.

Bryant, Christopher G. A. "Civic Nation, Civil Society, Civil Religion". In *Civil Society: Theory, History, Comparison*, ed. by John A. Hall. Cambridge: Polity Press, 1995. pp. 136–57.

Buci-Glucksmann, Christine. *Gramsci and the State*. London: Lawrence and Wishart, 1980.

Buell, Frederick. *National Culture and the New Global System*. Baltimore and London: Johns Hopkins University Press, 1994.

Burchell, Graham, Colin Gordon and Peter Miller. *The Foucault Effect: Studies in Governmentality*. University of Chicago Press, 1991.

Callinicos, Alex. *Against Postmodernism: A Marxist Critique*. Cambridge: Polity Press, 1989.

Carrier, James G., "Introduction". In *Occidentalism: Images of the West*, ed. by James G. Carrier. Oxford: Clarendon Press, 1995. pp. 1–32.

Chadwick, Owen. *The Secularization of the European Mind in the Nineteenth Century*. Cambridge University Press, 1975.

Cigar, Norman. "Serbia's Orientalists and Islam: Making Genocide Intellectually Respectable". *The Islamic Quarterly*, 38 (third quarter 1994). pp. 147–70.

Cole, Juan Ricardo. "Feminism, Class and Islam in Turn-of-the-Century Egypt". *International Journal of Middle Eastern Studies*, 13 (November 1981). pp. 387–405.

Coleman, James S. "The Development Syndrome: Differentiation–Equality–Capacity". In *Crises and Sequences in Political Development*, ed. by Leonard Binder *et. al.* Princeton University Press, 1971. pp. 78–9.

Connolly, William E. *Political Theory and Modernity*. Oxford and New York: Basil Blackwell, 1988.

——. *Identity/Difference: Democratic Negotiations of Political Paradox*. Ithaca: Cornell University Press, 1991.

——. *The Ethos of Pluralization*. Minneapolis: University of Minnesota Press, 1995.

Crone, Patricia. *Slaves on Horses: The Evolution of the Islamic Polity*. Cambridge University Press, 1980.

——. *God's Caliph: Religious Authority in the First Centuries of Islam*. Cambridge University Press, 1986.

Dahl, Robert A. *A Preface to Democratic Theory*. University of Chicago Press, 1956.

——. *Who Governs?* New Haven: Yale University Press, 1961.

——. *Polyarchy: Participation and Opposition*. New Haven: Yale University Press, 1971.

——, ed. *Regimes and Oppositions*. New Haven: Yale University Press, 1973.

——. *Dilemmas of Pluralist Democracy: Autonomy Versus Control*. New Haven: Yale University Press, 1982.

——. *A Preface to Economic Democracy*. Berkeley: University of California Press, 1985.

——. *Democracy and its Critics*. New Haven: Yale University Press, 1989.

Davis, Eric. "The Concept of Revival and the Study of Islam and Politics". In *The Islamic Impulse*, ed. by Barbara F. Stowasser. London: Croom Helm, 1987. pp. 37–58.

Dawood, N. J., ed. *The Muqaddimah: An Introduction to History*, trans. by Franz Rosenthal. London and Henley: Routledge and Kegan Paul, 1967.

Dekmejian, Hrair R. *Islam in Revolution: Fundamentalism in the Arab World*. Syracuse University Press, 1985.

Derrida, Jacques. *Of Grammatology*, trans. by Gayatri Chakravorty Spivak. Baltimore: The Johns Hopkins University, 1976.

Deutsch, Eliot, ed., *Culture and Modernity: East–West Philosophic Perspectives*. Honolulu: University of Hawaii Press, 1991.

Diamond, Larry, ed. *Political Culture and Democracy in Developing Countries*. Boulder, CO: Lynne Rienner, 1994.

Diamond, Larry, Juan J. Linz and Seymour Martin Lipset. *Democracy in Developing. Countries: Latin America*. Boulder, CO: Lynne Rienner, 1989.

——. *Politics in Developing Countries: Comparing Experiences with Democracy*. Boulder, CO: Lynne Rienner, 1990.

Dryzek, John S. *Discursive Democracy: Polities, Policy, and Political Science*. Cambridge University Press, 1990.

Dunn, John, ed. *Democracy. The Unfinished Journey: 508 BC to AD 1993*. Cambridge University Press, 1992.

Dwyer, Kevin. *Arab Voices: The Human Rights Debate in the Middle East*. Berkeley: University of California Press, 1991.

Eickelman, Dale F. *The Middle East: An Anthropological Approach*. Englewood Cliffs: Prentice Hall, 1989.

——. "Mass Higher Education and the Religious Imagination in Contemporary Arab Societies". *American Ethnologist*, 19 (1992). pp. 643–55.

Eickelman, Dale F. and Jon W. Anderson. "Print, Islam and the Prospects for Civic Pluralism: New Religious Writings and Their Audiences". *Journal of Islamic Studies*, 8 (1997). pp. 43–62.

—— and Kamran Pasha. "Muslim Societies and Politics: Soviet and US Approaches: A Conference Report". *Middle East Journal*, 45 (1991). pp. 630–44.

—— and James Piscatori. *Muslim Politics*. Princeton University Press, 1996.

Elster, Jon and Rune Slagstad, eds. *Constitutionalism and Democracy*. Cambridge University Press, 1988.

Esposito, John L., ed. *Islam and Development: Religion and Sociopolitical Change*. New York: Syracuse University Press, 1980.

——. *The Islamic Threat: Myth or Reality?* New York and Oxford: Oxford University Press, 1992.

—— and James P. Piscatori. "Democratization and Islam". *Middle East Journal*, 45 (summer 1991). pp. 427–40.

—— and John O. Voll. *Islam and Democracy*. New York and Oxford: Oxford University Press, 1996.

Fairclough, Norman. *Language and Power*. London: Longman, 1989.

Falk, Richard. "The Making of Global Citizenship". In *The Condition of Citizenship*, ed. by B. van Steenbergen. London: Sage, 1994. pp. 127–40.

——. "The World Order between Inter-State Law and the Law of Humanity: The Role of Civil Society Institutions". In *Cosmopolitan Democracy: An Agenda for a New World Order*, ed. by Daniele Archibugi and David Held. Cambridge: Polity Press, 1995. pp. 163–79.

Ferguson, Marjorie. "The Mythology about Globalization". *European Journal of Communication*, 7 (1992). pp. 69–93.

Ferry, Luc and Alain Renaut. *Heidegger and Modernity*, trans. by Franklin Philip. University of Chicago Press, 1990.

Finer, S. E. "Pareto and Pluto–Democracy: The Retreat to Galapagos". *The American Political Science Review*, 62 (June 1968). pp. 440–50.

Foucault, Michel. *The Archeology of Knowledge*, trans. by Alan M. Sheridan Smith. London: Tavistock Publications, 1972.

——. *Discipline and Punish*. New York: Vintage Books, 1979.

——. *Power/Knowledge*: *Selected Interviews and Other Writings, 1972–1977*, ed. by Colin Gordon. New York: Harvester, 1980.

——. "Truth and Power". In *The Foucault Reader*, ed. by Paul Rabinow. New York: Pantheon Books, 1984. pp. 51–75.

——. *The Use of Pleasure, The History of Sexuality*, trans. by Robert Harley. New York: Pantheon Books, 1985.

——. *The Care of the Self, The History of Sexuality*, trans. by Robert Harley. New York: Vintage Books, 1988.

Frank, Richard M. *Al-Ghazali and the Asharite School*. Durham, NC: Duke University Press, 1994.

Fraser, Nancy. *Justice Interruptus: Critical Reflections on the "Postsocialist" Condition*. New York and London: Routledge, 1997.

Fukuyama, Francis. *The End of History and the Last Man*. London: Penguin Books, 1992.

Fuller, Graham E. *The Democracy Trap*. New York: Dutton, 1991.

Gellner, Ernest. *Muslim Society*. Cambridge University Press, 1981.

——. *Plough, Sword and Book: The Structure of Human History*. London: Collins Harvill, 1988.

——. "Introduction". In *Europe and the Rise of Capitalism*, ed. by Jean Baechler, John A. Hall, and Michael Mann. New York: Basil Blackwell, 1988. pp. 1–5.

——. "Civil Society in Historical Context". *International Social Science Journal*, 129 (August 1991). pp. 495–510.

——. *Postmodernism, Reason and Religion*. London and New York: Routledge, 1992.

George, Jim. *Discourses of Global Politics: A Critical (Re)Introduction to International Relations*. Boulder, CO: Lynne Rienner, 1994.

——. "Realist 'Ethics', International Relations and Postmodernism: Thinking Beyond the Egoism–Anarchy Thematic". Paper prepared for the 36th Annual Convention of the International Studies Association, Chicago, IL, 21–25 February 1995.

Gerges, Fawaz A. "The Study of Middle East International Relations: A Critique". *British Journal of Middle East Studies*, 18 (1991): pp. 208–440.

Geyer, R. Felix, ed. *Alienation, Ethnicity, and Postmodernism*. Westport: Greenwood Press, 1996.

Ghoussoub, Mai. "Feminism—or the Eternal Masculine—in the Arab World". *The New Left Review*, 161 (January/February 1987). pp. 3–18.

Gibb, H. A. R. and Harold Bowen. *Islamic Society and the West: A Study of the Impact of Western Civilization on Muslim Culture in the Near East*. London: Oxford University Press, 1950.

Gibbins, John R., ed. *Contemporary Political Culture: Politics in a Postmodern Age*. London: Sage, 1988.

Giddens, Anthony. *The Constitution of Society: Outline of the Theory of Structuration*. Berkeley: University of California Press, 1984.

Gordon, David. "Orientalism". *Antioch Review*, 40 (winter 1982). pp. 104–12.

——. *Images of the West: Third World Perspectives*. Totowa, NJ: Rowman and Littlefield, 1989.

Gould, Carol. *Rethinking Democracy: Freedom and Social Cooperation in Politics, Economy and Society*. Cambridge University Press, 1988.

Gramsci, Antonio. *The Modern Prince and Other Writings*, trans. by Louis Marks. New York: International Publishers, 1968.

Gray, John. "Post-Totalitarianism, Civil Society, and the Limits of the Western Model". In *The Reemergence of Civil Society in Eastern Europe and the Soviet Union*, ed. by Zbigniew Rau. Boulder, CO: Westview Press, 1991. pp. 145–60.

——. *False Dawn: The Delusions of Global Capitalism*. London: Granta Books, 1998.

Green, Philip, ed. *Key Concepts in Critical Theory: Democracy*. New Jersey: Humanities Press, 1993.

Gusfield, Joseph R. "Tradition and Modernity: Misplaced Polarities in the Study of Social Change". *The American Journal of Sociology*, 72 (January 1967). pp. 351–62.

Hadar, Leon T. "What Green Peril?" *Foreign Affairs*, 72 (spring 1993). pp. 28–42.

Haddad, Yvonne Y. "The Islamic Alternative". *The Link*, 15 (September–October 1982): 1–14.

Hall, John A., ed. *Civil Society: Theory, History, Comparison*. Cambridge: Polity Press, 1995.

——. "In Search of Civil Society". In *Civil Society: Theory, History, Comparison*, ed. by John A. Hall. Cambridge: Polity Press, 1995. pp. 1–31.

Hall, Stuart. "The Local and the Global: Globalization and Ethnicity". In *Culture, Globalization and the World System*, ed. by A. D. King. Houndmills: Macmillan Press, 1991. pp. 19–39.

Hallaq, Wael B. *A History of Islamic Legal Theories*. Cambridge University Press, 1997.

——. "Was the Gate of Ijtihad Closed?" *International Journal of Middle East Studies*, 16 (1984). pp. 3–41.

Halliday, Fred. "Hidden from International Relations: Women and the International Arena". In *Gender and International Relations*, ed. by R. Grant and K. Newland. London: Open University Press, 1991. pp. 158–69.

——. "International Relations: Is there a New Agenda?" *Millennium*, 20 (1991). pp. 57–72.

——. "Orientalism and its Critics". *British Journal of Middle Eastern Studies*, 20 (1993). pp. 145–63.

Hatem, Mervat F. "The Paradoxes of State Feminism in Egypt". In *Women and Politics Worldwide*, ed. by Barbara J. Nelson and Najma Chowdhury. New Haven and London: Yale University Press, 1994.

Held, David. *Models of Democracy*. Cambridge: Polity Press, 1987. pp. 227–42.

——. "Democracy and Globalization". *Alternatives*, 16 (1991). pp. 201–8.

——, ed. *Prospects for Democracy*. Cambridge: Polity Press, 1993.

——. "Democracy: From City–States to a Cosmopolitan Order?" In *Prospects for Democracy*, ed. by David Held. Cambridge: Polity Press, 1993. pp. 13–52.

——. "Sites of Power, Problems of Democracy". *Alternatives*, 19 (spring 1994). pp. 221–36.

Hentsch, Thierry. *Imagining the Middle East*, trans. by Fred A. Reed. Montréal and New York: Black Rose Books, 1991.

Hirst, Paul. "Associational Democracy". In *Prospects for Democracy*, ed. by David Held. Cambridge: Polity Press, 1993. pp. 112–35.

——. "Associative Democracy". *Dissent* (spring 1994). pp. 241–7.

—— and Grahame Thompson. "Globalization and the Future of the Nation–State". *Economy and Society*, 24 (1995). pp. 408–42.

Hobbes, Thomas, *De Cive*, ed. by Howard Warrender. Oxford University Press, 1983.

Hodgson, Marshall G. S. *The Venture of Islam: Conscience and History in a World Civilization*, vol. 1: *The Classical Age of Islam*. Chicago and London: University of Chicago Press, 1977.

Holt, P. M., Ann K. S. Lambton and Bernard Lewis, eds. *The Cambridge History of Islam*, vol. 2A. Cambridge University Press, 1977.

Hooper, J. "Fundamentalists Sweep Algerian Elections". *Guardian Weekly* (24 June 1990). p. 11.

Hourani, Albert. *Arabic Thought in the Liberal Age, 1798–1939*. London: Oxford University Press, 1962.

——. *A History of the Arab Peoples*. London: Faber and Faber, 1991.

Hudson, Michael C., "The Political Culture Approach to Arab Democratization: The Case of Bringing it Back in, Carefully". In *Political Liberalization and Democratization in the Arab World*, vol. 1: *Theoretical Perspectives*, ed. by Rex Brynen, Bahgat Korany and Paul Noble. Boulder, CO: Lynne Rienner, 1995. pp. 61–76.

——. "After the Gulf War: Prospects for Democratization in the Arab World". *Middle East Journal*, 45 (summer 1991). pp. 407–26.

——. "The Possibilities for Pluralism". *American–Arab Affairs*, 36 (spring 1991). p. 4.

——. "Democratization and the Problem of Legitimacy in Middle East Politics". *Middle East Studies Association Bulletin*, 22 (December 1988). pp. 157–71.

——. *Arab Politics: The Search for Legitimacy*. New Haven: Yale University Press, 1977.

——, Louis Cantori *et al.* "The Possibilities for Pluralism". *American–Arab Affairs*, 36 (spring 1991). pp. 3–26.

Hume, David. *Political Essays*, ed. by Knud Haakonssen. Cambridge University Press, 1994.

Huntington, Samuel P. "Political Development and Political Decay". *World Politics*, 17 (April 1965). pp. 386–430.

——. *Political Order in Changing Societies*. New Haven: Yale University Press, 1968.

——. "The Democratic Distemper". *The Public Interest*, 41 (fall 1975). pp. 9–38.

——. "The Goals of Development". In *Understanding Political Development*, ed. by Myron Weiner and Samuel P. Huntington. Glenview, Illinois: Little, Brown and Company, 1987. pp. 3–32.

——. *The Third Wave: Democratization in the Late Twentieth Century*. Norman and London: University of Oklahoma Press, 1991.

——. "The Clash of Civilizations". *Foreign Affairs*, 72 (summer 1993). pp. 22–49.

Husain, Mir Z. *Global Islamic Politics*. New York: Harper Collins College Publishers, 1995.

Hussain, Asaf. "The Ideology Orientalism". In *Orientalism, Islam and Islamists*, ed by Hussain Asaf, Robert Olson, and Jamil Qureshi. Brattleboro, Vermont: Amana Books, 1984. pp. 5–21.

Ibn Khaldun, Abd al-Rahman. *The Muqaddimah [Prolegomenon]: An Introduction to History*, trans. by Frantz Rosenthal. Princeton University Press, 1967.

Ignatius, David. "Islam in the West's Sights: The Wrong Crusade?" *The Washington Post* (8 March 1992). c1–c2.

Jameson, Frederic. *Postmodernism: Or the Cultural Logic of Late Capitalism*. Durham, NC: Duke University Press, 1991.

Jansen, G. H. *Militant Islam*. London: Pan Books, 1979.

Jefferson, Thomas. *Democracy*, ed. by Saul K. Padover. New York: Appleton–Century, 1939.

Keane, John. *Civil Society and the State: New European Perspectives*. London and New York: Verso, 1988.

——. *Democracy and Civil Society: On the Predicaments of European Socialism, the Prospects for Democracy, and the Problem of Controlling Social and Political Power*. London and New York: Verso, 1988.

Keddie, Nikki R. *An Islamic Response to Imperialism*. Berkeley and Los Angeles: University of California Press, 1968.

Kedourie, Elie. *Democracy and Arab Political Culture*. Washington, DC: The Washington Institute for Near East Policy, 1992.

Kerr, Malcolm. "Arab Radical Notions of Democracy". *Middle Eastern Affairs* (St Anthony's Papers), 3 (1963). pp. 9–40.

Knox, T. M. "Translator's Foreword". In *Hegel's Philosophy of Right*. Oxford: Clarendon Press, 1942. pp. x–xi.

Kornhauser, William. *The Politics of Mass Society*. London: Routledge and Kegan Paul, 1965.

Krishna, Daya. *Political Development: A Critical Perspective*. Delhi: Oxford University Press, 1979.

Kymlicka, Will. *Multicultural Citizenship: A Liberal Theory of Minority Rights*. Oxford: Clarendon Press, 1995.

——. *The Rights of Minority Cultures*. Oxford University Press, 1995.

Lacoste, Yves. *Ibn Khaldun: The Birth of History and the Past of the Third World*. London: Verso, 1984.

Laffin, John. *The Dagger of Islam*. London: Sphere Books Limited, 1979.

——. *Holy War: Islam Fights*. London: Grafton Books, 1988.

Lambton, Ann K. S. *State and Government in Medieval Islam*. Oxford University Press, 1981.

Lapidus, Ira M. *A History of Islamic Society*. Cambridge University Press, 1991.

Lawrence, Bruce B., ed. *Ibn Khaldun and Islamic Ideology*. Leiden: E. J. Brill, 1984.

——. "Muslim Fundamentalist Movements: Reflections Toward a New Approach". In *The Islamic Impulse*, ed. by Barbara F. Stowasser. London and Sydney: Croom Helm, 1987. pp. 15–36.

Lawson, Fred H. "Political Economic Trends in Baathi Syria: A Reinterpretation". *Orient*, 29 (1988). pp. 579–94.

Lawson, Stephanie. "The Politics of Tradition: Problems for Political Legitimacy and Democracy in the South Pacific". *Pacific Studies*, 16 (June 1993). pp. 1–29.

——. *Tradition Versus Democracy in the South Pacific: Fiji, Tonga and Western Samoa*. New York, Cambridge University Press, 1996.

Lazreg, Marnia. "Gender and Politics in Algeria: Unraveling the Religious Paradigm". *Journal of Women and Culture and Society*, 15 (summer 1990). pp. 755–80.

Lefort, Claude. *Democracy and Political Theory*, trans. by David Macey. Cambridge: Polity Press, 1988.

Leftwich, A. "Governance, Democracy and Development in the Third World". *Third World Quarterly*, 14 (1993). pp. 605–24.

Lerner, Daniel. *The Passing of Traditional Society: Modernizing the Middle East*. New York: Free Press, 1964.

Levin, Michael. *The Spectre of Democracy: The Rise of Modern Democracy as Seen by its Critics*. London: Macmillan, 1992.

Levy, Marion J. Jr. *Modernization and the Structure of Societies*. Princeton University Press, 1966.

——. *Modernization: Latecomers and Survivors*. New York: Basil Books, Inc. Publishers, 1972.

Lewis, Bernard. *The Middle East and the West*. New York: Harper Torchbooks, 1964.

——. *The Political Language of Islam*. Chicago University Press, 1988.

——. *Islam and the West*. New York: Oxford University Press, 1993.

——. "Why Turkey is the Only Muslim Democracy". *Middle East Quarterly*, 1 (March 1994). pp. 41–9.

Lijphart, Arend. "Typologies of Democratic Systems". *Comparative Political Studies*, 1 (April 1968). pp. 3–44.

——. "Consociational Democracy." *World Politics*, 21 (January 1969). pp. 207–25.

——. *Democracies: Patterns of Majoritarian and Consensus Government in Twenty-one Countries*. New Haven: Yale University Press, 1984.

Lipset, Seymour Martin. "Some Social Requisites of Democracy: Economic Development and Political Legitimacy". *The American Political Science Review*, 53 (March 1957). pp. 69–105.

——. *Political Man: The Social Bases of Politics*. Baltimore: Johns Hopkins University Press, 1981.

Locke, John. *Two Treatises of Government*, ed. by Peter Laslett. Cambridge University Press, 1967.

Loen, Arnold E. *Secularization: Science Without God?* London: SCM Press, 1967.

Luciani, Giacomo, "Economic Foundations of Democracy and Authoritarianism: The Arab World in Comparative Perspective". *Arab Studies Quarterly*, 10 (fall 1988). pp. 457–75.

——, ed. *The Arab State*. London: Routledge, 1990.

Lyotard, Jean-François. *The Postmodern Condition: A Report on Knowledge*. Manchester University Press, 1984.

Machiavelli, Niccolo. *The Discourses of Niccolo Machiavelli*, trans. by Leslie Joseph Walker and Cecil H. Clough. London: Routledge, 1991.

MacIver, Robert M. *The Web of Government*. New York: Macmillan, 1947.

MacMillan, C. Michael. "Social Versus Political Rights". *Canadian Journal of Political Science*, 19 (June 1986). pp. 283–304.

Macpherson, C. B. *The Real World of Democracy*. Oxford: Clarendon Press, 1966.

——. *The Life and Times of Liberal Democracy*. Oxford University Press, 1977.

Maghraoui, Abdeslam. "Problems of Transition to Democracy: Algeria's Short-lived Experiment with Electoral Politics". *Middle East Insight*, 8 (winter 1992). pp. 20–6.

Mahdi, Muhsin. *Ibn Khaldun's Philosophy of History*. London: Allen and Unwin, 1957.

——. *Alfarabi's Philosophy of Plato and Aristotle*. Ithaca, NY: Cornell University Press, 1969.

Mardin, Serif. "Civil Society and Islam". In *Civil Society: Theory, History, Comparison*, ed. by John A. Hall. Cambridge: Polity Press, 1995. pp. 278–300.

Marsot, Afaf Lutfi al-Sayyid. "The Revolutionary Gentlewoman in Egypt". In *Women in the Muslim World*, ed. by Lois Beck and Nikki Keddie. Cambridge and London: Harvard University Press, 1978. pp. 261–76.

Martin, D. C. "The Choices of Identity". *Social Identities*, 1 (1995). pp. 5–20.

Martin, Josh. "Privatization Becomes Urgent". *The Middle East*, 220 (February 1993). pp. 33–4.

Marty, Martin E. and R. Scott Appleby. "The Fundamentalism Project: A User's Guide". In *Fundamentalisms Observed*, ed. by Martin E. Marty and R. Scott Appleby. Chicago and London: University of Chicago Press, 1994. pp. vii–xiii.

Marx, Karl. *Das Capital*. New York: International Publishers, 1967.

——. *The German Ideology*. New York: International Publishers, 1970.

Mathews, John. *The Age of Democracy*. Melbourne: Oxford University Press, 1989.

Matilal, Bimal Krishna. "Ethical Relativism and Confrontation of Cultures". In *Relativism: Interpretation and Confrontation*, ed. by Michael Kraus. Notre Dame University Press, 1989.

Mattoon, Scott, "Islam by Profession". *The Middle East*, 218 (December 1992). pp. 16–18.

Mayo, Henry. *An Introduction to Democratic Theory*. New York: Oxford University Press, 1960.

McGrew, Anthony, ed. *The Transformation of Democracy? Globalization and Territorial Democracy*. Cambridge: Polity Press, 1997.

McLellan, David. *Karl Marx: His Life and Thought*. London: Macmillan, 1973.

Mehden, Fred von der. "American Perceptions of Islam". In *Voices of Resurgent Islam*, ed. by John L. Esposito. New York: Oxford University Press, 1983. pp. 18–31.

Memon, Muhammad Umar. *Ibn Taimiya's Struggle Against Popular Religion*. The Hague: Mouton, 1976.

Mernissi, Fatima. *Islam and Democracy: Fear of the Modern World*, trans. by Mary Jo Lakeland. London: Virago Press, 1993.

——. *The Forgotten Queens of Islam*, trans. by Mary Jo Lakeland. Cambridge: Polity Press, 1993.

Miles, Angela R. *Integrative Feminisms: Building Global Visions, 1960s–1990s*. London: Routledge, 1996.

Miliband, Ralph. *Divided Societies*. Oxford: Clarendon Press, 1989.

Mill, John Stuart. *The Subjection of Women*, ed. by Susan Moller Okin. Indianapolis: Hackett Publishing Company, 1988.

Miller, Judith. "The Challenge of Radical Islam". *Foreign Affairs*, 72 (spring 1993). pp. 43–56.

Milson, Menahem. "Najib Mahfuz and Jamal Abd al-Nasir: The Writer as Political Critic". *Asian and African Studies*, 23 (1989). pp. 1–22.

Mitchell, Timothy. *Colonizing Egypt*. Berkeley, LA and Oxford: University of California Press, 1991.

Mlinar, Zdravko, ed. *Globalization and Territorial Identity*. Aldershot: Avebury, 1992.

Moghadam, Valentine M. *Modernizing Women: Gender and Social Change in the Middle East*. Boulder, CO and London: Lynne Rienner, 1993.

Mohaddesin, Mohammad. "There is No Such Thing as a Moderate Fundamentalist". *Middle East Quarterly*, 2 (September 1995). pp. 77–83.

Mohideen, M. Mazzahim. "Islam, Nonviolence, and Interfaith Relations". In *Islam and Nonviolence*, ed. by Glenn D. Paige, Chaiwat Satha-Anand and Sarah Gilliatt. Honolulu: Matsunaga Institute for Peace, University of Hawaii, 1993. pp. 137–43.

Morris-Jones, W. H. "The West and the Third World: Whose Democracy, Whose Development?" *Third World Quarterly*, 1 (July 1979). pp. 31–42.

Mortimer, Edward. *Faith and Power: the Politics of Islam*. London: Faber, 1982.

Murphy, M. Brian and Alan Wolfe. "Democracy in Disarray". *Kapitalistate: Working Papers on the Capitalist State*, 8 (1980). pp. 9–25.

Muslih, Muhammad and Augustus Richard Norton. "The Need for Arab Democracy". *Foreign Policy*, 83 (summer 1991). pp. 3–19.

Nasr, Seyyed Hossein. "Why was Al-Farabi called the Second Teacher?" *Islamic Culture*, 59 (October 1985). pp. 357–64.

Nehru, B. K. "Western Democracy and the Third World". *Third World Quarterly*, 1 (April 1979). pp. 53–70.

Nelson, Barbara J. and Najma Chowdhury, eds. *Women and Politics Worldwide*. New Haven and London: Yale University Press, 1994.

Netton, Ian Richard. *Al-Farabi and His School*. London: Routledge, 1992.

Norton, Augustus R., ed. *Civil Society in the Middle East*. Leiden: E. J. Brill, 1996.

Okin, Susan M. *Women in Western Political Thought*. London: Virago, 1980.

Olsen, Gorm Rye. "Africa and the Middle East in the New International System: Democracy, Aid and Security". *Journal of Developing Societies*, 10 (1994). pp. 125–47.

Ormsby, Eric L. *Theodicy in Islamic Thought: The Dispute over al-Ghazali's "Best of all Possible Worlds"*. Princeton University Press, 1984.

Ottaway, David B. "Saudi Liberals See Reforms Unlikely". *Washington Post* (16 April 1991). Al, A14.

Ovendale, Ritchie. *The Middle East Since 1914*. London: Longman, 1992.

Oweiss, Ibrahim M. "Ibn Khaldun, the Father of Economics". In *Arab Civilization: Challenges and Responses*, ed. by George N. Atiyeh and Ibrahim M. Oweiss. State University of New York Press, 1988. pp. 122–7.

Owen, John M. "How Liberalism Produces Democratic Peace". *International Security*, 19 (fall 1994). pp. 87–125.

Owen, Roger. *State, Power and Politics in the Making of the Modern Middle East*. London: Routledge, 1992.

Pangle, Thomas L. *The Ennobling of Democracy*. Baltimore and London: John Hopkins University Press, 1992.

Parekh, Bhikhu. "The Cultural Particularity of Liberal Democracy". In *Prospects for Democracy*, ed. by David Held. Cambridge, Polity Press, 1993. pp. 156–75.

Parens, Joshua. "Whose Liberalism? Which Islam? Leonard Binder's 'Islamic Liberalism'". *Political Science and Politics*, 27 (September 1994). pp. 514–15.

Pareto, Vilfredo. *The Transformation of Democracy*. New Brunswick: Transaction Books, 1984.

Parry, Geraint and Michael Moran, eds. *Democracy and Democratization*. London: Routledge, 1994.

Parsons, Talcott. *The Social System*. London: Tavistock Publications, 1952.

——. "Evolutionary Universals in Society". *American Sociological Review*, 29 (June 1964). pp. 339–57.

Pateman, Carole. *Participation and Democratic Theory*. Cambridge University Press, 1970.

——. *The Sexual Contract*. Cambridge: Polity Press, 1988.

Pennock, Roland. *Liberal Democracy: Its Merits and Prospects*. New York: Rinehart and Company, 1950.

Peterson, V. Spike, ed. *Feminist (Re)Visions of International Relations*. Boulder, CO: Lynne Rienner, 1992.

Phillips, Anne. *Engendering Democracy*. Cambridge: Polity Press, 1991.

——. "Must Feminists Give up on Liberal Democracy?" *Political Studies*, 40 (1992). pp. 68–82.

——. *Democracy and Difference*. Cambridge: Polity Press, 1993.

Piamenta, Moshe. *Islam in Everyday Arabic Speech*. Leiden: E. J. Brill, 1979.

——. *The Muslim Conception of God and Human Welfare as Reflected in Everyday Arabic Speech*. Leiden: E. J. Brill, 1983.

Pickles, Dorothy. *Democracy*. London: Methuen and Co. Ltd, 1970.

Pinkney, Robert. *Democracy in the Third World*. Buckingham and Philadelphia: Open University Press, 1993.

Pipes, Daniel. *In the Path of God: Islam and Political Power*. New York: Basic Books Inc., 1983.

——. "There are no Moderates: Dealing with Fundamentalist Islam". *The National Interest* (fall 1995). pp. 48–57.

Piscatori, James P. "The Roles of Islam in Saudi Arabia's Political Development". In *Islam and Development: Religion and Sociopolitical Change*, ed. by John L. Esposito. New York: Syracuse University Press, 1980. pp. 123–38.

——. *Islam in a World of Nation–States*. Cambridge University Press, 1986.

Plato. *The Republic of Plato*, trans. by Francis McDonald Cornford. New York: Oxford University Press, 1945.

Political Science and Politics. "Democracy, Islam, and the Study of Middle Eastern Politics", 27 (September 1994). pp. 507–19.

Przeworski, Adam. "Democracy as a Contingent Outcome of Conflicts". In *Constitutionalism and Democracy*, ed. by Jon Elster and Rune Slagstad. Cambridge University Press, 1988. pp. 59–80.

Putnam, Robert D. Robert Leonardi, and Raffaella Nanetti. *Making Democracy Work: Civic Traditions in Modern Italy*. Princeton University Press, 1993.

Pye, Lucian W, ed. *Communications and Political Development*. Princeton University Press, 1963.

——. *Aspects of Political Development*. Boston: Little, Brown and Company, 1966.

Rahe, Paul A. *Republics Ancient and Modern*. Chapel Hill: University of North Carolina Press, 1992.

Rahman, Fazlur. *Islam*. Chicago and London: University of Chicago Press, 1979.

Raphael, D. D. *Justice and Liberty*. London: The Anthlone Press, 1980.

Robertson, Roland. "Mapping the Global Condition: Globalization as the Central Concept". In *Global Culture: Nationalism, Globalization and Modernity*, ed. by M. Featherstone. London: Sage, 1990. pp. 15–30.

——. *Globalization: Social Theory and Global Culture*. London: Sage, 1992.

Robertson, R. and W. R. Garrett, eds. *Religion and Global Order.* New York: Paragon Press, 1991.

Rodenbeck, Max. "The Struggle Against Political Islam". *Middle East International*, 428 (26 June 1992). pp. 5–6.

Rorty, Richard. *Philosophy and the Mirror of Nature*. Princeton University Press, 1979.

Rosenau, James. "Citizenship in a Changing World Order". In *Governance without Government*, ed. by James Rosenau and E. Czempiel. Cambridge University Press, 1992. pp. 272–94.

Rosenthal, Erwin I. J. *Political Thought in Medieval Islam: An Introductory Outline*. Cambridge University Press, 1962.

Rotstein, Maurice. *The Democratic Myth*. The Florham Park Press, 1983.

Rousseau, Jean-Jacques. *The Social Contract*, trans. by M. Cranston. Harmondsworth: Penguin Books, 1975.

Rustow, Dankwart. *A World of Nations: Problems of Political Modernization*. Washington, DC: The Brookings Institution, 1967.

Sadowski, Yahya M. "The New Orientalism and the Democracy Debate". *Middle East Report* (July–August 1993). pp. 14–21, 40.

Said, Edward. *Orientalism: Western Conceptions of the Orient*. London: Penguin Books, 1978.

——. *Culture and Imperialism*. London: Chatto and Windus, 1993.

Salamé, Ghassan. "Strong and Weak States: A Qualified Return to the Muqaddimah". In *The Arab State*, ed. by Giacomo Luciani. London: Routledge, 1990. pp. 29–64.

——, ed. *Democracy Without Democrats? The Renewal of Politics in the Muslim World*. London: I. B. Tauris, 1994.

Salibi, Kamal Osman. *A House of Many Notions*. London: I. B. Taurus, 1988.

Sartori, Giovanni. *Democratic Theory*. Westport: Greenwood Press, 1962.

——. *The Theory of Democracy Revisited*. Chatham House Publishers, 1987.

Schuurman, Frans J., ed. *Beyond the Impasse: New Directions in Development Theory*. London and New Jersey: Zed Books, 1993.

Seligman, Adam B. *The Idea of Civil Society*. New York: The Free Press, 1992.

Shapiro, Michael J. *Language and Political Understanding: The Politics of Discursive Practices*. Michigan: UMI Out-Of-Print Books on Demand, 1981.

Sharabi, Hisham, ed. *The Next Arab Decade: Alternative Futures*. Boulder, CO: Westview Press, 1988.

——. "Introduction: Patriarchy and Dependency and the Future of Arab Society". In *The Next Arab Decade: Alternative Futures*, ed. by Hisham Sharabi. Boulder, CO: Westview Press, 1988. pp. 1–8.

Sharoni, Simona. "Gender Issues in Democracy: Rethinking Middle East Peace and Security from a Feminist Perspective". In *Building Peace in the Middle East: Challenges for States and Civil Society*, ed. by Elise Boulding. Boulder and London: Lynne Rienner, 1994. pp. 99–109.

Shils, Edward. *Political Development in the New States*. New York: Humanities Press, 1962.

Siffler, Eric. "A Definition of Foundationalism". *Metaphilosophy*, 15 (1984). pp. 16–25.

Sivan, Emmanuel. *Radical Islam: Medieval Theology and Modern Politics*. New Haven: Yale University Press, 1985.

Sklar, Richard L. "Developmental Democracy". *Comparative Studies in Society and History*, 29 (October 1987). pp. 686–714.

Sørensen, Georg. *Democracy and Democratization*. Boulder, CO: Westview Press, 1993.

Springborg, Patricia. *Western Republicanism and the Oriental Prince*. Cambridge: Polity Press, 1992.

Stowasser, Barbara F., ed. *The Islamic Impulse*. Washington, DC: Centre for Contemporary Arab Studies, Georgetown University, 1987.

Strauss, Leo. "Farabi's Plato". In *Essays in Medieval Jewish and Islamic Philosophy*, ed. by Arthur Hyman. New York: KTAV Publishing House, 1977. pp. 391–427.

Sullivan, Earl L. "Democratization and Changing Gender Roles in Egypt". *American–Arab Affairs*, 36 (spring 1991). pp. 16–18.

Sullivan, John. "A Market–Orientated Approach to Democratic Development: The Linkages". In *Promoting Democracy: Opportunities and Issues*, ed. by Ralph M. Goldman and William A. Douglas. New York: Praeger, 1988. pp. 139–83.

Tamadonfar, Mehran. *The Islamic Polity and Political Leadership*. Boulder, CO: Westview Press, 1989.

Taylor, Charles. *Human Agency and Language*. Cambridge University Press, 1996.

Tester, Keith. *Civil Society*. London and New York: Routledge, 1992.

Thompson, Edward P. "The Moral Economy of the English Crowd in the Eighteenth Century". *Past and Present*, 50 (February 1971). pp. 76–136.

Tibi, Bassam. *The Crisis of Modern Islam: A Preindustrial Culture in the Scientific–Technological Age*, trans. by Judith and Peter Von Sivers. Salt Lake City: University of Utah Press, 1988.

——. *Islam and the Cultural Accommodation of Social Change*, trans. by Clare Krojzl. Boulder, CO and San Francisco: Western Press, 1991.

Tickner, J. Ann. *Gender in International Relations*. New York: Columbia University Press, 1992.

Touraine, Alaine. *The Self-Production of Society*. Chicago University Press, 1971.

Triplett, Timm. "Rorty's Critique of Foundationalism". *Philosophical Studies*, 52 (1987). pp. 115–29.

Tucker, Judith E. *Women in Nineteenth-century Egypt*. Cambridge University Press, 1985.

Turner, Bryan S. *Weber and Islam: A Critical Study*. London: Routledge and Kegan Paul, 1974.

——. *Marx and the End of Orientalism*. London, Allen and Unwin, 1978.

——. "Orientalism, Islam and Capitalism". *Social Compass*, 25 (1978). pp. 371–94.

——. "Orientalism and the Problem of Civil Society in Islam". In *Orientalism, Islam and Islamists*, ed. by Asaf Hussain, Robert Olson, Jamil Qureshi. Brattleboro, Vermont: Amana Books, 1984. pp. 23–42.

——. "Postmodern Culture. Modern Citizens". In *The Condition of Citizenship*, ed. by B. van Steenbergen. London: Sage, 1994. pp. 153–68.

——. *Orientalism, Postmodernism and Globalism*. London and New York: Routledge, 1994.

Vatikiotis, P. J. *The History of Modern Egypt: From Muhammad Ali to Mubarak*. London: Weidenfeld and Nicolson, 1991.

Verba, Sydney. "Sequences and Development". In *Crises and Sequences in Political Development*, ed. by Leonard Binder *et. al.* Princeton University Press, 1971. pp. 283–316.

Warren, Mark. *Nietzsche and Political Thought*. Cambridge, MA: MIT Press, 1988.

Waterbury, John. *The Commander of the Faithful: The Moroccan Political Elite–A Study in Segmented Politics*. London: Weidenfeld and Nicolson, 1970.

Watt, W. M. "The Closing of the Door of Ijtihad". *Orientalia Hispanica*, 1 (1974). pp. 675–8.

Weber, Max. *The Theory of Social and Economic Organisation*, trans. by A. M. Henderson and Talcott Parsons. New York: Oxford University Press, 1947.

Weiner, Myron and Samuel P. Huntington, eds. *Understanding Political Development*. Glenview, IL: Little, Brown and Company, 1987.

Welch, Stephen. *The Concept of Political Culture*. New York: St Martin's Press, 1993.

Wilson, Richard W. *Compliance Ideologies: Rethinking Political Culture*. Cambridge University Press, 1992.

Wittfogel, Karl A. *Oriental Despotism: A Comparative Study of Total Power*. New Haven: Yale University Press, 1957.

Wright, Robin. *Sacred Rage: The Crusade of Modern Islam*. London: Andre Deutsh, 1986.

——. "Islam, Democracy and the West". *Foreign Affairs*, 71 (summer 1992). pp. 131–45.

Young, Iris M. "Polity and Group Difference: A Critique of the Ideal of Universal Citizenship". *Ethics*, 99 (1989). pp. 250–74.

——. *Justice and the Politics of Difference*. Princeton University Press, 1990.

Young, Robert. *White Mythologies: Writing History and the West*. London: Routledge, 1995.

Yusuf, K. Umar. "Farabi and Greek Political Philosophy". In *Comparative Political Philosophy*, ed. by Anthony J. Parcel and Ronald C. Keith. Delhi: Sage, 1992. pp. 185–216.

Yuval-Davis, Nira and Floya Anthias, eds. *Woman–Nation–State*. London: Macmillan, 1988.

ARABIC

ʿAalī, ʿAbd al-Salām Ibn ʿabd. al-. *Al-Falsafatu 'l-siyāsiyyah ʿinda 'l-Fārābī*. [*Al-Fārābī's Political Philosophy*] Beirut: Dar al-Taliʿah, 1986.

ʿAbbūd, Elias. *Judhūru 'l-dīmuqrāṭiyyah fī'l-mashriqi 'l-ʿArabī*. [*The Roots of Democracy in the Arab East*] Tripoli, Libya: Al-Markiz al-ʿAlami Li 'l-Dirasat wa Abhath al-Kitab al-Akhdar, 1990.

ʿAbd-Allah, Aḥmad, ed. *Al-Jaysh wa 'l-dīmukrāṭiyyah fi miṣr*. [*The Military and Democracy in Egypt*] Cairo: Sina Li-Nishr, 1990.

ʿAbd-Allah, Ismāʿīl Ṣabrī. *Miṣr allatī nurīduhā: Taqrīr siyāssī wa barnāmaj marḥalī*. [*The Kind of Egypt we Want: A Political Report and a Gradual Programme*] Cairo: Dar al-Shuruq, 1992.

ʿAlawī, Saʿīd Binsa ʿīd. al-. *Al- mujtamaʿu 'l-madanī fi 'l-waṭani 'l-ʿarabī wa dawruhu fi taḥqīqi 'l-dīmuqrāṭiyyah*. [*Civil Society in the Arab Homeland: its Role in Achieving Democracy*] Beirut: Markiz Dirasat al-Wihdah al-ʿArabiyyah, 1992.

ʿAllūsh, Nājī. *Al-waṭanu'l-ʿarabī: al-jaghrāfiyah al-ṭabīʿiyyah wa'l-bashariyyah*. [*The Arab Homeland: Human and Physical Geography*] Beirut: Markiz Dirasat al-Wihdah al-ʿArabiyyah, 1986.

Amīn, Muḥammad Ḥassan. al-. "Bayna 'l-shūrā wa 'l-dīmuqrāṭiyyah". ["Between al-shūrā and Democracy"] *al-Munṭalaq*, 98 (Rajab 1993). pp. 39–49.

Amīn, Samīr. *Ba 'ḍu qaḍāyā li 'l-mustaqbil: Ta'ammulāt ḥawla 'l-'ālam al-mu'āṣir.* [*A Few Questions for the Future: Reflections on the Challenges of the Contemporary World*] Cairo: Maktabat Madbuli, 1991.

'Aqqād, 'Abbas Maḥmūd. al-. *Al-Dīmuqrāṭiyyah fi 'l-Islām.* [*Democracy in Islam*] (Beirut: Manshurat al-Maktabah al-'Asriyyah, n.d.).

'Ashūr, Muḥammad al-Ṭāhir. Ibn. *Naqd 'ilmī li kitābi 'l-islām wa uṣūli 'l-ḥukm.* [*A Scientific Critique of the Book Islam and the Principles of Government*] Cairo: n.p., 1925.

'Awwā, Muḥammad Salīm. al-. "Al-Ta'ddudiyyatu 'l-siyāsiyyah min-manḍūr Islāmī". ["Multipartyism from an Islamic Perspective"]. *Al-'Arabī*, 395 (October 1991). pp. 30–6.

Bahā'u al-dīn, Aḥmad. *Shar'iyyatu 'l-sulṭah fi 'l-'arabī.* [*Legitimacy of Political Power in the Arab World*] Cairo: Dar Al-Shuruq, 1984.

Basharī, Tāriq. al-. *Dirāsāt fi 'l-dimuqrāṭiyyati 'l-miṣriyyah.* [*Studies in Egyptian Democracy*] Cairo: Dar al-Shuruq, 1987.

Bin Nabī, Mālik. *Wijhatu al- 'ālim al-Islāmī.* [*The Muslim World's Direction*], trans. by 'Abd al-Ṣabūr Shāhīn. Damascus: Dar al-Fikr, 1981.

——. "Al-Dīmuqrāṭiyyah fi 'l-Islām". ["Democracy in Islam"] *Ta'ammulāt.* [*Reflections*] Beirut: Dar al-Fikr al-Mu'asir, 1991.

Bīṭār, Fu'ād. *Azmatu 'l-dīmuqrāṭiyyah fi 'l-'ālami 'l-'arabī.* [*The Crisis of Democracy in the Arab World*] Beirut: Dar Birayt, 1984.

Faḍl-Allah, Muḥammad Ḥusayn. *Al-Malāmiḥu 'l-'ammah li lubnān fi 'l-niẓāmi 'l-ṭā'ifi 'l-ḥālī wa niẓāmu 'l-dīmuqrāṭiyyah al-'adadiyyah al-qā'imah 'ala mabda'i 'l-shūrā.* [*General Features of Lebanon's Political System Under Sectarianism and Pluralistic Democracy on the Basis of al-Shūrā*] Lebanon: [n.p.], 1985.

Faḍl-Allah, Muḥammad Ḥusayn. "Awlawiyyatunā 'l-dukhūl ila 'l-'aṣr". ["Our Priority is to Enter the Modern Age"] *al-'Ālam*, 425 (April 1992). pp. 36–7.

Farḥān, Isḥāq. al-. *Mushkilātu al-shabāb fi ḍaw'i al-Islām.* [*Problems of Youth in the Light of Islam*] Amman: Dar al-Furqan, 1984.

Ghalyūn, Burhān *et al.*, eds. *Ḥawla 'l-khiyāru 'l-dīmuqrāṭi: dirāsāt naqdiyyah.* [*On the Democratic Option: a Critique*] Beirut: Markiz Dirasat al-Wahdah al-'Arabiyyah, 1994.

Ghannūshī, Rashīd. al-. *Al-mara' al-muslimah fi tūnis: bayna tawjīhāti al-qur'ān wa wāqi' al-mujtama' al-tūnisī.* [*The Muslim Woman in Tunisia: Between the Instructions of the Qur'ān and the Reality of Tunisian Society*] Kuwait: Dar al-Qalam li al-Nashr wa al-Tawzi', 1993.

Ghazālī, Muḥammad. al-. *Azmatu 'l-shūrā fi 'l-mujtama'āti 'l-'arabiyyah wa 'l-Islāmiyyah.* [*The Crisis of al-Shūrā in Arab and Islamic Societies*] Cairo: Dar al-Sharq li al-Nashr, 1990.

Ḥāfiẓ, Ṣalāḥ al-dīn. *Ṣadmatu 'l-dīmuqrāṭiyyah*. [*The Shock of Democracy*] Cairo: Sina' Li-Nashr, 1993.

Ḥaddād, Al-Ṭāhir. al-. *Imra'atunā fī 'l-sharī'ah wa 'l-mujtama'*. [*Our Woman in the Islamic Law and in Society*] Tunis: Dar Busalama li al-Tiba'ah wa al-Nashr wa al-Tawzi', 1989.

Ḥaddād, Ibrāhīm. *Al-Shuyū'iyyah wa 'l-dīmuqrāṭiyyah bayna 'l-Sharqi wa 'l-Gharb*. [*Communism and Democracy Between East and West*] Beirut: Dar al-Thaqafah, 1958.

——. *Al-Dīmuqrāṭiyyah 'inda 'l-'arab*. [*Democracy Amongst Arabs*] Beirut: Dar al-Thaqafah, 1960.

Ḥamrūsh, Aḥmad. *Qiṣṣatu thawrat 23 yūlyū: al-baḥthu 'ani 'l-dīmuqrāṭiyyah*. [*The Story of the 23rd of July Revolution: The Search for Democracy*] Cairo: Dar Ibn Khaldun, 1982.

Ḥanafī, Ḥasan. *Al-Turāthu wa 'l-tajdīd*. [*Cultural Heritage and Regeneration*] Cairo: n.p., 1980.

——. *Muqaddimah fī 'ilmi'l -istighrāb*. [*Introduction to Occidentalism*] Cairo: al-Dar al-Fanniyyah, n.d.

al-Ḥasan, Khālid. *Ishkāliyyatu 'l-dīmuqrāṭiyyah wa l'-badīlu 'l-islāmī fī 'l-waṭani 'l-'Arabī*. [*The Problematic of Democracy and the Islamic Alternative in the Arab Homeland*] Jerusalem: Wakalat Abu 'Arfah li al-Sahafah wa al-Nashr, 1988.

Hāshimī, Al-Ḥusayn Ibn Ṭalāl. al-. *Khiṭābu 'l-'arsh fī iftitāḥi 'l-dawrati 'l-'adiyyati 'l-rābi'ah li-majlisi 'l-ummati 'l-urdunī 'l-ḥādī 'ashar*. [*The Crisis of Democracy in the Arab World*] Amman, Jordan: January 1992.

Hāshimī, Ibn. al-. *Humūmu al-mar'ah al-mulsimah wa al-dā'iyah Zaynab al-Ghazālī*. [*The Muslim Woman's Concerns and Preacher Zaynab al-Ghazālī*] Cairo: Dar al-I'tisam, 1990.

Haykal, Muḥammad H. *Al-Salāmu 'l-mustaḥīl wa 'l-dīmuqrāṭiyyatu 'l-ghā'ibah*. [*The Impossible Peace and the Absent Democracy*] Beirut: Sharikat al-Matbu'at li al-Tawzi' wa al-Nashr, 1988.

Hilāl, 'Alī al-dīn et al. *Al-Dīmuqrāṭiyyah wa ḥuqūqu 'l-insān fī 'l-waṭani al-'arabī*. [*Democracy and Human Rights in the Arab Homeland*] Beirut: Markiz Dirasat al-Wihdah al-'Arabiyyah, 1986.

Ḥuluw, 'Abdah. al-. *Al-Fārābī: Al-mu'allimu 'l-thānī*. [*Al-Fārābi: The Second Master*] Beirut: Bayt al-Hikmah, 1980.

Ḥussayn, Ṭāhā. *Al-Fitnah al-kubrā*. [*The Great Discord*] Cairo: Dar al-Ma'arif, 1958.

——. *Mustaqbalu 'l-thaqāfah fī miṣr*. [*The Future of Culture in Egypt*] Cairo: al-Hay'ah al-Misriyyah al-'Ammah li 'l-Kitab, 1993.

Huwaydī, Fahmī. *Al-'Islamu wa 'l-dīmuqrāṭiyyah*. [*Islam and Democracy*] Cairo: Markiz al-Ahram, 1993.

Ibrāhīm, Sa'ad al-dīn, ed. *Azmatu 'l-dīmuqrāṭiyyah fī 'l-'ālami 'l-'arabī* [*Crown's Speech: Opening of the Fourth Session of the Jordanian National Assembly, 1992*] Beirut: Markaz Dirasat al-Wihdah al-'Arabiyyah, 1987.

——, ed. *Al-ta'addudiyyatu' l-siyāsiyyah wa 'l-dīmuqrāṭiyyah fi 'l-waṭani 'l-'arabī*. [*Pluralism and Democracy in the Arab Homeland*] Amman: Arab Thought Forum, 1989.

Jāsim, Muḥammad 'Abd al-Qādir. al-. *Al kuwait…muthallathu 'l-dīmuqrāṭiyyah*. [*Kuwait…The Triangle of Democracy*] Cairo: Matabi' 'l-Shuruq, 1992.

J'ayiṭ, Hishām. *Al-Fitnatu 'l-kubrā: Jadaliyyatu 'l-dīn wa 'l-siyāsah fi 'l-islāmi 'l-mubakkir*. [*The Great Discord: The Dialectics of Religion and Politics in Early Islam*] Beirut: Dar al-Tali'ah, n.d.

Junblāṭ, Kamāl. *Aḥādīth 'ani 'l-ḥurriyyah: mukhtārāt*. [*Speeches on Freedom: Selections*] Al-Mukhtarah, Lebanon: al-Dar al-Taqaddumiyyah, 1987.

Kawākibī, 'Abd al-Raḥmān. al-. *Ummu 'l-qurā*. [*The Mother of Cities: Mecca*] Beirut: Dar al-Ra'id al-'Arabi, 1982.

——. *Ṭabā'i'u 'l-istibdād wa maṣāriu' 'l-isti'bād*. [*The Nature of Despotism: with an Introduction by As'ad al-Saḥmarānī*] Beirut: Dar al-Nafa'is, 1986.

Khaldūn, 'Abd al-Raḥmān. Ibn. *Muqaddimatu Ibn Khaldūn*. [*Ibn Khaldun's Prolegomenon*] Beirut: Dar al-Jeel, [no date].

Khālid, Muḥammad Khālid. *Muwāṭinūn lā ra'āyā*. [*Citizens not Subjects*] Cairo: n/p, 1951.

Khālid, Muḥammad Khālid. *Al-Dīmuqrāṭiyyah abadan*. [*Democracy Ever*] Baghdad: Maktabatu 'l-Muthannah, 1958.

Khālid, Muḥammad Khālid. *Min hunā nabda'*. [*Here we Begin*] Cairo: n.p. 1966.

Khālid, Muḥammad Khālid. *Difā'un 'ani 'l-dīmuqrāṭiyyah*. [*In Defence of Democracy*] Cairo: Dar Thabit, 1985.

Khālid, Muḥammad Khālid. *Al-Dawlah fi 'l-Islām*. [*The State in Islam*] Cairo: Dar Thabit, 1989.

Manīf, 'Abd al-Raḥmān. *Al-Dīmuqrāṭiyyah awwalan, al-dīmuqrāṭiyyah dā'iman*. [*Democracy First, Democracy Always*] Beirut: al-Mu'assassah al-'Arabiyyah li 'l-Dirasat wa 'l-Nashr, 1992.

M'Ghīribī, Muḥammad Zāhī. al-. "Al-thaqāfatu 'l-siyāsiyyah al-'arabiyyah wa qaḍiyyatu 'l-dīmuqrāṭiyyah". ["Arab Political Culture and the Question of Democracy"] *Al-Dimuqrāṭiyyah*, 3 (May 1991). pp. 6–11.

Muqaffa', 'Abd Allah Ibn. al-. *Kalīlah wa dimnah*. [*Kalilah and Dimnah*] (Beirut: Dar al-Fikr al-'Arabi, 1990).

Musṭafah, Muḥammad. *Al-Dīmuqrāṭiyyah wa 'l-intikhābāt*. [*Democracy and Elections*] Cairo: Dar al-Ma'arif, 1990.

Naqd, Muḥammad Ibrāhīm. *Qaḍāyā 'l-dīmuqrāṭiyyah fi 'l-Sudān*. [*Issues of Democracy in Sudan*] Cairo: Dar al-Thaqafah al-Jadidah, 1992.

Niẓām al-Dīn, 'Irfan. *Ḥiwārātun 'alā mustawā 'l-qimmhah*. [*Interviews at the Leadership Level*] London: Manshurat al-Mu'assassah al-'Arabiyyah al-urubiyyah li 'l-Nashr, 1988.

Nuʿmān, ʿAbd-Allah. *Al-ittijāhātu 'l-ʿalmāniyyah fi l-ʿālami 'l-ʿarabī*. [*Secular Trends in the Arab World*] Junih, Lebanon: Dar Nuʿman li al-Thaqafah, 1990.

Qumayr, Yūḥannā. *Falāsifatu 'l-ʿarab: Al-Fārābī*. [*The Arabs' Philosphers: Al-Fārābī*] Beirut: Dar al-Mashriq, 1986.

Qūrah, Nādiah Ḥāmid. *Tārīkhu 'l-mar'ah fī 'l-Ḥayāti 'l-Niyābiyah fī Miṣr Min, 1957 ilā 1995*. [*History of Woman in Parliamentary Life in Egypt, 1957–1995*] Cairo: al-Hay'ah al-Misriyyah al-ʿAmmah Li al-Kitab, 1996.

Quṭb, Muḥammad. *Madhāhib fikriyyah muʿāṣirah*. [*Contemporary Ideological Trends*] Cairo: Dar al-Shuruq, 1987.

Ramān, Ḥusayn. Abu., ed. *Al-mar'atu 'l-urduniyyah wa qānunu 'l-intikhāb*. [*Jordanian Woman and Electoral Law*] Amman: Sinbad Publishing House, 1997.

Salām, Fārūq ʿAbd. al-. *Azmatu 'l-ḥukmi fi l-ʿālami 'l-Islāmī*. [*The Crisis of Governance in the Islamic World*] Qalyub, Egypt: Maktab Qalyub li-Altabʿ wa 'l-Tawziʿ, 1981.

Samāwī, Aḥmad al-. *Al-istibdād wa al-ḥurriyyah fī fikr al-nahḍah*. [*Despotism and Freedom in the Thought of* al-nahḍah] Syria: Dar al-Hiwar, 1989.

Ṣāwī, Ṣalāḥ. al-. *Al-Taʿaddudiyyah al-siyāsiyyah fi 'l-dawlati 'l-Islāmiyyah*. [*Political Pluralism in the Islamic State*] Cairo: Dar al-Iʿlam al-Duwali, 1992.

Shābbī, Abū Al-Qāsim. al-. *Aghānī 'l-ḥayāt*. [*Life Songs*] n.p.: Dar al-Kutub al-Sharqiyyah, 1955.

Shaḥrūr, Muḥammad. *Al-Kitāb wa'l-Qur'ān: Qirā'ah Muʿāṣirah*. [*The Book and the Qur'ān: A Re-reading*] Beirut: Sharikat al-Matbu'at li-al-tawzi wa al-Nashr, 1992.

Shannāwī, Fahmī al-. "Al-Dīmuqrāṭiyyah wa 'l-shūraqrāṭiyyah". ["Democracy and *Shura*cracy"] *Al-ʿĀlam*, 380 (May 1991). pp. 36–7.

Sukkarī, ʿAbd al-Salām. al-. *Aʿḍam ḥiwār dīmuqrāṭī fī 'l-tārīkh: ʿUmar Ibn al-Khaṭṭāb maʿa Khālid Ibn al-Walīd*. [*History's Greatest Democratic Debate: ʿUmar Ibn al-Khaṭṭāb with Khālid Ibn al-Walīd*] Cairo: al-Dar al-Misriyyah li 'l-Nashr, 1992.

Sumayʿ, Ṣālah Ḥasan. *Azmatu 'l-ḥurriyyatu 'l-siyāsiyyah fi 'l-waṭani 'l-ʿarabī*. [*The Crisis of Political Freedom in the Arab Homeland*] Cairo: Al-Zahra' li 'l-Iʿlām al-ʿArabi, 1988.

Thānī, al-Ḥasan. al-. *Dhākiratu malik*. [*Memoris of a King*] Interviews by Eric Le Ran n.p. Kitab al-Sharq al-Awsat, 1993.

Ṭahṭāwī, Rifāʿah Rāfiʿ. al-. *Takhlīṣ al-ibrīz ila talkhīṣ bārīz*. [*The Extraction of Gold from a Review of Paris*] Tripoli, Libya: Al-Dar al-ʿArabiyyah li 'l-Kitab, 1991.

——. *Manāhiju 'l-albābi 'l-miṣriyyah fi mabāhiji 'l-adābi 'l-ʿaṣriyyah*. [*The Paths for Egyptian Hearts into the Joys of the Contemporary Arts*] Cairo: n.p., 1912.

Tūnisī, Khayr al-Dīn. al-. *Muqaddimat aqwām al-masālik fi ma'rifat aḥwāl al-mamlik*. [*The Surest Path to Knowledge Concerning the Condition of Countries*] trans. by Leon Carl Brown. Cambridge, MA: Harvard University Press, 1967.

Turābī, Ḥasan al-. *Al-ittijāhu 'l-Islāmī yuqaddimu 'l-mar'ah: bayna ta'ālīmi 'l-dīn wa taqālīdi 'l-mujtama'*. [*Islamism and Women: Between Religious Dogma and Social Traditions*] Jeddah: al-Dar al-Sa'udiyyah li al-Nashr wa al-Tawzi, 1984.

Ṭaḥḥān, Muḥammad Jamāl. "Al-Kawākibī bayna 'l-Islāmiyyah wa 'l-dīmuqrāṭiyyah." ["Al-Kawākibī Between al-Islāmiyyah and Democracy"], *Dirāsāt 'Arabiyyah*, 10–12 (August–October 1992). pp. 34–55.

'Umārah, Muḥammad. *Qāsim Amīn: taḥrīru 'l-mar'ah wa 'l-tamaddunu 'l-Islāmī*. [*Qāsim Amīn: The Liberation of Women and Islamic Urbanism*] Beirut: Dar al-Wihda, 1985.

——. *Al-mu'tazilah wa mushkilatu 'l-ḥurriyyatu 'l-insāniyyah*. [*The Mu'tazilite and the Problematic of Human Freedom*] Cairo: Dar al-Shuruq, 1988.

——. "Al-Islām wa 'l-ta'ddudiyyatu 'l-ḥizbiyyah". ["Islam and Multipartyism"] *al-'Arabī*, 403 (June 1992).

Zallūm, 'Abd al-Qādir. *Al-Dīmuqrāṭiyyah niẓāmu kufr: yaḥrumu akhdhuhā aw taṭbīquhā aw al-da'wah ilayhā*. [*Democracy is a System of Unbelief: It is Forbidden to Adopt, Practice or Call For*] n.p., 1990.

Zidānī, Sa'īd. "Iṭlālah 'ala al-dīmuqrāṭiyyah al-lībrāliyyah". ["Introduction to Liberal Democracy"] *al-Mustaqbil al-'Arabī*, 135 (May 1990). pp. 4–21.

FRENCH

Abdel-Malek, Anouar. "L'Orientalisme en Crise". *Diogène*, 44 (1963). pp. 109–42.

Arkoun, Mohammed. *Essais sur la pensée islamique*. Paris: Maisonneuve et Larose, 1973.

——. *Pour une critique de la raison islamique*. Paris: Maisonneuve et Larose, 1984.

Arkoun, Mohammed and Louis Gardet. *L'Islam. Hier-Demain*. Paris: Editions Buchet/Chastel, 1978.

Beauvoir, Simone de. *Le Deuxième Sexe*. Paris: Gallimard, 1949.

Djaït, Hichem. *La personnalité et le devenir arabo-islamiques*. Paris: Éditions du Seuil, 1974.

Etienne, Bruno. *L'Islamisme radical*. Paris: Hachette, 1987.

Foucault, Michel. *L'archeologie du savoir*. Paris: Gallimard, 1969.

Gardet, Louis. *La Cité Musulmane. Vie sociale et politique*. [*The Islamic City: Social and Political Life*] Paris: Librairie Philosophique J. Vrin, 1954.

L'Express. "Foulard, le complot: comment les islamistes nous infiltrent". ["Veil, the Plot: How Islamists Infiltrate us"] (17 November 1994). pp. 62–6.

Petit, Odette, *Presence de L'Islam dans la langue Arabe*. Paris: Librarie d'Amerique et d'Orient, 1982.

Philip, Bruno. "Taslima Nasreen, romancière maudite du Bangladesh". *Le Monde* (30 December 1993). pp. 1, 4.

Rodinson, Maxime. *L'Islam: politique et croyance*. [*Islam: State and Religion*] Paris: Librairie Arthème Fayard, 1993.

Tocqueville, Alexis de. *De La Démocratie En Amérique*. Paris: C. L., 1888.

Vatin, Jean-Claude. "Les partis démocratiques: perceptions occidentales de la démocratisation dans le monde arabe". ["The Democratic Parties: Western Perceptions of Arab Democratisation"] *Egypte/Monde Arabe* 4 (1990). pp. 9–24.

Waardenburg, Jacques. *L'Islam dans le miroir de l'Occident*. The Hague: Mouton, 1963.

INDEX

QM LIBRARY
(MILE END)